A Beowulf Handbook

Contributors

Theodore M. Andersson, Stanford University
Robert E. Bjork, Arizona State University
George Clark, Queen's University, Ontario
R. D. Fulk, Indiana University
John M. Hill, United States Naval Academy
Catherine M. Hills, University of Cambridge
Edward B. Irving Jr., Emeritus, University of Pennsylvania
Alvin A. Lee, McMaster University, Ontario
Seth Lerer, Stanford University
Donka Minkova, University of California, Los Angeles
John D. Niles, University of California, Berkeley
Anita Obermeier, Arizona State University
Katherine O'Brien O'Keeffe, University of Notre Dame
Alexandra Hennessey Olsen, University of Denver
Marijane Osborn, University of California, Davis
Ursula Schaefer, Humboldt-Universität zu Berlin
Thomas A. Shippey, St. Louis University
Robert P. Stockwell, University of California, Los Angeles

A
Beowulf
Handbook

Edited by
Robert E. Bjork
and John D. Niles

UNIVERSITY
of
EXETER
PRESS

First published in the UK in hardback in 1997
by University of Exeter Press.
This paperback edition first published
in the UK in 1998
by University of Exeter Press
Reed Hall, Streatham Drive
Exeter, Devon, EX4 4QR, UK.

© 1996 University of Nebraska Press

British Library Cataloguing in Publication Data
A catalogue record of this book is available
from the British Library

Hardback ISBN 0 85989 543 2
Paperback ISBN 0 85989 621 8

Published as a co-publication between
University of Nebraska Press and
University of Exeter Press

Printed in the United States of America

In memoriam

Daniel G. Calder

Contents

Preface

Beowulf scholarship has developed so rapidly during the modern era that few if any can hope to master all the work that has been done on the poem or to keep abreast of current developments in the field. Scholars from different disciplines employing a multitude of critical methodologies have studied *Beowulf*, thus making the work of understanding the poem more complex. This handbook lays the foundation for up-to-date, nuanced approaches to *Beowulf* by supplying a succession of analyses of all major aspects of it from the beginnings to 1994. After the first, introductory chapter, the individual chapters offer both a rapid glimpse at scholarly trends in the study of *Beowulf* and a more sustained exploration of selected problems. Each begins with a summary and an annotated chronology of the most important books and articles on the topic it treats, then presents an overview of scholarly interest in the topic, a synthesis of present knowledge and opinion, and an analysis of what remains to be done. We have structured the chapters to accommodate the needs of a broad audience: nonspecialists who wish to read *Beowulf* with a basic understanding of the major issues that concern the poem; graduate and advanced undergraduate students who, in scrutinizing the text of *Beowulf*, face a daunting task, although an exhilarating one; college or university instructors who teach *Beowulf* and are unfamiliar with all the problems attendant on this enterprise; and medievalists, whether Anglo-Saxonists or not, who wish to orient themselves in *Beowulf* scholarship either for their own research or for that of their students. The order of the chapters roughly suggests the order in which scholars began taking a strong interest in the particular topics.

In bringing this project to fruition, we have incurred many debts. We want to thank Willis G. Regier, former director of the University of Nebraska Press, for inviting us to undertake this challenging enterprise; the editorial board of the University of Nebraska Press for its stalwart support; the two specialist readers for the Press for their many constructive suggestions; the College of Letters and Science, Division of Humanities, Arts, and Cultural Studies, at the University of California, Davis, for subsidizing the publication of the illustrations for chapter 18; and the staff of ACMRS (the Arizona Center for Medieval and Renaissance Studies) at Arizona State University for its timely help on several aspects of this volume. Stephanie Volf and Irena Praitis invested many hours preparing the bibliography; Ms. Volf undertook the heroic tasks of preparing the index and producing the camera-ready copy; and T. Scott Clapp, Monica von Eggers, and Ann Matchette offered valuable assistance during the final stages of production. Plate 7 in chapter 18, *Beowulf and Nan-Zee,* is reproduced from "Beowulf " No. 3 Copyright © 1975 DC Comics. All rights reserved. Used with permission.

The dedication to this volume acknowledges a master in the field of Old English studies and a friend and valued colleague to nearly every contributor to this book. He is—and will continue to be—deeply missed.

Note: unless indicated otherwise, quotations from *Beowulf* throughout the text are from Klaeber 1950a, while quotations from other Old English poetic texts are from Krapp and Dobbie 1931–53. Except in chapter 4, where slashes are used for metrical notation, a double slash in quotations from the poetry marks line breaks, while a single slash marks the medial caesura.

A Beowulf Handbook

Chapter 1

Introduction

Beowulf, Truth, and Meaning

by John D. Niles

Readers of the poem that we call *Beowulf* are likely to have one desire in common with any seeker after truth: to cut through all misapprehensions in order to come to terms with the thing itself, as it really is. The attempt is as laudable as it is illusory. As soon as one reads a phrase in translation or looks up a single word in a dictionary, one is a participant in a hermeneutic process that is powerful and impersonal enough to subsume any attempt to circumvent it.

The present handbook is based on the premise—an uncontroversial one, since Jauss—that the understanding of a literary work is deeply implicated in its past understandings by prior generations of readers. Just as one cannot know what a word means until one knows what it has meant in the past, one cannot wholly separate a literary work from the meanings it has previously evoked: that is, its entire set of commentaries or glosses (from Greek *glossa*, "tongue"). This notion was readily accepted during the Middle Ages and there is little reason to resist it today. However misguided they may sometimes seem to us, the glosses of prior readers represent the tongues with which the work has spoken over time. There is no way that our own ears can attend to the poem, or our own tongues speak about it, without being affected by the cadences of this discourse.

Not every period has taken part in the making of *Beowulf*, however. Unlike many other masterworks of literature, this poem has had no unbroken history of reading. No one seems to have read it—or if anyone did, then no one left a record of any mental glosses on it—during a period of time extending from the twelfth century, or thereabouts, until the late eighteenth century. If the poem was read before that great hiatus, its reception then remains a mystery to us today. A few features of the manuscript in which the unique copy of the poem is preserved, such as the worn condition of folios 179 and 198, suggest that the poem was indeed read during the years before it fell into disuse, but these signs are subject to varying interpretations. Many scholars have surmised, perhaps on good grounds, that either *Beowulf* or poems resembling it were once performed aloud in some social context, but of such events we have no direct knowledge. For practical purposes, this handbook therefore takes as its subject *Beowulf* as that poem has come to be known since Thorkelin published the first modern edition in 1815.

From Thorkelin's time until now, a new and unintended audience (to use Haarder's name for it) has done its best to learn how to read the poem. *Beowulf* has become the hub of a critical discourse that extends around the world, now facilitated by electronic communications systems as well as by the media of print.[1] As it has been edited, translated, pored over, discussed, illustrated, and read or performed aloud by people in recent times, its features have been scrutinized with an intensity that the original poet and scribe might find odd, were they now in a position to observe it.

Opinions about the poem have kept pace with changing ideas both about the Middle Ages and about the nature and value of literature itself. Study of the critical reception of *Beowulf* can thus lead to instructive lessons in cultural history. Perhaps the main value of such a study is to promote humility on the part of authorities who wish to claim the final word concerning the poem's meaning and artistic effects. In a realm so far removed from the poem's original context, interpretive statements are likely to reveal as much about the interpreter as they do about the "authentic, true" poem, which is bound to remain an inscrutable object of desire. If the history of scholarship is indeed a history of error, as E. G. Stanley has acidly remarked (1975, 122), then it is at least a history that can put us in our place.

I have mentioned the year 1815, when the *editio princeps* of *Beowulf* was published, but the story of the modern interpretation of the poem does not begin then. Even though *Beowulf* played no part in the scholarly recovery of the records of Old English language and literature that began in Tudor England, its reception during the past two centuries can be seen as a development of the intellectual currents of earlier times. Those currents deserve brief notice here.

The text of *Beowulf* survives as the fourth of five vernacular works, three in prose and two in verse, that were copied out by two scribes about the year 1000. We know that the *Beowulf* codex came to light in the later sixteenth century, after the contents of most medieval libraries were scattered during the Dissolution of the Monasteries, for Laurence Nowell, servant to Lord Burghley, wrote his name and the date 1563 at its head. Since the works included in the codex had no bearing on the issues of church government and doctrine that were of pressing concern to Burghley and other men of power, they were not prepared for publication. Most people of Tudor England had little use for their Saxon forebears apart from combing old documents for evidence that could be cited for partisan purposes in contemporary religious debates. As Richard Harvey wrote in 1597, "Let them lye in dead forgetfulnesse like stones."[2]

Still the poem was saved from destruction. The name of the composite codex of which *Beowulf* now forms one part, British Library MS Cotton Vitellius A.xv, reflects its former place in the library of Sir Robert Cotton (1571–1631), where it was shelved as the fifteenth manuscript on the first shelf of a bookcase surmounted by a bust of the Roman emperor Vitellius. In 1700 the Cotton family presented its large collection of medieval manuscripts to the English nation. Humfrey Wanley summarized the poem's contents somewhat erroneously in 1705, not long before the codex narrowly escaped destruction in the Ashburnham House fire of 1731. Eventually, the Cotton collection of manuscripts found a secure home in the library of the British Museum, and visitors to the new British Library in London can now consult, or at least gaze on, the seared leaves on which all modern *Beowulf* scholarship is based. All these facts form part of the mass of "invisible glosses" that people of recent centuries have added to the poem, thereby affecting its reception much as visible glosses do.

Just as the poem played no part in the religious strife of the Reformation, it had no role in the political debates of the seventeenth and eighteenth centuries, when statesmen on both sides of the Atlantic believed they had found in Anglo-Saxon law and social institutions the bases on which a free democratic society could be formed (Hauer 1983; Frantzen 1990, 15–19, 203–7). Thomas Jefferson expressed the belief that the "happy system" of ancient Saxon laws constituted "the wisest and most perfect ever yet devised by the wit of man" (letter of 13 August 1776, quoted by Horsman 1981, 9, 22). Since *Beowulf* had no obvious part in that system, however, the poem remained unread.

Still, seeds for the appreciation of *Beowulf* as a work of art were being sown by the harbingers of the Romantic movement: Thomas Percy with his medievalism and his taste for minstrelsy and runes, Herder with his cult of *Naturpoesie*, Macpherson with his impudent Celtic forgeries. Soon anything that displayed the patina of British antiquity or embodied the purity of nature was prized. When Sharon Turner first called the attention of the scholarly world to *Beowulf* in the second edition of his *History of the Anglo-Saxons* (1807, 2:294), he praised it—somewhat astonishingly, in view of the stony forgetfulness in which it had previously lain—as "the most interesting relic of the Anglo-Saxon poetry which time has suffered us to receive."[3]

"Relic" is a keyword here in its suggestion of an almost religious aura. Antiquarianism and its loftier companion, art, were becoming the centerpieces of a surrogate religion. One of the temples of the new faith was the newly invented museum, then in the process of emerging into the institution as it is known today. Another was the "museum anthology" of literature, such as Percy's *Reliques of Ancient English Poetry* (1763), which served as a display case for antique texts of all description. The Anglo-Saxons were now praised as primitives, rude and somewhat childlike in their manners but of good blood. This primitivism fit in well with the evolutionary spirit of the times. According to the evolutionists, the Anglo-Saxons stood in relation to the modern age as the infant stands in relation to the man. Their poetry was wild and natural. The Middle Ages in general, as "the lost paradise of a simpler era" (Bloch 1990, 43), were gaining increasing attention as a field where nostalgia and fantasy could be indulged and whence art could draw its inspiration.

Nineteenth-century Anglo-Saxon studies received an unintended boost from the French Revolution and the Napoleonic Wars. British, Scandinavian, and German cultural patriotism surged in response to the French military threat. At the same time as scholars in France were discovering *La Chanson de Roland* to be that most coveted of properties, a national epic, and as German scholars were beginning to ascribe the virtues of their national character to the influence of the *Nibelungenlied* and the folktales of the peasantry, English-speaking scholars praised the pure Saxon spirit, bold and incorruptible, that they were quick to discern in such poems as *Beowulf* and *The Battle of Maldon*.

Thorkelin's chief motive for transcribing and publishing *Beowulf* was nationalism: Danish nationalism, to be precise (see Thorkelin 1815b). If scholarly accuracy was his aim, he failed. Superior editions of *Beowulf* were soon published in English, German, and Danish, however. The labors of N. F. S. Gruntvig over five decades of scholarly activity from 1815 to 1861 were of great value in establishing a standard modern text of the poem (see Haarder 1975, 59–88). All nineteenth-century editors and commentators were indebted to the science of historical and comparative linguistics that was being developed by such scholars as Rasmus Rask in Denmark and Jacob Grimm in Germany, in partial reaction to French cultural ambitions. *Beowulf* was now to be studied by correct German methods. It was prized as a work from the pure source of the Germanic race, of whom the English were considered to be one offshoot.

Nationalist biases of this period had a profound effect on the early reception of *Beowulf*, establishing intellectual houses that have remained habitable for the occasional reader despite their shaky foundations. Rather than accepting the poem as an Old English historical fiction dating from the tenth century, as might easily have been done given its language and manuscript context, early scholars took it to be a direct record of the Germanic Heroic Age of the fifth and sixth centuries. Thorkelin believed that the poem was originally composed in Danish, then later translated into Old English. German scholars posited a German original. Somewhat later, Chadwick made repeated efforts to fit the poem into an evolutionary social model according to which epic poetry was the natural expression of a prefeudal Heroic Age. What was of interest to most scholars at this time was the poem's connection to the ancestral *Heimat*. The true poem needed to be rescued from the poor, late Old English record in which it happened to be preserved.

The chapters of this handbook trace many of the quirks of nineteenth- and early twentieth-century *Beowulf* scholarship, with attention also to its many substantial achievements. Some of these quirks are notorious. The poem's Christian passages were effaced as supposed interpolations. The narrative was dissected so as to reveal the separate *Lieder* or "lays" that were believed to constitute its original parts, before the monks got hold of them. The meaning of the poem was sought in the realm of early Germanic mythology rather than in anything pertaining to Anglo-Saxon culture, and the work was mined for traces of pagan belief (Stanley 1975).

Not for some years did this search for a Germanic ur-poem come up emptyhanded. First Brandl (1908a), protesting the erosion of Christian passages, insisted that Christian doctrine and ideals had so infused the body of the poem that they could not be removed without killing the patient. Then Chambers, voicing similar misgivings about attempts to reconstruct an "original, pagan" *Beowulf*, approached the poem as we have it as a coherent work of art, "a production of the Germanic world enlightened by the new faith" (1921: 1959, 128). Patient research by Klaeber into the religious language of the poem (1911a, 1911b, 1912) demonstrated how thoroughly *Beowulf* participates in the devotional mode that is characteristic of almost all extant Old English literature. The publication of Klaeber's edition of the poem in 1922, with subsequent revised publication in 1928, 1936, 1941, and 1950, put a seal on a consensus that now seems as bland as toast, although occasional voices are still heard in dissent: that the work is a unified Old English heroic poem infused with Christian ideals.

Beginnings are never "merely given, or simply available," as Edward Said has remarked. "They have to be made for each project in such a way as to *enable* what follows from them" (1978, 16). Bypassing earlier scholarship, critics of the past fifty years have generally traced the current era of *Beowulf* studies back to 1936, when J. R. R. Tolkien published his eloquent and incisive essay "*Beowulf*: The Monsters and the Critics."

Tolkien's essay—actually more a midlife crisis for *Beowulf* criticism than a beginning—soon became a point of departure for scholars approaching the poem as an aesthetic unity endowed with spiritual significance. Tolkien saw the monster fights and the elegiac mood of *Beowulf* as expressive of the artistic designs of a deep thinker, religiously enlightened, who let his mind play over a lost heroic world of the imagination. In short, the author was a man like Tolkien himself, as we can say in retrospect. In his emphasis on the poet's melancholic vision and the characters' heroic fatalism, Tolkien finessed rather than superseded the dominant concerns of German Romanticism. To those qualities he added an idea that was just as dear to Romantic poets as it was to Homeric scholarship, which by the 1930s had taken a Unitarian turn: the notion of the individual poet as hero. One of Tolkien's legacies to *Beowulf* scholarship, as George Clark has remarked (1990, 8–13), is the myth of the poet as brooding intellectual, poised between a dying pagan world and a nascent Christian one. Tolkien's *Beowulf* may not be the same as the *Beowulf* of the Anglo-Saxons, but if not, it is a noble surrogate.

In the decades from the 1940s to the 1980s, criticism of *Beowulf* tended to take one of three scholarly directions, all of them philological in their foundations: the aesthetic, the patristic, and the oral-formulaic. Influential studies representative of each approach are discussed in the following chapters, but a brief overview may still be helpful here.

Aesthetic criticism tends to be formalist in its epistemology, for it is based on the reasonable assumption that the meaning of any statement depends partly if not largely on the way that that statement is made. Aesthetic criticism thus foregrounds questions of form, structure, tone, and style to the exclusion of other concerns. In North America, Old English scholarship of an aesthetic orientation developed in sometimes uneasy alliance with the New Criticism that dominated literary studies during the mid-twentieth century. One tendency of this approach was to de-historicize Old English literature and free its understanding from issues that pertain to ideology and personality. What mattered was the text, the whole text, and nothing but the text. Another tendency was to distinguish literary texts from subliterary ones (two categories that do not quite correspond to anything in Anglo-Saxon thought), to concentrate attention on poetry at the expense of prose, and to privilege elegy and epic over other poetic genres. A third tendency has been to search for multiple meanings, ironies, and ambiguities in a poetic work, with the tacit understanding that two meanings are better than one. An impressive amount of recent *Beowulf* criticism has started from the principle that a complex and unified work of art, or one that questions its own authority, is aesthetically superior to a transparent or disjointed one. Criticism of this kind tends to declare its mission accomplished when it finds evidence of complexity, tension, and hard-won structural unity in the poem, which is then found worthy of still closer aesthetic scrutiny.

Patristic criticism has tended to eschew such methods so as to concentrate on a single quest: to read the poem allegorically within the context of the writings of the Fathers. In practice, the usual method of patristic criticism has been to take up striking images from the text and relate them, via customary modes of exegesis, to one or more ecclesiastical sources. When source hunting has not been pursued as an end in itself, it has had the aim of disclosing how a privileged and, as it sometimes seems, an arcane theological system underlies what appear to be innocent details of the text, lending them symbolic or allegorical force. Patristic criticism has sometimes been attacked for being a machine that stamps out the same product, a coin whose two sides spell *caritas* and *cupiditas*, regardless of what kind of metal is fed into it. An excursus into patristics is always illuminating in itself, but the question may arise, Is the result of this inquiry something that functions in the poem in an integrated way, or is it a supertextual feature that pertains to intellectual history? Anything in either literature or life yields images that, when taken in isolation, can be analyzed in terms made familiar by patristic exegesis. Impatient scholars have therefore sometimes dismissed such exegesis as insensitive to the poem's literal meaning or as pursuing tangents that have little to do with literature at all; and yet in medieval aesthetics, symbolism is not only an omnipresent feature of the universe, it also sometimes gains force from its oddity. According to Pseudo-Dionysus, as Eco has remarked, "it was precisely the incongruity of a symbol that made it palpable and stimulating" (1986, 55). If one's world is a forest of symbols, then why not a symbolic *Beowulf*?

Oral-formulaic approaches to *Beowulf* have had one thing in common with patristic ones: the desire to stage a jailbreak from the prison house of the text of the New Criticism, with its strategies of interpretive confinement. For practitioners of either oral-formulaic or patristic criticism, what matters is not the isolated text but its literary tradition. This they have tended to hypostatize as something that either creates individual works or gives them the chief interest that they have. Drawing on the research of Parry (1980) and Lord (1960) into the techniques of Homeric composition, oral-formulaicists developed a theory of the poem's composition in performance. According to this view, the *Beowulf* poet was a gifted singer who made fluent use of formulaic phrases, set themes, and familiar plots to shape his narrative in the heat of oral delivery, much as skilled singers in the Balkans and elsewhere have been shown to do in recent times. Once again, as with Müllenhoff's *Liedertheorie* (1889) and Tolkien's unitarianism, Old English scholarship has blown with the wind of powerful work in the classics. Even though the oral-formulaic theory as stated by Magoun is an idea whose time has come and gone, research into the intersecting realms of medieval orality and textuality continues to offer insights into the hybrid culture that produced *Beowulf* and other Old English poems (see O'Brien O'Keeffe 1990; Doane and Pasternack 1991). Interest among critics has gradually shifted away from the originary moment of composition of a poem so as to engage more fully with what Peter Brooks aptly calls "the oral in the written" (1994, 76): that is, the residual imprint of oral techniques or oral-traditional modes of thought on works that were written out pen in hand. The question is worth raising if *Beowulf* is not a *tertium quid*: a new kind of literature, corresponding neither to usual literary standards nor to the norms of oral performance, that comes into being when people set out to make a textual record of a poem that would otherwise remain unwritten (Niles 1993c).

In sum, scholarly approaches to *Beowulf* over the past fifty years reveal an unresolved controversy as to how the poem is to be read. Some scholars—the formalists, we might call them—tend to read the poem's effects as essentially artistic. They have exhibited the poem's structural or stylistic features as admirable achievements that are worth knowing about for their own sake. Other scholars—the Christologers, they have somewhat uncharitably been called—have searched out sources for the poem in the literature of the Latin Middle Ages and have seen typology and allegory as keys to its meaning. Like the formalists, they assume that *Beowulf* was composed by a gifted individual author. In addition, they do not hesitate to identify this person as a monk or cleric writing for doctrinal ends. Still other readers—we might call them the neotraditionalists, to borrow a term from Menéndez Pidal (1959)—tend to see the poem as one outcome or expression of an Anglo-Saxon poetic tradition that had evolved, by the poet's day, to incorporate both Latinate learning and Germanic lore. They tend to look upon *Beowulf* the way that a geologist examines metamorphic rock: as containing elements of diverse origin that were fused into a complex amalgam through unknown heat and pressures acting upon an individual poet. They tend to read *Beowulf* less ironically than the formalists, more literally than the Christologers. If they find symbolism at work in the poem, then they see it expressed through culturally deep imagery, perhaps of ancient origin, that here operates within a Christian context.

Sometimes loosely coinciding with this controversy and sometimes cutting across it is a debate about ethics and values. Many readers have perceived a "great divide" between the poet's perspective and that of the characters in the poem. The effect of this gulf is to ironize the action and undercut the heroic ideals by which a hero like Beowulf lives and dies. This has been perhaps the dominant strain of twentieth-century *Beowulf* criticism from Tolkien to Fred C. Robinson (1985), who has taken this argument toward what would seem to be its limits. But critical consensus along these lines has never been firm. On one hand, not all religiously oriented readers see Beowulf as a flawed hero. Some see him as admirable, even as a figure meant to recall the Christian savior (e.g., Klaeber 1950a, li; McNamee 1960a). On the other hand, neotraditionalist scholars—including in this category such people as Irving (1989), Niles (1983), G. Clark (1990), and John Hill (1995)—tend to hold that the heroic world of the poem offers models for conduct in the world that the audience inhabited. Such scholars tend to see the poem's melancholy mood as part of a meditation on a world that is by its nature subject to violence, mutability, and death.

Surely there is merit in all these views, as incompatible as they may seem. For the *Beowulf* poet, the heroic past was both a grand and a terrible world. The poet depicts a kind of Germanic Old Dispensation, a time analogous to the fabled past of Old Testament history. Those were the days when mighty kings and heroes dwelling in the exotic lands of the Northeast vied with one another for fame, lavishing hospitality on one another, pursuing feuds to the utmost, and occasionally venturing their strength and courage in combat against giants and demonic monsters, watched over by the eyes of God. If the poet encourages the members of his audience to look upon the heroic past with awe, he also gives them reason to be thankful that they were not part of it.

There is little reason to suppose that during the next fifty years the reception of *Beowulf* will cease from its restless movement. No major part of the canon is likely to remain unaffected by the potent forces that are transforming humanistic studies at the present time. The scholarly understanding of *Beowulf* has already been affected by major trends in late twentieth-century thought. Widespread reflection on a social order that is becoming ever more pluralistic and multicultural has shifted attention toward *Beowulf* as a site for debate concerning ethnic or national identity, whether during the Anglo-Saxon period or in more recent times. In keeping with this trend, a growing self-consciousness as to how the current intellectual disciplines have emerged over time (see Foucault 1972; Graff 1987; Frantzen 1990) has encouraged research into the relation of *Beowulf* studies to socially-embedded phenomena such as aestheticism, medievalism, nationalism, and canon formation.

Surely these trends will continue. In particular, I suspect, Anglo-Saxonists will increasingly be attracted to the methods of what might be called literary anthropology. In a manner that has not been seen before, *Beowulf* will be found to have a relation to the discourses of power of a society whose institutions were very different from our own, and those discourses will be seen to be bound up in the whole text-making enterprise. Old English scholars will find reason to reject a simple cause and effect relation between literature and social forms. Instead, they will accept that everything in culture and society is knit together in a complex web of interdependency. When one pulls on even the smallest thread of this fabric, the whole structure vibrates. If one task of Old English scholarship will be to analyze how literary works like *Beowulf* created the culture by which they were created (cf. Montrose 1988, 56), another will be to investigate how, through a large system of education, such works continue to help shape the present-day culture that calls them to mind as past artifacts.

In short, future *Beowulf* studies are likely to reflect an increasing self-consciousness about both the historicity of Anglo-Saxon scholarship and the theoretical underpinnings of literary scholarship in general. However user-unfriendly the language of critical theory may sometimes be, however obscurantist its practitioners may sometimes take pleasure in being, the issues that it addresses will not go away. Scholars who resist theory in the name of empiricism, objectivity, or common sense run the risk of ignoring the fact that empiricism is itself a theory, while pure objectivity would be nice if it could be had. As for common sense, what it often boils down to is a refuge for people too impatient to search out the intellectual ground on which they stand.

The result of this self-reflective criticism will be to cast doubt on anyone's claim to have the power to name *the* meaning of *Beowulf*. To adapt a phrase from Geertz (1988, 141), there will be less of a pretense of seeing the poem as it really is, when only God is looking.[4] Rather than approaching the poem as if it were a hard thing whose meaning is apparent from certain fixed properties, we will be more apt to accept it as something more yielding: a text (from Latin *textum*, "a woven thing, web") whose appearance varies depending on how the light strikes it. As Eco has remarked, a text necessarily represents a complex set of filiations, "a network of different messages depending on different codes and working at different levels of signification" (1979, 5).[5] As scholars approach the poem in this way, they may find that it again takes on the guise it had a thousand years ago, when for its listeners (if my guess is correct and the poem did have listeners) it was not a document at all but rather a diaphanous fabric of words, a shimmering web of multiple significances.[6]

Shimmering web? Multiple significances? "This all sounds very Californian," I hear a voice say from somewhere farther east. "So you think that *Beowulf* can mean what any undergraduate says it means? Or have you set your feet against interpretation altogether?"

No, and no. What I wish to say is that the "meaning" of *Beowulf* may not be the most important thing about it. In time, I suspect, the quest for meaning in literary works may take on an almost quaintly period-specific look, as a phenomenon that was particularly characteristic of mid-twentieth-century critical moves. Other questions about literature, particularly ones that address its social functions, may come to appear just as important as "meaning" has been in the recent past. They may largely constitute meaning, in fact, as that term will come to be understood.

I do not think we can set the clock back to a time when literary meaning is taken to be something "out there," fully cooked and ready to be served. Instead, I expect that readers of *Beowulf* will conceive of meaning as something that darts and shifts at the convergence of two things: a source of information and an interpreter. Just as a person resides in the world he or she hopes to understand, a reader resides, temporarily, in the text that he or she reads. If specialized scholarship has a mission, it is to help readers deepen their knowledge and sharpen their perceptions of *every possible factor* that can have a bearing on the understanding of texts and readerly events. Such factors are virtually infinite. Our perceptions are only what they can be, given that we are historically conditioned human beings who are the products of a specific process of cultural evolution. So there is obviously work still to be done.

Then no: I am not speaking "against interpretation." It was not a Californian but a New Yorker who coined that phrase, anyway.[7] Nor do I suggest that every freshman should be given the same respect as E. G. Stanley (1963) or Stanley Greenfield (1985) when it comes to identifying the meaning of "soðfæstra dom." People earn credibility in these affairs through the sum total of their scholarship. Still, not even experienced scholars have a monopoly on good judgment—least of all, the present writer. Views will change and schools will drop out of favor, and soon every freshman may rightly view as comic many opinions that are now held dear.

So if respected critics disagree? Then they disagree. Their conflicting judgments are among the multiple significances to which I have referred. When two expert critics meet head on with neither one giving up ground, then the likelihood is strong that the reading that each one advocates has a basis in the text, that shimmering thing, as well as being historically conditioned as a product of its own time. Furthermore, we may reasonably suppose that some disagreements among current critics had their counterparts among members of the poem's original audiences as well. After all, why would a thegn's understanding of this poem tally with a monk's? A king's with a ceorl's? A man's with a woman's? A jaded old man's with a hotheaded boy's? A Dane's with a Saxon's? If the modern reception of *Beowulf* sometimes more closely resembles a kennel of yapping dogs than a massed chorale, then this lack of unison is understandable given that polyphony is an outstanding feature of the poem itself. Is Hrothgar's wisdom, the wisdom of old age and philosophical reflection, the same as the wisdom of Beowulf, who is never happy unless some high action is afoot? Is Beowulf's wisdom the same as that of Wiglaf, who regrets that his king did not leave ill enough alone? And none of these voices is autonomous. All are the work of our arch-ventriloquist, the narrator, who seems equally sympathetic to each point of view while at the same time he remains in possession of a superior wisdom grounded in both hindsight and Christian doctrine.[8] Some people, following Bakhtin (1981), may think that polyglossia went out of fashion in literature composed between late antiquity and the Renaissance. If so, they have not read *Beowulf*.

The future of *Beowulf* studies, I suspect, will not belong to those who just read the text, in the narrow sense of interpreting it. It will lie with those who also use and take pleasure in it, adapting it to their own purposes in the world in which they live, as the poet's own listeners and readers surely did. A reluctance to offer flat judgments about what *Beowulf* means may offer cold comfort to undergraduates needing to know what to write in their exam books; but in the long run, such diffidence may enhance the power of this work to speak past the ages and bring new readers under its spell of woe and wonder.

Notes

1. Many Anglo-Saxonists are linked now by ANSAXNET, a list-serve group on the Internet, and have the developing electronic facsimile of the *Beowulf* manuscript available to them on the World Wide Web (Kiernan 1993–). For a complete list of *Beowulf* publications to the end of 1972, see Greenfield and Robinson (1980, 25–197), supplementing Fry's well-indexed bibliography (1969). Short (1980a) offers a selective, chronologically arranged, annotated bibliography of *Beowulf* studies to 1978; Hasenfratz (1993), from 1978 to 1990. Hasenfratz (1994) brings the list of publications on the poem up to date, from 1979 to 1994, in his online, non-annotated bibliography. The early critical reception of *Beowulf* has been traced discursively by Haarder (1975), the more recent critical reception by Short (1980b) and G. Clark (1990, 1–25). Stanley (1981b) offers some useful supplementary perceptions.

2. Richard Harvey, *Philadelphus, or a Defence of Brutes, and the Brutans History* (London, 1593), p. 97, as quoted by Glass (1982, 91).

3. Turner, *History* (1807, 2:294), as quoted by Payne (1982, 164 n. 34).

4. Geertz here speaks of anthropologists looking at the world. His phrase could apply equally well to historians looking at history or literary scholars looking at a poem. Mitchell has recently made the same point in his own way. In speaking of "the folly of the idea that such a poem can have one 'meaning'"— a folly that he sees as based on the untenable assumption that the poem had only one kind of audience—he declares himself prepared for a multiplicity of interpretations: "What I cannot tolerate is the insistence that *this* is *the* meaning of *Beowulf*" (1988, 41–42).

5. Similarly, Chase calls attention to the possible coexistence of competing systems of value in a single work or a single person, "where they can, and will, produce dilemmas and tensions, but . . . one need not be invoked as a norm by which the other must be judged" (1985, 46).

6. The tactile metaphor here is familiar in the language of artistic expression from ancient times to the present: in the words of Cynewulf, "I *wove* [the song] with cunning verbal arts" (*wordcræftum wæf*, *Elene* 1237).

7. Susan Sontag spent a year at the University of California, Berkeley, but only a year (1948–49).

8. Pursuing the connection between literature and criticism, one might ask: Does the writer of literary history, or does the author of a synthesizing chapter such as the present one, not inevitably take on the role of such an arch-ventriloquist, modulating the voices of other speakers—here, other scholars and critics of various historical periods—into a single unitary discourse? Ideally such a person writes "in

possession of a superior wisdom grounded in hindsight," but more likely one hopes in vain for some vantage point that stands above or apart from the unfolding process that is being studied.

Chapter 2

Date, Provenance, Author, Audiences

by Robert E. Bjork and Anita Obermeier

Summary: Suggestions for when *Beowulf* was composed range from 340 to 1025, with ca. 515–530 and 1000 being almost universally acknowledged as the possible extremes. An early consensus favored ca. 650–800, but current thinking is balanced between roughly this view and the late ninth to early tenth centuries. Scholars have tried to specify provenance (Denmark, Germany, Anglia, Wessex), most preferring Northumbria or Mercia; they still debate whether the author, who remains anonymous despite sporadic attempts to discover his identity, was a layperson or cleric; and controversy continues as to the nature (e.g., secular or monastic) and number of the poem's audience or audiences.

Chronology

1815: Grímur Jónsson Thorkelin, first editor of the poem, asserts in his introduction that the author was an eyewitness to the deeds of Beowulf and presented the eulogy at Beowulf's funeral. The poem was composed, therefore, after 340, the year Thorkelin claims for Beowulf's death. Thorkelin also argues that the author and audience were Danish (1815b).

1817: N. F. S. Grundtvig identifies Hygelac as the Chochilaicus (d. 515–530) mentioned by Gregory of Tours. Identification implies a date after 550.

1820: Grundtvig, arguing for a date around 700, also suggests a companion of Cædmon or Aldhelm as author.

1826: John Josias Conybeare argues that the poem as we have it was written by a bard in the court of Cnut (1016–35) but attributes the original poem to the eighth or even seventh centuries.

1840: Ludwig Ettmüller dates the poem in the eighth century and proposes a Scandinavian source as well as multiple authorship.

1841: Grundtvig identifies "merewioingas" (2921) as "Merovingian."

1849: Joseph Bachlechner argues that "merewioingas" suggests 752 as the latest possible date for the poem, since the Carolingian line replaced the Merovingian then, and the poet probably would not refer to a dynasty long after it had fallen.

1862: C. W. M. Grein considers *Beowulf* a coherent work by one poet.

1869: Karl Müllenhoff, applying Lachmann's *Liedertheorie* (ballad theory) to *Beowulf*, concludes that it began as four independent lays, put together with interpolations before the time of Cædmon (657–680).

1883: Hermann Möller argues that *Beowulf 's* initial poetic form was a four-line stanza and claims that nonstanzaic parts are more recent interpolations. He dates the poem in the ninth, tenth, or eleventh centuries.

1883: Frederik Rönning, examining stylistic, historical, and linguistic details in the poem, rejects *Liedertheorie,* suggests the late eighth century as the date, Northumbria as the provenance, and a cleric as the author.

1884: Thomas Krüger examines the poem's historical and mythological background, backs Müllenhoff about six authors and a late seventh-century date.

1886–97: Gregor Sarrazin proposes that *Beowulf* was translated from a Danish original probably composed or reworked by Starkathr around 700 at Lejre, the Danish court of Ingeld. Argues that Cynewulf translated the poem and interpolated Christian material after writing *Christ A* and *B* but before *Elene* and *Andreas*.

1886: Eduard Sievers examines the thirty-six Scandinavian loan words cited by Sarrazin as proof for a Danish original and rejects thirty-four as either extant in Anglo-Saxon poetry or prose or part of a common Germanic heritage.

1888: Bernhard ten Brink elaborates Müllenhoff's conclusions and places the final redaction of the poem in Mercia in the eighth century.

1892: John Earle posits 775–800 as the date because of the Offa episode, lines 1931–62. Poem is therefore a political allegory for Offa's son, Ecgferth, by Archbishop Hygeberht of Lichfield.

1906: Lorenz Morsbach dates the poem to shortly after 700 on linguistic grounds (loss of final *u* after long root syllables and of postconsonantal *h* before vowels).

1912: Arguing mainly from the religious allusions in the poem, H. Chadwick postulates that the poem existed in its "full epic form" well before 650 and was later reworked by a Christian poet.

1917, 1923: Levin Schücking, on the basis of historical context, suggests 890–900 as the date, the Danish court in England as the provenance, since the poem is thoroughly Danish in orientation.

1920: F. Liebermann argues for a date of 725 and speculates that the poem could have been written at the court of Cuthburg, sister of King Ine of Wessex, queen of Northumbria and later abbess of Wimborne.

1922: Friederich Klaeber (1922a) claims a unified work by one poet, perhaps at Aldfrith's court.

1935: Ritchie Girvan argues for a 680–700 date in Northumbria on the basis of linguistic, historical, cultural evidence.

1935: W. A. Berendsohn offers an analysis of the poem similar to ten Brink's. Supports an eighth-century date. Last proponent of *Liedertheorie.*

1936: Alois Brandl, reading the poem as political allegory, dates it to the reign of Wiglaf of Mercia (827–838).

1937: C. C. Batchelor, discerning traces of Pelagianism in the poem, argues that it could not have been written much later than 705.

1943: George Bond, on the basis of onomastic evidence, links *Beowulf* to events in the reign of Beornwulf, 823–826, and Wiglaf, 828–838, of Mercia.

1948: Sune Lindqvist, on the basis of the Sutton Hoo discovery, argues for a date of ca. 700 and contends that the poem was written to honor a line of the royal Swedish house that descended from Wiglaf in the poem.

1951: Dorothy Whitelock suggests ca. 775–800, perhaps in the court of Offa of Mercia. Poem must be pre-835, when Viking raids began in full force.

1953: C. L. Wrenn suggests a pre-750 date because of what he says is an archaic instrumental, "wundini" (which is actually "wundum" or "wundnum," 1382).

1957: Robert Reynolds sees a connection between *Beowulf* and the *Wonders of the East* and argues for a tenth-century date (late ninth at the earliest).

1958,1963: Francis P. Magoun Jr. arguing for the presence of "an anthologizing scribe," distinguishes authors for three parts of poem: A (1–2199), A' (2009b–2176), B (2200–end).

1961–62: Gösta Langenfelt, arguing that the Scandinavian historical elements in the poem could not have been known in England before the late eighth century, posits an early ninth-century date.

1963: Paull F. Baum suggests that the poet was a "serious and gifted poet, steeped in the older pagan tradition from the continent." He mentions, but immediately discounts, the possibility of female authorship.

1966: Robert P. Creed (1966b) refutes multiple authorship, tries to explain Magoun's A' by suggesting a scribe wrote the epic down during performance.

1970: Arthur G. Brodeur attacks Magoun's (1958, 1963) theory of multiple authorship. Finds no evidence for the discrepancies Magoun asserts.

1977: Nicolas Jacobs, disputing Whitelock's theory, argues for a late ninth-, early tenth-century date.

1978: Patrick Wormald, exploring the historical and cultural backgrounds of the poem, argues for an eighth-century date, a clerical author.

1980: Richard J. Schrader hypothesizes that the *Beowulf* poet was a monk trained in the classical rhetorical tradition of Bede and that the poem is part of a literary tradition going back to Virgil.

1980: Louise E. Wright argues that "merewioingas" refers to Merovech, the legendary founder of the Merovingians identified in a chronicle not known in England before 751. The word supports a date after 751.

1981: Kevin Kiernan (1981a) posits two poems about Beowulf with the author of the second being the final redactor of the unified whole, ca. 1016–25.

1981: Ashley Crandall Amos casts doubt on the reliability of any of the linguistic or metrical criteria proposed for dating Old English poetry.

1981: Contributors to *The Dating of Beowulf* review many kinds of evidence for dating. Among them Thomas Cable, E. G. Stanley, Colin Chase, Walter Goffart, Alexander Murray, R. I. Page, Roberta Frank, and Kevin Kiernan either argue for a date later than the eighth century, an audience as late as the eleventh, or leave open those possibilities.

1981: W. G. Busse and R. Holtei, on the basis of historical criteria, chiefly the problem of loyal behavior to one's lord, date the preserved version of the poem to the reign of Ethelred (978–1016) and define the audience as Ethelred's thanes.

1981: David Dumville argues that there is no historical evidence to align date of manuscript and composition and that the poem has a monastic context.

1981: Patricia Poussa revives Schücking's argument for a date in the tenth century and an audience in the Danelaw.

1982: Frederic G. Cassidy proposes that the poet was a monk writing for a monastic audience; he was tolerated because of his "scholarly eminence."

1982: Horst Weinstock seconds Cassidy, opts for a later date, and theorizes that the poet might have written the epic for a monastic community engaged in missionary work to the Continental Saxons.

1982: Robert T. Farrell surveys Scandinavian contact with England 400–1000, concludes the poem was most probably composed in eighth-century East Anglia.

1982: Roberta Frank in one article finds that the poet's synthesis of religious and heroic idealism reflects attitudes current in the tenth century but not before. In another she argues that various Nordicisms in the poem point to a late ninth- or early tenth-century origin.

1982: Michael Lapidge, showing direct and indirect connections among *Beowulf*, Aldhelm's Wessex, and the *Liber Monstrorum*, suggests that the poem could have been composed in pre-Conquest Wessex.

1982: Michael Swanton, arguing that the poem reflects two systems of kingship, finds that the transitional period of the late eighth century is the most likely time of composition.

1983: John D. Niles argues that the poet's ambiguous depiction of the Danes fits in well with the hypothesis of a tenth-century date.

1985: Janet Bately, reviewing spelling patterns in the poem, concludes that it probably cannot be dated later than the early tenth century. An examination of "siþþan" in the poem supports the single-author theory.

1986: Karl Schneider, noting the transitional nature of the Christianity in the poem, dates it to 640–650 and places it in the court of Penda the Mercian. The poet "may be identical" with Widsith.

1986: Zacharias P. Thundy posits that the poem was written between 924 and 931 by Wulfgar, a retainer of King Athelstan.

1988: David Dumville, on paleographical grounds, dates the manuscript to the early eleventh century, not to the reign of Cnut.

1989: Audrey Meaney reviews the elements of the Scyld Scefing prologue to the poem and doubts that they came together before the early tenth century; she accepts the possibility that the *Beowulf* manuscript represents various layers of composition.

1990: Alfred Bammesberger reexamines *Beowulf* 1382a, "wundnum" and its suggested variants, as a means of dating the poem and concludes that it does not illuminate the dating question.

1992: R. D. Fulk applies Kaluza's law to the poem and maintains that *Beowulf* was most probably composed before 725 if Mercian in origin or before 825 if Northumbrian. Evidence favors Mercian origin.

1993: Sam Newton, on the basis of genealogical, orthographic, lexical, phonological, and archaeological evidence, argues that the poem may have been composed in eighth-century East Anglia for an audience of Danish extraction or familiarity with the East-Anglian Danish heritage.

1993: Niles (1993a) argues that the poem may reflect West Saxon politics and ideology during the period of nation building in the tenth century.

1993: Niles (1993c) posits that the text of *Beowulf* came into being as the result of a commissioned event (an "oral poetry act") staged by a patron for the benefit of a textual community.

"[It] will be clear to anyone," asserts Grímur Jónsson Thorkelin in his introduction to the first edition of *Beowulf* in 1815, that "our poem of the Scyldings is indeed Danish" despite its coming down to us in an Old English translation. The nameless Danish skald who originally wrote the poem "was an eyewitness to the exploits of kings Hrothgar, Beowulf, and Hygelac, and was the eulogizer at Beowulf's funeral," which Thorkelin unflinchingly fixes at 340, his earliest possible date for the poem's composition (Thorkelin 1815b). Though unequivocal, Thorkelin's contentions are demonstrably wrong or decidedly moot, mere curious footnotes to the whole bewildering debate about perhaps the most vexing problems in *Beowulf* scholarship: when was the poem composed, where, by whom, for whom?

Scholars responded quickly to Thorkelin. The first Danish reviewer (probably Peter Erasmus Müller in 1815) questioned Danish provenance for the poem and guessed at a date between the end of the seventh and the beginning of the eighth centuries (Cooley 1940, 51). The German Nicolaus Outzen claimed German provenance and intuited a date later than the fourth century because of the poem's Christian allusions and literary excellence (1816, 321). And the Dane N. F. S. Grundtvig (1817, 284–88) identified Hygelac in the poem with the historical figure Chochilaicus, the king mentioned by Gregory of Tours as having been slain in Frisia on a raid, probably between 515 and 530. The poem, therefore, had to be written in the sixth century or after. Grundtvig later suggested, in fact, that it was composed around 700, during what he thought to be the great flowering of Anglo-Saxon literature, probably by a companion of Cædmon or Aldhelm (1820, xxvii–viii). Independent of Grundtvig, John Josias Conybeare (1826, 156–57) corroborated this idea, at least in part. The original poem, he thought, probably did come from the eighth or even seventh century since, among other things, the poet displays such an intimate knowledge of Jutland before the eighth century. But the poem as we have it was probably produced by a bard in the court of Cnut (1016–35). Only then would the exploits of a Danish hero, which Conybeare believed Beowulf to be, have been popular in England.

What Grundtvig and Conybeare have provided us (the latter unwittingly) are the *terminus a quo* and *terminus ad quem* for dating *Beowulf*. The epic had to originate between the death of Hygelac and the date of the manuscript itself, which most scholars place at ca. 1000 and which could conceivably fall in the reign of Cnut (see N. Ker 1968, 45–46). Conybeare also raised for us—again unwittingly—a fifth perplexing question about the poem's genesis, and that is, What exactly are we trying to date? Is it the poem as preserved in the manuscript or some urtext, in whatever form or forms, that lies buried or dispersed in the Continental, Scandinavian, or Anglo-Saxon past?[1]

The early history of scholarship on these problems suggests the relatively unsystematized way investigators approach them, but as the history develops, the argument resolves into distinct, interrelated categories. Dating the poem by means of external and internal evidence can lead to knowledge of its provenance; knowledge of its date and provenance allows speculation about who may have written the poem and for whom. This chapter takes up these issues in turn.

I. Date and Provenance

Dating and locating the poem, impossible tasks, are nevertheless the simplest of the four and essential for approaching the questions of authorship and audience. Scholars have marshaled at least seven different kinds of evidence to try to place *Beowulf* in history and geography: (*a*) sources and analogues, (*b*) archaeology, (*c*) history, (*d*) literary history, (*e*) manuscript studies, (*f*) genealogies, and (*g*) linguistics, which itself has several categories.

(*a, b*) Sources and analogues and archaeology are examined in detail elsewhere in this handbook (chapters 7 and 15), so only two points need to be raised here. Although analogues tell us little about date, they do demonstrate that the Scandinavian material in *Beowulf* "is not derived from, nor influenced by, any known Northern tradition" (Newton 1993, 25) and the poem, therefore, is most probably "a peculiarly English expression" of the Germanic material (Andersson 1983, 300). Archaeological evidence, on the other hand, which is by no means conclusive because of the vague descriptions of artifacts in the poem, supports the possibility that the poem may have been composed as early as the seventh (more probably the eighth) but as late as the tenth century. The date of *Beowulf,* therefore, can be generally set in eighth- to-tenth-century England, assuming, of course, that the poem is a unified whole by a single author.

(*c*) For a more precise sense of when and where the poem was composed, scholars have turned to history. One particular reference in the poem has attracted the most attention for this purpose, "merewioingas" (2921, the sole appearance of the word in Old English poetry or prose). In 1841, N. F. S. Grundtvig conjectured that the word means "Merovingian" (497, 509), and, in 1849, Joseph Bachlechner, who is always credited with the identification, argued that the allusion suggests that the poem could not have been composed after 752 when the Carolingian line replaced the Merovingian. The poet, he reasoned, would not refer to a dynasty long after it had fallen. Some scholars (e.g., Liebermann 1920, 267; Chambers 1921, 487; Brandl 1929, 182) accepted the identification as proof of an early eighth-century date. Others, such as Friedrich Klaeber, did not. He stated that "no absolutely definite chronological information can be derived" from the mention of the Merovingian dynasty since the use of the name could have "continued in tradition even after" the dynasty's fall (1950a, cviii). Although Louise E. Wright implicitly agreed about the name's continued use, she disagreed about its value for dating the poem. She offered a convincing argument that "merewioingas" refers to Merovech, the legendary founder of the Merovingians uniquely identified in a chronicle not known in England before 751. The allusion, therefore, "can be used to fix, not a *terminus ad quem,* but rather a *terminus a quo*" and *Beowulf* can be dated "as late as the early ninth century" (2, 5). The reference could support a still later date, since Klaeber's observation about tradition applies to Wright's argument as well as Bachlechner's. "Merewioingas," therefore, helps little in specifying the poem's date.

Apart from focusing on this one allusion in the poem, scholars have employed three broad, overlapping historical approaches: searching for the source or justification for one or more element of the poem in external history; exploring periods of cultural transition and their possible presence in the poem; and reading the poem as political allegory. These approaches typically presuppose one of four periods and places of power and culture capable of supporting the production of such a sophisticated work of art as *Beowulf* is: seventh-century East Anglia (the age of Sutton Hoo), late seventh- to early eighth-century Northumbria (the age of Bede, 675–725), late eighth-century Mercia (the reign of Offa, 757–96), and ninth- to tenth-century England (the Danelaw and "English England"). Eleventh-century England (the reign of Cnut, 1016–35) has also been proposed.

The first, most amorphous approach embraces a wide range of considerations. In 1861, for example, noticing the similarity of word forms in *Beowulf* and "the Northumbrian monuments and the Durham Ritual," Daniel H. Haigh placed the composition of the poem in Northumbria and stated that "all the events [the poet] records, with two exceptions, occurred in this island, and most of them in Northumbria, during the fifth and sixth centuries" (3–4). The Dane Frederik Rönning in 1883 and the German Felix Liebermann in 1920 also argued for Northumbrian provenance. Rönning examined dialect features of the poem (91–98) and traced the path of the Scandinavian material in it from Sweden and Denmark to the north of England, where (he claims) the Grendel legend left its greatest mark (106). He concluded that the tale of the Gothic hero Beowulf originated in southern Sweden, then migrated either directly or with the Angles to northern England, where it was reworked into an epic whole by a Northumbrian poet, perhaps in the eighth century (107).[2] Liebermann argued for a more specific date, 725, speculating that the epic could have been written at the court of Cuthburg, sister of King Ine of Wessex, queen of Northumbria and later abbess of Wimborne. The social structure reflected in the poem fits that date better than it does a later date (267), and no historical evidence in the poem points to a date after 725 (270).

Likewise arguing for Northumbrian provenance is Ritchie Girvan, who in 1935 showed "a close correspondence between seventh-century conditions in Northumbria and the poem both in the material and intellectual side" (51). On the basis of linguistic and cultural evidence as well, Girvan set the date of composition between 680 and 700 (25). In 1937, while not arguing for provenance, C. C. Batchelor discerned traces of Pelagianism in the poem's vocabulary and therefore claimed that the epic could not have been written much later than 705, when the reign of Aldfrith ended and Aldfrith's opposition to "Roman formalism" was replaced by faith in Augustinian predestination (332). Dorothy Whitelock, however, stated in 1951 that we may look too readily to Bede's Northumbria for the origin of the poem and suggested that there are other possibilities, such as the court of Offa of Mercia, ca. 775–800, which would have been a fitting arena for the sophisticated Christian poet and audience that the poem requires (63). She was convinced that the epic must come from before 835, when Viking raids began in full force with ensuing deep Anglo-Saxon resentment of Scandinavians (25–26).

Scholars before and after Whitelock who concerned themselves with the poem's Scandinavian content have reached varied conclusions about it and its bearing upon the date. Gösta Langenfelt (1962, 34) posited an early ninth-century date, using Whitelock's findings and arguing that the Scandinavian historical elements in the poem could not have been known in England before the late eighth century, when they would have been brought back by missionaries to northern Germany. Robert T. Farrell (1982) surveyed Scandinavian contact with England from 400 to 1000 and concluded that the poem was most probably composed in East Anglia in the eighth century. Sam Newton (1993) concurred. He based his conclusion on a complex assessment of linguistic, historical, archaeological, and genealogical information, all of which conspire to locate the peculiarly English Scandinavian material in the poem in pre-Viking East Anglia.

Scholars drawn to a later period of Scandinavian influence in England appear as early as 1917. In that year, Levin Schücking tried to prove that a poem so thoroughly Danish in orientation could have been composed in 890–900 in a Danish court in England. During that time, he asserted, an appropriate mix of Anglo-Saxon and Scandinavian culture existed to give rise to the poem, and he speculated that a Scandinavian prince could have asked a famous English poet to compose it for the instruction of his children (407). His view did not gain much support, even before Whitelock, but in 1981 Patricia Poussa revived it. Neither Schücking nor Poussa "adequately explain the apparently pre-Viking background of the poem," however (Newton 1993, 56).

Other scholars favoring a later period of Scandinavian influence take on Whitelock directly, pointing to the fallacy involved in presupposing as homogeneous an audience as she does. Nicolas Jacobs (1978) reconsidered the possibility of date for the poem after 835 and concluded that "any periods in which political considerations may have discouraged the composition of *Beowulf* are likely to have been brief and at most intermittent" (42). R. I. Page (1981) offered an overview of Anglo-Saxons who had regular nonbelligerent contact with the Vikings (e.g.,

Athelstan of Wessex, Alfred) and argued that excluding the Viking age as a time when the poem could have been composed means assuming an "unsophisticated audience for a sophisticated poem" (113). Two of Page's co-contributors to *The Dating of Beowulf,* Alexander Callander Murray and Roberta Frank, shared his basic premise.

One more contributor to *The Dating of Beowulf,* Walter Goffart, argued for a late date for the poem, but did so by examining another of its historical features, the words *Hetware* and *Hugas*, traditionally thought to be ancient references to the Franks. Goffart sought to prove that the former derived from the eighth-century *Liber Historiae Francorum* (84–88) and that the latter reflected the name "Hugh" that was popular in the territories of the Franks in the ninth and tenth centuries only. *Beowulf,* therefore, seems to have been written "no earlier than the second quarter of the tenth century" (100). Since Goffart did not definitively negate other interpretations of *Hugas,* such as the traditional one, his theory opens a new avenue of inquiry but remains inconclusive.

The first historical approach to date and provenance then, which has the advantage of breadth, leaves us with a *Beowulf* from eighth-, ninth-, or tenth-century Northumbria, Mercia, or East Anglia.

The second approach, a bit more circumscribed than the first though overlapping with it, concentrates on periods of cultural or literary transition and the possible reflection of those periods in the poem. Three have been advanced as candidates thus far: the late seventh to late eighth centuries, the ninth century, and the tenth century. The first is the period of the gradual Anglo-Saxon conversion to Christianity and of the amalgamation of Germanic and Roman ideas of kingship. In 1928, analyzing the synthesis of Christianity and Mediterranean learning in the poem, William W. Lawrence dated it to 675–725 during the age of Bede (280). Likewise, in 1978, exploring the historical and cultural backgrounds of the poem and focusing on its peculiar mix of Christian and pagan elements, Patrick Wormald argued that it reflects the assimilation of the Anglo-Saxon church by the warrior nobility in the eighth century (57). In 1986, Karl Schneider found a similar, but earlier, assimilation. Examining what he termed "the camouflaged paganism" (199–232) in the poem, as well as its linguistic features, he claimed that it was most probably composed in Mercia between 640 and 650 during the reign of Penda (74). Michael J. Swanton, studying Germanic and Roman ideas of kingship—the former deriving governing power from the people, the latter from the king through God—discerned traces of both in the poem (1982, chapters 4–6) and assigned it to the late eighth century, when, he argued, a shift from one system to the other probably took place. Peter Clemoes, focusing on such matters as the use of figures and tropes in the poem and their reflection of the transition between an old and a new style that he noticed in Old English poetry around the ninth century, placed the poem between the oral poetry of Cædmon and the written poetry of Cynewulf, most probably in the second half of the eighth century (1981, 185).

The second period of transition—also literary—is the ninth century. Noticing the seemingly transitional nature of the poem as Clemoes did, Colin Chase focused on the "delicate balance of empathy and detachment" (1981b, 162) in it and compared it to Old English saints' lives and their early antipathy to and late attraction to Germanic heroic values. He concluded that the hagiographical evidence suggests that the poem "is likely to have been written neither early, in the eighth century, nor late, in the tenth, but in the rapidly changing and chaotic ninth" (163).

The poem seems to reflect yet a third period of transition, the shift from an Anglo-Saxon to an Anglo-Scandinavian ethos in the tenth century. Wilhelm G. Busse and R. Holtei (1981) noted this fact when they applied text pragmatics and reception theory to the poem to demonstrate that it operates within "a dynamic text tradition" that adapts itself to "changing social and political conditions" (277 [see also Busse 1987]). Not intending to date the "time of composition of *Beowulf*" (286) by this method, they did date the manuscript version of the poem to the reign of Ethelred (978–1016), chiefly because of the presence in it of the problem of loyal behavior to one's lord. Roberta Frank (1982a) found a peculiar synthesis of religious and heroic idealism in the poem that was current only in the tenth century and tentatively suggested that period for when the poem was composed. Similarly, John D. Niles (1983) argued that the poet's ambiguous depiction of the Danes, both flattering and unflattering, "reflects interests and attitudes that would have been prevalent among the aristocratic Englishmen in the early or middle years of the tenth century, but not earlier" (111). He subsequently elaborated that idea, offering "seven good reasons for locating *Beowulf* in the period of nation-building that followed the ninth-century Viking invasions" (1993a, 95). Besides the depiction of the Danes, he points to the Scylding connection with the West Saxon pseudo-genealogies, the affinity of the language of the poem with that of known tenth-century works, the presence of virtuous pagans, the evidence of Old Norse analogues, probable English allusions (Hengest, Offa, Wiglaf), and the role of the Geats (a tribe apparently confused with both the Getae and the Jutes during this period) (1993a, 95–101). While the evidence that Niles and others have assembled does seem to favor a tenth-century date for the manuscript version of the poem, cultural studies, like their predecessors, remain inconclusive.

The third historical approach to date and provenance promises the most specificity of all such methods of dating but is the least dependable. Six scholars, beginning with John Earle in 1892, have read the poem as historical allegory. Because of the mention in lines 1931–62 of Offa, the legendary late-fourth-century Angle, Earle (lxxxiii–c) tried to read the narrative as a complex allusion to events during the reign of Offa of Mercia (757–96). He equated Thryth and Eomer in the poem, for example, with Offa's queen Cynethryth and son Ecgferth in history. Similarly, in 1920 Liebermann thought the poem may allude to Cuthburg's marriage to a foreign prince, then her divorce and return home (275). In 1921–22, placing the poem in the reign of Aldfrith of Northumbria (685–705), Albert Cook theorized that Aldfrith is concealed beneath the name Offa. In 1936, because of Wiglaf's presence in the poem, Alois Brandl dated it to the reign of Wiglaf of Mercia (827–38), rooted out numerous references to Mercian history (e.g., Heremod represents Penda [ca. 632–55]), and placed the poem in the same class of *Tendenzdichtung* (politically-motivated writing) as Spenser's *Faerie Queene* and Swift's *Gulliver's Travels* (168). In 1943, George Bond, too, linked the poem with the history of Mercia (e.g., Heremod represents Ceolwulf [821–23]), arguing that the first half allegorizes the reign of Beornwulf (823–26), the second that of Wiglaf. Finally, in 1986, sensing allusions to the reign of Athelstan (924–39), including hints in Beowulf of Edward the Elder (899–924), Zacharias P. Thundy placed the poem firmly in Wessex between the years 924 and 931.

The flaw in the historical-allegorical approach to *Beowulf* should be manifest from the range of places (Mercia, Northumbria, Wessex) and dates (seventh, eighth, ninth, and tenth centuries) its proponents have established by its use. We simply do not have enough information about the poem's specific historical context in the first place, and the poem is not constructed in such a consistently symbolic way in the second, to substantiate a single allegorical reading. Although the first problem may someday be solved, the second will persist, so such interpretations remain primarily conjectural (see Whitelock 1949, 76–79).

(*d*) Literary history has also been employed to date *Beowulf* but mostly to place the poem in relation to other poems, which are themselves difficult to date. Klaeber (1910) embellished Sarrazin's argument (1886b, 1892) that the poem follows *Genesis A* and in his edition placed the poem between "the so-called Cædmonian group in the neighborhood of 700" and Cynewulf in the late eighth century (1950a, cxiii). In 1940, theorizing that *Beowulf* may be the first secular Germanic and Old English epic, Hertha Marquardt placed it after the Cædmonian poems with *Exodus*, as a Christian/heroic hybrid, in between (153–54). And, as we have already seen, in 1981 Peter Clemoes and Colin Chase focused on the transitional literary nature of the poem and placed it in the late eighth and ninth centuries respectively. Roberta Frank, however, compared the laments at the end of *Beowulf* with the Old Norse memorial eulogy (1982b, 3) and concluded that the similarities suggest an Anglo-Saxon/Scandinavian interaction and origin for the poem in the late ninth or tenth century (13).

(*e*) Manuscript studies for dating *Beowulf* focus on the content of the Nowell Codex (the unique manuscript containing the poem), the relation of that manuscript to others, and the codex's physical features. In 1957, comparing the monsters in *Beowulf* with those in *The Wonders of the East,* another of the five texts in the Nowell Codex, Robert Reynolds argued that both were composed in the late ninth or tenth centuries. In a complex 1982 study, Michael Lapidge showed direct and indirect connections among *Beowulf,* Aldhelm's Wessex, and the *Liber Monstrorum,* an English text mentioning Hygelac as a Geat, not a Dane as he is referred to in Continental sources, and datable to ca. 650–750. While not arguing for a specific date and place of composition, Lapidge concluded that the evidence he assembled "points to the south rather than the north of England, and suggests that a context for the poem's conception and especially its transmission can be discovered in and in the vicinity of pre-Conquest Malmesbury" (190). In 1981, Angus Cameron, Ashley Crandell Amos, and Gregory Waite tentatively compared the language of *Beowulf* with other Old English texts in order "to place the manuscript and possibly the text in the context of the surviving Old English literary and linguistic remains" (36). They found that the spelling system of the poem is matched closely by remaining texts in the same manuscript but not by others; that spellings in the poem show close affinity to those in *Exodus* and *Daniel*; that the vocabulary shows affinity to *Andreas* and *Judith* (36), and that "the mixed spellings in *Beowulf* are not necessarily to be explained by a long or complicated textual transmission, but may represent copying conventions or tolerances in a number of late tenth-century scriptoria" (37). They did not try to specify a date for the poem.

Also in 1981, returning to Levin Schücking's premise (1905, 11, 66) that "Beowulf's Return" had been composed and inserted by the final author as a connecting link between the Grendel part and the Dragon fight, Kevin Kiernan (1981a, 252–54) posited two poets for the poem with the second being the final redactor of the whole. Kiernan also returned to Conybeare's belief that the poem was probably written down during the reign of Cnut (15–23), but he made the radical assertion that the poem and the eleventh-century manuscript are contemporaneous (22). This point of view has occasioned—to say the least—lively debate. Scholars have attacked Kiernan's linguistic and codicological arguments (e.g., Amos 1982; Clement 1984; Newton 1993, 7–9) and have questioned the paleographical evidence placing the manuscript in the reign of Cnut (e.g., Dumville 1988; Gerritsen 1989). The latter ignore Neil Ker's point that Anglo-Saxon script from ca. 990 to 1040 is impossible to date closely (1968, 45–46). Although most would currently probably agree that the manuscript has little to tell us about the date of the poem (Fulk 1982, 357), the issue is far from settled (Kiernan 1983).

(*f*) Genealogies provide a sixth kind of evidence that scholars have called into play in an effort to date *Beowulf* and establish its provenance. Klaeber (1950a, 254–55) reprinted the relevant genealogical lists, the West Saxon containing references to Beo, Scyld Scefing, Scef, and Heremod in the poem; the Mercian to Garmund, Offa, and Eomer; the Kentish to Folcwalda and Finn. No one has used the Kentish genealogy so far, but scholars such as Earle (1892, lxxxvi ff.) and Whitelock (1951, 63) have regarded the parallels between the Mercian genealogy and the Offa episode in *Beowulf* as evidence of Mercian provenance, the reference being seen as a way to flatter King Offa of Mercia (757–96). Such claims, however, are speculative at best.

Alexander Callander Murray (1981), Michael Lapidge (1982), and Audrey L. Meaney (1989) all focused on the West Saxon genealogies. Murray pointed out that they were composed after the Viking invasions[3] and correspondingly display an unmistakable interest in blending Anglo-Saxon and Scandinavian traditions. The prologue to *Beowulf* seems clearly to be a Viking age genealogy that can be dated to the late ninth century (105), and so, therefore, can the poem. Lapidge, not trying to establish date, did use genealogies to argue for a possible provenance (Wessex) since Alfred extends his pedigree to include Scyld, Scef, Heremod, and Beow, thus indicating that a poem resembling *Beowulf* may have been known to him (187). And, after a complex analysis of the West Saxon genealogy of Æthelwulf dated 855, Meaney stated that "Scyld Scefing and his arrival from overseas cannot have become part of the prologue of *Beowulf* before 858, and almost certainly not before Alfred's reign" (21). That analysis, coupled with evidence from burial customs and hagiography, caused Meaney to assign the composition of the prologue to the years 924–55, during the reign of Athelstan (37). Finally, in trying to establish an early East Anglian provenance for *Beowulf,* Sam Newton (1993) examined both Mercian and West Saxon genealogies. He concluded that the reference to Offa in the Mercian example and *Beowulf* does not point exclusively to Mercia as a source for the poem's northern preoccupations and that the differences between West Saxon examples and *Beowulf* suggest that the poem was not influenced by them (chapter 3).

Genealogies, like much of the other evidence for dating examined thus far, prove mercurial. They seem to substantiate dates in the eighth through the tenth centuries as well as a provenance in Mercia, Wessex, or East Anglia.

(*g*) Finally the language of *Beowulf* has occupied scholars in their effort to place and date the poem. We know more, in fact, about dialect than date. Predominantly West Saxon (mostly late) with an admixture of mainly Northumbrian and Mercian elements, the poet's language also shows signs of Kentish influence. This blend naturally causes some difficulty for anyone seeking to define a specific place of composition, but most scholars have supposed the poem was originally composed in an Anglian dialect. The phonological evidence usually cited to support this conclusion is actually unreliable. For example, spellings like "waldend" (for late West-Saxon *wealdend,* "ruler") indicate not Anglian provenance but conformity to the koine in which nearly all Old English poetry is preserved (Tupper 1911, 248–49; Sisam 1953, 119–39). Fulk has argued, however, that a large body of Anglian morphological features, generally missing from poetry known to come from the south and otherwise conforming to the poetic koine, is found in *Beowulf* and other poems usually thought to be Anglian. Examples are the use of *hafo* in addition to southern *hæbbe* (have); *sægon* in addition to Southern *sawon* (saw); *fore* in addition to southern *for*; the use of the accusative as well as dative case after the preposition *mid*; of *sæ* as a masculine noun; of *fæger* with a long first syllable; and of accusative pronouns like *mec, þec,* and *usic* (Fulk 1992, 309–25). In addition, some Anglian vocabulary shows the same distribution, for example *oferhygd* (pride, arrogance) for southern *ofermod* (Schabram 1965b, 123–29), *in* for southern *on,* and *nymþe* or *nemne* for the conjunction *butan* (Jordan 1906, 46–48). Evidence for identifying the dialect of origin is thus sparse and should be viewed with caution. What there is of it does suggest "Anglian" provenance, but being more precise than that is difficult. Recent scholarship, however, favors the Midlands rather than the north (reversing a historical trend), with Newton (1993) arguing specifically for East Anglia.

Isolating date by linguistic means is another matter entirely. In their extensive review of the issue in 1981, in fact, Cameron, Amos, and Waite observed that "from our current understanding of the language of *Beowulf* we could not call any date in the Old English period impossible" (37). Scholars have nevertheless employed various tests to try to fix the date, relative or "absolute."

The syntactic and phonological-metrical tests for relative dating include the following: "Lichtenheld's test" of the weak adjective and definite article, the regular absence of the latter in *Beowulf* perhaps indicating an early date (Chase 1981a, 4; also Amos 1981, 110–24); the presence, as evidenced by metrical considerations, of earlier, uncontracted, dissyllabic instead of later, contracted, monosyllabic forms of words; the presence of "earlier long vs. later (analogical) short diphthongs in the case of the loss of antevocalic *h* after *r* (or *l*)"; and the presence or absence of parasiting (addition of an inorganic vowel to *l*, *m*, *n*, or *r* in later West Germanic, rendering an original monosyllable disyllabic) (Klaeber 1950a, cviii). In 1981, Thomas Cable applied a purely metrical test to the poem by calculating the combined percentages of Sievers's types C, D, and E verses in the poem and compared the percentages with those in other Old English poems.[4] Cable concluded that there is a decrease in the use of these verse types as the Old English period progresses (80), placed *Beowulf* in a middle group of poems (e.g., *Daniel, Exodus, Elene*), and found that it could have been composed in the ninth century (82). All these tests clearly fail to fix *Beowulf* in time, but philologists are in fairly consistent agreement that the phonological-metrical tests at least do seem to place it in an early "Cædmonian" group of poems (e.g., Klaeber 1950a, cix; Fulk 1992, 348–51).

Other tests for relative dating focus on the poem's vocabulary. Rönning (1883), for example, pointed to the use of the word "gigantas," a loan word probably from the Latin Bible, as evidence for an eighth-century date (89). Ritchie Girvan (1935) reached a similar conclusion, stating that the poem is "later than Cædmon, not earlier, that is, than about 670" (25). Whitelock (1951, 5) and Amos (1981) basically agreed, the latter noting that although this and other "ecclesiastical Latin loan words do not allow precise dating . . . they do provide a useful *terminus a quo*" (142–43). Kiernan focused on the words "here" and "fyrd," synonyms for "army," arguing that the first has positive connotations in the poem while the second does not. Since in the *Anglo-Saxon Chronicle* the situation is the opposite, with *here* referring negatively to the invading Danish forces, *fyrd* positively to the English, such a reversal could occur only in the reign of Cnut (1981a, 21–22). Phillip Pulsiano and Joseph McGowan (1990), however, reexamined the evidence for

Kiernan's claim and found that it was "not consistent and unambiguous under scrutiny" (12).

Likewise undermining Kiernan's and others' claim of a late date for the poem is the apparent absence in it of Scandinavian loan words and the presence of distinctly English spellings for Scandinavian names. Klaeber noted the first (1950a, cxvii), as did Frank, who, however, pointed out that a lack of "demonstrable Scandinavianisms . . . does not rule out a late date of composition," taking *The Battle of Brunanburh* from ca. 937, with just one loan word, as her example (1981, 123).[5] She went on in an intricate argument to explore the possibility that the poet's "interest in and knowledge of things Scandinavian was the result of the Danish settlements in England" and the subsequent influence of skaldic verse (124). Though the hypothesis is a compelling one, the evidence for it is inconclusive. "Some words could be cognate, and an occasional Norsism (*lofgeornost? bencðelu?*) could be borrowed from the spoken Norse language rather than skaldic practice" (Andersson 1983, 296). Fulk found a Viking age date unlikely because proper names in the poem do not reflect Scandinavian influence (1982, 343–44). Whether a Scandinavian presence would necessarily affect native onomastic traditions, however, is still a matter of dispute.

The linguistic tests for what is traditionally termed "absolute dating" are few. Lorenz Morsbach was the first to propose one in 1906, when he dated the poem to shortly after 700 by arguing that apocope of *u* (loss of final *u* after long root syllables) and loss of postconsonantal *h* before vowels did not occur until after that date. Since the poem will not scan correctly if one substitutes the earlier word forms for those in the manuscript, the poem has to have been composed after the phonological changes took place. Morsbach's conclusions about the dates of the sound changes and consequently the date of *Beowulf,* however, have been demonstrated to be unreliable (e.g., Amos 1981, 18–39; Fulk 1992, 369 ff.). Similarly, some scholars (e.g., Holthausen, cited in Klaeber 1950a, cix n. 7) suggested a date prior to 750 because of the presence of "wundini" (1382), an archaic instrumental "generally thought to be not later than *circa 750*" (Wrenn 1953, 27). The manuscript evidence for the word is equivocal, however (the word may actually be "wundum," "wundnum," "wundmi," "wundnu": see Stanley 1981a, 208; Kiernan 1981a, 31 ff.; Bammesberger 1990), and the word may represent either scribal error or stylistic choice (Klaeber 1950a, cx).

The most recent, meticulously argued, and seemingly reliable test for (relatively) absolute dating is by R. D. Fulk in 1992. Applying "Kaluza's law" to *Beowulf* (a "law" that states that early long inflectional endings differed metrically from short ones whereas later long and short endings had equal metrical value), he found that the poem is unique in its observance of that law (164). The evidence we have for the provenance of the poem, Fulk argued, suggests Mercia or Northumbria and favors Mercia. Therefore, since the distinction between long and short endings was being lost in the mid-eighth century in Mercia and in the mid-ninth in

Northumbria, Fulk maintained that *Beowulf* was most probably composed before 725 if Mercian in origin or before 825 if Northumbrian. It can even date from as early as ca. 685, "though such an early date is considerably less probable" (390).

Unfortunately, linguistic evidence obviously joins all other kinds of evidence in not fully substantiating a specific date of composition. Evidence suggesting Anglian provenance also suggests a time of composition between 685 and 825, but this does not rule out a later date. Advocates of a late *Beowulf,* however, must contend with the apparent absence of Scandinavian loan words in the poem, the presence of exclusively English forms of personal names, and "Kaluza's law."

II. Author

Early speculation on who wrote *Beowulf* was straightforward. Grundtvig, for example, concluded that since the poem was written after the death of Hygelac (ca. 521) and probably during a period of great learning in England, the age of Bede was the most likely time and a companion of Cædmon in Northumbria or Aldhelm in Wessex the most likely candidate (Schrøder 1875, 1–4; H. Chadwick [1912] and Cook [1921–22] make the same suggestion). The simplicity of such reasoning was demolished, however, when *Liedertheorie* (ballad theory) came into vogue. Not really a theory of authorship but of composition, it distinguishes various layers of authorial or scribal contribution to the poem as it separates blocks of pagan lays from Christian matter in the interstices. The theory had obvious ramifications for pinpointing who wrote *Beowulf:* almost everybody did.[6]

Modifications of the ballad theory, however, moved toward compromise and brought a single poet back into play, albeit at the end of a long process. In 1870, for example, Artur Köhler affirmed the composite nature of the poem but also asserted that "the Anglo-Saxon epic in its final form was without doubt fashioned by a single gifted poet" (1870b, 305). And between 1886 and 1897, striving to mediate between the ballad theorists and the advocates of unity and single authorship, Gregor Sarrazin (1886b, 545) argued that an Anglo-Saxon poet (interpolator B) translated and reworked a Danish original (a point refuted by Eduard Sievers in 1886 on linguistic grounds). Sarrazin identified the Danish author as the skald Starkathr, whom he placed around 700 at Lejre, the Danish court of King Ingeld (1888, 107), and made the bold claim that Cynewulf was both the translator of *Beowulf* and later the interpolator of moralizing passages (1886b, 543–44), an assertion refuted by Cook (1925c). On the basis of elaborate linguistic and metrical arguments, Sarrazin placed the time of composition of *Beowulf* between *Christ A* and *B,* and *Elene* and *Andreas* (1892, 415).

Other scholars, rejecting the ballad theory altogether, mostly on aesthetic grounds, continually maintained that *Beowulf* is both unified and the work of one author, a majority view by early 1900 that remains in force today. Grein (1862), Schrøder (1875), T. Arnold (1876), Schemann (1882), Rönning (1883), Fahlbeck (1884), Morsbach (1906), H. Chadwick (1907), Brandl (1908a, b), Smithson

(1910), Schücking (1917), Chambers (1921), Klaeber (1922a), and Tolkien (1936), for instance, all believed that the poem is the work of one man. While some scholars favoring individual authorship have not gone so far as to name the poet, they have tried to individualize him. Klaeber viewed the poet "as a man connected in some way with the Anglian court, a royal chaplain or abbot of noble birth or, it may be, a monk friend of his, who possessed an actual knowledge of court life and addressed himself to an aristocratic, in fact a royal audience." Such a person would be acquainted with Germanic, Scandinavian, and Old English verse, "a man of notable taste and culture and informed with a spirit of broad-minded Christianity" (1950a, cxix). Paull F. Baum similarly suggested that the poet was a "serious and gifted poet, steeped in the older pagan tradition from the continent" (1963, 365). And several scholars have speculated about whether the poet was a cleric or a layperson. Those adhering to theories of multiple authorship tend to favor a number of pagan lay singers and a final Christian redactor. Those advocating single authorship tend to see a unified work by a Christian author—whether a monk or a layperson—working with partially pre-Christian sources.

Rönning (1883), Wormald (1978), Schrader (1980), Dumville (1981), Lapidge (1982), and Cassidy (1982) all argued that the nature of the poem and its historical and cultural context indicate a cleric as author. Rönning asserted that the poem must have been authored "pen in hand" (89). Since opportunities for writing did not exist in the lay world, and since there are religious elements in the poem, the evidence "points toward the cloister" as place of origin and a monk as author (89). Wormald reasoned that since there was no independent lay epic and the poet shows evidence of a Christian-Latin education, he must have been "at the fringes of clerical society" (44), while Schrader, also regarding the evidence of classical learning in *Beowulf* as proof that the author had to be a cleric, probably in the age of Bede, felt that he was undoubtedly a monk (56).

Dumville continued this basic line of reasoning, arguing that Irish monasticism could have been favorably disposed to heroic literature and that *Beowulf* was either written or composed orally in a monastic setting or oral material was thoroughly changed in writing at that time by a Christian poet (146). Thus the author must have been a cleric, and the work must have been transmitted through the scriptorium, since, as Rönning pointed out previously, no other means of book production are known in Anglo-Saxon England (157, 156). Shifting the poem's provenance to Wessex ca. 700, Lapidge inferred that "a many-faceted scholar such as Aldhelm could have assisted at [*Beowulf*'s] composition" (157). Finally Cassidy considered the poet a careful crafter of words who practices the complex art of tectonic composition (9). He must therefore have been an extremely learned churchman whose monastic, unappreciative audience indulged his literary effort while he was alive (11).

The paltry evidence about who wrote *Beowulf* thus seems to suggest that a cleric is responsible. Not all scholars have accepted the conclusion, however. Work on traditional oral composition by Parry and Lord helped advance the argument that the *Beowulf*-poet was a singer of tales, an argument supported by Magoun (1953, 1958, 1963), Lord (1960), Storms (1974), Niles (1993c, 1993b), Irving (1989), and Foley (1990). Creed (1966b) makes the logical and necessary connection between the theory of oral composition and the extant epic in written form. He postulated a single singer of *Beowulf,* whose oral composition was recorded by a scribe (138). In 1983 and 1993, Niles elaborated Creed's idea by focusing on the performance of the epic, which could have been recorded on behalf of an aristocratic patron and thus could have become the basis for further dissemination either orally or scriptorally (1983, 112-13; 1993c). In 1991, Kendall opted to combine the lay and monastic theories of the author. He posited an "aristocratic" youth associated with a court and steeped in oral composition traditions who later entered a monastery, where he wrote down the oral literature he had heard and practiced previously (2-4).

Merely individualizing the *Beowulf* poet is difficult enough, so few scholars besides Sarrazin have actually tried to name him. In his 1892 allegorical interpretation, Earle claimed that Archbishop Hygeberht of Lichfield, closely tied to Offa, wrote the poem (xcviii). In 1971, categorizing the language of *Beowulf* as Old Phalian, which he said is still evident in Low German today, Wilhelm Tegethoff argued that the poem is the work of Adalbert of Bremen, the largely unappreciated eleventh-century German cleric whose praises are sung by church historian Adam of Bremen (i). And two authors in 1986, the second much more confidently than the first, ventured possible names. Noting the common reference to Offa in "Widsith" and *Beowulf,* Schneider suggested that the poet "may be identical" with Widsith (189). In his allegorical interpretation of the poem, Thundy assigned authorship to Wulfgar, a loyal retainer of King Athelstan named in a land grant charter "at Ham in Wiltshire on November 12, 931" (114).

One last possibility concerning authorship is that the *Beowulf* poet was a woman. Baum (1963) suggested that a learned abbess inspired by Hild of Whitby (Cædmon's abbess) or Hild herself may have written the poem, but his notion was advanced as an example of hypotheses that "do no harm if they are not taken too seriously" (359). Baum's did none apparently, since it was never mentioned again. In 1990, however, Fred C. Robinson revisited the possibility of female authorship of Old English poetry and took the idea quite earnestly. Referring to the "hints at possible [female] involvement in [Old English] versifying," the documented evidence of Christian-Latin women poets, and the substantiated activity of women poets in the rest of the Germanic world, Robinson argued that "there is reason to believe that women may have played as much of a role in Anglo-Saxon literary production as they have in the later periods of English literature" (62–63). This involvement would include, of course, *Beowulf.*

Provocative as it may be, complicated as it is, frustrating as it has always been, the search for the identity of the *Beowulf* poet seems largely futile, and what Thorkelin sagely observed in 1815 obtains today: "one might as well roll the rock of Sisyphus" as try to identify "our unnamed, unwept poet" (Thorkelin 1815b). Specifying what type of poet the author was, on the other hand (e.g., a singer of tales or a literate author, either layperson or cleric), remains an important, if elusive, enterprise.

III. Audiences

As with date, provenance, and author, opinions on the audiences of *Beowulf* inscribe an arc of waxing complexity from Thorkelin to our contemporaries. Scholars who agree on Mercia or Northumbria as the poem's provenance naturally try to locate an audience for the poem within that large geographical area. Some use internal and external evidence to establish something as simple as the poem's having been composed for Angles, not Saxons (Kier 1915, 12), others to show that the audience was secular or monastic, and yet others to prove that the audience lived at a particular time and the poem served a particular purpose.

Of the studies addressing the secular or monastic nature of the audience, more favor the former than the latter, a fact of mild curiosity since most scholars view the author as a cleric. Ten Brink (1888), for example, asserted that the cultural background of the audience must have been one of both a temperate heathendom and a temperate Christianity coupled with a positive nationalistic feeling (223). This mixture could have flourished best in Mercia after 650. The paucity of clergy and Christian institutions there at that time and the absence of Christian scholarship and poetry, ten Brink asserted, were favorable to keeping ancient tradition and ancient popular poetry alive and to maintaining a balance that would have been tipped toward a more radical Christianity in other parts of England (224). In 1906, taking the opposite view, Morsbach suggested that *Beowulf* could have been a literary reaction against the flourishing religious epic and the church's dogmatic stance against pagan traditions (276). Girvan, too, believed that the epic's audience had to be secular. The poet presents both traditional heroic material, such as ship burials, and glimpses of his own contemporary courtly life, alluding perhaps to the failed peaceweaving efforts of Oswiu's daughters (1935, 37, 47–48). Whitelock envisioned a Christian audience with enough knowledge to follow the biblical allusions and with an experienced ear for poetry (1951, 5–8). According to Whitelock, the poet wrote his "literature for entertainment" (20) for a lay audience of novice and veteran Anglo-Saxon warriors, who would also be sportsmen, listening to familiar things (19, 44). The poet, Whitelock presumed, would be "subtle and sophisticated," the audience "alert and intelligent" (99).

Expanding on Whitelock's notion, Baum maintained that such an audience must fulfill two prerequisites: it must have an interest in the "exploits of a heathen hero" and in Germanic history and lore and must be attentive enough to comprehend and enjoy a difficult and often cryptic narrative (1963, 360). Baum concluded that poet and audience had to be alike, and so the audience could not be the broad lay one of Whitelock but had to be a select and highly trained audience of a few ivory-tower listeners/readers (360–65). Both Mitchell and Storms rejected this idea. Mitchell pointed out that the depiction of "the ideal of Germanic heroic life" in the poem does not require specialized knowledge to recognize (1963, 128). Storms argued that a lay scop and lay audience in Northumbria would have a greater personal interest in the vicissitudes of political power than a more highly trained monastic writer and audience would have (1974, 22). For Busse and Holtei, too, the targeted audience was laymen, this time the thane class during Æthelred's reign, because thanes could appreciate the *comitatus* ethos in the poem (1981, 328–29). In 1981, contra Whitelock, Page argued for the possibility of a heterogeneous audience not necessarily in the Danelaw, and, in 1993, Newton favored a pre-Viking audience "already familiar with tales concerning the renowned Scyldings" (54–55).

Mostly because of the heroic content of the poem, monastic audiences have found less favor than secular ones. Wormald, however, gave considerable reason to doubt that the poem was designed for a royal court (1978, 52–58). Examining the amalgamation of spiritual and secular elements in the church during the age of Bede, he emphasized the phenomenon of *Eigenkirchen,* family minsters founded by, designed for, and controlled by aristocratic households. These minsters, Wormald argued, were places in which the boundaries between monastic and secular life became blurred (53). He suggested that such intertwined conditions could have fostered the composition of the epic. In 1982, Lapidge connected Wormald's *Eigenkirchen* theory with Liebermann's conjecture (1920) that *Beowulf* was written by a poet in the service of Cuthburg, the Northumbrian queen presiding over an *Eigenkirche* in Wimborne (156–57). Liebermann speculated that the poet may have returned to Wessex with Cuthburg, entered Wimborne with her, and finished the epic there. This view, Liebermann added, with its implications of the mixed tastes of a half-secular, half-monastic noblewoman, would explain why the epic contains court banquets, battle scenes, and biblical allusions (1920, 275; but see also Kendall 1991, 2–6).

Three other scholars, on the other hand, favored a more purely monastic audience for the poem. Dumville (1981) emphasized the literate nature of the work, assumed a monastic audience, and repudiated Whitelock's argument that literature of entertainment would be reserved for a lay audience. Cassidy proposed that the poet was a monk writing solely for a monastic audience and in such a rarified mode "that [the poem] was little understood" (1982, 10) and was probably "saved by benign neglect" after the poet's death (11). Horst Weinstock, commenting on Cassidy, posited a learned and well-read poet whose monastic audience would have been more "alert, intelligent, and congenial" than the lay audience at a secular court (1982, 23). He theorized that the poet may have written the epic for a monastic community engaged in missionary work to the Continental Saxons (23). Weinstock conjectured further that the manuscript copy was kept in the refectory for lections and recopied in the tenth century when it started to disintegrate (25).

Those arguing for a particular time for the poem generally assume a specialized genre for it or invoke an allegorical interpretation to support their view. At least five early scholars—Outzen (1816, 327), Earle (1892, xc), Schücking (1917, 399), Liebermann (1920, 275–76), and Andreas Heusler (cited in Schücking 1929a, 143)—considered the epic a *Fürstenspiegel,* a mirror for princes designed to instruct them in kingly behavior. Earle and Liebermann were even specific about the princes in question: Earle postulated Offa's son, Ecgferth (1892, xc), and Liebermann theorized that, if the poem originated in a royal monastery, it probably would have been noticed by a queen like Osburg around 854 and used in the education of her sons (276). Without arguing for a specific genre for the poem, Baldwin Brown (1915), Cook (1921–22), Whitelock (1951), and Wrenn (1953) also suggested the court of Offa or his successors as its birthplace. Bond (1943) made a case for the courts of Kings Beornwulf and Wiglaf and Lindqvist (1948, 139) for a court interested in honoring the royal house of the Uffingas.

None of the above interpretations of audience can be proved, and it is possible that all are wrong. As Baum observed in 1963, the poet may have written "a quasi-heroic poem to please himself, in the quiet expectation of pleasing also just that 'fit audience though few'" (365). Conversely, he or she may have gathered enough of everything into the poem to please everybody, making everyman its destined consumer. The question of audience, even in the presence of a firm grasp of who wrote the poem and when, is in the end exceedingly slippery, the most difficult of all such questions to answer.

From the intrepid certitude of Thorkelin in 1815 about the date, provenance, author, and audience of *Beowulf,* then, we arrive arduously at a cautious and necessary incertitude. Although we can discern a general trend in scholarship from early to late dating, from favoring northern to entertaining southern provenance, even from viewing the audience as secular to considering it monastic, reasoning about all four questions is based largely on probability, not on established fact. Until new facts surface, all we can say with assurance when asked when, where, by whom, and for whom the poem was composed is that we are not sure. The quandary we thus find ourselves in with these first, essential questions about the poem, of course, has serious ramifications for most, if not all other, interpretations of it. This, as Thorkelin would cavalierly have phrased it, "will be clear to anyone" who reads on in this handbook.

Notes

For their many invaluable suggestions for improving this chapter, we thank Theodore M. Andersson, R. D. Fulk, and John D. Niles. Bjork is primarily responsible for date and provenance, Obermeier for author and audiences.

1. On this issue, see Busse (1987, 9–140, 277–80).

2. Several German scholars stubbornly refused to see anything Scandinavian or British about the poem (Haarder 20 n.10). Heinrich Leo, for example, considered *Beowulf* the oldest German epic but preserved in the Anglo-Saxon dialect. He argued that since Hygelac died between 512 and 530 and Beowulf reigned after him for 50 years before his own death, the poem originated in Germany after 580

during the earliest German migrations to England (1839, 19). Cf. Karl Simrock's 1859 translation entitled *Beowulf: Das älteste deutsche Epos* and P. Hoffmann's 1893 translation entitled *Beowulf: Aeltestes deutches Heldengedicht.*

3. C. Davis (1992) concurs; but see Dumville (1977, 80–81), who marshals evidence that the genealogies were compiled as early as the seventh century.

4. For an explanation of Sievers's system, see chapter 4 below.

5. Newton (1993, 14) uses the same example to reach the opposite conclusion. The presence of loan words in *Brunanburh* and *Maldon* is evidence of Scandinavian/Anglo-Saxon assimilation in the tenth century; the apparent absence of Scandinavian lexical items in *Beowulf*, therefore, may imply "that the material which informs the poem was not derived from sources later than the Viking Age."

6. See chapter 8 for a discussion of *Liedertheorie.*

Chapter 3

Textual Criticism

by R. D. Fulk

Summary: In the nineteenth century there was greater diversity of attitudes and practices in regard to textual editing than there is now. But the proponents of liberal emendation had been defeated by the early years of this century, with the result that the texts in use today reflect, on the whole, moderate to conservative practices. In recent years the conceptual basis of even these texts has been challenged with increasing frequency, signaling the rise of a textual ultraconservatism that now seems to dominate in discussions of editing. In some ways this prevailing attitude conflicts with recent trends in general textual theory and brackets such issues as the relation of text to audience and the means of gauging probability in editorial decisions. Support for a lightly edited text does not reflect trust in the manuscript as much as distrust of editorial subjectivity; and so the dependence of liberal views on philological competence, when conjoined with this century's turn away from philology in Old English studies, ensures that conservatism will continue to dominate.

Chronology

1705: Humfrey Wanley transcribes lines 1–19 and 53–73 of the poem in his *Catalogus.*

1731: The manuscript is damaged by fire.

1787: Grímur Jónsson Thorkelin commissions a transcript of the manuscript. He subsequently transcribes it himself, as well.

1805: Sharon Turner transcribes forty-one lines from the manuscript in his *History.*

1815: Thorkelin publishes the first full edition of the poem, based on the 1787 transcripts, remarking in his preface on the negligence of the scribe (treated as singular), and claiming nonetheless to have copied as faithfully as possible, except in regard to division into verses, punctuation, word division, and use of final *ð/þ* (1815b).

1815: N. F. S. Grundtvig lists numerous errors in his review of Thorkelin's text.

1820: Grundtvig appends to his own translation (pp. 267–312) forty-five pages of corrections to Thorkelin's edition.

1824: Frederic Madden makes a collation of the manuscript with Thorkelin's edition.

1826: John Conybeare's 1817 collation of Thorkelin's edition with the manuscript is employed in his *Illustrations*, of which eighteen pages are devoted to correcting Thorkelin.

1833: John M. Kemble's text, the second to appear, is the first to employ German philological methods. His preface is highly critical of the scribes. The second edition of Kemble's work (1835–37) is more accurate; and there is a list of further corrigenda appended to the second volume (a translation).

1850: Ludwig Ettmüller edits several passages, proposing numerous emendations to Kemble's text.

1855: Benjamin Thorpe's edition is based on his 1830 collation of Thorkelin's edition with the manuscript.

1857: C. W. M. Grein's conservative text, though not collated with the manuscript, represents the first modern edition on scholarly principles.

1859: F. Dietrich proposes a number of "Rettungen" in defense of manuscript readings.

1861: Grundtvig's conservative edition is based on the Thorkelin transcripts and his own 1829 collation of the manuscript.

1876: E. Kölbing proposes more than twenty pages of corrections to the existing editions. A large number of his proposals have been adopted in subsequent editions.

1879: The fourth edition of Moritz Heyne's 1863 text employs Kölbing's collation with the manuscript, and throughout its many revisions has remained a conservative standard, especially in L. Schücking's and E. von Schaubert's later recensions.

1881: A diplomatic edition by Alfred Holder appears.

1882: Julius Zupitza's photographic facsimile includes a transcription collated with the Thorkelin transcripts.

1883: R. P. Wülcker's revision of Grein's text is a diplomatic edition.

1904: Moritz Trautmann's edition represents an extreme in conjectural editing and provokes a decisive conservative reaction.

1905: Ferdinand Holthausen's edition adopts Eduard Sievers's metrical findings as a rigorous standard and represents a "middle course" (R. W. Chambers) between Trautmann's and Heyne-Schücking's practices.

1910: Walter Sedgefield's heavily emended text employs a collation of the manuscript.

1914: Chambers' revision of A. J. Wyatt's edition (1894), collated with the manuscript, marks the ultimate victory of conservative over conjectural editing. Both editions are "ultra-conservative" (D. Short), though the emendations Chambers introduces into Wyatt's text are *metri causa*.

1922: F. Klaeber's first edition (1922a) appears and in time becomes the scholarly standard.

1938: A. H. Smith transcribes the damaged and badly worn last page of the manuscript with the help of new photographic technologies.

1951: Kemp Malone's facsimile of the Thorkelin transcripts appears.

1957: Norman Davis's revision of Zupitza's work (1882) includes a new photographic facsimile and a prefatory note containing accumulated scholarship on the final, damaged folio, along with additions and corrections to Zupitza's transliteration.

1963: Malone publishes a facsimile of the Nowell Codex.

1967: Tilman Westphalen discusses the manuscript and its textual problems and focuses on deciphering the badly worn final leaf.

1981: Kevin Kiernan argues that the poem is wholly or in part the work of the two scribes of the *Beowulf* manuscript (so that all but a minuscule amount of modern emendation is unjustified) and that gaps on folio 179 are the result of deliberate erasure.

1983: Birte Kelly traces the origins of emendations adopted in current editions and finds that most had been proposed by 1857 (two years before the first entry under the heading of textual criticism of *Beowulf* in the Greenfield-Robinson bibliography).

1986: Kiernan argues that Thorkelin's own transcript is younger by several years than his copyist's and considerably less reliable, despite appearances to the contrary.

The history of editing in regard to *Beowulf* begins with the scribes themselves, who introduced corrections to their own work as well as inadvertent changes to their exemplar. Subsequently, debate about textual criticism of the poem has tended to oppose the authority of these first known editors to that of modern ones. Historically, the question has been reduced to an excessively simple dialectic, asking whether the text of *Beowulf* is an abstraction, of which the manuscript is a representation, or a concretion represented only by what the manuscript says. One sort of evidence, and an exception to this narrow range of debate, is represented by the body of scholarship devoted to portions of the scribes' work that are no longer legible, first and foremost in regard to the parts of the manuscript that were burned in 1731. Some of the gaps can now be filled only by conjecture, but more often we have the witness of the two Thorkelin transcripts made in the later eighteenth century, when the burnt portions apparently were not as deteriorated as they are now. Kevin S. Kiernan (1986) has argued persuasively that the second of the transcripts (B), by Thorkelin himself, is more an edition-in-progress than a transcript, and its witness is thus less valuable than that of the first (A), the work of a copyist whose judgment was unprejudiced by even a rudimentary understanding of Old English.

Yet it is not so much the first copyist's ignorance of the language that ensures the superiority of A as the extraordinary unreliability of B: after all, despite its superiority, A nonetheless contains more than a thousand letter errors (Hall 1995a, based on Kiernan's findings). Ignorance of the language, rather, seems to have been the chief obstacle to accuracy in other early published excerpts: the rate of transcription error in the material published by Sharon Turner (1805) is no better than the dismal rate in Thorkelin's 1815 edition—better than one error for every two verse lines, to judge by Hall's figures. Even the two passages transcribed by careful Wanley (1705) contain several mistakes in just forty lines of verse; and Conybeare (1826), who collated Thorkelin's edition with the manuscript in 1817, has nearly as many letter errors as Wanley in the first forty lines he prints. Rather, any significant gains in accuracy awaited the appearance of an editor knowledgeable about the language and its philology. For the next edition to appear was that of John M. Kemble (1833), who was strongly influenced by German scholarship and particularly by the work of Jacob Grimm. The difference is striking: Hall finds that while there are nearly three hundred errors of transcription in the first five hundred verse lines of Thorkelin's edition, Kemble's first, less accurate edition has just twenty-one.

Though in their prefaces these earliest editors, Thorkelin and Kemble, sharply criticized the work of the Old English copyists, they at least claimed to be presenting the work of the scribes faithfully in all but the most minor details. The history of the poem's textual criticism in the nineteenth century reflects debate about the wisdom of such conservative practices. The impulse to emend the text derived originally from simple distrust of the scribes' work, an attitude with analogues in the Old English period itself.[1] But the impulse gained support from the example of classical scholarship, in which brilliant new methods of textual criticism, especially in the work of Karl Lachmann (1793–1851), had demonstrated what German philology could accomplish. And so although Kemble kept his suggestions for emendations (as opposed to conjectures about lost letters) out of the text, at the foot of the page, in the selections edited by Ludwig Ettmüller in 1850, it is the manuscript readings that are relegated to the apparatus, and this practice, with the attitude toward the Old English scribes' work that it implies, grows to be the standard.

The prevailing reasons for emending fall into a relatively small number of categories. Grammar is one of them. For example, all the most frequently cited editions emend manuscript "geōsceaft grimne" (1234a), since "geōsceaft" ought to be feminine, requiring "grimme" for proper agreement. That an inattentive scribe should have corrupted the passage is not unlikely because confusion of *mm* and *mn* is found elsewhere in the manuscript (1944b); because the reverse confusion ("grimme" for "grimne") is found at 2136a; and because (perhaps in all these instances) faulty expansion of an abbreviation may be involved: compare "grīme" (i.e., "grimme") twice in the work of the second scribe, who is not as averse as the first to the use of the mark of suspension of a nasal consonant.

Alliteration is a second reason for emendation, as in lines 948b–50:

> heald forð tela
> nīwe sibbe. Ne bið þē [n]ǣnigre gād
> worolde wilna, þē ic geweald hæbbe.

Here all the major editions negativize the indefinite pronoun in 949b for the sake of congruence with the alliteration on *n* in the on-verse. The scribal addition or deletion of negative particles seems common in verse (Fulk 1992, §331).

A third justification for emendation is poetic meter, as in "Werod eall ārās. / [Ge]grētte þā guma ōþerne" (651b–52). Here, like Klaeber's and Dobbie's (1953), even the very conservative Heyne-Schücking text in von Schaubert's seventeenth edition (1961) provides a prefix for the verb "grētte," because otherwise the verse would contain just three syllables, one of the less subtle in the range of possible metrical anomalies. Meter is the most controversial of these reasons to emend, and it is a relatively late addition to the list, since metrical theory did not have a firm enough scholarly footing until 1885, when Eduard Sievers published his first detailed study of Germanic meter.

The verses "Bær þā sēo brimwyl[f], þā hēo tō botme cōm, / hringa þengel tō hofe sīnum" (1506–7) illustrate a fourth reason to emend, which is the need to make semantic and pragmatic sense of the passage. Even though a word "brimwyl," meaning, perhaps, "sea-spring" (masculine) or "sea-wool" (feminine), is not attested elsewhere in Old English, it is not inherently implausible. But in this context it does not make much sense, where the word must refer to Grendel's mother, and so an *f* is added in all the major editions. Some other reasons for emending have been proposed—for example, Francis P. Magoun Jr. (1953, 458–59), proposes textual changes on the basis of formulaic parallels—but these four, grammar, alliteration, meter, and meaning, are the only criteria that have played a very significant role in guiding major editions of the poem. The examples cited illustrate that all four have been used in isolation as grounds for emending, but more usually two or more apply in concert, as in lines 953b–55a, in which the insertion of "dōm" marks an improvement in all four categories:

> þū þē self hafast
> dǣdum gefremed, þæt þīn [dōm] lyfað
> āwa tō aldre.

One objection that has been raised to these criteria is Kenneth Sisam's: "A defender of the manuscript readings . . . might well argue that the scribes were well trained, and that they knew more about Old English usage, thought, and tradition than a modern critic can" (1946, 37). Although he apparently devised this argument only to show its ineffectiveness, some more recent commentators have taken it up in earnest. It is certainly true that the scribes had a fuller and more natural grasp of the grammar and idiom of late West Saxon than we do. No one can seriously doubt this—least of all Sisam, who was an inveterate foe of philological complacency—and yet the practice of modern editors tacitly acknowledges that in some respects the advantage is actually ours. The language of Old English verse is a koine, not congruent with any scribe's own dialect. It is clear that the scribes were often puzzled by words that were rare and difficult, words of an archaic, poetic, or dialectal nature. Sometimes we are in a better position to understand such words, since we have access to comparative evidence. An example is found in lines 83b–85:

> ne wæs hit lenge þā gēn,
> þæt se *ecghete*   āþumswēoran
> æfter wælnīðe   wæcnan scolde.

In the manuscript the unfamiliar word "āþumswēoran" (son-in-law and father-in-law) has been trivialized by some scribe to "aþum swerian" (to swear with oaths)—requiring a human subject for the supposed verb "hete," and thus prompting the scribe to corrupt "ecg" to "secg," in the process spoiling the alliteration.

Similarly, the Anglian word *wærc* (pain) is rarely written as such in the surviving manuscripts of verse because the southern scribes did not recognize it. The modern reflex of the word is restricted to Scotland and the north of England. Southern scribes usually changed it to *weorc* (work), as seems to be the case at 1418b and probably 1638b and 1721b. Yet none of the major editions alters the manuscript spelling.

Perhaps most clearly, the scribes tended to change uninflected infinitives after *tō* to inflected ones. The verse "frēode tō friclan" (2556a) represents one of two uninflected examples in the poem, and "sæcce tō sēceanne," appearing just a few lines later (2562a), is one of several inflected examples. Except for the extra syllable added by the inflection in the latter, the two are metrically equivalent; and the inflection in 2562a renders the verse metrically anomalous. There are some fifteen similar instances in verse in which the inflection on the infinitive spoils the meter. Since the uninflected infinitive is almost never encountered in prose, the occurrence of two examples in *Beowulf* is itself a sign that the uninflected sort is natural in verse, either as an archaism or as a poeticism. The point is that the scribes' own language interfered with their copying, prompting them to write metrically incorrect forms because the forms in their exemplar were foreign to their own speech. In this respect we are probably less biased judges than the scribes. Although the scribes' knowledge of the late West Saxon dialect qualifies them as important witnesses, even their testimony demands a skeptical attitude.

Although doubts have been expressed about all the criteria for emendation mentioned above, objections to meter as an editorial tool have been commonest. Meter is, after all, the most complex of these criteria, and thus, because it is the least widely understood, it is also the least likely to engage the confidence of those who are not adepts. For the same reason it may be worthwhile to devote particular attention to the objections to meter. To begin with the most general criticism, some question whether our understanding of Old English meter is sufficiently reliable. To be sure, the dependability of metrical evidence is anything but uniform. The example of inflected infinitives illustrates the relative force of one sort of evidence: in the poem there are seventeen examples of such infinitives after *tō*, and in five of those instances the verse will not scan under Sievers's and related systems of scansion. If Sievers's analysis is incorrect, it can only be called an improbable coincidence that such a large proportion of verses containing inflected infinitives fall outside Sievers's patterns. But since these infinitives cause similar metrical problems in other poems, it is not very plausible to attribute the proportions to chance, and Sievers's system must be observationally (if not theoretically) correct, at least in general outline.

To take another example, both Alan Bliss (1967) and John C. Pope (1966) find that verses like "þæt se mǣra" (2587a), with the first overt stress on the penultimate syllable (or resolved pair of syllables), occur only in the on-verse. That this could be an accident is implausible, since even by Pope's more conservative reckoning there are in the poem at least forty-five verses of this sort (which Bliss labels type A). Consequently, regardless of how much or how little faith one invests in Sievers's metrical types, it would be obtuse not to suspect something amiss if a verse of this sort did happen to occur in the off-verse. Now, as it happens, there are in fact in the off-verse twenty-one verses of the sort "swā hē nū gīt dêð" (1058b) that might be analyzed as belonging to type A. Yet in every instance the vowel of the final syllable is the result of contraction (as indicated by Klaeber's circumflex diacritic), and decontraction always produces a verse type normally encountered in the off-verse. That all twenty-one exceptions to the rule should involve contracted vowels of course cannot be coincidence, especially as vowels that, historically, should have undergone contraction appear in the last syllable of the off-verse fewer than forty times. And so posing these twenty-one verses as exceptions to the restriction of type A to the on-verse would demand the assumption of an extreme coincidence—that all the exceptions just happen to contain a contracted vowel.

The implausibility of the coincidence thus furnishes strong evidence for the distributional restriction on type A (as well as for the assumption that historically contracted vowels may be decontracted in verse), which in turn reinforces general assumptions about stress placement and other aspects of metrical analysis, including the assumption that the off-verse must contain an alliterating lift followed by a nonalliterating one. I have made a similar point elsewhere (1992, §26) on the basis of the more striking evidence of Kaluza's law, to which *Beowulf* seems to conform with almost perfect accuracy. There is nothing in Sievers's metrical system to compel such conformity, since clearly other poems do not conform to the law. Such a degree of conformity as that found in *Beowulf* could not be achieved by accident, and if it is not accidental, then Sievers's analysis of meter must be right in essence if not detail, since our understanding of the operation of the law depends on Sievers's conclusions. The accumulation of evidence in instances like this (of which there are many), mainly through the rejection of gross improbabilities, leads to a set of strong probabilities that demands an analysis of Old English meter roughly corresponding to the set of assumptions that the analyses of Sievers, Bliss, and Pope have in common. The outright dismissal of metrical evidence for textual editing, on the basis of the argument that Old English meter is too poorly understood, thus contradicts too many strong probabilities.

From these examples it should also be clear why even the less extreme objection, that the rules of meter are not rigid enough to support emendation of the text, is uninformed (since, clearly, probability must be decided on a case-by-case basis), as is the assertion that even the most basic metrical rules cannot be applied with much confidence because the textual evidence on which metrical rules are built is so unreliable. Certainly the unreliability of the textual evidence is a strong argument against basing editorial decisions on conclusions about rare metrical types, but only in the sense that rare types ought always to be suspect: the assumption of poor textual transmission in fact strengthens the basic tenets of metrical theory, since it may explain the occurrence of verse types that are difficult to reconcile with Sievers's conclusions about meter. Some of the prescriptions of metrical theory are indeed firmer than others; but on the whole, few emendations *metri causa* in major editions have been based on anything but the broadest and least debated generalizations about meter. None of the major editions marks unmetrical inflected infinitives in any way, even by underdotting the endings. Neither, for instance, do they emend "Bēowulf Scyldinga" (53b), even though the meter has the support of the West Saxon genealogies in suggesting the name ought to be Beow rather than Beowulf. In contrast to the practice of earlier editors, nor do the current editions emend "secg betsta" (947a, 1759a) or "ðegn betstan" (1871b), though the verses seem to violate "the most basic and universal of the metrical rules" (Amos 1981, 15), that there must be at least four syllables to the verse, and though Klaeber remarks that the manuscript readings are not most likely the original ones. The editors could hardly be anything but cautious, since few editions have shown any very marked adeptness at metrical analysis. Even Klaeber makes some metrically poor judgments, as when he adopts Trautmann's (1904) emendation of manuscript "inne" to "īrne" (1141b) requiring trisyllabic scansion, as it would stand metrically for *īrenne* (cf. 802b, etc.), and when he writes "an wīg gearwe" (1247b) for what ought to be "anwīggearwe," since the on-verse, "þæt hīe oft wæron," ought to have stress on *oft*, demanding vocalic alliteration. The former example is particularly noteworthy, since it demonstrates that meter not only compels some emendations but also prohibits others.

In the final analysis, then, for the editors of the current major editions the pertinent question has been not whether meter should play a role in editorial practice, but how significant that role should be. Should the text ever be emended solely on the basis of meter? Some critics of the major editions say no, and yet this means, for example, that the emended reading mentioned above, "[Ge]grētte þā" (652a), would have to be discarded, even though the unemended verse seems anomalous, even to many who know relatively little about meter. And what of the verses "wīca nēosian" (1125b) and "dennes nīosian" (3045a), showing two examples of a metrical type that does not normally appear in the off-verse and that normally bears double alliteration when it appears in the on-verse? Sievers (1885, 233) would solve the problem by substituting verbs of the first weak class (*nēosan/nīosan*), and this solution derives support from the observation that the verb of the first class appears eight times in the poem, seven times as an infinitive, while these are the only two instances of the verb of the second weak class, aside from one metrically ambiguous example.[2] Once the small number of exceptions to the restrictions on this verse type are seen to have a transparent explanation, it may be said that the rule has about the same regularity as the rule that a verse must contain at least four syllables. So why is it that all the major editions adopt the emended reading "[Ge]grētte þā" but do not change "nēosian" to "nēosan"? Is it simply that the metrical rule applying to the former is transparent to everyone, while only those who know Sievers's metrical system well perceive the problem with the latter, even though it is no less insistent? To place unquestioning faith in the decisions of editors of course would be foolhardy, but it is no doubt equally dangerous to suppose that editing requires no particular expertise—that changes should be made on a democratic basis, only when their justification is obvious to everyone.

Up into the early years of this century, the debate over textual emendation was waged vicariously in the form of the editions themselves, which ranged from the extremely conservative (particularly Grein 1857b; Heyne -Schücking 1908; and Wyatt 1894) to the freely conjectural (Trautmann 1904). To illustrate the latter, the first few lines of the first fitt (53–58) in Klaeber's unemended version on the left may be juxtaposed with Trautmann's version on the right, a passage in which his changes are particularly heavy:

Ðā wæs on burgum Bēowulf Scyldinga,	Ðā wæs on burgum Bēowulf Scylding,
lēof lēodcyning longe þrāge	lēof lēod-cyning, longe þrāge
folcum gefrǣge —fæder ellor hwearf,	folcum gefrǣge. Fæder *eþel* hwearf,
aldor of earde—, oþ þæt him eft onwōc	ald*res*, on e*aforan*, *þē* him ef*ter* wōc:
hēah Healfdene; hēold þenden lifde	hēah Healfdene hēold, *oð hē* līo*rde*
gamol ond gūðrēouw glæde Scyldingas.	gamol ond gūðr*ōu*w, glæde Scyldingas.

Very likely it was the nineteenth-century consensus about the composite origins of *Beowulf* that provided the critical climate in which such *Konjekturfreudigkeit* was possible: the connection between the *Liedertheorie* and disregard for the surviving text is perhaps clearest in Hermann Möller's 1883 reconstruction of the "original" text in 344 quatrains and in Ludwig Ettmüller's 1875 edition in 2,896 lines, with the "Christian interpolations" excised.

Yet it would not be fair to say that conjectural emendation ever had the upper hand or that the range of opinions was even a balanced one, since, at the one end of the spectrum, Trautmann's edition (which was not in fact an edition for scholars, containing a facing-page translation and no explanatory notes) was universally condemned—Sievers himself was especially severe (1904, 305)—while at the other, very conservative editions like Grein's and Heyne-Schücking's garnered high praise and wide use, the latter, in its latest edition, remaining in use to the present day. And so even if the *Liedertheorie* had not sunk into disfavor it is likely that conjectural emendation would have suffered the same fate anyway. For textual conservatism can fairly be said to have won the field decisively with the repudiation of Trautmann's edition (see Lapidge 1993, 135–38). The result was that a decade later, in the preface to his revision of Wyatt's edition, Raymond Chambers could claim with justice that "wanton alterations of the MS . . . are now no longer tolerated: and even to argue against them would be an anachronism" (Wyatt 1914, xxiii). There was of course a variety of opinions on the Continent, but the triumph of conservatism was above all an English victory. The shortcomings of English scholarship in the nineteenth century were painfully apparent, so that in the same place Chambers would surprise no one when he deplored the former English "neglect of the earliest monuments of our literature" (Wyatt 1914, xxii). This is in part because German philology had never sunk very deep roots in England—it had in fact met some stiff opposition—and while philology was in ascendance Germany dominated *Beowulf* scholarship. But by the early years of this century England had produced a generation of scholars to rival the great names on the Continent, including Chadwick, Chambers, Sedgefield, and Skeat, whose scholarly accomplishments were not so firmly grounded in linguistic issues. The rise of English scholarship naturally tipped the scales away from philology and thus from textual methods that depend on philological study.

Not surprisingly, then, the further decline of philological study in this century has paralleled not only the entrenchment but also the deepening of conservatism in textual studies. As Michael Lapidge points out (1991, 45), textual criticism has in fact grown so conservative that the reverence accorded Old English manuscripts now extends inexplicably even to John Casley's eighteenth-century transcript of the now perished manuscript of *The Battle of Maldon*. And Peter S. Baker (1992) reports that the majority of those taking part in a recent debate on ANSAXNET favored editions that reproduce the manuscript text, with little editing.[3] Recent years have thus seen the rise of even more conservative positions than those that gained ascendancy at the outset of the century, with the result that editors formerly regarded as moderate in their views are now thought to occupy the most immoderate positions, and there have been calls for even more conservative editions than those currently available. Something like the most extreme position possible in this direction—more or less absolute reliance on the manuscript, except in regard to accidentals—has in fact been championed by Raymond Tripp, in his edition of the last third of the poem (1983), and is implicit in Kiernan's argument that the manuscript is an autograph copy, in which case nearly all editorial emendation must be rejected, and what is needed now is "a new, truly conservative, edition" (1981a, 278).

Although neither of these views ever gained much credence, their very existence suggests that it may yet be worth demonstrating why some emendation cannot be avoided. A good example appears in lines 2304–2306a:

> wæs ðā gebolgen   beorges hyrde,
> wolde *se* lāða   līge forgyldan
> drincfæt dȳre.

Manuscript "wolde fela ða" (for Klaeber's "wolde se lāða") lacks alliteration, proper meter, and sense, and it is most readily understood as the result of the scribe's misreading of an *s* in his examplar as an *f*, two nearly identical letters.[4] The example is particularly significant because this is not the sort of error a scribe could commit while either taking dictation or composing: it requires a written exemplar. Significant for the same reason is the verse "Gewāt him on naca" (1903b), emended from manuscript "nacan." Here apparently a scribe naturally enough took Beowulf to be the subject and assumed that an oblique ending was required in order for *naca* to serve as the object of the preposition *on*. Actually, the vocalic alliteration shows that *on* must be stressed—it is apparently an adverb—and so the ship is the subject. A similar instance occurs in lines 2769b–71a:

> of ðām lēom*a* stōd,
> þæt hē þone grundwong   ongitan meahte,
> wræ*te* giondwlītan.

Here "lēoma" is the subject of "stōd," so that the phrase means "from it a light arose." Manuscript "leoman" (for Klaeber's "lēoma") is apparently a result of the scribe's mistaking the syntax and, naturally enough, making the word the object of the preposition *of*. In the same passage the manuscript reading "wræce" (for Klaeber's "wræte") makes no very obvious sense and is best explained as a copyist's error, due to the similarity of the letters *c* and *t* in Anglo-Saxon scripts and to the familiarity of prosaic "wracu" and "wræc" in comparison to rare and poetic "wræt(t)." The same error in the same word is found in line 3060a. Similar confusion of letter forms seems to have affected lines 2881b–83:

> fȳr unswīðor
> wēoll of gewitte.   *W*ergendra tō lȳt
> þrong ymbe þēoden,   þā hyne sīo þrāg becwōm.

Manuscript "fergendra" (Klaeber's "wergendra") suggests that a scribe has mistaken *wynn* for *f*, two similar letters. The emendation corrects the faulty alliteration and makes sense of what appears to be nonsense.

It thus seems that certain kinds of emendation are unavoidable. It has of course been proposed that Old English poets could disregard alliteration at will, that metrical regularities are a philological fantasy, and that seeming obscurities of syntax and meaning are always due to our own deficiencies. Yet few are satisfied with blanket dismissals of the evidence, since they suggest gross improbabilities, not simply of a statistical sort (as with the metrical evidence discussed above), but, more important, of a textual sort, since it would otherwise be peculiar that textual incoherences of syntax or meaning are so often accompanied by alliterative and metrical difficulties, and vice versa. And so although Wilhelm Busse (1981, 202) argues that alliteration was not a strict requirement—and he is only the most expansive of a surprising number of like-minded critics—actually, more than half his examples of nonalliteration in *Exodus* also involve difficulties of another sort.

Such bald rejections of the requirement of alliteration as Busse's might at first seem implausible, yet Paul Zumthor (1984, 87–88) has argued that the nature of medieval oral works is such that we should not expect metrical regularity in them—a position that John D. Niles extends to alliteration, as well, and applies to the textual criticism of *Beowulf* (1994). The postulate here is that relative uniformity of meter and alliteration is a quality of literate texts, and so if it is found in recorded verse thought to be basically oral, it must be the result of scribal smoothing out of oral irregularities.[5] Yet the same obstacle of probabilism remains. In *Beowulf* itself, illegible words aside, out of 3,182 lines there are just thirty-seven that, unemended, would lack any alliterative link between the verses. It would be surprising if we did *not* encounter some such proportion, given the known unreliability of scribal transmission (see, e.g., Amos 1981, 171–96), and so this is not actually an anomaly that requires explanation, oral-formulaic or otherwise. But more important, in twenty-three of these thirty-seven nonalliterating lines, emending for the sake of alliteration also improves the meter, grammar, and/or sense. If nonalliteration were a poetic choice rather than the result of scribal change, it would be difficult to account convincingly for such a high coincidence of nonalliteration with other sorts of textual problems. The metrical and alliterative anomalies of the manuscript text are therefore less likely to be survivals of a formally irregular "original" than copyists' errors.

Still, the ascendancy of textual conservatism prevails to this day, with little dissent. Almost alone in his skepticism is Kenneth Sisam (1953a). He sets side by side parallel passages from the two versions of the Old English *Soul and Body*, and from the portions of *Daniel* and *Azarias* that overlap, as well as *Solomon and Saturn*, to show how different the versions are. Assuming the pairs derive from a single source, he deduces that Old English scribes felt no obligation to copy very faithfully when reproducing vernacular texts in verse. For most verse we have no proof, since almost all poems are preserved in a single manuscript; but this evidence, he says, suggests that we should not in any case assume that the text of *Beowulf* before us, or of almost any other Old English poem, closely resembles the "original composition." Sisam's conclusion is that textual conservatism is bad methodology, since the manuscripts before us are almost certainly corrupt and do not reflect the original creators' intentions: in proceeding conservatively, editors are lending authority to the textual corruptions of late and often obtuse scribes. Sisam recommends skepticism as an antidote to critical complacency, which most editions feed, admitting few emendations, and thereby giving the impression that the manuscripts are reliable.

For the most part, textual critics have neither accepted Sisam's conclusions nor managed to quash entirely the doubts he raises. Even if it is conceded that the *Beowulf* manuscript does reflect the effects of a substantial history of scribal intervention, it may still be argued that Sisam draws the wrong conclusion from his evidence—that what his parallel passages really demonstrate is that attempting to recover the poet's own work from under the layers of scribal interference is a vain project. Allen Frantzen (1990, 180–81), for one, expresses dissatisfaction with the idea that there actually existed a person we might justly refer to as "the *Beowulf* poet," and he advocates viewing the poem as the product of multiple authorship, calling for even more conservative textual practices than those currently employed. Katherine O'Brien O'Keeffe (1990) examines other parallel passages to demonstrate that the scribes did not simply copy vernacular verse mindlessly, making inadvertent alterations, but that they were steeped in a poetic tradition that licensed them to rewrite the text as they copied. This view would seem to imply that if there ever existed a unitary authorial text it may now be irrecoverable, since it has been altered in ways that we cannot detect. Douglas Moffat has countered O'Brien O'Keeffe's view with evidence that the scribes of the two versions of *Soul and Body* were not in fact sensitive and competent, but he still concludes that a poem should not be regarded as "the unified product of a single mind" (1992, 826). These scholars are hardly in agreement about editorial principles and practices, but their common view that a unified, original text cannot be recovered is associated to a greater or lesser degree with the idea that a manuscript text has a validity (or perhaps inevitability) of its own, a validity that, being more concrete, exceeds that of any reconstruction.[6]

The focus on the "original text" seems to me unfortunate, since it constructs a false dialectic in which the validity of an otherwise debatable position (that the manuscript text must be accepted as authoritative) is affirmed only by the patent absurdity of its opposite (that the "original text" can be recovered). In actuality, retrieving the original does not seem ever to have been the aim of the poem's editors, for otherwise they would have made considerably more extensive changes than they have, for example regularly altering the West Saxon spellings of the manuscript, substituting Anglian equivalents.[7] Despite even some editors' claims to the contrary, then, the purpose of the major editions cannot ever have been to recover a unitary original composition but only to mark likely sites of corruption and remove only those spurious accretions that can be identified with some certainty. If this is the case, the question of whether a unified original composition can be recovered is largely irrelevant. O'Brien O'Keeffe's views happily avoid the reductive thinking of the binarism that notions of an original text lead to, since she offers a suppler model of the manuscript text as a sort of performance, analogous, as A. N. Doane (1991) points out, to the oral-formulaic view of texts as records of performances. She is surely right that scribes could be involved, even intelligently involved, in rewriting the poems before them. There is an analogue, for instance, in the wide divergences among manuscript versions of some later medieval romances, such as *Beves of Hamtoun* and *King Horn*, which are due to the involvement of either minstrels (according to A. C. Baugh 1967) or scribes (according to Derek Pearsall 1985, 100–101) in recomposition of the works. I have myself argued elsewhere that at least one scribe in the course of this poem's transmission was aware of the meter (1992, §§279–80)—even if it can be shown that other scribes (or the same scribes in other places) were not, as demonstrated already by the examples given above. Of course it is true that in emending the text we might simply be restoring a reading that is itself an accretion. But as always, humanists must deal with relative probabilities, and well-motivated emendations like some of those given above are likelier to have authority than many clearly deficient manuscript readings. This should be fairly obvious, since scribes are at least not compelled to be aware of grammar, alliteration, meter, and sense as they copy, while, even if poets sometimes make mistakes, they still in general are obliged to observe the constraints of form and meaning. Moreover, elsewhere I have offered reasons to doubt the view that the text of *Beowulf* is so diverse or diversified in origin as to preclude rational metrical analysis (1992, §§32–33), and some of those reasons apply to these specifically textual arguments, as well. Particularly significant is the poem's nearly perfect conformity to Kaluza's law, when the law seems generally disregarded by other poets. Such a unique degree of conformity throughout the poem suggests a unified origin and generally only superficial scribal tampering. This is not to say that an original text can be recovered but that the text is probably not as thoroughly altered as some have feared.

The issue of authorial intent has been dealt with more effectively outside the field of Old English, and particularly in the work of Jerome J. McGann (1983, 1985, 1991), who has demonstrated that for some more recent texts the idea of a single set of final intentions on the author's part may be a chimera. For example, a text may exist in several states, perhaps published at different times, all with authorial sanction, the latest of which is not necessarily the most satisfactory; and a publisher's editorial changes may have been sanctioned by the author as improvements. (The former situation, at least, is best exemplified for the medieval period by the texts of *Piers Plowman* but perhaps also by Ælfric's *Catholic Homilies*.)[8] McGann's conclusion is that the production of a literary text is a social phenomenon and that we should be wary of editorial practices that continue to promote the Romantic view of the text as an ideal existing only in the mind of the author, of which the best expression in this imperfect world can only be the version least contaminated by interference with the creator's pure inspiration.

But this is not to say that authorial intent is irrelevant to the construction of a critical edition, and McGann rightly insists that even though an author's intentions may not be clear or simple, "texts can and must be analyzed in such a way as to distinguish author's intentions toward the works, or the degree of revision and correction which the various texts display, both authorial and nonauthorial" (1983, 122). What he advocates, then, is the construction of a "social text," one that distinguishes layers of revision and alteration—contrary to what most Anglo-Saxonists seem now to prefer. McGann's seems to me the solution that O'Brien O'Keeffe's arguments also implicitly demand, since the glass she holds up to Old English verse reveals texts that are layered products of authorial and scribal interaction, and an honest critical edition ought to reflect that polygeneity. For that purpose the least desirable text of *Beowulf* would be a diplomatic edition, which presents a single, late version as the only version with any authority.

In some ways the prevailing view on *Beowulf* thus seems to counter the direction that textual theory has taken in recent years, especially in regard to Anglo-Saxonists' desire for a textual absolute to replace the perpetual instability and editorial subjectivity that are part and parcel of the textual condition. Conservatism and liberal emendation both entail genuine dangers, and yet at the moment it seems to be the dangers of conservatism that are underrated. In addition to the general theoretical matters already mentioned, there are some practical difficulties of long standing that textual conservatism has not yet adequately addressed, not the least of which is that the lightly edited text draws attention away from issues of scholarly debate. In part the problem is simply typographical. Sisam remarks, "To support a bad manuscript reading is in no way more meritorious than to support a bad conjecture, and so far from being safer, it is more insidious as a source of error. For, in good practice, a conjecture is printed with some distinguishing mark which attracts doubts; but a bad manuscript reading, if it is defended, looks like solid ground for the defence of other readings" (1953, 39). Eric Stanley refers to a text "adorned with italics and various shapes of brackets" as "pedantically disfigured" (1984, 232); but however unaesthetic the visual display of the edited text might be, Sisam's point is well taken. The Anglo-Saxon Poetic Records (Krapp and Dobbie 1931–53), which represents such an unadorned text, seems particularly objectionable in placing manuscript readings at the bottom of the page without marking changes in the text itself, leading even the experienced to mistake emendations for scribal work.

By contrast, Klaeber's typographical choices make students aware not just of the conflicted nature of the text, but also of textual issues they probably would not otherwise recognize, as when he underdots excrescent vowels and circumflects uncontracted vowels and diphthongs, drawing attention to differences between manuscript and reconstructed versions without actually obscuring the scribal version. Such methods could be used in other instances, such as the treatment of inflected infinitives and the verb *nēosian*, mentioned above. Since few people now study the philological issues that underlie the construction of the text, such devices serve as an insistent visual reminder of the range of issues involved in debate about the nature of the text and promote more responsible scholarship by reminding students that many sorts of knowledge must be engaged before intelligent choices can be made one way or the other in establishing and interpreting the text. The semidiplomatic edition, on the other hand, promotes the illusion that interpretation is not constrained by philological issues. Teachers of *Beowulf* at American universities by and large do not have the training to serve as authorities for their students on many philological issues, and yet a largely unedited text forces readers to decide such matters for themselves. Peter Baker (1992) remarks that such "editorial democracy" discounts the value of the editor's expertise. Thus, in large part the debate over textual conservatism masks a less fully articulated debate over the issues of authority and specialization within Anglo-Saxon studies.

A consideration of probability is necessary in making intelligent editorial decisions, and this is roughly what recent textual theorists mean—even those as divergent in their views as G. Thomas Tanselle (1986, 2, 45–46) and McGann (1983, 104, 107)—when they insist on the relativity of all textual authority and upon the editor's obligation to engage in subjective decisions. Textual ultraconservatism seems to contradict this axiom of textual practice since, in varying degrees according to its different permutations, ultraconservatism amounts to an injunction for us not to interpret the poem: if we cannot make sense of what the manuscript says, the fault is most likely ours, and we should beware of imposing modern, ethnocentric cultural assumptions on the poem. Distrust of philology owing to its origins, for example, tends to this conclusion, enjoining us not to prejudice interpretation of the poem by rewriting the text on the basis of our own politicially and culturally suspect motives. But historians know that if the mere danger of ethnocentrism justified the refusal to interpret, there would be no historiography, since there is no place outside of history from which to view it: it simply is not possible to transcend one's own time and culture. One can only attempt to interpret historical material armed with a strong sense of the probable—and of course much textual evidence, including linguistic evidence, is historical in nature, too. In any case, it is as true in regard to *Beowulf* as other texts that every edition is by nature an interpretation. For example, among the major editions even the most conservative ones, and even Tripp's (1983), add punctuation, and this affects meaning, as in lines 669–72a, where Klaeber's punctuation resembles that of all the major editions:

Hūru Gēata lēod   georne truwode
mōdgan mægnes,   Metodes hyldo.—

Ðā hē him of dyde   īsernbyrnan,
helm of hafelan.

Yet the break after "hyldo" could be replaced by a comma, turning the next few verses into a subordinate clause. That is, the relation between the two clauses may be causal: Beowulf removed his armor *because* he trusted in God and his own strength. Any editorial decision in this case is a decision about meaning. Likewise, Klaeber's extraordinary glossary I think has exerted more influence on the interpretation of the poem than the sum of his textual changes. The purpose of a critical edition is to make the text accessible in ways that a facsimile does not, and so the relevant question is not whether an edition should interpret but how much it should interpret.

This question cannot be answered outside the context of the use to which an edition is to be put. Indeed, a prevalent assumption in current views of textual editing is that a critical edition is no less a social text than any other sort of text: it has aims suited to a particular purpose and audience and cannot be constructed effectively without the requirements of that purpose and audience in mind. McGann, for instance, would predicate the editor's choice of edition type (diplomatic, etc.) in part on whether the edited piece is regarded as a "text," a "poem," or a "work" (1991, 31–32). Thus, when, for example, J. R. Hall remarks, "To omit manuscript accents and to substitute modern for manuscript capitalization and punctuation is to set aside evidence on scribal tradition and reception" (1995b, 22), he is certainly right; but does this really mean that editors should never change the accidentals of the manuscript? He undoubtedly means this about something other than a students' edition of a verse text; but even in regard to a text for advanced scholars, different editorial practices will serve different research purposes, with metrists, for example, for most purposes preferring the marking of vowel quantities to the reproduction of manuscript accents. Word division is a similar problem. To offer a few of many examples: for "þysses" (806b) the manuscript reads "þys ses," for "ellenmærþum" (828a) "ellen mær þum," for "spel gerāde" (873b) "spel ge ra de," and for "þē ic geweald hæbbe" (950b) "þe icge weald hæbbe." Anglo-Saxon attitudes toward the relationship between morpheme spacing and juncture were clearly different from ours, and we can learn something about the language from observing the manuscript spacing. But such information is best gleaned from a facsimile, and examples like these demonstrate what difficulties students would encounter in a text really guided by the view that editors must not interpret.

Frantzen's (1990) quarrel with the existing editions leads in the opposite direction, for while his book admirably places the question in a pedagogical context, textual issues are considered from the standpoint of how editions influence the way the poem is taught rather than from the standpoint of how the demands of teaching and studying the poem influence the construction of editions. But even if this textual idealism, the desire for a text unencumbered by the influence of modern contexts, could be achieved, it could hardly be reconciled with the necessarily interpretive nature of critical editions. To use the "worldly" terms that Frantzen recommends, translating the entire poem in the course of a semester is a difficult enough task if there is to be any intelligent discussion as well. Is there really any good reason, for example, to compel students semester after semester to puzzle out the unmetrical nonsense word "swicðole" (3145a), an obvious error for "swioðole," when so many other matters of genuine importance must be accomplished in a semester?

This is not to say that the requirements of the classroom are the only ones that should be taken into account in the construction of a critical edition (though I doubt even the subtlest of Anglo-Saxonists could find much of interest to say about "swicðole"). But it might with fairness be said of philology as of learning in Alfred's England, "swā clǣne is hīo oðfeallenu," that it is a foolhardy scholar who would dare dispense altogether with an editor's guidance on philological issues. In a better world Klaeber's edition, which I suspect was at first intended as a students' edition, would be just that. As matters stand, though we all no doubt disagree with Klaeber at least in matters of detail, if not in more fundamental respects, to abandon an edited text and place faith in one's own editorial acumen would betray an enviable degree of self-confidence. This is not to say that editors are implicitly trustworthy: on the contrary, perpetual skepticism, as McGann rightly insists (1985, 187), should govern our attitude not only toward the text but also toward its critics. Yet *Beowulf* scholarship has perhaps never been farther from achieving a real balance between those two sorts of skepticism.[9]

Notes

I wish to thank Peter S. Baker, J. R. Hall, and John D. Niles for their generosity in sharing unpublished material with me. In addition, Robert E. Bjork, Alfred and Linda David, Michael Lapidge, John D. Niles, and John C. Pope read this chapter in draft and offered generous criticisms. To them I owe a debt of gratitude.

1. Ælfric twice expresses his distrust of scribes: "Nu ic bidde and halsige, on Godes naman, gif hwa ðas boc awritan wylle, þæt he hi geornlice gerihte be ðære bysne, þe-læs ðe we, þurh gymeleasum writerum, geleahtrode beon" (*Sermones*; Thorpe 1844–46, 2: 2–3); and "Ic bidde nu on Godes naman, gif hwa ðas boc awritan wille, ðæt he hi gerihte wel be ðære bysne, for ðan ðe ic nah geweald, ðeah ðe hi hwa to woge gebringe þurh lease writeras, and hit bið ðonne his pleoh na min: micel yfel deð se unwritere, gyf he nele his gewrit gerihtan" ("Preface to Genesis"; Crawford 1922, 80).

2. The ambiguous example is at 115a. In one other instance the Thorkelin transcripts read *mosum* (A) and *niosnan* (B). Klaeber emends to *fīonda nīos(i)an* (2671b), another metrical anomaly unless *nīosan* is substituted.

3. "The Animated Edition." Medieval Institute Conference. Kalmazoo MI.

4. Tripp's retention of the manuscript reading, translating "He would then with a lot of fire pay for / The precious drinking-cup" (cf. also Taylor and Davis 1982, 620, n. 6) of course is difficult to reconcile with normal assumptions about Old English syntax and semantics, as are his treatments of the following two examples.

5. Albert B. Lord found a very different situation among Balkan *guslari*: they have more difficulty composing normal verses when they are dictating than when they are merely performing, because slowing down the performance confuses the singer (1965, 126–27). This observation suggests another source of

formal irregularities in Old English verse. But even if *Beowulf* is an oral work (though one should then expect the incidence of abnormal verses to be significantly different in the literate works of Cynewulf), and if Old English verse was composed as rapidly as modern Macedonian song (Bede's account of Cædmon suggests otherwise, since Cædmon worked on his material overnight), probability still remains an obstacle: the co-occurrence of different sorts of formal irregularities suggests corruption in the course of scribal transmission.

6. This seems to be how Lapidge, too, understands the matter. He represents O'Brien O'Keeffe's view (1990), with which he differs, as leading to the conclusion that "every manuscript copy of an Old English poem is, in effect, a 'scribal version,' and as such deserves to be treated on its own" (1991, 41). Saying that the manuscript text is "inevitable" rather than "valid" perhaps better describes Moffat's position on textual conservatism, which he does not finally make very explicit. But he seems to be advocating increased conservatism when he deprecates the value of meter as an editorial tool. Examining eight parallel verses of *Daniel* and *Azarias* he finds "fairly consistent preservation of the meter" (1992, 826), and wonders, "How is one to detect skillful or even competent interpolation if only a single copy of a work remains?" (826). (Actually, of his eight examples two involve problems of meter or alliteration, *Daniel* 323a and *Azarias* 39a.) Ultimately his conclusions pertain to the validity of metrical analysis (and literary criticism in the form of close readings) rather than to textual criticism. But this objection is not new, and I have attempted elsewhere to deal with the issues and define the limits of the usefulness of metrical evidence (1992, §§25–33).

7. Most editors have agreed that the poem has been copied, either directly or indirectly, from an Anglian exemplar. For a review of the evidence, see Fulk (1992, chapter 11). A. S. Cook and Sievers did in fact attempt to rewrite some poetic texts into Anglian dialects: see the references given by Stanley (1984, 252, nn. 5–6). The failure of these experiments to influence general editorial practice supports the larger point.

8. Sisam argues that after their composition Ælfric "was constantly retouching the collection or adding to it at the suggestion of friends" (1953b, 179), and this is why the homilies exist in three discrete states.

9. This chapter was written early in 1993, when electronic media for the textual study of *Beowulf* were at a preliminary stage of development. Now, in mid-1996, there are several electronic editions and other computer resources under continuing revision and available on the Internet. The oldest of these is Patrick W. Conner's *"Beowulf* Workstation," a set of HyperCard stacks for the Apple Macintosh that provides a glossary for translation of the poem and a set of secondary materials, including critical studies, analogues, and digitized images of the Cotton mansuscript and some Anglo-saxon artifacts. "The Electronic *Beowulf,*" under the direction of Kevin Kiernan and Paul E. Szarmach as a project of the British Library, has made available detailed downloadable digitized images of the manuscript, the Thorkelin transcripts, and some early collations (Kiernan 1993–). The directors plan to continue work on enhancing images of obscured readings for their recovery. Several electronic editions of the poem are readily available, including Dobbie's edition (1953) and a text with a scansion by B. R. Hutcheson (as part of a larger corpus). Links to sites providing information on these and other resources may be found at the Old English Pages at http://www.georgetown.edu/cball/oe/old_english.html

Chapter 4

Prosody

by Robert P. Stockwell and Donka Minkova

Summary: Theories about the regularity of Old English meter are based on the assumption that verse is fundamentally different from prose. Even if one finds attractive Daunt's frequently cited suggestion that "Old English verse is really the spoken language rather tidied up" (1946, 64), the "tidying up" that eliminates common prose patterns from the poetic corpus needs to be addressed. Studies of the abstract structure of Old English meter fall into two camps. One camp focuses on regularities in syllable count (though not in the manner of post-Renaissance verse), and the other counts beats. Sievers initiated the former approach, and it continues in the work of Bliss, Cable, Kendall, and Fulk, among many others. Heusler initiated the latter one, and it continues in the work of Pope, Creed, and Russom, as well as among others, though perhaps not so many. The work of Sievers and Bliss has been refined into a theory of meter by Cable. The isochronous theory of Heusler and Pope was erected on a shaky linguistic foundation, which has been considerably buttressed by Russom. The use of scansion for the purpose of emendation depends on a precisely quantified theory, which is what Sievers and Bliss achieved. The notions of natural performable rhythms, on the other hand, may well depend on a large measure of isochrony, as theories of oral-derived verse would seem to entail.

Chronology

1703: George Hickes, basing his analysis of Old English verse on classical models, asserts that the meter is strictly quantitative.

1813: John Josias Conybeare (1826), against Hickes, denies that the verse was quantitative in nature, rather that periodicity of beats was fundamental.

1817: Rasmus Rask takes alliteration as the defining characteristic of the verse and classifies it in accord with a standard typology of Old Icelandic verse.

1848: Wilhelm Wackernagel proposes a two-beat theory in which 'feet' are dispensed with, defining a verse as consisting of two stressed syllables plus an unlimited number of weakly stressed syllables.

1876: Friedrich Rieger provides the first extended application of the two-beat theory to Old English verse.

1885: Eduard Sievers publishes the study that underlies all subsequent work in Old English metrics because of the precision and detail of its empirical foundation; devises a taxonomy of verse types A–E that no other system of scansion has been able to supersede as a "reference system."

1891: Andreas Heusler rejects Sievers's system and proposes a countertheory consisting of musical measures in which a foot is the distance from stress to stress and a verse is any two feet with proper alliteration. Allows any number of weak syllables between stresses, and allows silent ictus as well as silent drops where needed to generate isochrony.

1893: Sievers develops the 1885 system and applies it to all Germanic alliterative poetry.

1894: Max Kaluza clarifies the conditions under which the monosyllabic prefixes (*ge-, be-, ā-, on-, for-,* etc.) are extrametrical. Rejects Sievers's rising feet, though denies association of the feet with musical bars, which would entail isochrony.

1896: Kaluza discovers that failures of resolution, confined to metrical positions following a main stress within the same foot, are also governed by the etymological weight of the inflectional syllable in the resolvable sequence. The correlation between failure of resolution and inflectional weight is known as *Kaluza's law.*

1925: Sievers retracts the system of scansion for which he is most famous, because one can't beat time to it. He discards the most fundamental principle of alliteration, namely, that it is governed by the first foot of the off-verse. His retraction has been to a large extent ignored, justly.

1942: John C. Pope attempts to replace Sievers's theory with an isochronic theory of meter that rests on a notion of performance that is logically impossible to reconstruct. He rejects Heusler's earlier attempt at isochrony. Provides a complete catalog and a line index, both extremely useful.

1948: Samuel O. Andrew develops metrical criteria for interpreting syntax and style using *Beowulf* as his principal text.

1948: Paull F. Baum argues that the verses in the poem are fundamentally trochaic (not as a statistical observation but as a theoretical foundation: the former is correct, the latter is not), but the discussion is unsophisticated in respect to the Old English stress rules and therefore often imposes modern perceptions on a system that had a different basis.

1950: Jerzy Kuryłowicz claims that Sievers's system can be totally reduced to the scheme [w s w s w] (where "w" = "weakly-stressed syllable," and "s" = "strongly-stressed syllable") by suppression of the first [w], the second [w], the first [w s], or the first and third [w]'s. While this is true, in a purely mathematical sense, unlimited random suppression is not a theory of metrical form.

1956: Winfred P. Lehmann argues that the nature of the stress system of the language conditioned possible verse types, in particular requiring the "jagged effect" produced by D-types and E-types. Highly sophisticated comparative study of Anglo-Saxon epic verse with other Germanic epic literature.

1957: R. B. Le Page attempts to reconcile the theories of Sievers and Pope and in so doing argues in favor of violating the four-position rule.

1958: Jess B. Bessinger Jr. speculates on performance with a harp and in so doing tries to defend Pope's theory of isochronous rhythm.

1958: Alan J. Bliss expands Sievers's five verse types into 130 by elaboration of a system for characterizing the variation within each type. Discards the foot, replaces it with a quite different notion of caesural boundaries that are syntactically determined. Differentiates between light and heavy verses (based on number of strong stresses). Discards tertiary stress, arguing that it is functionally equivalent to weak. In part by virtue of its later use by Fulk (1992) in his monumental history, it is widely taken as the base for comparative metrical research in Old English.

1958: Lehmann and Takemitsu Tabusa produce an alphabetical list of alliterating words in the poem.

1959: R. B. Le Page demonstrates that "extra-alliteration has no stylistic significance in Old English poetry."

1961: Josef Taglicht argues that the meter of the poem was not isochronous but that the role of long versus short syllables was crucial. On this basis he proposes a system of scansion in which the measures are not of uniform length but are nonetheless measured beginning from each strong stress.

1962: Bliss clarifies differences between meter as found in Old English and meter as developed in English from the Renaissance onward.

1966: Robert P. Creed proposes minimal variation on Pope's isochronous theory.

1967: Rudolph Willard and Elinor D. Clemons modify Bliss's 1958 concept of light verses in favor of stressing finite verbs early in verses.

1968: Jan Cygan defends Kuryłowicz 1950, allowing even greater freedom such that several three-position verse types are recognized.

1969: Constance B. Hieatt analyzes hypermetric lines and develops a theory (in opposition to Pope's) in which each verse has three feet, a view generally accepted by subsequent metrists (except for Russom, who incorporates them into regular feet).

1969: Samuel J. Keyser develops a theory of meter that would make all lines in the poem metrical, a view generally rejected by subsequent metrists.

1970: Kuryłowicz argues that the alliteration rule derives from the Old English compound-stress rule.

1971: Thomas M. Cable argues that the first of two clashing stresses (i.e., consecutive stresses as in C and D verses) always receives the heavier stress. This view recapitulates the fundamental rule of Old English stress.

1972: Bliss explores the derivation of the Old English hypermetric line.

1972: Hieatt devises a convenient summary of Sievers's system, mainly, with comments on alternative systems and their possible virtues.

1974: Cable develops a new metrical-melodic theory of meter: given four metrical positions per verse, there are eight hypothetical metrical patterns; but given the condition that the second of two clashing stresses cannot be heavier, the eight hypothetical patterns are reduced to five. Suggests possible melodic analogs in the Gregorian chant.

1974: Eric G. Stanley examines A3 verses and classifies the more than 300 such verses in the poem.

1976: Spencer Cosmos reexamines the differences between stressed and unstressed verbs in the poem.

1976: John M. Foley bases a metrical analysis of the poem on the assumptions of isochrony and three stress levels.

1978: Jane-Marie Luecke applies the principles of Gregorian chant rhythm to the meter of the poem.

1985: David L. Hoover discusses, with insight, problems with all existing metrical accounts, especially with the traditional treatment of verses of type A3, and the related principles of resolution and anacrusis. Argues that Old English meter is neither stress-based nor rhythm-based; alliteration is the primary and only significant organizing principle.

1987: Daniel Donoghue, observing that only eight out of Bliss's fifty-five verses with anacrusis appear in the off-verse, violating the double alliteration condition on anacrusis, argues that such verses ([w s w s w]) could be reclassified as type C's with line-internal anacrusis, rather than the traditional A-type with initial anacrusis.

1987: Geoffrey Russom offers the first theory to propose a linguistic basis for the prosodic patterns that appear in the poem. This basis is taken to be that set of stress patterns that actually occur on regular Old English words.

1987: Wolfgang Obst presents arguments that require treating all half stresses as ictic, thereby expanding many lines to five feet and violating the four-position principle. Presents arguments that would disallow failure of resolution, claiming that a phonological rule of the language cannot be metrically ignored. The consequence of this argument is to create lines with only three positions. Allows no extrametrical syllables except anacrusis, which creates many additional expanded dips, often outside the first dip.

1990: Geoffrey Vickman provides an indispensable tool for metrists, a full concordance presented in the Bliss system of scansion. Provides instant access to all verses of any desired type.

1990: Creed continues Pope's work in isochronous interpretation, claiming that Kemble's system of lineation must have depended on the kind of isochronous foot and measure analysis that he (Creed) presents.

1990: Russom formalizes Kuryłowicz's 1970 suggestion about the fundamental nature of alliteration and demonstrates the relevance of foot constituency to the specification of alliteration.

1991: Cable refines his earlier work into a set of principles that generate all and only the Sievers's five types (and then goes on to show that these principles are substantially different from those needed to account for the verse form of the "Alliterative Revival").

1991: Calvin B. Kendall introduces a great deal of morphology and syntax into the notation of scansion with the intention of providing a stronger foundation for formulaic explanations of verse composition.

1992: R. D. Fulk authors a triumph of the Sievers-Bliss-Cable tradition, a comprehensive study aimed at identifying diachronic and diatopic metrical variation through the Old English period. Combines philological, linguistic, and metrical argumentation to establish what is perhaps as close as we can get to a linguistically definitive chronology of the Old English poetic corpus.

1993: Frank W. Whitman argues that the accentual alliterative verse of preclassical Latin was composed in a tradition related to that of Germanic.

1995: B. R. Hutcheson introduces a new wave of empirical accuracy into Anglo-Saxon metrics—by publishing commentary on a fully-scanned database (some 13,000 lines in a standard computer program—D-Base or Excel) in a notational system that is transparent (unlike Bliss), coherent, and easily mastered. His discussion highlights alliteration, formulaic diction, and syntax to a greater extent than the Bliss contingent has characteristically done.

Why develop a theory of meter? one may ask. From the point of view of the scop, surely the primary role of meter was its mnemonic value. If we believe that virtually all Anglo-Saxon verse was composed in accord with the conventions of what was originally an oral-formulaic tradition, then we must believe there was a set of metrical parameters that made it easy to recall set phrases and to construct new ones in the same patterns. Beyond this obvious primary function, the rhythm that results from the performance of metrical regularity is intrinsically pleasurable. The scops were not merely telling stories, and telling them in ways that were easy to recall and easy to elaborate; they were composing them in ways that were entertaining.

The idea of "performance" is nonetheless a hazardous one today. Even given all the metrical constraints Sievers, Heusler, and subsequent generations managed to figure out, we cannot know what an oral presentation of *Beowulf* sounded like, rhythmically. We can imagine performances that resembled the style of Gregorian chants (lacking isochrony), or we can imagine isochronous performances wherein the strumming of a harp filled the empty beats. There is no hard evidence either way, and the question of performance is moot.

There remains a need for understanding the meter. It is useful to discriminate, in discussions of prosody, between system and performance. In this chapter, we use the term *meter* to refer to the system and the term *rhythm* to refer to the performance. Rhythm depends on and can go far beyond the meter, but it cannot be recovered since it is intrinsic not to the language or to the verse but to the performance. Meter, which provides the basis of rhythm, derives from a set of intrinsic properties of language—recurrent variations of syllabic prominence and recurrent identities—either onset identity ("alliteration"), as in Old English, or coda identity ("rime"), as later. These intrinsic properties are universal in language, within a small range of variation, and the details can be substantially recovered from the orthographic record that remains to us.

Metrical studies have provided a rational basis for numerous emendations. These are singled out in all the standard editions. Such emendations may be challenged as circular, given that the metrical system is derived necessarily from the

existing (unemended) text and then applied back in a circle to remove "irregularities" that might not appear to be irregularities if one had figured out a better
metrical system. Surely the decisions one takes on such issues are based on
probabilities. If, to take a simple case, the vast majority of verses contain at least
four syllables, a verse like 947a *secg betsta* must be viewed as rationally emendable
to *secga betsta*. The possibility always remains open that some metrical theory will
be discovered that makes better predictions about emendation than existing theories,
and such a discovery would no doubt be quickly embraced. But it is not likely, for
example, just looking at the emendations *metri causa* that have been generally
accepted on the basis of the syllable-counting theory of Sievers, that a theory that
claimed that the meter of *Beowulf* consisted of alliteration plus four strong beats
with unstressed syllables scattered unsystematically among them could possibly
prevail, since such a view provides a weak probabilistic basis for emendation.

One would like to argue that the understanding of a metrical system provides
some specific kind of guidance to literary interpretation. We doubt that such a case
can be made persuasively; and it is even less likely that it can be made for Anglo-
Saxon metrics than for later metrics, since the essence of metrical excellence in
Anglo-Saxon terms is variation around a fixed set of norms, whereas at a later time
the essence is creating various forms of tension between the linguistic manifestation
of the rhythm, on the one hand, and the metrically prescribed alternation of
prominence levels on the other. The principal special effect that variation around
norms allows is for the scop to pick the shorter and heavier variants in a weighty
passage (e.g., in the funeral passages) and the lighter quicker variants in, for
example, fast action scenes. Just how much subtlety of effect is made possible by
these devices is open to dispute.

I. Approaches to metrics

The two main approaches to Anglo-Saxon metrics were enunciated clearly by
Sievers and Heusler at the end of the nineteenth century. Both positions share the
view, clearly expounded for the cognate tradition of Old Norse in the *Háttattal* of
Snorri Sturluson around 1220, that the two verses of a long line are linked by
alliteration. They differ in one central claim. In the Sievers tradition, the number of
weak syllables allowed to appear between strong syllables is strictly regulated, and
longer strings are limited to the first weak position. A consequence of this claim is
that a Sievers scansion does not "keep time," that is, does not have equally spaced
periodic crests. In the Heusler tradition, isochrony is mandated. One is given more
or less unlimited freedom to insert silent beats, and to speed up or to spread out the
weak syllables between beats, in order to achieve isochrony.

What we present below is a version of Sievers's theory that has been much
influenced by the work of Bliss and Cable but that follows neither of the latter in all
details. We recognize the legitimacy of certain central claims of the Heusler
tradition, especially as found in the work of Pope and Russom, and try to

incorporate them, at least as alternative scansions, below. What we present is therefore a new synthesis. Our approach preserves the notion of metrical feet, which Sievers had also, as the building blocks of the verse. Our principal innovations are to simplify the atoms of the metrical stress contours to a binary pair, strong and weak; to urge that more finely discriminated stress levels are both unnecessary and probably unsupported by the evidence; to insist that some form of "silent ictus" is unavoidable in scanning *Beowulf*; and to view the fine-grained subtypes of Sievers, Bliss et al. as nondistinctive and relatively uninteresting.

II. The stress rules of Old English

The one unifying and uncontroversial fact about Old English meter is the obligatory presence of alliteration, the primary linguistic means of creating an artistic effect. Since alliteration can occur only on syllables bearing stress, one must know the basic rules of normal stress assignment.[1]

(*a*) Stress the first syllable of nouns, adjectives, and adverbs whether that syllable is part of the root or of a prefix (except *ge-*, *be-*, which are never stressed, and *for-*, which is stressed only rarely, as in *Maldon* 156a). For example, *eorlas*, *sweotol, frēondlice, unblīþe, ætgædere, oferhygd*. Monosyllabic adverbs like *eft, nēah, ǣr* are generally stressed and can carry alliteration, for example 642 *þā wæs eft swa ǣr inne on healle.*

(*b*) Stress the first root syllable of lexical verbs, for example, *maðelode, gefremede, āsecgan*. Verbal prefixes are almost never stressed, the only exceptions being verbs that are derived from nouns, like *and̄swarian* and verbs with adverbial prefixes like *inn-gangan*. No other words (e.g., function words like prepositions, deictics, conjunctions, the negative proclitic *ne,* and the light auxiliary verbs like *bēon*) are normally stressed, though they can (rarely) be contrastively or emphatically stressed. The only reliable clue to stress in such instances is alliteration.

Unlike nouns and adjectives, lexical verbs sometimes lose their stress (i.e., get demoted) in some positions in verse, such as the first drop, for example, 1397: *Āhlēop ðā se gomela, gode ðancode*, where *Āhlēop* cannot be stressed (to stress it would violate the rules of alliteration). Compare it with 1384: *Ār īs, rīces weard, uton hraðe fēran*, where the imperative form of the verb clearly requires emphasis; or 1393: *Ic hit ðē gehāte, nō hē on helm losað*, where metrical environment (other words that are necessarily weaker) guarantees that the verb must be stressed.

(*c*) Assign cascading prominence[2] to compounds and to morphologically complex words—that is, those in which the second or third syllable is a recognizable derivational suffix like *-ing, līc(e), lēas, ness, end(e)*, for example, compounds like *búrhlòca, écghète, mórþorbèalo, míddangèard*, or derivatives like *dómlèase, grýrelìcne*. Assignment of cascading stress only to morphologically complex words entails that in disyllabic roots there will be no stress on the second syllable even when suffixed: for example, *éarfeþo, fǽderes*. The suffixes of second-class weak verbs (*-ode, -ian*) were apparently sometimes stressed and sometimes not: one must go with whichever choice produces the better metrical result in these instances.[3]

III. The falling prominence contour in language and verse

Rules *a–c* are actually manifestations of a general principle of falling stress. In falling stress patterns, the left member is the more prominent syllable of a pair. In the diagram below, each column may be thought of as representing a syllable. Two syllables of equal prominence (if there could be such a thing) would simply be represented by

$$\bullet \qquad \bullet$$

$$\text{syl} \qquad \text{syl}$$

The dot represents one level of prominence of stress, so that two levels are represented by stacking one dot on top of the other. Then the ordinary trochee can be represented like this, where we can think of the height of the column of dots as being like the relative height of a ball bouncing from syllable to syllable.

$$\bullet$$
$$\bullet \qquad \bullet$$
$$\text{gom} \qquad \text{ban}$$
$$\text{gyl} \qquad \text{dan}$$

Cascading stress, found in most trisyllabic words in Old English (all except those with disyllabic roots such as *altar-e, mihtig-an, gyfen-es, worold-e*), must have resembled what we hear in Modern English words like *caretaker, dilator, pulsating, retailing, pullover*. Cascading stress can be represented as "stair steps down":

$$\bullet$$
$$\bullet \qquad \bullet$$
$$\bullet \qquad \bullet \qquad \bullet$$
$$\text{care} \qquad \text{take} \qquad \text{er}$$
$$\text{un} \qquad \text{forh} \qquad \text{te}$$
$$\text{hel} \qquad \text{rū} \qquad \text{ne}$$

When the stress pattern appears otherwise in a polysyllabic word, it is because the root is disyllabic or because the word is a compound. That is, the falling prominence relation is extended from the word to the compound word, one level higher:

$$\bullet$$
$$\bullet \qquad\qquad\qquad \bullet$$
$$\bullet \qquad \bullet \qquad \bullet \qquad\qquad \bullet \qquad \bullet$$
$$\text{he} \qquad \text{te} \qquad \text{þanc} \qquad \text{fēa} \qquad \text{sceaft}$$
$$\text{eal} \qquad \text{dor} \qquad \text{lēas} \qquad \text{benc} \qquad \text{swēg}$$

All dissyllabic words except prefixed verbs, all compound words, most metrical feet, and all the metrical verses that contain two feet are falling. Using "s" for "strong" and "w" for "weak" we may say that typical bisyllabic words are trochaic [s w], for example, *gomban, gyldan,* as shown above. In verse, falling prominence is also extended to a phrase like adjective + noun, as in 836b *gēapne hrōf,* or genitive + noun, as in 1639b, *Grendles hēafod ,* where [s...s...] can be viewed as having the same trochaic [s w] relation at the phrase and verse level:

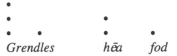

Grendles   *hēa*   *fod*

A verse is normally made up of two feet (about which more, below), and the first of these feet is stronger than the second: thus a verse like 13a *geong in geardum* [s w / s w] is realized rhythmically as

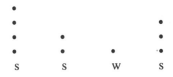

geong   *in*   *gear*   *dum*

The principal evidence that this is true is that if the on-verse has only single alliteration, it virtually always falls on the first of the two feet.

In short, any sequence [s (...) s] up to and including the full verse is read as if the left [s] is stronger than the right [s] on its own level: word level, derivational level, compound level, foot level, verse level.

Given this principle of falling stress at higher and higher levels of organization, it is possible to write simply [s s w / s] to represent complex surface sequences like

s   s   w   s

The simple binary notation, along with foot boundaries, contains all the information necessary for reading off these four rhythmical levels. Even in a sequence consisting of an iambic-like foot followed by a trochaic-like one, the fact that the first stress is stronger than the second calls for no special explanation: [w s / s w] in such verses as 4a *Oft Scyld Scēfing,* 170a *Þæt wæs wræc micel,* or 447b *gif mec dēað nimeð* is understood by the principle of falling stress as

$$\begin{array}{cccc} & & \bullet & \\ & \bullet & \bullet & \\ \bullet & \bullet & \bullet & \bullet \\ w & s & s & w \end{array}$$

In this simple binary formalism, we conclude, the regular stress patterns including half stress emerge quite naturally.

IV. Resolution and syllable weight in Old English

The binary formalism above does not, however, provide for a phenomenon called *resolution*, to which we now turn. Resolution is defined on the basis of the following metrical fact: to occupy the ictus of a foot, either a heavy syllable, or a light syllable plus the next syllable (whether heavy or light), is required. In our notation, resolution is marked by a hyphen: thus [s-w]. A light syllable consists only of a single short vowel, or short diphthong, along with any preceding tautosyllabic consonants: in *ealo, cyning, nama, seomian, werod,* etc., the stress falls on light syllables. A heavy syllable is any syllable that is not light—long vowels, long diphthongs, vowel plus one or more consonants in the same syllable. Syllable-initial consonants are irrelevant in determining the weight of a syllable. In *dǣd, hēafod, fæsten, sellan,* etc., the stressed syllables are heavy. This distinction is not necessary for any other purpose: as we saw above, syllable weight is in principle irrelevant to the placement of stress, which is dependent on morphology, not phonological structure[4].

In recognizing light syllables, it is very important to note the syllabification: (C)VCV[5] is syllabified as (C)V.CV in Old English, though not across word boundaries. Transparent compounds retain their precompound word boundaries: 78a *healærna* is syllabified as *heal.ær.na* and has a heavy first syllable for this reason.[6] Resolution is probably an artifact of prehistoric conventions of verse scansion, surviving as a fossil with rather trivial remnants in the regular phonological rules (e.g., high vowel deletion as in **wordu > word*). It is nonetheless a major complication in the prosody.

However, there is one condition under which resolution does not occur where, from the definition given above, it looks as though it ought to:

CONDITION ON RESOLUTION: If the light ictic syllable is immediately preceded by another ictic syllable, and if the weak resolving syllable is heavy (*monig* in 838b) or was historically heavy[7] (*cwida* in 1845a), then resolution does not take place:

$$\begin{array}{ccccccc} s & & s & & w & \Rightarrow & s & & s\text{-}w \\ | & & | & & | & & & \\ H & & L & & L & & & \end{array}$$

s	s	w	⇒	s	s	w
|	|	|				
H	L	H				

838b *guðrinc monig* [s s / s w], not [s s / s-w]
1845a *wīs wordcwida* [s / s s w], not [s / s s-w]
319a *wið wrāð werod* [w s / s w], not [w s / s-w]

Note that in 430a *frēowine folca* [s s-w / s w] resolution occurs even though the resolving [s-w] is immediately preceded by another ictic syllable (the first part of the condition above). This is because the weak resolving syllable *-ne* is light, that is, does not meet the second part of the condition; therefore resolution occurs as it normally should. Similarly, in 222a *brimclifu blīcan* [s s-w / s w]; examples could be easily proliferated. What it boils down to is, resolution is the unmarked norm, but if resolution creates a verse that would violate a higher norm, the four-position principle (discussed below), there must be a reason why it does so: this condition states that reason.[8] It does not, however, explain it: why should a heavy unstressed syllable be harder to resolve just in case it is preceded by two strong syllables, not one?

For the purpose of understanding the meter of particular verses, the main point to note is that resolution eliminates a large number of unstressed syllables from the metrical counting rules. Furthermore, it does so by a single generalization that has at least a fair amount of support from other aspects of the phonology of very early Old English. The exact phonetic nature of resolution remains unknown and mysterious to modern ears. The phenomenon died out, as a linguistic reality, in most Germanic languages by the eleventh century (surviving in Icelandic until the fourteenth). No one living has ever heard this phenomenon in any Germanic language. What we know is that, contrary to all modern English and Germanic intuitions about what can occupy a strong metrical position, in Old English two successive syllables commonly counted metrically as if they were only a single syllable if the first of the two was stressed but light in weight.

V. Notation systems for scansion

It is to be regretted that scholars have been quite divergent in the notational systems they have devised for Anglo-Saxon verse, even where there is no disagreement about the scansion. Most of the divergences result from their efforts to conserve every piece of information that they view as relevant to the goal of assigning each verse to a "type" for comparison to other verses: that is, a typology of well-formed verses. A comparison of all the varieties of notation is not in order here, since they range from a system of musical notes, or their equivalents, gathered into measures (Heusler and Pope) to a representation that indicates types of alliteration, compounds, word boundaries, and clause boundaries (Kendall). Sievers's system is used one way or another by everyone, including those who propose replacements. It includes an excess of detail also, though not so much as some others. The replacement that has gained greatest currency among "working metrists" is Bliss's, though there are serious problems with it; we summarize it below. The notation system used here is intended to be simple and minimal, though it does not lose much of the information found in other systems.

The most conspicuous piece of information that is explicitly noted in most systems derived from Sievers, but that is missing from the one presented here, is syllable weight. Sievers's representation of type A, for example, which in its prototypical form looks like a sequence of two trochaic feet [s w / s w], and which accounts for almost half of all the verses in *Beowulf*, is [$\acute{-}$x / $\acute{-}$x]. (Our replacement of Sievers's [x] by [w] is merely a matter of taste and mnemonic preference, especially in view of the fact that in much modern theoretical work on prosodic systems, [x] is used to represent *stressed* syllables.) The dash with accent above it is sometimes used to represent either a heavy syllable or a light one plus a resolved one. Sievers himself distinguished light syllables in a typographically rather awkward way. He represents a stressed light syllable plus an unstressed one by an accented breve and a tie line to x, thus: $\acute{\smile}$x . Notational variants aside, the real point is that heavy syllables are the default choice for ictus, whether in Old English or in Modern English. If the ictic syllable is light in Old English verse, we normally find resolution to compensate for it. In the usual case, then, if an ictic syllable is not resolved, it must be heavy. The presence of a resolved syllable is perceptually as well as representationally more salient than weight alone. Hence, if we represent resolved feet directly, syllable weight is a redundant fact that need not be marked in meter. It can be inferred from a metrical notation that indicates only alternation and resolution. Line structure is made coherent by alliteration; verse structure is made coherent by selectively abstracting a system of alternating prominence: [s] and [w], where [w] = [w (w)]. It is an unnecessary complication to encode both stress and weight in the notation, as Sievers did.[9]

Regardless of notation, the reference system presented here is basically Sievers's with minor modifications; in particular, most of his rather trivial subclassifications of equivalence classes are ignored. For single-ictus verses, we follow Bliss rather than Sievers: the latter forced his classification into a difficult corner trying to find two real peaks in verses like 22a *þæt hine on ylde*. From these two quite complex taxonomic systems, Cable (1974, 1991) has teased out underlying regularities that provide the easiest access to understanding how the scops might have intuitively calculated the prosodic regularity of their verses. We present Cable's rules later. We also summarize other theories, several of great interest. The ability of the scops, and of the appreciative and sensitive modern reader, to calculate regularity is what we seek to understand. We take it as the goal of any theory to enlighten us on the essence of this issue: What constitutes regularity?

Line Structure. The overarching structure of a line of Old English poetry is this:

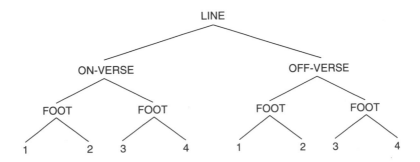

The details of this structure break down thus:

1. A line consists of two verses. The verses are linked by alliteration:

Alliteration requires identity in the beginning of the strong syllable in at least the first foot of each verse (or the second foot of the on-verse if the verse contains only one strong syllable). The rule is, the first foot of the on-verse must alliterate with the first foot of the off-verse (i.e., alliteration is governed by the first foot of the off-verse). The alliterating sound of the governing foot is called the "head-letter" (*Hauptstab*). The second foot of the on-verse may also alliterate, but the second foot of the off-verse cannot and does not participate functionally in the alliteration. In rare alliterative sequences of the type a b / a b, the b-alliteration is not functional: opinions differ as to whether it is a cultivated ornamentation. Any initial vowel can alliterate with any other initial vowel. Consonants alliterate only with themselves; and the consonant clusters ⟨sc, sp, st⟩ alliterate only with identical clusters (e.g., ⟨sc⟩ does not alliterate with ⟨s⟩). ⟨hr⟩ alliterates only with ⟨h⟩, except for two conspicuous exceptions, in 1390 and 1975, where it appears to alliterate with ⟨r⟩ (Klaeber underdots the ⟨h⟩ in the etymological *hraðe,* no doubt correctly).[10] Velar and palatal ⟨g⟩ alliterate freely with each other, likewise velar and palatal ⟨c⟩. Since, under the usual phonetic interpretations, these pairs sound very different to the modern ear, we must assume either that the alliteration of these consonants is purely traditional, or that palatalization was still non-phonemic, or both, at an early date. Occasionally, weak syllables appear to alliterate, but this is probably not even ornamental, just accidental.

2. Each verse contains two feet that jointly add up to at least four positions.

Each position is ideally filled by a single syllable and must be filled by at least one syllable (silent beats, though they must be assumed to exist, don't count in calculating positions—contrary to what a musician, e.g., would expect). There can be at most two feet per verse, but the two feet may be of uneven size and of differing internal composition because the ideal of one syllable per position is violated commonly in the first weak position. Some scholars[11] do not believe in "feet" and define the verse entirely in terms of four positions, ungrouped.

3. All feet except the first foot of the on-verse must contain an ictus (and even such feet, we argue, contain a silent ictus). The ictic syllables are called "lifts." They are grouped with weak (unstressed) syllables, usually called "drops" or "dips."

Many of the still unresolved controversies surrounding Anglo-Saxon verse concern the question of defining what combinations of lifts and drops should count as legitimate feet and what types of feet are permitted to be grouped into a single verse. The feet that occur in verse are metrical feet, units of scansion; in Sievers's theory, therefore, they need not correspond to linguistic feet, which for Old English we assume to have been left-headed, that is, always beginning with a stressed syllable. Some other theories, both early (Kaluza) and recent (Russom), require the metrical foot to be identical with, or to resemble very closely, a linguistic foot: that is, they would allow only falling metrical feet.

4. Nearly all verses are syntactic units at a fairly high level: they are often free-standing sentences, and they are at least noun phrases or prepositional phrases in the minimal instances:

Verses therefore could be spoken as independent units, rather easily separated by pauses. One naturally speculates that this fact is a corollary of the formulaic status of many verses, a status that requires that they be relatively free-standing units.

VI. Foot Types

With certain restrictions stipulated below, any foot can be of the following types:

(a) Regular left-strong, or "falling," all reducible to [s (w)]:
  (i) [s w (w...)] for example, *gomban, mōdig ond, sceaþena;*
  (ii) [s s] for example, *fēasceaft, mearcstapa;*
  (iii) [s !], with a "suppressed drop" or "empty syllable" after the lift, for example, 2a *þēodcyninga*[12] [s ! / s s w].
(b) Cascading left-strong, always trisyllabic[13] (plus resolved syllables), also "falling":
  (i) Regular cascading: [s s w] for example, *weorþmyndum, heaþodēorum;*
  (ii) Cascading down-up: [s w s] for example, *hylderinc, (arīs) rīces weard.*
(c) Right-strong, or "rising":
  (i) [(w...) w s] for example 109b, *nē lēof, ac hē hine feor (forwræc).*
(d) Suppressed[14] lifts (silent ictus):

(i) [! w (w...)] for example, 47a, *ða gyt hie him asetton* [! w w w w / w-s w].

Some theories eliminate rising feet from the system altogether (e.g., Pope, Russom), dealing with them by such devices as the insertion of suppressed beats. The arguments for eliminating rising feet from the system are fairly strong, and we return to them below and in a discussion of Russom's theory.

Given the foot types defined above, the following restrictions, along with the rules of alliteration, determine which kinds of feet can be combined with each other to form verses:

(a) Feet must be combined so as to generate exactly four positions in a sequence of two feet.

The four-position principle, along with the *Hauptstab* principle in alliteration, comes down to us from the first explicit writing on the subject of Germanic verse form, namely, the *Háttatal* of Snorri Sturluson, around 1220. For a recent enlightening commentary on the work of Snorri, see Lehmann (1982).

From the four-position principle it follows, for example, that two monosyllabic feet cannot be combined because only two positions would result. Two cascading feet cannot be combined because six positions would result. A rising foot cannot be combined with a cascading foot because five positions would result. Sievers defines two types of "normal" feet, [s w] and [w s] (i.e., trochees and iambs), but they may not combine in that sequence: [s w / w s]. When the sequence occurs, as in 2150a *lissa gelong,* it is generally taken as anomalous and in need of emendation on the basis of the four position principle.[15]

(b) Iteration of [w] is permitted only in the first foot of a verse.

This constraint requires that multiple weaks be included under a single weak branch in the leftmost foot. Thus, [w s] and [w w s] or even [w w w s] all scan as [w s]. Likewise, [s w] and [s w w] or [s w w w] all scan as [s w] provided that they are in the first foot of the verse. The constraint is equivalent to the one formulated in Cable (1991, 9 ff.), which states that only the first drop of a verse can be expanded[16], not counting verbal prefixes *ge-, wið-, be-on-, ā-,* etc. In all except the first weak position, that is to say, drops are limited to one weak syllable and a proclitic (the latter being extrametrical: see below). While there are exceptions to this generalization, like 2870a *ōwer feor oððe nēah,* the number is negligible.

This constraint further entails that except for resolution, a verse cannot end in more than a single weak syllable. There is a sense in which every verse achieves "right justification," to draw on the apt analogy first proposed by John Miles Foley (1982, 12): that is, every verse ends on [s] or [sw].

(c) There is a strong tendency, though it is not inviolate, to combine cascading feet with a monosyllabic falling foot, that is, [s !].

But the rest beat or suppressed syllable after the lift may be filled by one or two unstressed syllables: 223a *sīde sǣnǣssas* [s w / s s w]. When thus filled, the weak syllable counts as occupying a position: verses like 223a are therefore five-position verses (the so-called D*, discussed below). They are the only allowable exceptions to the four-position principle.

Verses with monosyllabic feet create a stress clash, either foot internally, that is, [s / s s w], or across feet, as in [s / s w s], where two [s]'s are contiguous: 164b *fēond mancynnes* [s / s s w]. The other source of stress clash is the juxtaposition of a rising foot with a falling one, that is, [w s / s w]: 556a *be ȳþlāfe*. Stress clashing is the phenomenon mainly responsible for the discomfort we feel when trying to read *Beowulf* rhythmically. The function of [!] in monosyllabic strong feet [s !] is to attenuate the clash. This jagged rhythm, as Lehmann (1982, 23) has called it, is inescapable unless one is willing to force the lines into isochronous feet, a choice that creates very severe further problems, to which we return below in our discussion of the theories of Heusler, Pope, Russom, and Creed.

(d) Feet with silent ictus [! w (w)] must be initial in the verse and can be matched only with falling feet.

This is a consequence of the fact that in a string of weak syllables we cannot tell where the end of the foot is until we reach the first (and only) lift of the verse, namely, the second lift. It is this logic that also accounts for the fact that off-verses never contain suppressed lifts (since the first lift governs the alliteration and therefore must be present).

VII. Principles of accommodation

Even with these constraints on the combining potential of the foot types, the system would still accommodate many ill-formed verses if there were not some other ways to discount a fair number of weak syllables in accommodations *a–e* below—and, in the case of contraction *f*, to add a weak syllable to provide grist for the four-position mill. The main principles of accommodation are these:

(a) Parasiting: A syllable that was a nonsyllabic resonant in West Germanic still counts as nonsyllabic even though it had been syllabically phonemicized by Anglo-Saxon times: for example, the *-or* in 611a *Ðǣr wæs hæleþa hleahtor* does counts not as a syllabic drop but rather as part of a final voiceless consonant cluster [-htr]. The vowel in all such examples is underdotted in Klaeber's edition.

(b) Elision: This phenomenon is common throughout the history of English verse and is generally believed to be no different in *Beowulf*, for example, 471a *sende ic Wylfingum*. When an elision vowel appears to have been dropped from the manuscript, Klaeber marks it with an apostrophe (e.g., 338a *wēn' ic*). But elision of the type that is probable in 471a is not marked by Klaeber or other editors because, as Klaeber says (1941, 280), "it admits of no positive proof." The metrical system will almost always allow an extra weak syllable.

(c) Extrametricality: The prefixes *ge-*, *be-*, *on-*, and the negative clitic *ne* (not the conjunction *nē*, however) are usually invisible to the scansion, whether on nouns

or on verbs; and all verbal prefixes are normally invisible. Occasionally, they have to be counted to get the obligatory fourth position (e.g., 210a *Fyrst forð gewāt*). Since extrametrical syllables are always cliticized to the stressed syllable that follows, we mark them with a hyphen preceding the [s] to which they are attached: thus [w-s]. (They are parenthesized in some other notations like Russom's.)

(d) Anacrusis: An initial falling foot in an on-verse may be preceded by at most two extrametrical weak syllables. The two lifts in such verses must alliterate. This phenomenon is similar to extrametricality, but it is restricted to line beginnings, and it is not limited to the light proclitics. In addition to *ne, ond*, and the verbal prefixes, almost any unstressed word—pronouns, conjunctions, monosyllabic adverbs—can be anacrustic: for example, 93b *swā wæter bebūgeð*, 2247b *nū hæleð ne mōstan*. But by far the majority of anacrustic syllables are the same ones that tend to be extrametrical in verse-internal positions: 2703a *gewēold his gewitte*, 2878a *ætgifan æt gūðe*.

(e) Resolution: This is discussed sufficiently above, but it should be remembered that the main metrical effect of resolution is to dismiss a weak syllable from the scansion. Like extrametricality, resolution is marked with a hyphen, but following the [s] to which it is attached: thus [s-w].

(f) Contraction: Certain Old English words contain prehistorically contracted forms that have to be restored metrically to their (earlier) uncontracted form (i.e., they have to count as two syllables): for example, 25b *man gepēon* [s w / s w]. These are all marked in Klaeber's edition by a circumflex accent over the two vowels.

VIII. Verse Types

Given the constraints and principles of accommodation above, Sievers defined five main verse types (actually six, since type D contains two rhythmically distinct variants). We introduce these first with modern equivalents (not translations) alongside an example of each type, to get a feel for the jaggedness and common stress clashing that characterize Anglo-Saxon meter:

Type A.	Arnie's army	[s w / s w]	83a *lāðan līges*
Type B.	in briny baths	[w s / w s]	511a *nē lēof nē lāð*
Type C.	by cost-cutting	[w s / s w]	1073a *beloren lēofum*
Type D$_1$.	dumb dogcatchers	[s ! / s s w]	3133a *flōd fæðmian*
Type D$_2$.	dry daisy-chain	[s ! / s w s]	2885a *eall ēðelwyn*
Type E.	egg-laying hen	[s s w / s !]	2285a *fēasceaftum men*

The essence of scansion is to show that a verse contains a string of syllables that are equivalent to one of these types. "Equivalence" is defined by appealing (1) to the basic foot types and (2) to the principles of accommodation listed above. The determination of equivalence can be shown in diagrams like these:

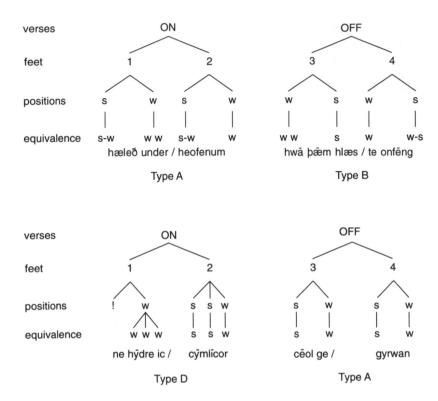

Type A

Type A consists of a sequence of two falling feet. Many such verses look like familiar trochaic sequences in classical and Renaissance traditions of metrical analysis. But to look at Anglo-Saxon verse in that way is a mistake, since the unstressed syllable may be fairly freely expanded to two or three or even four (the parenthesized (w) in our foot types such as [s w (w)] means "zero, one, or more weakly stressed syllables"). The examples below are arranged in an approximately ascending order of complexity. Note that the basis for classing them together is that all are metrically equivalent to [s w / s w].

> [s w / s w] 121a *grim ond grǽdig,* 366a *wordum wrixlan,* 1897b *hringedstefna*
> [s w w / s w] 1907b *wind ofer ýðum,* 1699b *swīgedon ealle,* 2622a *eorlscipe efnan,* 560a *prēatedon pearle*
> [s w / s s] 1522a *grǽdig gūð-lēoð*
> [s w w / s s] 1161a *beorhtode bencswēg*

[s w / s-w s] 558a *mihtig meredēor*
[s s / s w] 1033a *scūrheard scepðan,* 306a *Gūðmōd grimman*
[s s / s s] 1881a *gūðrinc goldwlanc* 1719a *brēosthord blōdrēow*[17]
[s s / s w] 973a *fēasceaft guma*
[s-w w w / s-w w] 52a *hæleð under heofenum*
[s-w w w w / s-w w] 310a *receda under roderum*
[w-s w w / s w] 1169a *onfōh þissum fulle,* 1549a *wið ord ond wið ecge*
[w-w-s w w w / s w] 109a *ne gefeah hē þære fæhðe*
[s-w s w / s s] 608a *gamolfeax ond gūðrōf*[18]

In verses with anacrusis, such as 1169a and 109a, the two lifts must alliterate.[19] In verses with expanded internal drops, such as 52a, double alliteration is obligatory. Verses that have a silent ictus in the first foot and a falling second foot are categorized as A3 by Sievers, on the basis of the fact that the second foot is the normal falling foot of type A. To classify them as belonging to this type, Sievers had to upgrade some weak syllable at the beginning of the verse in order to manufacture a first ictus (but nonalliterating). It seems better to agree with Bliss's classification of verses that have only one true strong syllable. He characterizes these as "light verses," verses in which the first stress is "suppressed," or, in our terms, has a silent ictus, labeling them with the corresponding lowercase letter: thus "type a, type d, type e." We will keep Sievers's numbers with the letter classification, however, because the label "a3" (= A3) is widely recognized for this type. There is considerable controversy over the question whether finite verbs in the first foot of such verses are stressed (and therefore ictic). The most widely accepted position, challenged vigorously by Kendall (1991), is that they are ictic if they alliterate. If they are not ictic, as Kendall argues, then the number of a3 verses is substantially increased. Here are verses that everyone would categorize as a3 exemplars (the silent ictus can be ignored if the reader is more comfortable with the unadorned "light foot" concept of Bliss's later work; however, the notion of "equivalence class" is considerably obscured by ignoring the silent ictus):

[! w w w / s w] 9a *oð þæt him æghwylc*
[! w w w / w-s w] 28a *hī hyne þā ætbæron*
[! w w w w / s s] 168a *nō hē þone gifstōl*

Type B

Type B consists of a sequence of two rising feet. While this pattern looks superficially like a familiar iambic sequence, it should not be thought of that way. If there is anything clear about Anglo-Saxon metrics, it is that verses like 469b and 1585b below cannot be taken as "iambic" in any sense speakers of modern English can understand. For this sort of reason, type B (and similarly type C) has caused considerable controversy, to the point where the existence of the rising foot type itself has been challenged vigorously by Pope and Russom, among others. There are no stressable words in Old English with the rising foot pattern (discounting prefixes like *be-*, *ge-*, and *on-*). If, as Russom has argued, the available metrical patterns found in ordinary words define the metrical possibilities, then there should be no rising foot type in the metrical inventory. All type B exemplars are open to alternative analyses, the favored one being a first foot with a suppressed ictus and the second foot cascading down-up. Thus, Sievers's [w s / w s] would be replaced by [! w / s w s] in the concocted Modern English example *in briny baths*.

With this warning, that all type B and type C verses are dubious at the very core of Sievers's analysis, we proceed with a range of examples to show the kinds of verses the B type is intended to include. On the left we cite the traditional Sievers analysis. On the right we cite a basic representation of the alternative equivalent scansion (Pope, Russom) that disallows rising feet. It should be understood here only as an alternative whose virtues are worthy of study: it is not in any sense an interpretation of Sievers's theory, as the other scansions are.

Sievers   = Pope-Russom

[w s / w s] 511a *nē lēof nē lāð*   = [! w / s w s]

[w w s / w w s] 7b *hē þæs frōfre gebād*   = [! w w / s w w-s]

[w w w s-w / w s] 66b *oðð þæt sēo geogoð gewēox*   = [! w w w / s-w w-s]

[w w w s / w s] 75b *geond ðisne middangeard*   = [! w w w / s w s]

[w w w s / w s] 114b *hē him þæs lēan forgeald*   = [! w w w / s w s]

[w w s-w w / w s] 469b *se wæs betera þonn(e) ic*   = [! w w / s-w w s]

[w w w w w s / w w-s] 1585b *tō ðæs þe hē on ræste geseah*   = [! w w w w w / s w w-s]

Type C

Type C always introduces a stress clash, a "jagged" effect, since it juxtaposes a rising foot against a falling foot (very roughly, iamb + trochee). The first of the two adjacent strong stresses is, as normal, stronger than the second; and scholars who do not go along with the iambic aspects of Sievers's system analyze such verses as containing a cascading foot beginning with the first stress (shown to the right, below). Thus, instead of [w s / s w], they assign the value [! w / s s w], which of course sounds almost the same. Note a nontrivial drawback, however: it puts the alliteration into the second foot, which is certainly disallowed in off-verses; and, in on-verses, it assigns double alliteration inside a single foot. Neither of these obstacles is insurmountable to such a theory, but they require a less elegant characterization of alliteration.

Sievers   = Pope-Russom

[w s / s w] 1297b *be sǣm twēonum*   = [! w / s s w]

[w s / s w] 4a *oft Scyld Scēfing*   = [! w / s s w]

[w s-w / s w] 21b *on fæder bearme*   = [! w / s-w s w]

[(w) w w s-w / s w] 190b *ne mihte snotor hæleð*   = [! (w) w w / s-w s w] [w w w s / s w] 1654b *þē þū hēr tō lōcast*   = [! w w w / s s w]

Verses of type C very commonly meet the condition for nonresolution. 190b above is an example: when resolution fails to occur in such instances, the unresolved ictus is in the second foot and is preceded immediately by another ictus, as the condition requires.

Type D

Type D is divided into D_1 and D_2 on rhythmic grounds: they feel very different. They share the label *type D* only because they share the formal property that the first foot is falling (including especially the monosyllabic falling foot with an empty second position) and the second foot is cascading. This is the most jagged of all Old English verse types, often with three stresses in a row.

[s ! / s s w] 621b *dæl æghwylcne,* 469a *bearn Healfdenes,* 449b
unmurnlīce, 1653a *lēod Scyldinga*
[s-w / s s w] 445a *mægen hrēðmanna,* 432b *Heorot fælsian*
[s ! / s-w s w] 286a *Weard maþelode,* 1847a *hild heorugrimme*

Type D_2 is less jagged than D_1 because the cascading down-up foot has an intervening weak stress in the second foot that removes some of the jagged effect. The drop in the middle of the second foot is always either monosyllabic or a weak syllable plus a light proclitic (Duncan 1993, 501).

[s ! / s w s] 2138a *holm heolfre wēoll,* 1926b *Hygd swīðe geong*
[s-w / s w s] 1646a *hæle hildedēor*
[s ! / s w w-s] 2774a *eald enta geweorc*

The jaggedness is very commonly relieved by the presence of a weak syllable in the first foot: these varieties are labeled D*. Verses of this type have five positions, a fact that is merely stipulated and must be viewed as problematic, given the importance of the role that is normally assigned to the four-position principle within the Sievers school.

[s w / s s w][20] 1154a *Scēotend Scyldinga,* 1727a *eard ond eorlscipe*
[s w / s-w s w] 2136a *grimne gryrelīcne*
[s w w / s s w] 1790a *deorc ofer dryhtgumum*

As in type A, anacrusis is permitted; in nearly all instances, the anacrustic syllables are proclitics:

[w-s / s s w] 2930a *ābrēot brimwīsan*
[w-w-s w w / s s w] 2628a *Ne gemealt him se mōdsefa*

Finally, there is a "light" version of type D in Bliss's classification, as there is of type A. Here the only justification for the *d* label is the fact that the second foot is cascading—so the *a* label would be inappropriate. But type d verses do not feel like regular type D verses at all, because the number of initial weak syllables may be as many as four or five; Bliss theorized that there was a necessary and proper correlation between the suppression of the initial ictus and the increase in the number of weak syllables possible (for both d and a). We view the classification as being strictly formal. The number of type d verses is very substantial, however: it was clearly well-recognized and acceptable. In Sievers's classification, which does not include the notion "light verse," type d examples go in type C. We therefore provide the alternative scansions below, the one on the right corresponding to Sievers's.

[! w w w / s s w] 38a *ne hȳrde ic cȳmlīcor* [w w w s / s w]
[! w w / s-w s w] 665b *Hæfde Kyningwuldor* [w w s-w / s w]

Type E

Type E is the rarest of all verse types in *Beowulf*, less than 5 percent of the total. The second foot is most commonly monosyllabic or resolved. The cascading first foot is almost always trisyllabic except for resolution and extrametrical proclitics. Because he does not discount verbal prefixes, Bliss finds a fair number of E* verses, like 697a *wīgspǣda gewiofu*, but we find no good reason not to treat these as ordinary type E verses. He also finds a small number of type E verses that have but a single final stress in the verse (e.g., 262a *Wæs mīn fæder*): these are probably all to be viewed as a3's without resolution (irregular), and type E should be deemed nonexistant. There are only seven of them, anyway.

[s s w / s !] 150b *undyrne cūð*
[s-w s w / s !] 236b *meþelwordum frægn*
[s s w w / s-w]²¹ 343b *Bēowulf is mīn nama*
[s-w s w / s-w] 667a *seleweard āseted*

Hypermetric Verses

Although hypermetricality is quite common in the rest of the Old English verse canon, only twenty-three of over 6,300 verses in *Beowulf* are hypermetric. Most of them occur in three clusters: 1163a–68b, 1705a–07b, and 2995a–96b. In addition, there are two hypermetric verses, 2173a and 2297a. The whole lines are printed by Klaeber and other editors offset on the left margin so they can be easily spotted. These verses violate the basic organizational principles: they have more than two feet and more than four positions. Where they occur in a line together, they add up to six feet and twelve positions. They are not subject to any persuasive analysis in terms of types. Rather, one can say, in terms of the feet of which they are composed, they have an additional falling foot (including the possibility of silent ictus) at the beginning of the verse. Russom (1987, 63) tries to accommodate them as normal verses, but his attempt is not conspicuously successful. Also, his explanation for their existence is only slightly better than the shoulder shrugging that other metrists engage in, such as arguing that one or another syntactic structure that the poet wishes to use simply won't fit into a verse of normal length. Examples:

[s w w / s w / s w] 1163a *gān under gyldnum bēage*
[s w / s w / s w] 1163b *þǣr þā gōdan twēgen*
[! w w w w w / s w / w-s w] 2996b *syððan hīe ða mǣrða geslōgon*

IX. Variations on the reference system

Cable's generalizations

Cable (1991) converts the Sievers reference system into principles that may be thought of as lying behind the system, as being somehow part of the intuitive knowledge of the scop (who surely did not know anything remotely like the Sievers or Bliss classifications). He argues that the view is wrong, though widely held, that Old English verse can be characterized as "strong stress meter", in which the only syllables that "count" are stressed, and weak syllables can be scattered more or less randomly. He argues that Old English verse was a syllable counting meter, though in a way very different from later syllable counting. The crucial difference is that there was a variable position, as we have seen above, which could be expanded fairly freely, namely, the first drop in all verse types. He set forth principles that enable one to measure metricality without actually making a determination of "type" in the sense of Sievers. In effect, he replaced a taxonomy by a set of principles from which the members of the taxonomy can be derived. Here are his principles:

a) The four-position rule of Snorri.
b) Expandability of only the first weak position (the "strong dip").
c) Extrametricality of *ge-, be-, on-,* and *ne,* plus verbal prefixes.
d) Conditions on resolution (roughly as above).
e) Never more than one final weak syllable in a verse (entailed by rule b).
f) The first of adjacent strong syllables stronger than the second.

Bliss's elaborations of the reference system

In 1958, A. J. Bliss published his interpretation and enrichment of the Sievers system. His account is not at all easy to read. His full classification includes 130 types, and he provides a catalog giving his scansion of every verse in *Beowulf*. This system, as Fulk says (1991, 29), is "now indisputably the most widely used" by practicing metrists. It has at least three highly controversial features: (a) it does not distinguish tertiary from weak stress in its classification of types; (b) by conflating tertiary with weak, it allows some verses to have only three positions (since two adjacent w's count as a single position—e.g., [s w w s] or [s s w w]); and (c) it requires the notion of verse-internal caesura to make certain discriminations among verse possibilities made with tertiary stress in other systems. For comparative prosody, it is the ultimate codification of types in the Sievers sense. It is the system used in Vickman's *A Metrical Concordance to Beowulf* (1990) as well as by Fulk in his *History of Old English Meter* (1992); we therefore summarize the system here to provide easier access to those fundamental resources.

Bliss's type labels have a minimum of three digits (i.e., XXX, where X is either a number or a letter of the alphabet) and a maximum of five. The first alphabetic character, either lowercase or upper, in a Bliss label corresponds to the standard Sievers type. Thus, Bliss 2A3b designates a type A, and likewise a2c, 1A1c, 1A*2a(i), etc. That is, no matter how much other apparatus there is, look for the first letter in the sequence to determine which one of the basic five types Bliss assigns the verse to. If there is an arabic numeral preceding the first letter, it will be 1, 2, or 3—nothing else is permitted. Bliss claims to be marking "breath groups" with these numbers, but in fact it seems clear that he is usually marking syntactic constituent boundaries (like, say, the boundary between a subject and a verb, or between a noun and a prepositional phrase that modifies it), which often correspond to foot boundaries and roughly even to the notion "caesura" in later verse. The number 1 means the shorter constituent is at the left edge (i.e., an early caesura), the number 2 means they are balanced in size (a mid-verse caesura), and the number 3 means the shorter constituent is on the right edge (a late caesura). If there is only one ictus in the verse (i.e., it is a "light" verse, or has a "suppressed" first ictic position, what we have called a "silent ictus"), then the letter designating the verse type is lowercase (a, b, c, d, e), and no arabic numeral is allowed to precede it: thus, type a1b designates a "light" Sievers type A, and it has no caesura. Caesuras are permitted by Bliss only between lifts; since the light verses have only one lift, they have no caesura.

Up to this point, Bliss's system is easy: type 2A is a syntactically balanced trochaic verse; 1A is a trochaic verse in which the first dip is syntactically associated with the second lift. 3A does not exist: in fact, 3's exist only in verse types B and E, because only these allow the possibility of a lift at the end of the verse, which will necessarily, if the caesura immediately precedes it, be a monosyllabic syntactic constituent (or its resolved equivalent), as in 1133b *oþ ðæt ōþer / cōm.*

The third digit in Bliss's representation of normal verse types is merely an arbitrary designation (following Sievers's equally arbitrary system) of the linguistic stress level of the syllable that fills the various dips: that is, half stressed or unstressed. Thus, 2A1 is [sw/sw], 2A2 is [sw/ss], 2A3 is [ss/sw], and 2A4 is [ss/ss]. We need not spell out further details of the third digit. Since the principle of falling stress within any foot of the form [ss] assigns ictus to the first of the two s's, the third digit never provides information of consequence to the basic metrical typology.

The fourth digit in normal verse types (the third in light verses) is filled by one of the early letters of the alphabet: these represent, in alpha-numerical sequence, the number of weak syllables occupying the first dip: thus, 1A1c designates [swww/sw] in which c = w w w. This information is not generally very useful except in the "light verses", where we encounter up to seven initial weak syllables (including, arguably and in disagreement with Sievers, finite verbs) represented as type a2g, that is, [w w w w w w w s s], which we would have to break into two feet, both slightly bizarre, namely, as [! w w w w w w w / s s]. There is only one such verse, 2172a: *Hȳrde ic þæt hē ðone healsbēah.*

The final noteworthy feature of Bliss's system is carried over from Sievers's and somewhat extended, namely, the use of the asterisk to designate "expansion" of any single-syllable foot to include a dip: thus, D*, we have seen, is a type D [s/ssw] in which the first foot is expanded to [sw], giving [sw/ssw], a five-position verse. Bliss also allows A*, but this is an artifact of his caesural system. His type 1A* [sw/wsw] (where the slash represents a caesura in his system) is actually an ordinary type A with an expanded first dip [sww/sw] in a foot-based account like Sievers's.

Vickman's concordance marks single alliteration with a single underline, double alliteration with a double underline of the verse line number. While Bliss discusses alliteration extensively, it is not represented in his notation, nor is it in Sievers's. It is in fact not difficult to devise a far better system of representation than Bliss's—for example, that of Hutcheson (1995), which has the advantages of theory neutrality and considerable transparency. But Bliss, like Sievers, has been there for a long time: his system, given the opacity of it, should be replaced but is not likely to be immediately, just because it has been adopted by so many metrists.

Kendall's elaborations of the system based on syntax

At least from the time of Francis P. Magoun's influential essay on the oral-formulaic aspects of Old English poetry (1953), most scholars have been persuaded that though the *Beowulf* epic was certainly not composed orally in the form that now exists, it has many properties that can be explained best on the assumption that it appeared near the end of a long oral tradition that had created many formulaic verses readily incorporable into any performance, going back hundreds of years into Germanic prehistory. It is hardly novel to suggest that a major virtue of any prosodic scheme is that strings of words that conform to it are more easily remembered than strings that don't. Oral-formulaic composition is almost inconceivable without some sort of regular prosodic underpinning.

Basing his arguments on some observations of Hans Kuhn's about the positioning of finite verbs, Kendall argues that the prosodic underpinning was much richer even than the Bliss enrichment of the Sievers system. The essence of his very substantial contribution goes far beyond what anyone ever before has been willing to include under the heading *scansion* or *prosody*, however. On the basis of a combination of prosodic and syntactic properties, Kendall classifies all verses into three types: those that can only initiate a clause, those that can never be in initial position, and those that can occur in any position. The "position suitability" of a particular formula is surely a central piece of information that one can reasonably speculate was within the solid grasp of a good scop. No theory of the composition of *Beowulf* along the lines initiated by Magoun can fail to be enriched by Kendall's arguments. Like Bliss, Kendall provides a full catalog, scanning every verse in *Beowulf* in his own quite complex system. It is an elaboration of Sievers's, and it is in most ways more transparent than Bliss's. It certainly contains a great deal more information. Still, the system goes deeply into morphology and syntax and cannot count as prosodic analysis in any well-understood sense. For this reason, it seems unlikely that it will come to be generally used, in the way that Bliss is used, or as Hutcheson certainly can be, for the study of comparative prosody.

The linguistic foundations of Old English metrics: Russom's theory

We have stressed that Old English verse form depended on a specifically controlled kind of alliteration, on a system of stress assignment that differed from that of modern English, on the four position principle, and on a very wide range of variation in the equivalent surface manifestations of the underlying foot types. Until recently, no one had suggested an explanation for this wide range or its limits. Russom brings a new light to bear on the explanation of the range and its limits. The range is defined simply: every possible foot is identical to the stress pattern of a possible word; that is, feet must mimic words. In this sense, the phrase *blōde fāh* (which is a possible foot in 1594a, a D-verse) "mimics" *middangeard* in its stress pattern. The limit on the range of variation is then simply this: if it is not (like) a possible word, then it is not a possible foot.[22]

Since all Old English stressed words received stress on the first syllable of the root or on the first syllable of a compound word (treating nominal and adjectival prefixes as roots, such that the compounding rule applied to them exactly as to all other roots, namely, assigning stress to the leftmost syllable), it is obvious that B-verses and C-verses, both of which begin with unstressed syllables, must be eliminated from the list of possible foot types. They cannot possibly "imitate" or be a calque on an existing word stress pattern. The consequence of discarding all rising feet is that there will be many instances of feet containing only unstressed syllables. All C-types (prototypically [w s / s w]) will turn into a cascading foot preceded by a foot with a silent ictus and some number of weak syllables [! w / s s w], and B-types will turn into the same structure with the cascade down-up [! w / s w s]. But Sievers's system is deeply entrenched, and Russom's scansion is (on the surface) not easy to see as possessing much rhythmic promise, or at least not more than Sievers's. His nine foot patterns and twenty-five allowable foot pairings, plus quite complex rules of extrametricality, provide an apparatus that is almost as formidable as that of Bliss. Nonetheless, it is a genuinely innovative metrical theory, one that makes metrical and linguistic sense—as distinct from atheoretically-imposed rhythmic performance—of the aspirations of isochronous theories like Pope's. One may hope that it provides a basis, still not fully unexploited, for reconciliation between metrical typology (which is the basis for many brilliant emendations) and foot-tapping rhythm (which is, arguably, what the Anglo-Saxon audience somehow perceived).

Notes

We have benefited from extensive critiques of an earlier draft of this chapter by Thomas Cable, Edwin Duncan, Robert Fulk, Rand Hutcheson, Herbert Penzl, and a group of UCLA medievalists including Karl Hagen, Angel Gulermovich, Terri Bays, and Cathy Sanok. Research assistance provided by the UCLA Academic Senate and the UCLA Center for Medieval and Renaissance Studies is also gratefully acknowledged.

1. We use the word *stress* to refer to intrinsic linguistic prominence. By *normal* we mean "unless special conditions obtain." Such conditions include, e.g., contrastive stress, which in Old English as in Modern English can override other factors. We use the word *ictus* to refer to metrical prominence.

2. That is, creating a stair-step effect with peaks on the roots that make up the compound, exactly as in Modern English compounds like *caretaker, beefeater, moneylender, storyteller.*

3. We sweep under the rug here a complexity in the relation of stress to ictus for which we have no coherent explanation, namely that heavy medial syllables (like the second syllable of *hláfordes* or of *slǽpende*) occupy the second [s] of a cascading foot, whether they are morphologically recognizable or not (we take it that the second syllable of *hláfordes* was no longer recognizable as cognate with *weard*). Light medial syllables, on the other hand, are ictic only in the second foot of a verse, as, e.g., the second-class weak verbs (e.g., *-ode* is not ictic in 922a *tryddode tīrfæst* [sww/ss] but must be ictic in 725b *féond treddode* [s/ssw]). This difference is analyzed in detail by Fulk in his discussion of the "rule of the coda" (1992: 201 and passim), which asserts that "suffixes like *-scipe* and *-sume*, with an etymologically short high vowel in the penultimate syllable, count as two metrical positions in the coda of a verse; otherwise they count as one." *Coda* means "the last full lift and all subsequent syllables," which seems to be equivalent to "second foot." In our scansions, we follow this rule, as did Sievers and Bliss. But since it introduces a phonological weight constraint into a system of morphologically-based stress assignment rules, the result is incoherent. We believe this incoherence is a function of the time depth of the Germanic metrical tradition: a metrical practice has been preserved here long after some sort of regular phonological distinction had ceased to exist. We are grateful to Robert Fulk for pointing out our inconsistency on this point in an earlier draft. We want to be very clear, however, that such solutions as "the rule of the coda" and our equivalent version, which might be called the "cascading second foot rule," are a cludge, not a solution. (We view Bliss's three exceptions to the cascading second foot rule in *Beowulf*, namely, 612a, 1727a, and 2751a, as unexceptional examples of type D [Fulk's suggestion] rather than type A, as scanned by Bliss.)

4. As Lass remarks (1992, 86), the rule of stress placement "is blind to weight and syllable count, and pays no attention to anything except the location of the first syllable of the root."

5. "C" stands for "consonant" and "V" stands for "short vowel or short diphthong." Parentheses in a formula indicate that the enclosed segment may be present or not, without the generalization's being affected.

6. This should be noted carefully, since it is quite contrary to modern English intuitions: it is possibly due to the presence of glottal stops as the initial sounds of words that apparently begin with vowels—i.e., there may have been no smooth vowel onsets in stressed syllables in Old English, which possibly explains both vowel alliteration and the fact that word-final consonants never resyllabify with the first vowel of the following word (see Hutcheson 1991, 47), thereby maintaining the underlying weight

of word-final syllables. This is contrary to the rules of syllabification in the classical languages, where word boundaries are ignored in syllabification: *ab oris* is metrically *a.bo.ris*.

7. This historical condition (Kaluza's law) has been discussed extensively in Fulk, because it is very consistently true in *Beowulf* but less so at later dates, suggesting an important linguistic criterion for relative chronology in the poetic corpus.

8. This explanation is based on Cable (1994).

9. The view is mistaken, in our opinion, that phonemic vowel length played a timing role in the verse structure, producing alternations of length (as in the quantity-based verse of classical antiquity) rather than of prominence. The metrical alternations depend on prominence, which always favors heavy syllables, but does not require them. Old English prominence must have been marked by the same conglomerate of features—weight, pitch obtrusion, length, stress—that continue to this day to mark prominence. There is no evidence that suggests we should believe otherwise.

10. We assume the alliteration on *r-* in these lines is possibly the consequence of instability of this cluster in pronunciation; see Lutz (1993, 305). We are not prepared to take these two examples as a potential refutation of the much more solidly based philological claims for the "earliness" of *Beowulf* and the overwhelmingly regular alliteration of *h-* with *h-*.

11. Most notably A. J. Bliss, who in one of his several departures from Sievers's taxonomy replaced "foot boundaries" by "caesuras" between breath groups (actually syntactic phrases); and Thomas Cable, who, in striving for the simplest possible account of the scop's intuitive "rules of prosody," simply found no evidence that satisfied him that feet were units necessary to characterize the properties of Old English verse. We argue that feet are universal units of prosody that cannot be eschewed by the analyst's choice. Feet are necessary "constitutive" units. We assume that metrics must be more than merely descriptive, that it must try to say something about the atomic units and the molecular formation rules—in other words, it must be explicit, which is to say it must be generative. To be explicit in this generative sense, as distinct from after-the-fact descriptive, we do not think it is possible to avoid feet as second-level constituents.

12. The "empty syllable" is the rest beat after *þeod* that buffers the stress clash. In musical notation, it would be a quarter rest in 2/4 time. We believe that the shape [s !] is the correct interpretation of all monosyllabic strong feet, but if readers in their own wisdom feel we have erred on this point, all our scansions can still be made to work in a normal Sievers-Bliss style by removing the [!] wherever it appears in the configuration [s !]. The [!] cannot be removed when it appears initially in the foot, however, without destroying our understanding of feet containing suppressed lifts.

13. These trisyllabic feet cannot be further reduced, e.g., to a binary structure in this manner:

The phonetic effect would be the same, of course, but not the equivalence relations. They are genuinely tripartite feet at the most abstract level, and must be, if one is to preserve, as we believe is necessary, the four-position principle discussed below in the text.

14. This understanding of "suppression" differs slightly from that of Bliss, though it comes out to the same scansions in all instances (barring notation, of course).

15. There are at least two dozen verses for which emendations have been suggested on this account. But see Bliss (1967, 76), who argues that the presence of a caesura between the two weak syllables is sufficient to allow such verses to count as type E (indeed, Bliss says, they represent "the simplest and most fundamental variety"). This conclusion has not generally met with the favor of subsequent metrists. The even more obvious violations are the three-syllable verses like 947a *secg betsta*, for which there is no possible scansion in any theory that respects the principles set forth by Snorri.

16. Cable calls these expanded drops "strong dips." By his count, only 2.7 percent of the 6,342 verses in *Beowulf* have such drops outside the first foot.

17. Such verses are extremely rare (there is one more in *Beowulf*, with resolution at the beginning of the second foot), which suggests that demotion of **both** secondary [s]'s to metrically weak status was in principle disallowed. As the examples immediately above show, however, it was common to have to demote a secondary [s] in one foot or the other.

18. This subtype is extremely rare (there is one other in *Beowulf*). Like other five-position verses it is marked with an asterisk to indicate which type it belongs to, exceptional though it is: in this instance, A*.

19. For a very useful discussion of the constraints on weak-stressed syllables in general and especially in anacrusis, see Duncan (1993). For an earlier very thorough discussion of anacrusis in Type A verses, see Cable (1974, 32–43). We do not agree with Duncan's view that the constraints on weak positions suggest that there were two different phonetic levels of weak stress—a weaker level for the "light proclitics"—verbal prefixes, *ne*, and *ond*—and a stronger level for all other unstressed syllables. The reason we disagree is that the two classes are morphologically distinct, which is sufficient. Proliferation of "levels of stress" is not a good move, in any theory, because there is too much evidence that the ear does not make such fine phonetic discriminations in matters of relative prominence. Putting this point aside, Duncan's view of the constraints on weak positions seems to be correct.

20. Note that 432b, above, looks just like 1154a except for the resolution of the weak syllable in the first foot. To a modern ear they sound identical. It should be noted that in verses of the type D*, there is always double alliteration; hence, they appear only in on-verses.

21. Note that the first drop, even in type E, can apparently be expanded. However, except for proclitics, this is rare to the vanishing point. It occurs here and in one other verse (2882b). We do not believe it should be considered a regular verse possibility.

22. Kuryłowicz stated the essence of this idea in two or three places in his extensive poetic studies over many years (e.g., in Kuryłowicz 1979, 119, with references to earlier work), but he never developed it with the kind of responsible following out of all the consequences and implications that in our opinion gives Russom unique claim to this innovative theory.

Chapter 5

Diction, Variation, the Formula

by Katherine O'Brien O'Keeffe

Summary: Apart from interest in individual words and semantic fields, study of the diction of *Beowulf* has focused on synonyms, compounds, and kennings (a particular form of compound) from both aesthetic and functional perspectives. Variation, a term open to restrictive and loose definitions, is generally regarded as a technique, characteristic of *Beowulf*, that permits numerous descriptive elements (with the same grammatical structure) to be piled up. The study of "formula" (a concept borrowed from Homeric scholarship) has focused on continuing redefinition to accommodate the particulars of Old English metrics, the written evidence of the poetic tradition, and the complex question of aesthetics.

Chronology

1925: Henry C. Wyld treats poetic diction and imagery under three main headings: poetic words and phrases; metaphors and epithets; words used with striking originality.

1929: William F. Bryan argues the artistry of the *Beowulf* poet in his choice of epithetic compound folk names in the face of metrical and alliterative requirements.

1934: John O. Beaty discusses repetition of words or root syllables in five categories of simplices and compounds.

1937: C. C. Batchelor contends that the poet is "conditioned" psychologically by his religious training; he attempts to use diction to refute Blackburn's thesis on the "Christian coloring" of *Beowulf*.

1952: Caroline Brady attempts to determine which of the forty words and phrases for *sea* are synonyms, which are literal, which are metaphors.

1953: Drawing on Parry and Lord, Francis P. Magoun Jr. argues for the oral composition of *Beowulf*.

1955: Stanley B. Greenfield, in a broad consideration of conventional aspects of the theme of exile in Old English poetry, treats *Beowulf* 721a, 1274b, 1275a, 1352b, 2368a, 3018b, 3019b.

1956: Claes Schaar questions Magoun's assumption that formulaic poetry must be oral.

1956: E. G. Stanley explores Old English poetic diction in general.

1957: Adrien Bonjour argues against Magoun's theory of oral composition using the beasts-of-battle theme.

1957: Robert P. Creed examines *Beowulf* 258 and 340 as part of a formulaic system, arguing that it is a "verse-pair system designed to make a whole line of song."

1959: Arthur Gilchrist Brodeur argues against Magoun for the literate poet's originality in diction by analyzing the poem's mode of compounding and use of the kenning. He offers two appendices on poetic compounds.

1959: Douglas C. Collins considers the importance of the kenning and the difficulty of its use.

1959: Robert P. Creed illustrates his thesis that composition was a "process of choosing rapidly . . . *not* between individual words but between *formulas*"; he offers his own composition of Old English verse.

1960: David K. Crowne argues that themes are not necessarily expressed by similar formulas: the "hero on the beach" theme consists in a "concatenation of four imagistic details."

1960: Albert B. Lord analyzes the oral process of composition and applies it (in chapter 10) to *Beowulf,* finding the poem oral in origin but a single composition.

1961: Robert P. Creed sketches an aesthetics of reading *Beowulf* as an oral poem.

1961: William Whallon investigates the formulaic aspect of *Beowulf*'s diction by comparison to Homeric diction.

1962: Robert P. Creed, by focusing on three passages in Beowulf that describe a singer at work, discusses the poet's use of formula and theme.

1962: Robert D. Stevick analyzes shortcomings in the articulation of oral theory for Old English and in the practice of that criticism; he urges greater systematization.

1963: Randolph Quirk considers the lexical, metrical, and grammatical environments of complementarity and parity (= variation) as well as the audience's expectations about them.

1963: James L. Rosier makes dictional clusters of feasts and hands illustrate some ways in which the poem revises scenes for different purposes.

1965: Frederic G. Cassidy highlights the syntactic dimensions of formula in examining the freedom of the Anglo-Saxon scop in his use of individual formulas.

1965: Robert L. Kellogg examines the formulaic character of the *Heliand* and its similarity to that of the Anglo-Saxon tradition to argue the continuity of the South Germanic alliterative tradition.

1965: William Whallon (1965a) modifies his 1961 views on formulaic diction: "the formulaic kennings for the heroes of *Beowulf* are true to generic character but significantly appropriate to context."

1966: Larry D. Benson demonstrates that oral composition of *Beowulf* cannot be proved on the basis of the presence of formulas.

1966: Stanley B. Greenfield analyzes the function of series and variation in 221–23a in presenting a view of the Danish coast.

1966: R. F. Lawrence surveys the history of oral-formulaic theory.

1966: H. L. Rogers questions the oral-formulaic research of Parry, Lord, and Magoun on linguistic grounds and argues that the Parry-Lord definition of formula in Homeric poems is not applicable to Old English.

1967: Donald K. Fry offers an important summary of approaches to defining formula and presents new definitions of formula and system.

1968: Donald K. Fry argues (against Whallon 1961, 1965a) that since variation is essential to Old English poetry, the concept of thrift or economy is not applicable to Old English verse.

1969: Thomas Gardner believes that the kenning is not Germanic in origin but seeks its roots in the Christian dialogue tradition.

1969: Ann Chalmers Watts presents a detailed review and analysis of Parry on Homer and Magoun on *Beowulf*; she finds that Magoun did not rigorously apply the Parry-Lord thesis and did not evaluate the analogy between Greek and Old English.

1971: Lars Lönnroth compares the deaths of the hero in *Beowulf* and *Hjálmar's Death Song,* finding that *Beowulf* has more formulas and formulaic systems.

1972: Thomas Gardner reviews common definitions of *kenning* and proposes instead that a kenning "must contain a metaphorical base and an associating link."

1972: Stanley Greenfield argues the importance of determining the aesthetic qualities of the formula, their "dictional expectations," and the limitations on our knowledge.

1973: Thomas Gardner maintains that the *Beowulf* poet manipulated formulaic material to achieve "conspicuous" variety.

1974: Albert B. Lord offers a review of oral traditional scholarship and some comments on its applications to Old English.

1976: John Miles Foley defines a level of "purely metrical" formula below verbal structure, which generates 94 percent of the lines in *Beowulf.*

1976: Jeff Opland studies passages on poetry and poets and on the basis of their references to the scop, suggests that the Yugoslavian *guslar* is not an exclusive model for the scop and that African tradition may provide more useful analogues.

1977: James L. Rosier defines and explains "the process of the habit of contiguous recurrences of forms" in *Beowulf* as generative composition. (This treatment acknowledges and supersedes that of Beaty 1934).

1978: Geoffrey R. Russom examines violations of economy, concluding that the Parry-Lord hypothesis is "fundamentally wrong."

1979: Caroline Brady analyzes nominal compounds, genitive compounds, and simplices for *weapon* to determine their meanings and the use to which they were put in the poem.

1979: Fred C. Robinson offers an important definition of variation (variation is considered apposition if apposition is extended to include adjectives, verbs, and phrases).

1980: John Miles Foley offers a definition of formula that meets Old English metrical requirements.

1981: Robert P. Creed applies Peabody's four tests of orality to *Beowulf* and finds they confirm his hypothesis that *Beowulf* is "a copy of a recording of a performance."

1981: Francelia Clark finds that the low incidence of repetition in the flyting in *Beowulf* (vs. high repetition in the *Song of Bagdad*) indicates that the Lord definition of theme does not apply to *Beowulf.*

1981: John Miles Foley presents an important bibliographical review of the application of oral traditional theory to Old English.

1981: Joanne De Lavan Foley extends Fry's conception of formulaic system and describes a larger superstructure in Beowulf of systems generically related through the collocation of feasting and sleeping.

1981: R. W. McTurk compares various patterns of parallelism and variation in Old Norse and Old English poetry, concluding that variation is not a valid marker of chronology.

1982: A. Leslie Harris offers a useful overview of earlier work preparatory to her examination of variation and parallel as part of the poet's strategies for slowing or accelerating the narrative.

1982: Valerie Krishna examines necessary enjambment and thrift to assess the degree to which *Beowulf* and the *Alliterative Morte Arthure* may be considered traditional.

1982: Hiroto Ushigaki considers epithets applied to the good king, specifically to Hrothgar, Beowulf, and Hygelac, and offers an appendix listing these epithets.

1983: Caroline Brady examines the meaning of the 101 nominal compounds or genitive combinations for *warrior* to establish their contextual use, whether informative, traditional, stylistic, or artistic.

1983: Calvin B. Kendall adapts Kuhn's laws to describe a metrical grammar of *Beowulf*, concluding that whether lettered or oral the poet worked within the half-line units of traditional composition.

1983: John D. Niles applies and develops Fry's concept of Old English formula, concluding that nearly two of three verses in the poem are members of identifiable formulaic systems.

1985: Anita Reidinger proposes new definitions for formula, system, and set.

1985: Fred C. Robinson surveys the polysemous nature of the poem's terms for God and argues that the poem's appositive style keeps alive both primitive and Christian meanings in traditional diction.

1986: René Derolez argues that several passages with variations contain not synonyms but words with distinct meanings.

1986: Roberta Frank examines the meanings of "mere" and "sund" and the implications of their drawing in particular circumstances on meanings otherwise found only in prose contexts.

1986: Robert P. Creed discusses alliteration and its relation to the verse line and to memory.

1986: Paul Beekman Taylor considers seven categories of words for treasure; he finds "etymological associations between treasure goods and the life forces believed to reside in them."

1987: Roberta Frank examines *Exodus* and *Beowulf* for evidence of Scandinavian stylistic devices, concluding that Unferth's rhetoric seems to call on Skaldic as well as Old English rhetorical technique.

1988: John S. Miletich concludes that the low density of formulas in *Beowulf* indicates that it is the product of "learned written-style technique."

1988: Geoffrey Russom finds that the use of compounds in verse translations from Latin shows neither unambiguous orality nor literacy; he objects to Niles's conclusions on combinatives.

1990: Andrew Galloway analyzes the language of choice and its meaning within the political realm.

1990: Eric Jager explores descriptions of speech from the chest, suggesting that spoken words are conceptualized as physical events or objects.

1990: Gillian R. Overing defines kenning and descriptive epithet in terms of the definition of metonym; she explores the metonymic function of poetic diction in *Beowulf*.

1990: Paul Beekman Taylor demonstrates some semantic contours of epithets in context and the semantic weight an epithet may be given.

1991: John Miles Foley adapts reception criticism in an exploration of how oral and oral-derived poems (including the epics of the South Slavs, the *Iliad*, and the *Odyssey*) convey meaning.

1991: Albert B. Lord discusses formula clusters (with the sentence beginning in the b-verse) in introductions to speech; he responds to Benson 1966.

1992: John D. Niles outlines seven features of early European oral heroic poetry and seven features of oral composition by the scop as prolegomenon to an Anglo-Saxon oral poetics.

In the last forty years or so, no single critical movement has changed the face of *Beowulf* scholarship more than oral traditional criticism. In Old English, the concept of the formulaic nature of oral poetry was borrowed initially from the researches of Milman Parry and Albert B. Lord into the Homeric and South Slavic epic traditions, and it quickly captured the imaginations of numerous students of the poem while raising the ire of many others. Oral traditional criticism seemed to offer both a unified theory of the production of oral poetry and an account of compositional and stylistic features in an anonymous tradition that promised to connect the earliest English verse with its counterparts on the Continent. But the application of oral traditional criticism to Old English verse, and, in the present instance, to *Beowulf,* meant rethinking many assumptions about the poem, its composition, its contemporary audience, and the techniques a modern audience could use to read and understand it. The impact of oral traditional criticism has been particularly noticeable on the study of two elements in the style of the poem—diction and variation—and the introduction of the notion of formula as a compositional technique.

I. Diction

When J. R. Clark Hall concluded his entry for *hlæst* (burden, freight, load) in *A Concise Anglo-Saxon Dictionary* by citing *holmes hlæst* and glossing *finny tribe,* he provided at once a rare instance of humor in an otherwise sober lexicographic project and a glimpse at a fairly early approach to Old English poetic diction. *Finny tribe,* of course, had been coined in the eighteenth century within a particular understanding of what might constitute appropriate poetic language: elegant circumlocution made it possible to avoid the hopelessly mundane word *fish.* Insofar as the language of Old English poetry reserved to itself a set of words that do not appear in prose and delighted as well in using compound nouns and adjectives in periphrasis for more ordinary expressions, the comparison seemed useful to early scholars of the poem. For W. W. Lawrence "Anglo-Saxon verse was, of course, as much confined by 'measures and rules' as that of Dryden or of Pope" (1928, 3). While both intrigued and repelled by what he saw as similarities to the elegant artifice of eighteenth-century poetic diction, Henry Cecil Wyld (1925) still found much in Old English poetic diction that appeared "genuine."

The diction of *Beowulf* has attracted a good deal of attention over the last century on a variety of fronts. Numerous scholars have written on individual words and semantic fields.[1] Considerable work has been devoted to defining and exploring the nature of compounds in the poem and refining the definition and applicability of the word *kenning* for a class of those compounds. There have been important studies of the simplices and compounds for specific concepts (such as *sea* or *warrior*) and the question of whether the words within such groups may legitimately be considered synonyms. But all such studies may be plotted on two sets of axes, depending on the critical perspective their authors bring to the problem. Studies of diction may be author based, by which I mean their paramount interest lies in demonstrating the ability of poets either to manipulate traditional materials or to invent their own, or they may be audience based, that is, driven by a desire to examine the affective component in the language of *Beowulf*. Although the audience-based approach is not univocal, author-based studies may be plotted on a further set of axes, depending on whether the investigator regards the *Beowulf* poet to be a writer or a singer and the poem to be a literate or oral production. (The section on formula will deal with the difficulties inherent in regarding "oral" and "literate" as the terms of a dichotomy.) The discussion that follows groups the scholarship on diction according to these broad guidelines.

During the course of his appreciative study, Wyld wished for a more precise understanding of the shades of meaning of the diction he discussed. As if in answer, in three fundamental studies, Caroline Brady investigated words for *sea, weapon,* and *warrior* in *Beowulf* (Brady 1952, 1979, 1983). Throughout, her purpose was to ascertain which of the apparently equivalent words in a class might actually be synonyms and which were not; which individual words were used literally, which metaphorically. What distinguishes Brady's approach from the majority of early studies of diction (whose "endless lists" Brady regarded as "worthless" [1979, 80]) is its commitment to analysis of the words or expressions in context. Individually she examined simplices, nominal compounds, and genitive combinations for precise shades of meaning. The distinction among these is most easily illustrated by the following set of related ideas: *yð* (wave) is a simplex; *yðgewinn* (tossing water) is a nominal compound; *yða gewinn* (tumult of the waves) is a genitive combination. (More recently Fred C. Robinson has demonstrated some possible syntactic relations between the elements in the compounds in *Beowulf* [1985, 16–18]). Of the words for the sea, Brady concluded that "the metaphorical content in the sea-vocabulary of *Beowulf* is negligible. . . . In depicting the sea this poet is no artificer mechanically piling up synonyms and conventional metaphors, but an artist who knows how to use a variety of words and phrases" (1952, 44). Brady's other two studies focused on nominal compounds in context, and she was much concerned to refute the critical assumption that all expressions that might be grouped under a general heading such as *spear* or *warrior* are synonyms. In her view, an "obsession with synonyms" (1979, 80), a failure to distinguish between determinatives[2] and true circumlocutions, and an imprecision in classifying figures of speech had led to an undervaluing of the precision of diction in *Beowulf*.[3] While Brady focused exclusively on metaphor (cf. the discussion of Overing, below), her approach was philological in the traditional sense and was very much affected by her conviction that the *Beowulf* poet was literate in the traditional understanding of that word.

Perhaps the most extensive study of diction in *Beowulf* is that of Arthur Gilchrist Brodeur in his influential 1959 *The Art of Beowulf.* Brodeur was concerned to demonstrate the *Beowulf* poet's artistry, not only his mastery of traditional conventions but his originality within the medium. Quite obviously, Brodeur's approach to diction was through the poet, here too conceived of as a literate author. While he was willing to concede that the poet was trained as a "professional scop" (4), he argued that only the assumption of literacy on the part of the author could explain the brilliance of *Beowulf* in comparison to other long poems in Old English. The fervor with which he argued the poet's literate ability can be understood only in the light of the position Brodeur argued against.

In 1953 Francis P. Magoun Jr. rocked the world of *Beowulf* scholarship with an essay in *Speculum* that argued that the long poem in Old English was totally formulaic. Magoun relied heavily on the extensive work of Milman Parry on Homeric epic, and he applied the categories Parry had developed for analyzing Greek formulas to the analysis of Old English verse. From the distance of forty years, this first attempt at understanding the orality underlying surviving Old English verse seems oversimple and overargued. But the consequence of his argument was stunning. In a way much different from the methods of Foucault and Barthes some twenty-five years later, Magoun had managed, nonetheless, to kill the author of *Beowulf.* If the diction of the poem was completely formulaic, then there was really no author of the poem, only a scop who performed, and the question of originality seemed silly indeed when individual choice disappeared under the weight of traditional formulas. There had never been a name in the author slot, but now the man and his art were being made to disappear.

Brodeur perceived the threat from this approach to understand Old English verse, and his response was a chapter on diction that met Magoun head on. Quite unlike Magoun's unlettered singer, Brodeur's author of *Beowulf* was educated and literate, familiar with the Old Testament and some patristic writings. And Magoun's assertion that those compounds called "kennings" were specifically "traditional and formulaic" (Magoun 1953, 452) was the particular issue of diction that Brodeur chose to challenge: "In both diction and manner the conventional element is indeed strong; it is the element which we may safely presume to be original that determines the quality of the diction and style of *Beowulf*" (1959, 6). In his treatment, Brodeur analyzed diction by the structure of the substantives, whether simplices or compounds. Each may be literal or figurative, as a ship might be termed a *sæbat* or a *wegflota*, in the latter instance drawing on the metonymy of the simplex *flota*. Brodeur simply noted that compounds may be metonyms or metaphors; this important distinction would be fruitfully considered later by Gillian Overing (1990; see below).

Brodeur took issue with the relative looseness of the definition of *kenning* (See also Collins 1959; Gardner 1972; Overing 1990). In Brodeur's treatment, "kenning" is restricted "to those periphrastic appellations in the base-word of which a person or thing is identified with something which it actually is *not*" (18). Brodeur used the term *kent heiti* to refer to those periphrastic expressions that describe the referent in terms of what it *is*. Thus *yða full* (cup of the waves) is a kenning, while *yða geswing* (tumult of the waves) is a *kent heiti*. (This conceptual distinction has not been widely accepted.) This distinction, however, allowed Brodeur to compare the kennings in *Beowulf* with those in other longer poems and to conclude that the poet of *Beowulf* is more precise and more restrained in his use. The variety and force of the poem's diction are, in Brodeur's view, evidence of its (and the poet's) originality.

In the thirteen years following Brodeur's book, the landscape of Old English studies was changed by inroads from two powerful critical forces: oral formulaic criticism and formalism. While the decade of the 1960s saw a proliferation of studies on the formula, type-scene, and oral composition, it also experienced a dramatic upsurge in the number of essays using the techniques of formalist analysis for Old English verse. Such approaches were at loggerheads. Although both approaches focused on the text, formalist analysis presupposed an author, a written text, and a reading audience; formulaic analysis assumed precisely the opposite. Quite apart from their differences over the circumstances of composition and reception, the two approaches differed on the question of art: while the oralists emphasized the beauty in the tradition, formalists objected that the oral traditional model made individual choice (thus original art) impossible.

This is the mine field Stanley Greenfield negotiated in his 1972 *Interpretation of Old English Poems*. While Greenfield argued that it was mistaken to look for the dictional precision of modern poetry in Old English verse, nonetheless, he disputed Creed's contention that formula was crucial in Old English verse, not diction. (The distinction here construes "diction" as word *choice* and "formula" as traditional, hence *preexisting*, phrases.) Greenfield urged a different procedure: "It seems critically valid to evaluate, if not the originality of the phrasing, the aesthetic qualities *in situ* of the conventional formula" (1972, 36). As Greenfield read Old English poetic diction, context exerted a more powerful force on its meaning than did any expectation of individual word meaning. Thus, while he weighed the force of "dictional and formulaic semantic expectations" against context, he generally maintained the power of context over "expected" word meaning. In this his criticism flew the formalist flag rather than the oral traditionalist.

A decade later John D. Niles approached the question of diction from the opposite perspective (1983). In an important change of direction, Niles put aside the vexed question of aesthetics to focus on the *function* of a specific feature of the language of *Beowulf*—compound diction. As Niles pointed out, compounds are an extraordinary dictional feature, occuring over fifteen hundred times in the poem, and their density of occurrence is greater in *Beowulf* than in any other Old English poem, save *Exodus.* Niles viewed compound diction as part of a flexible system of composition with a traditional formulaic vocabulary. (On formulas, see below.) A few of the words used to describe Hrothgar illustrate the system of compounding: Hrothgar may be described by "cyning" (king) or "dryhten" (lord), "weard" (guardian), or "hyrde" (guardian, keeper) or by a number of other simplices. By forming nominal compounds—"heahcyning," "þeodcyning," "sigedryhten," "winedrihten" (great king, king of a people, victorious lord, friendly lord)—or genitive combinations—"folces hyrde," "rices hyrde," "beahhorda weard" (guardian of the people, guardian of the kingdom, guardian of the ring hoard)—on the basis of old formulaic patterns, the poet could negotiate fluidly the local demands of both meter and alliteration. Hrothgar might be called "sigedryhten" when alliteration on *s* was needed (see 391b) but "winedryhten" to accommodate alliteration on *w* (see 360b). Within a traditional poetry, compounding allowed the poet considerable flexibility in working with an inherited word hoard and meter. Niles pointed out that function does not obviate aesthetics. Agreeing with Brodeur that the poem shows both splendor of language and the work of a great artist, Niles nonetheless offered a corrective within the oral traditional understanding of composition. The *Beowulf* poet, he argued, was not "an individual genius chafing against the limits of an inherited form . . . [but] an accomplished poet who brought an inherited form to a fine stage of fulfillment" (1983, 151).

Niles's attention to the function of compounding within the diction of *Beowulf* offers a useful entrée into a more specifically linguistic consideration of the diction of the poem, that is, how one might describe and explain the numerous repetitions of simplices (either as a simplex or as an element in a compound) within small numbers of verses. In an early study, John O. Beaty termed such recurrences "echo-words" and suggested that repetition of a word could be explained by the "pleasure of echoing its identical sound in a different meaning" (1934, 366). Beaty's study, interested only in sound as an element of poetic style, had no explanatory power and essentially trivialized the phenomenon. In 1977, James L. Rosier examined from a specifically linguistic perspective pairs of simplices or simplices plus compounds in what he called contiguous lexical recurrence. The process of their recurrence he termed "generative composition," since the process involved using a simplex again a few lines later, or reusing it as part of a compound (see, e.g., *Beowulf* 2017b–22b: "flet," "fletsittende" [floor of a hall; sitters in a hall]). Far from being random, this lexical recurrence was part of the nature of the language itself and was very much determined by the conservative nature of the Old English lexicon and by the tendency of Old English to form new words by compounding and affixation (1977, 202). Although Rosier confined his study to *Beowulf,* the process of generative composition can easily be seen in other Old English poems, particularly *The Wanderer* and *The Seafarer.*

As the implications of the oral traditional approach to Old English developed, a number of studies used a comparative approach to illustrate the nature and degree of formulaic diction in *Beowulf*. In several studies, William Whallon compared the diction of *Beowulf* to that of the Homeric poems (Whallon 1961, 1965a, 1969), concentrating mainly on kennings. In the earliest study, when Whallon accepted criteria of oral composition derived from the *Iliad* and *Odyssey* as universal, he found the diction of *Beowulf* wanting and certainly lacking the economy characteristic of the Homeric epics. He modified in the 1965a study, judging what he calls "the formulaic kennings" appropriate to their context (96, italics removed; see formula below).

Whatever their local disagreements about aesthetics, composition, or the nature of the author, earlier considerations of diction agreed in making the focus of their attention the connection between the author and his text. Gillian Overing offered a dramatic departure from this tacit agreement by considering *Beowulf* from a specifically postmodern perspective. Here the closure of meaning implicit in the appeal to authorial intention is rejected in favor of a continuing openness generated by a focus on the relationship of audience to text: "The reader has to be prepared to put meaning 'on hold,' but in this reciprocal space between text and reader, I shall argue . . . that the text holds sway. The primarily metonymic Old English poetic text engages, perhaps demands, a metonymic response from the reader" (1990, 10). Overing argues that meaning in *Beowulf* is not metaphoric but rather metonymic. The difference is crucial. Metaphor works by transferring meaning to another term; metonymy works by substituting meaning. Overing illustrates with the use of *goldwine* (gold-friend) as a term for lord. "Gold-friend" substitutes for "lord" and the two terms coexist, but independently. While metaphor operates in a world of controlled meaning, metonymy prohibits closure. Overing argues that this refusal of closure is responsible for the immediacy of effect that the diction of *Beowulf* (and of Old English poetry in general) has on its audiences.

Rather than make Brodeur's distinction between kenning and *kent heiti,* Overing collapses the two categories in order to focus on their shared metonymic function. What she loses in the distinction of metaphoric force, she gains in broadening the scope for considering the operation of metonymy in the poem. "Instead of looking at the kenning in terms of metaphor, I suggest that a working definition for the kenning and descriptive epithet (both of which I will call simply compounds) is that applied to the metonym: 'a figure of speech which consists in substituting for the name of a thing the name of an attribute of it or something closely related' (OED)" (1990, 16).

II. Variation
Variation is perhaps the most distinctive feature of the style of *Beowulf,* and depending on whom you talk to, it is either the element responsible for the deeply resonant texture of the poem or a cause for despair in the novice translator. Take,

for example, the description of the helmet Beowulf puts on when he prepares to enter the mere and fight Grendel's mother:

> ac se hwita helm   hafelan werede,
> se þe meregrundas   mengan scolde,
> secan sundgebland   since geweorðad,
> befongen freawrasnum,   swa hine fyrndagum
> worhte wæpna smið,   wundrum teode,
> besette swinlicum,   þæt hine syðþan no
> brond ne beadomecas   bitan ne meahton. (1448–54)

[But the shining helmet protected the head, (the helmet) which had to disturb the bottom of the lake, to seek out the surging water, adorned with treasure, encircled by splendid bands, just as in days gone by the weaponsmith had made it, formed it wonderfully, adorned it with the likenesses of boars, so that neither sword nor battle swords might bite it.]

This is not a narrative style for the impatient. If one were to try to reduce this little passage to its bare bones, one might try: "A splendid helmet protected Beowulf's head when he entered the mere." Unfortunately, such a reduction merely cartoons the passage by trimming away so many details—the suggestion of the difficulty of Beowulf's task, the nature of the ornamentation on the helmet, the suggestion of its history, its purpose and mettle as armor. Variation as a stylistic device gives texture to the narrative; as the story moves forward, the elements in variation give us information often at odd angles to the main line of the narrative. In this passage, in the present moment of arming, the description takes us out of the present (the helmet being donned) into the future (Beowulf's imminent penetration of the lake) back into the present (the current appearance of the helmet) into the past (the efforts of the smith) and back into a looming future (the helmet was fashioned so that swords might not harm it). But this account examines only the temporal aspect of this kind of variation. A closer grammatical examination of the passage will illustrate how variation affects the poem's diction.

What are the terms in variation? They include accusative nouns ("mere-grundas" and "sundgebland," each paired with infinitives—"mengan" and "secan"—dependent on "scolde"), past participles ("geweorðad" and "befongen," each modified by a dative noun "since" and "freawrasnum"), and preterite third singular indicative verbs ("worhte," "teode," and "besette," the last two modified by another pair of dative nouns, "wundrum" and "swinlicum"). There are also the nominatives "brond" and "beadomecas," producing the Modern English pleonasm of "sword and swords." In this passage, the parallels are very tight, and points of description come in twos. The helmet has to be good because the job is difficult. The listener or reader of the poem is expected to consider supplementary (but not equivalent) pieces of information. In the first phrase, the helmet (as a metonym for

Beowulf's head) must do the disturbing ("mengan" = 'to disturb') at the bottom of the lake; in the second phrase, the verb is neutral but its object is not. That is, in the variant, the helmet seeks out what is already disturbed (surging water ["blandan" = 'to mix,' 'to blend,' 'to mingle']). In this way, the variation offers the audience of the poem two aspects of Beowulf's journey. Similarly, the helmet is presented as a costly object adorned by treasure ("since") but also prudently reinforced by lordly bands. It is at once described as being beyond the everyday (its smith fashioned it *wondrously*) but also adorned by recognizable and functional images (the smith set it about with swine likenesses [cf. *Beowulf* 303b–06a]).

Such variation often complicates the process of translating the poem into modern English, as the ambiguous placement of "adorned with treasure" in the translation above will attest. The inflectional endings of Old English make the grammar of "geweorðad" clear and helped the native speaker of Old English distinguish the terms in variation. In Old English there is no difficulty in separating "se hwita helm" from its modifier "since geweorðad" four half-lines away; in fact such a separation actually allows this portion of the poetic description of the helmet to encircle the head, as is the helmet's real job. Often a translator will add redundant words, precisely to keep the variations clear. In the translation above, the extra "helmet" supplied for 1449a above—". . . [the helmet] which had to disturb"—forces the reading that "se þe" refers to "helm" and not "hafelan." But the effect is rather pallid. At other times, translators subtract words. The combination of "brond" and "beadomecas" similarly loses its effect in translation because, with its impoverished vocabulary for swords, modern English presses the translator either to reduce the variety the poem offers or change the force of the second noun. (On the question of synonymy in variation, see Brady [1952, 1979, 1983] and Derolez [1986].) Despite the number of excellent translations of *Beowulf* available, variation is best appreciated in Old English.

Variation as a technique has been approached variously. Brodeur (1959, 40) refined Paetzel's 1913 definition of variation to distinguish between variation and parallelism: "I should prefer to define variation as a double or multiple statement of the same concept or idea in different words, with a more or less perceptible shift in stress: one member of a variation may state the thought either more generally or more specifically than the other; or the second member, while restating essentially the same concept or idea, may do so in a manner which emphasizes a somewhat different aspect of it. While the members of a variation possess the same grammatical structure, they constitute a parallelism as well as a variation; but not all variations are parallelisms, nor are all parallelisms variations." Thus, Brodeur did not accept the last lines of the poem as variation:

cwædon þæt he wære wyruldcyninga
manna mildust ond monðwærust,
leodum liðost ond lofgeornost. (3180–82)

[They said that of kings of the world he was mildest of men and the gentlest, kindest to his people and most eager for praise.]

Rather, he discerned here a parallelism among four superlative adjectives, what he called "eloquent enumeration of his virtues" (1959, 68). Fred C. Robinson (1985), on the other hand, reads this series as a clear example of apposed epithets.

A permeable boundary between variation and enumeration is not the only difficulty besetting an analysis of the poem's technique. If we take, for example, the lines "flota wæs on yðum // bat under beorge" (the ship was on the waves, the boat under the cliff, 210b–11a), we will notice that Brodeur did not accept them as an example of variation because the prepositional phrases have different referents. But Stanley Greenfield (1972) suggested that such a distinction draws the lines too fine. In his general study of the uses of variation in Old English poetry, Greenfield suggested a productive loosening of the terms: "I propose that though such elements as the adjectives, parts of compounds and prepositional phrases are not identical in their referents, that the syntactic parallelism plus the variational quality of the rest of the expression effectively *does* equate, or at least link, the disparate elements: . . . the boat's being beneath the cliff indicates that, in addition to the difference in perspective, it is equally on the waves." (1972, 74). For a further difficulty, Brodeur did not limit variation to elements in the same grammatical constructions (as, e.g., in *Beowulf* 1–2, "þrym" and "hu"), but most discussions of variation do so. On the difficulties of definition and the many practical problems of distinguishing variation, parallelism, and enumeration in the poem, see A. Leslie Harris (1982).

The phenomenon of variation in *Beowulf* has been studied from a variety of perspectives, quite apart from studies of individual passages (as, e.g., Greenfield 1966; Taylor 1986) or themes (Taylor 1967). C. C. Batchelor (1937) focused on variation to advance the proposition that the poet was "conditioned" psychologically by his religious training, producing, it would seem, a kinder, gentler Beowulf. In the early days of oral-formulaic researches, variation in *Beowulf* came to pose something of an embarrassment. In the formulations of Parry and Lord (based on analysis of the Homeric epics), a primary characteristic of oral epic was the principle of thrift or economy. For the *Iliad* and the *Odyssey*, "economy" meant that the oral poet did not multiply entities—he tended to use the same epithets for a particular character in the same metrical positions. Since economy was considered to be a quality of mature epic, *Beowulf*, in the light of its unthrifty variation, was judged to be lacking (Whallon 1961, 318-19). Whallon softened this view in a subsequent essay (1965a), and Donald K. Fry (1968b) put the question to rest by pointing out that the terms of the argument were incorrect. Another attempt to use variation as a marker, this time for dating the poem, was made by Rory McTurk (1981). Working from precisely the opposite assumption from Whallon, McTurk tested the hypothesis that the greater the amount of variation, the later the poem, given the model of Old Norse-Icelandic evidence. However, as he notes, such comparison yields only negative evidence: the amount of variation cannot provide a means for dating an Old English poem.

In perhaps the most far-ranging study of the nature and function of variation in *Beowulf,* Fred C. Robinson offered an analysis of the fundamentals of variation and an argument for its determining role at every level of the poem. This use of variation he termed *Beowulf*'s "appositive style": "What is essential, apparently, is that the two elements in an appositive construction be the same part of speech, have the same referent, and not be connected except by syntactic parallelism within the sentence in which they occur. 'Appositive' in this broad sense describes fairly accurately what Anglo-Saxon scholars term 'variation' in Old English poetry" (1985, 3). Robinson's approach to variation, considered under the umbrella term *apposition,* would extend the concept throughout the various layers of the poem: to possible ambiguous meanings for individual words, to the composition and understanding of compounds, as well as to the paratactic arrangement of words and phrases. Robinson argued that the appositional quality of nominal compounds (where the relation between the two elements must be deciphered by the audience) contributes to the syntactic openness of the poem, what he calls its "inferential demands" (1985, 14). In Robinson's view, apposition is the fundamental mode of the poem, allowing the poet to treat the delicate interrelations of paganism and Christianity. In this argument, he deftly connects the preeminent element of the poem's style with what many have regarded as its overarching theme.

III. The Formula

In 1953, Francis P. Magoun Jr. instilled new vigor into the tired term *formula* by a form of intellectual cross-fertilization. The term, used by German scholars of the nineteenth century in research into the circumstances of authorship, was by then out of fashion, and the ideas associated with it—stock phrases, repetition, *Liedertheorie,* all vaguely embarrassing to *Beowulf* scholarship after Tolkien—were relegated to the stacks of dry-as-dust scholarship (Watts 1969; Foley 1981a). Magoun did not rehabilitate the concept of "formula" in Old English scholarship; he transformed it by adapting the fruits of the researches of Milman Parry and Albert B. Lord (for an account, see Lord 1960) into Homeric and South Slavic epics. Magoun's application of the Parry-Lord thesis to *Beowulf* affected *Beowulf* criticism more than perhaps any other single modern work of scholarship, and its influence continues today. If the predominant metaphor in this description of Magoun's work on the oral formula draws on the propagation of plants, there were many contemporary scholars of the poem who were prepared to view Magoun less in the role of Luther Burbank than Dr. Frankenstein. The controversy over the oral-formulaic analysis of *Beowulf* begun by Magoun, remarkable in its vigor, has been extremely productive for *Beowulf* scholarship.

Using Parry's definition of the formula—"a group of words which is regularly employed under the same metrical conditions to express a given essential idea" (1953, 449)—Magoun analyzed the first twenty-five lines of the poem (fifty verses) for evidence of formulas. By his count, more than 70 percent of the half-lines were matched elsewhere in the canon, and he believed that were the canon of surviving poetry larger, the 30 percent not matched would prove to be "formulaic" after all. For Magoun, these statistics constituted conclusive proof that the poem had been orally composed. Parry's work with the living oral tradition of South Serbia had led him to conclude that oral poetry was formulaic. Magoun extended this contention to assert for Old English that all formulaic poetry is oral. On the vexing question of Cynewulf (whose self-conscious epilogues, manipulating the runes for his name, suggested literate authorship), Magoun, somewhat lamely, allowed that whatever the origin of the epilogue, Cynewulf had to have composed the narrative of his poems in traditional fashion.

As the chronology above demonstrates, reaction to Magoun's essay was swift. Stanley Greenfield (1955) explored formulas constituting the theme of exile. Robert Creed's unpublished 1955 Harvard Ph.D. dissertation analyzed the entire poem for its formulaic content. In subsequent essays, Creed (1957) explored the function of a formulaic system for *andswarode,* composed his own "oral" verse as part of a demonstration of the possible process of composition (1959), and argued that *Beowulf* was composed by an oral poet (1962). But reaction was also negative. Maintaining a lettered origin for Cynewulf's poems on the basis of what he considered literate borrowings, Claes Schaar (1956) attacked the faulty logic in Magoun's conclusion that formula was an accurate test for orality. As Schaar devastatingly pointed out, the converse of a proposition is not necessarily true. Robert D. Stevick (1962) found Magoun's application unsystematic. H. L. Rogers argued that the Parry-Lord hypothesis was not applicable to Old English, that its definitions were too loose, and that, in any event, they were inadequate on linguistic grounds. He further objected that the hypothesis pictured the poet producing his formulas without thought (1966). Adrien Bonjour took Magoun on from another stance. Concerned that oral theory denied the poet creativity, Bonjour argued that the poem's use of the beasts of battle demonstrated the poet's originality (1957a). In his view, the question of the poet's literacy or lack of it could not be decided. The gentlemanly battle lines were drawn.

Among the most potent of the arguments against the Magoun thesis (and in its own right an argument with comparable staying power) was Larry Benson's study of the "literary character" of Old English verse (1966). Benson targeted Magoun's claim that the presence of formula in verse was a guarantee of the oral origin of that verse. Benson drew on several poems with apparently written origins (e.g., *The Phoenix,* Exeter Riddle 35, *Meters of Boethius*) and demonstrated their high percentage of formulas. From this he inferred that "not only can literate poets write formulaic verse, they can write it pen in hand in the same way any writer observes a literary tradition" (1966, 337). Although there is an element of overstatement in Benson's conclusion, since the features of literacy in Anglo-Saxon England are not identical to our own, his demonstration dismantled a crucial tenet of Magoun's argument. No longer could the presence of identifiable formulas in Old English verse be accepted as signs of oral provenance. Later scholars drawing on Benson include Russom (1978, 1987b) and F. H. Whitman (1975).

To understand the dimensions of the response to this groundbreaking essay, it will be useful to back up a bit and look at the features of the Parry-Lord hypothesis before they were grafted onto the poem. The first of these is Parry's definition of the formula (quoted above); the next is the concept of thrift (or economy). The latter describes the condition of formulaic language in Homeric verse, where there is "a noun epithet formula to meet every regularly recurring need. And what is equally striking, there is usually only one such formula" (quoted in Foley 1981a, 31). The formula and thrift that Parry described were hypothesized initially from Homeric Greek. Later, Parry and Lord would field test this hypothesis in the Balkans. But it is important to realize that the Homeric line is a hexameter and the South Slavic line is decasyllabic, because these verse shapes are very different from the alliterative metrical lines in Old English. This crucial difference has given rise to many attempts to modify the definition of the formula to fit the particular metrical demands of Old English verse. As more work was done on oral formulaic analysis, further difficulties with the applicability of the Parry-Lord hypothesis appeared. Not only differences in the particulars of verse form but also historical questions of the applicability of a theory modeled on the circumstances of classical Greek culture to the circumstances of early medieval England posed problems. Further, the binary terms of the argument (that a culture or an individual was either oral or literate) cartooned the history of literacy and misrepresented the practice and impact of reading (O'Brien O'Keeffe 1990).

Formulaic repetition, as emphasized in Magoun's initial study, as well as the question of thrift became important points for criticism of the theory and modification of it. Variation, that defining feature of *Beowulf*'s style, now plays a crucial part in the arguments over oral-formulaic theory. Variation is not simply the juxtaposing of appositives to slow down a narrative advance; variation is intrinsic to the poet's ability to meet the demands of alliteration. For example, Hrothgar is six times described as "wine Scyldinga" (friend of the Scyldings), a D-type verse providing alliteration on *w*. But he is also described as "frea Scyldinga" (lord of the Scyldings), "helm Scyldinga" (protector of the Scyldings), "eodor Scyldinga" (protector [or prince] of the Scyldings), "þeoden Scyldinga" (lord [king] of the Scyldings), and so on. All of the latter are also D-type verses whose varying elements adapted to the demands of alliteration. This feature could be illustrated at random throughout the poem. Now given Parry's (and later Lord's) definition of thrift or economy (a feature Parry had claimed to be a defining marker of oral composition), it becomes obvious that the principle of thrift is stunningly inapplicable to *Beowulf* and to other Old English long narrative poems. William Whallon (1961) pointed out the difficulty with thrift in *Beowulf*, and since he accepted the criteria of oral composition derived from the *Iliad* and *Odyssey* as universal, Whallon concluded that *Beowulf* shows earlier (i.e., more primitive) compositional development. In 1965a Whallon corrected his 1961 *PMLA* argument, considering "the formulaic kennings for the heroes of *Beowulf* . . . true to generic character but significantly appropriate to context" (96; italics removed).

The crossing of *Beowulf* scholarship with the Parry-Lord hypothesis had proved fertile, but the volume of scholarship on the oral character of the poem was consistently pointing out serious difficulties with the application. A definition of formula (and formulaic system) built on the exigencies of quantitative verse proved unwieldy in its application to English verse, which was accentual in nature. While early on repetition was emphasized as essential to the formula, Lord (1960) offered a more relaxed definition, where phrases could be formulaic if they followed "the basic patterns of rhythm and syntax and have at least one word in the same position in the line in common with other lines or half-lines" (1960, 47). Further refinements by other scholars followed, although the idea of the formula as a ready-made phrase still held. In 1965, Frederic G. Cassidy considered the "freedom" of the scop in formulaic composition. He noted that while repetition has been a stressed feature of formulaic theory, the repeated phrases need not be identical. What indeed constitutes repetition? What qualifies as "the same"? Cassidy called attention to the limited number of syntactic patterns used in the half-lines of *Beowulf* (originally analyzed by Godfrey L. Gattiker in an unpublished 1962 Wisconsin dissertation), analogizing from biology: "Each of the latter [oral formulas] is a species of which the syntactic form is the genus; and the genera are the survivors of a process of natural selection" (81). This understanding of the production of formulas makes formulas more interesting than mere prefab parts and restores to the performer a creative originality. Thomas Gardner (1973) argued that, far from being a prisoner of the formulaic system, the poet manipulated formulaic material to achieve "conspicuous" variety.

In two important articles, Donald K. Fry rethought the difficulties posed by Homeric definitions of formula and thrift. The results made possible a more productive phase for formulaic analysis. Fry proposed definitions of formula and formulaic system that emphasized the productive relation between the two. In his view, a system is "a group of half-lines, usually loosely related metrically and semantically, which are related in form by the identical relative placement of two elements, one a variable word or element of a compound usually supplying the alliteration, and the other a constant word or element of a compound, with approximately the same distribution of non-stressed elements" (1967, 203; italics removed). The formula, then, is "a group of words, one half-line in length, which shows evidence of being the direct product of a formulaic system" (204; italics removed). In the next year, Fry argued against Whallon (1961, 1965a) that thrift is not applicable to Old English verse (1968b).[4] John Miles Foley approached the formula from the perspective of metrics, defining a level of "purely metrical" formula lying below the verbal structure. In his estimate this metrical level generates 94 percent of the lines in Beowulf (1976; see further Foley 1980). He made further extensive consideration of the importance of meter in defining formula in *Traditional Oral Epic* (1990). Working also with formula and metrics, Calvin B. Kendall adapted Kuhn's laws to describe a metrical grammar of *Beowulf*. He argued that whether lettered or unlettered, the poet worked within the half-line units of traditional composition (1983, 1991).[5]

A number of scholars have stressed the flexibility of the poet's diction. Working from Fry's definition of formula and formulaic system, and making important modifications in it, John D. Niles presented a new definition of the formula within the formulaic system (1981b, 1983). In his new definition, "a formula in Anglo-Saxon poetry may be considered a rhythmic-syntactic-semantic complex one half-line in length" (1983, 126; italics removed). In this compact definition, Niles incorporated the various strands of thinking on the modification of "formula" for the exigencies of Old English verse. The result is a definition that stresses the flexibility of formulaic systems. He then applied this definition to the first twenty-five lines of *Beowulf* in an instructive reply to Magoun's original analysis thirty years before. To summarize his results in brief, reiterated verses accounted for 16.9 percent of the total (very close to Creed's 1955 figure of 16.7 percent). However, Niles estimated that nearly two of three verses in the poem are members of an identifiable formulaic system (1983, 128). Working with "feasts and anti-feasts," Joanne De Lavan Foley (1981) extended Fry's conception of formulaic system and described a larger superstructure of systems generically related through the collocation of feasting and sleeping. Anita Reidinger offered an additional refinement on Fry's definition by connecting theme and formula and distinguishing a "set" as a subgroup within a formulaic system (1985).

While the presence of formulas in *Beowulf* seems virtually to have become the consensus position, a number of scholars still caution that the link between the formula and oral composition must not be taken for granted. On the basis of the use of necessary enjambment and thrift, Valerie Krishna found that *Beowulf* appears less traditional than the *Alliterative Morte Arthure* (1982). Working across cultures, Francelia Clark compared the flyting in *Beowulf* with the rebuke in the *Song of Bagdad* (1981). She concluded that the low incidence of repetition in *Beowulf* suggests that Lord's definition of the theme did not apply to *Beowulf*. Similarly, studying *Beowulf* within the context of Muslim oral epic, John S. Miletich concluded that the low formulaic density of *Beowulf* indicates that it was a product of learned, written technique (1988).

In the light of the evolution of oral-formulaic studies in Old English, one of the most interesting current developments has been a concern with the ways the modern audience can read a possibly orally derived *Beowulf*. As early as 1961

Robert P. Creed asked the question, "How can a tissue of formulas, of repeated verses and significant parts of verses, be a great poem?" (98). Phrased in the hard-line terms of early oral theory, this essay on the necessity of developing an aesthetics of reading *Beowulf* as an *oral* poem preached mostly to the choir. Edward B. Irving Jr.'s groundbreaking *A Reading of Beowulf* (1968) had little use for oral theory. However, his 1989 *Rereading Beowulf* demonstrates both the changes in oral-formulaic theory and the Old English community's accommodation to it. There he argues: "A literary critic's first job is to understand how rich and powerful meaning can be expressed in an oral-derived style subject to such narrow limitations of range, if we compare it in this respect to the more familiar styles of written literature. To do this we must move from seeing the oral-derived style as a crippling restriction to perceiving it as generating through its very conventions the unmistakably high quality of the verse" (1989, 7–8). Addressing questions of aesthetics from a different direction, John Miles Foley adapts the techniques of reception theory to the art of an oral culture (1991). Focusing on the "traditional referentiality" of oral traditional art, Foley stresses the crucial metonymic function of oral and oral-derived poetry. In contradistinction to the way a modern, literate work means (where meaning is largely conferred by its author), meaning in an oral traditional work is "inherent." Since any performance of an oral traditional work calls on the whole tradition, its meaning functions metonymically (cf. Overing 1990).

The adaptation of Homeric and South Slavic oral traditional theory for the special circumstances of Old English poetry has proved remarkably productive, as the continuing studies of the last four decades attest. Its effect may be seen in virtually all aspects of *Beowulf* criticism, but our understanding of the poem's diction, the nature and purpose of variation, and obviously, the presence of formulas have undergone the most spectacular development. The oral traditional approach to the poem continues to adapt and to draw from other disciplines and other critical theories; the cross-fertilization of oral traditional theory with reception theory promises to be productive indeed in developing an aesthetics for a traditional *Beowulf.*

Notes

1. Since this section is on diction in general, I do not include single-word studies in the following discussion.

2. "The great majority of compounds in *Beowulf*, however, are determinatives, in which the first element stands in a case or prepositional relationship to the second, although some are appositional" (1979, 82). Brady illustrates her point with two related compounds: *wælsceaft* (slaughter-shaft), a circumlocution for *spear*; *wælsteng* (corpse-pole = pole being used for the slain), a determinative usually mistranslated as "shaft of a spear."

3. Another approach to the same problem is offered by W. V. Quine in a discussion of "meaning": "If the meaning of an expression is to be sought in its use, what is it for two expressions to have the same meaning? They cannot have exactly the same use, for when we use one we are not using the other. One wants to say rather that they have the same meaning if use of the one in place of the other does not make any relevant difference. The question of sameness of meaning, then, comes down to the question what to count as relevant difference" (1987, 131).

4. In the same year, Fry (1968a) offered new definitions for the theme ("a recurring concatenation of details and ideas, not restricted to a specific event, verbatim repetition, or certain formulas, which forms an underlying structure for an action or description" [53; italics removed]) and type-scene ("a recurring stereotyped presentation of conventional details used to describe a certain narrative event, requiring neither verbatim repetition nor a specific formula content," [53; italics removed]). While Lord accepted the usefulness of Fry's definition of the type-scene (1974), he found the definition of theme too general. Emphasizing that the theme contains a repeated narrative element and verbal expression, he refined its definition so that a theme "tells a certain repeated part of the narrative, measurable in terms of lines and even words and word combinations" (206). Although questions of theme and type-scene are clearly related to the concept of formula, their study is beyond the scope of this chapter. For further studies, see Greenfield (1955), Diamond (1961) Magoun (1961), Taylor (1967), Anderson (1980), Heinemann (1987), and especially Crowne (1960).

5. In the last twenty years, Foley has been at the forefront of oral-formulaic studies, particularly in his comparative studies of oral traditional composition in Serbo-Croatian and Old English. For an important bibliographical review of work on oral tradition in Old English see Foley (1981a, 27–122).

Chapter 6

Rhetoric and Style

by Ursula Schaefer

Summary: Examination of the poem's rhetoric and style started out with investigating common Germanic features. On the other end of the scale, attention was given to a possible Latin influence on the poem's style. Recently, there have been reconsiderations of autochthonous traditions linked mainly with the analysis of larger narrative patterns.

Chronology

1875: Richard Heinzel for the first time applies the notion of *variation* to Old Germanic and hence Old English style.

1888–89: E. Nader identifies *apo koinou* constructions in *Beowulf*.

1899: Bernhard ten Brink characterizes Anglo-Saxon poetic style as being better able to describe than to narrate.

1935: Adeline Courtney Bartlett discusses envelope patterns, parallelism, incremental repetition, and other rhetorical patterns.

1937: Frederick Bracher categorizes the figure of understatement according to both type and function.

1938: Joan Blomfield proposes a circumscribed field of material presentation, in which the themes are drawn out by a center of attraction; structure is thus circumambient.

1940: Samuel O. Andrew argues for a periodic style, not a paratactic one.

1945: Fernand Mossé enumerates four types of "disjunction."

1948: Andrew discusses the poet's use of temporal clauses, the syntax of speeches, gnomic sentences, litotes, parallelism, anaphora.

1953: Francis P. Magoun Jr. claims oral-formulaic composition of Anglo-Saxon narrative poetry, thus pleading for traditional rather than individual style.

1955: George J. Engelhardt presents a study of *peribole* (dilatation and abundance), *effectio*, and *corruptio*.

1959: Arthur G. Brodeur emphasizes the individual stylistic achievements of the *Beowulf* poet.

1960: Kemp Malone takes the *Beowulf* gnomai as evidence for the "poet's skill in handling the inherited stylistic features," assigning to them a structuring function as introductions and conclusions.

1960: Baird Shuman and H. Charles Hutchings discuss *litotes* achieved by adding the prefix *un-* to words.

1962: Harry and Agathe Thornton discuss the appositive mode of expression.

1962: Alistair Campbell believes that the new epic style was developed from that of the lays rather than from Latin verse.

1963: Randolph Quirk discusses the poetic effects inherent in the relations between alliterative and lexical collocations.

1967: Stanley B. Greenfield (1967a) focuses on "the interaction between grammar and meaning, between formal meaning and lexico-semantics."

1967: Greenfield (1967b) examines the poet's manipulation of meter, syntax, and diction in Grendel's approach to Heorot.

1969: Ewald Standop deals with *disjunction* (and *conjunction*), *parallelism*, and *chiasm* as rhetorico-stylistic criteria for classifying the various types of variation.

1970: Michael Cherniss argues that the poet uses the reference to Beowulf's inglorious youth for immediate rhetorical effect with regard to a listening audience.

1970: Fred C. Robinson (1970a) warns against the lexicographer's reluctance to acknowledge synaesthesia, paronomasia, and the frequent use of *lyt* for understatement.

1972: Greenfield, in his chapter "Verse Form, Syntax and Meaning," views Old English poetry in terms of general critical theory and practice.

1975: Bruce Mitchell insists on the priority of linguistic arguments over interpretative speculation in arriving at an understanding of Old English verse.

1975: Robert B. Burlin sees the function of the narrator's gnomic passages in *Beowulf* as giving "both shape and scope to his utterance."

1975–76: Joshua Bonner argues that the "rhetorical devices" made out in Anglo-Saxon poetry by several scholars are actually grammatical figures and that there may be a Germanic poetic tradition independent of Latin influence.

1976: Greenfield sees as one of the functions of the gnomic passages in *Beowulf* that of decreasing the distance between story and audience.

1978: Jackson J. Campbell suggests that the *Beowulf* poet has thoroughly assimilated the disciplines of the Latin poetic and rhetorical tradition.

1979: Peter Clemoes sees as the effect of priority of nouns and adjectives over finite verbs the identifying of "action as part of the doer."

1979: Daniel G. Calder gives a comprehensive survey of the study of style in Old English poetry.

1979: John D. Niles shows the "ring composition" of *Beowulf* on the micro as well as the macro level of the organization of the poem.

1980: Bruce Mitchell warns that modern editors' punctuation may "eliminate options" and blur "alternative connections and associations."

1980: Eric G. Stanley argues that the "patterns of narrative in *Beowulf* build a structure of action out of a universalizing statement."

1981: Niles (1981a) stresses utility (alliterative concerns) over aesthetic subtlety in assessing the poet's choice of one compound over another; he concludes that the poet might have been versed in an oral tradition.

1985: Fred C. Robinson presents a study on the appositive style, which he distinguishes from variation by "its lack of an expressed logical connection between the apposed elements" and extends metaphorically toward narrative structures and themes.

1985: Clare Kinney discusses the concept of narrative foregrounding, where the poet brings to the foreground a different narrative mode or focus and thus links audience and poem.

1986: Stanley reviews the controversy concerning whether periodic sentences can be attributed to the influence of the church.

1986: Morton W. Bloomfield argues that because of the "sequentiality" of narrative, the interlace image, which suggests simultaneity, is not a useful criterion in verbal art.

1986: Alain Renoir pleads for a "tradition of oral-formulaic rhetoric" evidenced, e.g., in *Beowulf* and *Andreas*.

1988: Ward Parks further elaborates on the "ring structure" of *Beowulf*.

1988: A. Leslie Harris argues that litotes is associated with the characters' values.

1988: Peter S. Baker reevaluates Anglo-Saxon attitudes towards rhetoric; he asserts that "oratory, like battle, is one of the warrior's arts."

1989: Edward B. Irving Jr. discusses style, starting with Leyerle's notion of "interlace," insisting that the poem is "oral-based."

1990: Catherine Karkov and Robert T. Farrell attribute to the gnomic passages in *Beowulf* the structural function of linking one episode to the next.

1990: John Miles Foley compares the traits of traditional oral epic in the *Odyssey*, *Beowulf*, and the Serbo-Croatian Return Song.

1991: Foley takes a reception-oriented stance to explore the conveying of meaning in oral and oral-derived epic.

1992: Ursula Schaefer sees specific "exordial formulaicness" in the Old English elegies and in *Beowulf* and attributes to the gnomes in *Beowulf* a structuring function.

1992: Robert D. Stevick thinks that the notion of interlace is useful as a metaphor only for certain types of syntactic variation, as a synonym for "discontinuous," or to refer to "fragments of background matter appearing now and then."

1993: Stanley denies *apo koinou* the status of a rhetorical device in *Beowulf*.

Before I offer a review of research into the rhetoric and style of *Beowulf,* a few clarifications are in order, as both *rhetoric* and *style* are problematic categories to begin with. First, even a cursory look reveals—by no means only with regard to *Beowulf*—that scholars only vaguely agree what these categories refer to. The smallest common denominator in their use (either in everyday or in scholarly application) is that *style* refers to the "linguistic how" of a verbal utterance while *rhetoric* deals with the question of "to what end" that "linguistic how" is used. The two categories are often blended, since it is evident that this separation into the linguistically "factual" and the linguistically "effective" can be only a heuristic one.

Second, *style* is a notion that has undergone historical change. Thus the concept of the *individual style* has been established only since the middle of the eighteenth century.[1] Subsequently, with the pervasive realization of the historicity of cultural phenomena, the nineteenth century also conceived of style as modes of expression particular to specific *periods*. We will see that both concepts of style underlie—more often than not only implicitly—the various scholarly statements on and analyses of *Beowulf*. Additionally, we have to take into account a third concept of style, one that may be termed *generic style*. For *Beowulf,* this is evidently the "epic style." This type of style may, in its turn, be linked to the individual poet who has chosen—more or less individually—to follow the basic stylistic rules of a given genre, or an individual verbal work of art may be seen as being cast in the style of a specific genre for a specific period.

Third, in particular, with regard to an (alleged or given) individual style of any verbal utterance, statements tend to become evaluative: note, for example, the criteria "clearness, effectiveness, beauty" listed in the *Oxford English Dictionary* (s.v. *style*). Here, the unobjectifiable element of an individual reader's feeling for the language (*Sprachgefühl*) intrudes, the reliability of which must needs decrease with increasing historical distance. A similar caveat is necessary when determining certain rhetorical effects. For *Beowulf,* such a case in point is the difficulty of ascertaining whether particular diction is meant to produce comic or ironic effects.

In approaching *Beowulf,* we need to be aware of these divergencies and (potentially) subjective undercurrents as they usually may be traced back to fundamentally discrepant convictions that pertain to other fields of research on this poem. If, for instance, Arthur Brodeur in his 1959 *The Art of Beowulf* speaks of "a large element of originality in the poet's diction" and of "the poet's choice and combination of words" (6), he conceives of an individual poet who has composed *Beowulf* and understands *style* as "the individual poet's style." Compare to this, for instance, Friedrich Klaeber's statement that "the Beowulfian stylistic apparatus (taken in its widest sense) was to a great extent traditional, deeply rooted in time-honored Germanic, more particularly West Germanic practice" (1950a, lxvi). By using the somewhat vague periphrasis of "the Beowulfian stylistic apparatus," Klaeber does not commit himself to postulating single authorship (although later on [cvii, at the end of the section titled "Genesis of the Poem"] Klaeber does speak of "the author"), and he thus implicitly refers to a different type of style: the poetic style of "a culture" or, more narrowly, the style of a genre in that culture (here, that of the [West] Germanic epic).

Behind the concept of single, individual authorship and style (as opposed to generic style or even the style of a culture) lie strong convictions as to the provenance of *Beowulf*. As has already been pointed out in chapter 5 of this handbook, Brodeur in 1959 responded vigorously against Francis P. Magoun Jr.'s

1953 article "The Oral-Formulaic Character of Anglo-Saxon Narrative Poetry." However, there was little new about the idea that, in view of its diction, *Beowulf* is not the unique, individual achievement of one single author. As we have seen (and Brodeur had also noted), Klaeber refers to the "traditionality" of the style of *Beowulf*, taking up ideas presented by Bernhard ten Brink as early as 1877.

Let me quote ten Brink at some length.[2] Ten Brink states not only that the Angles and Saxons had brought with them language formed in meter, but also adaptable to the purpose of individual expression:

> [They possessed] simultaneously a rich treasure of ready-made expressions and arguments which could be used for the higher purposes of speech, a treasure of words and formulae, i.e., of *audible* signs of intellectual achievement. From within the language of everyday life and remaining in the closest relationship and most lively interaction with it, such a language had been formed which, like the former, was common property on which anyone could draw freely, yet which everyone in a position to do so was also allowed to increase, and in whose application the *creative spiritual power* [of a poet] could reveal itself. (1899, 446–47; italics added)

It should be noted here that ten Brink found a diplomatic compromise: although he presupposes an inherited treasure of words and formulae that is "common property," he also allows for the apt individual who, by drawing on this treasure, may display his own "creative spiritual power." We should remember that the idea of the *Formelvorrat* (stock of formulas) was discussed in the later nineteenth century by other scholars such as Johannes Kail (1889). Kail was reacting to Sarrazin's endeavor to prove individual authorship by those formulas. As Kail put it, "Sarrazin bases his theory on the assumption that parallel phrasings [*Parallelstellen*] are characteristic of a particular author" (30). Kail, on the other hand, showed that these parallel phrasings are omnipresent in Anglo-Saxon and other Germanic poetry. He therefore rightly asked, "Now, if [these parallel phrasings] are the common property of all the poetry, how can they be characteristic of one particular poet?" (30).

But let us return once more to ten Brink, who—rather casually—raises yet another pertinent question when dealing with the formulas. He expressly points at *oral* tradition when he speaks of those "words and formulae" as "*audible* signs of intellectual achievement" (my italics). Ten Brink thus refers not only to the traditionality of the words and formulas that are found in the "general stock," as it were, but also to their orality and aurality. Evidently, ten Brink's era was not yet the time to investigate aural aesthetics. This step was only taken about a century later as a modification of Magoun's oral-compositional approach by including consideration of the aural-receptive side of oral performance.

In a 1970 article, Michael D. Cherniss argues that in order to deal with *Beowulf* appropriately with regard to rhetorical effects, the question of oral composition need not be decided "once and for all." He continues, "We need accept only two modest assumptions: first, that the *Beowulf*-Poet intended that his poem be delivered orally; and second, that he was a conscious craftsman who knew what he was doing when he composed his poem and whether he composed orally or otherwise, was aware that his audience was a listening audience" (1970, 216). While modern readers may—literally—look at *Beowulf* as a whole, while they may freely move forward and backward in the fixed script, an "Anglo-Saxon listening to the poem for the first time . . . would experience its elements sequentially, one element at a time" (216). John Niles has gone in very much the same direction in his "Compound Diction and the Style of *Beowulf* " (1981a), though he also puts great emphasis on the traditional character of the poet's diction due to oral inheritance and hence unites the "compositional" with the "receptional" view.

Finally, we should be aware that, from a quite different angle, the question of the way in which the *Beowulf* poem as we know it came into existence implies preconceived stances determining a certain kind of research devoted to the poem's *rhetoric* (in the sense of rhetorical devices). I am referring here to those scholars who claim that the *Beowulf* poet must have been intimately acquainted with classical rhetoric and thus must have been an educated monk.[3] Scholars who detect in *Beowulf* an indebtedness to classical rhetoric are very often also partisans of a theory of the poem's origin that holds that an epic of the size of *Beowulf* was a fairly late achievement in the history of Germanic narrative poetry.

Here I shall divide my discussion into four parts according to the following headings: "Basic Stylistic Features," briefly surveying criticism concerning the general features of Old English poetic style as illustrated in *Beowulf*; "Specific Features of Epic Style," such as the prevalence of nouns, parallelism in the device of variation, enumeration, and parataxis; "Classical Rhetoric," surveying the few contributions that adduce evidence of *schemata* and *tropes* in *Beowulf* directly derived from classical rhetoric; and "Rhetorical Patterns," reviewing those features of the diction of *Beowulf* to which structuring effects are attributed.

I. Basic Stylistic Features

In *Beowulf,* we can identify linguistic devices that are also found in other Old English poetry (and some of them also in prose). From the analytic point of view, they may be divided into lexical and syntactic devices. To the former category belongs a linguistic characteristic that appears particularly striking to the novice reader of *Beowulf*: the doubling of expressions in various ways. To the category of syntax belong "unusual word order," "obscure" syntactic correlation, and—situated between lexis and syntax—the tendency for litotic expression of actions, states, and ideas.[4] I will be concerned here with those kinds of lexical repetitiveness that may be characterized as recurrent collocations, often alliterative ones. As we may surmise that the contemporaneous audiences of *Beowulf* heard a number of performances of this epic in one or another variant form, this device deserves attention both from the compositional and from the receptional point of view. The same observation may hold true for verbal repetition, not of a formula, but of clusters of words, sometimes over a long distance, and—closely associated—the repetition of words of identical sound but different meaning.

In 1963, Randolph Quirk suggests a definition of the formula as "a habitual collocation, metrically defined, . . . a stylization of something which is fundamental to linguistic expression, namely the expectation that a sequence of words will show lexical congruity, together with (and as a condition of) lexical and grammatical complementarity" (1963, 150–51). Quirk names, for instance, the frequent collocation of "mod" and "mægen" (151), as in Hrothgar's words to Beowulf: "þu eart mægenes strang, / ond on mode frod" (thou art strong in thy strength and wise in thy mind, 1844). This collocation, as Quirk points out, is found in other Old English poems (*Gifts of Men* 98; *Elene* 408; *Paris Psalter* 144.5 and 150.2) and also in the Old English version of Bede's *Historia Ecclesiastica* (1.16). Another such pair is "dom" and "deað" as in lines 1388a and 1491 of *Beowulf*. As an extreme form of such collocations we may consider what Meyer in 1889 aptly called "twin collocations," that is, synonymous or antonymous words, often alliterating, that recur as pairs. Thus, the pair *to have and to hold*, still surviving in Modern English, is found in *Beowulf* in line 658, "Hafa nu ond geheald / husa selest" (have now and hold the best of houses), and reversed in line 2430, "heold mec ond hæfde / Hreðel cyning" (King Hrethel had me and held me, i.e., kept me and watched over me). The same collocation is found in *Daniel* 198 and *Christ* 1648. As Meyer already showed, such twin collocations occur throughout Germanic poetry, and we must add that they are by no means restricted to poetry.[5] In view of the audience's reception of such collocations, Quirk has remarked that there is "evidently a primary satisfaction in the propriety of like belonging with like, of traditional correspondences" (1963, 153).

Another type of repetition, called "echo" by John O. Beaty, is the "repetition of a word for the pleasure of echoing its identical sound in a different meaning, connotation and association" (1934, 366). Examples are the repetition of "ful" from line 1192a in 1208b and of "aldre" from line 1434b in line 1447b. As another kind of echo, Beaty identifies the joining of "words of different roots or of widely different meanings" (369), as in line 421: "yðde eotena cyn, / ond on yðum slog" (laid waste the tribe of giants, and on the waves slew).

As an extension of habitual collocations or "long distance echoes," we may regard groups of words recurring in different passages of the poem. Recently, Thomas Gardner has elaborated on the finding that, for instance, the words "geneðde" (ventured, 2133b), "eacnum" (mighty, 2140a), and "unsofte" (with difficulty, 2140b) recur in lines 1655–63 in slightly different order ("unsofte" in 1655; "geneþde" in 1656; "eacen" in 1663). Gardner's main concern here is to point to a compositional technique that, to his mind, is "unthrifty" and hence, in his view, "is not amenable to oral composition" (1993, 222).

On the syntactic level, as early as 1875 Richard Heinzel investigated a phenomenon that he characterized as "deviations" from the "order of thoughts and words which seems natural to us" (1875, 14). He makes the observation that not only in the syntactic arrangement of *Beowulf,* but also in Old High German, in Old Norse, and in Vedic poetry, "direct relations are separated by other parts of speech." An example is lines 251b–52a of *Beowulf:* "Nu ic *eower* sceal // *frumcyn* witan" (now I must know your lineage), where the modal "sceal" splits the possessive "eower" from the noun "frumcyn." Entire clauses may split, as happens with verb and direct object in lines 452–53a: "*Onsend* Higelace, / gif mec hild nime, // *beaduscruda betst*" (Send to Hygelac, if the fight carries me off, the best of war-garments).

Heinzel argues that such "deviations" only partly resemble the "free word order"—or *hyperbaton*—of Greek or Latin poetic speech. Rather, Heinzel thinks, "they seem to correspond to a state of mind in which two ideas are almost simultaneously present, permeating and intertwining with each other. There is no real successiveness" (14). In later analyses, this feature has been termed *disjunction* (Mossé 1945; Standop 1969), yet these analyses have largely remained descriptive. A new appreciation has been initiated by Lydia Fakundiny (1970). She presents a thorough investigation of the indefinite article of quantity, possessive pronouns, demonstrative adjectives, and prepositions with regard to their "flexible nature both syntactically and metrically" (131). Fakundiny refers to the phenomenon of disjunction as "interception" and argues convincingly that in cases like "Nu ic *eower* sceal // *frumcyn* witan" (251b–52a) "the separated possessive stands in an off-verse constituting the beginning of a clause . . . with the possessive in the head-stave" (137). In view of "the generally proclitic use of sentence-part-particles" in Old English prose, she shows that departure from this norm "can . . . be seen not as expedient aberrations but as part of a larger rhetorical design" (261). Fakundiny argues that "contextual emphasis and displacement create stylistic variety and richness" (264).

While Fakundiny thus is able to assign to disjunction a stylistic and rhetoric function, the possible stylistic and/or rhetorical function of syntactic arrangements such as *apo koinou* or *amphiboly* are still under discussion. Modern editions gloss this problem over as they disambiguate ambiguous syntactic relations by punctuation. Without capitalization and punctuation, lines 1233b–38 read as follows:

> wyrd ne cuþon
> geosceaft grimme   swa hit agangan wearð
> eorla manegum   syþðan æfen cwom
> ond him Hroþgar gewat   to hofe sinum
> rice to ræste   reced weardode
> unrim eorla   swa hie oft ær dydon.

The problem here is how to interpret "syþðan" (1235b). If we take it to be a conjunction, it introduces an adverbial clause that is subordinate to what syntactically precedes:

> They did not know their fate, their fierce, long-determined destiny, as it befell many of the nobles when the evening came and Hrothgar went to his house, the mighty one to rest. The host of nobles guarded the building, as they often had done before.

But if "syþðan" is interpreted as the temporal adverb (introducing a main clause), we read, "as it had befallen many of the nobles. Then the evening came and Hrothgar went. . . . " There are a number of such instances where—if we disregard the modern editor's punctuation—problems of this kind arise. As early as 1888–89 E. Nader identified a number of such instances as *apo koinou*, that is, constructions where a clause is syntactically related to both what preceeds and what follows. Bruce Mitchell (1980, 1985) allows for a number of *apo koinou* constructions in *Beowulf*, while Eric G. Stanley has recently rejected *apo koinou* as "a figure in Rhetoric" in Old English (1993, 181). For him, the notion of *apo koinou* "is not a solution to a syntactical or stylistic problem, but a term used to conceal failure to find a solution" (182); he appeals to our realization that the "means of connecting clauses are often loose in *Beowulf*" (207).

This issue touches on a general problem that we face when evaluating features of diction. Is a specific wording chosen purposely in order to produce a specific effect? Is it the individual poet's choice, or does tradition impose this diction? These questions have also been asked with regard to litotes, a specific form of understatement common in epic narrative and elsewhere. Frederick Bracher treats "rhetorical understatement" and attempts "an investigation of its origin, occurrence and uses" (1937, 228). He counts ninety-four occurrences of understatement in *Beowulf* (233) and asks whether "this stylistic mannerism" was inherited "from an earlier, possibly common-Germanic, poetic tradition" or whether it was "the result of borrowing from the Latin literature," where litotes is quite common. In view of its high frequency "in the early, 'heroic' [Old English] poetry" (242), he decides in favor of Germanic provenience (249), a thesis that is corroborated by the occurrence of understatement in medieval German and Old Norse poetry (245, 249). The conclusion that "this figure has its roots in a common Germanic poetic tradition" (249) is again supported by Alistair Campbell (1962, 18–19).

Bracher also reviews previous criticism analyzing the intended or achieved effects of understatement. To "mocking irony" (in hatred or aversion), "humor," and "emphasis" he adds the effect of "moderation, or tempering, of an expression" (1968, 235). In particular with regard to possible humorous effects, he concedes that these remain uncertain, since we lack "knowledge of the full connotations of words," a knowledge always essential for an appreciation of verbal humor (237). On the morphological level, Shuman and Hutchings (1960) have seen a "Germanic means of irony" in the use of the *un-* suffix, and Godfrid Storms speaks of the "suggestive mood" (1963, 173) of the *Beowulf* poet in his analysis of adjectives in *-leas*.

In his *Postscript on Beowulf*, a syntactic description of the poem, Samuel O. Andrew also states that "sometimes the understatement is ironic" (1948, 94), referring explicitly to *Beowulf* lines 1018 and 1575. Moreover, Andrew draws our attention to the use of "not many" as a frequent litotes for "none at all" (95), one such example being in lines 2736b–39a, in Beowulf's retrospective speech before death (italics added):

> Ic on earde bad
> mælgesceafta,   heold min tela,
> ne sohte searoniðas,   *ne* me swor *fela*
> aða on unriht.

> [I at home waited for my destiny, held mine (own) properly, neither
> sought quarrels nor swore many oaths unrightfully.]

One may add to this example the litotic use of "lyt" (little) for "none." Robinson pointed to the fact that a dictionary entry such as "not at all" for "lyt" (1970a, 109) obscures this stylistic figure. However, the litotic use is noted in the glossary of the Heyne-Schücking *Beowulf* edition (1961; glossary, s.v. "lyt"). One may compare lines 2897b–99 on the unnamed messenger's report of the king's death (italics added):

> *Lyt* swigode
> niwra spella   se ðe næs gerad,
> ac he soðlice   sægde ofer ealle. . . .

> [Little was (he) silent about the news, the one who rode up the bluff,
> but he truly said over all. . . .]

Here the litotic use of "lyt" is made clear by the juxtaposition of the verbs "swigode" and "sægde."

In 1988, A. Leslie Harris addressed the use of litotes in *Beowulf* and combined it with an analysis of the use of the superlative in the poem because, although "superlatives may be seen as the semantic opposite of understatement, they are only the opposite side of the coin" (8). For Harris, the overall effect of this stylistic device is that of underlining "the distance between the narrative voice and the characters." Superlatives, he contends, achieve much the same effect, since a "heroic world incorporates the hyperbolic in its frame of normality" (9).

Harris thus supports a view advanced several times in the past two decades, that some stylistic features have this distancing effect (cf. Greenfield 1976; Robinson 1985). This observation has a very important consequence pertaining to the "implied audience" of *Beowulf* and to the date of composition. If the author intentionally chose this distancing device, he addressed an audience that was no longer part of the world depicted in the narrative. And if we believe in the ironic effect of some litotic passages, we may suppose this distancing eventually to merge with criticism of the values depicted in the text. These arguments, however, lose some of their substance if we merely attribute litotes to a common Germanic tradition of poetic diction.

It is evident that even with these basic stylistic features a number of aspects have to be taken into consideration that by far transcend simple linguistic analysis. As to disjunction—which Heinzel also showed to be a phenomenon not restricted to Old English poetry—metrical analysis can support the conclusion that such an "irregularity" had an intended stylistic function. As to *apo koinou,* our difficulties as modern readers may be, as Eric Stanley and—a little earlier in connection with other syntactic "oddities"—Herbert Pilch (1979) have argued, the result of our insufficient concept of Old English syntax, rather than the poet's "faulty" syntax.

Attributing a specific function to a conspicuous type of wording is, as we have seen, particularly difficult with litotes. Any discussion of this subject must take into account the modern reader's inability to specify what the effect of such a wording would have been on the contemporaneous audience. The problem is aggravated by the difficulty of identifying this "original audience" socially as well as temporally. As litotic expression seems to be a common Germanic feature, its evaluation is even more difficult. This point holds for all other stylistic features if such a common origin appears likely. Although the search for the origins of stylistic phenomena is certainly of historical interest, conclusions that go beyond this—for example, to extrapolate a certain mental bent—must needs be speculative.

II. Specific Features of "Epic Style"

The main stylistic features that have been described as characteristic of epic style are a reliance on nominal style, parallelism in the device of variation, enumeration of elements in a series, and a largely paratactic syntax. The first three of these features are so closely related that they will be treated here jointly.

In his planned contribution on medieval English literature for Paul's *Grundriss der germanischen Philologie,* Bernhard ten Brink made the following remark on Old English poetic style: "The quality of the Anglo-Saxon thesaurus of words and formulae—in particular the preponderance of the noun over the verb—clearly points already to the direction in which Anglo-Saxon poetry tended to move. . . . It takes more care in the presentation of characters and objects or situations than in the presentation of events; it is better able to describe than to narrate" (1891, 449). Ten Brink has thus very aptly characterized the "static" impression of *Beowulf* on a modern reader. Almost a century later, Peter Clemoes makes a similar observation: "Movement in *Beowulf* is not portrayed as a detachable outward concept: it merely identifies action as part of the doer; action belongs to him as an innate, inherent attribute" (1979, 155). Clemoes also refers to the prevailing use of nouns: "Priority of nouns and adjectives over finite verbs works to the same effect: 'æfter leodhryre' (after prince-fall, 2030a), twins actor and action as 'after a prince has fallen' does not" (156).

Fred C. Robinson opposes this view by drawing our attention to "the wealth of verbal action which is implicit in the seemingly static nominalizations of Old English poetic diction" (1985, 17). He finds examples in such nominal and adjectival compounds as "beadurun" (battle-rune, 501a) or "lifbysig" (966a; paraphrased by Klaeber as "struggling for life, in torment of death"). Robinson stresses that in view of such findings "we become aware that the often-remarked static quality of *Beowulf* is partly an illusion created by the chosen style" (17).

Evidently, the "static, additive" character of *Beowulf* is strongly enhanced by the pervasive element of *variation* (see chapter 5 in the present volume). In Arthur G. Brodeur's understanding of variation, or "the fondness of the poet of *Beowulf* for grouping together different poetic appellations for a single referent," each individual "appellation" in such a group expresses "one aspect of the referent" (1959, 41). Thus, "the sum of members of the variation presents a total description or characterization" (41). Ewald Standop, in his turn, has called this procedure *rhetorical diaeresis,* in which one notion is split into several other notions (1969, 57). Syntactically, he distinguishes between the following types of succession in variation: *abab* (parallelism), *abba* (chiasm), *ab* (conjunction), *axb* (disjunction), and *ba* (inversion).

Parallelism has long been identified as a feature in Old English poetry in general and of *Beowulf* in particular. Heinzel spoke of an emphasis on "notions, ideas, and judgements" that is achieved through repetition of an "expression consisting of one or more words," varied "with the same parts of speech and in a certain parallel form" (1875, 9). Brodeur claims that parallelism is not a necessary, let alone sufficient, condition for variation: "not all variations are parallelisms, nor are all parallelisms variations" (1959, 40). An example of parallel variation is for him (though not for other interpreters) the opening of *Beowulf*:

Hwæt, we Gardena in geardagum,
þeodcyninga þrym gefrunon,
hu ða æðelingas ellen fremedon! (1–3)

[Lo, we heard—in days of yore—of the glory of the Speardanes, of the people's kings, how the nobles achieved deeds of valor.]

In his view of the syntax of this passage, "þeodcyninga" is not dependent on "Gardena" but rather varies "Gardena" with a parallel structure (both are genitive plurals). In turn, the clause "hu ða æðelingas ellen fremedon" is the object of the verb "gefrunon," together with / "þeodcyninga þrym." The clause is a variation of the noun phrase, though its structure is vastly different.

Under parallelism in general we may also subsume the long-observed paratactic structure of *Beowulf*. Ten Brink's observation that Old English poetic style is "better able to describe than to narrate" (1891, 449) has been mentioned. Immediately following this remark he turns from diction to syntax: "The rhetorical syntax matches this characteristic. Remember the mostly paratactic and usually asyndetic syntax" (449). Klaeber similarly sees evidence of "a primitive or, perhaps, 'natural' method of expression" in the poet's "simple way of connecting sentences by the monotonous *þā* or of dispensing with connectives altogether" (1950a, lxvii).

In 1948, Samuel O. Andrew contradicts the claim that "so-called paratactic sentences" constitute one of the essential characteristics of *Beowulf* (viii). He attributes this misconception to modern editors' punctuation, which makes the complex syntax of *Beowulf* disappear. Andrew counts, for example, thirty-three instances of "*ða*-sentences with conjunctive order" (5), that is, end positioning of the (finite) verb, as in Modern German subordinate clauses. Through their choice of punctuation, modern editors have presented these passages as independent sentences, but Andrews identifies them as subordinate clauses of various sorts. One such example (in Klaeber's edition and hence also exemplifying Klaeber's syntactic "misinterpretation" by his punctuation) is the following passage:

> ne wæs hit lenge þa gen,
> ðæt se ecghete   aþumsweoran
> æfter wælniðe   wæcnan scolde.
>   Ða se ellengæst   earfoðlice
> þrage geþolode. . . . (83b–87a)

[it was not yet very long until the time when sword-hate (= war) among fathers- and sons-in-law should wake in the manner of deadly hostility. Then for a while the great monster impatiently suffered distress. . . .]

From Andrew's point of view, the editorial indentation of line 86 aggravates misinterpretation, since he understands lines 86b–87a as a causal subordinate clause with *ða* as a subordinating conjunction (6). He would probably translate the passage as follows: "it was not yet very long until the time when the sword-hate [= war] among fathers- and sons-in-law / should wake *since* the great monster / impatiently suffered distress. . . . "

Bruce Mitchell opposes this kind of syntactic interpretation. Resisting "superstitions about word order" (1975, 13), he remains "unconvinced by arguments that . . . the word order Subject-Noun Object-Verb proves that a clause in poetry must be subordinate" (13). This remark pertains, for instance, to Andrew's interpretation of lines 86a–87b as a subordinate temporal clause. For a convincing counterexample, Mitchell refers to lines 1–2 of *Beowulf,* which, despite their SOV word order, certainly represent a principal clause. In 1980 Mitchell repeats his skepticism about Andrew's belief in extensive hypotaxis in *Beowulf,* but he also—though for different reasons—warns that "modern punctuation produces modern sentences," thus also "eliminating options and blurring alternative connections and associations" (1980, 411).

In German, the notion of *epische Breite* (epic expansiveness, breadth) nicely expresses these specifics of the style of *Beowulf.* In his revision of ten Brink's *Geschichte der englischen Literatur,* Brandl says that "the epic style affords elaboration in greater detail" (ten Brink 1899, 24). One could modify this claim to say that "the epic style *is* elaboration in greater detail." The pace of the narrative is usually slow, if not stagnant. As has been observed by Adeline C. Bartlett, the "progression" of the narrative is that of two steps forward and one step back, evoking in the modern reader what she has called "the non-narrative feeling of Anglo-Saxon 'epic'" (1935, 108).

III. Classical Rhetoric

Identifying—or failing to locate—figures of speech, schemata, and tropes that are derived from Greek and Latin rhetoric in an early medieval vernacular poem such as *Beowulf* is an activity as old as philological concern with it. If, owing to the (purported) lack of such figures, Old English poetry was regarded in the eighteenth and the early nineteenth century as "a rudeness preserved," as Andreas Haarder has so well phrased it (1975, 33), this judgment reflects the implicit standards of the age of neoclassicism. If, on the other hand, later in the nineteenth century, philologists concentrated on tracing stylistic elements in Germanic poetry to their common Germanic roots, they did what philologists were wont to do in a discipline that was still relatively new. Bartlett sees "Teutonolatry" at work there (1935, 36), although she herself relies heavily on scholars of that disposition. However, a scholar like Heinzel concedes to the Anglo-Saxons a "relative richness" with regard to the use of "similes and colorful [*malerische*] expressions," and he attributes this richness to the possibility that "the model of Roman taste here suggested itself more strongly" (1875, 25).

Andreas Heusler (1929) claims a strong indebtedness of Germanic epic poetry to classical models, in particular to Virgil. However, this debt concerns the overall structure—even conception—of a "large epic" (*Grossepos*) much more than its diction and rhetoric. Thus, in 1935, Bartlett rightly observes that "many students appear unwilling to admit even the possibility of Latin influence on Anglo-Saxon poetic form" (111).

It was not until some thirty years after Heusler that the first thorough analysis of *Beowulf* in terms of "classical rhetoric" was proposed by George J. Engelhardt. Following Heusler—and others—in the opinion that in "the Germanic past, narrative poetry had been confined to the heroic lay" (Engelhardt 1955, 825), that is, a narrative form much shorter than *Beowulf.* Engelhardt contends that the *Beowulf* author was led "to reach beyond the native tradition" by the Christianiza- tion of the Anglo-Saxons (825–26). While the native narrative tradition of the short lay was characterized by what the ancient rhetoricians called *syntomia,* "brevity," this poet employed *peribole,* that is, "superabundance" (826). The poet also exploited the *loci argumentorum* (= Greek *topoi*), one such *locus/topos* being *epimone,* that is, "'to dwell upon' a subject, repeating the thought and recurring to it while varying the words" (828). Engelhardt thus analyzes the narrative of *Beowulf* under the preconception that the poet "dilated," or augmented, a short narrative by using rhetorical devices and prescriptions handed down to the Middle Ages by Priscian, Donatus, and Isidore of Seville.

Jackson J. Campbell's repeated attempts to demonstrate the presence of learned rhetoric in Old English poetry were at first an explicit reaction to what he called the "neoprimitive school" represented by Francis P. Magoun Jr. While the latter saw *Beowulf* as a product of oral-formulaic composition, Campbell contends that the scop as a *poet* "discovered that writing had changed the conditions of his profession" (1966, 189). This change had been brought about by a Latin education in which *grammatica* and *rhetorica* were, so to speak, the "grade school disci- plines." Campbell therefore concludes that any Old English poet who was able to read Latin "would also have had some basic instruction in the figures of speech as taught by the grammaticians" (1966, 192).

In 1967, Campbell further elaborates on the arguments advanced in 1966, yet in 1978 he observes that the "careful study of Old English literature from the point of view of classical rhetoric has little more than begun" (1978, 197). He still—probably correctly—insists that an Old English poet availed himself of some kind of Latin education and therefore must also have used "all his skill from whatever source" when he was "retelling an ancient heroic tale" (189–90). An example at stake is variation, the core characteristic of Anglo-Saxon poetic style. Though Donatus and Isidore of Seville treat variation under the headings of *synonymia* and *schesis onomaton* (191), Campbell cannot exclude the possibility that variation could also be an autochthonous poetic tradition inherited from Germanic prehistory. Thus all that is left to him is a feeling that "an influence of some kind from the Latin poetic tradition was working on the Old English poet [of *Beowulf*]" (196).

In 1975–76, Joshua H. Bonner rejects the "scribal theory" that "conscious artistry . . . can only be a product of written composition" (220). He draws our attention to the observation that what we today identify as "rhetorical" devices were not part of the ancient system of rhetoric but rather part of grammatical training and were hence regarded as grammatical figures (224). To Bonner's knowledge, however, "classical systems of rhetoric were not taught comprehensively in the monastic schools" (224).

As Campbell has remarked, it is also difficult to demonstrate whether the rhetorical rules of *dispositio*—the ordering into *exordium* (justifying introduction), *confirmatio* (substantiation of the argument), and *peroratio* (concluding appeal)—were followed. Campbell concedes that Old English poems "do indeed have clearly defined beginnings, middles and ends" that may be identified in those terms. Yet he argues that "beyond this, rhetorical structure is doubtful" (1978, 190). However, lines 1–3 of *Beowulf* may be regarded as some kind of rule-oriented *exordium*, all the more so as we find very similar openings in the Old English *Andreas* and *Exodus*. Described in terms of exordial rhetoric, the first three lines of *Beowulf* introduce the topic with the words "Gardena . . . þeodcyninga þrym" and its heteromorphic variation "hu ða æþelingas [in geardagum] ellen fremedon." With "in geardagum" the story is placed "firmly in the past in 'days of yore'," as Robinson has remarked (1985, 28). Moreover, these introductory lines state how the story dealing with this topic has manifested itself: "we . . . gefrunon."

It is futile to argue over whether the opening lines of *Beowulf* are the "original" exordium of which those of *Andreas* and *Exodus* are just "imitations." With special regard to this and other obvious parallels between *Andreas* and *Beowulf*, Kennedy in 1943 speaks of "conscious imitation of the *Beowulf*" (279), while Hans Schabram insists that the parallels "do not allow us to conclude—still less impose on us—that the author of *Andreas* must have known *Beowulf*" (1965a, 218). Instead of inferring intertextual dependencies, it is probably much more reasonable to account for these similarities in terms of a native "poetical heritage," as Greenfield put it (1965, 104), and hence to presuppose, in Alain Renoir's words, a "tradition of oral-formulaic rhetoric" (1986, 70). Elsewhere, I have suggested taking the three openings as evidence for some Old English exordial tradition, be it old and indigenous or relatively recent and shaped along classical models (Schaefer 1992, 133–43).

The question of the degree of classical influence on *Beowulf* depends on explicit or implicit preconceptions with which one approaches the poem. Moreover, the kinds of stylistic questions that readers pose depend on the scope of the preliminary questions they ask. Thus, Bonner's contribution to the problem shows that broader cultural studies may help us assess certain aspects of the cultural conditions more adequately. Even if these were not the conditions in which *Beowulf* was first composed, they certainly must have been the conditions affecting the production of the *Beowulf* manuscript that has come down to us.

IV. Rhetorical-Structural Patterns

In 1935, Adeline Courtney Bartlett published her small, yet substantial *The Larger Rhetorical Patterns in Anglo-Saxon Poetry*. Here she proposes "to abandon the theory . . . that nothing in Anglo-Saxon poetry can be of any historical significance or any poetic value unless it be 'altgermanisch'" (1935, 4). Indeed, such works as Heinzel's saw *altgermanische Poesie* in its entirety and very often proceeded by comparative methods with the aim of arriving at its "common roots." Bartlett, by contrast, sets out "to establish the outlines of rhetorical devices which actually appear in Anglo-Saxon poetical records." Noting the "dominance of the rhetorical unit over the metrical unit" (6), she detects in Old English poetry an "Envelope pattern" consisting of "any logically unified group of verses bound together by the repetition at the end of (1) words or (2) ideas or (3) words and ideas which are employed at the beginning" (9). Such a group of verses must form a unity of content or be logically complete. As two fine examples of envelope pattern Bartlett gives the beginnings of Hrothgar's speech after Grendel's raid into Heorot and Beowulf's speech in reply. Hrothgar commences (the "envelope" is italicized):

> Ne frin þu æfter sælum! Sorh is geniwod
> Denigea leodum. *Dead is Æschere,*
> Yrmenlafes   yldra broþor. . . .
>   Swy(lc) scolde eorl wesan,
> [æþeling] ærgod, *swylc Æschere wæs!* (1322–29)

> [Ask not about joy! Sorrow is renewed for the people of the Danes. Dead is Æschere, Yrmenlaf's elder brother. . . . So should a man be, a hero good from old times [= preeminent], such as Æschere was!]

To Hrothgar Beowulf replies ("envelope" italicized):

> Ne sorga, snotor guma! *Selre bið æghwæm,*
> þæt he his freond wrece,   þonne he fela murne.
> Ure æghwylc sceal   ende gebidan
> worolde lifes;   wyrce se þe mote
> domes ær deaþe;   *ðæt bið drihtguman*
> unlifgendum   *æfter selest.* (1384–88)

> [Grieve not, wise man! It is better for everyone that he avenge his friend than that he mourn much. Each of us shall see the end of worldly life; may he who may acquire glory before death; that is afterwards best for the warrior once he is dead.]

Bartlett remarks that each of these passages "becomes formal with the Envelope, the earlier a dirge, the later a gnomic outburst; after the Envelope each passage again becomes more conversational" (12). She is able to show that patterns of this kind can be found in other Old English poems and that there are long passages that are framed by an envelope, such as the Finn episode (1063–1162a). Moreover, Bartlett gives examples of what she calls the "Parallel pattern," where words, phrases, and sentences come in pairs (30). Almost indiscernable from the parallel pattern, as Bartlett concedes, is what she calls the "Incremental pattern," in which "the narrative proceeds by a series of more or less parallel steps which have a cumulative force" (49). A good example of this is the approach of Grendel to Heorot (702b–36a), a scene that has also been extensively analyzed with regard to diction and syntax by Stanley Greenfield (1972, 122–30).

Another kind of structural pattern that—like Bartlett's envelope—has since become an established notion, and not only in *Beowulf* scholarship, is John Leyerle's concept of interlace. But while Bartlett has made out rhetorical units that are a "content unity" or display "logical completeness" within the envelope pattern (1935, 9), Leyerle stresses the "interwovenness" of the structure of *Beowulf*. Thus, an "episode cannot be taken out of context . . . without impairing the interwoven design" (1967, 8). The term interlace is borrowed from the visual arts to support Leyerle's view that the structure of *Beowulf* is "the poetic analogue of the interlace designs common in Anglo-Saxon art of the seventh and eighth centuries" (1). Almost a century before Leyerle, Heinzel had already spoken of "this restless emerging and submerging [*Auf- und Untertauchen*] of ideas" (1875, 4)[6]—the same concept that Leyerle captures with the image of interlace.

Leyerle's suggestion has not remained unchallenged. In 1985, Clare Kinney sees in Leyerle's insistence on interlace structure the danger that "we overemphasize the synchronicity of *Beowulf*" (1985, 297). Morton W. Bloomfield also finds fault with Leyerle's emphasis on simultaneity, pointing out that there is a basic difference between visual and verbal art, since in the latter "neither the creator nor the audience can follow two different lines at the same time" (1986, 50). In other words, "Verbal art cannot indicate simultaneity simultaneously" (52). Edward B. Irving Jr., however, thinks that the concept of interlace is still "insufficiently exploited by Leyerle himself and by subsequent critics" and moreover argues that "it is also adaptable to the more recent ideas about the nature of oral-based poetry" (1989, 80). Robert D. Stevick, in his turn, has recently warned that the notion of interlace is used in an inflated manner, observing that "to apply the same metaphor of interlace to syntactic variation, discontinuous increments, and thematic resemblances is only to loosen the connection between 'interlace' and the form of the poem" (1992, 5). He thus thinks the notion helpful only as a "metaphor for some patterns of syntactic variation or as a very loose equivalent to 'discontinuous' or 'fragments of background matter appearing now and then'" (9).

In 1983, John Niles takes up the idea of ring composition in *Beowulf*, "a chiastic design in which the last element in a series in some way echoes the first, the next to the last the second, and so on" (1983, 152). As a fine example of this kind of composition Niles quotes lines 12–19:

> Ðæm eafera wæs   æfter cenned
> geong in geardum   þone Gode sende
> folce to frofre;   fyrenðearfe ongeat,
> þe hie ær drugon   aldor(le)ase
> lange hwile;   him þæs Liffrea,
> wuldres Wealdend   woroldare forgeaf,
> Beowulf was breme   —blæd wide sprang—
> Scyldes eafera   Scedelandum in.

Niles's translation:

> To him in time   a son was born,
> young in the land,   whom the Lord sent
> to comfort the folk;   He knew the dire need
> they had suffered earlier,   lacking a king
> for a long time.   The Lord of life,
> Ruler of glory,   granted them grace for this.
> Beo[wulf] was famous,   his name rang widely,
> Scyld's son,   in the lands of the North. (153)

As the frame of this "self-contained verse paragraph" Niles identifies the word "eafera" (son). The second element is the description of Scyld's son, Beo[wulf], in 13a and 18a; the third is "the equivalent of the phrase 'God sent him as a blessing to the people' (13b–14a, 16b–17)," and the "kernel" passage is "the reference to the Danes' long years of misery before the coming of Scyld (14b–16a)." Niles is well aware of possible doubts as to the effect of this structural-stylistic device if the poem were presented to a listening audience (161). Yet we should account for the specific contemporaneous reception of the poem not only in terms of the medium. As Niles puts it: "An audience that had heard a story told often, with variations, might have become sufficiently discerning to appreciate even subtle instances of thematic echo" (162). Similarly, in 1988 Ward Parks conceives of ring structure as a "binary and chiastic ordering device" that takes care of "narrative integration through the interfacing of narrative units" and that is "often found in oral or residually oral literature" (237). It is, therefore, an "integral mechanism" (241) that can work, however, only if the feature used to serve this purpose is sufficiently salient, "so that the listening audience can recognize its recurrence at the conclusion of the framed passage" (243). Parks thus convincingly shows the possibility of connecting "digressive material with the narrative contexts in which it occurs" (247) with regard to the so-called "Song of Creation" (lines 91–99), for example, as well as the "Lay of the Last Survivor" (lines 2247–66).

Such investigations into the larger rhetorical patterns of *Beowulf* make us sensitive to designs that are not at once conspicuous to the reader trained in modern literature. Yet again, we must take care not to arrive at conclusions too rashly. Such patterns were successful in that they aptly conveyed the narrative. Still, we must keep in mind that they are not icons of the mind-set of the composer or the audience of *Beowulf* but merely symptoms of this mind-set.

For some scholars, an investigation into the rhetoric and style of *Beowulf* may seem an inadequate approach to the poem, since it requires criteria that are anachronistic in their application to this text. This brief survey shows, however, that, as long as scholars control their heuristic premises and tools, such investigations may uncover linguistic techniques that otherwise would remain unnoticed by the modern reader. Evidently, in a work of art rhetorical and stylistic techniques need not be conspicuous in order to enhance the audience's aesthetic experience. If it is the analytic task of literary historians to reveal these techniques for any text, this task is the more difficult as the text recedes in time.

Notes

1. For this and the immediately following observations on style, I am indebted to Hans-Martin Gauger's recent article "Zur Frage des Stils" (1992).

2. I translate from the appendix of the second edition of the *Geschichte der englischen Literatur*, vol. 1, issued in 1899, the main text of which was edited by Alois Brandl. The appendix to this volume renders ten Brink's own words.

3. Such a claim obviously touches on several other fields of research on *Beowulf*, such as "Date, Provenance, Author, Audiences," "Sources and Analogues," and particularly "Christian and Pagan Elements" (chapters 2, 7, and 9 in the present volume).

4. The lexical device of repetition known as *variation* will not be dealt with here *per se*, as it is treated in chapter 5 of this handbook.

5. Compare, e.g., the pair *biddan—bodian* = "to order and establish," which is found in Old English charters. Wulfstan's *Sermo Lupi* abounds in twin collocations.

6. Leyerle also conceives of interlace in a larger sense as "an organizing principle closer to the workings of the human imagination proceeding in its atemporal way from one associative idea to the next" (1967, 14). This is very similar to what Heinzel had said about the use of *hyperbaton*, which to him seems "to correspond to a state of mind where two ideas are almost simultaneously present, permeating and intertwining with each other. There is no real succession" (1875, 14).

Chapter 7

Sources and Analogues

by Theodore M. Andersson

Summary: Scholars have adduced sources and analogues from every conceivable time and place but chiefly from Norse, Irish, and classical literature (mainly Homer and Virgil), church tradition (including biblical, apocryphal, and patristic material), and other Old English texts. Despite the voluminous literature on these matters, almost everything is in doubt. Among the Norse analogues only *Grettis saga* seems convincing to most students, although the recently emphasized two-troll tale in the Icelandic *fornaldarsǫgur* may suggest a North Sea tale type underlying *Beowulf*. The Irish analogues have been subject to equal measures of conviction and skepticism. Homer has been dropped from the discussion, and, although Virgilian parallels are attractive, they command no consensus. Ecclesiastical influence seems ubiquitous in spirit but undemonstrable in detail. The strongest case for an Old English source is Klaeber's argument in favor of borrowings from *Genesis A*.

Chronology

1852–54: Gísli Brynjúlfsson makes a plea for more English recognition of their cultural community with Scandinavia and notes in passing the similarity between the missions of Beowulf and Bǫðvarr bjarki.

1878: Guðbrandur Vigfússon calls *Grettis saga* "a late version of the famous Beowulf Legend," which spread in two branches from its Scandinavian home to England and Iceland. He indicates that he first observed the correspondence in 1873.

1880: Hugo Gering welcomes G. Vigfússon's discovery that the Beowulf story was known in Iceland and translates chapters 64–67 of *Grettis saga*.

1888: Gregor Sarrazin argues for a Scandinavian original of *Beowulf* and surmises that it was composed at the court of King Ingeld at Lejre around the year 700.

1903: George Lyman Kittredge notes in passing that the Irish "The Hand and the Child" belongs to the same story type as that found in Beowulf's adventure with Grendel.

1909: Max Deutschbein stresses the deviations from Germanic heroic poetry in *Beowulf* and traces the monster stories to Irish lore, especially *Fled Bricrend*

(*Feast of Bricriu*). He locates the epic at the court of King Aldfrith of Northumbria (ca. 680–705).

1910: Friedrich Klaeber presents a model case for the priority of *Genesis A* in relation to *Beowulf.*

1910: Friedrich Panzer revolutionizes *Beowulf* studies by placing the Grendel story in the broad international folktale context of "The Bear's Son Tale."

1911: Klaeber (1911a) publishes the best study to date on the possibility of Virgilian influence on *Beowulf.*

1912: William W. Lawrence argues that Grendel's mere was originally characterized by a waterfall rather than marsh or seaside. In the wake of Panzer (1910) he believes that *Beowulf* and *Grettis saga* may have common Märchen origins but that in addition the first may have influenced the latter directly.

1913–14: Oscar L. Olson rebuts Deutschbein (1909) and denies categorically that there is any influence on *Beowulf* from *The Feast of Bricriu.*

1916: Olson criticizes the attempts to link *Beowulf* to the legend of Hrólfr kraki and concludes "that the dragon story in the *Hrólfssaga* has no connection whatever with the Grendel story or the dragon story in *Beowulf.*"

1918: Klaeber weighs the parallels between *Beowulf* and *Exodus* and is inclined to accept Schücking's view that *Exodus* is anterior.

1920: Gustav Neckel offers a deeply informed if speculative reconstruction of the lay underlying the Sigemund reference in *Beowulf* 884–97 and surmises a Geatish origin. He considers Beowulf's dragon fight to be a variant of this original.

1921: R. W. Chambers provides an indispensable compilation of study materials, including an extensive collection and translation of historical and narrative sources and analogues.

1923: Carl Wilhelm von Sydow (1923b) provides the best exposition and sharpest critique of the analogues in the Hrólfr kraki legend and *Grettis saga.* He rejects Panzer's derivation of the Grendel story from "The Bear's Son Tale" and briefly restates his belief in an Irish prototype related to "The Hand and the Child."

1927: Heinz Dehmer argues that the Grendel story derives from the Irish "The Hand and the Child" and that *Grettis saga* goes back to some form of the English Grendel story.

1927: Klaeber carefully compares the funeral descriptions in *Beowulf* and Jordanes's *Getica*, concluding that the two accounts are most likely independent of each other and the similarities coincidental.

1927: Alexander Haggerty Krappe finds an overall parallel to the Grendel story (including the severed arm) in Somadeva's eleventh-century *Ocean of Story.*

1928: Alois Brandl converts to a thoroughgoing belief in the *Aeneid* as a model for *Beowulf* and argues in particular the parallelism of Beowulf's adventure in Grendel's mere and the Cacus episode in book 8 of the *Aeneid.*

1929: Levin L. Schücking (1929a) defends his view that *Exodus* 56–58 provided the model for *Beowulf* 1408–10.

1931: Tom Burns Haber builds on Klaeber (1911a) in an attempt to maintain Virgilian influence on *Beowulf.*

1935: Walter A. Berendsohn attempts the last large-scale "analytic" prehistory of *Beowulf*, distinguishing a Geatish heroic Ecgtheow poem (along with several other lost poems), a Geatish Grendel poem, and an Anglian redaction. In the process, he compiles a good deal of useful material on style and tone.

1936: Alois Brandl equates the plot of *Beowulf* with events in Mercian history and identifies Heremod with King Penda, Scyld with King Wulfhere, and Wiglaf with King Wiglaf.

1937: Brandl argues that *Beowulf* and the *Aeneid* are analogous epics about the salvation of a people and are closely related in narrative sequence: heroic missions, swimming episodes, arrivals at court, encounters with monsters, momentary relief, descents into the underworld, and so forth.

1939: Ingeborg Schröbler assembles an interesting collection of verbal and motival correspondences between Homer and *Beowulf* but is unsure how to interpret them.

1950: Felix Genzmer makes the last attempt at an "analytical" reconstruction of the lost sources, a Geatish tale of Beowulf the Bear's Son, a Danish tale of Beowulf the Geat, a tale of the "Hrethlings," and an account of the final Anglo-Saxon *Beowulf* with ample latitude for Irish influence.

1950: Klaeber (1950b) argues that the phrasing in *Beowulf* 1408–10 derives from the *Aeneid* 2.524–25 and that the same phrasing in *Exodus* must be derivative from *Beowulf.*

1951: Leonard J. Peters provides a very thorough review of the proposed borrowings from *Beowulf* in *Andreas* and considers them to be inconclusive.

1952: Calvin Claudel criticizes Colgrave (1951) and Panzer (1910), warning against the practice of merging too many disparate variants in an ancient prototype that is apt to be an imaginary abstraction.

1952: A. R. Taylor connects Grettir's encounter with the *haugbúi* (barrow-dweller) Kárr and a bear in Norway with Beowulf's adventures.

1954: Francis P. Magoun Jr. abstracts the content of a Hygelac lay that may have entered East Anglia from Sweden.

1955: James Carney argues that the parallels with *Grettis saga* are exaggerated and obscure the Irish parallels, which include three sources: the folktale of "The Hand and the Child," Irish ecclesiastical material on the monstrous progeny of Cain, and the eighth-century *Táin Bó Fraích* (Cattle Raid of Froech).

1959: Nora K. Chadwick reviews the monster analogues in the *fornaldarsǫgur* and argues that the *Beowulf* poet based his narrative on a traditional Scandinavian story that might have been introduced by the East Anglian Wuffingas.

1961: G. V. Smithers emphasizes the multiplicity of *fornaldarsaga* analogues in *Beowulf* and argues that the dragon episode is a transmuted version of the barrow-dweller adventure peculiar to that genre.

1966: P. G. Buchloh analyzes the transformation in composition and meaning undergone by *Beowulf* in the evolution from short narrative to epic.

1968: G. N. Garmonsway and Jacqueline Simpson include many Scandinavian parallels with their translation of *Beowulf.*

1969: Ursula Dronke argues that *Beowulf* is predicated on the same sort of larger life—death—rebirth cycle that we find in Norse mythology.

1970: Larry D. Benson reflects on the advantage of a hero with no historical burden (apart from a swimming contest with Breca) and minimizes the importance of quasi-historical traditions in an effort to refocus attention on the poet's originality.

1971: Alistair Campbell argues that the *Beowulf* poet is almost alone in using the Virgilian technique of inserted narrative not only to summarize events but also to illuminate the narrator.

1972: Richard J. Schrader argues for analogies between Beowulf's funeral pyre and the funeral pyres in Statius's *Thebaid.*

1975: Peter A. Jorgensen identifies the "two-troll" variant of the Grendel story in two *fornaldarsǫgur.*

1979: Ruth Mellinkoff compares the Cain material in *Beowulf* to the monster lore in the Book of Enoch and the "Noachic tradition."

1979: Martin Puhvel assembles his observations on Celtic parallels and concludes that Irish tradition has a definite role in the creation of *Beowulf.*

1980: Carol J. Clover explores the morphology of Beowulf's confrontation with Unferth and relates the form of the quarrel to the flyting in Norse poetry and prose.

1980: Ruth Mellinkoff traces the idea that the giants survived the Deluge in Jewish and apocryphal legend.

1981: David N. Dumville is skeptical of the Irish analogues to *Beowulf* and confines himself to a review of the contacts between Ireland and England.

1981: Karl P. Wentersdorf adduces a number of ecclesiastical documents tending to show that relapse into heathen practices was common enough even among the contemporaries of the *Beowulf* poet. He argues plausibly that "Metod hie ne cuþon" means only that the Danes ignored God.

1982: Roberta Frank (1982a) analyzes the *Beowulf* poet's ability to project the remoteness of history and distills the essence of the Virgilian spirit in the poem.

1982: Richard Mark Scowcroft minimizes the analogies to *Grettis saga* and reemphasizes the role of "The Hand and the Child" in the narrative of *Beowulf.*

1983: John D. Niles argues that *Beowulf* does not have any of the essential features that we would expect in a work influenced by Virgil.

1985: Joseph Harris restates his theory of *Beowulf* as a *summa litterarum* and considers a point of origin in East Anglia at the end of the seventh century.

1986: Anatoly Liberman reviews the discussion of *Beowulf* and *Grettis saga* in great detail and offers his own reconstruction of the underlying story.

1988: Gernot Wieland argues that the *Beowulf* poet draws on the Old English *Exodus* and that the Beowulf figure is predicated on Moses.

1992: Joseph Harris (1992a) places Beowulf's last words in the context of a hypothetical Germanic "death song," which he extrapolates chiefly from Eddic analogues.

1992: J. Michael Stitt gathers and translates or summarizes the Scandianavian two-troll stories identified to date.

1993: Sam Newton capitalizes on archeological, genealogical, onomastic, and quasi-historical evidence to argue that the matter of the poem is pre-Viking. He connects Beowulf with the Wulfings of southwestern Sweden and the Wuffings of East Anglian dynastic history in the time of King Ælfwald (ca. 713–749).

The quest for Beowulfian sources and analogues has been long-standing, earnest, and surprisingly (perhaps revealingly) barren. Ever since Guðbrandur Vigfússon noted the correspondence to *Grettis saga* (1878, 1, xlix; also Vigfússon and Powell 1883, 2, 501–3), the search has gone on unabated. There is, however, some evidence that the institutional memory in *Beowulf* studies is about an even century, because we now appear to be rediscovering the parallels that have been pointed out repeatedly in the past. In 1982, McConchie rediscovered the "neglected" analogue of Grettir's fight with a *haugbúi* (barrow-dweller) noted by Danielli (1945, 242), A. R. Taylor (1952, 13–14), Smithers (1961, 12), Benson (1970, 28–29), R. Harris (1973, 31), and Jorgensen (1979, 86). In 1985, Wachsler reintroduced Grettir's fight with a bear as a "neglected analogue," although it had been observed by Klaeber (1922a, xiv, n.3), Lawrence (1928, 187), Danielli (1945, 242), A. R. Taylor (1952, 14–15), Arent (1969, 189–99), and Jorgensen (1979, 86). This cycle illustrates not so much the inevitable limitations of bibliographical consciousness as the need for occasional bibliographic updates. The question of *Grettis saga* has in fact been surveyed in imposing breadth and depth by Liberman (1986), but other matters have been less fully reviewed. They cannot be accounted for exhaustively because there are myriad references to sources and analogues in the many monographs, general books, and text editions devoted to *Beowulf* and other Old English texts. The following survey is therefore largely confined to the periodical literature and refers to only about two hundred and fifty studies.

Aside from a small grab bag of exotica—analogues from Japan (Kittredge 1903, 228; Oshitari 1988), Mexico (Colgrave 1951; Claudel 1952; Barakat 1967), Burma (Woolf 1947), China (Maeth 1987), India (Krappe 1927; Clark 1964; Thundy 1983a), Armenia (E. Anderson 1981), Russia and Wales (Whitbread 1945), Finland (Magoun 1960), Kirghiz epic (Reichl 1987), the *Theodosian Code* (E. Anderson 1982), *Tom Sawyer* (Belden 1918), C.S. Lewis's *Perelandra* (Musgrove 1945), and James Bond fiction (Webb 1968)—the search has concentrated on five distinguishable sets of texts that may have some real relation to *Beowulf*, sometimes offered as sources, but more often to be understood as significant parallels perhaps implying something about the sources. In the order of expended effort—there is no order of conclusive results—these categories may be designated as follows: Scandinavian parallels, classical sources (Virgil, Homer, and others), Irish sources and analogues, ecclesiastical sources (biblical, apocryphal, patristic), and echoes in other Old English texts (notably *Andreas, Exodus*, and *Genesis A*).

I. Scandinavian Parallels

The peculiarity that *Beowulf* is an English poem about the fortunes of Scandinavians in Scandinavia engaged the interest of Scandinavian scholars at an early date and, not unnaturally, prompted the idea that *Beowulf* was a translation from a lost Scandinavian original (Thorkelin 1815b). That idea now provokes only a consensus of mirth, but it survived until the end of the nineteenth century in the writings of Gregor Sarrazin. Writing against Eduard Sievers, Sarrazin (1886a) defended his view that a number of words and phrases were derived from Norse, and he ended the second chapter of his 1888 study with the following bold conclusion: "In all probability the Scandinavian original on which *Beowulf* is based was composed or reworked by the *þyle* (skald) Starkaðr at the court of the Danish king Ingeld at Lejre around the year 700" (107). (For a general but flawed account of Sarrazin's theories, see Luehrs 1904, and for an explicit refutation, see von Sydow 1923a.) Thereafter the idea of a Scandinavian original died quietly, though as late as 1897 Sarrazin persisted in believing that *Beowulf* was translated (at least orally) from Scandinavian versions. There is now a consensus that it is in fact one of the peculiarities of *Beowulf* that it contains no Scandinavianisms (e.g., J. Harris 1985, 264), although one scholar has raised anew the possibility of a few loans (Frank 1981, 1987).

The abolition of a Scandinavian original was not, however, tantamount to rejecting a Scandinavian source. About the time that Sarrazin's voice became solitary, Vigfússon's discovery of the poem's likeness to *Grettis saga* breathed new life into the speculation on Scandinavian antecedents. Hugo Gering (1880) greeted the news with delight, translated the relevant chapters of *Grettis saga*, and expressed amazement that the discovery had not been made earlier, for example, by Jacob Grimm (87). But the matter was far from closed. In 1903, Axel Olrik expressed skepticism about the age of the Scandinavian examples and opened the way for the belief that *Grettis saga* was merely a reworking of *Beowulf* (248; omitted in Hollander's translation [1919, 400]; cf. Liberman 1986, 356). As early as 1909 we find William W. Lawrence groaning under the burden of the growing scholarly literature (1909, 221). He too attributed the correspondences between *Beowulf* and the saga to a knowledge of the poem in Iceland (238). Thus, Thorkelin's idea that *Beowulf* was Scandinavian had evolved a century later into the idea that the relevant sections of *Grettis saga* were, in a manner of speaking, English.

In the wake of Panzer (1910) and the location of both *Beowulf* and *Grettis saga* in the context of international folktale type 301B ("The Bear's Son" or "The Three Stolen Princesses"), Lawrence altered his view in 1912 to the extent of believing that the waterfall of *Grettis saga* was more original than the mere in *Beowulf.* He believed that the two texts might have common antecedents in folktale form but that there was still room for the direct influence of *Beowulf* on *Grettis saga.* The close resemblance between the two texts was reaffirmed by Stedman (1913–14), and by the time Lawrence's 1928 book appeared, Lawrence subscribed more completely to Panzer's derivation from folktale. Although there is a residual sentence on the possibility of literary influence (1928, 182), the discussion focuses on independent derivation from "The Bear's Son." At this point the development of Icelandic literature was familiar enough to make the influence of an Old English poem on an Icelandic saga quite implausible. In 1929, R. W. Chambers supported Lawrence's view, at the same time agreeing that a second analogue in *Samsons saga fagra*, which Lawrence argued in 1928 and 1929, was also significant. With the notable exception of von Sydow (1923b), there now appeared to be a consensus (also supported by Klaeber 1922a, xviii) on a folktale source for *Beowulf* and *Grettis saga*. (In an altogether different vein, Gustav Hübener [1927–28, 1935] used *Grettis saga* to argue that Beowulf's "cleansing" of Heorot is based on a Germanic tradition of demon exorcism.)

But the consensus eroded somewhat ten years later when W. S. Mackie (1938) argued against Lawrence and Klaeber that Grendel's mere is described not as an inland pool but as a landlocked saltwater inlet, with no hint of a waterfall. That had the effect of compromising the comparison with *Grettis saga.* Lawrence (1939) issued a quick rebuttal (cf. Liberman 1986, 360), but twenty years later Kemp Malone (1958) again argued that Grendel's mere was not an inland lake but a seascape misconstrued by critics because of a false analogy to *Grettis saga.* He averred that the landscape was originally hellish and surreal and was naturalized only when the story migrated to Scandinavia and Iceland.

Despite this curious debate over landscape features, there is not much doubt of some connection between *Beowulf* and *Grettis saga.* Even in his debunking of the analogue industry, Larry D. Benson allowed for a common source to explain the correspondences and offered a rough approximation of what the source may have looked like (1970, 27). Most important, Anatoly Liberman provided a detailed review of the problem, including a bibliography of 213 relevant items and a different (but not irreconcilable) reconstruction of the common source (1986, 380). Benson devoted the last ten pages of his paper to a fine analysis of the *Beowulf* poet's original development of his meager sources, but the implications of the analogues may still not be exhausted, and I will return to the general issue below.

In the meantime, a considerably more checkered reception was in store for another Scandinavian analogue from the Skjoldung (Scylding) legend of Hrólfr kraki (the Hrothulf of *Beowulf*) preserved in a variety of texts including Saxo Grammaticus's *Gesta Danorum* (ca. 1200), a *fornaldarsaga* entitled *Hrólfs saga kraka,* and a late Icelandic verse rendering called *Bjarkarímur* (the latter two texts from ca. 1400). The correspondence between incidents in the Danish material and *Beowulf* was first observed by Gísli Brynjúlfsson (1852–54, 130) and has haunted the handbooks ever since (e.g., Chambers 1921 and later eds.; Garmonsway and Simpson 1968). Because there is an extensive coincidence of legendary (even quasi-historical) names in the English Scylding and Danish Skjoldung dynasties, it was tempting to look for some narrative link as well, particularly in an era when Scandinavian scholars looked to *Beowulf* for some light on their own prehistory. It seemed like a stroke of extraordinary good fortune that the richest and best-documented Danish heroic legend should turn up with analogous names in the English *Beowulf* several centuries before the earliest Danish versions. It could hardly be dismissed as happenstance when *Hrólfs saga kraka* (and the *Bjarkarímur*) told of a Bjarki ("little bear"—hence the identification with Beowulf, "bee wolf "

= bear) coming from southern Sweden (*Beowulf*'s Geatland?) to Lejre on Zealand (Hrothgar's putative home) and killing a winged monster posing a threat to the royal hall there. The early phases of this discussion were reviewed by Oscar L. Olson (1916, 7–12).

Although Scyldings and Skjoldungs are easily equated, the narrative analogue never carried great conviction. The preeminent authority on the Danish Skjoldung legend, Axel Olrik, was among the most skeptical (1903, 134–37; 1919, 247–51). He complained that only a merging of all three combats in *Beowulf* produced any likeness at all and that the closest analogue was found in the latest and least authentic Scandinavian source, the *Bjarkarímur*. A much fuller refutation was undertaken by Oscar L. Olson in his University of Chicago dissertation of 1916, privately printed and distributed by the University of Chicago Libraries and simultaneously printed in *Scandinavian Studies*. Olson (31–35) derived Bjarki's slaying of the monster not from Skjoldung pseudohistory but from a folktale in which a troll attacks a house on Christmas Eve. Since then the identification with Grendel's maraudings has been kept alive mostly by the inclusion of the Danish materials in the semipopular collections of sources and analogues. The texts were gathered and translated into German by Paul Herrmann (1905) and into English by R. W. Chambers (1921, 129–46, 182–86). Chambers (57–61) doubted that Olrik and Olson had made their case and agreed with the scholars who believed there was some connection, notably Lawrence (1909) and Panzer (1910, 364–86). In Germany, Hermann Schneider (1934, 21–24) and, in exile, Walter A. Berendsohn (1935, 213–28) also maintained the connection. A few years later, James R. Caldwell (1940) supported Olson in the view that the *Bjarkarímur* are secondary to *Hrólfs saga kraka* and created a new distance from *Beowulf* by aligning the story of Bǫðvarr bjarki not with Panzer's "Bear's Son Tale" but rather with "The Two Brothers." The association of *Beowulf* and *Hrólfs saga kraka* lived on in the later editions of Chambers's *Introduction* (1932, 1959) and in Garmonsway and Simpson (1968), but it was not until 1970 that the problem was reassessed by Larry D. Benson.

Benson devoted five corrosive pages (1970, 15–19) to the perceived parallels and concluded: "In short, only in its latest developments does the Bjarki story look anything like the story in *Beowulf*, and even the latest versions, I must stress, do not look all that much like our poem." For the last twenty-five years there has been no further comment. Whereas the analogues in *Grettis saga* are still in litigation (Richard Harris 1973; Jorgensen 1973; J. Turville–Petre 1977; McConchie 1982; Wachsler 1985; Liberman 1986), *Hrólfs saga kraka* has vanished from the docket. This cannot be attributed to Benson's critique, which appeared inconspicuously in a collection of papers on many topics; it is rather the result of the intrinsic inconclusiveness of the comparison.

In the late nineteenth century, the discussion was still fueled by the ambition to reconstruct national history, especially in Scandinavia (e.g., Levander 1908).

Beowulf promised an almost magical step back in history to a time not illuminated by Scandinavian sources. Hence an obsession with shreds of genealogical and dynastic matter and a rash of ingenious attempts to reconcile *Beowulf* with Saxo Grammaticus or the very sparse evidence on early Swedish history. Oddly enough, the most indefatigable reconstructor of such legendary history in this century was the American Kemp Malone (e.g., 1927, 1930, 1939, 1939–40, 1942, 1954, 1959), but there were others as well (e.g., Detter 1893; Weyhe 1908; Belden 1913; Klaeber 1922b; Boberg 1942–43; Magoun 1954). Such studies are now too complicated and the correlations too tenuous to offer any edification. That is, it would seem, also the fate of the Hrólfr kraki parallels. They must be argued with such ingenuity and such a suspension of disbelief that they can no longer hold an audience. If there is some ancestral connection, it is not clear enough to be useful. The larger point of Benson's paper was that in the absence of any clearly profiled sources we would do better to study the poet's manifest originality rather than some unascertainable degree of indebtedness (1970, 33–43).

　　Grettis saga and *Hrólfs saga kraka* have been the focus of the debate. Attempts to locate other Scandinavian analogues have not been successful enough to provoke further discussion. In *Flóres saga konungs ok sona hans* Margaret Schlauch (1930) located a hero entering a dragon's cave only to be abandoned by his companions. Paul Beekman Taylor (1964–65) used the description of Odin's funeral pyre in *Ynglingasaga* as evidence that the *Beowulf* poet was working from an old Germanic tradition. George Clark (1971) and Jeff Opland (1973) argued more independently than convincingly for a parallel to Beowulf 's dragon fight in chapter 119 of *Njáls saga*. In 1983, Helen Damico tried to reconstruct a mythological source for the Hama episode in *Beowulf* with the aid of *Sǫrla þáttr*, and in the same year Fredrik J. Heinemann tried to elucidate the *ealuscerwen* crux from a passage in "Baldrs draumar." Finally, in 1989 R. D. Fulk wrote a learned piece in the tradition of Magnus Olsen comparing Scyld Scefing to Bergelmir being loaded on a *lúðr* (vessel or container of some sort) in *Vafþrúðnismál* 35 and in *Snorra Edda*.

　　The impression conveyed by this outline may be that the initial harvest was more apparent than real and that there has been very little in the way of a second harvest, but the outlook is not altogether bleak. We need to shift our focus from the quasi-historical or legendary materials in the Skjoldung traditions to the folktale line of inquiry initiated by Panzer (1910). Panzer's reorientation liberated the study of sources and analogues from the rather fruitless historical perspectives and at the same time put an end to the curious idea that the author of *Grettis saga* was subject to literary influence from *Beowulf*. Panzer broadened the scope of the inquiry by placing *Beowulf* in the context of the international tale type 301B and providing an extensive repertory of occurrences. The weakness of his new context is that it is too universal, and this weakness was no doubt instrumental in some of the more exotic quests noted in the second paragraph of this chapter. Scholars were diverted from the immediate context of the poem in favor of a more amorphous categorization that revealed little about the real sources of *Beowulf* (see von Sydow 1923b; Claudel 1952; Szövérffy 1956, 104; Chambers 1959, 374; Rosenberg 1991, 46). Such an approach detracted from the explanatory force of the analogues in *Grettis saga* rather than reinforcing them. But *Grettis saga* is so much more apposite than any other analogue that it is surely more reasonable to view the matrix of *Beowulf* as North European rather than "Indo-Iranian" (Panzer 1910, 245).

This realization has accrued only gradually as further Old Icelandic parallels have been pointed out, all tending to show that *Grettis saga*, and by extension *Beowulf*, belong to a Norse "ecotype" in which a hero enters a cave and kills two giants, usually of different sexes. This type is referred to by Jorgensen (1975) and subsequently Stitt (1992) as the "two-troll tradition." The gradual identification of the tradition can be traced in the handbooks on sources and analogues. The first edition of Chambers's *Introduction* (1921) included, in addition to *Grettis saga*, only *Orms þáttr Stórólfssonar*, but the second edition from 1932 added passages from *Þorskfirðinga saga* (or *Gull-Þóris saga*) and *Samsons saga fagra*. To this repertory Garmonsway and Simpson (1968) added passages from *Þorsteins þáttr uxafóts* (see Binns 1953–57) and *Þorsteins saga Víkingssonar*. But that was only the beginning.

In a series of papers, Peter A. Jorgensen added a number of new parallels. In 1975, he pointed out the two-troll variant in *Hálfdanar saga Brönufóstra* and *Gríms saga loðinkinna*. In 1979, he explored variants in *Hrana saga Hrings, Fljótsdæla saga, Hálfdanar saga Eysteinssonar,* and *Gunnars saga Keldugnúpsfífls,* with special reference to the presence of effective and ineffective weapons. Finally, in 1986, he added some partial analogues from *Egils saga einhenda, Göngu-Hrólfs saga, Þórodds þáttr Snorrasonar,* the Arnljótr episode in *Óláfs saga helga,* and *Ála flekks saga*. These variants become increasingly remote, but they clearly belong to the same two-troll monster story that underlies Beowulf 's encounters with Grendel and his mother. Much of this material was assembled and translated by Stitt (1992). There is consequently ample evidence of a Scandinavian monster story with which *Beowulf* is closely associated. It remains to assess what it means that *Beowulf* is not so much a narratively deformed account of legendary Danish history (as in *Hrólfs saga kraka*) as it is a variant of a Scandinavian monster tale. Alois Brandl (1932, 193) once asked a little impatiently, "Should we not for once make the experiment of understanding the cannibal and the fire-breathing dragon as the original layer, with the historico-geographical setting understood only as a later disguise?" Jorgensen and Stitt have provided a broader base for such an experiment.

II. Irish Parallels

Although Hugo Gering (1880, 87) expressed surprise that Jacob Grimm had not observed the analogues in *Grettis saga*, Richard Mark Scowcroft (1982, 479) credits Wilhelm Grimm with first linking *Beowulf* to Irish lore. In point of fact, the passage in question (Grimm and Grimm 1826, cxix–xx) mentions Grendel only in connection with the German "Schrätel und Wasserbär." The exploration of such parallels developed very slowly. Ludwig Laistner (1889, 25), Albert S. Cook (1899), and George Lyman Kittredge (1903, 222–28) noted similarities in passing, but the first to present an academic argument, in the form of an inaugural lecture, was Max Deutschbein (1909). He dismissed the Norse analogues and proposed that the Irish *Feast of Bricriu* underlay the plot of *Beowulf.* But Oscar Olson (1913–14), who would also choose the role of spoiler with respect to the parallels in *Hrólfs saga kraka,* soon rebutted Deutschbein's contention and denied categorically that there was any influence from *The Feast of Bricriu* on *Beowulf.*

In the same year, 1914, the distinguished Swedish folklorist Carl Wilhelm von Sydow took a much more favorable view of Irish influence, and ten years later in two separate publications he pursued the argument. He refuted Gregor Sarrazin's theory of a translation from the Norse, stating that even if it were a translation, that translation would, according to medieval practice, have to be of the loosest kind (1923a; cf. Benson 1970). But the idea of a translation was in any case quite impossible because *Beowulf* is a fundamentally Christian poem written at a time when any Norse tale would have been thoroughly pagan. Furthermore, von Sydow asserted, the source is in fact not Norse but Irish. Presumably, the tale was picked up by an Englishman at an Irish center of learning ("university") together with a knowledge of Virgil. Von Sydow pressed the matter further, sharply criticizing the validity of the analogues in *Grettis saga* and *Hrólfs saga kraka* and rejecting Panzer's derivation from the "Bear's Son Tale." He reasserted his belief that *Beowulf* is best explained as a variant of the Irish tale called "The Hand and the Child," a story in which a monster stretches his arm in through the roof only to have it detached by the hero (1923b).

A few years later, Heinz Dehmer (1927, 51–69; 1928) renewed the Irish initiative (cf. Berendsohn 1935, 232–33). He proceeded by minimizing the resemblances between *Grettis saga* and *Beowulf* and arguing that the decisive difference between the two texts was the motif of the monstrous arm, precisely the motif that aligns *Beowulf* with "The Hand and the Child." It was under the influence of the argument advanced by Dehmer (not von Sydow, who is only listed in the bibliography) that Chambers included a few pages on "The Hand and the Child" in the second edition of his *Introduction* (1932, 478–85), but he was not convinced that the Irish story displaced *Grettis saga* as the primary analogue.

On Dehmer's heels, Samuel J. Crawford (1929) found a new approach in the form of a note from the Irish *Lebor Na Huidre* (Book of the Dun [Cow]) indicating that Cain's monstrous progeny expired in the Deluge (cf. *Beowulf* 107–14). In 1949, Howard Meroney produced Irish analogues to the classical "Quid genus? Unde domo?" formula that seems to reverberate in *Beowulf,* lines 237–57, and, in 1950, Charles Donahue resurrected Crawford's idea that the Cain lore in *Beowulf* is "at home in an early Celtic Christian climate of opinion" (174).

Up until this point, the theory of Irish origins amounted to little more than stray notes, but in 1955 James Carney devoted a full chapter in his *Studies in Irish Literature and History* (77–128) to "The Irish Elements in *Beowulf*." Carney's theoretical point of departure was an opposition to "nativist" views of early literature tending to militate against the idea of borrowing across national or linguistic boundaries. He found that the inner-Germanic links between *Beowulf* and *Grettis saga* were exaggerated and apt to obscure the Irish parallels. Carney himself believed in three Irish sources: the previously adduced folktale of "The Hand and the Child," Irish ecclesiastical material on the monstrous progeny of Cain, and an eighth-century Irish *Táin Bó Fraích* (Cattle Raid of Froech).

The Celtic derivation of Cain lore and the model provided by *Táin Bó Fraích* have not received much support in the last forty years (but see Scowcroft 1982, 498–508). Niilo Peltola (1972) pointed out that Bede derives giants from the daughters of Cain and thought that this might explain Grendel's descent from Cain (cf. Pulsiano 1985). An English source for the presence of Cain in *Beowulf* would of course be more attractive than an Irish source. Stephen C. Bandy (1973) summarized the moral status of giants in book 15 of *The City of God* with reference to *Beowulf*. Most important, Ruth Mellinkoff placed the question on a much broader base in two interlocking studies (1979, 1980). In the first, she aligned the characteristics of Grendel and his mother with the monster lore in the Book of Enoch (see also Kaske 1971) or, more generally, the "Noachic tradition." In the second, she explored traditions about surviving giants after the Deluge. The value of her studies is not that she pinpoints particular sources but that she demonstrates how widely disseminated such lore was. She notes (1979, 157) that it is not "inherently unlikely" that Jewish lore might have reached Anglo-Saxon England but does not insist on bookish transmission. Word of mouth may have sufficed (1979, 161). The effect of Mellinkoff's material is to make it less likely that an individual Irish source underlies the Cain motif in *Beowulf*. With respect to Carney's comparison of *Beowulf* to *Táin Bó Fraích,* even the advocate of Irish connections R. M. Scowcroft concludes: "The remarkable series of parallels that Carney sees between *Beowulf* and *Táin Bó Fraích* conceal major structural differences, and the relationship between the two texts must remain uncertain" (1982, 504).

Outside the mainstream lies an interesting paper by Angus F. Cameron (1969), who found a good parallel to Scyld's sea burial in a Latin life of St. Gildas. On that basis, he argued that the practice was probably Celtic rather than Germanic. On the other hand, John Lindow (1993) has recently made the case that the Gotland picture stones may depict a Germanic belief that the dead were conveyed to the next world by ship.

The most persistent advocate of Irish influence in a long series of articles has been Martin Puhvel (1965, 1966, 1969, 1971, 1980, 1983). In contrast to those who have observed parallel narrative structures in Irish texts or folktales, Puhvel worked more in terms of motifs. In 1979, he drew his observations together in a book with brief chapters on a variety of these motifs, for example, the more powerful giant mother (Grendel's dam), the mysterious light in the cave, the melting of the sword in blood (cf. Princi Braccini 1984), the phenomenon of battle rage, swimming prowess, combat with water monsters, underwater adventures, and the bear-hug style of wrestling. In a longer concluding chapter, he reverts to the more general consideration of a narrative model. Like Dehmer he minimizes the similarities to *Grettis saga* and finds them outweighed by "The Hand and the Child": "All in all, it is apparent that the Grendel story in *Beowulf,* far from being derived from ['The Bear's Son Tale'], exhibits far less parallelism with this folktale than with ['The Hand and the Child']" (101). Again: "On balance, the Celtic folktale of 'The Hand and the Child,' or a tale very closely related to it, appears to be the most plausible candidate for the role of skeletal source of—or chief inspiration for—the struggle against Grendel and his mother" (125). At the last moment, however, Puhvel leaves open the possibility that a Scandinavian folktale "may have fused in England with somewhat similar Celtic folktale elements and possibly elements of Anglo-Saxon folklore, such as those considered above, to provide the basic plot of the Grendel story" (137).

Even with this moderate approach Puhvel may not have won the day. In 1981, David N. Dumville, who had not yet seen Puhvel's book, began his study on a skeptical note: "I think it fair to say that the proposed links have always seemed tenuous or imaginary and have not been taken seriously by most students of the Old English poem" (109; cf. C. Wright 1993, 30 n.122). Dumville's own contribution was to summarize (109–21) the historical evidence of contacts between Ireland and England, including missionary, monastic, and linguistic contacts. The body of the paper is, however, concerned with a more aggressive probing of linguistic stages prior to the *Beowulf* manuscript. Only at the conclusion does Dumville adduce Celtic precedent in arguing that *Beowulf* was not intended for a lay audience (Whitelock 1951) but was an entirely ecclesiastical project. In 1982, Joseph F. Nagy expressed skepticism about Carney's findings and explored an analogue to Beowulf's combat with water monsters in the myth of Fergus mac Léti only in terms of a common Indo-European heritage.

That analogues are nonetheless always a matter of judgment was confirmed in the same year by R. M. Scowcroft's Cornell dissertation. Scowcroft again reduced the importance of *Grettis saga*: "The lack of comparable analogues earlier than *Grettissaga* in any Germanic area other than Iceland, or at all commensurate to the full Grendel episode, leaves this axis between *Beowulf* and Iceland problematical. We cannot, in any case, reconstruct a Germanic prototype from only two constituent traditions, or a prototype of any kind from only two variants" (1982, 498). Consequently, Scowcroft attaches more importance to "The Hand and the Child" (or "The Hand and the Hall"). But Liberman, who was cognizant of Scowcroft's arguments, once again summarized the Irish hypothesis and noted in passing: "Not a single Irish parallel discussed by *Beowulf* scholars is specific enough to be of real value" (1986, 362).

III. Classical Influences

In the early study of classical prototypes, there was as much emphasis on Homer as on Virgil. Once again a Grimm stands at the beginning. In a one-page note, Jacob Grimm (1856) compared Beowulf 's barrow on a promontory with Patroclus's tomb on the shore of the Hellespont (*Iliad* 23.239–56). But it was not until fifty years later that J. Wright Duff (1905–6) undertook a general comparison of Homer and *Beowulf,* without, however, suggesting any direct connection. No such inhibition characterized the work of Albert S. Cook (1926a), who returned to the topic again and again, no fewer than four times in the year 1926. In his first discussion (1925c, 385–406), his comparison of *Beowulf* to the *Odyssey* was merely an addendum to an argument denying that Cynewulf had any hand in *Beowulf,* but he later argues the Odyssean parallels separately and concludes: "Are we to believe, then, that the author of the *Beowulf* was acquainted with the *Odyssey?* This is a difficult question, but one which it would be scarcely safe to answer in the negative" (1926c, 228). In addition, he finds parallels to the Herakles legend and assumes, on the basis of Tacitus's reference to Ulysses in *Germania* (chapter 3), that the legend may have been passed down to the *Beowulf* poet in oral tradition. He also argues (1926b) that the "x maðelode" formula in *Beowulf* is a borrowing from the equivalent formulas in Homer, compares the "rim" (for shield) and "ash" (for spear) metonymies in Homer and *Beowulf* (1926d), and uses the analogy to Telemachus's voyages and his own view of the departure and arrival points in Beowulf 's voyages to calculate the length of time needed for the passage (1926a). Cook's faith in Greek sources culminated in 1928 when he argued that "heahcyning" in *Beowulf* 1039 derived from the Greek *archibasileus,* which occurs (only once!) in a Persian request for safe-conduct addressed to the Byzantine government ca. 619.

A belief in Homeric influence may seem quite extravagant now, but it was sufficiently prevalent in the 1920s that even the sure-footed Klaeber elected an agnostic formulation in his edition (1950a, cxxi). In 1930, James A. Work gave a paper the straightforward title "Odyssean Influence on the *Beowulf.*" He compared the encounter between Beowulf and Unferth with the encounter between Odysseus and Euryalus in books 7–8 of the *Odyssey,* noting that the common features were an attack on the hero's athletic prowess and a display of good sportsmanship on the part of the loser. As late as 1939, the respected Germanist Ingeborg Schröbler assembled an intrinsically interesting collection of verbal and motival analogies but remained quite uncertain about how to explain them.

At some point, the idea of Homeric influence succumbed to the inherent unlikelihood that Homer was known in Anglo-Saxon England. By 1963, we find John Nist returning to a general, though brief, comparison of *Beowulf* with Homer and Virgil coupled with a stout denial of any direct influence from either. His point is that *Beowulf* shares a lifelike naturalness with Homer that could owe nothing to the Schopenhauerian "dead concept" of Virgil (1963, 260). A few years later, the parallels were perceived only in terms of "comparative literature." Nancy Rose (1967) compared Nestor's sacrifice in book 3 of the *Odyssey* with the Danes' heathen sacrifice in *Beowulf* and argued that the purpose of both sacrifices is to provide characterization through religious posture. Perhaps there is at least some residual illumination of the *Beowulf* poet's sensibilities implicit in the oddity that almost all the comparisons have paired *Beowulf* with the *Odyssey* rather than the *Iliad*.

The question of Virgilian influence on *Beowulf* is more complex and more difficult to resolve. The very act of writing something like a secular epic in the Germanic world seems contingent on Virgil. Yet a really credible case for an imitation of the *Aeneid* has never been made. The initiation of the debate is frequently attributed to Georg Zappert in a paper entitled "Virgil's Fortleben im Mittelalter" (1851), but this is somewhat misleading. Zappert did no more than assemble a variety of motival and situational analogies in the style of nineteenth-century cultural history and in a number of disconnected medieval texts, including *Beowulf* (50–51, 53–61, 63, 65, 68–70). There is no question of tracing links or establishing anything about the nature of *Beowulf*. The debate can more properly be dated from a two-part study by Friedrich Klaeber (1911a).

Klaeber cites the cautious assessment in Brandl's literary history (1908b, 1008) and proposes to strengthen the case for influence significantly. He begins with the commonsense arguments having to do with the decisive status of the *Aeneid* in the development of secular epic. Virgil seems to be the most logical point of departure for any epic venture such as *Beowulf*. Klaeber notes the general motival similarities (in part echoing Zappert) in such matters as battles and voyages, court scenes, gift giving, contests, solemn speeches, genealogies, descriptions of weapons, and burial rites in conjunction with mourning and funerary monuments. He also finds analogies in the value systems and singles out a few verbal echoes. In particular, he emphasizes the apologue pattern ("nachholende Erzählungs-weise"—cf. Alistair Campbell 1971). Following Brandl, he believes that the clearest case of imitation is to be found in the narrative of Beowulf's arrival in Denmark.

In a rather longer continuation, Klaeber adduces a large number of more specific parallels. He finds analogies in characterization between Aeneas and Beowulf (similar sensibilities and a "characteristic touch of melancholy"), Evander and Hrothgar, and Unferth and Drances. Both poems have a decorative streak, a fondness for moral statements, and a certain sentimentality, all illustrated by Klaeber in detail. Finally, he attempts to locate similarities in phraseology and construction, even outright Latinisms, such as a predilection for the passive. It is not far from the truth to say that the exploration of Virgilian echoes began and ended with Klaeber, because not much has been added since 1911.

The most creative collaborator was Alois Brandl, who converted from his initial caution to a far-reaching interpretation of Virgilian influence. In 1928, he arrived, independently of Cook (1926a), at the idea of an influence from the legend of Hercules and compared details of Beowulf 's combats with the Cacus episode in book 8 of the *Aeneid*. Far more radical was the notion, put forward in 1937, that the *Aeneid* and *Beowulf* are analogous epics about the salvation of a people with very similar narrative structures, for example, the dispatching of a hero, swimming episodes (Palinurus!), descriptions of arrivals at court, encounters with monsters (Polyphemus = Grendel), a comic interlude (*Aeneid* 5 and the celebrations at Heorot), a descent into the underworld, and so forth.

Rather less original was Tom Burns Haber (1931). His most interesting chapter ("Non-Germanic Influence in the *Beowulf* ") seeks to distinguish the style of the poem from other Old English or Germanic pieces in order to establish what features require explanation from a differing tradition. Otherwise, his method follows Klaeber's study of 1911a closely, though with expanded details: a chapter on "The Popularity of Vergil in Britain," another on "Broad Similarities," a third on "Parallels in Phraseology," and a final one on "Parallels in Motif and Sentiment." Haber developed the material but without altering the approach or increasing the likelihood of direct influence. Whitbread added a not very compelling source in 1945, and in 1951 Klaeber himself compared *Beowulf* 3116–17 with *Aeneid* 11.431 and 12.284.

It was clear by this time that the compare-and-derive strategy had been exhausted without providing anything like a consensus on Virgilian influence. It was also in the early 1950s that Magoun's paper on oral-formulaic composition (1953) began to raise doubts about whether *Beowulf* was by its very nature a literary epic that was susceptible to classical influence. As a result comparison took a new turn, notably in two papers by Alain Renoir (1966, 1974). Renoir reacted against the preoccupation with literary influence and focused on the distinctive techniques in the *Aeneid* and *Beowulf*. In 1966, he argued for new techniques of comparison appropriate to orally composed poems, and, in 1974, he compared Virgil's description of Avernus with the depiction of Grendel's mere in lines 1357–76, emphasizing the still-life quality of the former and the dynamic, realistic, even cinematographic style of the latter. Richard J. Schrader (1983b) later followed up on Renoir by suggesting that the mere was conceived not as hell itself but rather as "a place meant to suggest the familiar locale of 'devil-worship' as Bede commonly calls pagan rites (e.g., *HE* [*Historia Ecclesiastica*] I,7)" (81).

Others adhered to a belief in literary influence and attempted to find new ways to isolate the Virgilian heritage in *Beowulf*, beyond the compilation of verbal echoes. Alistair Campbell (1971), adverting to Klaeber's suggestion (1911a, 46), argued that the apologue technique (Beowulf 's account of his own past) is so distinctively Virgilian and so infrequent in the epic tradition apart from Virgil that the poet could hardly have hit upon it without reference to Virgil. Andersson (1976) suggested that Virgil's scenic techniques are innovative in relation to Homer, survive only in the close Virgilian imitations of the Carolingian period, and disappear in the reworkings of the *Aeneid* in the twelfth century, never to be revived in epic. When the same techniques can be identified in *Beowulf,* it is therefore probable that they derive from the Virgilian model.

Roberta Frank astutely formulates the intuitions of those scholars who continue to believe in Virgilian influence: "Both the *Aeneid* and *Beowulf* are in some sense historical novels, mythically presented, philosophically committed, and focused on the adventures of a new hero. Both poets project onto the distant past features of the society of their own day, consciously and deliberately, in order to provide a sense of continuity. Virgil's Rome is grounded in an earlier Rome; the *Beowulf* poet anchors the West Saxon *imperium* in a brilliant North Germanic antiquity" (1982a, 64). But the following year John D. Niles (1983, 78–79) offered a telling list of what we might expect to find in *Beowulf* if the poet had truly been influenced by Virgil (cf. Trnka 1981; Andersson 1992). At this point the question is therefore moot.

There have been only very occasional attempts to find classical or late Latin echoes in *Beowulf* apart from the *Aeneid.* Sivert N. Hagen (1904) provided an extravagant etymology in the style of Sophus Bugge, deriving the name *Grendel* from Latin *grandis* with an English nominal suffix and thus equating that monster with the Lernaean Hydra. Albert S. Cook (1902, 1907) offered various parallels to the dreary landscape of the mere in *Beowulf* from three Seneca plays, Silius Italicus, Ovid's *Metamorphoses,* and Virgil's fourth *Georgic* (cf. Cornelius 1927). Since evidence is often by analogy, it should not be forgotten that Rudolf Imelmann (1920, 188–238) also combed the Old English elegies for classical echoes, though with no greater success than inheres in the Virgilian parallels to *Beowulf.* Coolidge O. Chapman (1931) thought to find significant analogies in the welcoming scenes of *Apollonius of Tyre.* A much fuller case was mounted for analogies between Beowulf's funeral pyre and the funeral pyres in Statius's *Thebaid* by Richard J. Schrader (1972), (see also Schrader 1984). More recently, A. G. Rigg (1982) discovered a "mere" analogue in Alexander Neckham's *De Laudibus Divinae Sapientiae* (ca. 1200), including the element missing in Cook's classical analogues—fleeing animals that fear to enter the water. Rigg speculates that there may have been local lore about certain bottomless lakes.

To these stray observations might also be appended the discussion of a possible influence from the description of Attila's funerary rites in Jordanes's *Getica* on the corresponding episode in *Beowulf.* Edward Schröder (1921–22) issued a categorical denial that there was any connection, arguing that the accounts were quite different in detail and that Jordanes's description is in any case Hunnish, not Germanic. Klaeber (1927) provided a more circumspect discussion of the problem but tended on the whole to believe that the similarities are coincidental and that the *Beowulf* poet is independent of Jordanes. That conclusion was supported by Puhvel (1983).

IV. Scriptural and Patristic Echoes

It was probably not until the appearance of Klaeber's edition (1922a) that the recognition of *Beowulf* 's fundamental Christianity struck firm roots. The search for Christian sources therefore began late and has produced a rather thin trickle, probably because the influence is more conceptual than textual. Here I will confine myself to a few textual observations and leave the underlying Christian outlook of the poem to chapter 9, "Christian and Pagan Elements." The very thinness of the yield is illustrated by two notes from the pen of Albert S. Cook. In 1924, he found parallels to the internal rhyme "flod blode weol" (1422) in Aldhelm's *De Virginitate,* which he therefore took to be a terminus a quo. The following year he associated the "mistige moras" of *Beowulf* 162 with the "montes caliginosi" in Jeremiah 13.16.

Samuel J. Crawford (1928b) was a little closer to the mark with a good parallel to "no he þone gifstol / gretan moste" (168–69) from Gregory's *Dialogues* and (1928a) a passage from Job 26.5 to parallel Cain and his attendant water monsters (lines 107–14, 1258–67, 1689–93). A.C. Bouman (1959) argued a model for the bereaved father's lament (lines 2444–62) from Samuel 2:18. On the basis of parallels in *Andreas,* Thomas D. Hill (1966) equated the dragon with the "draco malitiae" and detected the "puer senex" topos in Hrothgar's praise of Beowulf. Robert E. Kaske (1968) provided a useful summary of general interpretations, restated his *sapientia et fortitudo* thesis, and pointed out Christ-like attributes in Beowulf. Specifically, he compared *Beowulf* 942–46 with Luke 11:27 (cf. Klaeber 1922a, 166–67), aligned Beowulf's twelve companions with the twelve apostles (cf. Neckel 1920b, 126), and likened him to Christ trampling lion and dragon. In 1971, Kaske located parallels to Beowulfian giant lore, the pagan sacrifice to demons, and so forth in the Book of Enoch, and this comparison was substantially enlarged by Ruth Mellinkoff (1979). Stephen Morrison (1980) pointed out that the collocation "frofor ond fultum" in *Beowulf* 698a and 1273a echoes an Old English rendering of "adiutor et protector" in several psalms.

In line with Christ's trampling of the beasts, Sylvia H. Horowitz (1978) offered a typological interpretation of the Beowulf figure based, perhaps surprisingly, not on his encounter with the dragon but on his encounter with Grendel. We might expect to find an obvious hunting ground for ecclesiastical parallels in Bede, but aside from Peltola (1972) and Schrader (1983b), already mentioned, only John C. McGalliard (1967) has addressed the topic. He stated from the outset that he had "no reason to suspect an influence in either direction" (103), and his collection of cultural analogies is in fact quite meager. Malcolm Andrew (1981) explained "Grendel in hell" (101b) from the Augustinian idea, elaborated by Gregory the Great and familiar to Bede, that sinners are in hell and hell in them. Vaughan Black and Brian Bethune (1984) traced similarities between Beowulf's adventure in the mere and the liturgical events of Easter week. In the same vein, André Crépin (1987) drew some very general analogies between the structures of *Beowulf* and liturgical rhythms. William Helder (1987) argued that the "song of creation" should be seen in typological relation to *ecclesia*, which in turn finds its secular and literary expression in Heorot. Finally, Alan K. Brown (1980) surveyed the biblical and astronomical lore that might underlie Beowulf's dragon.

The most interesting discussion has focused on the Danes' curious reversion to pagan sacrifice during Grendel's ravages (lines 175–88). A. D. Horgan (1970) tried to square such pagan appearances with Christian doctrine by adducing Saint Paul's idea of natural religion in Romans and equating the Danes with "noble heathens" (independent of Benson 1967). Donald W. Lee (1972) argued the specific influence of Lactantius on the episode, and some such account of idolatry seems quite likely as a background for the passage. Karl P. Wentersdorf (1981) provided a very satisfactory solution of the apparent contradiction between pagan rite and Christian community. He adduced a variety of contemporary ecclesiastical documents tending to show that relapse into heathen practices was common enough even among the contemporaries of the *Beowulf* poet, and he argued very reasonably that the famous crux "metod hie ne cuþon" (180) means only that the Danes ignored God, not that they were ignorant of Him. Andersson (1985), missing Wentersdorf, adduced a parallel from Rimbert's *Life of Ansgar* to illustrate the interactions in a mixed pagan and Christian community. Finally, Roberta B. Bosse and Jennifer L. Wyatt (1987) extracted a paradigm of slow, halting conversion in certain other Old English poems in order to explain Hrothgar's apparent relapse.

V. Old English Sources and Analogues

Logic and convention might seem to dictate that the most immediate sources of a poem should be considered first, English sources in the case of an English poem. In the present survey, they appear last because they have figured only at the periphery of the discussion. This anomaly can be explained by the anomalous position of *Beowulf* in Old English literature. It is the only secular quasi-epic and, as such, has no narrative overlap with the rest of the Old English corpus. On the other hand, there are similarities in phrasing that have been the focus of considerable interest. The most persuasive cases for verbal borrowing have linked *Beowulf* with *Andreas, Exodus,* and *Genesis A*.

The least resolved discussion surrounds *Beowulf* and *Exodus*. Levin L. Schücking (1915, 37–44) upset an older consensus in favor of *Beowulf*'s priority by arguing that the key echo in *Beowulf* lines 1408–10 and *Exodus* lines 56–58 ("enge anpaðas / uncuþ gelad") was a rendering of the biblical "per viam deserti" and must therefore be original in *Exodus*. Klaeber (1918) was inclined to accept that view and concluded that *Daniel, Exodus,* and *Genesis A* were all earlier than *Beowulf*. But shortly thereafter Imelmann (1920, 408–20) responded at length and traced the phrasing to *Aeneid* 11.524–25 ("tenuis quo semita ducit / angustaeque ferunt fauces aditusque maligni"), so that *Beowulf* must be primary and the Virgilian echo in *Exodus* secondary. Klaeber (1926, 202–3) fell in line with that view, but Schücking (1929b, 213–16) quickly restated his view and was supported by Hertha Marquardt (1940). Klaeber (1950a) then reasserted the primacy of *Beowulf*. Edward B. Irving Jr. saw no way out of the impasse and concluded "that there was no direct influence either way, that the parallel passages are essentially coincidental" (1953, 25–26). But the identity of phrasing remains haunting, and in the most recent well-informed and broadly conceived argument Gernot Wieland (1988) maintains that the *Beowulf* poet drew on *Exodus* and equated Beowulf with Moses.

Not much more conclusive is the relation between *Beowulf* and *Andreas*. Albert Cook (1922–24, 270–76) agreed with the then-prevailing view (esp. Fritzsche 1879, 493–95) that the *Andreas* poet was dependent on *Beowulf*. Klaeber concurred in a brief note from 1938–39, arguing that the *Andreas* poet misunderstood the crucial "ealuscerwen" passage in *Beowulf* (769) and must therefore be secondary. Leonard J. Peters (1951) went over the ground in considerable detail and found the correspondences in phrasing to be inconclusive. In his edition of *Andreas*, Kenneth R. Brooks (1961, xviii–xxvi) finds the verbal similarities to be weighty but stops short of considering them decisive. He quotes Dorothy Whitelock to the effect that "one can make a case for the influence of *Beowulf* on *Andreas*, . . . but it stops short of proof" (xxvi). Hans Schabram (1965a) was even more doubtful. He tested two of the ten echoes that Claes Schaar (1956) had still found compelling and judged that they did not document direct borrowing. On the other hand, Arthur G. Brodeur (1968) discounted Peters's skepticism and continued to believe that the *Andreas* poet had *Beowulf* in mind. Most recently, John M. Foley (1990, 223, 230) assumes without argument that the correspondences are formulaic.

The least disputed correspondence connects *Beowulf* with *Genesis A*. In a full and systematic paper from 1910, Klaeber established a large number of similarities. Since many are predicated on the Vulgate Genesis, it seems clear that the priority lies with *Genesis A* and that the *Beowulf* poet is the borrower. In his edition of 1978, A. N. Doane does not review the question but offers no deviation from Klaeber's view (37). If this dependence can be regarded as fairly established, the implications may not have been sufficiently appreciated. The connection suggests something about the *Beowulf* poet's literary culture and monastic models. If, in addition, *Andreas* or *Exodus* (or both) drew on *Beowulf*, that would tell us something about the reception of *Beowulf* in learned and monastic circles.

A learned context does not of course exclude popular models. James R. Hulbert (1951a) once reacted edgily against the literary consensus building up among Klaeber, Chambers, and Lawrence. He was not certain that *Beowulf* should be considered unique, literary, and Virgilian: "It is possible that he [the poet] used as models long heroic poems which had been produced by English poets but . . . improved on them" (1176). That suspicion anticipated the hypothetical oral epics ushered in two years later by Magoun's oral-formulaic theory. Those who credit such a theory believe not so much in a few literary models as in oral models, as many as there were occasions on which they were performed.

Oral epics in Germanic are of course a point of contention, but there were almost certainly short popular forms. P. G. Buchloh (1966) showed very interestingly how the epic *Beowulf* evolved in both form and meaning from the Germanic short forms. Even Benson's acerbic account of the source situation (1970) speculated, on the basis of Breca's appearance in *Widsith*, that there may have been a lost story about Beowulf's youthful swimming contest with Breca. Others have focused more on the poet's generic repertory in addition to the heroic lay. Clover (1980) argued from analogies in Beowulf's encounter with Unferth to flyting forms documented elsewhere in the Germanic world that the poet must have been familiar with the flyting as a literary entity. J. Harris (1982; 1985, 260–72) went further and argued for an understanding of *Beowulf* as a generic compendium. More recently (1992a) he has derived the concluding sequence of *Beowulf* from a hypothetical Germanic "death song" documented chiefly in Eddic poetry.

A small subset of such speculations has probed the connection between *Beowulf* and the Nibelung or Volsung legends. A curiosity is L. W. Smith (1917), written in the latter phases of World War I. The author argues that *Beowulf* and the *Nibelungenlied* embody the differing national characters of England and Germany (much to the detriment of the latter). He notes with concern that at this time American students were more often likely to read the *Nibelungenlied* than *Beowulf*. At the opposite scholarly extreme, Gustav Neckel (1920a) produced a probing reconstruction of Sigemund's dragon slaying, which in turn underlay Beowulf's dragon fight and was of Geatish origin. Sixty years later, Thomas D. Hill (1982) returned to the topic, speculating that the *Beowulf* poet may have known the Volsung legend in approximately the same shape in which it appears in *Vǫlsunga saga*. He surmised that Beowulf's dying claim to be innocent of unrightful oaths and the murder of kin is a reaction against Volsung heroism. In 1983, Annelise Talbot speculated that Beowulf as dragon slayer might be identified with the historical Batavian chieftain Civilis mentioned by Tacitus. A. E. C. Canitz (1986) drew a very general comparison between *Beowulf* and the *Nibelungenlied* in terms of "the gradual decline in importance of personal prowess as a preeminent qualification for successful kingship" (118).

A wholly different line of comparison has been the sporadic attempt to anchor *Beowulf* in English history, as a kind of historical allegory. Brandl (1936) equated the plot with events in Mercian history, matched Heremod with King Penda, Scyld with King Wulfhere, and Wiglaf with King Wiglaf. George Bond (1943) produced similarities in names and events connecting *Beowulf* with the reigns of Beornwulf (823–826) and Wiglaf (828–838) in Mercia. Francis P. Magoun Jr. (1954) abstracted the content of a historical Hygelac lay that may have entered East Anglia from Sweden. Finally, Zacharias P. Thundy (1986) found echoes of events in the time of King Athelstan and dated the composition of *Beowulf* between 927 and 931.

On the basis of these analyses and speculations—textual, oral, and historical—it is difficult to assert that the English context of *Beowulf* is any less nebulous than the Scandinavian, Irish, classical, or Christian backgrounds.

I. Future Directions

Earl R. Anderson's Armenian analogues (1981) suggest that the comparative material is far from exhausted, but the future focus is more likely to narrow than to broaden. The only analogue that has commanded a fair consensus is *Grettis saga*. At the same time, attempts to find a folktale context have shifted away from the international "Bear's Son Tale" and toward the specifically Scandinavian two-troll ecotype. The result is to reemphasize the Scandinavian character of the underlying tale. That should come as no surprise considering how deeply *Beowulf* is embedded in Scandinavian matter in every respect. With the folktale matrix somewhat clearer, future scholars may wish to reformulate the literary question. If the Grendel tale per se and the historical frame of reference are Scandinavian, can the literary form of *Beowulf* as a whole be connected with some Scandinavian prototype? The verse form and the quasi-epic dimensions are definitely not Scandinavian, but the tragically tinged heroic biography, which is quite distinct from the dramatic conflicts of Germanic heroic poetry, has occasionally been compared to the Norse *fornaldarsaga*. Felix Genzmer (1950, 24–25) defined the tale in *Beowulf* as a "Kämpensaga," by which he meant something very much like a *fornaldarsaga,* and G. V. Smithers (1961, 13) was even more specific. He noted that the *fornaldarsǫgur* "may contain material of considerable though unspecifiable antiquity" and that it may not be "outrageous to use them to elucidate an OE poem at least five hundred years older." More recently, Thomas Klein (1988) included references to *Beowulf* in his distinction between "classical" heroic poetry and the style of legendary heroism that supersedes the heroic lay, for example, in the *fornaldarsaga.*

Such a comparison has made no headway for at least two good reasons. The *fornaldarsaga* is the latest and least admired saga genre, most remote in both time and literary interest from *Beowulf.* Furthermore, the closest analogue, *Grettis saga,* is classed as a family saga, not a *fornaldarsaga.* But both of these objections may be more apparent than real. The Icelandic scholar Bjarni Guðnason (1963, 267) has distinguished between the late fantastic *fornaldarsǫgur* and earlier *forneskjusǫgur* with a historical ambience and ambition. The prime example of the *forneskjusaga* is *Skjǫldunga saga,* which Guðnason dated around 1180, but which may be dated more conservatively around 1200. It antedates most of the "classical" kings' sagas and possibly all of the family sagas. The object of *Skjǫldunga saga* was to resurrect the Danish legendary history of the Skjoldung dynasty. It therefore exhibits the same combination of heroic adventure and quasi history that we find in *Beowulf.*

As for *Grettis saga,* though it is classified as a family saga, it is notoriously the family saga that most closely verges on the *fornaldarsaga,* and those episodes that are regularly compared to *Beowulf* are the ones that most resemble the motival stock of the *fornaldarsaga.* We do not of course know how long the quasi-historical heroic adventure story existed in Scandinavia before it was transformed into what we now know as the *fornaldarsaga,* but it appears to be as old as our oldest Scandinavian sources. One of the breakthroughs in the study of Germanic heroic poetry was the recognition that the "classical" heroic lay probably did not exist in a pure, isolated form but must have been embedded in saga-like adventure tales. Thus, the heroic lay *Bjarkamál,* recast in Latin by Saxo Grammaticus, must have emerged from some quasi-historical lore about the Skjoldung dynasty, lore of the sort that eventually evolved into *Hrólfs saga kraka.* Although *Hrólfs saga kraka* is not much use as a historical analogue, it may still serve as a generic analogue.

There must have been heroic adventure tales about the Skjoldungs going back to the sixth century, and it is this narrative matrix that explains the emergence of *Bjarkamál,* Saxo's tales, *Hrólfs saga kraka,* and *Beowulf* as well. The heroic life was the narrative vehicle for all these writers, but it was a heroic life in the sort of quasi-historical setting that we find in both Saxo and *Skjǫldunga saga.* It appears to be a peculiarly Scandinavian form, and the form may well have been brought to England with the narrative itself. With respect to the folktale and historical layers, it probably makes little sense to speculate on which was older since monster tales and legendary kings and heroes may have been inextricably meshed in the anterior narrative tradition.

When the Scandinavian adventure tales underlying *Beowulf* came to England is uncertain, but it could not have been as late as the tenth century because Alcuin notoriously knew about Ingeld at the end of the eighth century. The heroic lore of Scandinavia was therefore available from the eighth century on and could have been developed in epic form at any time. One attractive hypothesis that takes Sutton Hoo into account is a port of entry in East Anglia. The idea was clearly stated by Nora K. Chadwick (1959, 203), who suggested that "the poet is composing a Scandinavian theme for a Scandinavian dynasty in a milieu in which both had become thoroughly English. Perhaps it was the East Anglian royal family, the Wuffingas, who introduced the original story relating to their ancestors in Gautland, and naturalized it among their own subjects in East Anglia."

Joseph Harris (1985, 265–66) was attracted to the same hypothesis. In an archaeological survey, Martin Carver speculated interestingly on the strained position of East Anglia between the Roman Christian missions from the west and traditional affiliations with the Scandinavian countries to the east: "East Anglian royalty thus vacillated between these positions, at one time building an exaggerated pagan monument at Sutton Hoo as a sign of ideological defiance and solidarity with the North. Indeed, it may be that East Anglia never fully abandoned its sympathy with Scandinavian lands" (1989, 158). That *Beowulf* may also belong in this cultural context has now been very fully developed in book form by Sam Newton (1993). Whether the hypothesis stands to gain or lose ground in the ongoing debate remains to be seen, but it accords well with the evidence from the Scandinavian sources and analogues.

Chapter 8

Structure and Unity

by Thomas A. Shippey

Summary: In the early years of *Beowulf* scholarship, the poem was seen as so structurally flawed that it must be a product of multiple authorship. Once the poem's unity was conceded, various theories were developed to account for its sudden changes of time and its many episodes or digressions. It was seen as bipartite, tripartite, arithmetically structured, or deeply affected by folktale; the dominant theory in recent years has, however, been that of interlace, though this approach is still not fully accepted.

Chronology

1815: N. F. S. Grundtvig (1815a) declares that the poem is a beautiful and tasteful whole.

1817: On closer inspection, Grundtvig decides that the poem is a spiritual whole but not properly arranged.

1820: Grundtvig criticizes the poem for lack of both external and internal unity and for the use of episodes.

1826: John Josias Conybeare censures the poem for use of digressions and for continuing too long.

1836: John M. Kemble introduces the idea, further repeated in Kemble (1837b), that the poem consists of layers of different date and origin.

1840: Kemble finds further corroboration for his preexisting myth theory in a Wiltshire charter.

1840: Ludwig Ettmüller argues that the poem is an inartistic patchwork and distinguishes original from interpolated lines in his German translation.

1849: Karl Müllenhoff (1849a) attempts to identify the original myth at the heart of the poem.

1862: C. W. M. Grein insists that the poem is the work of a single, skilful poet.

1869: Müllenhoff creates a complex theory of multiple authorship, distinguishing four authors, an author/interpolator A, and a final interpolator B.

1870: Artur Köhler (1870a and b) distinguishes art poet from folk poem in the episodes of Scyld and Heremod.

1877: Hermann Dederich asserts that single authorship is unthinkable.

1877: Bernhard ten Brink sees the poem's lack of national spirit as a result of its diversified origins.

1883: Hermann Möller goes beyond Müllenhoff by declaring that the poem was originally written in four-line strophes and attempts to recover this structure.

1883: Frederik Rönning analyzes and rejects the arguments for composite authorship; his work is reviewed by Heinzel (1884) and supported by Fahlbeck (1884).

1884–85: John Earle insists that the poem possesses "absolute unity" and was created with a single didactic purpose, expanding his views in 1892.

1888: ten Brink sees the poem as composed of different sections but argues that each of them is itself a conflation of different versions.

1891: M. Jellinek and Carl Kraus follow Rönning and Heinzel in explaining apparent contradictions.

1897: W. P. Ker declares that in spite of faults in structure the poem deserves to be appreciated as it stands.

1904: Ker calls the poem structurally weak, even preposterous.

1905: James Routh sees episodes and parentheses as part of poetic style.

1905: Levin L. Schücking argues that 1888–2199 are a connecting link between two originally separate poems.

1908: Alois Brandl (1908a) insists that if *Beowulf* is stylistically and structurally mixed, it is nevertheless the work of a single poet.

1909: W. W. Lawrence rejects belief in a preexisting myth underlying the poem.

1910: H. Bradley contrasts the poem's lucid core with its general impression of chaos.

1912: Richard Boer divides the poem into at least eleven stages of development.

1912: Ker criticizes the poem for want of proportion and feebleness of plan.

1912: Lawrence explains discrepancies in the poem as the result of a single author handling varied material.

1915–16: Bradley considers the poem's numbered sections as a clue to its origin.

1916: Enrico Pizzo sees the poem as aesthetically unified by its interest in monsters.

1921: R. W. Chambers defends the poem's unity against Schücking but still finds parts of it inapposite.

1922: While accepting the poem's unity, Friederich Klaeber denies that it achieves any superior unity of structure.

1925: Chambers sees the poem as possessing a folktale plot, with epic relegated to its digressions.

1928: Defending the poem as a work of art, Lawrence explains its digressions as deliberate ironic juxtaposition.

1935: Walter Berendsohn notes the demise of *Liedertheorie* while arguing for the poem's stylistic inconsistency.

1936: J. R. R. Tolkien insists on respect for the poem as it stands and puts forward a theory of structural unity in balance.

1949: Adrien Bonjour defends the unusual narrative mode of the Grendel's mother story as artistic and deliberate.

1950: Bonjour extends the method of Bonjour (1949) to many sections of the poem.

1952: T. M. Gang severely criticizes Tolkien's idea of balance, answered by Bonjour (1953).

1953: Arthur G. Brodeur points out the critical and pivotal role of Hygelac, expanding his views in 1959.

1955: H. L. Rogers sees a consistent pattern of decline in the poem, which is, however, not perfectly executed.

1955: Jan van Meurs criticizes Tolkien for too readily accepting the poem's perfect structural unity.

1958: Francis P. Magoun Jr. argues that 2009b–2176 are the relic of a separate poem. He extends his view in 1963, is supported by Creed (1966b), answered by Brodeur (1970).

1958: John Nist introduces the idea of pointillist narration.

1961: George V. Smithers argues that the poem's unity is inherited, rather than the result of individual art.

1965: John Leyerle sees the poem as presenting individual failure through contrasted roles and introduces the idea of interlace structure.

1965: Kenneth Sisam argues that the poem is not structurally unified but may have been a serial in three instalments.

1966: P. G. Buchloh sees the poem as structurally similar to Norse heroic lays, but amplified in epic style.

1967: Leyerle develops further the idea of interlace structure and rejects the use of such terms as *digression*.

1967: Eamonn Carrigan argues for a complex diagrammatic structure based on the poem's numbered sections.

1968: Edward B. Irving Jr. sees the poem's unity as emotional rather than structural.

1969: Sherman Kuhn shows that references to the hero's life are scattered but internally consistent.

1969: T. A. Shippey applies Propp's folktale theories to the poem.

1970: Using a method similar to Shippey (1969), Daniel R. Barnes reaches more extensive but similar results.

1971: Lawrence Fast follows Brodeur in seeing Hygelac as a focal point in the poem.

1972: Gwyn Jones continues to see the poem as structurally flawed.

1974: David Howlett produces a complex diagram similar to Carrigan (1967).

1975: Constance B. Hieatt indicates envelope patterns in the poem, not always related to numbered sections.

1975: Kathryn Hume sees the poem as possessing both bipartite and tripartite structures.

1976: David M. Wells expresses skepticism about the relevance of section openings to the poem's structure.

1977: H. Ward Tonsfeldt notes chiastic structures in the poem and sees in its technique a combination of repetition and stasis.

1978: Whitney F. Bolton compares the poem's forty-three sections to those of the Alfredian Boethius.

1978: Martin Stevens assumes the poem's unity but sees its progress as entropic.

1978: Brian Shaw sees two paired sets of speeches surrounding a pivotal speech in 1384–96.

1980: Eric G. Stanley remarks on the poet's detailed narrative skills.

1980: Theordore M. Andersson sees in the poem an oscillating pattern on both small and large scales, with emotional as well as narrative intentions.

1980: Jane Chance (Nitzsche) foregrounds the Grendel's mother episode as of pivotal structural importance.

1981: Thomas Hart finds symmetries in the poem surrounding the use of numerals.

1981: On codicological grounds, Kevin Kiernan (1981a) revives Schücking's 1905 suggestion that the poem consists of two once distinct works, connected by a collaborative link.

1981: Leonard Boyle replies to aspects of Kiernan's (1981a) thesis.

1982: Joseph Harris suggests that the poem is a compendium of literary genres.

1983: John D. Niles draws on recent research on oral poetry to explain previously controversial aspects of the poem.

1984: Bernard Huppé sees a clear, mathematically ordered structure in the poem.

1985: Janet Bately demonstrates, in reaction to Kiernan (1981a), that the poem is grammatically unique and consistent in all parts.

1985: Fred C. Robinson views microstructure and macrostructure alike as built on apposed segments.

1986: Morton W. Bloomfield insists that verbal art cannot be properly compared to the visual technique of interlace.

1988: Ward Parks shows how ring structures can integrate digressions with main narrative.

1989: Edward B. Irving Jr. indicates incremental circling on both small and large scales.

1990: Gillian Overing praises elements of irresolution and interplay within the poem's structure.

1991: Allen J. Frantzen condemns attempts to make the poem speak with a single voice, seeing these as editorial and critical constructs.

1991: James Earl proposes a psychological shift as part of the poem's movement.

1992: Paul Sorrell notes oral features within the poem, such as the dominance of local effect over narrative unity.

The issue of the overall structure of *Beowulf* did not seem of special importance to early commentators on the poem. This indifference was partly the result of mistaken ideas of what a heroic or epic poem ought to be (a macro-problem), partly by inability at first to understand the vocabulary, grammar and even nomenclature of the poem (a series of microproblems). Thus, a question that has concerned many later commentators is why the poem should begin, as it ends, with a funeral, and the funeral of a character no more than distantly related to any of the major figures of the poem. This was, however, not a problem to the poem's first editor, Grímur Jónsson Thorkelin (1815a), because he failed to realize that the "Scyld Prologue" describes a funeral. He thought it was about the start of a raid or campaign, partly (one imagines) because that would coincide better with the start of the *Iliad* or *Aeneid,* but partly also because in line 26 he failed to recognize the name *Scyld.* When N. F. S. Grundtvig insisted in a review (1815a) that the poem *did* begin with a death and a burial, Thorkelin (1816) refused to admit his error. None of the other six reviewers of the first edition had the knowledge or confidence to correct Thorkelin's text and Latin translation, which were especially misleading with regard to the poem's many flashbacks or asides. One may say in brief that the whole question of the allusive or episodic nature of the poem was passed over by most early commentators through failure to recognize or to accept it.

The exception to that statement is the work of the Dane Nikolai Grundtvig, "easily the most important link between early criticism of *Beowulf* and modern literary debate," as Andreas Haarder (1975, 88) has said.[1] Grundtvig wrote on the poem for almost fifty years, and his views changed several times. Thus in 1815, in the review mentioned above, he praised the poem as "a beautiful, tastefully arranged and ornamented whole." This seems, however, to have been a first enthusiastic response. Two years later, in a longer piece, Grundtvig's praise was more qualified and more directed. He wrote, "The poem is a spiritual whole, only not rightly arranged artistically." With characteristic confidence, Grundtvig suggested both what the poet intended and how he could have better achieved his intention. Since his aim was "to present the life and achievement of three great heroic families, the Scildings, the Scilfings and the Waegmundings, so that the Waegmundings were in the centre as the warrior tribe proper," it would have been better not to have forgotten the Scildings entirely once the scene of the poem changed but to have "made their lamentations sound together with Wiglaf's over the dead body of Beowulf." Grundtvig would also have relocated the references to the Scilfings in ways less "intricate and abrupt." Three further years later, in his Danish translation of the poem (1820), Grundtvig went on from these criticisms to say that he could rate the poem no higher than "a work of art, half-miscarried," for three reasons: its blending of folktale and history, which forfeits "internal unity"; its "lack of external unity," in the joining of the Grendel and dragon fights only through the hero; and its use of episodes, some of which Grundtvig defended in surprisingly modern terms, while dismissing others as clumsy or indefensible. Grundtvig's overall opinion, as expressed in the pieces cited already and in his long review of scholarship in 1841, may be summed up in the phrase he used in 1817: "The eye saw rightly, but the hand made mistakes." He deeply admired the poem and understood its structure far better than any other early commentator; however, like many later commentators, it seems that he would have preferred a different poem, more tightly-constructed and probably much shorter.

It was Grundtvig's fate, writing in Danish, to receive less attention and less credit than was his due. Nevertheless, his unease about the poem's structure, and still more its unity, was soon felt independently elsewhere. In a posthumously published work of 1826, J. J. Conybeare remarked that the poem would have shown "unity of plan" if it had stopped at line 2207 (65) and complained that the Messenger's speech (2900–3027) "like most other episodes of the same nature . . . is extremely obscure" (76). Conybeare summed up his view of the poem by saying, "If we except perhaps the frequency and length of the digressions, the only considerable offence against the received canons of the heroic muse is to be found in the extraordinary interval of time which elapses between the first and last exploits of the hero" (81). Since Conybeare was, for instance, still under the impression that the Finnsburg Episode related "a successful expedition of Halfdane against the Frisians, a Finnish tribe" (50), his criticisms were not always well-grounded. More ominous for the future was his assertion that the poem is above all "an antiquarian document," valuable for what it reveals rather than what it is (81). Such beliefs received strong implicit support from Wilhelm Grimm (1829) and from Mone (1836), who further censured the poem's abrupt *Sprünge*, or leaps, and lack of "epic calm and constancy." One might say that almost as soon as the allusive nature of the poem was recognized, scholarly interest began to switch to the material in the allusions, as opposed to their function. No serious attempt was made to "see the poem whole" for many years, other than by Grundtvig.

This trend was accelerated by the genuine discoveries of John Mitchell Kemble, the poem's first great English editor. Kemble brought out his first edition in 1833 and in the preface discussed the poem entirely as history. On 17 July, 1834, however, Kemble wrote to his hero Jacob Grimm in great excitement recording his discovery of two manuscripts giving a version of the story of "Scyld Sceafing" and linking similar names with one "Boerinus" (see Wiley 1981, 61–64). From these and other accounts, Kemble drew far-reaching conclusions about the poem's deepest structure. He insisted that the various name forms of late genealogies derived from an original "Beo," to be identified with the poem's Beowulf son of Scyld, and that the poem's hero, Beowulf son of Ecgtheow, was a further reflection of this originally divine figure. Kemble put forward these views in a pamphlet of 1836, written in German, and in a postscript to the preface of his 1837 translation of the poem explicitly retracted his conclusions of 1833. The poem contained historical figures but was fundamentally mythical, resting on stories about a god, Beow, as well as a hero, Beowulf. Kemble in short gave a strong lead to the idea that the poem as we have it consists of strata from different periods, mythical at bottom, historical on the surface, and that the duty of scholarship was to "archae-ologize" the strata. The view was strengthened by Kemble's further discovery of a charter of 931 that seemed to associate the names "Beowa" and "Grendel" independently of the poem (see Kemble 1840).

Kemble's view was readily seized on in Germany. Jacob Grimm accepted it in his *Deutsche Mythologie* of 1835, as did Heinrich Leo in his commentary of 1839. In 1840, Ludwig Ettmüller found in the opening myth of Scyld, so loosely connected to the main story, decisive proof that "the *Beowulf* poem was not organically constructed by one poet but was put together from separate folk poems."[2] In his view, one should also "grant to the uniter of the separate poems no great artistic skill," for he makes no attempt in his opening lines to use the Scyld myth to present the relationship between Geats and Danes. Ettmüller thus, in the introduction to his German translation of the poem, established what was to be the dominant mode of structural criticism for several generations: *Liedertheorie,* the theory that the poem of *Beowulf* was not an intrinsic unity but a composite of different "lays" or *Lieder,* whose junction points could still be seen. In the pages of the translation itself, Ettmüller distinguished original from interpolated lines by indenting the latter. In extreme forms of this theory, any unity the poem possessed was adventitious, while only its structural failings were of interest, as guides to its complex history.

*Liedertheorie*soon came to be associated with the dominating figure of Karl Müllenhoff. In two effectively consecutive articles (Müllenhoff 1849a, 1849b), he established a view of the poem as mythic allegory that was to dominate the field for many years. But the structural corollary of this view was that anything which did not support the allegory was dismissed as later accretion. In an article of 1869, Müllenhoff set himself to decide the question of the poem's structure once and for all. His findings were, he said, "simple enough." The poem consisted of an introduction plus four parts numbered 1 to 4. What had happened was that there had been originally two *alte Lieder* or "old lays," by different authors, one on Grendel (preserved in part 1, 194–836) and one on the fight with the dragon (embedded in part 4, 2200–3183). To the Grendel lay had been added, by different authors again, first a sequel (the fight with Grendel's mother, part 2, 837–1628), and then the introduction (1–193). Yet a fifth author had then added on part 3, "Beowulf's homecoming" (1629–2199). This fifth author, however, whom Müllenhoff described as "A," not only had added his section but also had gone through all the sections available to him (everything up to 2199), interpolating passages of his own into the work of three preceding authors. Finally, a sixth author, Müllenhoff's "B," had taken the work of A, added to it the old lay of the dragon, and once more worked through all his predecessors, interpolating heavily, especially with theologizing additions and pieces from other "legend-cycles."

The bulk of Müllenhoff's 1869 article consists of a section-by-section commentary on *Beowulf,* in which he indicates lines of division and detects and rejects the interpolations of A and B. His criteria are never explicitly stated, but he relies heavily on a very close literalist reading. Müllenhoff notes (to give only one specimen of his method) that Wealhtheow is introduced at line 612 and sits down at line 641. Her departure is never indicated, but she seems to be absent by 664. At 1175–76 Wealhtheow speaks as if she had not been present to hear Hrothgar's words of 946–48, whereas line 923 shows that she had. After 1232, she is once more "sunk without trace." All this, in Müllenhoff's view, is the result of incompetent patching by A. In the end, Müllenhoff rejected all but 1,788 lines of the poem as interpolations and reduced his two "old lays" to 643 lines (Grendel) and 984 lines (the dragon). Müllenhoff repeatedly uses such phrases as "without doubt," "undoubtedly," and "with complete safety"; he gives exact line references and line counts for all his six authors, interpolators included; the work of B especially is written off again and again as "bad," "heartily bad," "unbelievably badly expressed" (902b–05). Against this crushing display a few voices were raised in protest, but for the most part Müllenhoff's "archaeologizing" method and his deep belief that the poem was not structurally unified were accepted as securely established.

Conviction on this point was often expressed in remarks strongly disparaging of the poem. "As we have the poem now, it is like a ruin," wrote a Danish translator, Adolf Hansen, in 1901 (see Haarder 1975, 89). W. A. Berendsohn, writing from the Western Front in 1915, declared angrily that it was inconceivable to take *Beowulf* as a poetic high point or as a unity: it was a *Stilwirrwarr,* "a stylistic mish-mash," in which some hostile ecclesiastic had too often covered over the true *Volks-dichtung* or "folk poetry" with tedious *Geschwätz* or "chatter." Other authors at least framed more interesting questions, their attention often falling on the poem's tendency to have incidents told and then retold. Did these double versions of the same thing, critics wondered, not show internal contradictions or *Widersprechungen* of the kind one might expect if two different poets had tried to tell the same story? The year after Müllenhoff's "Inner History" article of 1869, Artur Köhler wrote two once more effectively consecutive pieces on "The Introduction of the *Beowulf*-poem" (1870b) and "The Two Heremod-Episodes" (1870a). In the former, Köhler insisted, counter to Müllenhoff, that the poem had been finally shaped by "a single poetically-gifted poet" and had been "worked together," *zusammengearbeitet,* rather than just "put together," *zusammengestellt,* the word Ettmüller had used. Nevertheless, he had no doubt that the final "art poet" was working from preexisting *Lieder,* and he was happy to distinguish art poetry from earlier folk poetry. In lines 1–52, for instance, Köhler gives the art poet twelve lines in three sections, the other forty coming from the older "lay of Scyld." In the same way lines 901–15 are "popular" in tone as lines 1709b–22a are not, but both betray the influence of a previous Heremod poem inexpertly reworked by the poem's final creator. At one point Köhler declares that "anyone who finds everything smooth and orderly there is blind to the natural history of poetry."

Several similar arguments could be cited, with an authoritative summary given by Richard Wülker in 1885: the poem definitely consists of old *Lieder,* the dragon fight was definitely originally separate and Grendel's mother probably so, the poem as we have it was *umgedichtet* or "recomposed" ca. 650, but (tolerantly) one should not blame the final poet for all discrepancies. Two major variations on Müllen-hoff's thesis were meanwhile made by Bernhard ten Brink and Hermann Möller. In 1877, ten Brink put forward the Kemble-derived theory that a historical Beowulf had become prominent in the sixth century and then been confused with an earlier hero of myth, the separate origins showing themselves in nationalistic confusions: the poem was accordingly "not a national poem and not an epic in the strict sense." Eleven years later (ten Brink 1888), he produced a much more detailed work in which he argued that the poem contained four "adventures" (much the same as Müllenhoff's four parts) but that three of these at least, namely the three major fights, had at one time existed in two versions, while the Breca episode had also been a major element in the early Beowa myth. Ten Brink's detailed analyses reveal that he saw the poem as a kind of complex "interleaving"—though this would now be taken as a feature of the "appositive style" (see the discussion of Robinson 1985 below) rather than as proof of composite authorship. Hermann Möller's thesis of 1883 was even more extreme: he deduced that the original *Beowulf* had been written, not in its present continuous verse form, but in four-line strophes like the *Nibelungenlied.* Müllenhoff had taken only what was impossible out of *Beowulf,* said Möller; he would take out the improbable as well, and what was left would be the true kernel. Möller held to Müllenhoff's overall thesis, finding the "mythic core" more strophic than the later historical "episodes," and ascribed the abandonment of the strophic form to Müllenhoff's much-blamed "Interpolator B," the Christianizing ecclesiastic who in most views of the time had "put together" or "worked together" or "recomposed" the poem.

For a "lowest common denominator" summary of *Liedertheorie* views on the unity of *Beowulf*—its structure still hardly an issue—one might, however, turn to the unlucky figure of Hermann Dederich. In 1877, he produced a volume of studies on the poem in which he disarmingly stressed his youth and professed his admiration for Müllenhoff and his longing for "the real tasty smell of German folk poetry." He summed up the results of scholarship by declaring, with a sarcastic air now difficult to translate: "That in *Beowulf* we do not have before us a unified and artistic product, [the work] of a poet who has with creative power taken the popularly-transmitted material into himself, made it fully the possession of his own independent creative poetic spirit, poured it into its external mold of meaning, and shaped it into an epic—of this, after the shrewd investigations of modern scholars, there can now be no further doubt" (Dederich 1877, 6). Müllenhoff characteristically responded to this touching discipleship with a long, scathing review in which he advised Dederich never to write on this subject again. Nevertheless, Dederich had well expressed the consensus of his time.[3]

There had during this period been some signs of resistance to *Liedertheorie.* In 1862, Christian Grein wrote on the poem's "historical relationships," but defied the dissectors by observing that however scattered the references to history were, they nevertheless remained consistent; the episodic mode of the poem did not make its matter incoherent:

> now a singer sings in the drinking hall of the deeds of the fathers; now events that occurred only after the actual scenes of the poem are prophesied as likely; now it is a treasure or a weapon, of which it is told in what circumstances an earlier owner bore it; now an earlier event is slotted in by mention of a person or a deed which stands in relation to it; now finally reference is made to someone of evil memory, to make the famous deeds or splendid qualities of another stand out more brilliantly by contrast. If we try, however, to put together the scattered announcements and order them chronologically, we receive a consistent historical picture stretching over a fairly considerable period. (Grein 1862, 261)

Grein goes on to defend the much-criticized prologue as sensible and original and to declare it "a real component of the poem, which I can really only consider, as it lies before us, as the consistent work of a single poet." Grein continued to accept that the poem contained both a historical and a mythical Beow(ulf). Yet even the suggestion of a single poetic vision was enough—Grein believed—to produce another bitter review from Müllenhoff for his later editions and concordance. Grein died without ever receiving a university teaching appointment.

Other assertions of the poem's unity were made by Ludvig Schrøder (1875) and Johannes Hornburg (1877), but both were made outside a university context, while the former work was strongly marked by Grundtvig's Danish (and anti-German) nationalism. Frederik Rönning's *Beovulfs-kvadet* of 1883, however, engaged more deeply with Müllenhoff and was taken more seriously by German academics. Rönning examined the innumerable "contradictions" discovered by this time by scholars and reduced them to three, the first being, for instance, the query (by no means inexplicable in itself) as to whether Beowulf beheaded Grendel or Grendel's mother (compare 1590 and 2138). Rönning allowed this and the other two to stand but pointed out that similar slight errors might be found in works of undoubted single authorship from *Paradise Lost* to Scott's *The Antiquary.* Rönning noted also that while the poem's style did seem to change, there was no decisive turning point, nor would the poem's two main sections make easy sense independently. Rönning's view was supported in Sweden by Fahlbeck (1884). An unsympathetic review could be expected from the Müllenhoff-dominated journal *Anzeiger für deutsches Altertum,* and duly appeared from Richard Heinzel (1884). However, Heinzel's own interest in style made him in several ways skeptical of *Liedertheorie*; his review of Rönning was picked up a few years later by two followers of his, M. H. Jellinek and Carl von Kraus (1891). They accepted a number of apparent contradictions in the poem but agreed with Rönning that these did not necessarily prove multiple authorship, being rather "stylistic peculiarities" of the poet or of Old English poetry. This greater receptivity to questions of style was ultimately to affect views of unity and structure, as can be seen also from Routh (1905), the second of whose *Two Studies on the Ballad-Theory* (i.e., *Liedertheorie*) explained "Irrelevant Episodes and Parentheses as Features of Anglo-Saxon Poetic Style," drawing parallels with many other undissected poems, including *Exodus, Andreas,* and *Genesis B.*

The only other noteworthy assertion of the poem's unity during the nineteenth century came from an unexpected quarter: England, where since Kemble there had been no Beowulfian scholar other than the Scandinavian-oriented Thorpe and the chronically indecisive Thomas Arnold. In 1884 and 1885, however, there appeared in *The Times* three anonymous articles whose substance was later brought together in the long introduction to John Earle's 1892 translation, *The Deeds of Beowulf.* In his piece of 25 August 1884, Earle followed Grein in asserting "the absolute unity of the poem . . . a unity arising from the design of a single poet using for his purpose what materials he found available." On 30 September 1885, Earle repeated that the poem "showed the strong and delicate touch of a master working with a purpose, and what that purpose was is the problem of the 'Beowulf.'" On 29 October 1885, he declared that it was the reference to Offa (1949–62) that "contains the secret. The praise of Offa gives a centre." Earle's explication of this "secret" is discussed in chapter 2 in this volume, but he should be given credit for bravely giving part 3, section 6 of his 1892 introduction the then-provocative title "The Unity of the Poem." Earle further identified the poem's "centerpiece" as Hrothgar's speech of 1700–84, and its theme as "Mutual dependence is the law of human society." Many critics have followed Earle in giving the poem a moral purpose and a social perspective. Nevertheless, there is a certain irony in locating the key to the meaning of a unified poem in exactly that passage—the account of Hygd, Thryth, and Offa (1925–62)—that still seems the least well integrated part of it. German reviewers treated Earle with tolerant contempt as a dilettante.

Beowulf scholarship in England achieved no respect abroad until the time of W. P. Ker, and he was little readier than his predecessors to "see the poem whole." Ker wrote three times on *Beowulf,* in 1897, 1904 and 1912. Over this fifteen-year period, Ker's opinion of the poem seemed to go down, while his ability to find the trenchant phrase went up. Thus, in 1897, one finds Ker conceding to the poem "at least an apparent and external unity" and declaring that it "deserves to be appreciated as it stands." Nevertheless, its "faults of structure" would have been apparent to Aristotle: an epic poem should not be held together just by its events happening to the same person. Furthermore, given that "the essential part of the poem is the drama of characters," and given that these characters are often not part of the main story, we have a "constitutional weakness": the poem puts its weight on the wrong place, the "old wives' tales" of monsters and dragons rather than the heroic stories of Finn or Heremod, Ingeld or Ongentheow. By 1904, while still insisting that the poem was "the work of educated men," exuding an "air of libraries and learning," Ker went so far as to say that in *Beowulf* there is "nothing much in the story," that it is structurally "curiously weak, in a sense preposterous," with "its irrelevancies in the centre." By 1912, the poem was "over-valued . . . not a particularly interesting story . . . The story is commonplace and the plan is feeble." Ker continued to insist that the poem had great merits but seemed at the same time to be *disappointed* by it. Where Müllenhoff wanted to strip the historical accretions away from the "mythic core," Ker conversely wanted a main plot based on the episodes, not the monsters. The two critics took entirely different views of the poem's origins and unity, but both agreed that the final compiler/composer had done the wrong thing.

Determined rebuttal of Ker was to come from Tolkien in 1936. However, major change in the climate of opinion was to come first from Alois Brandl and then from an international triumvirate of scholars, Friedrich Klaeber, W. W. Lawrence, and R. W. Chambers. Before considering this change, though, it might be as well to consider what it was that led to the eventual abandonment of *Liedertheorie,* the dominant view for some fifty years. One reason might be that its practitioners seemed able to go only in the direction of ever greater complexity: from Müllenhoff to ten Brink to Möller and then on to R. C. Boer, whose *Altenglische Dichtung* of 1912 ascribes the poem, in a diagram (126), to at least eleven different poems/poets/compilers, and follows up (127–31) by assigning every single line of the poem to one or the other. Just as significant was the "outflanking" of the subject by discoveries in other fields that challenged its basic assumptions. Walter Berendsohn, in a sense the *letzter Ritter* of *Liedertheorie,* shrewdly pointed in 1935 to the effects of Heusler (1905), which sharply distinguished *Lied* from *Epos* and made it more than ever unlikely that an epic could be formed by assembling four, eleven, or any number of *Lieder,* and to Klaeber's demonstration (1911b, 1912) that the poem's "Christian elements" were too widely spread and deeply rooted to be simply discarded. Berendsohn thought, however, that Sievers's metrical studies had perhaps delivered the heaviest blow, for "Five-Type" analysis showed no serious metrical variation within the poem at all.[4] His own views are discussed briefly below, but it is clear that, for all his own preferences and his dogged refusal to accept any stylistic consistency in the poem, Berendsohn nevertheless could by 1935 view *Liedertheorie* only elegiacally.

Brandl's (1908a) account of *Beowulf* was meanwhile to be remembered more than forty years later by an American scholar, J. R. Hulbert (1951a), as a personal liberation, perhaps because of its appearance in the authoritative pages of Hermann Paul's *Grundriss der germanischen Philologie.* This immense co-operative work had been begun as early as 1891. The section on English literature was entrusted to ten Brink (see ten Brink and Brandl 1891), who died without completing it; the replacement of his incomplete account by Brandl's in the second edition (Brandl 1908a) was accordingly a major scholarly landmark. Brandl was to modern eyes less than iconoclastic: he continued to distinguish Beow from Beowulf; he entertained the idea that lines 2200 ff. were markedly different from the rest; he felt that part 1 was "rounded off" in a way that suggested part 2 had not been preplanned; he commented on what he called the poem's *Sprunghaftigkeit,* its erratic abruptness; while noting also its epic discursiveness, he denied that any "organically new architecture" had been raised on its expanded foundations. Yet Brandl decisively rejected the Müllenhoffian attempts, not just to believe in earlier *Lieder,* but to attempt to find the text of them, dismissing ten Brink's theory as "more than Alexandrine." His summary of the problems of structure ran: "I therefore consider the *Beowulf* as basically the work of a single poet, who, however, wavered between two styles, that of the artful epic, to which he aspired, and that of the minstrel lay, to which he was still connected and from which he could not entirely free himself. It is not the text that seems to me—in the main—to be mixed, but the structure" (Brandl 1908b, 1008–09). The assertion of unity had at least made it possible for doubts to be raised about the poem's structure, no longer seen as merely accidental (if still seen as misguided).

In the twenty years after Brandl, a new consensus grew up in *Beowulf* studies. In this a major figure was the German émigré Friedrich Klaeber, who left Berlin for Minnesota in 1894. Klaeber's edition of 1922 is still the basis for the main scholarly text of the poem, section 5 of the introduction to which shows a view similar to Brandl's. Klaeber retains the basic criticism made from Conybeare to Ker, that "the poem . . . consists of two distinct parts joined in a very loose manner and held together only by the person of the hero" (li), and notes like Brandl that part 2 (after 2200) refers to part 1 only twice. He did see a kind of planning in the "remarkable gradation" of Beowulf's three fights: they get steadily harder. Yet in other respects Klaeber did not move far from the traditions of his teachers. He titled one subsection of section 5 "Lack of Steady Advance" and remarked on the poem's "rambling, dilatory method" (lviii). He accepted unity of authorship but still felt that "the author had no complete plan of the poem in his head when he embarked upon his work" (cvi) and that "a superior unity of structure was never achieved" (cvii).

Klaeber's moderate stance was repeated with variations by the other major scholars of the 1920s. R. W. Chambers discussed "Theories as to the Structure of *Beowulf*" in his book of 1921 but spent most of his space on rejecting earlier notions. He concentrated in particular on Levin L. Schücking's monograph *Beowulfs Rückkehr* of 1905. In this Schücking had argued that lines 1888–2199 were a link specially composed to join two separate poems and marked once more by *Widersprechungen* (contradictions) as well as peculiarities of language. Chambers dismissed this thesis as "not proven."[5] Nevertheless, he repeated and amplified Ker's criticism of the poem, insisting that its plot is inferior, the central folktale having driven "into episodes and digressions the things which should be the main stuff of a well-conducted epic" (Chambers 1925, xxvi). Meanwhile, the American W. W. Lawrence had since 1909 been writing a series of articles in *PMLA* that came to have a prominent effect on later studies. It is a straw in the wind that early in his career this scholar had launched a determined attack on Kemble's theory of an early myth of "Beowa" and Grendel and on the charter evidence that Kemble had offered in support (Lawrence 1909). "Beowa" had nothing to do with "Beowulf," Lawrence maintained; "Grendel" might not even be a proper name in the charter; the name "Beowulf" (16 and 53) is simple scribal error, proving nothing about mythical and historical layers. In 1912, Lawrence went on to see in the "contradictions" of the "haunted mere" section, not multiple authorship, but different conceptions brought together by a single author. In his book of 1928, he repeated that the poem was a "well-considered work of art, composed according to strict rules by a well-trained poet" (3). Even more influentially, he expanded on an article of 1915 to suggest that the "Finnsburg Episode" might have been chosen to bring its queen Hildeburh "designedly into connection with the tragedy in store for Queen Wealhtheow" (1928, 126). Like Chambers and Klaeber, Lawrence was impressed by the Scandinavian analogues accumulated over the years; he used them to suggest a poem united by a deliberate use of ironic juxtaposition, in which the episodes, far from being excrescences or interpolations, were the major proof of the poet's art. He also introduced interdisciplinary metaphor to the study of the poem: "Against the main themes of the epic there run, contrapuntally, minor themes, and the effect is mixed, as in an elaborate piece of polyphonic music, when the attention is centred wholly upon the outstanding melodies" (Lawrence 1928, 27).

By the 1930s, it might be said that the battle for Beowulfian unity was over. Assertions of unity had been made by Pizzo (1916) and Du Bois (1934), besides those mentioned above, while it had been suggested by Bradley (1915–16) that the poem's forty-three sections might represent only the original poet's loose leaves. But though the poem was increasingly accepted as unified, it was rarely felt, except by Lawrence, to be much of a structural success. In his 1910 article for the eleventh edition of the *Encyclopaedia Britannica,* Bradley had contrasted the "lucid and well-constructed story" at the poem's core with the "general impression . . . of a bewildering chaos" made by the work as a whole, and his opinion remained unchanged in the fourteenth edition of 1929. Du Bois (1934) could see *Beowulf* only as "a pageant drama," which Adeline Bartlett (1935) varied to "a tapestry . . . a series of panels." Trying in the same year to retain something of the results of *Liedertheorie* after its demise, Berendsohn offered an image of an aged poet by a littered desk, whose feeble memory could no longer separate what was original from what was copied.[6] One might say that a dominant thesis about the nature of the poem had been decisively defeated, but a satisfactory new one had not taken its place. This uncertain situation was radically altered by J. R. R. Tolkien's British Academy lecture of 1934, published in 1936, "*Beowulf*: The Monsters and the Critics"—the most influential essay ever written on the poem.

Two of the qualities that made it so influential are its aggression and its humor. In one allegory after another, Tolkien presents the poem as Cinderella taken over by a series of domineering fairy godmothers, as a victim of "the jabberwocks of historical and antiquarian research," and as a tower looking out on the sea. Yet comic though they sometimes are, his allegories contain an element of literal truth. From what has been said already in this essay, it will be clear that when Tolkien sees the poet's friends (i.e., the critics) knocking down the tower (i.e., the poem) to look for buried antiquities and saying simultaneously "This tower is most interesting" but also (after pushing it over) "What a muddle it is in!," he is giving a reasonably fair account of the whole dissectionist school. The word *muddle* had not actually been used by scholars; but they had called the poem a "ruin" and a *Wirrwarr,* though the evidence for their terms of abuse was entirely the product of their own critical theory. Tolkien mocked this theory derisively; but he reserved special ire and verve for his countrymen and immediate predecessors Ker and

Chambers. He cited them carefully and respectfully, but concluded, "There is something irritatingly odd about all this." The poem is praised by Ker and Chambers for all kinds of qualities; yet it seems that the critics think the poet was wasting his time, had simply *written the wrong poem.* How much better, Tolkien proposed, to assume that he knew what he was doing and to try to discover what it was. The major achievement of Tolkien's essay was to insist on the poem's autonomy and its author's right to create freely, regardless of critical canons.

On the poem's structure, Tolkien's main point was once more a rejection, this time of Klaeber's "lack of steady advance": "But the poem was not meant to advance, steadily or unsteadily. It is essentially a balance, an opposition of ends and beginnings. In its simplest terms it is a contrasted description of two moments in a great life . . . It is divided in consequence into two opposed portions, different in matter, manner, and length: A from 1 to 2199 (including an exordium of 52 lines); B from 2200 to 3182 (the end). There is no reason to cavil at this proportion . . . it proves in practice to be right" (Tolkien 1936, 271–72). If the poem has a structural weakness, Tolkien suggests, it lies in the long recapitulation of Beowulf's voyage to Hygelac, the "Return" of 1888–2199 (already singled out by Schücking and defended by Chambers), but even this can be explained. If one needs an image of the poem's "total structure," it is the Old English metrical line, two halves of "roughly equivalent weight . . . more often rhythmically contrasted than similar." Tolkien concludes—still arguing down the Ker/Chambers thesis that the poem should have concentrated more on the human tragedies of its episodes—by sketching a poem without monsters, based on Anglo-Saxon history. Such a poem would, he argues, lack the "cosmic" dimension created precisely by keeping the monsters in the foreground and telling the hero-stories only through allusion, prophecy, or flashback.

Tolkien's defense of the poem as something existing in its own right was in a sense long overdue. It was seized on eagerly, even gratefully, by generations of critics, among them Blomfield (1938), O'Loughlin (1952, responding to Imelmann 1920), and H. Wright (1957). Tolkien's most influential supporters, however, were the Swiss Adrien Bonjour and the American Arthur Brodeur. Bonjour wrote on the poem in 1940 and in 1949, but his major work was his 1950 monograph, *The Digressions in Beowulf.* In this Bonjour took in sequence all the poem's major "episodes" and argued that their abruptnesses, discrepancies, or doubtful relation to the main narrative were in every case deliberate, the signs of a conscious artist working by irony and by contrast, here casting a shadow of vulnerability, there pointing an implicit moral. Meanwhile Brodeur (1953) directly addressed the question of "structure and unity." Once again Tolkien's view of "balance" was praised, as was his repudiation of Ker and Chambers: if the poet had concentrated on historical heroes rather than mythical monsters, Brodeur declared, "we should have gained a kind of English *chanson de geste,* and lost the world's noblest *Heldenleben*" (1959, 73–74). To the view that the character of the hero was a major unifying factor, Brodeur added an attractive twist. He suggested that during the poem Beowulf advanced from being an ideal retainer to being an ideal king. The event on which this change pivoted was the death of Hygelac, and the mentions of him became (again in musical terms) a leitmotiv. Brodeur stresses that the poet could have centered his whole poem on this story, and if he did not, it was because he wished to "subordinate" historical record rather than sacrifice it. In his 1959 book, Brodeur repeated his conviction that the poem and all its details were the work of a "great artist." Largely by the efforts of Brodeur and Bonjour, this view, set in motion by Tolkien and strongly opposed both to the early German tradition and to the questioning attitudes of Klaeber, Ker, Chambers, and (to a lesser extent) Lawrence, became the dominant one in *Beowulf* studies.

Tolkien, however, had his detractors. Major objection was raised to his views by T. M. Gang (1952). Tolkien had asserted that the poet, clearly able, must have done what he set out to do. How can we know? asked Gang. To say this is to refuse to consider any possibility of error or failure. Specifically, Gang felt that the loose comparison of the poem's "balance" to the Old English alliterative line was unhelpful, while the dragon was not a fair counterpoise to Grendel, for it was more provoked, less evil. Furthermore, Gang could not see that dragons were more of a universal theme than Swedish invasions. If the monsters were symbolic, as Tolkien had insisted, he could not see what they symbolized. Gang also noted Tolkien's eclectic use of Norse tradition to explain an English poem and argued acutely that Tolkien was trying to impose a twentieth-century understanding on a much earlier poem. Adrien Bonjour predictably replied to Gang the following year, but Gang's criticism continued to carry weight. It was echoed by H. L. Rogers (1955), who insisted that the poet was not entirely successful in imposing himself on his material but nevertheless put forward an idea later popular, that the "gradation" in the poem was downwards: success is inversely proportional to the hero's reliance on weapons, desire for treasure, or need of help. In the same year, J. C. van Meurs felt that "important objections may be raised against a theory which assigns a perfect structural and artistic unity to the poem" (129–30). Van Meurs did not scruple to compare Tolkien with Müllenhoff: both had been too readily believed.

Two further opponents of Tolkien should be noted, their fates very different. John A. Nist published two papers on the poem in 1957 and 1958, and repeated their findings in Nist (1959). His views were of limited circulation, but he did extend metaphorical descriptions of the poem's structure by suggesting that it was marked by "fugal variation," the allusions being "contrapuntal," while the hero's life was told "in a *pointillist* manner" (1959, 22). In the end, Nist decided that the poem had eight intentions, giving rise to ten motifs, which he outlined—an omen of the future—in a diagram too detailed to carry general conviction (1959, 23–24). Kenneth Sisam, by contrast, published his short monograph on *The Structure of Beowulf* with the Clarendon Press in 1965 and was in consequence widely read. Sisam—he had been Tolkien's unsuccessful rival for the Oxford Chair of Anglo-

Saxon forty years before—was as immune to Tolkien's spell as anyone alive and, furthermore, was unimpressed by the post-Tolkien industry of artistry detection. He rejected outright the generally accepted view of ironic allusion to the fall of the Scyldings, via Hrothulf and Wealhtheow and the parallel with Hildeburh; no audience, he thought, would be "ingenious enough to detect" such hints (Sisam 1965, 39). He repeated Schücking's view of the "Return" section as a weakness (29–32), dismissed the Thryth episode as a "crude excrescence" (49), and scorned the Ongentheow tale as reading "almost like a caricature of the practice of digression" (13). In essence, he suggested, the poem consisted of a work and two sequels, or a serial in three instalments, the transitions or poetical "recapitulations" quite clearly marked. It had "enough high qualities without the claim to structural elegance" (66). Sisam in effect challenged Tolkien's view of a brilliant eccentric poet, seeing the poem as something more functional, if not exactly "commonplace." A further objection to Tolkien was made by Moore (1968), who dismissed the whole theory of "balance" as "general to the point of banality" (293).

In the background of this Tolkien-centered debate, it should be said, some stubborn scholars continued even after World War II to work along older lines, among them Sune Lindqvist, with his Ettmüller-like *Beowulf Dissectus* of 1958, and Francis P. Magoun Jr. in two papers of 1958 and 1963. Magoun's use of terms like *folk poem* and *folk variant* show the German ancestry of his dissectionist views—*Volksdichtung* and *volksmässig* had been major terms of praise for the nineteenth century. Though Magoun was loyally supported by his former pupil Creed (1966b), who gave an oral-formulaic slant to a theory not dissimilar to Sisam's "serial" view, Brodeur, with fifty years of Anglophone scholarship behind him, had little difficulty in refuting Magoun point by point in 1970. A much more original "holdout" was Geoffrey Smithers, whose 1961 inaugural lecture "The Making of *Beowulf*" ignored the "Tolkien revolution" and returned to the question of how the poem arose. Smithers remarked that the poem was "full of puzzles and loose ends" (5). However, he believed that these were caused not by different authorship, but by one author proving unable to control material he had inherited, the character of which could be estimated by considering the poem's many analogs in Icelandic. An unexpected point made by Smithers was that the analogs seemed to show that the three-fight sequence was found in essence elsewhere. The story as we have it had been a unity, therefore, *before* it was recomposed by the poet; *Beowulf*'s unity is inherited, not individual. P. G. Buchloh (1966) also attempted to compare the structure of *Beowulf* with that of Norse Eddic poems and saw it as similar but affected by epic "amplification."

Nevertheless, in spite of these cross-currents and back eddies, the tide of *Beowulf* criticism was still flowing in the direction pointed by Tolkien, as one may see, for instance, in Edward B. Irving Jr.'s 1968 study, which supports the poem's unity but finds it "an emotional unity hard to analyse and describe . . . a unity based on the very fact of diversity" (193). This critical tide was, however, about to flow a good deal further up the beach than Tolkien probably would have preferred. The mood of the time was expressed most clearly and influentially by John Leyerle, in two articles of 1965 and 1967. In the earlier of these, Leyerle put forward two ideas. The main one, expressed in the title, "Beowulf the Hero and the King," was a corollary of the "ironic" tradition established by Lawrence et al. and denied by Sisam; but it went from saying that the poem indicated tragedy in the Scylding or Hrethling families to saying that the tragedy is general. The poem's theme was "the fatal contradiction at the heart of heroic society" (89). Structurally speaking, the poem showed a successful hero becoming not an ideal but a failed king, through inability to realize that indomitable will needs to be subordinated to the common good. Leyerle's second major idea was to say that the poem presented this theme and this gradation not overtly or consecutively but through a series of comparisons and contrasts that Leyerle related to the "interlace patterns" of early English art. This second idea was taken up in the later article of 1967, in which Leyerle related the poem to the art of Sutton Hoo, the Lindisfarne Gospels, or the Bewcastle Cross. The similarity between verbal and graphic arts lay in their unnaturalness. In the poem, a story was told in nonchronological order; in jewelry, manuscript illumination, or sculpture, images were presented not naturalistically but as design. The difficulty of following a single thread of story in the poem was paralleled by the difficulty of following a line in sculpture or picture through weavings seemingly designed to distract. The interlaced design of the poem, Leyerle claimed, revealed "the meaning of coincidence, the recurrence of human behavior, and the circularity of time, partly through the coincidence, recurrence and circularity of the medium itself" (1967, 8). Critics should never have expected to find one clear line through the maze, for "understatement . . . is inherent in interlace structure" (8). Leyerle repeated that the theme expressed was "fatal contradiction." Once this was grasped it would be seen that "there are no digressions in *Beowulf*" (13).

Most of what Leyerle said was latent in earlier criticism. The "gradation" of the three fights had been seen by Klaeber and Rogers; the idea of youth versus age had been foregrounded by Tolkien; the word *interlace* was a cross-medium metaphor like *polyphony* or *pointillism*; to say there were *no* digressions in *Beowulf* was only an extreme form of Bonjour's opinion; the praise of "interlace" could be seen as a reversal of the complaints about "barbarian" art made by Imelmann in 1920 and rejected by O'Loughlin in 1952. The last point could furthermore rely on increasingly strong feelings about cultural relativism; it has remained *de rigueur* (at least in theory) to attempt to see *Beowulf* in its own terms instead of imposing later cultural ideals on it. There have been attacks on the very idea of "interlace," notably by Morton Bloomfield in 1986, who reminds us that the word is only a metaphor, misleading if it makes one think that verbal art, inevitably linear, can approach the effect of visual art seen as a simultaneous whole. Nevertheless, Leyerle's composite notions of "fatal contradiction" and "interlace structure" tended to dominate interpretation for twenty years. They did, however, leave it open for critics to position themselves at different points along two different axes. *How* critical was the poet of the society he presented? How far was his method traditional, how far consciously artistic? These issues left ample room for discussion.

Sherman M. Kuhn thus made a strong point in his "study in epic structure" of 1969. The hero's life, he pointed out, could be divided into five parts, told in over fifty sections, some long, some short, and told in no evident chronological order. Though scattered, they were consistent (a point made by Grein more than a century before); the mode was highly unlike classical epic. Lawrence Fast made a similar point with reference to another character in 1971. Following on from Brodeur's 1953 discussion of Hygelac as a pivot for the poem, Fast reviewed the three dozen mentions of Hygelac and concluded that he was indeed a "focal point," in spite of the scattered nature of references to him. These two articles perhaps indicated "pointillism" rather than "interlace," but they made clear the poet's ability to integrate a mass of detail. But how, one might ask, did the poet do it? Different positions on the art/tradition scale were taken by, for instance, Gradon (1971), Liggins (1973), Oshitari (1974), Burlin (1974), and Nicholson (1980). Meanwhile, the "fatal contradiction" view was extended or modified also by Palmer (1976), Dragland (1977), Locherbie-Cameron (1978), and Shippey (1978).

Two articles, however, put the post-Leyerle consensus as well as any. Kathryn Hume (1975) rejects Brodeur's *Heldenleben* idea, asking us to think of all the things about the hero's life that we never learn; she points also to the poem's asymmetries and the critical inability to decide between a two-part and a three-part structure; and she concludes—with a certain resemblance to John Earle ninety years before—that the poem's theme is "threats to social order," a different one indicated by each monster. This tripartite structure is action based, but there is also a bipartite structure that is hero based. The two structures, or ways of looking at structure, are by no means incompatible. This subtle and flexible piece may be compared with Martin Stevens's article of 1978, which represents the "common denominator" of views at that time. It sees the poem as tightly-unified, without digressions, proceeding firmly in the direction (one might sum up) of entropy: towards ashes, rust, and silence. Stevens's opening remarks may be cited as similar in conviction, if totally opposed in content, to those of Hermann Dederich a century before: "Few scholars today would take issue with the view that *Beowulf* is a tightly-unified poem in which the two major parts are conjoined to develop a narrative contrast between the youthful hero . . . and the aged king. . . . Few, I believe, would even admit that the notorious digressions are, in fact, 'digressions.' . . . It is safe to say, then, there is wide agreement on the general proposition that the poem is a unified work of art" (Stevens 1978, 219). Finally, one can see that the debates over "interlace" and "fatal contradiction" continue to be productive from such pieces as Jane Chance (Nitzsche)'s 1980 article on "structural unity" and Grendel's mother; or Edward B. Irving Jr.'s 1989 *Rereading Beowulf,* which contradicts Leyerle over his "crypto-Christian" approach to heroic society but nevertheless tends to agree with him over interlace, detected in both the poem's smaller and larger structures. Fred Robinson further associates "microstructure" and "macrostructure" in his 1985 monograph *Beowulf and the Appositive Style,* seeing both as "built on apposed segments."

Two further debates on the poem's structure had meanwhile continued throughout the "post-Leyerle" phase, in a way on opposing flanks of it. One looked not at the poem's integrations but at its discontinuities, so tending to cast doubt on the Bonjour/Brodeur/Leyerle view of a poet in total control of his material, while the other tended by contrast to see more and more precise symmetry in the poem, arguing arithmetical or geometric modes of composition, as well as literary. The former sequence contains only three contributions, two of them very similar to each other. Shippey (1969) and Barnes (1970) not only hit on the same idea, of applying Vladimir Propp's well-known views on the morphology of folktale to *Beowulf,* but more surprisingly also reached very similar conclusions. Both writers saw the poem as tripartite, so agreeing implicitly with Smithers (1961), and both explained the puzzling figure of Unferth as a "donor" (of the eventually useless sword Hrunting). Unferth's repeated actions and appearances in the poem had not been convincingly explained as "conscious artistry," and the suggestion was that his role in some earlier folktale version had not been perfectly integrated by the poet. Meanwhile, in a wide-ranging work of 1972, Gwyn Jones saw the poem as derived from folktale and inherently tripartite, compared it with works in Middle Welsh and Old Norse, and declared it "structurally, to a modern eye . . . less than perfect" (4).

By contrast, a group of scholars from 1967 on saw the poem as produced in a hyperliterary way. Their starting point is the numbered sections into which the poem is divided in manuscript, forty-two of them plus the unnumbered prologue about Scyld. In 1967, Eamonn Carrigan organized these into a complex and symmetrical thirteen/seventeen/thirteen diagram, with the fight against Grendel's mother taking a central or pivotal place. David Howlett offered a five-part structure of similar type in 1974, also attempting to see the poem as divided according to the rule of the "Golden Section," in Howlett's calculation at line 1962. A more thought-provoking attempt to see geometry in *Beowulf* was made by T. E. Hart in 1981, an article that did indeed note surprising symmetries in the poem's use of numerals. Meanwhile, both Whitney Bolton (1978) and B. F. Huppé (1984) saw significance in the one plus forty-two patterning, the former relating it to Alfred's Boethius translation (also a prologue followed by forty-two sections), the latter claiming that "the rhetorical interlace of narrative design and verbal ambiguity is supported by a clear mathematically-ordered structure" (Huppé 1984, 89). Huppé's structure is a bipartite one, breaking at line 1887. Such theories faced immediate skepticism, for instance, from David M. Wells (1976)—maybe the sections begin where they do because the scribes grew tired of repeating capital Ð or Þ—and Constance Hieatt (1975). Hieatt returned to Bartlett (1935), showed many clear "envelope patterns" in the poem, but noted their lack of consistent relation to numbered sections. One might note also that any complex work is likely to develop symmetries. Brian A.

Shaw's 1978 article counts fifteen speeches in the poem that receive no reply and sees them as two paired sets of seven, with a pivotal speech in Beowulf's imperatives to Hrothgar. He argues that this marks a turning point from retainer to king and is in the poem's central section (21). Yet Beowulf is little different immediately after the speech than immediately before.

In any case, a much more scrupulous and long-overdue examination of the manuscript finally appeared in Kevin Kiernan's important *Beowulf and the Beowulf Manuscript* (1981a). Several of Kiernan's linked theses lie outside the scope of this chapter, but as regards structure, he throws special stress on the eleventh gathering of the *Beowulf* codex, the pages begun by scribe A (1874–1939) but completed by scribe B (1939–2207). These pages contain not only the transit from youth to age, and from Denmark to Geatland, but also most of the inconsistencies and contradictions noted by Schücking in 1905. Kiernan suggests that this section, "Beowulf's Homecoming," could have been "first composed to join together two different Beowulf MSS" (257) and that the extant manuscript may indeed show us the two scribes collaborating in the composition. He suggests further that scribe B deliberately erased a page after the end of this section (folio 179, 2207–52) and three further lines a little later (2275–77), in order to write his own lead-in to the last part of the poem, possibly omitting parts of his original at the same time. Unfortunately, the scribe did this on still-damp vellum, which accounts for the damaged state of folio 179. From these and other observations, Kiernan proposes that the poem as we have it could be "an amalgamation of two originally distinct poems" (249), though the poem "as it has come down to us is now unquestionably unified" (250). Quite what this last statement might mean was probed by Janet Bately's article of 1985, which demonstrated that in the grammar of its *sippan* clauses *Beowulf* repeatedly "differs in its usage from the rest of the [poetic] corpus," while "all three [of its major] parts share these unique features" (428). Bately's results do not exclude complex origins or possible interpolations, but they do seem to indicate at least a detailed rewriting of the poem into one poetic idiolect. Boyle (1981), meanwhile, dismissed the "palimpsest" page as rainwater damage. Nevertheless, Kiernan and Boyle together have created a realistic picture of two scribes working under difficulties to create the manuscript copy since almost lost beneath editorial decisions.

At this stage, it may be helpful to review the structural problems as perceived by scholars during the 180 years of *Beowulf* scholarship to date.

1. First on the list must be the unease felt from Conybeare to Kiernan over the sudden movement from the hero's youth to his old age (2200 ff.): "fiftig wintra'" passed over in barely ten lines. If unity is to be asserted in spite of this abrupt transition, all scholars have agreed that some connecting principle needs to be found, whether Tolkien's "balance" or Brodeur's *Heldenleben*.

2. With this first problem must be connected the doubt over whether the poem is fundamentally bipartite (so Tolkien and Kiernan, in their different ways) or tripartite, as urged, for instance, by folktale scholars.

3. A third area of doubt lies in the poem's many episodes or digressions (for a full discussion, see chapter 10 in the present volume). Whatever these are called and however they are explained, it is true that the poem contains many historical "flashbacks" as well as prophetic "flash-forwards," often introduced with striking abruptness. The most evident case is the Hygd/Thryth "comparison" (1931), but this differs only in degree from a dozen other sudden introductions. There is some justice in Brandl's term *Sprunghaftigkeit,* whatever artistic justification one finds for the quality.

4. Yet at the same time one has to note a frequent quality of leisureliness about the poem. Parts of the narrative are not only told but retold, and the poet shows no reluctance to spend considerable time on courteous civilities. Whether one calls this *Geschwätz* or "chatter," with Berendsohn (1915), or epic "amplification" with Buchloh (1966), it forms a striking contrast with problem 3 above.

5. A final internal problem that received relatively little attention until recently is the poem's use of significant (?) silences. In the "ironic" view of the poem now well established, one could say that its most significant figure is Hrothulf: his relations with his uncle, aunt, and cousins, as reconstructed from Scandinavian story, are vital to the whole post-Leyerle school of "fatal contradiction" critics. Yet, as Sisam pointed out most forcefully in 1965, in the whole poem Hrothulf is never introduced, never says a word, and never lifts a finger. Similar points could be made of several other characters.

6. More doubtfully relevant is the ongoing problem of the poem's numbered sections. These have been asserted as authorial from the time of Bradley. Yet the acceptance of them as secure data has halted serious consideration of their nature. They often bear little relation to the intuitions of modern editors, a contrast that has not been probed. If the German and English scholars before Tolkien were overready to "colonize" the poem, their successors have often seemed compensatingly deferential. As a result, many questions have remained unanswered, some unasked.

In the most recent period of *Beowulf* criticism, no clear consensus has emerged of the post-Leyerle kind. Nevertheless, there have been several interesting ventures, in which one may see a certain common direction, beginning with Theodore Andersson in 1980. Andersson diagrams the poem—much more simply than Hart or Carrigan—as a series of ups and down, disasters and recoveries. He shows this oscillatory pattern working on both large and small scales and concludes that while modern scholars have often seen the poem's structure as "a problem in pertinence," the poet was aiming above all at "a persistent cultivation of mood and emotional resonance," "communicating an experience" rather than "telling a story" (93–94).

In this he was assisted by having available "a certain inventory of conventional situations"—a point taken further by Joseph Harris (1982). Harris argues that the poet had in hand a certain number of "marked genres" (found inside the poem, like the "Creation Hymn" or the heroic lay of Finnsburg) as well as "unmarked genres" alluded to or presented vestigially (like the genealogical table or the death song). Harris suggests that *Beowulf* is in effect a compendium, like the *Canterbury Tales,* and like them at once a new literary form and oriented towards its own past—even, Harris suggests, harking back to Grundtvig's last work on *Beowulf* 120 years before, a kind of literary "barrow" for a passing heroic society.

Literary criticism of the past is also drawn on by Eric G. Stanley (1980). Stanley repeats Klaeber's often-quoted criticisms and opposes to them a term used originally by Wilhelm Grimm, *Unbefangenheit*. What Stanley means by this (see problem 4 above) is perhaps that the poet seems under no pressure to explain himself or to reach narrative turning points. His skill is seen in the good, often grim endings to sections, in the links made between passages of narrative, in the way in which action is related to "universalizing wisdom": skills of mood rather than of adventure fiction. Chapters 7 and 8 of one recent authoritative work on *Beowulf,* John Niles's book of 1983, likewise show points of agreement with Andersson, Harris, and Stanley. In chapter 8, "Barbaric Style," Niles takes up the accusation made by Imelmann in 1920 and finds it true but praiseworthy. Much of the poem, he notes, is nonrepresentational (Wiglaf speaking to men who have fled, Beowulf's anxious thanes falling asleep in Heorot); these features are there, however, to satisfy immediate narrative needs—needs that create the *Widersprechungen* of a previous age. Niles also uses the idea of the "truncated motif" (172), something mentioned but not used, like Grendel's "glof" (2085), or more provocatively the curse on the dragon's treasure, or the hints at Hrothulf's treachery. Niles draws on recent research on oral poetry to argue that such works tend to achieve "a unity that might be called inorganic . . . based on consistencies of theme" (169). As for the overall structure of the poem, it "can be described in terms of a series of major and minor pairs" (159), some narrative, some thematic. Niles's indication of success/failure as a major pair, leading to a tone of "realistic fatalism," comes close to Andersson's formulation of 1980.

Niles's suggestions cut through many of the knots of *Beowulf* criticism by making it permissible to praise the poem in terms alien to those of later literature ("*inorganic* unity . . . consistencies *of theme*"). In his chapter 7, he also draws on the notion of "ring composition." This had been introduced to *Beowulf* studies some years before by H. Ward Tonsfeldt (1977). Tonsfeldt follows recent trends in Homeric scholarship, in which it has been pointed out how often Homer organizes motifs in a chiastic rather than a parallel structure: not A B C, $A^1 B^1 C^1$, but A B C, $C^1 B^1 A^1$. Tonsfeldt finds a number of such "ring structures" in *Beowulf* and states that "the repetitious arrangement of narrative agents within a nearly static structure is the essence of the poet's technique" (452). Ward Parks's article of 1988 gives further examples and notes that a major function of ring structures is to integrate digressions with main narrative by linking the two or by framing a "core episode"; ring systems provide both bridges and interfaces, and create an effect not of disclosing narrative so much as unfolding it from within. Like Niles, Parks and Tonsfeldt deal with old criticisms of the structure of *Beowulf* not by denying them but by seeing them as features of a different, nonclassical rhetoric exemplified also in the recently acquired records of oral epic. A further step in this direction is taken by Paul Sorrell (1992). This follows Niles in noting "truncated motifs" and in seeing "local effects" as taking priority over "narrative unity"; the "oppositional expansions" detected in the episode of Wiglaf's sword are again similar to Niles's "major and minor pairs" or Tonsfeldt's "repetitious arrangement of narrative elements."

One might sum up by saying that the more relaxed attitude taken to narrative art and organic unity in the past fifteen years has led to a dissolution of problems 3 and 4 on the list above, abruptness and leisureliness, or in other terms *Sprunghaftigkeit* and *Unbefangenheit*; while problems 2 and 6, the two- or three-part structure and the poem's numbered sections, are no longer seen as directly relevant. The problem of the poem's "broken back," or more politely its sudden "fifty-winter" transition, continues to cause unease, with Kiernan's thesis of a deliberately rewritten connecting link still unrebutted. One is left with problem 5: the poem's "gaps" or "silences."

These have been foregrounded, in different ways, by three recent critics, Allen Frantzen, Gillian Overing, and James Earl. Each has written an essay or article that functions also as a chapter in a book, respectively Frantzen (1990, 1991a), Overing (1987, 1990), and Earl (1991, 1994). All three authors are in strong agreement on the gap between previous criticism and the poem itself. Frantzen points out that the poem is in some places literally unreadable, the conventional critical text being a later invention of scholars. This philological urge for definition has, however, extended also to attempts to create a unified narrative, an epic voice (or an anti-epic voice), a single statement for the poem to make (see, e.g., Earle 1892; or Hume 1975). Frantzen argues in reply that we should be more alert for the suppressed voices within the poem, accept the "illusive and allusive nature" of writing and reading within the poem, and hold back both from "acts of closure" and the unifying strategies of conventional criticism. Frantzen has here certainly indicated one of the weak points created over the years by the need of professional academics in the Old English field to have a "masterpiece" with which to stake their claim to classroom time. It is less clear what Frantzen means by writing that acceptance of the poem's intertexts "is a return to the premise of *Liedertheorie* . . . but it is not the *Liedertheorie* made new" (180). It seems that, rather than advocating actual composite authorship after the manner of Müllenhoff or Berendsohn, Frantzen sees the poem as a "dialogized" or even "repressive" text, single authored, but signaling the author's uncertainties and accommodations rather than the unifying grasp so long propounded.

Overing similarly condemns acts of critical closure, the urge to find one single structural overview, and the tendency to see the poem's structure merely as "a problem to be solved" (33). She reaffirms the "essentially nonlinear" (35) nature of the narrative and stresses "the irresolution and dynamism of the deconstructionist free play of textual elements" within it (xiii). She feels that the impasse between Leyerle's and Bloomfield's views of interlace can, however, be escaped by using C. S. Peirce's theory of signs; and she shows such repeated elements as cups, rings, and swords recurring in the poem in a mode balanced between "the dynamic viscerality of the index and the collected synthesis of the symbol" (64). Overing's views are based on observations not dissimilar to those of Wright, Liggins, or Oshitari discussed above, but her and Frantzen's critiques strive to resist the urge of previous critics to assimilate the poem by interpretation. Finally, James Earl also sees critics imposing themselves on the poem's silences and projecting onto it their own scholarly neuroses. Understanding *Beowulf,* in his view, "shades into the problem" of understanding oneself. One suggestion made is that the shift of Beowulf from "hero" to "king" would have been perceived by an audience of warrior-aristocrats as a shift from ego to superego, the latter "revealing by his very existence our inadequacy" (1991, 85); critics have felt a similar inadequacy before the poet and the poem.

It may be that study of the poem's unity and structure is about to make another major turn similar to the one at the start of this century, but this time away from the view that *Beowulf* is an artistic unity with a single purpose (if only we could discover it) and towards acceptance of its inner diversity (though on some less literal level than the Müllenhoffian one). To this a major challenge may, however, come from attempts, in the manner of Kevin Kiernan, to determine what may yet be learned from the study of the poem as artifact, in its one surviving manuscript. Scientific codicological study may not perform an act of "critical closure," but it may nevertheless set productive bounds to the area in which imagination may play.

Notes

1. The following account of Grundtvig is substantially drawn from Haarder's remarks on him (1975, 59–88 and 281–85), and the translations from Grundtvig's Danish are his also.

2. This and all subsequent translations from German are my own.

3. It is striking how totally Dederich and Martin Stevens a hundred years later contradict each other (see the discussion below), yet each author believes he is expressing settled and noncontentious fact.

4. One might note the similar riposte given by Bately's grammatical study of 1985 to the incipient dissection of the poem hinted at by Kiernan (1981a).

5. It has attracted new interest in recent years; see the commentary on Kiernan's thesis below.

6. It is only fair to note that Berendsohn wrote under tragic personal circumstances. Dismissed from his university post in 1933 by the Nazis (Berendsohn was Jewish), he found physical refuge in Denmark and spiritual consolation in his study of *Beowulf*. He was especially unfortunate in that his quasi-Darwinist account of the poem's growth through heroic and folktale stages should appear almost simultaneously with Tolkien's essay; he indeed proposed (1935, 71) that the "original" Beowulf must have met his end in a

Swedish war, the view that Tolkien was to treat as a *reductio ad absurdum*. Berendsohn, however, escaped to Sweden in 1943, had a distinguished later career, and lived to be one hundred.

p. 153 - Grundtvig
154 - Kemble
① 155 - Liedertheorie + Mütterhijff
❸ 157 · early resistance
❸ 160 - Brandl — resistance to multiple authorship,
161 - Klaeber — but agree not unified still.
161-2 - Lawrence, well-considered work of art.
           ironic juxtaposition
162 - J.R.R. Tolkien - his 'balance'.
163 - Bonjour, worked by many + contrast.
164 · Brodeur, Beowulf's development
       Gang, H.L. Rogers opposed (inwards, gradations,
       Nist, Sisam   dragon, half-lines)
166 · Leyerle - 'ironic' trad.; tragedy; interlace.
       Interlace? His aftermath   No digressions
168 · ████████ Total control? Unferth
       Hyperliterary way.
169 - Kiernan + the join between the 2 sections
       REVIEW
p. 170 - Andersson, ups + downs
171 - Harris, Canterbury Tales
       Stanley, Leisurely, skills of mood
       Niles, nonrepresentational, inorganic unity,
       consistencies of theme, any or mixed?
172 - Condemning of acts of critical closure
       lean more toward acceptance of
       inner diversity.

Chapter 9

Christian and Pagan Elements

by Edward B. Irving Jr.

Summary: *Beowulf* tells a story of a secular hero in pre-Christian times, but the poem is unmistakably cast in terms familiar to a Christian audience. Earlier scholars tried to make the poem fundamentally pagan in ethos and message, while in this century there has been an equally vigorous attempt to read it as a cleverly masked theological work. Most recently, scholars have tried in various ways to describe a complex blending or balancing of the two traditions, with the honored values of an older heroic society placed in a familiar Christian context, creating a logical impossibility but an outstanding poem.

Chronology

1840: Ludwig Ettmüller suggests that certain passages in the poem are Christian interpolations.

1897: F. A. Blackburn maintains that the poem once existed with no Christian allusions.

1911–12: Friedrich Klaeber demonstrates in detail that the Christian elements are integral to the poem and cannot be detached from it.

1912: H. M. Chadwick insists that the Christian elements are not integral parts of the poem.

1928: Bertha Phillpotts claims that the poet modifies traditional epic plot to satisfy demands of a recently converted audience.

1929: Levin L. Schücking in "Das Königsideal" argues that the poem is influenced by Saint Augustine's concept of the ideal king.

1934: Arthur E. Du Bois accuses Beowulf of the sins of pride and avarice.

1936: J. R. R. Tolkien sees the poem as basically Christian, even though it invokes the Germanic myth of the final battle of gods and men.

1946: Marie P. Hamilton argues that the poem shows the influence of the theory of divine grace and is basically Christian in thought.

1950: Charles J. Donahue considers the possible influence on *Beowulf* of the Irish concept of pre-Christian virtue and the noble heathen.

1951: D. W. Robertson Jr. argues the centrality to the poem's meaning of the Augustinian pattern of *caritas* and *cupiditas*.

1951: Dorothy Whitelock offers evidence that the poem was composed for an audience of fully converted Christians.

1952–53: Ernst Leisi maintains that gold in the poem is a Germanic measure of honor and in no way associated with Christian ideas of avarice.

1955: Allen Cabaniss sees a parallel between Beowulf's descent into the mere and Christ's death, descent into hell, and resurrection.

1955: J. C. van Meurs, disagreeing with Tolkien, doubts that the Anglo-Saxons had any knowledge of the late myth of the Twilight of the Gods.

1958: Robert E. Kaske views *Beowulf* as fundamentally Augustinian/Christian, with the theme of *sapientia et fortitudo* at its center.

1958: Kemp Malone points out that Grendel's abode shares several features with the Christian hell described in Blickling Homily 17.

1959: Arthur G. Brodeur sees a fusion of ancient paganism and Christian culture in the poem, with true Christianity embodied in Beowulf himself.

1960: Margaret E. Goldsmith sees the poem as essentially Christian in all its themes.

1960: Maurice B. McNamee believes the poem is an allegory of Christian salvation.

1962: William Whallon sees evidence only of a very simple form of Christianity in the poem.

1963: Morton W. Bloomfield pleads for recognition of patristic exegesis in the poem.

1963: Eric G. Stanley sees the poet as feeling compassion for the hopeless state of the pagan characters.

1963: Robert D. Stevick thinks the poet was handling oral poems about Beowulf that had already absorbed some Christian elements.

1963: Stanley chronicles scholars' search for pagan features, in their long-lasting attempt to deny the fundamental Christianity of the poem.

1965: Charles Donahue sees similarities between *Beowulf* and Celtic Christianity and believes that Beowulf is a Christ figure.

1967: Larry D. Benson claims paganism is a deliberate addition to the poem in the context of Anglo-Saxon missions to the continent.

1967: Charles Moorman maintains that the poem is pagan/heroic and the Christian features merely non essential detail.

1969: Lars Lönnroth points out that Icelandic sagas often represent pagan heroes as noble and admirable.

1972: Michael D. Cherniss sees Christian piety as incidental to the poem, which is basically a strong assertion of secular heroic values.

1974: Robert Hanning views the poem as a Christian author's attempt to display both the attraction and the serious limits of paganism.

1978: Marijane Osborn sees an outer frame of Christian understanding surrounding a story told within a native Germanic frame of reference.

1978: Patrick Wormald argues that the poem's audience may have been members of aristocratic families who had entered a heavily secularized church.

1981: Robert L. Kindrick sees wisdom elements drawn from a Germanic context, not solely a Christian one.

1982: Paul C. Bauschatz sees the concept of time in the poem as being as much Germanic as Christian.

1982: James W. Earl argues that the poem is a moving act of mourning for the necessary loss of the pagan world in a Christian culture.

1982: David Williams sees the poet as attributing all violence and evil to the Cain tradition, thereby dramatizing the failure of the feud-ridden pagan society.

1983: John D. Niles sees the poet finding a common ground between pagan heroic virtues like courage and loyalty and Christian ideals of altruism and restraint.

1984: B. F. Huppé sees the hero caught in "the iron circle of heroic error" as an inhabitant of Augustine's earthly city.

1984: Edward B. Irving Jr. analyzes the distribution and nature of the Christian elements, finding them significantly bunched in part 1 of the poem.

1985: Fred C. Robinson sees the poet as constantly punning on secular and Christian meanings, with the purpose of showing the pathetic state of the characters.

1986: Thomas D. Hill sees blending of pagan myth and ideas of Christian kingship in the Scyld Scefing passage.

1986: Karl Schneider argues at length that the poem is camouflaged paganism with only a deceptive Christian overlay.

1988: Charles Dahlberg reasserts strongly the Augustinian interpretation of the poem.

1988: Gernot Wieland maintains that the characterization of Moses in *Exodus* passed on to *Beowulf* the idea that a hero can be *manna mildost*.

1990: Daniel Pigg views the audience's Christian heritage as furnishing a frame for understanding the shadowy heroic past.

1991: James W. Earl sees the poem as "postheroic, Christian but secular."

1993: John D. Niles in "Rewriting *Beowulf* " distinguishes the rich and supple style of *Beowulf* from what we find in Old English monastic verse.

1993: Alvin A. Lee, opposing exegetical critics, calls the poem pre-medieval, an instance of Northrop Frye's "first phase" mythical language.

Although *Beowulf* deals with ancient Germanic stories and heroes clearly dating back to a time before the Anglo-Saxons or their Continental cousins were converted to Christianity, in its style throughout its narrator and characters seem entirely comfortable with the conventional Christian phrases found elsewhere in Old English poetry, phrases deferring at all times to a recognizably Christian order. There are references to God's creation of the universe, the story of Cain, Noah's flood, devils and hell, and the Last Judgment. At least since 1951, when Dorothy Whitelock's influential *The Audience of Beowulf* appeared, readers have generally agreed that the poet of the text we have was a Christian composing for a Christian audience. Many scholars, and perhaps most ordinary readers, have simply accepted this odd blend of pagan story and Christian teller as perhaps illogical and somewhat puzzling in purpose and implications, but nonetheless the way the poem is. To many other scholars over the years, however, the combination of pagan and Christian elements has seemed a problem demanding clearer resolution.

We ought first to clarify our key term, since *pagan* is a word used in at least three different senses in discussing this problem: the literal, the vestigial, and the ethical. The first sense is the most precise, since it refers to the actual practices and beliefs of a pre-Christian religion in which Germanic peoples participated. For a general account of this religion, see Owen (1981), Wilson (1992; largely archaeological evidence), Polomé (1989), and Niles (1991). *Beowulf* contains descriptions of pagan religious rituals. Most striking are the three accounts of pagan funeral rites, of a kind known to be frequently condemned by Christian authorities: there is an odd version of a ship burial (odd since the funeral ship is not buried in a mound but pushed out to sea) in the funeral of Scyld (26–52), a ceremonial pyre for the casualties in the Finn Episode (1107–24), and Beowulf's own cremation funeral at the end (3134–82), all three rites accompanied by rich grave goods. Discovery in 1939 of a sumptuous ship burial, almost certainly a royal one, at Sutton Hoo in the former kingdom of East Anglia, datable within a few years of 625, and thought by some to be the tomb of King Rædwald, has provided a clear picture of the nature of such pagan funerals on English soil, a picture consonant with the descriptions in *Beowulf,* so much so that some have tried, though without any striking justification, to tie this archaeological find directly to the poem (see Frank 1992, and, for a full account of the find, Bruce-Mitford 1975–83; see also Pearson, van de Noort, and Woolf 1993 and, for a recent discussion of the possible relation of *Beowulf* to East Anglia, Newton 1993).

Then at one point (and one point only, in 175–93) the Danes, despairing of any other remedy for Grendel's attacks, are said to engage in the actual worship of heathen gods, for which the poet roundly condemns them, though realizing with some sympathy that they cannot help their ignorance. Though the Danes of the poem (and indeed all its characters) were pagans both before and after this event, we never otherwise see them engaging in actual worship of any kind (though they may voice vaguely Christian-sounding expressions of gratitude to God), no pagan gods are ever referred to elsewhere, and there is no other explicit mention of their being pagans.

Thus, this curiously isolated passage, the so-called Christian Excursus, was early seized on by scholars who saw it as an obvious reader's interpolation (e.g., Ettmüller 1875), perhaps an outburst of offended piety touched off by some earlier version's more offhand reference to pagan worship. The passage is out of keeping with the dominant strategy of the poem, which might be summed up as "let's assume these old heroes were much like us in their beliefs." Those sensitive to tone will note that in style the passage very much resembles the language of Old English religious and homiletic texts but has few stylistic parallels elsewhere in *Beowulf* itself; one such parallel might be the description of the curse on the dragon treasure (3069–75), curious in that it describes a pagan curse in unmistakably Christian language.

A second "pagan" area is less clearly defined and may be the least important in the controversy, though it was much investigated in earlier years when there was great interest in turning up every trace of paganism. Much of it, perhaps most of it, is what we might call fossil paganism, where an expression we can now identify as originally pagan has been preserved in a poetic formula that may well have lost any such specific meaning. The Germanic gods live every day now in the names of the days of the week, but no one notices it. Like an attic, language, especially the highly stereotyped language of Old English verse, preserves much forgotten lumber. For instance, warriors in *Beowulf* wear helmets with images of boars on them (303b–06a). The boar was an animal sacred to the Germanic god Freyr, and thus its image was once seen as powerful protection, but probably later Anglo-Saxon poets merely inherited a verbal convention that saw boar images as appropriate for heroes' helmets and had no special thought of Freyr. Brief references to magic spells and "battle runes" ("onband beadurune," 501a) probably fall into the same category (but for the persistence of some pagan practices even in late Anglo-Saxon England, see Wentersdorf 1981). Doubtless some of the much-discussed phrases concerning Wyrd or Fate, especially when it seems to be personified, were also such fossil expressions, and not evidence for any still viable religious beliefs in a god or goddess of Fate (the curious should consult references to *wyrd* in the glossaries, and see Phillpotts 1928 and Kasik 1979). There is not enough evidence to conclude that the hanged son for whom the old father mourns, in the famous passage in Beo-wulf's last long speech (2444–59), had been hanged as a human sacrifice, as some have speculated; he might simply have been executed by royal command for some crime. But the recent discovery of mutilated bodies, perhaps hanged, surrounding what might have been a large tree in the cemetery at Sutton Hoo does make the possibility of human sacrifice among the pagan Anglo-Saxons seem more vivid.[1]

The account of the mysterious arrival by boat of the child Scyld Scefing and his ceremonial departure after death seems to be derived from a pre-Christian myth, perhaps an important fertility myth. R. D. Fulk (1989) believes it to be a genuine pagan myth preserved in oral tradition and thus evidence of the antiquity of *Beowulf*. But the story is certainly not offered here as an object of living belief; indeed, any suspicion of such pagan taint is removed by having the Christian God himself deeply involved in the sending of Scyld to the Danes' rescue (12–17; see the comments of Osborn 1978, 973–74).

Another pagan institution that may have left an important imprint on the poem (though a difficult one to detect) is the "cult of kingship" described by Chaney (1970; see also Swanton 1982; Bauschatz 1982; T. Hill 1986; Rollason 1989). In this view of royal sacral authority, the Anglo-Saxons typically blended pagan and Christian beliefs, but such details as the representation of Scyld as "luck-bringing" savior, the rather priest-like role of King Hrothgar, the emphasis placed on King Beowulf's burial mound, which seems almost to be constructed for his people to venerate, even the depiction of God as above all a royal figure, all may be powerful pagan themes that were, as Chaney makes clear, modified and continued by the church, for instance, in the veneration of militant royal saints like Edmund and Oswald. For a general consideration of Germanic modifications of Christianity, see Russell (1994).

A third sense of *pagan* lies in the realm of ethics and morality, and this is the area that has caused the most argument. Here matters might often be clarified if we used terms like *secular* or *non-Christian* (or possibly *Germanic* or *heroic*) for *pagan,* since we clearly do not know enough about truly pagan ethics, the explicit recommendations of pagan priests, for example, to talk reliably about the subject.

The fundamental ethical code of the poem is unmistakably secular: it is the warrior code of the aristocracy, celebrating bravery, loyalty, and generosity, with the hero finding his only immortality in the long-lasting fame of great exploits carried out in this world. It is not fundamentally different from the code found in Homer's *Iliad.* Katherine O'Brien O'Keeffe (1991) provides a good summary of the values of this code. In later Scandinavian mythology, a similar code is sanctioned by the warriors' god Odin (Woden in Old English), who rewards his followers with a place in Valhalla, but we cannot assume that such beliefs were current among Anglo-Saxons, though they sometimes thought it important for their kings to claim descent from Woden (doubtless thinking of him as an ancient hero rather than as a god). The code could clearly have gone on existing, however, without such elaborate supernatural sanctions—as in fact it did.

In certain strict Christian contexts, on the other hand, some of these secular virtues can be seen as vices: especially pride in the frank display of strength and the open pleasure taken in material wealth. Wealth was to the Germanic people ordinarily a positive value, a symbolic measure of a man's worth (see Leisi 1952–53 and Cherniss 1972), but in Christian thinking wealth led too quickly to the deadly sin of avarice. And it was always the case that strict Christians might elect to view these pagans, however obedient they may have been to their own code, as ignorant of the true God and thus having before them only the prospect of damnation.

Before we conclude too hastily, however, that such a secular heroic code is incompatible with the ethics of Christianity, as some have done, we should remind ourselves that a very similar heroic ethic coexists famously with noisily explicit Christianity in other early-medieval heroic poems like *The Song of Roland.* There the Frankish heroes cheerfully alternate mass with massacre, the supposedly noncombatant Archbishop Turpin stoutly cleaves pagan knights in twain, and Roland himself glories in his pride, only sporadically aware of any higher responsibility than to the heroic code involving himself, his fellows in the comitatus of the Twelve Peers, and the Emperor Charlemagne. If in some sense Roland is condemned for his reckless secular pride, he is also loved for it, or there would have been no point in composing the poem or celebrating its hero.

The history of this controversy over "Christian and Pagan" is long, complex, and central to succeeding interpretations of the poem; every general essay on *Beowulf* has been obliged to deal with the problem. I should trace the course of the discussion briefly before focusing on recent attempts to reconcile the apparent polarities.

The earliest nineteenth-century readers of *Beowulf,* most of them northern Europeans, were involved in the Romantic search for national origins and in a revolt against Mediterranean traditions; hence they tended to welcome, and exaggerate, any pagan elements as authentically Germanic and to discount the Christian elements. In his prefatory remarks to the first edition of *Beowulf,* Thorkelin (1815b) had such readers in mind when he wrote: "Some will claim this epic cannot be genuine since it is full of Christian doctrine concerning the one and only God." Thorkelin believed the poem to have been composed by a Danish poet and then imported to England and slightly Christianized, possibly by King Alfred. "Nothing in this poem, I venture to say, would smack of Christianity had mention not crept in, à la Alfred, of the brothers Abel and Cain and his descendants, the Jutes or giants, those destroyed by the Flood, and of the satyrs and monsters. To these intrusions, if you like, add the lament about the Danes' ignorance of God, their worship of Odin, and the pagan spirits doomed to hell" (Thorkelin 1815b).

Ten Brink in 1883, to choose one instance of these early paganizers, speaks of the poem as being based on "the myth of Beowa, the divine hero who overcame the sea-giant, Grendel. . . . He is essentially Frea [i.e., Freyr] in a new form, the bright god of warmth and fruitfulness."[2] It will be noted that here the initial story of Scyld and Beow or Beowa (a name, most commentators now assume, converted erroneously though understandably by some scribe or editor into "Beowulf ") is jumbled together with the main plot of the poem, a common practice in earlier years, with the hero Beowulf being identified with the old god Beow(a). To such readers *Beowulf* seemed a self-consistent and gloriously "pagan" poem by a "folk" poet, but a work that had subsequently been tampered with by Christian scribes and interpolators. This way of thinking accorded with then prevalent ways of reading the Homeric poems as layers of different versions, interpolations, and revisions, in a process that tended to obscure the purity of some earlier, more primitive, and thus more valuable ethnic expression. In the case of *Beowulf,* it was sometimes believed that, before its scribes copied such inflammably pagan material, the church had to add some "Christian coloring" (to use a now famous phrase) to mask and justify the process (see Blackburn 1897; Chadwick 1907; Moorman 1967).

There were certainly precursors of Christian interpretations of the poem, but for this century we might focus on Klaeber, who published in 1911 and 1912 a series of articles that studied and documented the Christian elements in the poem, responsibly and in great detail. He made the indisputable claim that the so-called Christian coloring was not laid late and lightly on the surface but was worked deeply into the very tissue of the poem at every point and could not be surgically removed without the death of the patient, and his majestic and universally admired edition of the poem (1950a) stressed the same point. The student will find Klaeber's own summary in the section of the introduction to his edition entitled "The Christian Coloring" (xlviii–li). It should be agreed by all that, like Klaeber, we can deal responsibly only with the single text we have, even though we are of course free to speculate about possible earlier versions of the poem, whether written or in purely oral form, that might have been less Christian or not Christian at all (for interesting speculations about such earlier strata, see Stevick 1963).

A few others (Schücking 1929a; Du Bois 1934) joined Klaeber in stressing these Christian elements, but it was Tolkien's renowned essay of 1936 that somewhat paradoxically started a powerful new wave of Christian interpretation—paradoxically because Tolkien made much of later pagan Scandinavian mythology, especially the Final Battle and Defeat, Ragnarok, the Twilight of the Gods, as a source for the pessimistic tone of the poem, at the same time seeing the poet as a mature Christian who would have viewed the world of the poem as "heathen, noble, and hopeless (265)." Nowadays, there is more skepticism than Tolkien felt about whether the Anglo-Saxons themselves even knew of such a final battle, since it is only recorded several centuries later in Iceland (van Meurs 1955). Still, the emotional similarity holds true enough: both the poem and the later Scandinavian eschatological myth must be seen as profoundly tragic in tone.

A still fairly cautious and temperate Christian view was that of Marie P. Hamilton in 1946: she envisioned a poet, influenced by Augustine's *City of God,* who saw signs of God's grace operating in pre-Christian Scandinavia, with the poem showing "the Germanic tradition ennobled by the new theology, as by a light flashed backward into the heroic past" (309). A similarly moderate attempt to deal with the likelihood of the poem being fundamentally Christian, though in a severely limited way, was that of William Whallon in 1962, who held that the poet displayed "a primitive form of Christianity" and saw Beowulf and Hrothgar as Christians of the poet's own kind, though having only "a slight grasp of Christianity as we understand it" (82).

But 1963 can be remembered for several much more radically Christian interpretations. In 1951, D. W. Robertson Jr. had included the poem within his all-embracing Augustinian frame of reference as a poem dealing with *caritas* and its opposite *cupiditas,* in an article that led to the movement often named "Robertsonian." In 1960, Margaret E. Goldsmith published "The Christian Theme of *Beowulf*" and continued along the same lines in several articles culminating in her 1970 book, *The Mode and Meaning of Beowulf.* She finds teachings of Augustine and Gregory in Hrothgar's "sermon" (1770–84) and views the poem as a kind of Christian historical novel, with selected bits of paganism deliberately laid on as "local color," such as the references to fate or Wyrd. Of the hero, she writes: "As king, we admire his strength and fortitude. As man tempted, we share his agony of spirit. As soul aberrant from truth, 'reflected against the stainless mirror of the real,' we can only pity him. For he is supremely brave, supremely heroic in suffering, and supremely wrongheaded" (1963, 83). In the same Brodeur festschrift, E. G. Stanley (1963) writes of the certainty of Beowulf's damnation in the eyes of any Christian poet and severely judges the hero's final moments in these Christian terms: "He is a pagan, virtuous, all but flawless. His flaw being this, that ignorant of God he, in the hour of his death, could think of nothing other than pelf and a cenotaph; avarice and vainglory" (203). Still, this "flaw" is immense in any serious Christian context and overshadows whatever pagan virtues the hero may have revealed; the fundamental verdict on Beowulf is crushingly negative. The influential anthology of critical studies edited by Lewis E. Nicholson also appeared in 1963; most of its articles simply start from the assumption that *Beowulf* is an explicitly dogmatic Christian poem.

Another series of short articles published in 1964 and 1965 by Stanley, and later collected in 1975 as *The Search for Anglo-Saxon Paganism,* recounts, often amusingly and with copious quotations, the stubborn and long-lasting attempt by many scholars and critics, extending well into this century, to deny utterly the Christian nature of poems like *Beowulf.* The quotations tell their own undeniable and embarrassing story, but Stanley's study has since often been used by others to accuse any contemporary scholars who refuse to read *Beowulf* as an orthodox Christian tract of being as pigheaded and self-deluding as the older paganizers. This seems an inappropriate extension of Stanley's useful research.

The assertion that *Beowulf* is a seriously didactic Christian poem was now being restated by many scholars (see, e.g., Kaske 1968), and took several forms. An early interpretation was to identify the hero with Christ and to read the poem as an allegory like book 1 of Spenser's *Faerie Queene,* where the Christ figure Saint George also slays a dragon (Cabaniss 1955; McNamee 1960b). This view now seems to have been generally discarded, but another attempt to preserve Beowulf as a basically good and moral hero within a Christian framework is the "noble heathen" approach. For this, one must first posit a more tolerant form of Christianity than we usually find in the early Middle Ages.

Such an attitude is to be found in the more liberal Irish attitude toward noble heathens among their ancestors that has been stressed by Charles J. Donahue; it is a known fact that Irish missionaries had much to do with converting the northern English (Donahue 1950, 1977; see also McCone 1990). But Anglo-Saxonists have unfortunately always been slow to accept the reality of any important influences from the Celtic cultures, and, although this view is a tempting one, it has not attained general acceptance. Taking another approach, Larry D. Benson (1967) pointed out that the Anglo-Saxon missionaries to the Continent in the seventh and eighth centuries felt great sympathy and admiration for the yet unconverted Franks and Frisians and that the poem's positive attitude toward its heathen characters might have reflected that context.

More recently, scholars have brought in the analogy of the Icelandic sagas, in which the action often takes place before the conversion of Iceland about the year 1000 and where pagan characters may be represented as unquestionably admirable. A well-known example would be Gunnar Hamandarson in *Njáls saga,* a noble and glamorous warrior, co-hero with Njal in the saga, who lives and dies a pagan and is given pagan burial. After discussing such Old Norse parallels, Lars Lönnroth

(1969) states that "the whole drama of *Beowulf* seems to be based upon a conflict between noble and monotheistic pagans, dwelling in a world of light and order, and godless heathen monsters" (1969, 7). Richard North (1991) deals chiefly with Icelandic works in discussing "pagan words and Christian meanings"; he sees Gunnar as sympathetic in almost Christian terms.

Such are some of the defenses offered for Beowulf's character, but it has also been under heavy attack from some of the Christianizers, who claim that, far from being a figure of Christ, Beowulf is an active sinner who deserves damnation not merely for the unlucky technicality of being unconverted but for his own evil deeds. Margaret Goldsmith has already been mentioned in this context. Her book of 1970, its footnotes thick with Biblical and patristic references, accuses Beowulf of two deadly sins, pride in recklessly volunteering to fight the dragon alone and cupidity in longing for the dragon's treasure, and similar accusations have since been echoed by others. Two examples of more recent books taking a more moderate "exegetical" view are Huppé (1984) and Dahlberg (1988). Huppé views Beowulf as not so much actively evil as helplessly "caught in the iron circle of heroic error" (38) and sees the conclusion as demonstrating the failure of the "ancestral way" of the English (40). Dahlberg, who is heavily Augustinian in his developing of a Christ-centered theory of kingship applicable to the poem (26–35), finds in it a "sense . . . of constant uncertainty and apprehension" (35). Like Robinson (1985), he stresses what he sees as the poet's careful critical distancing from pagan ideals and behavior.

Aside from often occasioning truly major distortions of the poem's meaning, such interpretations usually demand that we see the poet as a serious cleric, if not a theologian, and his or her audience as one familiar with many patristic niceties. But many studies of this exegetical school tend to be ominously more full of claims like "the audience would instantly have recognized" and "any Anglo-Saxon Christian would know" than full of any evidence for such knowledge. The charge of arguing in a circle is often brought, fairly, against this kind of interpretation. Since the poem is assumed to have hidden meanings, it must have had readers who could recognize them. But such hidden meanings may be visible only to the faithful.

Arguments that introduced a Latin vocabulary into the discussion by that very fact tended to tilt the interpretation of the poem noticeably toward a Latin/Christian/literate context, rather than a secular/Germanic/oral one. Such arguments were those of Bloomfield (1949–51) who wished to see the name *Unferð* as being a translation of *Discordia* and the poem thus resembling Prudentian allegory, and of Robert E. Kaske (1958), who insisted on using the Augustinian terms *sapientia* and *fortitudo* in a long (and quite valuable) critique. But the Anglo-Saxons had plenty of words of their own for these two qualities (Kindrick 1981). Fitting *Beowulf* into such Latinate contexts inevitably makes it seem more "Christian" than it may actually be; unfortunately, we have no equivalent oral/heroic "documents" to support the poem's other components, because such documents never existed.

Opposition to the more extreme Christian interpretations has been steady and sometimes acrimonious. John Halverson (1966) attacked some of the articles in the Nicholson anthology, maintaining that *Beowulf* "is primarily a secular poem with a secular hero" (275) and holding that one may be "suspicious of glowing claims about the thoroughness and sophistication of Anglo-Saxon Christianity" (276). In the following year, Charles Moorman published "The Essential Paganism of *Beowulf*," asserting that the principal Christian elements (which he lists as allusions to free will, Hrothgar's sermon, Beowulf 's moderate behavior and gratitude to God, and assigning the troll Grendel to the race of Cain) are all quite peripheral to the main story itself, in which the "pagan" features (listed as pessimism, a sense of unyielding fate, the heroic code, the praise of heroism, and the celebration of prowess and courage) are central. G. V. Smithers (1970) also speaks of the poet's interjecting of some Christian values into the poem but holds that it is the inherited pagan heroic ethos that matters.

Michael D. Cherniss (1972) sounds many of the same notes in a longer work, its title, *Ingeld and Christ,* an allusion to Alcuin's famed remark, *Quid Hinieldus cum Christo?* (what does Ingeld have to do with Christ?), allegedly reproving the monks of Lindisfarne for listening to secular poetry about the pagan hero Ingeld, a minor character in *Beowulf* (see also Levine 1971). It has been recently argued with some force, however, that Alcuin's letter was not intended for monks at Lindisfarne or elsewhere but directed at a more secular "mixed" audience at a bishop's feast (Bullough 1993). In countering the attribution of covetousness to Beowulf, Cherniss spends much time explaining the positive or heroic Germanic concept of treasure visible in the poem, where it is used to define honor and worth, with no ironic undertone.

Before we venture some tentative conclusions on this controversy, we should first be sure we get everything we can in the way of evidence out of the poem itself, with as few preconceptions as possible. Some years ago (Irving 1984), I made a modest attempt to do so and will summarize a few conclusions. I used a rough quantification of what are generally accepted as Christian references: biblical allusions; references to "Metod" and "Dryhten" and the like; allusions to hell or the Last Judgment. To give a better sense of relative densities, I counted single words, so that "ece" and "Dryhten" registered as two units rather than as a single phrase (for an earlier study of the Christian language of the poem, see Batchelor 1937).

One important finding was that lines 1–1887 of the poem contain one hundred forty-two such references while lines 1888–3182 contain only thirty-six—that is to say, there is one Christian reference for every thirteen lines in the Danish part of the poem and one for every thirty-six in the Geatish part. Several possible reasons for the difference suggest themselves. The most thoroughly Christian speaker of the poem, Hrothgar, is absent in part 2; he averages twice as many Christian references as the narrator in the poem as a whole. Then too the symbolic structure of part 1 is amplified in Christian terms in a way that part 2 is not: it is in part 1 that Grendel is said to be descended from Cain, associated with devils, and either resident in or destined for hell, and it is here that the pious Hrothgar thanks God for sending his champion in the person of Beowulf. But the final fight with the dragon is never put in symbolic terms like these, though prolonged and strenuous attempts have been made by a number of exegetes to relate him to Satan, the great dragon mentioned in chapter 12 of the Book of Revelation.

If the difference between the two parts in this respect is significant, any full account of the Christian/pagan problem might then have to deal fairly and separately with both parts of the poem. It seems likely that the version of *Beowulf* we have may have been patched together from two or three earlier stories. If so, it seems plain that the Danish story (or perhaps two stories: "Grendel" and "Grendel's Mother") was given a much more thorough Christian treatment than the final story of Beowulf 's death fighting the dragon. Why this uneven distribution of Christian references remained in the final composite version is unclear. Osborn offers one possible reason: "There is no need for further scriptural references after the two kinsfolk of Cain have been destroyed" (1978, 979). One may even speculate that the final poet believed that, whatever his heroic virtues, the pagan Beowulf 's death had better not be surrounded by too much Christian language, lest it raise awkward questions.

In the same study, I concluded that the kind of Christianity that *Beowulf* displays is distinctly limited: not so much primitive (though critics may once have seen it as the Christianity of those recently or barely converted) as either deliberately or unconsciously tailored to the dimensions of heroic poetry. Thus, God is not associated with prayers, angels, saints, and miracles (or with the never-mentioned Christ) but is the great and austere King of Heaven, perpetually at war with an evil force of trolls and demons and using the heroic power of Beowulf to accomplish his ends. Preserving the safe and brightly lit human world God has created is clearly a moral goal, but the means he uses are less spiritual than physical. Yet the vitality of this royal, monotheistic God is genuinely felt in the poem; we can still respond to its presence today. In 1984 I wrote: "God is truly felt as a living presence only at those moments when we feel the surges of heroic power in Beowulf. In this special sense the hero is indeed God's agent, for he is the only way we can be aware of God and of how he acts in the world of men we know" (18).

The "mixed" or "blended" nature of the poem is now agreed on by almost everyone, but scholars differ in how to describe it or account for it—and will always continue to do so, in the absence of more knowledge. One way to explain it is to posit some kind of mixed audience. In 1978, the historian Patrick Wormald published an important study of such a mixed audience (see also Wormald 1991). He amasses much evidence to argue that the early Anglo-Saxon church was heavily secularized, with churches and monasteries often the property of aristocratic families, whose members became bishops and monks. He concludes that Christianity "had been successfully assimilated by a warrior nobility, which had no intention of abandoning its culture, or seriously changing its way of life, but which was willing to throw its traditions, customs, tastes and loyalties into the articulation of the new faith" (1978, 57). Thus, a poem like *Beowulf,* which celebrated the greatness of their noble ancestors, would be exactly what representatives of such a secularized culture would demand and would produce. Members of this kind of audience might refuse flatly to concede that their traditional heroes were unworthy of respect or even of some form of salvation. Wormald's view has received support from Lapidge (1982) and Niles (1983, 115; 1993c, 146), among others.

Other readers have made much of a more subtle kind of mixture within the poem itself, namely, the unmistakable contrast in tone between the exultant Danish section, where so much is achieved, and the deep sadness and sense of loss of the last section on Beowulf's death. They tend to take this sense of loss as a form of Christian message. Earl (1982) sees the poem as a statement of deep and necessary mourning (in the psychiatrist's sense) for a great heroic past now irrevocably destroyed by the coming of the new faith. Benson (1967), Frank (1982a), and Robinson (1985), as well as others, view the poem as a kind of historical novel, similar to the Icelandic sagas, in which a conscious and painstaking effort is made by a Christian author to recreate the pagan heroic world, perhaps chiefly to show its limitations as well as its appeal. Thomas D. Hill (1986) echoes Hanning (1974), who speaks of the gloom deriving from "history as yet unillumined by the promise of redemption" (86).

Yet it should be pointed out here that there are readers in our own post-Christian century who have never seen history so illumined and may feel themselves perfectly at home with the "existential" gloom and bleakness of Beowulf's last end. They may find it simply a realistic view of mortal life. They may believe that, like other epic heroes, Beowulf goes in unflinching courage, in the words of Wallace Stevens, "downward to darkness, on extended wings."

This kind of blending of the two traditions, where a work produced in an unmistakably Christian context seems able to tolerate large admixtures of the secular with no sense of incongruity, is not easy to describe. A bold but not entirely persuasive attempt to describe in serious philosophical terms the kind of universe the poet envisions is that of James Earl (1987). His title suggests his basic approach: "Transformation of Chaos: Immanence and Transcendence in *Beowulf* and Other Old English Poems."

The better-known recent attempt of Fred C. Robinson (1985) to define such blending, however, seems to me misguided and unsuccessful, perhaps because he tries so hard to eliminate the very incongruity rather than accepting it as a fact of the poem. While Robinson acknowledges the secular side of the poem, describing it as the poet's wish to honor "lost ancestors" (13), the very word *lost* can be pushed a little farther into meaning *damned*, and we are not surprised to find that he holds to most of the usual "exegetical" interpretations as well (e.g., the dragon = Satan, the characters are "lost eternally").

Robinson tries to resolve these flat contradictions between "heroic" meaning and theological demands by assuming an extraordinary number of puns and deliberate double meanings, where a word or phrase is ostensibly "pagan" but is also sending hidden "Christian" meanings to the audience. Thus, the poet is seen as constantly wigwagging secret messages to his Christian audience over his characters' heads. Robinson here resorts to a desperate expedient, since such punning is no feature of the oral-derived style. It is rather a way of reading inherent in the Latin exegetical tradition of interpretation, where the nut of any word must be forcibly cracked to extract the church's kernel.

Finally, and perhaps most important, the tone he attributes to the poem seems entirely inappropriate: the poet is shown as constantly pointing to, or perhaps gloating over, the pitiable or pathetic condition of the benighted characters. This is in no way the *Beowulf* most of us think we know.

Yet Robinson's approach is a valid attempt to deal with the problem of a double audience, though his method is not successful. Earlier scholars apparently did not really discriminate clearly between what the fictional characters know and what (Christian) knowledge seems to be shared by poet and audience. A fine place to see this distinction is the scene where Hrothgar examines the hilt of the giant sword Beowulf has just brought up from the depths of Grendel's mere.

Hroðgar maðelode— hylt sceawode,
ealde lafe, on ðæm wæs or writen
fyrngewinnes, syðþan flod ofsloh,
gifen geotende giganta cyn,
frecne geferdon; þæt wæs fremde þeod
ecean Dryhtne; him þæs endelean
þurh wæteres wylm Waldend sealde. (1687–93)

[Hrothgar spoke, looked at the hilt, the old relic, on which was written the beginning of the long-ago struggle, when the flood, gushing ocean, struck the race of giants (they suffered terribly); that was a nation alien to the Lord; for that the Ruler gave them their final reward through the surge of water.]

Does Hrothgar read this biblical story? Represented on the hilt (written? carved in runes [the "runstafas" of 1695]? just possibly [the word *writan* has this meaning] drawn as a picture?) is the story from Genesis 6:1–2, describing the "giants on the earth in those days"; mention of them immediately precedes God's decision to destroy all life in the Deluge. A *post hoc, ergo propter hoc* logic can easily see the Flood as directed specifically at the giants. We must say that Hrothgar is here quite illiterate. It is impossible for him to "read" this story, as it was impossible at the beginning of the poem for the assembled Danes in Heorot to "hear" the story of Cain and Abel the poet tells us as a natural sequel to the scop's account of Creation, which the Danes *did* hear. (For further discussion of this aspect of the poem, see Osborn 1978).

John D. Niles has spoken in several places (1983; 1991) of the "tempering" of the strong secular themes of the poem with Christianity, a better way to describe what happened. Something like this takes place, but we may still feel a certain uneasy incongruity. We have a classic example of such strange pairing in the Franks Casket, where a panel showing Weland, a pagan hero of a tale of bloody vengeance, as offering a vessel made of a skull to his captors nestles symmetrically beside one showing the Magi offering gifts to the Christ Child. Did an Anglo-Saxon examining the casket feel that these were similar gifts, both part of equally powerful and interesting stories from the past? So the artist seems to suggest; there is no indication in the *picture* that the Christian story is to be favored. We can never answer that question with any assurance, but it is likely that the Anglo-Saxon's answer would not be ours.

But we should return to safer ground in our own time. Though it is currently unfashionable to assert that literary works are founded on some basic and apparently universal aesthetic principles, I believe they are so founded and that such principles can be applied to *Beowulf*. Since I have tried to carry out this application at some length elsewhere (Irving 1968, 1989), I will here mention only one of the simplest of such inductively derived principles: what a poet talks about and gives full attention to well over 95 percent of the time is what he or she is interested in and what the poem is chiefly about, and thus it is what readers and critics should give their attention to.

From this point of view, *Beowulf* is, in overwhelming mass, an admiring account of heroic action, focused with special intensity on a single figure (there is nothing in the poem that is not directly related to Beowulf), and a somewhat less admiring account of the heroic world in which action takes place. This overwhelming mass, the towering bulk of the poem, has been ignored or brushed aside by those who have clung to the now moribund view of the poem as flat-out Christian sermon; they concentrate on a tiny number of details widely scattered in the poem—surely making up no more than 1 percent of the poem. But it is simply wrong to let details wag the dog.

Yet it would be fair, and an appropriate conclusion that will bring us back closer to the words of the poem, to look at some of these hot spots of past discussion of our topic, these hooks on which so much has depended.

One famous spot is Hrothgar's "sermon" (1700–84). Calling his speech a sermon may prejudge the issue, of course; the term was originally jocular, before the humorless took it over. Hrothgar's chief point is that we should all remember that we are vulnerable to fate and death or we will suffer dire consequences, a valid warning that might be made by any Christian or any pagan. Some readers (e.g., Stanley 1979, 62) have taken the speech to be a theme statement of which the poem is almost an exemplification, but the actual warning is so broadly couched and all embracing that it is hardly a real theme, though appropriate generally to any work with a gloomy ending. It might have been a real theme if Beowulf had turned arrogant or believed he would never die, but that never happens. It is true that Hrothgar's sermon contains some notably Christian imagery (of the evil spirit shooting arrows to wound the sinner), but this agrees with Hrothgar's usual preaching tone and the high ratio of Christian language in his speeches. Furthermore, Hrothgar may not be entitled to make a theme statement about the poem's main business (the nature of heroism), since he is not at all the hero of the poem (for unheroic aspects of his character, see Irving 1989).

A second hot spot is the phrase "ofer ealde riht." News is brought to Beowulf that the dragon has destroyed his royal hall. His reaction is as follows:

> Þæt ðam godan wæs
> hreow on hreðre,   hygesorga mæst;
> wende se wisa   þæt he Wealdende
> ofer ealde riht   ecean Dryhtne,
> bitre gebulge; breost innan weoll
> þeostrum geþoncum,   swa him geþywe ne wæs. (2327b–32)

[For the good one that was grief in the breast, greatest of sorrowful emotions; the wise one believed that against old law he had bitterly angered the Ruler, the eternal Lord. His breast welled up inside with dark thoughts, as was not his custom.]

This seems to be the only time Beowulf feels himself estranged from God's purposes or support, however briefly. He concludes at once that this must be because he has offended God in some way, "against old law." Is that phrase, "ofer ealde riht," a reference to a Christian law (see Goldsmith 1963, 78), or the "old law" of the Old Testament, or "natural law," or a pagan law (Moorman [1967] thinks it might be the heroic code itself), and if so, what does it mean here? Might it just mean vaguely "in a wrong way" in a formulaic phrase dating back to the oral stage of poetry? We cannot furnish certain answers to these questions. It is certainly hard for us to see how Beowulf has had anything to do with the dragon's sudden attack. Beowulf may blame himself for it (he is a super-responsible king, and it happened under his administration), but if we blame him, we turn the whole poem from then on into something it so very clearly is not—a conventional study of crime and punishment rather than a moving tale of a hero's last battle and courageous death.

An even more problematic passage occurs immediately after Beowulf speaks his last words to Wiglaf.

> Þæt wæs þam gomelan   gingæste word
> breostgehygdum,   ær he bæl cure,

hate heaðowylmas; him of hræðre gewat
sawol secean soðfæstra dom. (2817–20)

[For the old man, that was the last word from his inner thoughts, before he chose
the pyre, the hot hostile flames; from his breast his soul went to seek the judgment
of the righteous.]

The last two words occur elsewhere in clear religious contexts and normally refer
to the favorable judgment made on the virtuous at the time of their death, usually
implying their admission to heaven (see Greenfield 1985). Here Beowulf's body
is said to "choose" the flames of the pagan pyre; his soul, however, escapes this fate
and travels to find "the judgment of the righteous." But if he is not a Christian, how
can his soul enter heaven? This question can be answered either by exerting very
considerable pressure on the phrase "soðfæstra dom" or by putting up with the
inconsistency of what is implied. In the first case, the phrase *might* be forced to
mean the opinion of good secular men (though why would his *soul* seek that?),
rather than God's judgment, but that would be a distortion of ordinary meaning. In
the second case, we must accept the poet's casual assumption that so good and great
a king obviously deserves heaven, if anyone does—whatever ecclesiastical
bureaucrats may say. Earlier we were told that King Hrethel of the Geats "chose
God's light" when he died (2469). The phrases slide neatly and quietly into place;
poet and audience seem to agree that these are the appropriate and expected phrases
for the death of good men—unless you are talking about extreme cases of
wickedness, like those who fall back on worshiping idols (178b–83a) or like
Grendel, hell dwelling, man eating, Cain descended (805b–08). They unmistakably
go to hell, and, in the heat of the flyting between them, Beowulf predicts the same
destination for the brother slayer Unferth (588b–89). Obviously, the virtuous—the
soðfæst—Beowulf cannot go where those people go, and his soul goes somewhere.
It goes to heaven. Yet perhaps it is also just as true that his "pagan soul" is placed
in the barrow up above the sea in the course of a pagan's funeral and wins the
pagan's reward of eternal fame on earth. We may be looking at the paradox of the
Franks Casket once again.

Examples like these reveal a few of the underlying reasons for the long
controversy over the poem's religious dimension. Apparently a consensus is now
forming, or has formed, on the subject: namely, that *Beowulf* is at all points a
smooth *blend* of pagan/secular elements with Christian ones, with its chief purpose
to express and celebrate the heroic ethic (see, e.g., John 1974; Tietjen 1975; Earl
1983; Niles 1983). Many believe that the poem is a "swan song," a conscious
memorial tribute to a vanished, or vanishing, culture, and this is certainly what the
historical context would suggest it might be, but people may differ on what that
implies. Some share the views of Hanning (1974, 99): that the poem is "a
devastating commentary on the hero, and the history, of an age possessed of

grandeur but denied the knowledge of Christ from which alone could come understanding and control of its destiny." Here Hanning's word *devastating* seems to throw the emotional balance quite off; nothing in the poem devastates this hero. Others would insist that so strong a statement of ultimate Christian meaning is merely what some think *should be* in the poem, but in fact is not. It is necessary to say at the end of this discussion that such differing *personal* beliefs are unlikely ever to be fully reconciled with each other. And so there will be no end to this discussion.

It hardly needs pointing out, finally, that the Christian/pagan question is tightly connected to other problems dealt with elsewhere in this volume. I will mention here only the unsolved problem of dating the poem. To simplify greatly, we are most likely to find a Christian poet interested in stories from a pagan past in either of two periods: in the time well after the conversion of the English but before the Viking invasions, roughly in the eighth century; or in the later Benedictine revival period of the late tenth and early eleventh centuries, when so many manuscripts were being produced, including the *Beowulf* manuscript. Looking at the problem strictly from this chapter's standpoint, in favor of the earlier period are these factors: the oral tradition is fresher and stronger and the stories are better remembered and admired; some generations have passed since the conversion, but memories or traces of paganism are still present; courts like that of King Offa of Mercia, with some imperial pretensions, or aristocratic monasteries like those described by Wormald have arisen that might furnish suitable "mixed" audiences, with a strong interest in celebrating a heroic past (see Howe 1989). In favor of the later period are these factors: an apparent urgent need to incorporate the culture of the newly converted Danish settlers, who had brought along their own stories of Scylding heroes, into a united national epic tradition; Alfred's well-known encouragement of vernacular literature; enough distance from the pagan English past to enable a poet to recreate it sympathetically; perhaps keener awareness of classical epics like the *Aeneid* as models for a long heroic poem; possibly even new infusions of stylistic features from Old Norse poetry. On these grounds alone, however, we can make no firm decision about the date.

Notes

1. At a session of the Medieval Institute at Western Michigan University in 1993, Martin Carver, director of the Sutton Hoo archaeological project, suggested (with great tentativeness) such an interpretation of the evidence.

2. Quoted in Calder 1981, 214. The reader is referred to this valuable outline of the earlier criticism of Old English poetry, especially up to 1870, and to similar surveys of criticism relevant to this chapter by Rollinson (1973), Donahue (1977), and Short (1980b). George Clark (1990, 13–21, 45–46) has an excellent and up-to-date summary of the matter.

Chapter 10

Digressions and Episodes

by Robert E. Bjork

Summary: Earliest commentaries considered digressions and episodes clumsy breaches of decorum, extraneous matter interesting chiefly for historical reasons, or proof of the poem's multiple authorship. Later commentary, particularly but not exclusively after 1936, viewed them as deliberate parts of an organic whole. The current trend is to regard the approximately twenty-eight digressions and episodes as appropriate in terms of the poem's non-Aristotelian aesthetics and of their cultural function during the poem's time of composition. The Scyld Scefing prologue, for example, once considered a separable entity reflecting vegetation myths, is now considered integral to the poem and responsive to the cultural and political realities of its epoch. Unferth, once thought to symbolize feud, now is seen as a champion participating in a traditional Germanic verbal contest. Finnsburg and Unferth are the most scrutinized digressions, followed by Hrothgar's "Sermon," Scyld Scefing, Sigemund-Heremod, Offa-Thryth, and the Lay of the Last Survivor.

Chronology

1772: Jakob Langebek concludes from Wanley's account of the poem and transcription of lines 1–19 and 53–73 from 1705 that Scyld Scefing is the Skiold of Danish tradition.

1815: N. F. S. Grundtvig conjectures that the Old English account of Scyld predates the Danish; he straightens out the Hrethel episode and clarifies the Swedish wars.

1820: Grundtvig states that the episodes are tasteless intrusions, one of the poem's three major flaws; the others are bipartite structure and blending of history and folktale.

1826: John J. Conybeare states that the frequent, lengthy digressions and the fifty-year gap between the hero's first and last exploits are the poem's only flaws.

1869: Karl Müllenhoff points to what he considers the irrelevant Finnsburg digression as support for his *Liedertheorie*.

1875: Ludvig Schrøder is the first to view the digressions and episodes as participating in the aesthetic unity of the poem.

1877: Hermann Suchier considers the Thryth digression a ninth-century Mercian interpolation to honor the memory of Cynethryth.

1884: Pontus Fahlbeck views the digressions and episodes as integral parts of the poem, products of an aestheticizing consciousness.

1903: Axel Olrik maintains that Unferth ("unpeace, feud") was not created for the Beowulf story, where he is noble, but for the Scylding story, where he is not.

1904: W. P. Ker criticizes the poem's "preposterous" construction with the important material (digressions and episodes) surrounding an irrelevant core.

1904: Edith Rickert distinguishes between the historical Offa of Mercia and the Offa of a lost saga and tries to indicate the content of the saga.

1905: James Routh Jr. demonstrates that episodes are a common feature of Old English style, not proof of the composite authorship of the poem.

1910: Henry Bradley considers the digressions and episodes disruptive additions.

1912: Richard C. Boer argues that the final, "episode" poet of *Beowulf* tried to integrate the episodes and digressions, which are unrelated to the main action.

1917: Harry M. Ayres argues that Hengest is torn between avenging Hnæf and keeping his oath to Finn.

1921: R. W. Chambers analyzes the background and function of a number of digressions, including Scyld, Finnsburg, Offa, and the Heathobards.

1922: Friederich Klaeber (1922a) itemizes the digressions and episodes, which provide "a magnificent heroic background" to the poem.

1924: R. A. Williams explores the possible relation between the Finnsburg episode and the second part of the *Nibelungenlied*.

1926: Kemp Malone finds a parallel between Hildeburh and Hengest in the Finnsburg episode.

1928: J. Schick locates sources for the Offa-Constance legend, not in England, but in the Greek-Hellenistic world.

1929: Carl Otto Fast believes that Scyld was a king in the Göta River region near Göteborg and thus was Swedish, not Danish.

1930: Malone, following Olrik, argues that when Beowulf relates the Heathobard episode, he speaks of past, not future, events.

1930: J. M. Steadman Jr., *contra* Malone, argues that Beowulf's story of the Heathobards is prophetic.

1934: Svetislav Stefanović argues that *Beowulf* contains the oldest form of the Offa legend, which is later fully expressed in the *Life of Offa I*.

1936: D. E. Martin-Clarke maintains that Unferth is an exorcist who fails in ridding Heorot of Grendel.

1937: Alexander H. Krappe affirms Hickes's contention that the Offa-Constance legend is of Byzantine origin.

1943: Arthur G. Brodeur sees revenge as a central theme of the Finnsburg episode.

1949: Henry B. Woolf argues that the poet helps characterize Beowulf through Unferth's move from hostility to silence to admiration.

1949–51: Morton W. Bloomfield views Unferth as an allegorical representation of discord.

1950: Adrien Bonjour writes the first full analysis of all the digressions, offering aesthetic justification for each. He validates the organic unity of the poem.

1959: Arthur G. Brodeur focuses on the Finnsburg, Unferth, and Ingeld episodes, demonstrating how each serves the poem's organic unity.

1959: Robert E. Kaske outlines how the Sigemund-Heremod and Hama-Hygelac episodes are complementary, illustrating the themes of *fortitudo* and *sapientia*.

1962: Norman F. Blake examines the Heremod passages and concludes that Heremod was consigned to torment in hell for his transgressions.

1962: James L. Rosier, on the basis of evidence from Old English and Old High German glosses and Old Norse sources, argues that Unferth is treacherous.

1963: Norman E. Eliason argues that Unferth is the scop in Heorot and that his altercation with Beowulf is a traditional Germanic flyting.

1963: Stanley B. Greenfield explores the ways in which the historical material in the poem contributes to its epic quality.

1964: J. D. A. Ogilvy, *contra* Rosier, argues that Unferth is a champion, not scoundrel, whose challenge allows Beowulf to demonstrate prowess.

1965: Norman E. Eliason asserts that Hygd and Thryth are one person and that the Offa-Hygd-Hygelac matrix connects English audience and Geatish subject matter.

1968: Robert E. Kaske shows that the digressions amplify the theme of *sapientia et fortitudo*.

1969: Angus F. Cameron explains Scyld's non-Germanic funeral by pointing to an Irish saint's life where the funeral vessel was likewise set adrift and not set on fire.

1969: Adelaide Hardy sees Unferth as a heathen priest opposing the Christian Beowulf.

1970: Daniel R. Barnes, using Proppian analysis, shows that Unferth is important as a tester of the hero.

1970: Larry D. Benson argues that the Unferth digression allows the poet to magnify the stature of Beowulf, an obscure hero in the legendary past of the audience.

1970: Fred C. Robinson interprets Unferth's name to mean "nonsense, folly."

1971: Geoffrey C. Britton draws a parallel between Unferth, a renowned hero, and Grendel since both are guilty of fratricide.

1972: Greenfield establishes Beowulf's syntactic superiority over Unferth.

1972: Thomas E. Hart shows numerically disposed relations between the Finnsburg episode and others; this underscores the persistence of feuding in Germanic society.

1974: Donald K. Fry argues that Hengest deliberately spends the winter with Finn to exact revenge.

1976: Ida M. Hollowell interprets Unferth as an important member of the court, perhaps a wizard, who is petulant but not treacherous.

1976: Bruce Moore affirms Ayres's claim that Hengest is torn between revenge and keeping his oath. He opposes Fry.

1976: M. F. Vaughan argues for retaining the manuscript form "Hunferth" and for avoiding interpretations of the character on the basis of his name.

1977: John F. Vickrey holds that Hengest stays with Finn voluntarily and that the story of his revenge is told twice.

1979: Eliason argues that Hygelac, not Beowulf, had an inglorious youth.

1979: Joseph Harris finds the pattern of the Old Norse *senna* in the Beowulf-Unferth exchange; the fratricide charge may be traditional.

1980: Earl R. Anderson detects a Germanic type-scene behind the Finnsburg episode, the Danish-Heathobard feud, and part of the *Nibelungenlied*.

1980: Carol Clover develops a morphology of the Old Norse flyting to provide a Germanic context for the Beowulf-Unferth exchange.

1981: Martin Camargo contends that the Finnsburg episode undermines the revenge ethic.

1984: Jean Haudry contends that the historical digressions exemplify decadence that will lead to catastrophe.

1984: Constance B. Hieatt claims that the names Thryth and Heremod are anagrams of each other and that the characters are mirror images.

1986: Jonathan Evans asserts the non-Aristotelian nature of medieval aesthetics and the centrality of the episode to medieval narrative art.

1986: Thomas D. Hill maintains that the Scyld prologue illustrates the importance of orderly royal succession.

1986: Ward Parks sees in the Beowulf-Unferth exchange a contract for Beowulf to prove his courage by fighting Grendel.

1987: R. D. Fulk rejects etymological and allegorical interpretations of Unferth's name, a normal name with Germanic analogues.

1989: Stephen Glosecki sees vestiges of a shamanistic charm in the Lay of the Last Survivor; the charm ensures Beowulf's defeat.

1989: Parks maintains that digressions functioned as mnemonic devices for both poet and audience.

1990: Catherine Karkov and Robert T. Farrell argue that digressions give concrete examples of gnomic wisdom.

1990: Richard North views the Finnsburg episode as an example of a calculated game rather than as "a case study on heroic honour."

1990: Eric G. Stanley asserts that no single, factually consistent story can be derived from the Finnsburg fragment and episode.

Interest in the "digressions and episodes" of *Beowulf,* like interest in nearly all other aspects of the poem, grew out of the passion of late eighteenth-century Danes for knowledge of their own past. In 1772, Jakob Langebek, not having seen the poem himself, although Thorkelin (1815b) claims he tried to, was the first to link it to Danish history. After reading Humfrey Wanley's brief description of the poem and transcription of lines 1–19 and 53–73 from 1705 (Hickes 1703–5, 2:218–19), Langebek placed Scyld Scefing in the English and Scandinavian chronicle traditions and identified Scyld as the Skiold of Danish legend (1772, 9n. r; 44n. e). In his 1815 review of Thorkelin's first edition of the poem, N. F. S. Grundtvig observed further that the Old English poem probably preserves an older version of the story than Danish sources do since they do not mention Scef. Grundtvig thus started the debate on the notorious Scyld problem in *Beowulf* (1815a, no. 65, col. 1027; cf. Grundtvig 1820, xxxvi–xxxix).

In the same article, Grundtvig laid the groundwork for a great deal more *Beowulf* scholarship, groundwork he himself would be the first to build on. Specifically related to digressions and episodes are his rescuing the name *Sigemund* from Thorkelin's mistranscription ("si gemund") and his recognizing the dragon fight in the Sigemund episode (no. 65, col. 1009); his pointing out that Hygelac's campaign against the Franks and Frisians is different from the Swedish wars; and his straightening out the poet's depiction of the Swedish wars themselves. Later in

1815, in a follow-up article, he also rescued the name *Heremod* from Thorkelin's treatment of it (1815b, col. 1142). He would uncover more names and clarify more narrative as his knowledge of the poem and the language increased. As characters and events emerged from Thorkelin's misreadings, the possibility of interpreting the digressions and episodes emerged as well.

Two years later, in 1817, for example, Grundtvig published what is considered his most comprehensive interpretation of the poem, a synopsis of and commentary on it as a prelimary treatment to his Danish translation of the whole work. There, among other things, he compared the scop's song of creation in lines 90–98, both in content and style, to Cædmon's paraphrase (220), thus laying the groundwork for his argument about date and author. He also talked briefly and contemptuously about Unferth, an ostensible spokesman for the Danes but really merely a warrior angry that anyone could be more famous than he is (229, 231, 242). Hrothgar, said Grundtvig, is rightly annoyed by Unferth's rude conduct. Most importantly, however, at least four comments from 1817, and a couple from a study Grundtvig published in 1841, show that he was developing a theory of the episode in *Beowulf*. That theory, which began as generally critical, would remain so by the time he published his edition of the poem in 1861.

The Finnsburg episode "is absolutely in its right place," he wrote in 1817, because it shows that the Danes lacked the massive physical strength, not the courage or manhood, necessary to defeat Grendel (239).[1] Conversely, he went on to say a few pages later that the story of Freawaru and the Heathobard feud interrupts the tale of Grendel without the slightest reason (249). The stories of the Swedish wars and the Nameless Messenger in part 2 are likewise disruptive, even if they do augment our knowledge of history (266). In fact, the episodes in part 2, said Grundtvig, constitute the principal matter and needlessly obscure the narrative (251). These four statements led to his assertion in 1820 (li) that the episodes are tasteless but that the art of *Beowulf* is still remarkable for its day.

In 1841, Grundtvig allowed that art to extend to a digression or two beyond the Finnsburg episode. The Unferth episode, for example, cannot be deemed an aesthetically pleasing one, he wrote, but Beowulf's boastful behavior justifies it (516). The Sigemund episode, on the other hand, does not offend one's sensibilities where it is, but it probably would have been better placed near the dragon fight—if, that is, part 2 were not characterized by the intrusion of irrelevancies (512). In Grundtvig early medieval art and eighteenth-century decorum meet. The two do not mix well, and although Grundtvig finds *Beowulf* superior to the saga of Starkathr or the tragedy of the Volsungs (1861, xxx), his general criticism of the poem was unshakable: the episodes, on the whole skilfully but tastelessly woven into the fabric of the poem, constitute one of its major flaws. The other two flaws are its bipartite structure and its blending of history and folktale (1820, li).

Grundtvig established the early boundaries for *Beowulf* criticism, particularly for the Scandinavian branch. Arguments about the role of the digressions and episodes implicitly rested on Aristotelian aesthetics as scholars either criticized the poem for not adhering to unity of action, time, and place or praised it for using the digressions and episodes to create an organic whole. Grundtvig is the most often consulted of these scholars and has been said to anticipate Tolkien (e.g., Malone 1941a, 135; S. Bradley 1993, 57). Other Scandinavians, however, do so even more.

In contrast to Grundtvig, for instance, despite his dependence on and veneration for him, is the utterly neglected Danish scholar Ludvig Schrøder, who wrote in 1875 and whose view of the episodes (and poem) is relatively coherent, sympathetic, and Aristotelian.[2] He commented on just a few of the episodes, and, although he could not always perceive why certain ones appear, he believed the poet put them and other seemingly extraneous matter where he did for good reason (73), namely, to establish Beowulf's heroism and to advance the poem's major themes. He saw, for example, that the Breca episode confirms Beowulf's swimming prowess, which would be of importance later (31), that Sigemund and Sigurd are relevant because Beowulf, too, would become a dragon slayer (81–85), and that the Offa and Thryth episode increases the stature of Beowulf, who is implicitly compared to Offa, the great and noble warrior (80–81).[3] Episodes such as these, felt Schrøder, awaken the memory of past glory and link it to present reality, all to underscore the greatness of Beowulf's achievements (64).

A major theme in the poem—the relative weakness eating at the heart of Danish society—is likewise emphasized by the poet's use of episodes. The hint in lines 1160–69 that strife would erupt between Hrothgar and Hrothulf carries with it the suggestion, said Schrøder, that Unferth somehow is the source of that strife; it is a definite weakness in Hrothgar to trust such a man, and he will pay dearly for that weakness (56). Further indications of Hrothgar's weakness and the fragility of his court lie in his willingness to use his daughter Freawaru to buy peace (61) and in the Finnsburg episode, which the poet uses to give specific historical cause for the present weakness: the emigration from Denmark during the reign of Halfdan, an emigration represented by Hengest (91) and creating a vulnerability in the Danes to monsters like Grendel. In all these instances, Schrøder clearly believed that the poet subordinates all his disparate material to specific artistic ends.

A few years after Schrøder, in 1884, the equally neglected historian Pontus Fahlbeck took a particular interest in *Beowulf* and produced the first Swedish commentary on the poem. Fahlbeck's focus was primarily historical, but he too treated digressions and episodes as part of a coherent aesthetic developed by a single *Beowulf* poet. Fahlbeck acknowledged a loose connection between the Beowulf story and historical material, but whatever connection exists the poet himself, whose concept of art differs from ours, establishes. Beowulf occupies the world of legend, which reflects the real world embodied in the historical material in the poem; the historical in *Beowulf,* said Fahlbeck, localizes the poem in time as well as space (75). The Unferth episode, for example, and the description of Beowulf's burial both seem irrelevancies, but both represent historically accurate

accounts of Germanic customs and constitute, he thought, some of the best material
the poem has to offer (76). They are artistically employed, deliberately plucked
from the poet's own imaginative universe to create a believable Germanic world.
Similarly in the cases of Sigemund, Heremod, and Thryth the poet illuminates and
intensifies the nobility of Beowulf by insisting on a comparison between them and
him (79). The Finnsburg digression, too, is manifestly unrelated to the original
Beowulf story but is likewise clearly inserted by the poet for specific aesthetic ends,
that is, to change pace and to supply ornamentation (79). For Fahlbeck, as for
Schrøder, digressions and episodes are the fruits of an aestheticizing consciousness
(79).[4]

These early Scandinavian voices seem not to have been heard by subsequent
generations of scholars; if they were, they were entirely forgotten in the wake of the
hugely influential and atomizing *Liedertheorie* (ballad theory) of Ettmüller and
Müllenhoff, which rendered the digressions and episodes repositories of what
Joseph Bachlechner described in 1857 as the oldest indigenous traditions of
Germanic Scandinavia.[5] The Aristotelian point of view the Scandinavians
represented, however, would emerge again, particularly after Tolkien's 1936 lecture
to the British Academy, and would come to dominate thinking on the digressions
and episodes in *Beowulf*.[6] Before taking up some of the episodes and digressions
as critics tend to—individually—it will be useful to look quickly at those few
scholars who take a global view.

To date only one scholar has devoted a full-length study to the function of all
the digressions and episodes in *Beowulf*. Adrien Bonjour, observing that "few other
features are more characteristic of the *Beowulf* than the use of numerous digressions
and episodes" (xi), produced a monograph that was New Critical in orientation and
that thoroughly elaborated a brief conclusion reached by Adeline Courtney Bartlett.
That is, that "of all the so-called episodic material, only the Finn lay can be said to
be a real digression from the principal narrative; and it, of course, is by no means
unwarranted in epic style. All the other passages have some narrative, even some
dramatic significance. Not only are they not interpolations, they are not even mere
ecphrasis" (Bartlett 1935, 88; cited in Bonjour 1950, xvi). The digressions and
episodes, wrote Bonjour, have two main advantages: their number and variety make
the background of the poem alive (71), and they enrich the main theme (73). All are
"artistically justified"—although in different degrees—a fact that inevitably
suggests unity of authorship (75–76). In 1955, J. C. van Meurs rebuffed both
Bonjour and Tolkien for imposing twentieth-century perspectives on the poem, but,
in the main, Bonjour's concept of the organic unity of the poem (and unity of
authorship) has remained unshaken. In 1959, for example, in his influential *The Art
of Beowulf*, Arthur Brodeur "wholeheartedly" agreed with Bonjour (132), and the
vast majority of scholars has concurred until the present day.

Several other scholars have offered alternative means of viewing the
digressions and episodes in *Beowulf*. Morton W. Bloomfield, for instance, sought

to define the difference between the narrative strategies of epic and romance and did so by concentrating on the role of episodes and digressions. In the former, digressions tend to be rationally motivated or "completely sensible within [the poem's] own premises" (1970, 102). In the latter, they are not. Bloomfield used *Beowulf* as an example of "the almost universally adequate motivation" of episodes in the epic (127). André Crépin, also looking for motivation for the digressions, suggested that the organization, rhythm, and composition of the poem are reminiscent of the divine office (1987, 58), so the digressions and episodes stand in an antiphonal relationship to the main narrative. Clare Kinney, too, along with Catherine Karkov and Robert T. Farrell, argued that digressions have a structural function. Kinney maintained that, like other "narrative moments," the digressions achieve a "fleeting autonomy within the overall linear drive of the exemplary heroic life" (1985, 311), and Karkov and Farrell asserted that they give concrete examples of the gnomes that permeate the poem and define its structure (1990, 303). Finally, two other scholars should be mentioned. Ward Parks claimed that the poet uses the digressions to indicate "the style of relationship obtaining between the *Beowulf*-story and other tales in his tradition" (1989, 28). They are mnemonic devices through which the poet "situates his story of Beowulf in a world of songs" for both poet and audience (32). Less persuasively, Hans-Jürgen Diller (1984) categorized the digressions according to Roman Jakobson's theories of speech pathology and style psychology, finding that the different (metaphoric or metonymic) styles of the digressions confirm the dual authorship of the poem (1984, 78).

The most innovative look at the episode in medieval narrative has been taken by Jonathan D. Evans, who contended that in our evaluation of texts from the early middle ages, we must divest ourselves of an Aristotelian bias, since Aristotle's *Poetics* was not known until the sixteenth century (1986, 127) and could not have influenced those texts. When we do so, we can see that digressions and episodes are not mere troublesome features of medieval narrative that need to be fitted to an organic whole but are the central structural unit of medieval narrative that needs further exploration (130). Although he did not mention *Beowulf,* his analysis has clear, albeit general, relevance to the poem. "In confronting the episodic character of medieval narratives," Evans stated, "we at last address the salient feature that marks the fundamental difference between medieval poetics and the Aristotelian tradition in its proper dimensions—that is, as a difference not merely of accidental textual structure nor of poetics isolated from other spheres of human expression, but universally as a full-fledged semiotic phenomenon" (128–29). The episodic structure of medieval narratives gives "evidence of the cultural patterns creating and sustaining them and investing them with meaning" (134). Future work on the digressions and episodes of *Beowulf* should proceed along the lines suggested by Evans and should probably relinquish the concept of digression itself. Since the poem is demonstrably non-Aristotelian, John Leyerle may well have been correct in stating that "there are no digressions" in it (1967, 13).

Whether or not the poem actually digresses, the terms *digression* and *episode* are commonplaces in the scholarship on it. And within that scholarship, a minor debate has taken place about the precise number of digressions and episodes: Ettmüller (1869) found eight, Bonjour (1950) seventeen, Klaeber (1950a) twenty-eight, and Diller (1984) twenty-nine. In this chapter, I adopt Klaeber's categories (1950a, liii),[7] but, since I obviously cannot thoroughly discuss all twenty-eight items, I have selected three major ones. These present a range of scholarly and interpretive problems and are crucial to our understanding of the poem as a whole: Scyld Scefing, Unferth, and the Lay of the Last Survivor. Many of the other digressions and episodes are touched on elsewhere in this volume (e.g., those containing Christian elements in chapter 9), and I have listed in the chronology the most important statements about those that are not, particularly the most scrutinized of the digressions, Finnsburg and the related Heathobard episode. The scholarship on these two episodes is conveniently assessed by Nellie S. Aurner (1917) and Donald K. Fry (1974a, 1974b). A good starting point for a study of any digression or episode, however, is always Bonjour (1950), which can be supplemented by reference to Short (1980a) and Hasenfratz (1993; 1994).

I. Scyld Scefing, Lines 4–52

Beowulf begins with an enigma for modern readers, who must wonder who Scyld was and how the episode containing him relates to the rest of the poem. Scholars generally agree with Langebek, Grundtvig, and others that Scyld ("Skjǫldr" in the Scandinavian tradition) is "the eponymous ancestor of the Skjǫldungar" (Klaeber 1950a, 121), the royal Danish line called "Scyldingas" in *Beowulf*. Numerous Scandinavian documents support this identification (see Klaeber 1950a, 256–63; Benediktsson 1957–61; Garmonsway and Simpson 1968, 118–23), especially Saxo Grammaticus, whom Klaeber quotes in his commentary on lines 4–52, 6b, 12 ff., 18 f. and 20 ff. Scholars also generally agree that both Scyld and his son Beow (erroneously "Beowulf" in the manuscript) have mythic, not historical, origins. Scyld is undoubtedly a personification of protection (shield) but probably also, by association with Sceaf ("Scefing" = son of Sheaf), reflects vegetation myths.[8] Gustav Neckel and Maire McHugh, for example, found evidence of a vegetation myth behind the episode. Neckel, recognizing the Germanic origins for several Finnish deities, argued for a Finno-Ugric source for the myth, claiming that the Finnish vegetation divinity Sämpsä (see *The Kalevala,* poems 2, 16 [Magoun 1963b]) is identical with Sceaf (1910, 678–79). McHugh, on the other hand, was more general in claiming simply that Scyld Scefing is an unspecified vegetation god while his son Beow (etymologically connected to "barley") is akin to "Pekko," the Finnish personification of the barley god (1987, 17–18; see also Chambers 1959, 87–89, and Fulk 1989; von Sydow 1924, 76 ff. denies any mythic background). At least one scholar has argued for the historicity of Scyld. Carl Otto Fast claimed that Scyld was Swedish, not Danish. The flow of the genealogy, Fast claimed, follows the flow of expanding power south from Bohuslän (the area around Gothenburg) through Halland and Skåne (southern Sweden) to Sjælland in Denmark. Scyld was a king in the Göta River region near Gothenburg; Beow expanded his inherited influence south to Skåne; Halfdan continued the expansion south through Sjælland, where Hrothgar solidified it (1929, 15 ff.; 1944, 64–68). Fast's argument has not been generally accepted.

In trying to identify Scyld, scholars beginning with Langebek and Grundtvig have looked to Scandinavian and Anglo-Saxon genealogies. A major point of interest is that the genealogies by Æthelweard (died c. 1000) and William of Malmesbury (died 1143) both have Sceaf, not Scyld, arriving in a boat while Saxo Grammaticus—the major source of information about Scyld (Scioldus)—does not mention a boat at all. What appears to have happened is that the "arrival-by-boat" motif, found in the Finno-Ugric vegetation myths and transferred to Sheaf in the English accounts, was conflated with the Scyld story in the Scandinavian accounts. Chambers felt that all this "becomes straightforward if we allow that Scyld and Sceaf were both ancient figures standing at the head of famous dynasties. Their names alliterate. What more likely than that their stories should have influenced each other, and that one king should have come to be regarded as the parent of the other?" (1959, 86). Thomas D. Hill, however, considered "the attempt of an earlier generation of *Beowulf* scholars to separate Scyld from Scef and to speculate about the diverse origins and significance of these figures" to be misguided. The peace (shield) and the abundance (sheaf) represented by Scyld Scefing's name, Hill asserted, simply reflects a formula of Anglo-Saxon coronation rituals, *pax et habundantia salutatis* (1986, 41). Likewise deviating from that earlier generation is Joseph Harris. In discussing *Beowulf* as an anthology of literary genres, he placed the Scyld prologue in the tradition of the Old Norse royal genealogical poems from the ninth, tenth, and twelfth centuries. We find an emphasis on the death and burial of rulers in the tradition as well as the same "element of mystery that attends Scyld's passing" (1982, 238). The *Beowulf* poet adapted the genre to his needs as he "integrated the genealogy into his poem as a whole" (239).

Other scholars interested in the genealogical tradition focus on the date of the Scyld Scefing story in *Beowulf,* and Grundtvig's notion that it must be early has not gone unchallenged. Alexander Callander Murray in 1981 and Audrey L. Meaney in 1989 both argued that it is in fact probably late. Murray pointed out that the West Saxon genealogies were arguably composed after the Viking invasions (but see Dumville 1977, 80–81). They show an interest in blending Anglo-Saxon and Scandinavian traditions, as does the prologue to *Beowulf,* which must also therefore be a Viking age genealogy (105). Meaney, likewise noting the blend of Scandinavian and Anglo-Saxon as well as Celtic traditions in the prologue, tried to establish the prologue's dependence on the West Saxon genealogy of Æthelwulf dated 855, where we find the first mention of Scyld's arriving from across the sea. On the basis of this evidence, Meaney concluded that "Scyld Scefing and his arrival from overseas cannot have become part of the prologue of *Beowulf* before 858, and almost certainly not before Alfred's reign" (21).

Scyld's arrival by sea has intrigued scholars, and so has his ship burial, which does not have an analogue in the Germanic tradition. The relevant analogues reprinted in Garmonsway and Simpson (1968, 340–49)—Old Norse parallels and Ibn Fadlan's account of the Rus (c. 922)—include cremation of the dead, but the account of Scyld's burial does not. Scholars have tried various methods for explaining why. C. W. von Sydow maintained that the poet does not actually mention Scyld's death, so Scyld's departure should not be construed as a death journey but rather the leave-taking of the superior, god-like being who arrived mysteriously in the first place (1924, 71). Another scholar, accepting the departure as a death journey, unpersuasively suggested emending "aldor of earde" (lord from the land, 56) to "aldor ofer ade" (lord on the pyre) to solve the problem (Whitbread 1968). And two others found analogues in other cultures for the burial. A. F. Cameron pointed to the Celtic Latin *Life of Saint Gildas,* where "instructions for a ship burial which is very similar to that of Scyld can be found" (1969, 242; adopted by Meaney 1989), and Giulia Mazzuoli Porru, referring to Wulfstan's description of Estonian burial practices in the Old English *Orosius,* argued that Scyld's ship's being covered with ice may reflect a Baltic tradition of freezing the body to preserve it for the death journey (1985, 265–66).

Another way of explaining the unusual burial involves placing the episode in the context of other myths. Without actually mentioning the burial problem, Paul C. Bauschatz saw the iconography of Urth's well in the episode (1982, 103), iconography that would not include fire. Similarly, Jean Haudry maintained that the poem as a whole concerns the cycles of creation and that the first part of the poem is dominated by water and water crossings, symbolic of winter and the danger inherent in it: Scyld's arriving and departing by sea, Beowulf's arriving and departing by sea, Beowulf's swimming prowess and his fighting water monsters, Beowulf's descent into the mere, and the mention of the deluge (1984, 46). Fire would once again be out of place, one could argue, in such a myth and in this part of the poem.

In comparison with identifying Scyld and accounting for the details surrounding his incarnation in *Beowulf,* determining how the prologue relates to the rest of the poem seems relatively uncomplex. The adherents of the *Liedertheorie,* of course, considered the prologue a separable entity, partially proving their theory of the composite nature of the poem. Henry Bradley, for example, found the prologue a "strangely out of place" irrelevancy and postulated a second version of the poem that does not include it (1910, 759). Such reasoning fell into disfavor after Tolkien (1936) and vanished completely after the publication of Bonjour's *The Digressions in Beowulf* in 1950.

Bonjour offered a convincing analysis of the artistic function of the prologue (1950, 3–11). Acknowledging Klaeber's appreciation of the prologue's relation to part 1 or the Danish part of the poem (Klaeber 1950a, cvi), Bonjour extended that relation to the entire text. Not only does the prologue establish the glory of the Danish dynasty, but it also establishes a parallel between Scyld and Beowulf. Both come across the sea to save the Danes. Furthermore, the glorious past of the Scyldings makes Beowulf's undertaking all the more glorious, and the rise of the Scyldings is the prologue to the historical swell of the epic; the expected fall of the Geats is the epilogue. Finally, the prologue offers Scyld's funeral; the end of the poem offers Beowulf's. The poem's beginning thus already contains its end as the opening lines cast a shadow of doom and inevitability over all the subsequent action. At the same time, Scyld's funeral, which is a glorious apotheosis, suggests a brilliant start for a whole race, whereas Beowulf's funeral, which is a gloomy, depressing close to a magnificent life, suggests a terminus, "the end of a glorious past, while the future is fraught with black and uncanny forebodings" (11).

For the most part, scholars after Bonjour have simply added details to his argument or have shifted its focus slightly. Edward B. Irving Jr., for example, contended that "the brief proem that tells of Scyld does what the poem as a whole does: it defines [memorable strength and courage], shows them in action, and perhaps even tests them" (1968, 44). Similarly, Pamela Gradon argued that "the fundamental pattern of the poem can be seen in the Scyld prologue," which contains "the arrival, the rise to fame, and the death of the hero. All the rest of the poem is a development of, and a comment on, this schema" (1971, 128). Earl R. Anderson, on the other hand, unearthed a fresh connection between the prologue and the poem proper, discerning the metaphor of the mead hall underlying the description of Scyld's conquests. The metaphor receives concrete expression in the building of Heorot (1972, 4; see also Irving 1989, 137). Jean Haudry, too, perceived the connection between prologue and Heorot, observing that the hall represents the culmination of the mythical golden age initiated in the Scyld story (1984, 46).

While some scholars implicitly accept Bonjour's premises, they have taken them in slightly different directions. Lewis E. Nicholson imposed a typological reading onto the prologue, maintaining that its setting (and the whole poem's) is antediluvian. Baptismal symbolism permeates the narrative. Scyld Scefing's association with Sceaf and water and Sceaf's traditional association in the genealogies with Seth, the son of Adam, begin the sacramental imagery (1964, 159 ff.), and Scyld's funeral rites become a *figura* for baptism: "the pagan ceremony of ship burial described here bears a striking resemblance to the sacramental typology of baptism developed by the Patristic writers" (185). Not adopting a typological scheme, Marijane Osborn nevertheless discerned two levels of knowledge in both poem and prologue, "that bound by the secular world of the poem and that perceived from our initiated Christian perspective" (1978, 973). Scyld's past glory is known to the audience within the poem but his destiny only to listeners or readers outside it (974).

In trying to determine the relation of prologue to poem, three other scholars have examined overarching patterns. Thomas A. Shippey employed Proppian analysis of the fairy-tale structure of the poem and suggested that the Scyld prologue contains the first two components of such a structure: it introduces the requisite family of a folktale and the requisite absence of one of its members, Scyld (1969, 4–5). Thomas D. Hill maintained that the Scyld prologue "articulates one of the main ideological concerns of the poem, the importance of true kingship and orderly succession" (1986, 44). And James W. Earl contended that the famous parable of the sparrow from book 2, chapter 10 of Bede's *Ecclesiastical History of the English People* (Colgrave and Mynors 1969) underlies the structure of the episode. Like the sparrow, Scyld comes in from and exits to the unknown and has a glorious existence while he lives (180). The poem, too, manifests the same pattern. "The world of the parable is the world of the poem—a hall in a storm, besieged, promised to ruin, distinctly material, strongly determined, wholly immanent. Here the transcendent is simply unknown, everywhere bordering the world of the known as the ocean surrounds the earth" (1987, 180–81).

II. Unferth, Lines 499–606

Unferth has concerned critics since Grundtvig, who eventually saw him as fulfilling a dramatic purpose (1841, 516). Most studies after Grundtvig have focused on the characterization of Unferth and the role he plays in the poem; virtually all of these rest on an underlying assumption of dramatic verisimilitude in the text. Axel Olrik considered Unferth to be a divided character, reflecting the possibility that the poet did not create him but rather retrieved him from legend. In the Scylding part of *Beowulf,* where Unferth is the instigator of evil and Beowulf's antagonist, Unferth lives up to his legendary origins; in "the Beowulf episodes," his villainy is unnecessary, and he graciously lends Hrunting to a superior warrior (1903, 55–58; cf. Klaeber 1950a, 150; Ogilvy 1964). One of Unferth's main functions in the Scylding part of the poem, wrote Olrik (58), is to allow the poet "an opportunity to give an account of Beowulf's youthful exploits" (see also Rosenberg 1969, who put this function in a folkloristic context).

Unferth's villainy seemed obvious to many scholars besides Olrik. Schrøder, for example, considered Unferth an untrustworthy scoundrel (1875, 56); Chambers declared him "evil" (1959, 27); Henry B. Woolf deemed him the least heroic Dane, the least like Beowulf (1949, 52); Brodeur did not doubt his "ultimate treachery" (1959, 153); and Geoffrey Hughes labeled him "a failed warrior, an empty boaster, a treacherous fratricide and a figure of ominous discord" (1977, 395). Other scholars, however, have been less condemnatory (e.g., Bonjour 1950; Ogilvy 1964; Barnes 1970; Benson 1970; Britton 1971; Gingher 1974), viewing Unferth as a noble warrior who voices the misgivings of the Danes about Beowulf's abilities (Bonjour 1950, 17). Sisam's comments sum up this point of view quite well: "For the part he plays, [Unferth] must be eminent . . . an active champion . . . a brave man, short of being a match for Grendel: that would have spoiled the story. There is no evidence that he had the part of a traitor or evil counsellor in a time of strife between Hrothulf and Hrothgar's family" (1965, 41).

Along with an emphasis on Unferth's character came an interest in specific details of the poet's description of him and his exchange with Beowulf. The manuscript reading for Unferth's name is "Hunferth" (499a, 530a, 1165b, 1488a), for instance, but scholars since Olrik have maintained that "the alliteration proves that it ought to begin with a vowel: *Unferð*. Reducing this to the form it must have had at the time when *Beowulf* was composed we obtain the form *Unfrið*. The name signifies 'unpeace, feud'" (1903, 56). Olrik's formulation contains three considerable leaps—from emendation[9] to metathesis of vowel and consonant to allegory—but critics have accepted it nonetheless. Klaeber simply repeated it (1950a, 148), and Morton W. Bloomfield (1949–51) embraced it to construct a complex allegorical reading of the poem wherein the Christian Beowulf conquers the heathen *discordia,* personified in Unferth.

Although other scholars rejected "unpeace" as the meaning of Unferth's name, they still found symbolism in it. In a brief onomastic study, Fred C. Robinson interpreted several names in *Beowulf.* The unmetathesized meaning of *Unferð* or *Unferhð* would be "unmind" or "nonsense" or "folly" (1970b, 46; see also Robinson 1974, 127–32). Stanley B. Greenfield likewise reasoned that the unmetathesized form was preferable to scholars' reconstruction but took the *un-* prefix "as an intensifying particle rather than the negative (or we may even retain the manuscript *Hun* = 'giant')" (1972, 106; see also Roberts 1980). *Unferð* could thus mean "great heart" or "giant heart."

Niles found Greenfield's argument sound but did not think "Hunferth" needed emendation in the first place (1983, 82–83). Other scholars have been more insistent. Lewis E. Nicholson claimed that the manuscript reading "Hunferth" for "Unferth" should be retained, since *h* plus a vowel may alliterate with other vowels in Old English (1975, 51–52), and M. F. Vaughan also wanted "Hunferth" restored, since the name as spelled was a common Anglo-Saxon one, he claimed (1976, 42 ff.). He, like Nicholson, also insisted that the *h* in the name may not have been pronounced. Restoring the "Unferth" to "Hunferth" would remove the traditional symbolic connection between character and name (see also Silber 1980; Kiernan 1981a, 188; Taylor and Davis 1982, 619; and Daldorph [= Dahlberg] 1986). In a richly documented article, R. D. Fulk likewise argued that "Unferth" is "a normal Germanic hero's name," though not Anglo-Saxon (1987, 113), and he also dismissed allegorical readings of that name because its commonality argues against its symbolic nature. But the urge to restore the manuscript spelling of "Hunferth" he dismissed as well since *h* plus a vowel does not alliterate with vowels in any other place in *Beowulf* (119 ff.). As Niles and others have pointed out, however, editors have changed a number of *h*-initial words in the manuscript, "where they make good sense" (1994, 458), to vowel-initial words. In the case of Hunferth, this is unfortunate since "an intelligible and well-attested Anglo-Saxon proper name—one that in the context of this poem may carry somewhat sinister overtones, connoting 'the one of Hunnish spirit'—is rendered into a name of debated meaning . . . or no particular meaning at all" (459).

For the time being, the dispute over Unferth's name seems unsettled, although it has moved away from Christian allegoresis. The meaning of Unferth's position as "þyle" (1165a, 1456b) who "æt fotum / sæt frean Scyldinga" (sat at the feet of the lord of the Scyldings, 500, 1166a) likewise remains unsettled. Some scholars have tried to determine the meaning of *þyle* in a broad context (e.g., Vogt 1927) but usually in connection with what was thought to be the symbolic nature of Unferth's name. The results are predictable. Those with a bad opinion of Unferth find a perjorative meaning for the term; those with a good opinion find a good one. James L. Rosier's highly influential study from 1962 is the best example of the former. Basing his argument on evidence from Old English and Old High German glosses and from Old Norse, Rosier concluded that the word has a negative sense in *Beowulf* that accords well with Unferth's treacherous actions in the rest of the poem (1–3). Only a "drunkard, scurrilous accuser, fratricide, and coward" (4) could have committed them. J. D. A. Ogilvy questioned Rosier's interpretation of his evidence (1964, 370–71), arguing instead that Unferth is a champion warrior "of some reputation" (374) who is a foil to Beowulf, and I (Bjork 1980) questioned Rosier's evidence itself, pointing out, for example, that Rosier found glosses for compounds of *þyle,* not *þyle* as a simplex. Rosier's argument, shaky as it is, continues to have influence, however, even if those attending to it may find it questionable (e.g., Fulk 1987, 116 n. 16; Jack 1994, 99 n. 1165).

A positive interpretation of *þyle* can likewise derive from examination of Old English glosses and Old Norse literature, however. Ida M. Hollowell found that Scandinavian sources indicate the priest-like function of the *þyle* (1976, 243–45) and that the Old English glosses cast a "favorable light" on the term (251). Unferth is a wise and important man carrying out an important function in the pre-Christian world of the poem.

Attempts to clarify the role of *þyle* in *Beowulf* are attempts to define the cultural underpinnings of the epic, and other scholars have searched for those underpinnings as well. D. E. Martin-Clarke, for example, described Unferth as a hero-exorcist, prophet-priest or shaman, or sage (1936, 63), who happens to have failed in ridding Heorot of Grendel (see also Hardy 1969; Baird 1970; Hollowell 1976). Malcolm M. Brennan, on the other hand, analyzing the governmental structures revealed in Hrothgar's court, stated that Unferth's functions resembled "those of a public prosecutor" examining a petitioner to the court (1985, 10). Interesting and useful as such studies are, those with a broader focus—the Germanic context of the episode—seem to offer more complete explanations for Unferth's role in the poem. Many critics, such as Rosier (1962) and Eliason (1963), have observed that the Beowulf-Unferth exchange is an example of a Germanic flyting, a verbal battle traditional in heroic verse. Joseph Harris expanded the observation, placing the scene in *Beowulf* in the context of twelve *senna* (quarrel) passages in Eddic poetry, finding among other things that Beowulf's accusing Unferth of fratricide may be a traditional part of such duels (1979, 69). Carol J. Clover's 1980 *Speculum* article, however, has proved to be definitive on this subject. Clover provided a taxonomy of the flyting in all its manifestations in Old Norse (the *senna*, the *mannajafnaðr* [man-comparison], and *nið* [sexual defamation]), focusing on setting (447–52), structure (451–53), content (453–59), and outcome (459–63), and demonstrated that the relation of the episode in *Beowulf* to the Old Norse examples "is immediate and detailed." It lacks only the sexual element, but then "the *Beowulf* poet is not known for developing the erotic dimensions of his gothic tale" (466). Clover's study has clarified much about the Unferth episode. It explained Unferth's seemingly rude behavior that receives no reprimand and occasions no apology. It accounted for "the unusual rhetorical features of the speeches." Through it, "the seemingly abrupt and anticlimactic ending (Unferth's silence) is likewise accounted for. The Hel curse may be regarded as a traditional element requiring no further explanation." Clover also rendered unnecessary the need to allegorize Unferth's name. If it is meant as an abstraction, the abstraction "is by way of embellishment, not explanation" (467; see also Parks 1986, elaborated in Parks 1990, 42–95).

Central to the flyting, as Clover noted, are the "unusual" speeches, which Klaeber claimed "show the style of the poem at its best" (1950a, 150). Several critics have demonstrated how. Stanley B. Greenfield examined the syntax of the exchange, pointing out that Beowulf's speech contains numerous subordinating conjunctions, which help make it "measured and thoughtful" and differentiate it from the unsubordinated, aggressive, emotional speech of Unferth (1972, 130–31). Livia Polanyi, focusing on lexical sets "with their synonyms, antonyms, homonyms, and semantically near neighbors" in the two speeches (1977, 25), found that Beowulf's superior manipulation of those sets makes him "an intelligent and skilled orator as well as a mighty fighter" (34), a point more fully developed by Baker (1988, 11–19) and others. Patricia Silber, for example, analyzed the classical and Germanic rhetorical schemes in the flyting to support her view that the debate is "not over physical valor, but rather over ready wit, eloquent speech, and telling allusions" (1981, 473). Beowulf wins. And I noted Beowulf's superior use of stylistic devices important in the poem as a whole. Beowulf's speech contains two instances each of chiasmus and maxims, six of enjambed alliteration, and one of a bracketing pattern of auxiliary and verbal. Unferth's contains one instance of chiasmus and one of enjambed alliteration (Bjork 1994, 1012). Future work on these speeches is unlikely to turn the tables on Beowulf.

III. The Lay of the Last Survivor, Lines 2247–66

Interest in the so-called "Lay of the Last Survivor" focuses on its generic characteristics, its thematic relevance, its structural features or function, and its speaker. Most scholars have viewed the Lay as an instance of the Old English elegy, comparing favorably with such examples as *The Wanderer* or *The Ruin* (e.g., Ernst Sieper 1915; Klaeber 1950a, liv; Greenfield 1966, 142–43). Levin Schücking argued that generically it lies midway between the "death lament" (what Schücking considered to be the oldest form of elegiac poetry in Old English) and the elegy proper (1908, 11–13). Other scholars have discerned generic elements beyond the elegaic in the Lay as well. Robert P. Creed (1989) sensed a ritual incantation in "Heald þu nu, hruse, / nu hæleð ne m[o]ston, // eorla æhte" (Hold now, earth, now that men cannot, the possessions of noblemen, 2247–48a). The ritual called into effect here is a general one of the circle, argued Creed, that we still see in such commonplace expressions as "ashes to ashes, dust to dust" (164). As men took gold from the earth, the Last Survivor returns it, and Beowulf's survivors "repeat the Last Survivor's ritual as the poem draws to its close" (165). Stephen O. Glosecki was more specific still in discerning vestiges of a shamanistic charm in the lines, which are "a literal command, identical to the imperatives used in fully recorded charms" (1989, 105). The charm seals Beowulf's doom, "since the enchanted gold is bound to kill the man who wins it from the dragon" (106).

Scholars have also tended to view the Lay as serving a clear thematic purpose, almost unanimously agreeing with Bonjour that the lyric reflects the dominant grieving mood at the end of the poem (1950, 68). Bonjour also maintained that the destruction of the Last Survivor's people foreshadows the destruction of the Geats (69). Subsequent scholars have added weight to Bonjour's analysis. Edward B. Irving Jr., for instance, pointed out that the passage moves steadily "toward a state of total rest," both for the treasure and "the living society for which it stands" (1968, 213); Martin Green drew a connection between the Lay and the poem's apocalyptic imagery (1975, 515–18); and James W. Earl (1979, 82) and M. A. L. Locherbie-Cameron (1978, 6) focused on the Lay's retrospective qualities, which emphasize the theme of transience. A number of scholars before and after Bonjour have compared the Lay with the Father's Lament (2444–62a), an elegy likewise conjuring up images of futility and doom, and at least two (Locherbie-Cameron 1978, 6; Niles 1983, 231–32) have seen similarities connecting those two passages with the equally sorrowful Messenger's Prophecy (3014b–27). The last part of the Lay also "compares closely with the passage in Hrothgar's sermon that directly confronts Beowulf with his own death (1757–68)" (Chickering 1977, 357).

Less attention has been paid to structural features of the Lay and to the identity of the Last Survivor than to the Lay's thematic relevance. In the first instance, four scholars have looked at the Lay's ring structure or its presence within such a structure. Adeline C. Bartlett pointed out that the lyric itself is an example of an envelope pattern, although she found it a crude one (1935, 24); both Constance B. Hieatt (1975, 256) and Niles (1983, 157) noticed a "minimal" envelope beginning with the Lay and ending with an observation by Wiglaf (2864–91); and Ward Parks offered a detailed account of how the Lay is central to a complex ring pattern that "consists of three rings: an external ring (A) narrating the five-step process of the dragon's arousal, a boundary ring (B) describing the concealment/discovery of a treasure hoard, and an internal ring (C) that presents the theme of human society and human happiness in its negative (anti-typal) form." The ring system "yokes together the digression with the story that follows, just as Grendel's arousal earlier connected the Song of Creation with the narration that followed it" (1988, 250).

Since the Lay of the Last Survivor strikes such a universal note of gloom, the speaker's identity has not seemed important to many critics. Even so, diverse scholars beginning with Ettmüller (1840, 177) have pondered the problem and have held that the warrior was transformed into the dragon after consigning the treasure and himself to the earth. G. V. Smithers felt that such a conclusion was both ineluctable and necessary for explaining the presence of the Last Survivor in the poem that "would otherwise be both puzzling and pointless" (1961, 11). Raymond P. Tripp Jr., too, felt that the dragon was originally the warrior, but his interpretation of the digression differs from all others. Tripp maintained that in the unemended text of *Beowulf,* there is neither a Last Survivor nor a dragon (an animal). The two are actually "a single evil king, most likely Heremod himself, who became a dragon and later, for reasons of hateful greed, like Grendel before him, attacks a good king." Tripp felt that eliminating emendations from the text would also eliminate the ancient curse, which is instead "a contemporary prohibition placed by the Geats themselves upon any further abuse of treasures as a means to survive against God's will" (1983, ix). Tripp's views have not been influential.

IV. Conclusion

The three digressions discussed here offer up a considerable variety of content and a complex range of scholarly conundrums. Those that cannot be discussed because of limitations of space participate in a similar complexity. For example, the Breca episode (419–24), nested within the Unferth episode, attests to Beowulf's ability to complete his task in Denmark and can be seen adumbrated in his slaying giants in his youth (see Lawrence 1913; Bonjour 1950, 13, 17–22). Beowulf's youth (2183b–89) may or may not have been inglorious, and the fate of Heorot may or may not have been sealed (81b–85). Similarly, Thryth, usually considered a negative contrast to Hygd (Eliason 1979 and 1980), may actually be Hygd in her youth (Eliason 1965), and the story of Sigemund (874b–97), which scholars have viewed as much earlier than its Old Norse analogues, may be more nearly contemporary with them (Frank 1981, 130–31). Finally, Hama (1197–1201) may be a legendary Germanic hero or a cricket, a manifestation of "Loki's fly personality" (Damico 1983, 231).

The cumulative effect of all the possibilities inherent in each digression is to affirm both the mercurial, polysemous nature of each and the non-Aristotelian character of the early medieval world that Evans described (1986). In an aesthetic sense, the individual episode seems a microcosm of the poem, with a dazzling, complex depth that renders it prism-like, reflecting variegated light and layered meaning with each twist. In concert, the episodes partially account for what might best be described as the kaleidoscopic effect of *Beowulf*. There is, after all, no still point in this turning poem, and as we enter it through the first enigmatic reference to Scyld, we inhabit as much the world of Virginia Woolf as of *Beowulf*. For neither life nor this epic is "a series of gig lamps symmetrically arranged; but a luminous halo, a semi-transparent envelope surrounding us from the beginning of consciousness to the end" (Woolf 1925, 212). The digressions and episodes in *Beowulf* constitute a large part of that envelope and become a dominant means of conveying "this varying, this unknown and uncircumscribed spirit" (213).

Notes

1. In 1841, Grundtvig said that the episode is appropriately placed to emphasize the likeness of Hildeburh and Hrothgar, both of whom exact revenge on their enemies (516 ff.).

2. For a fuller treatment of Schrøder in the context of Scandinavian Anglo-Saxonism, see Bjork (1997).

3. Schrøder anticipated Adrien Bonjour's conclusion that Offa's successful career "may give us a kind of prefiguration of Beowulf's own future successful leadership" (1950, 55).

4. Another Dane (and Grundtvig's student) was Frederik Rönning (1883), who argued specifically against *Liedertheorie* and likewise found unity in *Beowulf*. Chambers points out that fifty years after Rönning made his neglected argument, it was generally accepted (1959, 400).

5. For a full discussion of ballad theory, see chapter 8.

6. The few definitions of digression and episode that scholars have formulated testify to the strength of that implicit point of view, for all clearly imply the subordinate status of both. Bartlett, e.g., wrote that digressions are "elaborated narrative passages which would appear to be present . . . as much for their own sake as for the sake of furthering the progress of the principal narrative" (1935, 85). Bonjour described the episode as "a moment which forms a real whole and yet is merged in the main narrative [e.g., Finnsburg], whereas a digression is more of an adjunction and generally entails a sudden break in the narrative [e.g., Offa and Thryth]" (1950a, xi). And Diller considered a digression "a piece of text which interrupts the chronological progress of those events which make up the main story, by telling or summarizing (sequences of) events outside that story" (1984, 71).

7. In part 1 the digressions and episodes are: (1) Scyld Scefing, 4–52; (2) the fate of Heorot, 82b–85; (3) the song of creation, 90b–98; (4) the story of Cain, 107b–14, 1261b–66a; (5) Beowulf's slaying giants in his youth, 419–24; (6) the settling of Ecgtheow's feud, 459–72; (7–8) the Unferth episode (plus Breca), 499–606; (9) the Sigemund and Heremod episodes, 874b–915; (10) the Finnsburg digression, 1069–1159a; (11) the stories of Eormenric and Hama, 1197–1201; (12) the fall of Hygelac, 1202–14a; (13) the Deluge and destruction of the giants, 1689b–93; (14) Heremod's tragedy, 1709b–22a; (15) Hrothgar's "sermon" against pride, 1724b–57; (16) the Thryth and Offa digression, 1931b–62; (17) the Heathobard-Dane feud, 2032–66; and (18) Beowulf's inglorious youth, 2183b–89. In part 2 they are (19) the Lay of the Last Survivor, 2247–66; (20–21) Geatish history: Hygelac's death, Beowulf's swimming match, and Heardred and the second Swedish wars, 2354b–96; (22–25) the stories of Hrethel

and Herebeald, the earlier Swedish wars, and Dæghrefn, 2428–2508a; (26) Weohstan's slaying of Eanmund in the second Swedish wars, 2611–25a; (27–28) Hygelac's fall, and the battle at Ravenswood in the earlier Swedish war, 2910b–98.

8. For a full discussion, see chapter 11.

9. The emendation was first suggested by Max Rieger (1871, 414).

Chapter 11

Myth and History

by John D. Niles

Summary: Nineteenth-century interpretations of *Beowulf*, particularly in Germany, fell under the influence of the nature mythology that was then in vogue. More recently, some critics have related the poem to ancient Germanic or Indo-European myth and cult or to archetypes that are thought to be a universal feature of human consciousness. Alternatively, the poem has been used as a source of knowledge concerning history. The search for either myth or history in the poem, however, is attended by severe and perhaps insurmountable difficulties. More useful may be attempts to identify the poem as a "mythistory" that confirmed a set of values among the Anglo-Saxons by connecting their current world to a fabulous ancestral past.

Chronology

1833: John Mitchell Kemble, offering a historical preface to his edition of the poem, locates the Geats in Schleswig.

1837: Kemble corrects his preface to reflect the influence of Jakob Grimm; he identifies the first "Beowulf" who figures in the poem as "Beaw," the agricultural deity.

1849: Karl Müllenhoff (1849b), also inspired by Grimm, identifies the poem as a Germanic meteorological myth that became garbled into a hero tale on being transplanted to England.

1861: Daniel H. Haigh, in a fanciful study, discovers historical models for the action of *Beowulf* in fifth-century Northumbria.

1884: Pontus Fahlbeck argues that the poem's Geats are the Jutes of history; his thesis provokes debate for almost fifty years.

1889: Karl Müllenhoff restates his mythological theories: Grendel and his mother represent the North Sea in its spring floods; the dragon represents the sea driven by autumn storms.

1907: Henrik Schück, writing against Fahlbeck and others, argues that the poem's Geats are the Gautar (modern Götar) of southern Sweden.

1909: William W. Lawrence attacks various mythological interpretations of the poem.

1921: R. W. Chambers foregrounds the poem's historical elements and finds them based on fact, accepts the identification *Geatas* = *Gautar*, and speculates that the *Beowulf* story came to England via Geatish exiles in Angeln.

1925: Kemp Malone, building on Chambers's suggestion, surmises that Geatish exiles established a state in Jutland after their kingdom was overthrown by the Swedes.

1928: W. W. Lawrence, while repeating his antimythological arguments, builds on the poem's internal hints and allusions to develop a complex account of the poem's substratum of history.

1932: R. W. Chambers, in the second edition of his *Introduction*, comes down hard against the Jute theory, closing this debate for the time being.

1936: J. R. R. Tolkien, inaugurating an age of aesthetic criticism, argues against scholarship of a narrowly historical, archaeological, or philological kind.

1950: Friedrich Klaeber's third edition of the poem (1950a) confirms the Chambers/Lawrence consensus: mythological theories are of little value, but the poem probably contains much true history.

1951: Samuel F. Johnson initiates a wave of neomythological criticism by isolating aspects of Indo-European culture in the poem: a tribal coronation rite, rites of passage, and a totemic hero.

1959: Joseph Fontenrose identifies the poem as a variant of the ancient Apollo-Python combat myth.

1964: Carl Meigs analyzes the poem in terms made familiar by Frazer, Weston, and Campbell and sees in it "the mythical progress of a world hero."

1965: Kenneth Sisam argues against two firmly-entrenched notions: that the Geats are destroyed after Beowulf's death and that Hrothulf betrays Hrothgar's faith and usurps the Danish throne.

1966: Paul Beekman Taylor, taking the hall Heorot as both a figure of the macrocosmos and a counterpart to the Asgard of Old Norse myth, finds that the poet writes at a point where Christian and pagan eschatology merge.

1967: Jane Acomb Leake, identifying the Geats as the legendary *Getae* rather than any historical tribe, argues that the poem presents a fanciful "geographical mythology."

1968: Jeffrey Helterman presents a mythic interpretation of the poem indebted to Jung and Eliade and argues that the tragedy of the poem arises as the hero passes from myth (in part 1) into history (in part 2).

1969: A. Margaret Arent, drawing on archaeological evidence, maintains that the hero's life and deeds reflect ancient archetypes and cult practices.

1969: Ursula Dronke finds that the poem is a euhemerized version of the Germanic myth of Ragnarok; the hero is a secularized counterpart to Thor/Thunor.

1969: Amy Page and Vincent H. Cassidy, seeing Beowulf as a man-god who must descend to the netherworld, pursue parallels with ancient Sumerian, Greek, Hebrew, and Christian myth.

1970: Terry A. Babb finds in the poem a myth of creation and dissolution, here turned to elegiac purposes.

1970: Janet H. Dow discovers in the poem an archetypal myth, laden with psychological significance, whereby a savior-hero confronts his shadow self and the Great Mother.

1972: Alvin A. Lee, pursuing archetypal criticism of the kind associated with Northrop Frye, analyzes the interplay of four myths in *Beowulf*: cosmogony, fratricide and crime, the heroic redeemer, and the return to chaos.

1972: Robert T. Farrell disputes the accepted idea that the Geats of history suffered tribal dissolution soon after the era described in *Beowulf*.

1977: John Miles Foley, basing his argument on Jung and Neumann, argues that the poem served as a psychohistory for the Anglo-Saxons: the hero represents the nascent ego, Grendel the Terrible Father, the monsters' mere a pool of chaos and the unconscious.

1979: Martin Puhvel finds the most likely source of many supernatural features of *Beowulf* in Celtic myth and folktale.

1980: Albert B. Lord identifies the poem's debt to two intersecting narrative patterns of Indo-European origin.

1980: Michael N. Nagler interprets the victory over Grendel's mother in terms of ancient cosmogonic myth, Old Testament myth, and timeless psychological struggles.

1982: Paul C. Bauschatz argues that the banqueting scenes in *Beowulf* recall primal myths of the Norns' nurturing functions.

1984: Helen Damico finds that Wealhtheow is a reflex of the Old Norse figure of the valkyrie.

1986: Lars Gahrn, reviving an old argument about the Geats and their destiny, declares the poem of no value as a source for history.

1986: Karl Schneider offers an atavistic reading of *Beowulf* as a pagan poem incorporating Germanic cosmogonic lore.

1986: Thomas D. Hill explores the Scyld Scefing episode as an aetiological myth that established the legitimacy of Scyld-descended kings in Denmark and speculates that it had a similar role in England.

1989: R. D. Fulk connects the figures of Scyld and Beow to the Old Norse myth of Bergelmir as told in *Vafþrúðnismál* and to Finno-Ugric agricultural myth and rite.

1989: Nicholas Howe finds that the poem makes "assimilated and allusive" use of the Anglo-Saxons' Myth of Migration through its evocations of the geography of their Continental homeland.

1993: Sam Newton tentatively identifies Wealhtheow and her son Hrothmund, a Danish fugitive, as legendary founders of the East Anglian line of kings.

1994: Seth Lerer sees in Grendel's glove a reflex of Indo-European rituals of repast and sacrifice and a link to the Eddic tale of Thor and his escape from Skrýmir's glove.

1994: James W. Earl, relating *Beowulf* to the period of the historical Conversion, finds that the poem mourns the loss of the heroic age by appropriating the mythic eschatology of the Germanic peoples and historicizing it through the story of the Geats' destruction.

1994: Gillian R. Overing and Marijane Osborn reflect on their attempt to retrace Beowulf's sea journey to Denmark, thereby providing the poem with a concrete geographical locale.

Anyone delving into the annals of *Beowulf* scholarship will find examples of the mythic fallacy, or what Walter J. Ong has called "the myth of myth" (1962, 131–45). This is the conviction that primal stories underlie features of a literary text and give this text its chief significance and value. These master narratives, or myths, are believed to derive from a deeper or more elemental source than the text in question, whether this source is located in the remote past or the unchanging human psyche.

Myths in this sense are unlike allegories in that they are not normally encoded in texts by authorial design,[1] nor is their presence announced through transparent labels (such as Christian and Faithful meet Mr. Money-love while fleeing the City of Destruction). Scholars must infer their presence in a given literary work by probing its plot, patterns of imagery, and the like as well as through the study of names and their possible etymological meanings. To discover a myth in a text is a privileged scholarly enterprise that naturally lends that text added value, if not an almost magically therapeutic force, for myths are commonly thought to express enduring wisdom about the human condition. Texts come and go; myths are thought to be coherent and to have high truth value. Myths are therefore prized in and of themselves as well as being of heuristic use as keys that will unlock the secrets of literature. To put the matter another way, the typically modern condition of *amythia,* or a world stripped of its myths (to use a term favored by Loyal D. Rue [1989]), is a post-Nietzschean spiritual wasteland from which escape must be found if human culture is to survive.

While the quest for secret meaning in *Beowulf* has often gravitated toward myth, whether of a pagan or a Christian kind,[2] it has also turned to history. With no less energy than the myth seekers, scholars of a historicist orientation have scrutinized the text and ransacked external sources either to provide a real-life identity for the characters and tribes who figure in the poem or to locate features of its landscape and plot in the actual world. A historicist fallacy has thus arisen side by side with the mythic fallacy, whether in tandem with it or opposed. History, like myth, assumes a high truth value for those who believe in it. Just as some critics use the poem as a means of discovering a "myth to live by," others respond more vibrantly to the complex and tragic history that they believe to be secretly woven into *Beowulf* than they do to the plain story itself.

Beowulf begins with a genealogical prologue that sets the main action of the poem against the background of Danish dynastic history from the time of Scyld Scefing, the eponymous ancestor of the Scyldings, to that of Hrothgar, his great-grandson. Since Scyld is generally taken to be a mythical king while Hrothgar is thought to be historical, readers must soon confront a question posed by Claude Lévi-Strauss in the context of North American Tsimshian myths: "The problem is: where does mythology end and where does history start?" (1978, 38). The reader's desire to distinguish between two different modes of past time, the fabulous and the factual, runs headlong into the obstacle of the storyteller's blank refusal to admit such distinctions. Such an impasse naturally spurs reflection as to how adequate the reader's categories are.

Lévi-Strauss's question has an obverse side—"Where does history end and where does mythology start?"—that is worth posing for its bearing on the poem's main plot. This plot takes us from the shadowy land of the hero's people, the "Geats," to Hrothgar's brightly lit Denmark, then back again to "Geatland," with stops at two fabulous locales, Grendel's mere and a firedrake's barrow. Again and again in the history of *Beowulf* criticism, scholars have tried to convert the more fabulous elements of this plot into the terms of a myth whereby a godlike savior or Everyman-like hero is pitted against adversaries suggestive of primeval chaos, death, or the unconscious. Alternatively, the poem's putatively historical elements have been taken as factual and, indeed, as amounting to a master narrative, myth-like in its functions,[3] that explains one or more features of either the Scandinavian or the Anglo-Saxon past.

Treading such slippery turf, and unsure that anyone among us has unmediated access to the truth about the past, some contemporary historians no longer claim that a firm distinction between myth and history either can or should be made. In his *Mythistory and Other Essays* (1986), William H. McNeill describes the task of the historian as a never-ending process of "historiographical myth making and myth breaking." At its best, in his optimistic view, the process of historiography results in "ever-evolving mythistories [that] become truer and more adequate to public life" (20).[4]

It was chiefly to combat the entrenched habits of naive historicist thinking that J. R. R. Tolkien went out of his way in 1936 to defend the narrative text of *Beowulf* ("the monsters," in his synecdoche) against the trivializing gestures of academic criticism ("the critics"). For Tolkien, the question of the historicity of the elements of *Beowulf* was a distraction from the text as an example of magnificent fiction. Tolkien initiated a revolution in *Beowulf* studies that continued strong through much of the century. Historicist claims about *Beowulf* have still been heard, but by being presented as facts, not interpretations, they have stayed outside the precincts of criticism. Only in the past ten or fifteen years, thanks in part to controversy concerning the date of the poem, have the biases of positivist historicism and literary aestheticism been challenged strongly enough for a fresh critical approach to *Beowulf* to emerge. This approach, which as yet has no name but is associated with the New Historicism,[5] focusses less on issues of historicity or literary value *per se* than on questions of how a given text serves as an agent of social ideology, a means of collective self-fashioning, and a participant in period-specific tensions and tropes.

My purpose in the main body of this chapter is to review selected examples of first mythic and then historicist criticism of *Beowulf,* having now briefly set them into a wider context. I will then briefly offer reasons for regarding the poem *as* a myth or, better, as an example of mythistory: that is, as a narrative that, by telling about a formative period of the ancestral past, served the Anglo-Saxons as a charter for contemporary institutions of kingship and thaneship while also reinforcing a wide range of culturally-specific beliefs and values. Skepticism is my keyword here, however, and I will conclude by suggesting reasons to question some aspects of the argument that I myself have posed.

I. The Quest for Myth

The term *myth* means many things to many people. Notoriously, the word covers a range of meanings that extends from "sacred narrative" or "the highest form of truth" to "false idea" or "lie."[6] When used in a scholarly context, it is usually a neutral term denoting a story about gods, heroes, and the like, set in ancient times, viewed as true, and serving to explain important features of the natural world. Although the term appears often in *Beowulf* criticism, it is seldom defined. Although often used neutrally, sometimes it has been used in the approving sense that it carries in Jungian psychology; *myth* then refers to an archetypal story, akin to dream, that encodes a message relating to personal spiritual growth. Sometimes this positive connotation spills over to the former usage, as if it were by nature a good thing for a poem, novel, or play to have a mythic dimension, or as if one were showing something final about it when one demonstrates that it resembles a myth.

It is now over a century and a half since Karl Müllenhoff (1849a, 1889), inspired by the nature mythology that was then in vogue, offered a meteorological interpretation of *Beowulf* that was in keeping with late Romantic ideas concerning the character of primitive literature. According to Müllenhoff, *Beowulf* was a symbolic drama whose action signified human beings' struggle for existence in a hostile physical environment over which they had little control. Nineteenth-century scholars looked for traces of primitive nature myths in *Beowulf* with results that varied with each investigator (for reviews of this scholarship, see Klaeber 1950a, 25, and Chambers 1959, 46–47). The appeal of Müllenhoff's approach to *Beowulf* was due partly to its invocation of a specific northern geography.

Müllenhoff found it essential that the main action of *Beowulf* takes place in the North Sea coastal zone in and around Jutland, the ancestral homeland of the Angles. Grendel, Grendel's mother, the dragon, and the Breca episode all represent personifications of the North Sea in its devastating storms and floods. Since there is a seasonal aspect to the strife of sea versus land, calm weather versus storm, the hero's death represents the demise of the sun in winter, while the winning of the dragon's hoard signifies that the resources of the whole vegetative kingdom have been secured for human benefit for another year. The whole story is thus a localized myth of the seasons. How did what was originally a legend featuring a local hero figure (*Localsage*) come to take on the characteristics of myth? Müllenhoff found the answer to this question in onomastics: the adventures that the poet ascribed to the Geatish warrior Beowulf were attached to him by mistake, for they once properly pertained to the agricultural god *Beaw* or *Beow,* who is introduced into the poem under the erroneous name "Beowulf" (18 and 53). The Anglo-Saxon poem preserved a primitive myth in displaced and somewhat garbled form.

Müllenhoff's theories were the orthodoxy of their day. Nature myths were so arbitrarily defined that they could not well be refuted, only ignored. It was thus predictable that as new intellectual movements emerged during the early decades of the twentieth century, the mythographic impulse began to fall of its own weight to earth. Still relevant to *Beowulf* studies are the devastating criticisms that W. W. Lawrence leveled against Müllenhoff and other mythologists (1909; 1928, 129–60). As Lawrence saw, readings of *Beowulf* as a displaced nature myth left themselves open to charges of *a priori* methods and reductive thinking. Their main disadvantage was that they stifled inquiry. By chasing phantoms of the prehistoric imagination, such theories explained little about the particulars of the poet's account of the hero's specific conduct in Denmark and his homeland.

The waning of nature mythology did not mean the end of the mythological impulse in *Beowulf* criticism. Given that *Beowulf* is the only early Germanic epic on a secular theme to have survived virtually intact, and taking into account also its many marvelous features and its apparent indebtedness to an ancient folktale pattern (Panzer 1910), scholars inevitably have continued to search the poem for evidence bearing on early myths and cults. In addition, some critics have developed new models for the understanding of *Beowulf* based upon the search for psychological archetypes.

Some of the mythic connections that have recently been posited pertain specifically to Germanic terrain. The ravens that feed on the dead, for example, are thought to be reflexes of Odin's birds (Huntley 1981). The rites of drinking and cup bearing in Heorot have been likened to the nurturing of the tree Yggdrasil, one of the central activities of the Norns (Bauschatz 1982, 85–116). The Danish hero Hengest, featured in the scop's song of Finn and Hengest, has been linked, with his brother Horsa, to early Germanic and Indo-European myths of divine twins (Turville-Petre 1953–57; Joseph 1983). The Heathobard chief Froda has been found to be a displaced figure of the god Frey (Ebenauer 1976). The poet's allusion to the story of the arrival of Scyld as a helpless foundling has been linked, by a circuitous path, to tales of the Eddic giant Bergelmir and the Estonian agricultural deity Pekko (Fulk 1989; cf. Neckel 1910). According to Karl Schneider (1986), the whole poem is based on a putative Germanic creation myth about a Primary God, otherwise figured as a hermaphrodite giant named Hegil, who sacrificed himself for the sake of the cosmogony. Schneider's neopaganism runs the risk of burlesque in that he finds that "Cædmon's Hymn" too was composed in honor of Hegil, who is none other than the ithyphallic giant carved into the chalk hill at Cerne Abbas. Helen Damico (1984) has advanced complex etymological arguments to support the claim that Wealhtheow, Hrothgar's queen and a cupbearer in Heorot, has a vestigial relation to the valkyries of ancient Germanic belief. She arrives at a composite speculative portrait whereby Wealhtheow is imagined as "a female of noble birth, southern in origin, who undergoes a period of enslavement" and who also has martial and priestly qualities (64–65). Any of the studies mentioned in this paragraph are open to the same criticism as Müllenhoff's: by ignoring the possibility that a pagan myth may adopt a different semiotic code when taken up by a Christian author (see Clunies Ross 1989, 8–9), they still tell us little about *Beowulf* as a literary creation. At best, such arguments can shed light on the complex matrix of myth and rite from which the poem developed.

Other connections between *Beowulf* and Old Norse myths known from the *Elder Edda* or Snorri Sturluson's *Prose Edda* have been argued from time to time, although never with definitive results, partly because of the difficulty of knowing if authors and audiences in Anglo-Saxon England were familiar with the Norse myths in question. The chief of these connections are the accidental slaying of Herebeald by Hæthcynn, a tragedy that has been likened to Baldr's death; the relation of the ending of the poem, with its images of impending desolation, to the Norse concept of Ragnarok; and the resemblance of Beowulf as dragon slayer to Thor, particularly with regard to that god's combat against the Midgard Serpent.

The Baldr connection, raised repeatedly in the critical literature (see Klaeber 1950a, xli n.5; also Nerman 1913a, 70–71; and Neckel 1920b, 141ff.), has a sound linguistic basis in that the second element in the name of Hrethel's son *Herebeald* is cognate with Old Norse *Baldr,* while the first element in the name of Herebeald's slayer *Hæðcyn* is cognate with Old Norse *Hǫðr,* Baldr's slayer. Herebeald and Baldr die in analogous ways—Herebeald is killed by an errant arrow, Baldr by being struck with a thrown dart—and each death inspires great grief and desolation. A vestigial connection to the myth is therefore plausible, yet the link remains delicate. The reason Baldr is grieved so intensely is that he is the fairest of all the gods, while nothing is said about Herebeald's appearance. All nature grieves for Baldr, while it is the aged Hrethel alone who suffers suicidal grief for Herebeald. The Norse myth is a fully elaborated story that features Loki's treachery and disguise, Baldr's lavish ship cremation, and Hermoð's arduous journey to Hel, three themes that have no analogues in the Herebeald episode from *Beowulf.* While the myth of Baldr may be echoed vestigially in the poem, it has been altered almost beyond recognition.

Some readers of *Beowulf* have followed Tolkien (1936) in linking the last part of the poem, with its warnings of impending warfare and tribal dissolution, to the Norse concept of the end of the world in a final combat of gods and men against the hostile hosts of monsters. Since one cannot be sure that the myth of Ragnarok was known to the Anglo-Saxons, those who pursue these traces must postulate that the myth as told in *Vǫluspá* is early and pan-Germanic in origin rather than being a late development influenced by Christian concepts of apocalypse. Ursula Dronke (1969), accepting *Vǫluspá* as early, argues that the *Beowulf* poet's account of the building of Heorot is based on pagan creation myth; she finds in both sources the theme of a menaced creation faced by approaching destruction. Paul Beekman Taylor (1966) argues that the poet develops a three-fold parallel between Heorot, the whole created earth (as in the Christian myth of Genesis), and Asgard (as in the cosmogonic myth related in *Vǫluspá*). Pagan and Christian myths thus reinforce one another. The connection between *Beowulf* and Norse myth remains impressionistic, however, for the ending of *Beowulf* falls short of apocalypticism. The funeral of a beloved leader, one who sacrificed his life to defend his people, is attended by expressions of grief that spring in part from fears of worse days to come. In other words, things are as they should be, dramatically speaking. One would not have wanted the Geats to rejoice at this moment. The muted ending of *Beowulf* confirms the note of pessimism that permeates this philosophical poem throughout, lending the dragon episode in particular a melancholy air. To look beyond this pessimism for echoes of pagan myths is to shift into an associative realm where Wagnerian strains prevail.

Ever since N. F. S. Grundvig praised *Beowulf* as "a heroic poem of Thor" (1820, 1), critics have wanted to see the hero of the poem as a displaced figure of the great warrior god of Norse mythology. Both Dronke and Taylor point out parallels between Beowulf as dragon slayer and Thor as slayer of the Midgard Serpent, a connection that was urged by Müllenhoff (1889, 4) despite its inherent incongruities on the side of both the dignified hero and his scaly, apparently nonaquatic opponent. Freshening up the Thor connection and turning it to new ends, Seth Lerer (1994) has recently argued that in the passage telling of Grendel's marvelous dragon-skin glove, the *Beowulf* poet trades on his audience's familiarity with the Eddic tale of Thor's escape from the giant Skrýmir's glove, at the same time as he presents an unconscious reflex of an ancient pattern of ritualistic dismemberment. Counting against conscious allusion is the same problem already cited: claims about literary debts run up against the difficulty of knowing whether the Eddic myths were known to the Anglo-Saxons. As for a connection to ancient rites, such arguments remain impressionistic in the absence of evidence concerning what such rites were and who practiced them, when and where.

Given the origins of *Beowulf* in the Isle of Britain, it is natural that the Celtic realm too, with its rich array of myths, should be searched for parallels to the story. The search has met with only partial success. In a book that draws on a set of previously published articles, Martin Puhvel (1979) postulates Celtic origins for such features of *Beowulf* as the unusual might of Grendel's mother, the hero's marvelous swimming prowess, the "sword of light" that the hero wields against the demoness, and the subsequent melting of that giant blade. Although the parallels are fairly close and their sum total impressive, they remain somewhat disjointed, for there is no one myth or even one coherent body of myth to which the poem can be related. Puhvel deals in isolated motifs only, and these can surface in folk literature of all description.

Going beyond Germanic and Celtic mythology to a deeper European past, some scholars (like Lerer, discussed above) have found evidence linking *Beowulf* to myths or rites that are believed to be embedded either in the Indo-European tradition or in a more capacious ancient context. Studies by Joseph Fontenrose, Albert B. Lord, and Alvin A. Lee are cases in point.[7]

In his *Python: A Study of Delphic Myth and Its Origins* (1959), Fontenrose casts his comparative net widely enough to catch both Beowulf and Thor in it as Germanic manifestations of a basic and far-flung story pattern celebrating the victory of a divine or semidivine hero figure over a dragon or chaos demon who guards a life-giving spot. Only a loose fit can be found between the local contours of *Beowulf* and the general pattern that Fontenrose isolates, however. Working in a similar mode, Lord (1980) has made the more cautious claim that *Beowulf* includes vestigial elements of two narrative patterns that play a major role in various ancient epics. These are a pattern of the hero's "withdrawal, devastation, and return," including the death of a surrogate figure, and a hero's escape from a male monster and thwarting of a female monster who wishes to keep him in an otherworld locale. Lord's arguments have the attraction of accounting for features of the text that might otherwise go unexplained, like the necessity of Hondscio's or Æschere's death. Although his line of investigation is intriguing, his comparisons are based on too small a body of evidence to be compelling. In a recent article (1993), Lee has revived a type of mythological criticism that is associated with Northrop Frye and that Lee developed in his earlier *The Guest-Hall of Eden* (1972). Lee sees the poet as drawing obliquely on Christian myths of Creation and Doomsday to create an image of Heorot as *imago mundi,* brilliant but destined to fall. If the dominant myths here—"the myth of a hero destroying monsters that attack by night from beyond the light-filled human centre" and "the myth of the death of the hero and the return to chaos" (1993, 202)—have features in common with Christian doctrine, Lee still sees no symbolism at work in *Beowulf* but rather a merging of mythic conceptions in a poem that came to life in a no-man's land stretching between pagan and Christian belief.

One claim about *Beowulf* that has surfaced persistently during the second half of the twentieth century is that the poem is indebted to ancient rites of passage or, alternatively, an ancient hero pattern, whose ultimate source is a set of archetypes in the unconscious mind. The controlling ideas of this neomythological school first surfaced in a note published by S. F. Johnson (1951); they have been argued subsequently, with variations, by a small parade of critics, including Carl Meigs (1964: Hrothgar is a sacral king, Beowulf a healing quester, Wiglaf a re-emergent savior), Jeffrey Helterman (1968: Grendel is the hero's shadow self, while Wealhtheow and Grendel's mother represent two aspects of the Great Mother), Terry A. Babb (1970: the poem is a combat myth telling of creation and dissolution), Janet Dow (1970: the poem mirrors initiation rites, symbolic of psychological processes, so as to reaffirm man's place in the cosmic rhythm of all nature), A.

Margaret Arent (1969: the poet secularizes ancient mythic motifs and cult practices that are based on universal patterns buried in the human psyche), Amy Page and Vincent H. Cassidy (1969: the poet tells of a man-god who is sacrificed for the universal good), John Miles Foley (1977: Hrothgar and Grendel represent two opposing aspects of the Good/Terrible Father, while the hero represents the ego involved in a deadly Oedipal struggle), and Michael N. Nagler (1980: the poem embodies a hero-quest archetype portraying the victory of a savior over the forces of chaos). In a similar vein but with impressively detailed anthropological support, Stephen O. Glosecki (1989) has gathered evidence linking *Beowulf* to accounts of shamanic initiation. For Glosecki (1989, 152–210), *Beowulf* includes reflexes of many ancient initiatory elements: the hero as "healer" and "apprentice shaman," Grendel as a "disease spirit," the hero's byrnie as symbol of his link to "a mythic father initiator," and the descent through Grendel's mere as entry to "a dangerous dreamtime."

All these studies, even Foley's and Glosecki's, could be called essentially Jungian in inspiration, whatever other factors they may stir into the soup (a dash of Freud, a large chunk of Eliade, a shake of Joseph Campbell, an old chestnut deriving from James Frazer or Jessie Weston). The appeal of Jungian approaches to literature is their apparent ability to explain so much that is important; their drawback is their reductive and totalizing method. For Jungians, a story is taken to be an expression of certain archetypes lodged deep in the human psyche. The meaning of the story is revealed when these archetypes and their relations are named. Since archetypes are prelogical, they cannot be explained rationally but surface only in symbolic form in myths, dreams, fairy tales, and the like. There is no need to prove their existence; it is enough to know that individuals have access to them through the work of interpreters. Thus we arrive at the role of the literary critic as analyst. The reader of literature, like the hero, is involved in an initiatory journey that arrives, to no one's surprise, at the desired end of spiritual satisfaction.

This is essentially the method that Helterman, Babb, and Dow employ and that the other critics cited above implicitly rely on. Grendel is taken to be Beowulf's shadow self. The physical combat between these two fearsome opponents is taken to represent an inner struggle between two opposed psychic principles, one of which is associated with our moral being, the other with those dark impulses that civilized people normally suppress (Freud's ego or superego and id, respectively, whether or not these terms are invoked). To approach *Beowulf* in this manner is to read its action as a psychomachia whereby fearsome antisocial impulses threaten to overwhelm consciousness but are ultimately overcome and integrated into an expanded self. Foley (1977) takes this argument and converts it to communal history: the integration in question was a cultural one for the Anglo-Saxons as a people.

There remains a question as to whether such studies as these, with their broad and familiar categories of opposition, tell us much that is specific about either the contours of this literary text or the mental world of the people who made it. Any approach to *Beowulf* that reduces a long, involuted narrative action into a single pattern of initiation or a single clash of demiurges is missing too much. If a reading has nothing to say about a variety of matters that were of importance to the poet, to judge from the number of lines he devotes to them—the logic of the feud, for example, or the protocol of gift giving, or issues of dynastic succession, or the demands of leader-thane loyalty, or problems that are inherent in the institutions of exogamy, fosterage, or wergild—then again, it is missing too much. Perhaps the most important question relating to any Jungian approach to *Beowulf* is not "Is it a true account of the poem?" but "Is it a complete enough account of the poem's particulars to satisfy our desire for period-specific, socially-grounded understanding?"

In the end, the neomythological school that was active during the period from 1950 to 1990—roughly the period of the Cold War, as it happens—cannot be refuted. Like the nineteenth-century school of nature myth to which it at times adverts, it can only fall to ground of its own weight at such time as it ceases to offer answers to the kinds of questions that critics are increasingly inclined to ask.

II. The Quest for History

Beowulf has always been taken as a poem that includes history. Few people, however, have paused to contemplate what history means when filtered through a literary work of this character. Most of the debates about historicity that have dominated prior scholarship are posed in terms foreign to the conceptual world of the Anglo-Saxons. When historians ask chronological questions from oral tradition, as David P. Henige has remarked in his *The Chronology of Oral Tradition: Quest for a Chimera* (1974, 1), they are usually seeking information that those sources were never designed to provide. Even when historians turn from chronology to genealogy and try to ascertain basic facts about a person's ethnic identity, no agreement from their sources may be forthcoming, for the legalistic distinction between "historical fact" and "useful and commonly accepted idea about the past" may be a foreign one except to certain technicians of the written word.

During the period that followed the modern discovery of *Beowulf,* critics were chiefly interested in appropriating the poem so as to magnify one or another nation of Europe through what the poet had to say about the early history of the Germanic peoples. Scholars thus posed such questions as "Where was Heorot located, and when and how was it destroyed?" "Who are the *Geatas*?" "Who are Hygelac, Ongentheow, Onela, and the other kings who are prominently named in the poem?" and "When were the *Geatas* wiped out by the Swedes?" Among the debates that ensued, none was fiercer than the one concerning the tribal identification of the *Geatas*: Are they Jutes? Are they Goths? Are they the tribe known in Old Norse as Gautar and in modern Swedish as Götar? Neither the Geatish Question, as it might be called given its former prominence, nor any other debate concerning history admitted the possibility that modern concepts of time, space, and historical truth may not apply to a poem of this character.

There is a delightful quaintness about the nationalistic biases that inspired some of the Old Historicism of that time. Who today, for example, would call *Beowulf* a German heroic poem that happens to have been preserved in an Anglo-Saxon copy, as H. Leo did in 1839? Or who would venture the confident assertions that Daniel H. Haigh makes in his 1861 study *The Anglo-Saxon Sagas: An Examination of Their Value as Aids to History?* Here we learn that the action of *Beowulf* was localized in northern England. The hall Heorot (or *Hart*) really once stood at *Hartlepool,* near Durham. The Scylding kings lived here, hard by the coast of Northumberland, while Ingeld held a principality in York. As for Grendel, he was no monster. That was the poet's hyperbole. He was a man, an outcast who ranged freely in the wastes of that region.

Local boosterism of this kind is easy to dismiss. But to what extent do historicist fallacies still govern the current understanding of *Beowulf?*

Chiefly because no historical prototype can be found for the poem's hero, great excitement attended the discovery that the name of the hero's uncle—Hygelac, king of the Geats—corresponds phonologically to the Chochilaicus, king of the Danes, who figures in the chronicle of Gregory of Tours and in the anonymous *Liber Historiae Francorum.* A network of events known only from *Beowulf* is thus set into an absolute chronology ranging from the accession of Healfdene ("445," according to Klaeber, 1950a) to the death of Hrothulf ("545").

It is worth stressing that no date is part of the fabric of the poem itself. In the poem, the past is the past. The narrative action takes place "in geardagum" (in days of old), not in the kind of history that is the creation of annalists and chroniclers. And yet Klaeber is so driven by a sense of chronological exactitude that he even invents a character who is found necessary on temporal grounds. This is Hygelac's "first wife," whom Klaeber introduces into Geatish history because of his belief that the wife that the poet does attribute to Hygelac, Hygd, must have been too young to have been the mother of the princess who was given in marriage to Eofor as a reward for Eofor's killing of Ongentheow (1950a, xxxviii). If one sets out to subtract mythological ghosts like Beaw from the text of *Beowulf,* one would also be advised to subtract historical ghosts such as this bride.

Just as Klaeber encourages a chronological fallacy, calibrating the *Beowulf* poet's past so as to impose the rhythms of a metronome on it, he contributes to a cartographic fallacy as well. Every advanced student of *Beowulf* is familiar with the map entitled "The Geography of *Beowulf"* that Klaeber includes as part of the front matter of his edition (1950a, viii). Nowhere in the poem are spatial relations spelled out with anything resembling the specificity of this map, with its gridwork of Greenwich-meridian latitude and longitude, its exact charting of the coastlines of Scandinavia and Germany, its location of Heorot on the isle of Zealand, and its prominent labeling of the homeland of the *Geatas/Gautar* in what is now southern

Sweden. Nowhere does the *Beowulf* poet tell us where either Heorot or the land of the Geats is located. He speaks of both Danes and Geats as inhabiting lands that border on the sea but omits telling us what lands or what sea or seas he is thinking of: the North Sea, the Kattegat, and the Baltic, we assume, but these are our names, not his. Nor does the poet say whether the Geats lived north, south, east, or west of the Danes. One geographical detail he does provide has caused discomfort among critics, for again and again he states that a body of water separates the Geats from the Swedes, who must seek them out "ofer sæ" (across the sea), "ofer sæ side" (across the wide sea), "ofer heafo" (across the open sea), or "ofer wid wæter" (across the wide waters). These statements are awkward if the Geats are taken to be the Gautar. The poet's claim about a sea voyage must then either be taken as a reference to inland seas—not a very convincing explanation either philologically or nautically—or treated as a mistake. A less arbitrary response is to take the Geats as one of a number of tribes who figure in what Leake (1966) has called the "geographical mythology" of *Beowulf.*

Historicist fallacies concerning *Beowulf* are hard to kill. Hrothulf's supposed treachery comes first to mind. Lawrence (1928, 73–79) offers the following summary of the story of Hrothulf as the central element of a tale that might be called "The Fall of the House of Hrothgar." To paraphrase his theory:

> The immediate danger confronting the Danes is the incursions of the demon Grendel. But the king faces troubles more serious than this. His sovereignty, won by disregarding the legitimate successor, Heoroweard, is challenged by his scheming nephew Hrothulf, aided, it would appear, by his treacherous counsellor Unferth. Hrothulf usurps the throne, but he is not to go unpunished. The rightful heir to the throne, Heoroweard, wins the crown by slaying Hrothulf in his own hall.

Here we have the elements of a fiction, constructed from scattered sources, that has been repeated so often that it has come to take on the semblance of fact. Lawrence is idiosyncratic in believing that Hrothgar assumed the throne unfairly and that Heoroweard eventually avenged this insult by killing Hrothulf. His speculations about Hrothulf's schemes and crimes, however, have become firmly entrenched in the critical literature (see, e.g., Malone 1927, 269; Hoops 1932b, 153; Klaeber 1950a, xxxii; Chambers 1959, 25–29; Brodeur 1959, 153–57; Bonjour 1965, 30–31).

Although Kenneth Sisam attempted to exorcise the ghost of Hrothulf's treachery (1965, 80–82), the notion of Hrothulf's blood guilt and usurpation has remained unaffected by the *Beowulf* poet's failure to provide information about such crimes. Nor does any other source mention Hrothulf's guilt; it is entirely a product of critical extrapolation from a few lines of text (1013–19, 1163–65) that can just as well be taken to refer to something completely other than Hrothulf's supposed usurpation. An outsider to the realm of *Beowulf* criticism might here suspect an example of the ironic fallacy—the idea that two literary meanings are better than one, especially if one of them is sardonic.

A second historicist notion that has become entrenched in the critical literature is the idea that the ending of *Beowulf* refers to the literal annihilation of the Geats, who are the Gautar of southern Sweden (an identification that is essential to this view). In a classic example of the tragic fallacy—the notion that tragedy is the highest form of literature, especially when it is based on *hamartia,* or the fatal flaw of a high-ranking person[8]—Beowulf's death is taken to be the prelude to the extinction of the Geats as a people, and this supposed catastrophe is then blamed on the rash judgment of Beowulf himself. The hero's fatal flaw is his "understand-able, almost inevitable pride" (Leyerle 1965, 89; cf. Goldsmith 1960, 1963, 1964, 1970; and Huppé 1984, 40). Entranced by the lure of high tragedy, and giving literal value to dire prophecies made by several speakers near the end of the poem, scholars too numerous to mention have taken these prophecies as relating to history and have dated the actual destruction of the Geats to one or another period before the poem was composed. Lawrence (1928, 85–106), elaborating on the theory, speculates that the defeat of the Geats, whose leaders at that time were Heardred and Wiglaf (!), spurred the development of legends concerning a fictive savior named Beowulf and hence led to the creation of our epic. This is guesswork run riot. As both Sisam (1965, 51–59) and Robert Farrell (1972, 28–43) have noted, critics have spun out such theories in the absence of historical evidence either that the Gautar disappeared at any time during the first millenium or that their eventual absorption into "greater Sweden" was the result of wars of conquest. The modern equation of the *Geatas* with the Gautar rests almost exclusively on the phonological correspondence of these names, together with some *Götterdämmerung*-style thinking.[9]

In a similarly speculative mood, some critics have succumbed to the temptation to extrapolate from the poet's narrative and wonder what happened in history after the narrative of *Beowulf* leaves off. Where did the wretched Geats go, once driven in exile from their homeland? Chambers (1959, 400), repeating a hypothesis raised by F. Rönning (1883) and varied by Malone (1925) and Girvan (1935, 80), suggests that a group of Geatish exiles crossed the sea to Angeln, there to sing nostalgic lays about the great days of the Geatish kingdom; the Angles then migrated to Britain with these stories in tow, hence the existence of our *Beowulf* as an epic poem incorporating what is believed to be reliable Geatish history. Thomas Hill has recently helped keep such imaginings alive (1986, 46–47). While Geatish refugees have no place in James Earl's thinking, Earl bases a theory of the poem and its deep motivating psychology on three aligned ideas, each one of which is open to question (1991; 1994, 46–47, passim). These ideas are that the historical Geats suffered annihilation long before the poem was composed, that the fall of the Geats is symbolic of the death of civilization, and that the death of civilization (as in *Vǫluspá*) was a controlling myth for the Anglo-Saxons. Earlier I raised the problem of using the Norse concept of Ragnarok to explicate features of *Beowulf.* Going one step further than other critics, Earl weds northern apocalypticism to a historicist fallacy concerning the Geats and their destruction. The result, though eloquently argued, seems to mirror more closely the Freudian anxieties of the nuclear era than the orthodox Christian doctrines of the world that produced *Beowulf.*

Chasing a related will-o'-the-wisp, some critics ask: "What happened to the wretched Danes who went into exile once Hrothulf had done his dirty work?" In his recent *The Origins of Beowulf and the Pre-Viking Kingdom of East Anglia,* Sam Newton looks into the connections between Wealhtheow, her son Hrothmund, and their tribe the Helmings or Wulfings, on the one hand, and Anglo-Saxon kings of the East Anglian royal line, on the other. He finds that the East Anglians cultivated a foundation legend—now lost, like so much else—that told of their descent from Wealhtheow's line of Scylding kings (1993, 77–132). This guess leads to a special theory of the poem's composition: it was produced in East Anglia (Sutton Hoo country) during the first half of the eighth century (1993, 133–45). Meditations of this kind thus move seamlessly from supposed dark hints of treachery in *Beowulf,* to a master narrative about history, to a theory of the poem's genesis, with all that such theories imply.

Arguments like these could not well be advanced without the aid of maps. As cartographers are aware, however, no map is neutral; each one encodes a way of looking at the world. By defining one group's boundaries and relations to other groups, maps can be a valued means of naturalizing that group's sense of identity (and, sometimes, its hegemonic ambitions or pride of place).

Gillian R. Overing and Marijane Osborn's recent *Landscape of Desire* (1994) is a case in point. Here the authors report on a sailing expedition they undertook from Sweden to Denmark in an effort to retrace Beowulf's route from his homeland to Hrothgar's court. Any attempt to map the spatial itinerary of a character from ancient legend—an Agamemnon, an Odysseus, a Beowulf—itself runs the risk of taking on some of the qualities of myth. Since Overing and Osborn have no doubt that "the *Beowulf* poet had a sound sense of the history and material culture of the period of his poem" as well as sound nautical knowledge, they are able to project into space a definite homeland for the Geats, who are revealed to be a subgroup of the Gautar dwelling along the coast of western Sweden in what is now the province of Bohuslän. The authors' desire is focused so exclusively on medieval Scandinavia that there is no place for Britain on their maps. Their geographical conclusions are made poignant by the tragic fallacy that plays over nearly all historicist readings of the poem. The Geats suffered tribal dissolution, and Geatish exiles—here, sorrowing women—carried the story of this tragedy abroad, perhaps to the very headlands visited by the authors. This is a book self-consciously, artfully, full of daydreams and salt spray. Even if it cannot place its readers a yardarm closer to

Hronesness, it can at least provide temporary vicarious respite from the dry winds of amythia.

In sum, those who turn to *Beowulf* in search of hard knowledge about the past may be asking it to provide more information than it can yield. A more productive question to ask is: "What use does the poet make of the elements of an imagined past?" This is the question that Bonjour raises again and again in *The Digressions in Beowulf* (1950), a book that remains valuable precisely because the author analyzes the poem's episodes and digessions as examples of narrative art rather than trying to use them to uncover facts about history. The same is true of Stanley Greenfield's nuanced discussion of the poet's use of Geatish history to establish epic breadth and a tragic mood in part 2 of the poem (1963a). Paradoxically, studies of the historical elements in *Beowulf* are likely to be most productive when they are willing to let history go.

III. The Poem as Myth and as Recalcitrant Text

The landscape of myth criticism is littered with the bones of dead theories. Wherever one looks in this lunar dreamscape, one stumbles across elements of the unreal: weather gods, Terrible Fathers, chaos demons, rites of passage, ritual dismemberments, shamanic dream travel, phallic swords, uroboric wombs, and the like. A dim light suffuses everything with an eerie glow. The aura of the holy is enhanced by reeking altars dedicated to Jung, Frazer, or other High Gods of modern mythography. The ground is otherwise bare. What a relief to return to that other land of heart's desire, the landscape of history! This ground at least seems brightly lit, with reassuringly familiar contours. But look: what monstrous people inhabit it! Wherever one turns, one finds cutthroats, schemers, backstabbers. Intrigue leads to usurpation, usurpation to vengeance, vengeance to disaster, murder, annihilation. It is a land where nothing seems to happen but treachery and death. Still, at the core of all these mythic or historical accretions, the poem remains what it has always been: a grand, magnificently ornamented account of heroism and devotion, of proud acts and of loss that strikes to the heart.

How are we to read *Beowulf,* then, if the search for its historical contents seems only another manifestation of the search for its underlying myths?

One response to this question may be to reconceive of *Beowulf* as a poem that did work in its time as both a product and an agent of complex cultural transforma-tions. What is of primary interest from this perspective is not the *historicity* of its narrative, in the sense of its capacity to yield hard information about the past, but rather its *mythicity,* in the sense in which that term has been introduced.

It is not wild speculation to suppose that the discourse of heroic poetry, as a special instance of what Robert W. Hanning has called "heroic history" (1974), subsumed some of the functions of myth for the Anglo-Saxons. Myths, in the neutral sense of sacred narratives about the actions of gods and heroes *in illo tempore,* are commonly understood to have the function of "chartering" a society's institutions while validating certain culturally specific attitudes and beliefs.[10] They can do cultural work in their own time and place by projecting current ideology back into the past and associating it with founding figures. In a manner similar to myth, a heroic poem like *Beowulf* may have provided Anglo-Saxons with a model for current institutions of kingship and thaneship, a means of validating power relations among Saxons, Mercians, Danes, and other groups, and a justification for a wide range of attitudes and values about such matters as kinship obligations, the need for generosity on the part of kings and loyalty on the part of thanes, the dangers of greed and unchecked violence, and the sacredness of one's word. As should go without saying, myths can also establish emphatic differences between the present world and the more primitive world of the past. The setting of *Beowulf*—Denmark and adjoining regions of Northern Europe during the Heroic Age of the Germanic peoples—lent itself well to the mythopoeic impulse, for this was regarded as the point of origin for the English people, the pagan Egypt for their Christian Canaan.

As I have stressed, this remote setting was a country of the mind. In defiance of modern chronology, its various legendary inhabitants—Hrothgar, Hygelac, Ongentheow, Ingeld, and the rest—rubbed shoulders with one another regardless of when they "really" lived according to latter-day reckoning. *Beowulf* creates its own history, chronology, and geography that are operative only within the confines of the poem and that cannot be related directly to anything outside it. No one can navigate this country using the latitude and longitude of Greenwich meridian space, for, as Nicholas Howe has remarked, the poet thinks of Germania "less as a region to be mapped than as one to be evoked" (1989, 143). The lands of the Danes, the Geats, the Swedes, and the other tribes that are mentioned in the poem are nowhere set into clear relation to one another. Routinely, these tribes are separated from one another by a sea, and the coastlines along which they live have headlands. *Sea* is a trope that indicates distance, not just water. *Headlands* denotes a political border or threshold, not just a range of promontories. Those utterly conventional geographical details are the only ones the poet chooses to give.

Ancient Germania as it figures in *Beowulf* was a vague *then*, not a *now*, a capacious *there,* not a *here.* Its inhabitants were people of extraordinary size, strength, and courage who were *those legendary ones,* not *us*; and yet from those people we have derived much of our character, or so the origin myth affirms. The Germania of *Beowulf* has what Robert Kaske has called a "strangely Old Testament tone" (1958, 273), as if it were a northern counterpart to the biblical past of Moses and Abraham (see also Tolkien 1936, 28; Wieland 1988). The ancient Continental homeland of the English was a site where huge and unruly forces clashed under the watchful eye of God. The kings and heroes of this realm were not just more wealthy, more courageous, more generous, or more ferocious than the people of subsequent generations; several of them were literally gigantic, as Hygelac was reputed to be and as the young Beowulf seems to impress the Danish coastguard as being (247b–49a). By invoking this imagined realm of the past, the Anglo-Saxons saw themselves reflected as if in a convex mirror, far larger than life. As Howe has suggested, through *Beowulf*—and, surely, through other poems like it that did not happen to survive—they were able to give flesh to one of their cherished ideas, that there once existed an Old Dispensation of the Germanic peoples before their migration to Britain and their conversion to the Gospel of Christ had transformed the terms of their existence.

As one can see, the response I am suggesting to the question "How shall we approach *Beowulf*?" invokes yet another master narrative: the story of how the English became English, in the full sense of that term. There are dangers in this approach as well. To add another item to a list of fallacies that now includes the mythic, the historicist, the chronological, the cartographic, the ironic, and the tragic, this critical impulse could be called the nationalist fallacy. Those critics who flirt with it tend to assume that the idea of nationhood (or, at least, a generalized sense of nationalistic pride and identity) was as important to the inhabitants of medieval Europe as it is to most people today. Motivating such research is the central faith that *Beowulf* derives from a time and place when what historian Benedict Anderson (1983) has called an "imagined community" was under construction, so that the poem must have some relation to a story that has England as hero. Perhaps the idea of nationhood was important to high-ranking persons living in the poet's day. Perhaps it was not. Most people of that time, even if they lived in the tenth century, may often have felt more passionate about local issues and loyalties than about national ones.

The nationalist impulse in *Beowulf* criticism springs from the conviction that encoded in the narrative of *Beowulf* is a set of allusions to well-known figures from the English past (Niles 1993a, 98–101): Hengest, the founding father, particularly of the kings of Kent; Offa the Great, contemporary of Charlemagne and ruler of a powerfully united Mercia; his grandson Wiglaf, the last king of an independent Mercia before that kingdom became absorbed by the kings of Wessex; Wealhtheow, the queen whose family seems somehow wrought up in East Anglian traditions; the Geats themselves as one of the three founding tribes of England, according to the West Saxon translator of Bede. It should go without saying that every one of these allusions must be inferred. The poet never mentions England directly. Even if these inferences are justified, the wish to find them so should be seen as one manifestation of a current scholarly desire for a *Beowulf* that relates to the period of nation building that followed, step by step, once King Alfred had gained moderate success in his wars against the Danes.

We are left with a curiously recalcitrant text. Despite all efforts to unlock its meaning, it has remained equally resistant to mythomania and historicist ferreting. Perhaps in no other area of *Beowulf* studies is the truth clearer that literary meaning, as defined by the critics, is a product of literary theory rather than of literature itself. Understandably, few critics of *Beowulf* have been willing to take it at its face value, as an epically elaborated account of how a certain warrior named Beowulf, nephew of the king of the Geats, ventures to Denmark to free that kingdom from the depredations of two cannibalistic giants, then meets his death in combat against a dragon after having ruled in his homeland for fifty years. That, plus a great deal of lore and legend about the Germanic past, is what the poem is about: not solar heroes, not Ragnarok, not initiation rites, not the passion of Christ, not the struggles of the human psyche, not any of the other subjects discussed in this chapter. If we insist on discovering hidden meaning in *Beowulf,* we may be forgiven for wishing to anchor our appreciation for that poem in a master narrative that seems to us worthwhile. Anyone, after all, may at times feel an undeniable urge to swim in that ocean of stories, that bath of primal narrative elements, out of which this particular work emerged when a gifted poet gave it firm shape. We will spin out such theories, all the same, at the risk of having them seem quaint to future eyes.

Notes

1. There are many exceptions to this generalization, especially in the modern period with the appearance of such works as Eliot's *The Waste Land* and Joyce's *Ulysses.*

2. The role of Christian myth or allegory in the poem will not be my concern here, as that topic is treated by Alvin A. Lee in chapter 12 ("Symbolism and Allegory").

3. Compare Lévi-Strauss (1978, 42–43): "I am not far from believing that, in our own societies, history has replaced mythology and fulfils the same function."

4. McNeill chooses not to address a contrary, equally plausible view: that the process of historiography can result in ever more firmly-entrenched errors, as long as those errors are adequate to public life.

5. A brief orientation to work of this character is provided by the anthologies edited by Veeser (1989, 1994).

6. For a set of essays illustrating chiefly anthropological approaches to myth, see Dundes (1984); for literary uses, see Ruthven (1976) and the essays included in Vickery (1966); for approaches from the perspective of sociology and oral history, see Samuel and Thompson (1990). This last book plays a variant on the title of a well-known book by Joseph Campbell (1972), the foremost contemporary practitioner of Jungian approaches to myth. Lewis (1976, 121) has stated succinctly why one word, *myth,* can carry such a wide range of meaning: "Myths proclaim great truths by telling great lies!"

7. I shall leave aside David Bynum's study *The Daemon in the Wood* (1978), for Bynum's interpretation of the "two trees" of *Beowulf* (analogous to the two trees in the Garden of Eden) hinges on a philological error: *wudu* in lines 1364 and 1416 means "woods," not "a tree."

8. Here I am using the phrase *tragic fallacy* in a manner that is deliberately somewhat tangential to that of Joseph Wood Krutch in an essay of that title (1970). For him, the term denotes the false ascription of the name *tragedy* to mundane modern dramas of a melancholy nature. His own essay exemplifies the term as I am using it, to denote critics' quasi-religious veneration for Aristotelian models of tragedy as the highest form of literary art.

9. There is one other reason to accept that equation, however: the fact that Bǫðvarr Bjarki, the counterpart to Beowulf in the analogous part of the Old Norse *Hrólfs saga kraka,* is identified as one of the Gautar. For discussion, see Chambers (1959, 54-61).

10. Functionalist accounts of myth are associated above all with Bronislaw Malinowski (e.g., 1926, 1932, 1935). Malinowski has been criticized, however, for minimizing the extent to which myth can adapt in response to social pressures.

Chapter 12

Symbolism and Allegory

by Alvin A. Lee

Summary: Although a consensus has emerged that *Beowulf* is not an allegory in a formal, structural way, there is wide recognition that it is strongly thematic and that it shows allegorical tendencies. Over the last six decades, vigorous and often controversial attempts have been made by numerous scholars to interpret the poem by reference either to ancient/medieval or to modern/postmodern structures of ideas and events. Such commentary or allegoresis divides into three broad, typical forms that are focused, respectively, on the poem and concepts, the poem and history, and the poem and consciousness.

Chronology

1815: Grímur J. Thorkelin thinks the few Christian references in *Beowulf* were intrusions by King Alfred, as part of an English appropriation of a Danish poem composed by a Danish bard (1815b).

1817: N. F. S. Grundtvig interprets Grendel as the evil in time and the dragon as the evil in nature. In 1861, he says that the dragon symbolizes Roman domination of the Danes.

1875: Ludvig Schrøder, following Grundtvig, says that Grendel represents the lethargy that destroys a civilization; the dragon symbolizes the violence at the center of Germanic society that makes inevitable its destruction.

1934: Arthur E. Du Bois sees the dragon as a symbol of discord and Beowulf as succumbing to pride, sloth, and avarice.

1936: J. R. R. Tolkien thinks *Beowulf* is firmly located in the physical world and composed in the language of myth and symbol, not of allegorical homily, as it deals with the great temporal tragedy of man's life on earth.

1946: Marie Padgett Hamilton provides the first important Christian doctrinal allegoresis of the poem.

1951: Morton W. Bloomfield sees conscious use of personified abstraction in Unferth (*Discordia*) and in Beowulf (the *rex justus*).

1951: Charles J. Donahue sees in *Beowulf* Augustine's two cities; he sees also (from Irish tradition) a third city of natural goodness for those like Beowulf outside the Christian scheme.

1951: D. W. Robertson Jr., using Augustine's doctrines of *caritas* and *cupiditas,* thinks Beowulf is shown as acting in imitation of Christ to purify society against the forces of cupidity.

1955: Allen Cabaniss concentrates on Beowulf's descent into the mere and the fight with Grendel's mother to delineate seven motifs paralleling the liturgy of baptism.

1958: Robert E. Kaske sees as the controlling theme of *Beowulf* the ancient concepts of *sapientia et fortitudo.*

1960: Margaret E. Goldsmith begins a series of commentaries (ending in 1970) meant to show the poem as a Christian allegory of the life of man in contest with the Enemy.

1960: Maurice B. McNamee sees the poem's unity in theological dogma and in references to scriptural events.

1962: William Whallon opposes the growing trend to see Christian allegory or typology, citing lack of evidence in the poem.

1964: Lewis E. Nicholson, with an emphasis on baptism, argues for conscious use by the poet of biblical types and symbols.

1966: John Halverson recognizes few Christian references in the poem and no clear evidence of allegorical intention.

1968: Jeffrey Helterman, helped by Eliade and Jung, describes a total narrative action in *Beowulf* that moves from sacred, mythic time to profane, historical time.

1968: Edward B. Irving Jr., in opposition to Kaske and Goldsmith, interprets the mythic symbolism of Heorot and the hero with the help of Eliade's concept of sacred time and space.

1970: Margaret E. Goldsmith brings together in book form her carefully developed Augustinian interpretation of the mode and meaning of *Beowulf.*

1970: Philip Rollinson provides a useful clarification of the two patristic senses of a narrative text, the *litteralis* and the *spiritualis.*

1972: Michael Cherniss describes the ideological framework of Germanic heroic poetry and sees this as controlling *Beowulf,* making its pervasive Christianity incidental.

1974: Kathryn Hume thinks moralistic negative readings of hall life in *Beowulf* are wrong and that the audience is meant to respond positively to the hall values, however flawed.

1975: John Gardner sees the poet as constructing an allegory of the heroic soul, composed of three virtues: *arma, virum, primus.*

1975: Martin Green interprets Grendel as a paradigm of apocalyptic beasts, the dragon as an embodiment of the apocalypse, and the treasure in part 2 as the central symbol of doom.

1975: Bernard F. Huppé reads *Beowulf* as a poem about a hero without Christ, as a revelation that the heroic in itself is empty.

1975: Alvin A. Lee, in relation to Old English poetry, explores connections between the theory of four-level exegesis and major preoccupations of modern criticism.

1976: Stanley B. Greenfield describes an "authenticating voice" in the poem, by which the audience is meant to understand. He contrasts this with the patristic exegetical mode of thought.

1977: Raymond P. Tripp accepts Robinson's restoration of the manuscript reading of 67b–70, and sees Heorot and its builders as models of heroic excellence, not as emblems of pride.

1977: Willem (William) Helder traces in part 2 of the poem eschatological references associated with Christ.

1978: Whitney F. Bolton identifies much more biblical material in *Beowulf* than has previously been done but sees no continuous allegorical structure.

1978: John C. McGalliard describes six classes of comments on the narrative by the poet that are useful for consideration of thematic elements or allegorizing tendencies within the poem itself.

1978: Marijane Osborn sees two complementary frames of reference, one heroic and knowable through natural pagan wisdom, the other cosmic and involving revealed Christian knowledge.

1978: Patrick Wormald looks to a secularized Anglo-Saxon church in the age of Bede, not to the ideology of Western Christianity, for light on the religious character of *Beowulf.*

1979: James W. Earl sees the poem as concerned with divinely permitted evil and suffering (cf. Job), instrumental in leading Hrothgar and Beowulf to hard-earned wisdom.

1980: Alan K. Brown examines various meanings of *dragon* and identifies a patristic one, the fiery Leviathan that destroys God's enemies, to show that Beowulf fails and is damned.

1981: Thalia Phillies Feldman rejects, for identifying Grendel, Christian and most Judaic connotations of the race of Cain and turns to a broad range of possible Germanic ancestors.

1981: Katherine O'Brien O'Keeffe traces ambiguities, especially in the presentation of Grendel as spirit, man, and monster with whom Beowulf merges without succumbing to the monstrous.

1981: Robert L. Kindrick offers a Germanic model of heroic *sapientia* to supplement the work of Kaske.

1982: David Williams sees *Beowulf* as a secular allegory that makes extensive metaphorical use of Cain lore and of Augustine's concept of the two cities.

1983: André Crépin makes credible, as a modern allegorization, what initially seems unlikely, that the poem is the odyssey of the conscious mind against the forces of the unconscious.

1983: James W. Earl provides a stimulating Freudian reading of *Beowulf* as an act of mourning for, and acceptance of, the replacement of the old heroic superego by the Christian one.

1983: Raymond P. Tripp, with timely iconoclasm about many of the editorial accretions and scholarly misreadings, emphasizes multiple meanings and paronomasia in the text.

1984: Bernard F. Huppé considers *Beowulf* not an allegory but rather a critique of the heroic code within an inescapable Augustinian frame of reference.

1984: Edward B. Irving Jr. sees a Christian dimension to the poem but rejects use of the Fathers to explain its treatment of its primary subject, the lasting values of the heroic world.

1986: Robert Lawrence Schichler thinks the patristic traditions of dragons and harts are built into the structure of the poem.

1987: Ian Duncan makes good use of certain deconstructionist techniques to read *Beowulf* as a contest of narratives, mythological and historical, the latter being privileged and the winner.

1987: James W. Earl's exploration of symbols of immanence and transcendence in Old English poetry leads to important insights into the main *Beowulf* metaphors of hall, hero, and monsters.

1987: Willem (William) Helder thinks *Beowulf* need not be read typologically but is enriched when it is, for example, in interpreting the scop's Song of Creation.

1988: Charles R. Dahlberg brings to *Beowulf* Augustine's concept of the unlikeness of the spiritual and earthly kingdoms. He sees King Beowulf as like both Christ and the kings of the world.

1988: Kenneth Florey sees the poem as beginning in myth and moving into history, as encouraging a belief in absolutes and then showing them to be illusory.

1988: Gernot Wieland thinks *Beowulf* shows influence from the Old English *Exodus* in its depiction of a Moses-like Beowulf.

1990: George Clark considers Tolkien's willingness to see spiritual meanings beneath the poem's secular surface as having encouraged too much subsequent searching for polysemy.

1990: A. Leslie Harris examines suggestions in the poem of events outside it and thinks there are enough of these to guide interpretation.

1990: Daniel F. Pigg sees Christian elements in *Beowulf* as biblical riddlings and symbolic touches, not as evidence of allegory, in a reconciliation of Germanic and Christian ideals.

1990: E. G. Stanley gives thoughtful scrutiny to the relation between history and fiction in *The Finnsburg Fragment* and the Finnsburg episode.

1991: James W. Earl makes judicious use of Freudian theory to explain the act and effect of reading the silences and reticence of the text.

1992: Raymond P. Tripp challenges what he sees as unconscious assumptions underlying many interpretations of *Beowulf*.

1993: John D. Niles (1993a) views *Beowulf* as a projection of two great desires in tenth-century England: for a distinguished pan-Germanic ethnic origin and for a unifying Christian ethical origin.

In criticism, a symbol is any word, phrase, or motif in a literary text with some kind of special reference beyond itself. *Beowulf* is a verbally complex work of human imagining, culturally remote from modern readers and containing various kinds of special references that must be considered if we are to understand the poem. The most important of these are set out in the chapter divisions of this *Handbook*. Delineation, in this way, of the range of possible frames of reference and meaning indicates that *Beowulf* criticism has now become, *inter alia,* the identification and systematizing of the different kinds of symbolism discernible in the text. The more such understanding of the poem has grown, the clearer it has become that we have arrived at a concept of a sequence of contexts within which to consider the text, based on a recognition of phases of meaning in *Beowulf* itself, not on all the things we can attach to it. This suggests to me that in *Beowulf* studies the principle of manifold or "polysemous" meaning is no longer a theory but an established fact, established by the different scholarly approaches and schools of criticism focused on different aspects of the poem, each of these approaches having made its distinctive choice of symbols for analysis and commentary.

As this critical development shows, *Beowulf* is not a simple, easily accessible communication but a richly symbolic poem from a thousand or more years ago, still doing its work in later times and places and in a variety of cultures. Because of what it once was, for some unidentified poet or poets and for unknown listeners or readers, because of what it has become, as it has exercised the minds and imaginations of readers in the last three centuries, and because of the significance it will still generate as it continues to function, each particular reading of it is part of a larger whole. No one interpretation or commentary can afford to present itself with the smugness of a solved puzzle. Although the writings cited and discussed in this chapter are diverse (those in the whole handbook more so), it is obvious that neither separately nor all together are they the end of the matter.

If one selects a broad enough definition of symbolism, the one common in ordinary, nonspecialist usage, anything (including all words) that signifies something else is symbolic. If one narrows the definition to the meaning found most often in literary discussion, by which symbols are words or images in a text used in thematically significant ways, the range of reference is still too large for this chapter. For practical purposes, then, the principle of selection here is whether a particular bibliographical item is recognizably part of the ongoing discussion of the poem's symbolism in relation to the question of possible allegorical meanings in the text, Christian or otherwise.

It was suggested above that there is a *de facto* consensus among *Beowulf* scholars and critics that the poem is symbolic, provided the term is not delimited too sharply. For good and understandable reasons, however, there is no broad agreement that *Beowulf* is an "allegory," in any of the senses of that problematic word. Every work of literature has both a fictional and a thematic aspect, and all formal allegories have, in their composition, a strong thematic interest, but thematic emphasis in itself does not make a particular work an allegory. Nor does the emergence of thematic interpretation turn it into one, though the commentary may and does allegorize the text. We have allegory when the events of a fictional narrative obviously and continuously refer to another simultaneous structure of ideas, events, or things, whether moral or philosophical or theological ideas, historical happenings, or phenomena in nature. When a writer (Prudentius, *Psychomachia*; De Meun, *Roman de la Rose*; Dante, *Divina Commedia*; Langland, *Piers Plowman*; Spenser, *Faerie Queene*; Bunyan, *Pilgrim's Progress*) explicitly indicates the relationship between the images in the narrative and a set of precepts and examples, thus trying to show through the mode of composition itself how understanding and interpretation should proceed, we have actual allegory.

For example, in the Prudentian allegorical interiorization of epic called the *Psychomachia,* the first battle encounter described (Prudentius 1966, 21–39) is between *Fides* (Faith) and *Veterum Cultura Deorum* (Worship-of-the-Old-Gods). To a considerable extent the imagery of *Fides*'s bare arms and weaponless state symbolizes the power that enables her to crush underfoot and strangle her enemy, but, in case the intended meanings are not clear, the capitalized, personified names make them explicit. In Spenser's *Faerie Queen,* (Spenser 1952) the first two lines of the first canto proper—"A Gentle Knight was pricking on the Plaine, / Y cladd in mightie armes and siluer shielde"—are followed by a description of "the old dints of deepe wounds" still on the knight's armor from previous battles, his angry steed with "foming bitt," and the "bloudie Cross he bore, / The deare remembrance of his dying Lord." But we have not been left unguided to puzzle over the possible meanings of these images, to engage, so to speak, in our own private allegories of reading. We have already been told twice who this knight is, allegorically or conceptually: in the title, "The First Booke of the Faerie Queene, Contayning The Legende of the Knight of the Red Crosse, or of Holiness," and in a prefatory stanza, beginning "The Patron of true Holiness, / Foule Errour doth defeate" (3–4). Writers are working allegorically when it is clear that they are saying "by this I also [Greek *allos*] mean that." Genuine allegory, then, is a structural matter; it has to be there and cannot be added by critical interpretation (allegoresis). If the allegorical reference is continuous, as it is in all the works cited above, we have an allegory; if it is sporadic or intermittent, it can be said that the work has allegorical tendencies.

Because of a widespread recognition among critics, including numerous interpreters of *Beowulf,* that there can be varying degrees of allegorical composition both within a particular work and from one text to another, there is controversy about where, if at all, *Beowulf* sits within the allegorical spectrum. There is general agreement that structurally the poem is not formal allegory, in the way that the *Psychomachia* and the other works cited above are. At the same time, because of the poem's seriousness of tone and the frequent (apparently didactic) expressions of ethical and religious concepts, because also of the way it conveys a sense of large reserves of understanding and wisdom, it continues to invite thoughtful consideration of those tendencies in it that plausibly can be called allegorical. Still, it is obvious that these exemplary elements are powerfully balanced, I would say outweighed, by the strong, sinewy story itself and by the vivid imagery (much of it highly figurative) that pervades all parts of the poem. In my view, it is these primary elements that are the source of whatever meanings *Beowulf* has.

It is not always realized that, in a general sense, all interpretive commentary is allegorizing, the attaching of ideas to the structure of images. It seems to be in the very nature of critical interpretation to see works of the imagination as potential allegories of ideas and events or, in modern times, of psychic or cultural realities. It may well be that it is because *Beowulf* is not structurally or formally a sustained allegory but a richly symbolic poem, with many of its subtleties of meaning suggested but not made explicit, that it has attracted such a sizable library of criticism, by writers devoted to bringing out aspects of its significance that might not occur to other readers. It is at least arguable that it is because the numerous gnomic comments and other typifying or exemplary pointers in the text are so firmly subordinated to the dominant imagery and narrative that *allegoresis* or allegorical interpretation has been relatively free to flourish, with widely different and often conflicting readings. The poet has signaled some directions, clearly, but has left a great deal unexplained. For some scholars, that is where the matter should rest. For others, the text actively invites and rewards intensive, sustained pondering and energetic interpretive response.

Within the total corpus of *Beowulf* studies to date, the subdivision that includes symbolic interpretations of an allegorizing kind has loomed large only during the last six decades. Within this body of writings three broad, typical forms of commentary can be discerned: *poem and concept,* or those focused on overt or latent doctrinal or conceptual content, to be drawn out and explained in relation to other texts, known or possibly known, in Anglo-Saxon times; *poem and history,* or those focused on the narrative and meaning of *Beowulf* in relation to history, either sacred scriptural history or events or situations in the ancient Germanic or Anglo-Saxon periods, as these latter are known by modern historians; and *poem and consciousness,* or those that interpret the poem as psychological or cultural allegory, by reference to dreams and the unconscious and to myths and rituals. These three forms of commentary, it need hardly be said, are major emphases, not exclusive categories, and a number of studies embrace more than one of the three. Underlying all such interpretations, of course, and rendering each one hypothetical to some extent, lies the large, intractable problem that we do not know by whom (singular or plural), where, when, why, or for whom *Beowulf* was composed. The wide range of possibilities surrounding such questions, and the much narrower one of probabilities, has always to be kept in mind, as a caution against overconfidence in any reading.

I. Poem and Concept: Phase 1 (until the Early 1970s)

Some of the motivation for the conceptual and historical allegoresis that *Beowulf* has attracted in recent decades appears to be to defend the seriousness and profundity of the poem against scholars unable or unwilling to take seriously the centrality of a hero with the strength of thirty men in his hand grasp pitted against monsters. Tolkien (1936) describes some of the attitudes and historicist assumptions of earlier scholars troubled by the main subject of the poem. His long since famous 1936 lecture to the British Academy is a rhetorically powerful call for scholars and critics to catch up to students and those others who are willing to read *Beowulf* not as an antiquarian quarrying ground but as a poem with a profound appeal, because it "glimpses the cosmic and moves with the thought of all men concerning the fate of human life and efforts" (277). Tolkien sees *Beowulf* as written in the language of myth and symbol, not of allegorical homily, and as firmly located in the physical world, even as it conveys a sense of many-storied antiquity in the ways it deals "with the great temporal tragedy" (265) of man's life on earth. It is probably fair to say that, along with Klaeber's edition of the poem (1922a), Tolkien's manifesto and interpretation have had more influence on readers than any other single study, even though it has been challenged on just about every one of its major points. For our purposes here, it is the distinction that Tolkien draws between the presentation of great themes in the language of symbol and myth rather than as abstract allegory that is important. In this, whether as a causal influence or simply as a particularly eloquent early modern example, the 1936 lecture can be taken as the starting point for those interpretations that see the poem as held together and informed by means of concrete symbols and thematically significant images, rather than by the controlling concepts or historical exempla favored in conceptual and historical allegoresis. In a major way, most of the studies discussed in this chapter (including one by Tolkien himself) have tended to undercut the important distinction he draws in 1936 between allegory, on the one hand, and symbol and myth, on the other. The tradition of criticism true to the early direction is discussed in chapters 8, 9, 10, and 11.

The first major attempt to account for the themes of *Beowulf* in the form of conceptual allegoresis is Hamilton's "The Religious Principle in *Beowulf*" (1946). This is an intellectually lucid study of how the poet might have seen and appraised heathen narratives from the Germanic past in the light of two doctrines familiar in Anglo-Saxon England: that of a Providence in which God has governed all humankind since the time of the Creation and that of election and grace, by which the divine mercies never were reserved exclusively for the Christian or Old Testament faithful. These two, says Hamilton, provide the central religious principle of *Beowulf* and underlie the numerous references to grace and divine favor; they also help explain Beowulf as both a pagan and a member of the society of the just (*Civitas Dei,* book 15) and the Scandinavian monsters from old legend as figures of evil and members of the society of reprobates. Hamilton does not think that *Beowulf* is an allegory, nor that the monsters are purely symbolic. What she is consciously doing, in the history of *Beowulf* studies, is accepting Klaeber's challenge of trying to find "a formula which satisfactorily explains the peculiar spiritual atmosphere of the poem" (1950a, cxxi, n.28). Although at times her critical vocabulary ("merely employing a metaphor," "with any save figurative intent," "if the utterance is more than a faded proverb") betrays a rationalist uneasiness with the imaginative language of *Beowulf,* her study still stands as a classic of early conceptualizing allegoresis. In various ways the background for it had been established by O. F. Emerson, S. J. Crawford, R. W. Chambers, W. W. Lawrence,

C. W. Kennedy, Friederich Klaeber, J. R. R. Tolkien, A. S. Cook, and J. D. A. Ogilvy, all cited by her.

Donahue (1949–51) also sees the Augustinian doctrine of two societies or cities as underlying the poem's conception of good and evil, but he would add, from Irish tradition, a "third city" whose pre-Christian inhabitants (e.g., the Old Testament patriarchs and prophets and Beowulf) follow a principle of natural goodness in their battles against evil. Robertson (1951) continues but considerably intensifies the Augustinian doctrinal emphasis, reformulating it in terms of the contrast between *caritas* and *cupiditas*. He uses these two concepts to read the details of Grendel's mere as the evil garden of medieval iconography and the stag or hart as the hart of Psalm 42, traditional symbol of the human soul aspiring to union with God by seeking him in the Living Waters. In Robertson's exegesis, Grendel is the militant heretic, and Beowulf, who is not Christ but acts in imitation of him, is the one able to purify a human society from the forces of cupidity. Robertson suggests, in perhaps too homogenizing a way, that although *Beowulf* is not formal allegory, it shares "the allegorical quality of literature and art from Prudentius to Spenser" (25). This means that, like the Bible and all serious literature, it should be searched for hidden layers of spiritual meaning.

At the same time as Donahue and Robertson's articles, Bloomfield (1949–51), trying not to overemphasize the role of allegory, suggests that in two specific instances the poet consciously uses the model of personified abstractions from Christian Latin literature of the Prudentian kind: in patterning Unferth (*Discordia*) and in the conception of Beowulf as the *rex justus* or ideal king pitted against the discord that destroys societies. A year later, O'Loughlin (1952), reading thematically but not arguing that the poem is allegory, interprets it as concerned primarily with feuds, in a Germanic secular aspect (the ideal of making peace by resolving feuds) and in a Christian religious one (uncompromising war against inhuman forces of evil). Chaney (1961) focuses on the Germanic idea of sacral kingship to explain Grendel's destruction of the peace and sanctuary embodied in the king, his throne, and his hall.

Kaske's "*Sapientia et Fortitudo* as the Controlling Theme of *Beowulf*" (1958), with later elaborations (1959, 1960, 1963, 1968), is the most illuminating early example of conceptual allegoresis applied to *Beowulf*. Erudite in texts from Greek and Roman times and in those of biblical, patristic, and Germanic tradition as well as in Anglo-Latin and Old English writings, Kaske explores in detail the resonances in *Beowulf* of the ancient theme of *sapientia et fortitudo*. He sees this old ideal of heroism as the point of synthesis in *Beowulf* between Christianity and Germanic paganism. Because he recognizes ambiguities and avoids doctrinaire or tendentious thinking and keeps the whole poem in mind while considering any part of it, he presents an interpretation able to accommodate the view, still held by many even in our so-called age of irony, that this *is* a poem about a hero who is presented as behaving wisely and bravely according to two coexisting codes, one embracing the ideal of eternal salvation, the other that of earthly glory.

Two other critics make significant contributions to the early phase of conceptual allegoresis. T. Hill (1966) identifies a patristic commonplace, the *draco*, as a symbol of the *malitia* in the mind of the wicked and sees this idea at work in the flames from the bestial, physical dragon in *Beowulf* 2881–82. J. Gardner (1970; recast 1975) explains the heroic theme in the light of Fulgentian allegory, not necessarily Fulgentius's actual commentary on the *Aeneid* (it may not have been available to the *Beowulf* poet), but the same allegorizing tradition. For Fulgentius, heroism is composed of three virtues, *arma, virum,* and *primus,* associated with the three parts of the soul, the irascible, the rational, and the concupiscent. These three, respectively, inform the poet's conceptions of Scyld, Beowulf, and Hrothgar and also of the three main monsters. Grendel is "cosmic unreason," his mother is "wrong irascibility," and the dragon is "perverse concupiscence." Although, according to Fulgentius, earthly happiness comes from a correct understanding of the tripartite soul, the poet does not think such *felicitas* possible and so presents his hero as successful against the Grendel kin but defeated by the dragon.

II. Poem and History: Phase 1 (until the Early 1970s)

Paralleling and at times overlapping with conceptual allegoresis of *Beowulf* is the development of "historical" allegorizing, the attaching of the images and narrative of the poem to what are thought or were thought in Anglo-Saxon times to be actual events and circumstances. This kind of commentary divides into two very different streams, one based on a modern sense of historiography, the other on an early medieval one. In the former, the working assumption is that the text contains nuggets of reliable information about ancient and early medieval Germania or about Anglo-Saxon England, or both; in the other, images and events of the poem are placed in the context of scriptural or sacred history. The first of these flourished in the nineteenth and early twentieth centuries and was often based on an assumption of close correspondence, in a representational or descriptive way, between the words of the text and the actual natural and social world within which the poem was composed or is thought to have been set. As a relatively late example, Lawrence (1928, 1939), involved in a controversy with Mackie (1938) about whether Grendel's mere has an inland waterfall setting or is a body of landlocked sea water, shows no awareness of his naturalistic, low mimetic assumptions about the nature of the poem's fiction. In contrast, Mackie stresses the imprecision and lack of verisimilitude in the description of the mere, pointing out that the poet is interested not in making the supernatural appear natural but in creating an eerie atmosphere of strangeness and horror. A parallel example, which tries to relate the poem to very specific events in history rather than nature, is Bond (1943). With a historicist confidence few critics could now muster, he links the poem with names, situations, and political concerns involving the Mercian kings Beornwulf (823–826) and

Wiglaf (828–838). A different example, this one pointing from the poem back to ancient Germania, is Herben's "Beowulf, Hrothgar and Grendel" (1938), in which the story of Heorot is seen as connected with the fertility cult of the Earth Mother, the goddess Nerthus (told about by Tacitus in *Germania* [1935, 40]), the main parallels being human sacrifice, a taboo on weapons, Beowulf's ability to forgo them, and the behavior of Grendel (the enraged priesthood of Nerthus).

Another, more influential, form of historical allegoresis can be seen pervasively at work in Klaeber's edition, especially in the many notes and the glossary translations of Old English words that indicate an inability or unwillingness to let figurative language do its work. Although Klaeber gives plenty of room to what he calls "the fabulous elements," he also notes what he calls "a scarcity of conscious metaphors, by the side of the more numerous ones of faded and only dimly felt metaphorical quality" (lxiv), and he clearly favors explanations that reflect a confidence that things and events in the phenomenal or actual world of nature and history are somehow fairly accurately represented.

The kind of allegoresis that more closely parallels and sometimes overlaps with conceptual readings of *Beowulf* is the exegesis that treats the narrative as having important connections, explicit or latent, with parts of the scriptural story about God and his Creation. In a number of such commentaries, the biblical story is extended to include hexaemeral accretions, patristic interpretations, and liturgical or other uses of scripture. As with the doctrinal readings, so here, earlier scholars (Blackburn 1897; Chambers 1921; Klaeber 1950a; and others) have laid the groundwork by identifying as Christian a large number of elements in the poem. Emerson (1921), for example, had probed a motif that was to become a major scholarly preoccupation, the connection between the devilish, Cain-like Grendel and his murderously envious biblical forebear, neither of whom can stand the joy and innocence of those enjoying the Creator's favor. But it is not until the 1950s, and after, that such materials of sacred history become part of an extensive allegorizing account of the events of the poem.

Cabaniss (1955), concentrating on the fight with Grendel's mother, documents seven motifs that seem to show the poet's familiarity with the liturgy of baptism and a significant paralleling of two sets of events: Beowulf's descent into the mere, underwater battle, and reemergence; and Christ's death, harrowing of hell, and resurrection. These baptismal echoes, in turn, Cabaniss sees as being placed within widening concentric circles by the allusions to Cain, the Deluge, and Creation. His carefully stated conclusion is that the central narrative part of the poem is, "at the least, a reflection of the liturgy of baptism; at the most, an allegory of it" (200). McNamee (1960b) thinks the poem's unity is theological, not literary, and sees both doctrine (what he calls New Testament theological dogma) and scriptural event in the poem's three main battles. Takayanagi (1961) suggests that the poet, conditioned by symbolic and liturgical influences and by the allegorical temper of the times, found the Christian sense of history important (perhaps as shaped by allegorizations of the *Aeneid*) and that he thought of Beowulf as a Christ figure. Nicholson (1964), with an emphasis on baptism, expands on what he sees as the poet's conscious use of biblical types and figures and of christological and sacramental symbolism. He constructs an argument that the action of the poem is set before the Flood. Sutherland (1964) sees *Beowulf* as based on the Gospel of John as set out in the liturgical lectionary. Delasanta and Slevin (1968) argue for a christological purpose by which the poet seeks to perfect the pagan heroic ideal through submerged references to Christ. Ziegelmaier (1969), like several others, sees liturgical symbolism of baptism at work, in the context of a poem that shows a thoroughly Christian symbolization of nature, especially in its use of sea imagery.

With the publications by Goldsmith (1960, 1962, 1964, 1970), allegoresis, both conceptual and historical, takes a sharp U-turn. Goldsmith thinks that the poem presents Beowulf not as "an ideal exemplar" (1970, 3) but as someone who, "wanting in the supernatural strength of the *miles Christi*" (239), is defeated by the pride and cupidity that are his legacy as a son of Adam, despite his earlier achievement as a just man fighting the good fight against monstrous embodiments of evil. Goldsmith's reversal of the overall meaning of Beowulf 's life, and also of the newly created Heorot, so that ultimately they become symbols of human sin and corruption, does have a historical predecessor and also a nonreligious contemporary companion. Du Bois (1934) saw the Scyldings of Heorot as weak, guilty of pride and treachery, and deserving punishment by the Grendel kin. He interpreted the dragon as the symbol of internal discord in Geatland. He also saw Beowulf (like Hrothgar before him) not as an emblem of the unity of his people but as someone who finally succumbs to pride, sloth, and avarice. Tolkien (1953) says that, apparently because of a "chivalric" desire for praise, Beowulf goes beyond heroism and wrongly decides to fight the dragon single-handedly. Leyerle (1965), not much interested in religious significance, sees the major theme of the poem as a "fatal contradiction at the core of heroic society" (89) by which, the greater the hero's individual magnificence and bravery, the more likely it is that he will be subject to pride and so fail to exercise mature leadership. The problem with this interpretation, held in some form by several critics, is that it implies that Beowulf, protector and king of his people, should somehow have tried to avoid the deadly creature that has come spewing flames, burning "the bright dwellings, to the horror of men," and intending to destroy there every living thing (2312–15). Beowulf, with Wiglaf's help, does after all kill this destroyer before it sets on fire the whole of Geatland.

Goldsmith picks up and elaborates the rigorously moralistic Du Bois theme, thus helping set the scene for what, from a perspective in the 1990s, can be seen as the beginning of "deconstructionist" readings of *Beowulf*, that is, interpretations that do not accord with what Hamilton (1946) calls "the prevailing tenor" of the poem. In Goldsmith's extended exegesis, the poem's dominant symbols, Heorot and treasure, are the Christian poet's way of showing the Christian audience the rewards available to heroism. But the listeners or readers also are shown, "in the longer perspective" (1970, 96), that attachments to such things are "fundamental sins which tie the carnal man to earth" (96). For Goldsmith, although this poem is not as abstract as formal allegories of a Prudentian or Fulgentian sort, it is nonetheless "a Christian allegory of the life of man" (4) concerned with one aspect of human life, "the contest with the Enemy" (76). The main problem with Goldsmith's interpretation is that it assumes, in ways simply not supported by the text, that the poet is consciously and thoroughly, from the outset, intent on developing a contempt-of-the-world theme in a didactic work primarily about pride and covetousness. It is certainly possible that an ascetic, anagogically inclined Christian from any time in the Anglo-Saxon period might have brought such a rigorous, judgmental attitude to the heroic matter of the poem. But such an interpreter would have had little in common with the kind of imagination responsible for shaping the images and events in the text we have, so that the memory of the initial splendor and *dream* (joy) of Heorot, and of the God-given heroic energy and generosity of the man Beowulf, is never allowed to fade entirely from the tragic vision.

Not surprisingly, given the numbers and, in some cases, the zeal of those who would see *Beowulf* almost as naive allegory or as a disguised form of doctrinal catechizing, a sizable negative reaction emerges in the 1960s. Whallon (1962) argues that the poem knows little of Christianity (only two stories from Genesis, but these are made good use of) and that there is no evidence either of a sophisticated Christian perspective or of traditional allegory or typology. In 1965, he makes the claim that, since the apparently Christian vocabulary of the poem comes mainly from Germanic poetic diction, it in itself does not indicate Christian background (1965b). Halverson (1966) recognizes few Christian references in the poem and no clear evidence of allegorical intention. He attacks not only the interpretations of Hamilton, Cabaniss, McNamee, and Goldsmith but also the widely accepted view of Whitelock (1951, 21) that the audience was "steeped in Christian doctrines" and familiar with "the terminology of Christian vernacular poetry." It is instructive to note that Whallon and Halverson's minimalizing of the poem's Christianity was anticipated as early as 1815 by Thorkelin, in the first modern edition of the poem (with a translation into Latin), in which the Danish scholar says that there is nothing of the gods and religion in *Beowulf* that is not present in the epics of Homer and Virgil and in the *Eddas*. Thorkelin claims that the Christian references, to Abel and Cain and to the giants destroyed in the Flood, were intruded by Alfred the Great into what had been a Danish poem before it somehow came into the possession of the English (Thorkelin 1815b).

Rollinson (1970) provides a useful theoretical clarification of the two fundamental patristic senses of a narrative text, the *litteralis* and the *spiritualis*. The former embraces not only literal or historical meanings but also the full range of "human" language, including figurative expression, in contrast with the meanings called *spiritualis*. These latter are made known through the language of revelation, divine language, on the three levels traditionally designated as allegorical, tropological, and anagogic. In Rollinson's view, *Beowulf* conveys its themes on the literal level and makes itself easily comprehensible there, with the help of certain christological overtones that increase the significance of the literal actions. Cherniss (1972) identifies Germanic heroic traditions, with reference to concepts of loyalty, vengeance, treasure, and exile ("the ideological framework upon which the heroic poetry of Germania was built," 120), to show how in Old English poetry these Germanic traditions are combined with Christian Latin ones. In this conceptual context, he seeks to define "as precisely as possible in what way and to what degree *Beowulf* is a Christian poem" (125). After a careful review of scholarly opinion, he examines the allegedly Christian elements in the poem itself and concludes that, although the Christianity is pervasive, it (like the few traces of Germanic paganism) is "coloring" and incidental; the conduct of the action is controlled by Germanic heroic ideals (149–50).

Greenfield (1972, final chapter) cautions against excess in finding allegory in Old English poetry. In 1976, he articulates an idea meant to place exegetical interpretation of the poem in a broader critical context: the voice that records the narrative events also validates how it understands them and how it wants its audience to do so. It does this in four "authenticating" ways: temporal distancing, to make the story seem like history for the poet and his audience; contemporizing, to make this history relevant for them; moralizing, about human behavior in a continuum from past to present; and, finally, showing an epistemological and eschatological concern for the limits of human abilities and knowledge and "a concomitant awe at the unfathomable beyond" (60). Clearly, there are close parallels between these four perceived ways of directing interpretation and those of traditional four-level polysemy. Greenfield of course recognizes this, but he insists that there is a crucial difference between what he sees as the "literalness" of the "authenticating voice" and the "symbolic or typological or allegorical value-adding" of "the patristic exegetical mode of thought" (61). He makes the interesting suggestion that the important difference lies in the fact that the patristic mode "is but a sub-species of a more universal way of viewing human experience, a way embedded in the narrative mode itself" (61). In my judgment, Greenfield is on the verge here of an important insight, which partly eludes him.

It is not the opposition seen by Greenfield—between what he describes as the literalness of the authenticating voice and the symbolic or allegorical accretions supplied by exegesis—that is the problem. The real problem has two aspects. First, from most modern or postmodern perspectives, the three spiritual levels of the ancient-medieval theory of polysemy are just as "literal," even "historical" in the old sense of a true sacred story, as the first or literal level is. In a confessional context of Christian belief, the four irreducible "facts," causally related in the four-level scheme, are these: what you read; what you believe; what you do (because you read and believe); and what result follows for your soul, eternally (because you have read, believed, and acted according to the rule of *caritas,* or not). The problem for modern interpreters is not, as Greenfield thinks, that three of the old levels are too symbolic or allegorical but that they are too literal, not symbolic enough, for those of us who inhabit a post-Hegelian world and cannot be placed back in a believing early medieval community. The second matter was identified by Rollinson (1970): the literal or historical level of the old schema includes the figurative meanings (what we think of as the particularly "literary" or imaginative ones) that much of modern criticism values in poems like *Beowulf*. As a substantial body of commentary recognizes, there is wide scope on this level for the play and power of words. Whoever imagined *Beowulf*, and shaped its verbal patterns, included in the literal narrative many things that now have to be understood as highly fictional and figurative. (I develop this idea in Lee 1975).

By the 1960s and the early 1970s, the battle had been joined on whether *Beowulf* is to be read allegorically and, if so, by what particular structure of concepts or events it is to be interpreted. Within the conceptualizing commentaries, the main thrust is toward some part of the large body of Christian doctrine established in the early centuries of the church and thought to be known by the poet, either consciously and directly or less consciously through cultural conditioning. But other allegorists, hampered though they inevitably are by the paucity of early documents, prefer a Germanic frame of reference. The most versatile and learned writers of conceptual allegoresis, like Hamilton and Kaske, allow a large place for both sources but keep the main emphasis of the poem itself in the foreground. Historical allegoresis, unassisted by any real knowledge among us about the date of the composition of *Beowulf*, either makes certain assumptions and becomes very specific or has to be content with generalities potentially relevant to several centuries of Anglo-Saxon history—or else turns to the revelation of the nature and meaning of history as set out in the same scriptural stories told to Cædmon. Since that body of lore is in fact one of the most powerful mythologies in world history, as well as the one that largely created and shaped Anglo-Saxon Christian culture, it not surprisingly has proved a rich hunting ground for those who would understand the poem's intricate but powerful fusion of northern stories in an old poetic language with biblically accrued meanings. From the early 1970s on, despite vigorous controversy (see, e.g., Whallon et al. 1973; Oshitari 1974; Joyce Hill 1975), each of the two kinds of allegoresis has continued to flourish according to a program of inquiry already established in its essential outlines.

III. Poem and Concept: Phase 2 (since the Early 1970s)

Conceptualizing commentary continues to be divided on whether the poem presents the hero and heroic life as good and admirable, however limited, or as negative in its fundamental values. Within each of these views there is considerable variety of emphasis, which can be appreciated only by reading the documents themselves. Critics in the positive group include Thundy (1973), Hume (1974), A. P. Campbell (1974, 1975a), Donahue (1975), Hieatt (1975), Earl (1979), Tripp

(1977), Bolton (1978, 1979), Finnegan (1978), McGalliard (1978), Damon (1980), Kindrick (1981), D. Williams (1982), Dahlberg (1988), and Florey (1988). A strong, recent statement by G. Clark (1990, 7–21) holds Tolkien largely responsible for the numerous critics in recent decades that let a modernist antiheroic bias shape their view of the poem. Continuing the negative judgments articulated earlier by Du Bois, Goldsmith, and Leyerle are Crook (1974), Huppé (1975, 1984), Bandy (1976), Bliss (1979), and Bosse and Wyatt (1987). Particularly influential in this group is the view of Huppé that *Beowulf* is not an allegory but a critique of the heroic code from an Augustinian perspective: "Beowulf is a hero without Christ and reveals that the heroic in itself is an empty ideal" (1984, 40). The fundamental problem with this reading is that Beowulf is never presented in the poem as "the heroic in itself." He is presented as the most powerful of men between the seas because God has made him that and as himself knowing throughout the whole of his life that God has given him his strength and is in control of his fate at each stage (227b–28, 440b–41, 555b, 569b–75a, 669–70, 685b–87, 963–70a, 977b–79, 1270–74a, 1655–66a, 2327b–32, 2352a, 2524b–28, 2736b–43a, 2794–2801).

In recent years, Irving has been one of the most prominent and vigorous opponents of the use of patristic doctrines or any strict theology, external to the poem, to interpret it. In 1989, he attacks what he calls "Robertsonian exegesis," while earlier (1984) he examines the Christian references and tabulates them according to the frequency of their use by different characters: the narrator, Hrothgar, Beowulf, other speakers. In this accounting, Hrothgar emerges as the one outstandingly pious character, followed by the narrator, and then Beowulf. Irving points out that Christian references drop off sharply in the last third of the text, in favor of an emphasis on what he calls the lasting values of the heroic world. He claims that God is "seen from earth's viewpoint as an absentee landlord, remote and isolated" (16). The first four words of the statement are accurate, in my view, but the others are a contradiction of the very references he has tabulated, most of which recognize the immediacy of God's involvement in the affairs of the *middangeard* and his complete and final control of them. It is the remote, isolated Drihten of more transcendentally focused or anagogic works that is absent from *Beowulf.*

IV. Poem and History: Phase 2 (since the Early 1970s)

Because of the interpretive pressure felt by certain readers to pass from the immediate sense of the primary story of *Beowulf* to some other sense of the progression of actual events over time, historical allegoresis has continued. Again, this commentary has found its main outlet in exegesis focused on parts of sacred history thought to be explicit or suggested in the text. At the same time, and even with the intractable problems that arise from our ignorance of the specific historical origins of *Beowulf,* there are those who continue to seek clarification of the poem's meanings by linking it with particular historical situations or events. Perhaps the most valuable efforts of this kind in recent years are by Wormald (1978), Frank

(1982a), and Niles (1993a). Wormald dates *Beowulf* in the period of Bede and reasons that the religious character of this "great secular poem about the pagan kings of the past" (58) is not to be explained by searching the ideological heritage of Western Christianity. Rather, he would have us see it in the context of a secularized Anglo-Saxon church within which the warrior aristocracy had successfully resisted cultural assimilation, by establishing in the church their own traditions and codes. Frank, equally plausibly, would place *Beowulf* in the period of Alfred and his tenth-century successors, when generous celebrations of paganism were more possible and various accommodations of piety and the heroic life had been arrived at. Niles, like Frank, favors a late date for the poem (without being dogmatic about it) and cites seven reasons for locating *Beowulf* after the ninth-century Viking invasions, in the period when an English nation was emerging for the first time and "reinventing the ancestral past in the light of Christian doctrine and the Danish presence" (107).

Other historical contexts seen as relevant are described by Anderson (1978), Thundy (1983b, 1986), and Damico (1984). A. Harris (1990) approaches questions of history and the poem by looking inside the text itself at the passages of prediction that anticipate later events. These vatic or prophetic statements indicate historical understanding and character; Beowulf's predictions, for example, are more insightful and accurate than those of Wealhtheow. Harris thinks, moreover, that there has been scholarly overemphasis on how much knowledge of the Danish past the audience of *Beowulf* might have had or needed. Within the poem itself there are enough suggestions about events outside it to guide interpretation, and the passage of history since the events of the poem would have given the audience ironic distance. Stanley (1990) articulates an idea important for anyone trying to interpret *Beowulf* by reference to actual historical events and situations. By thoughtful scrutiny of the relation between history and fiction in *The Finnsburg Fragment* and the Finnsburg episode in *Beowulf,* he demonstrates how the *Beowulf* poet's imagination makes unhistorical use of the material we know from history. Stanley deftly defines the trap in thinking either that historical allegorization of a poem is a reliable guide to history or that history is a reliable guide to meanings in a work like *Beowulf.*

As becomes clear in the first phase of historical allegoresis of *Beowulf,* up until the early 1970s, explication of the text in terms of sacred history has major advantages compared to the other stream of historical commentary. First, the poem does assume a cosmos in which God is in control of events, including the giving of extraordinary powers to such a man as Beowulf, to allow him to intervene when monsters and other forces threaten the order of the human world. Whether we call this a mythological conception of history (a modern way of putting it) or a sacred conception (assumed in virtually all texts from the period), there is no avoiding the fact that heaven, hell, and middle earth are intimately interconnected in the poem. *Beowulf* (and the rest of the Anglo-Saxon poetic records) knows nothing of the sacred/secular split that modern thought forms and scholarship have imposed on it. Second, the explicit uses of biblical materials in the text itself provide an explanation of events as part of sacred history, in the words of the narrator and Hrothgar. This does not mean, however, that interpretation must go in the direction of doctrinal or conceptual allegoresis. The biblical references can be treated as evidence of poetic, not theological, thought, as myths and metaphors that identify things, people, monsters, places, and events in the poem with biblical symbols and types, while at the same time reidentifying the Christian elements by recasting them in the poetic language and cultural forms of heroic Germanic tradition.

In the last two decades, commentary assisted by biblical references has focused on four parts of the poem—Heorot, Grendel and his mother, Beowulf, and the dragon—in what can be seen as an overall pattern of creation (or Creation), the undoing of creation (or Creation), heroic rescues, and final victory/defeat. Golden (1976) suggests that even as Grendel is Cain so Heorot is a type of the heavenly city, which Grendel-Cain continually attacks. Osborn (1978) describes two perspectives, one heroic and one cosmic, by which the audience is linked with both the heroic world and the Christian biblical one. Helder (1987) notes that in Bede, Ambrose, and the liturgy, the Creation of the world with which Heorot is associated is taken to prefigure the formation of the church and that Cain's victim Abel, like Grendel's victim Heorot, is a type of the church. Ball (1971), arguing that "feond" in these lines (99–101) is Satan, not Grendel, suggests that the "drihtguman" (driht-men) who live in blessedness are the original inhabitants of Creation, not the Scyldings.

The figurative connotations and lineage of Grendel and his mother have received extensive commentary by Britton (1971), Kaske (1971), Peltola (1972), Bandy (1973), D. Williams (1975), Malmberg (1977), Mellinkoff (1979, 1981), M. Andrew (1981), and Feldman (1981). The only one of these critics to see Beowulf himself as a culpable member of the society of Cain's descendants is Bandy.

Three recent articles cite biblical or Bible-inspired references in support of interpretations of the events of Beowulf's life as parts of an idealizing pattern of meaning: Schichler (1986) identifies Beowulf with the hart or stag of biblical and bestiary tradition, enemy and destroyer of monsters; Wieland (1988), with backing from the poem *Exodus,* sees Beowulf as in a typological relationship to God; Pigg (1990) sees christological elements in *Beowulf* not as evidence of allegory but as "biblical riddlings and symbolic touches" (601) that are helpful to the poet in reconciling Germanic warrior ideals with Christian ones.

Three other articles link the dragon and its treasure with the biblical Doomsday. M. Green (1975) sees the fated hoard as the central symbol of doom that hangs over part 2 and the dragon as the embodiment of the Apocalypse. Helder (1977) traces eschatological resonances surrounding the Christ-like actions of Beowulf as he achieves victory over the dragon, before his passing in the Doomsday of the poem. Diametrically opposing Helder's view of Beowulf is A. K. Brown (1980), who links the dragon and the flames of the funeral pyre with the fiery Leviathan that consumes the deeds and souls of the wicked. Less ferocious but more illuminating is Duncan (1987), who reads the poem as a contest of narratives (mythological and historical) in which the historical narrative wins, by revealing human failures and recognizing human achievements instead of by the externalizing of internal social problems into monsters that can be defeated. Duncan also gives us a sentence worthy of gnomic status: "Secrecy in itself generates malignity, breeds dragons" (123).

V. Poem and Consciousness

The conceptual and historical allegorizations of *Beowulf* delineated above are rationalizations of an imaginative fiction. As such they seek to do with *Beowulf* what, from late antiquity on, had been done with Homer and Hesiod, with the Jewish Bible, and with the Christian Bible: they take a fabulous and mythical story interspersed with historical reminiscences (and permeated with an ancient sense of an interconnected three-tiered cosmos) and translate it into a vehicle of moral and religious teaching. Allegorization, like creeds, seeks to smooth out the discrepancies in mythical and metaphorical structures by making images and narratives defer to some other structure, of ideas or events, for their real authority. By doing this, it tries to establish or defend the thematic weightiness of what otherwise might be dismissed or undervalued. Since, however, the commentaries on *Beowulf* just discussed all point primarily to structures of ideas and events far in the past and deal only in a secondary way (and often unconsciously) with twentieth-century thought forms, a third kind of allegoresis has developed, to assist in appropriating an old poem into thought forms and cultural constructs believed to be more comprehensible and meaningful to modern and postmodern readers. This branch of *Beowulf* criticism, like the studies of the poem as a work of art, starts with an interest in structure, motifs, and patterns but goes beyond such enclosing New Critical or structuralist concerns and follows the images and story of the poem into wider cultural contexts of myth, ritual, and dream, as these are described by modern anthropology, comparative religion, and psychology. In this development, *Beowulf* criticism is of course part of that much larger twentieth-century literary enterprise in which, since Frazer's *Golden Bough* (1890), Freud's *Interpretation of Dreams* (1900), and Jung's *Psychology of the Unconscious* (1916), many works of literature are read as psychological allegories of latent psychic drives or conflicts or as myths containing and at the same time revealing the meaning of rituals and ceremonies. Unlike most conceptual and historical allegoresis, this form of allegorical interpretation usually assumes unconscious rather than deliberate concealment of the allegorical allusions.

Helterman (1968) combines influences from Eliade and Jung in an interpretation of Heorot as both the sacred or hierophantic center of the ordered cosmos and the microcosm or body of Beowulf. This center is plunged into chaos but restored to order by the hero, even as he triumphs over his shadow self. Helterman sees a conflict between Beowulf 's deeds as symbolic actions and their functions as events in history, in a total narrative action that moves from sacred, mythic time to profane, historical time (cf. Osborn 1978 and Duncan 1987). Irving (1968, chapter 3), in strong disagreement with the allegoresis of Kaske and Goldsmith, effectively combines New Critical close reading of patterns in the text with Eliade's concept of sacred time and space to interpret the mythic symbolism of Heorot and the hero. Dow (1970) also uses Eliade to read Beowulf as the hero of an archetypal, pre-Christian myth about a savior who suffers, dies, and experiences rebirth.

Influenced by Jung and Neumann, Foley (1977) interprets Hrothgar and Grendel as competing male symbols, Hrothgar being the good, benevolent, productive part of the male principle, versus Grendel the threatening, destructive part. Beowulf's victory over Grendel is seen as a mythic projection of the ego's first step towards resolution of the Oedipal conflict. Foley's overall idea is that, through oral performance and aural reception, *Beowulf* was a conscious forming of symbols of unconscious processes, to provide Anglo-Saxons with a handbook of counsel for social and psychological growth. Dragland (1977) sees the poem as pointing to an ultimately fatal darkness in the human mind, symbolized in the close association of man (including Beowulf, who "contains this shadow") and monster. In another example of psychological allegoresis, Chance (1980) sees the ideal roles of queen and mother (symbolized in the poem by Hygd) as parodied in the monstrously masculine mere-wife, who, in the depths, attempts a kind of savage sexual intercourse with her hall guest. Vaught (1980) discusses the cosmological, psychological, and social significance of a narrative sequence in which Beowulf becomes stronger by entering the center of society in Heorot and fighting Grendel but then must alienate himself and enter an unknown symbolic landscape of the unconscious and irrational. O'Keefe (1981) develops the idea that, in references to his mental states, Grendel is more closely identified with human beings the closer he gets to Heorot and that his nature, deeply ambiguous, prepares the audience for his being merged with Beowulf in their battle. Nonetheless, Beowulf, protecting a humanity that depends on living in community, defeats the uninvited "hall-thane" without succumbing to monstrousness.

Crépin (1983) raises a question not usually thought relevant about the "pre-psychological" literature of the early Middle Ages: If heroism is going beyond oneself, the negation of limits, weaknesses, and those other things that define individuality, is consciousness of self at all compatible with the heroic ethos? He sees in the text indications of a consciousness guiding Beowulf 's actions and reads the poem as the odyssey of the conscious mind against the forces of the unconscious, symbolized by the three main monsters. Earl, in three important articles, assisted in interpreting *Beowulf* by Freud's (1930) study of the nature of aggression and its effect on civilization, makes astute, nonreductive use of psychoanalytical concepts of group identity and the Oedipus complex. In Earl (1983), he gives an account of the psychological development of Anglo-Saxon culture from a primitive tribal stage to a civilized one: first comes competition between a male warrior culture (symbolized by the hall) and a feminized system of kinship-revenge (symbolized by the domestic hut); then domination (in postmigration England) by the male hall culture; and, finally, a stage in which Christianized Anglo-Saxons reject but mourn the culture of the hall. Earl sees traces of this cultural evolution in *Beowulf*: the world of the poem is that of the hall and male, warrior values; the domestic or feminine-dominated world is all but suppressed, but present in Grendel's mother. Beowulf is an "ego ideal," and the poem as a whole shows the superseding of the old superego hall values by those of the new Christian superego. In Earl (1987), he describes the world of human existence inside the hall in *Beowulf* as a symbol of safety and immanence, in contrast with the mysterious chaos of the outside, the transcendent unknown. As in Bede's simile of the sparrow, Beowulf goes into the darkness with only the barest glimpse of his destination, in a poem that stoically refuses to look beyond the threatening borders of the immanent. In Earl (1991), he points out two heroic codes in *Beowulf*, one for the lord and one for the thanes, but does not psychoanalyze the text itself. Instead, with considerable subtlety and insight, he seeks to understand how the text, "with its deep, uninterpretable silences," can be placed in the position of an analyst psychoanalyzing the audience ("then and now") by serving as a screen for its projections (1991, 66). Earl assumes that we are meant to link our egos with the thane's code, not the lord's, so that by the end of the narrative we are identifying with Wiglaf, not Beowulf, who is beyond us. As lord and hero, Beowulf is the superego, "terrifying in his heroic freedom and superiority" (85).

Kroll (1986) argues that *Beowulf* is primarily political and temporal, not temporal and spiritual, as indicated in the poet's ignoring of the sin of Adam and Eve in favor of Cain's crime, brother slaying being a failure of loyalty and civility. Kroll reads Beowulf (who is his brothers' keeper) and the monsters as doubles or second selves, each playing out the drama of Cain. Butts (1987) sees the mere as an extended metaphor or dreamlike landscape, with features corresponding to a psychological state (terror) that is beyond description. John M. Hill (1989) explicitly rejects Christian allegoresis as a way of interpreting the poem in favor of the id-ego-superego theory from psychoanalysis. He reads the monsters as externalizations of human impulses and thinks that the heroic world in *Beowulf* is at an early stage of the dissolution of the Oedipus complex, with a hero who imposes superego control over the libidinal forces of Grendel and his mother but is killed by the dragon because he is unable to rise above his own primitive desire for treasure and gifts.

I began this chapter, about the numerous allegorizations of *Beowulf* that have emerged mainly in the last six decades, by welcoming the scholarly acceptance of polysemy that this handbook implies. Not surprisingly, then, while considering particular interpretations and their overall accumulation, my mind frequently has been pulled away, in two opposite directions: either to some other kind of critical approach or back into the language and experience of the poem itself. This is not to diminish or undervalue the host of illuminating insights that can be gained from the articles and books in question. On the contrary, I am convinced that most of these commentaries have value, and I regret that the brevity of my summaries inevitably strips away much of the richness and subtlety found in the critical writings themselves, leaving only an abstract digest of what lively intelligences have presented.

That having been said, I confess a long-held bias against allegoresis as such, especially when applied to *Beowulf*. The translating of imagery into examples and precepts (ancient or medieval, modern or postmodern) is a quite distinct process from following images around in a poem, to find what they might mean in it. It is distinct also from following those same images into other poems (especially Old English ones) or from other poems back into the one you have started with, to see what the words might mean in any one of the passages considered. Structurally and formally, *Beowulf* is not an allegory, though it does have pronounced thematic emphases that plausibly can be called allegorical tendencies. Still, the primary challenge for criticism is to confront the structure of images as a product of poetic thought and imagining, from a very particular mind working in a particular set of verbal conventions. The biggest and most difficult critical task (as, e.g., Tripp [1992] recognizes) is knowing what the Old English words are doing, poetically, at any particular place in the text. Here, in my view, we still need to pay attention to Tolkien's main point, that in *Beowulf* we are dealing with myth presented in the concrete language of metaphor and that the poet's concern is with such realities as a dragon who "wields a physical fire," "covets gold not souls," and "is slain with iron in his belly" (265–66). Allegoresis encourages us to think of the words of the text as designating or signifying something beyond themselves, and no doubt they do, but as soon as we start to say what they point to outside the poem (and even outside of Old English poetry), a process of abstraction begins to take over, and shortly we are translating into another *langage* (of description, concept, or even preaching), which is not the *langage* of *Beowulf*. In the poem itself we are dealing with words of power that are and act, before they mean.

Chapter 13

Social Milieu

by John M. Hill

Summary: Readers have discussed various Germanic social customs, values, and structures found in *Beowulf*: gift giving, boasting behavior, revenge and feud settlement, lordly generosity and munificence, the keeping of genealogies, kinship ties, warband loyalties and reciprocities, the function of peace brides, and queenly peace weaving in the hall. But these matters have usually been discussed in relative isolation from each other, rather than receiving an ethnologically integrated viewing that would allow us to see *Beowulf* as a world that works rather than, in effect, as a partly misunderstood assortment of customs, values, and relationships the poet busily transcends.

Chronology

1892: John Earle in passing notes that the controlling idea of *Beowulf* is that mutual dependence is the law of human society.

1909: Vilhelm Grønbech surveys the social values of Germanic gift giving, relying largely on the Old Norse poem *Hávamál*.

1911: Frederic Seebohm, drawing from *Beowulf*, reviews the blood feud in terms of customary controls as well as heated emotions. He concludes that there is no feud within the kindred, marriage between kindreds is a common way of closing feuds, and the wife does not pass entirely out of her kindred into her husband's.

1912: H. Munro Chadwick surveys *Beowulf* from an anthropological perspective as marking a stage when lordship ties overtake kinship ties.

1916: Alexander Green interprets the Finn episode as a dramatization of Danish prowess.

1922: Friedrich Klaeber (1922a) publishes *Beowulf and the Fight at Finnsburg*. Social information appears in the extensive introductions, notes, and glossaries.

1929: Levin L. Schücking (1929a) argues for the melding of Christian and Germanic cultural values in *Beowulf*.

1934: Stefán Einarsson demonstrates the living reality in *Beowulf* of a pre-Christian ritual: the consequential, drink-induced boast or vow.

1952–53: Ernst Leisi discusses the congruence of riches, generosity, and moral worth in *Beowulf*.

1952: J. L. N. O'Loughlin, concentrating on the theme of settled and unsettled feud, sees Beowulf as a just king rightly proud of never having slain his kin.

1955: Margaret Pepperdene comments on the diplomatic protocol of Beowulf's progress toward Heorot.

1955: H. L. Rogers treats weapons and treasure in *Beowulf* as having negative connotations.

1958: Lorraine Lancaster presents a schematic account of Anglo-Saxon kinship terms and relationships.

1959: Morton W. Bloomfield argues for the relevance of the idea of divinely judged trial by combat in Beowulf's fights.

1959: Arthur G. Brodeur comments on Beowulf's noble kingship when compared to the kingships of other Germanic heroes.

1959: Thomas Garbaty ties the heroic oath to reciprocal, feudal contracts.

1962: James L. Rosier comments negatively on drinking behavior in the hall and in reference to Unferth.

1963: Alain Renoir remarks on the absolute nature of the heroic boast.

1965: D. H. Green produces a landmark study of the warband's legal, ethical, and reciprocal vocabulary.

1966: E. Talbot Donaldson translates *Beowulf,* characterizing feud as an almost inescapable net in the poem.

1968: Inspired by E. Leisi, Michael Cherniss shows the honorable nature of material gain in *Beowulf.*

1968: Edward B. Irving Jr. discusses the courtly decorum of Beowulf's approach to Heorot, the often public nature of gift giving, and Wealhtheow's fragile peace weaving.

1969: John Halverson elaborates what he sees as a politically unstable ethic of personal, individualistic loyalty in *Beowulf.*

1970: William Chaney argues for the sacral character of the gift seat in *Beowulf.*

1970: John Golden shows the legal purport of "hafa nu ond geheald" (have now and hold) and focuses on the opposition between kinship and warfare as well as the social importance of gift giving and liberality in *Beowulf.*

1972: Stanley J. Kahrl argues for the interminable nature of feud in *Beowulf.*

1973: Elizabeth Liggins argues that there is no general critique of revenge in *Beowulf.*

1973: Richard Palmer surveys the moral qualities, especially boldness and liberality, of good kings and heroes in *Beowulf.*

1974: Harry Berger Jr. and H. Marshall Leicester Jr. interpret social institutions in *Beowulf* as deeply self-destructive.

1974: Stanley B. Greenfield comments on the positive valence of gold in the poem.

1975: Citing Marcel Mauss, Charles Donahue reviews munificence and continuing gift exchange in *Beowulf.*

1977: Ellen Spolsky comments on the ambiguity of archaic, compounded kinship terms in *Beowulf,* focusing especially on "suhtergefæderan" and "aþum-sweoras."

1978: T. A. Shippey suggests that the social and semantic system of *Beowulf* differs greatly from our own.

1979: Eric G. Stanley (1979a) asserts the figurative nature of legal language in *Beowulf.*

1980: Rolf H. Bremmer produces a comprehensive overview of the uncle-nephew bond in *Beowulf*.

1980: Jeff Opland brings a comparative ethnological dimension to the study of Anglo-Saxon oral poetry and performance.

1980: Barbara Nolan and Morton W. Bloomfield show the social context of boasting behavior in *Beowulf*.

1981: Martin Camargo raises the view of feud as interminable to a thematic level for *Beowulf*.

1981: While arguing for its profoundly sociocentric nature, Dwight Conquergood also notes the temporal dimension of boasting behavior in Anglo-Saxon poetry.

1981: Robert Kindrick emphasizes the congruence of moral values in *Beowulf* with native, Germanic traditions.

1981: Hermann Moisl shows the traditional character of Anglo-Saxon and Germanic genealogies.

1982: Robert T. Farrell (1982a) elaborates the mixed social and political relations between Geats and Swedes.

1982: John M. Hill discusses the social drama of complex gift giving in Heorot and in Hygelac's hall.

1982: Thomas D. Hill focuses on the refinement of Beowulf's kingship in pointed comparison to the Volsung kings.

1982: Michael J. Swanton, while eventually characterizing Beowulf's kingship as touched finally by vainglory, also notes the legal implications of *treow,* suggesting that the word hardened away from an earlier sense of reciprocity.

1983: John D. Niles argues for the centrality of a communitarian theme in *Beowulf* and comments on the dramatic contrast between Hrothgar's shell of a kingship and Beowulf's active old age.

1984: Helen Damico argues for a Valkyrie-like background to Wealhtheow's forcefulness, enlarging our sense of her social roles.

1985: James Bellman Jr. addresses social questions of institutionalized feud, gift exchange, and heroism.

1985: Malcolm Brennan underscores the political tensions in Beowulf's approach to Hrothgar.

1985: Hugh Magennis corrects misconceptions about drinking among retainers, showing its socially cohesive purposes.

1985: Fred C. Robinson emphasizes the relation between drinking and serious boast.

1986: Hugh Magennis reveals the social and elegiac elements in images of sitting in *Beowulf*.

1988: Michael Enright indicates the importance of Wealhtheow's and Hygd's cup-bearing roles for ritually developed, hierarchical cohesion within the warband.

1988: Nicole Gardiner-Stallaert surveys the concept of loyalty in Old English heroic poetry in terms of a developing idea historically of transcendent loyalty to God.

1989: Stephen O. Glosecki underlines the archaic nature of special weapons and underwater journies in *Beowulf*.

1989: Edward B. Irving Jr. argues for a characterization of Hrothgar's aged kingship as impotent, pathetic.

1989: Wade Tarzia discusses the hoarding ritual in Germanic life and in *Beowulf* as the removing of cursed prestige goods from circulation.

1991: John M. Hill applies Dumézil's distinctions between the war gods Tiu and Odin (war as law and war as frenzy, respectively) to kings in *Beowulf.*

1992: Catherine Carsley meditates on the tenuous inventions of cultural pasts in *Beowulf* in the face of blood feud.

1993: John D. Niles (1993a) argues for *Beowulf* as a tenth-century, Anglo-Danish kingdom's incorporating myth.

As the preceding chronology clearly shows, there has been no lack of significant commentary on such social institutions and behaviors in *Beowulf* as the lord-retainer relationship, the uncle-nephew bond, kinship terms, boasting, revenge and feud, gift giving, and the use of genealogies. Too often, however, while these commentaries are observant, they lack an integrative view of social features in *Beowulf.* Moreover, many of them import distorting literary plots to the poem, usually those of tragedy. However, when we step back and consider *Beowulf*'s social institutions as interconnected in a dramatized social system, such as we find constructed in ethnographies of noncentralized peoples, a very different *Beowulf* emerges. The poem takes on an idealized, as well as socially and temporally comprehensive, cast that suggests its role in its Anglo-Saxon present. It is part, this chapter will argue, of its society's social myth: a dramatization set in the past of living values and encouraged behaviors.

Early in this century, a number of anthropologically informed scholars used heroic poems as evidence for early Germanic social life. When H. Munro Chadwick did so, he eventually expanded his focus comparatively, defining a heroic age that parallels similar ages (occupying different historical moments) in Greece, Ireland, India, and Russia and that one can glimpse even in the modern poetry of Serbo-Croatians and Tatars (1912, 725–49). For him, the heroic age had a particular social organization, centered on individual, often aristocratic warrior-heroes. It was transitory and eventually evolved into something more communal. In that shift, for Chadwick, it recouped something of the past out of which it had evolved. In the Germanic context, Chadwick saw the evolution of life into a heroic age as a movement away from family ties reckoned on both parents' sides, with inheritance favoring the sister's son, to descent through males at the kindred's expense. In turn, he saw the family as giving way to the warband.

Thus in *Beowulf,* among other things, he notes the lord to retainer tie but downplays kinship when he mentions kingly generosity. Without considering social contexts, he simply asserts that warriors will render gains to their lords, citing Hygelac's supposed coming-of-age gift to Beowulf as historically accurate, while missing that gift's dramatic context (a return gift). Because of the lordship theme, furthermore, he sees Beowulf's final gifts to Wiglaf as yet another instance of familial inheritance absorbed by the lord to retainer relationship. Thus, heroic poetry supports an anthropologically presumed change in social structure. That poetry is not looked to for re-created social dramas.

However, when we think of *Beowulf* as an integrated social world dramatized by the poet, nearly everything Chadwick focused on changes. We begin to see the economy of honor and gift giving as open to social complexity, competitiveness, and possibilities for manipulation. We see the social tensions and legal issues addressed in Beowulf's progress to Heorot: his nighttime stewardship of the hall comes into relief, bringing the jural dimensions of heroic action into focus. We find that feud relationships become more functional and less a sign of social dissolution than they have seemed. And we can even see the genealogical and temporal indicators in the poem differently as they suggest the poem's incorporating rather than distancing role. An integrated ethnological approach of this kind has not been tried in the literature on such matters as kinship and the special ties between maternal uncle and nephew, reciprocal ties of loyalty between lord and retainers, gift giving and the acquiring of wealth, boasting behavior, feud and revenge, legalistic vocabulary, the institution of kingship, the role of the hall and of cup-bearing queens, and the poet's perspective on the heroic past. In these matters, the history of *Beowulf* commentary is largely a history of atomization, one that distorts the poem's social drama.

To begin with one of the most commented on institutions, gift giving has been generally understood at least since Vilhelm Grønbech (1909, 47–59) surveyed the nature of the gift in Germanic contexts, particularly in the Old Norse *Hávamál*: gift exchange identifies friend to friend; friends exchange gifts; gifts look for a return. In the late 1960s, Edward B. Irving Jr. and John Halverson write about the communal joys of the hall in *Beowulf*, among which is gift giving, treated by Irving (1968, 131) as a public act and thus open to either approval or criticism. The good king's liberality becomes a commonplace for scholars, as does the idea that gifts establish bonds of loyalty between lord and retainers.

Harry Berger Jr. and H. Marshall Leicester Jr. invoke Marcel Mauss's and Marshall Sahlins's anthropological work to suggest the competitive and even conflicted possibilities for gift giving in *Beowulf*. They see the heroic institutions in the poem as destructive and inherently doomed (1974, 56–59). In contrast, Charles Donahue (1975, 25–26), also inspired by Mauss, deepens an idealizing tradition by referring lordly munificence and retainer loyalty to ancient ways of feeling. He thinks of gift exchange in *Beowulf* as a kind of potlatch—a misnomer because nothing like an aggressive giving away appears in *Beowulf*. But crucially he notes that we misunderstand gift exchange and munificent gesture if we think in terms of modern goods and services. Donahue also sees gift exchange as a continuing affair open to various purposes: suitable reward, policy and alliance, and an expression of affection (1975, 27, 28, 39). But in overlooking competitiveness he misses possibilities for social drama, for the revising of intentions, for unstated invitations and alternative offers (as when Wealhtheow counters Hrothgar's gifts to

Beowulf)—issues I address elsewhere (1982, 187–93) in terms of complex gift giving in Hrothgar's and Hygelac's halls.

To seek material wealth seems vainglorious to some (Rogers 1955, 339–42) and honorable to others. Inspired by Ernst Leisi, who cites Grønbech, Mauss, and Malinowski (Leisi 1952–53, 271–73), Michael D. Cherniss (1968, 475–76) corrects misunderstandings generated by our own, as well as medieval Christian, censoriousness. Militarily gaining treasure manifests the possessor's worthiness as warrior or as king; thus, the rightful possession of treasure marks honor. In this respect, Beowulf's interest in the dragon's gold is not vainglorious, not something we must either excuse or condemn. Gold has positive valence when appropriated for social purposes, negative when hoarded (Greenfield 1974, 113). Negativity infuses hoards seen as prestige goods ritually taken out of circulation and socially cursed against reappropriation. Without a clear understanding of hoards, one might nevertheless feel a superstitious need to redeposit a disturbed hoard as soon as possible—hence Wiglaf's deposition of the hoard in Beowulf's mound (Tarzia 1989, 115).

Munificence embraces exchange and the establishing of loyal ties between lord and retainers. The theme of loyalty within the warband appears early in the scholarly literature and receives periodic attention down to the present, especially in readings (perhaps indebted to H. M. Chadwick [1912]) that see a weakening of kinship bonds and a corresponding strengthening of ties to lords and the warband—reciprocal ties modeled on those of kinship in part, although entered into freely for some (Golden 1970, 54) and a mixing of kinship and retainership for others (Halverson 1969, 598). In turn, because mutable, these ties might suggest that transcendent tie to the Lord of all (as argued in Nicole Gardiner-Stallaert's 1988 survey of reciprocal loyalty in *Beowulf* and other heroic poetry). But in itself personal loyalty rarely seems problematic, although Halverson (1969, 606–08) sees it as making for weak institutions.

Berger and Leicester (1974, 61–64) handle this point through their interpretation of social doom, such that Beowulf finally gives so much of himself that his people cannot reciprocate and thus manifest their loyalty. In this, as in other matters, heroic institutions are analyzed as inherently fractured or else destructive. Here, revenge feud is seen as the most obvious manifestation of poison within the institutions of competitive gift giving and loyal service. Much as a warband leader must take from others before giving to his own, within the warband envy and greed can move one from the reciprocities of receiving and giving to the violence of taking (or withholding). This violence generates treachery and jealousy within the warband and feuds within families, within dynasties, and between neighboring peoples. Indeed, revenge feud has long tainted *Beowulf*'s world for modern readers not approaching feud in terms of potentially stabilizing rules, such as those Frederic Seebohm (1911, 71–72) mentions: that there is no feud within the family when kinsmen slay each other; that murder within the family is followed by outlawry; that marriage between peoples is a common if chancy way of settling feuds; and that in marriage a wife still has close, even legal ties to her father's people. Aside from an occasional comment early in the century—see Alexander Green (1916, 760) on Danish prowess and the Finn episode—and excepting Elizabeth Liggins's argument for no critique of revenge in *Beowulf* (1973, 213), modern readers overwhelmingly respond to feud in the poem as a vicious circle or net from which there is little prospect of escape (Donaldson 1966, x–xi) and even as something interminable (Kahrl 1972, 198).

Focusing especially on the Finn episode, Martin Camargo (1981, 132–34) gathers such responses into an examination of the revenge ethic. He finds that ethic terribly wanting and argues that here the otherwise exemplary Beowulf fails a Christian ideal the poet embraces. But, as I will illustrate later, revenge feud in *Beowulf* can look different, incident by incident, when approached anthropologically (although overviews of societies that practice the feud can come to very different conclusions about feud as a mode of relationship, competition, self-help, and settlement between groups). Indeed, feud takes on a different look when seen as part of a system of exchange no more inherently conflicted or contrary than any other social system.

Whether born or (re)made through fosterage, adoption, or else the mutualism of violent support, people bound in kinship help each other in feuds. Many readers have noted the special kinship Tacitus emphasized in the *Germania* between sister's brother and sister's son, a bond that both explains Beowulf's love of Hygelac (his mother's brother) and makes the deaths of maternal uncle and nephew in the Finn episode so grievous. Bremmer's (1980) convenient overview of uncle-nephew ties in *Beowulf* makes the Finn feud even seem unnatural to some, such as Camargo (1981, 128). Two other, uniquely named ties in Beowulf are the ones between Hrothgar as paternal uncle and his brother's son, Hrothulf ("suhtergefæderan"), and between son-in-law and father-in-law ("aþumsweoras"). Lorraine Lancaster's schematic account of Anglo-Saxon kinship terms (1958) suggests the generality of some terms and the ambiguity of others—an ambiguity Ellen Spolsky (1977, 234–35) investigates closely in *Beowulf.*

Spolsky notes that *suhterga* can indicate either a brother's son or an uncle's son, one's cousin: thus, the seemingly archaic compound, "suhtergefæderan," which crosses generational lines, not only appropriately covers Hrothgar's relationship with Hrothulf, his brother's son (nephew), but also embraces the tie between Hrothgar's sons and Hrothulf (their cousin). "Aþumsweoras" joins two terms connecting in-law relationship and possible consanguinity (*sweor* as either father-in-law or cousin) as well as cross-generational ties (*aþ*, tie by oath, can indicate either a son-in-law or a brother-in-law). Those two compounds argue, then, that comradeship in arms and mutual welfare define aristocratic relationships more importantly than do considerations of age or generation.

Along with feud, readers may also censor competitive behavior in the hall, especially when associated with drinking. Thus, Unferth's challenge and various references to drink and drinking have taken on negative connotations for James L. Rosier (1962, 5) and have troubled many readers and translators. Hugh Magennis (1985, 161–64) and Fred C. Robinson (1985, 75–76) correct matters, with the former noting that drinking in the hall usually symbolizes cohesion for the group and properly accompanies verbal challenges, while the latter particularly links drinking and the oath. Although Beowulf rebukes Unferth for speaking about Breca's adventure while flushed with beer, there is no overt critique of drinking in the poem. Beowulf's point is that Unferth, who may think he speaks seriously, actually does not know the truth. Taking these points together with Helen Damico's comments on the power of cup-bearing queens like Wealhtheow (1984, 166–67), we can see taking the *ful* (cup) and drinking in general as having sacral possibilities and as solemnizing vows, promises, and perhaps even flytings.[1] The latter become authorized in a more serious way than they would be if simply excused as drink induced. Here too the queen as peace weaver in the hall takes on a different cast if seen as socially and politically regulative rather than as pathetic. Damico (125–32) notes Wealhtheow's forceful style, adding that Wealhtheow supports Hrothulf as a "mother-aunt" would support a nephew—thus correcting the many characterizations of Wealhtheow as a brave or fragile, incantatory or future-fearing speaker in Heorot (e.g., Irving 1968, 139–45; Chance 1986, 99). Damico may overargue her case, but on balance Wealhtheow is a stronger presence than even Enright admits while convincingly arguing for the socially important ways in which queens ally families as well as religiously sanction hierarchical relationships within the warband, doing so through the drink and cup-bearing ritual (1988, 191, 201). Enright argues that here queens are extensions of their lords, having little power of their own. They become cultishly important only during periods of doubtful succession, when they become extensions of the kingless warband. Of course their paternal families could no doubt influence what happens to and through them.

To similar effect, a social view can correct misapprehensions about Beowulf's boasting behavior as excessive in some way, a view not shared by Stefán Einarsson (1934) in his demonstration of the boast-drink ritual or by Dwight Conquergood, who notes that boasts are valued, deeply meaningful speeches to Anglo-Saxons (1981, 26). Moreover, in heroic poetry, boasts express temporal and social continuity by projecting violent engagement publicly in terms of past action and given group values (28, 30). Thus, boasts are not egocentric. Through boasts individuals stand out, to be sure, but in profoundly sociocentric ways (30). Barbara Nolan and Morton Bloomfield (1980, 500, 511) argue similarly that boast words and boasting speeches are traditional forms of public speech, and of vow or promise, that the community requires of its aspiring heroes. Boasts also in part define the hero's purposes, establish his social identity, and suggest a kind of word magic over the future. In these distinctions, Nolan and Bloomfield improve on both general invocations of the heroic oath (Renoir 1963, 239–40) and efforts to link heroic vows to feudal contracts (Garbaty 1959, 11–12). Nolan and Bloomfield point to the social and ritualistic contexts in which actions occur or are proposed—contexts that interrelate the political and the poetical, much as the series of challenges through which Beowulf passes outside and in Heorot involves political threat and the negotiating functions of Hrothgar's officialdom (Brennan 1985, 3–6). Thus, those challenges become more complex than earlier views of Geatish and Danish protocol and courtly decorum suggest (Pepperdene 1955, 409–19; Irving 1968, 51–60). Protocol here involves a language of juridical right that Klaeber (1950a, 272) and E. G. Stanley (1979, 76–82) take figuratively. But that language may well become literal when seen as part of the warrior's juridical functions and when attended to for legalisms inherent in the ethical vocabulary and public injunctions of the comitatus, such as "hafa nu ond geheald" (have now and hold) (D. H. Green 1965, 142–62; Golden 1970, 75). I partly address this issue for Hrothgar and Beowulf elsewhere (1991, 169–71).

Kingships change also when seen in social contexts and within ideas of the juridical, not just as strong or weak or indebted to self and folk, rather than to God. While both Niles (1983, 110) and Irving (1989, 59–63) note the complexity of Hrothgar's character, they stress his weakness in contrast to Beowulf's kingship, and M. J. Swanton (1982, 141) sees Beowulf adjuring both folk and God in his prideful challenge for the dragon's gold. But, as we see it foregrounded, Hrothgar's kingship seems more "legislative" than martial (J. Hill 1991, 169–71), whereas Beowulf's is both. The poet idealizes good kings, perhaps mixing his understandings of Germanic and Christian virtues (Schücking 1929a, 151–54). Although the poet does not suggest a Christ figure in *Beowulf* (Klaeber 1950a, li), he may well depict a nobler kingship in *Beowulf* than one finds in Germanic heroic tales (Brodeur 1959, 76). Perhaps this nobility is especially evident in contrast to stories of violated kinship and reckless aggression among such figures as the Volsungs (T. Hill 1982, 175–76). Thus, the poet seems little interested in some archaic idea of the sacral king (Chaney 1970, 121–56; opposed by Golden 1970, 100). Instead, he seems to dramatize a renovated conception of kingship, with or without firm commitments to succession. The language in which Beowulf's people praise him draws in part from the vocabulary of kinship amity—a vocabulary missing from Hrothgar's aged kingship of laudable munificence and harmony-inducing custom.

Nolan and Bloomfield (1980, 516) also move us toward a fuller understanding than we previously had of "the central social function a poem like *Beowulf* would have played in defining values as well as recording tribal history"—an understanding that informed Bloomfield's (1959) earlier work on divine sanctions for Beowulf's combats and that increasingly informs Niles's view of a communitarian theme both in (1983, 224–26) and around *Beowulf* (1993a, 106–07). A hint of that theme appears early in *Beowulf* scholarship, as in John Earle's remark that the theme of the poem is the need for mutual dependence in a strong society (1892, lxxxvii–viii). But the incorporating work the poem does in its possibly tenth-century, Anglo-Saxon present—work combining the heroic past with an

Anglo-Danish, Christian present—has only recently been emphasized. Such views redirect us away from Tolkien's concept of the poet's detached perspective, according to which the poet sympathized deeply with the heroic world but remained emphatically separate from it.

Seeing *Beowulf* as incorporative in its work requires an all-embracing time scheme as well as a genealogical sense of social identity: that is, identity forms out of a sense of rights and values in an inheritor-like relationship with forebears (Meany 1989, 37–38: the Scyld Scefing genealogy suggests a tenth-century patron's identification with Danish ancestry). This makes the concept of time one of descent more than of clocks and numeration. Time becomes an extended or specious present rather than an array of past, present, and future wherein the past is alienable and the future redemptive.

In this genealogical sense, the poet looks back to a mythically heroic past, to myth in the sense in which Malinowski (1932, 327–28) characterizes stories accepted or else modified and posed as truth, bearing the sanction of righteousness and propriety in virtue of their "preterity and universality," and thus possessing "the normative power of fixing custom, of sanctioning modes of behavior, of giving dignity and importance to an institution." The poet seamlessly establishes a basic continuity with such a past. He projects a fundamental sameness of moral and ethical values. This sameness frames both his sense of difference from some customs (especially prayers to devils) and, as established in his dual perspective, the limited but clear-eyed theism his noble characters express. As his tie to the heroic past is inclusive, his sense of time becomes structural, rather than given over to ideas of alterity.

As the poem's time schemes establish an incorporating moral frame, we should expect everything social in the poem to illuminate moral issues in some interconnected way, yielding significant fruit when approached as an integrated world rather than seen piecemeal or as a congeries of customs, values, and institutions. This approach especially matters for all of the friendly as well as violent relationships between people and monsters. Those relationships fall further into two large categories: feuding and legal or customary settlement and gift and marriage exchanges. Insofar as some exchanges are fruitful, no particular exchange is necessarily baleful. Insofar as feud settlements do occur, no instance of feud necessarily argues for unending vendetta in the world of the poem. This principle holds also for acts of requital or repayment, which categorically unite feud relations with gift exchanges. The result is a dynamic, comprehensive system of exchange across time—a system expressive of social values and order in this world, while revealing desires and behaviors that reverse prominent values and threaten social order.

Many evolving nuances aside, the world in *Beowulf* operates by at least four nearly symmetrical social principles, those in turn generating a central imperative: continuing gift and marriage exchanges create peace, kinship, and alliance, opposing feud; continuing feuds forbid all kinship possibilities, opposing gift and marriage exchanges; settling external feuds enhances internal group life and opposes baleful strife between peoples (which can reach the level of Odinesque terror and the desecration of bodies); and stopping gift exchange within the hall destroys hall kinship and invites treachery, enmity, fratricide, and broken or else false oaths. These relationships are only approximately symmetrical because gifts always carry something of their giver's wishes. Competitive gift giving, for instance, can define the kinds of kinship desired and look for a return, while gift exchange always involves temporary inequalities within relationships of support and dependency. Strongly marked oppositions are unstable as well in that something of each pole exists in the other; no opposition is exactly polarized in all respects. The central event in this world, then, is exchange. The crucial imperative is the settling of feuds and the continuation of fruitful exchange, the latter creating or else intensifying further kinship between individuals and peoples.

Those points are general but crucial to a social reading of *Beowulf*. Yet without some concrete illustration their force may not be apparent to the many readers who see the poem's social institutions and behaviors in atomized terms and through tragedy-enhancing lenses. Thus, in the following pages, I elaborate several of those points briefly in relation to portentous moments in the poem, concentrating on instances of revenge and feud settlement, on the idea of warfare as law, and on gift giving and receiving. The disturbing story of Hildeburh's sorrow is a good place to begin.

Told in Heorot after Beowulf's victory against Grendel, this tale, a Danish victory song, strikes many readers as ironic pathos because it movingly stresses Hildeburh's undeserved suffering. But does this story indeed indict revenge? We do not know why Frisians attacked their Danish guests and in-laws, but we do know that a surviving party of Danes, linked in a winter pact with Finn and some of his surviving Frisians, avenges their leader's death in the spring. Finn and his men perish, Finn's treasures are taken, and Hildeburh returns to her people. The ending thus settles a grievous wrong rather than indicts revenge, and Hildeburh at least can assume a once familiar place in the world, where her legal status in fact has remained.

One might object to this settlement by noting that nothing erases our sense of Hildeburh's sorrow when in the morning light she beholds all her joys dead, her brother and son both. Nor can we easily forget the grim pathos of uncle and nephew devoured side by side on the funeral pyre—together in fiery immolation much as the uncle-nephew, sister's-son tie would have socially linked them in life. These points are provocative. Yet, turned around, they substantially define just how grievous is the disaster Hildeburh suffers—a disaster that more than justifies the complete settlement Hunlafing urges upon Hengest in the Danish spring.

Even the case of Freawaru's marriage to Ingeld and the story of resumed feud, as delineated prospectively by Beowulf, speaks to something other than the revenge ethic itself: rather, Beowulf would have us contemplate the question of just how we would ally two peoples when there has been little time for the cooling of hot blood. Beowulf has already established continuing exchange and support between Geats and Danes–who once exchanged enmities rather than friendship—and so he might favor such an arrangement between Danes and Heathobards.

We think of revenge as extralegal, as something to replace with systems of payment or some other form of nonlethal settlement, such as outlawry. But for many societies, including Germanic ones, revenge can be jurally definitive. Even when urged by an old, grim-hearted warrior, as in the Heathobard allusion, revenge can have jural respectability. After all, the Dane-Heathobard scenario is the just-minded Beowulf's.

The poet sometimes does seem ambivalent about violent exchanges, especially in his comment that that exchange was not good when Grendel's mother slew Æschere. But complaint arises here mainly because Grendel's death did not settle the feud definitively. Indeed, Beowulf's vow to seek Grendel's mother wherever she might go meets with Hrothgar's joyful approval; and even God, we are told, takes his revenge upon those who warred against Him.[2]

From justified feud settlement, to the more disturbing, to the malignant—this is largely the range of feud relationships morally calibrated in *Beowulf*. Hengest's revenge, Beowulf's opposition to Grendel, the mother, and the dragon, and God's requital of giants who warred against him—these mark justified settlements: that is, revenge for criminal slaughter and feud as self-help. Baleful feuding is violence that seeks no settlement, countenancing only the continued slaughter of its objects. Such is the feud Grendel has with Hrothgar's Danes, the kind Swedes open up against Geats (for which settlement eventually occurs at Ravenswood), the kind the dragon enacts against humans in its fiery joy, and the kind the messenger, reacting unstably to great fatality, expects once news of Beowulf's death reaches Swedes and Frisians. Against such potential disasters people can arm themselves, as Wiglaf expects the Geats to do, and advance the good of kinship amity and righteous settlement.

Violent requital can be jural, a legal response that may well involve a vocabulary of right, just, and proper behavior. That behavior can include appropriate deliberation or council in the hall and aims for definitive settlement. Seeing *Beowulf* in such a context moves us from the usual accounts of his early journey as the undertaking of a hero-adventurer. Instead, we can see him socially as coming to assert what is right against an unimaginably savage creature, hoping to enact the law out of friendly, honorable feelings.

The difficult social context into which Beowulf intrudes, uninvited, and within which he twice meets a vigorous challenge, sports a mixed vocabulary we have too often either overlooked or undertranslated. That vocabulary speaks of reciprocal favoring (*hold, ar*), counsel (*ræd*), urgent petition and possible refusal (*ben, forwyrnan*), juridical meeting and settlement (*meþelword, sacu, þing, þingian*), law in the sense of rights or of what is right (*riht*), entrusting (*alyfan*), and special office (*sundornytt*). In the ensuing social drama, Beowulf reveals his jural mind.

Arriving as the strong hand of law, he must nevertheless win his way into what becomes a unique guardianship of Heorot. Each turn in his progress involves assemblies, interpreted in legalistic terms. Arriving without permission, Beowulf must first meet the coast watch's challenge by explaining himself, which he does by naming his people and his lord, paying tribute to his father, and then stating the genuineness of his loyal heart ("holdne hige," 267a) toward Hrothgar. He then immediately volunteers that he has come to offer counsel concerning Grendel's predations—a slaughter the poet has already framed legalistically in lines that have Grendel contend against "riht" (144b), engage in continual and implicitly illicit strife ("singale sæce," 154a), and refuse peace, settlement, or compensation (154a-58b). The collocation of "sæce" (strife) and lack of "sibb" (peace) strongly underlines Grendel's lawlessness.

After three other meetings Beowulf eventually receives the blessing of Hrothgar, who adds that never before since he could raise hand and shield has he entrusted the best of houses to any man, except now to Beowulf. Hrothgar entrusts Beowulf with stewardship of the hall, something he has not done before. Therefore, now he formally intones that Beowulf "have and hold" the best of houses, be its guardian (658).

With victory comes celebration as Heorot is put right and Hrothgar begins his unparalleled show of munificence. Hrothgar has mentioned reward twice in the course of Beowulf's progress toward stewardship, but his actual, extraordinary giving expresses desires not announced beforehand—as though he has progressively revised his intentions with each new situation. Wealhtheow also gives gifts independently, in a powerful move by which she would deflect the purport of Hrothgar's giving, thus blunting his invitation to Beowulf, for she knows he would have Beowulf as an adopted son and may fear that he would invite Beowulf into the line of succession. I have discussed this social drama elsewhere and so now will mainly focus on how Wealhtheow would replace Hrothgar's invitation to close kinship and succession with her own idea of kinship and social order.

Having already committed Hrothgar to the "ful" (cup), and thus to the arrangements she urges should Beowulf agree, she approaches Beowulf in good will ("est") outside warband reciprocity. She expresses herself in words and with gifts, bringing among other rings the greatest of necklaces the poet has heard of since Hama carried away the necklace of the Brosings, fleeing Eormenric's terror and instead choosing long-lasting counsel. Her gift, we then learn, later goes with Hygelac on his ill-fated raid into Frisia, where Frisians strip it from Hygelac's body. Perhaps this complicated, extended aside is a kind of voiceover on Wealhtheow's behalf, suggesting a doubled intention in her giving: she would have Beowulf use the necklace as Hama did, not Hygelac—choosing the better counsel (Hama's and hers), thus avoiding enmity and perhaps death. Beowulf accepts her "ful" and listens to her words, by which she would have him declare his prowess only through gentle counsel to her boys, for which she will reward him. Thus she proposes an ongoing relationship outside the warband but within terms invoking a kinship different from Hrothgar's proposal ("liðe" [kind, 1220a] and "gedefe" [gentle, 1227a])—an amity in fact echoed at poem's end in one of the superlatives by which Beowulf 's Geats remember him.

By his silence, and presumably by joining in the renewed drinking, Beowulf, in effect, chooses Wealhtheow's way and remains unimpeachably loyal to Hygelac. Here and elsewhere Beowulf consistently refuses precedence over other qualified people, even treating his own retainers as less than obligated (by defending them in Heorot and dismissing them before the dragon fight). That Wiglaf responds anyway speaks less to obligation than to generosity, although Wiglaf signifies his impelled move in terms of reciprocity for great kindnesses shown.

Thus, something new appears in this poem in the person of Beowulf: a retainer standard that internalizes kinship amity rather than pride of place and a kingship standard as much built on the same kinship amity as on the ethical foundations of lordship. In these respects especially, those readers who hear something Christian in the superlatives by which the Geats praise their interred king are not deaf, however amiss they might go in their further interpretations. Compared to Hrothgar, who abides well by the old customs, Beowulf responds partly in a new way, replacing munificence with magnanimity and imbuing lordliness with the kinship values of brotherly kindness and support: he is generously lordly in being "mildust," kindred-kind in being both "monðwærust" and "liðost," and extraordinary in the fame he seeks in those terms (3180–82).

The social world in *Beowulf*, then, is dynamic and in fact transactional. Relationships and intentions can change in the course of events. Feud relationships can be justifiable or malignant and can go from one to the other. Revenge is unexceptionable if the avenger's motives and turns of mind are ethical. Family lines can be altered through fosterage or adoption, and a retainer's identity can thus change, even as he embodies a kind of loaned identity in virtue of what he has accepted from his lord, to be used on his lord's behalf. This social world rises above any Anglo-Saxon one we know of from historical documents in terms of the ideals insisted on by the noble characters and in fact revised through Beowulf 's and Wiglaf 's actions. But the poem is not thereby rendered otherworldly, its values set off in a separate realm. Rather, the poem operates, I would argue, as an idealized incorporation of past and present, of noble behavior then and now—all projected large in both good and inverted or evil manifestations. *Beowulf* is part of an Anglo-Saxon culture's social myth.

Notes

1. The connection between mead, poetry, and wisdom is an ancient one, especially commented on in Scandinavian contexts by E. O. G. Turville-Petre (1964) and Georges Dumézil (1973): "the Germanic legend presents 'Kvas' as a benefactor from the beginning, well disposed toward men—a sort of martyr—and his blood, properly treated, produces that most valued thing, the mead of poetry and wisdom" (Dumézil 1973, 23).

2. Anglo-Saxon "friendship" can imply legal responsibility. But here Beowulf seems to state a moral good, much as seems the case among the bilateral Tausug (Kiefer 1972, 60), who form friendships for mutual support and who thus establish a kinship-like relation between two men, who would then exchange, but in a competition of increasing values. Supporting a friend is a moral need, although friendships can change, even drastically, such that today's friend is tomorrow's enemy. Such a change would in turn alter the already shifting compositions of allied groups for feud purposes, given that ties exist between individuals (who may bring along armed collaterals and clients), not between groups. Although nothing as fluid as this appears clearly in *Beowulf*, something like it may very well underlie relationships between Danes and Frisians, Danes and Heathobards, and Geats and Swedes.

Chapter 14

The Hero and the Theme

by George Clark

Summary: The poem opens with an illustration and assertion that success is achieved only by praiseworthy deeds and closes commending the hero's pursuit of fame. In youth, the hero asserts that fame is best after death and reaffirms that truth in age again facing mortal battle. The poem's creation of Beowulf gives its theme ethical force. He is seen, though externally, as a person living from childhood to youth to age, in a family, a kin group, a people, and in a world the audience can recognize. Beowulf has human qualities—he is wise and shrewd, brave, cheerful, humorous and ironic, sympathetic, an alert hearer and artful teller of tales. The poem's three great stories lead the audience from an assured vision of a benevolently ordered world to the existential world of its minor stories where only the heroic will can achieve a lasting value, the memory and fame of praiseworthy deeds.

Chronology

1817: N. F. S. Grundtvig suggests that *Beowulf* may continue the story of the "warfare that the devil and the old giants waged against God."

1892: John Earle sees the pursuit of praise as a royal norm, compares the hero to Lancelot, Henry V, and Arthur, and concludes that the last word, "lofgeornost" (most eager for praise), praises Beowulf.

1922: Friedrich Klaeber (1922a) believes that Beowulf's virtues and his final self-sacrifice make him reminiscent of Christ.

1929: Levin L. Schücking (1929a) finds Beowulf modeled not on Christ but on an ideal of kingship fusing stoic-Christian and Germanic-heroic norms.

1933: Schücking concludes that pride and desire for fame are central to the heroic ethos, which is in conflict with the Christian value of humility.

1936: J. R. R. Tolkien claims that Grendel unites the Nordic troll and biblical Cain to signify evil in the individual, that the dragon signifies evil in "heroic life" and in "all life."

1946: Marie Padgett Hamilton believes that Beowulf's life suggests the "Scriptural drama" of evil defeated by a self-sacrificing hero.

1948: Kemp Malone finds Beowulf ideal as retainer and king battling "the forces of evil" and characterizes part 1 as "cheerful," part 2 as "sad."

1949–51: Charles Donahue argues that the poet's tolerant view of his characters suggests Irish notions of ancestors as natural monotheists not beyond salvation.

1952: T. M. Gang argues that Tolkien (1936) was wrong to treat the dragon as a symbol of "evil" like Grendel.

1952–53: Ernst Leisi argues that in the poem's world riches indicate social and moral worth and at once signify and demand the owner's virtue.

1953: Tolkien finds heroes blamable for reckless courage to which their natures and "aristocratic tradition" incline them and finds the term "lofgeornost" to be "ominous."

1955: Allen Cabaniss claims that Beowulf's descent into the mere and battle there parallels Christ's death, harrowing of hell, and resurrection.

1958: Robert E. Kaske argues that Beowulf embodies the heroic—and Christian and patristic—ideal of *sapientia et fortitudo* (wisdom and strength).

1959: Arthur G. Brodeur concludes that *Beowulf* has a unified action, a humanized hero, and a tragic theme: "a doomed king has died to save a doomed people."

1960: Maurice B. McNamee (1960a) claims that Beowulf illustrates the "Christian concept of magnanimity" and the poem's action parallels the story of redemption.

1960: Margaret E. Goldsmith finds Beowulf, like David and Sampson, a great but imperfect hero; Beowulf suffers a moral decline, but his "old Germanic virtues" serve God.

1962: Goldsmith argues that old Beowulf falls into the errors Hrothgar warned him against and dies "blinded by arrogance and desire for the [dragon's] treasure."

1963: Eric G. Stanley argues that the poem casts doubt on Beowulf's salvation and represents the heroic ideal as futile; the last word, "lofgeornost," blames the hero.

1965: G. N. Garmonsway concludes that *Beowulf* recognizes diverse forms of heroism and the perspective of the "world of common sense and nonheroic norms," which the hero exceeds.

1965: Charles Donahue argues that the poem records Beowulf's "spiritual growth" and death (as a Christ figure) in an unconscious "state of grace."

1965: John Leyerle asserts that Beowulf illustrates a "fatal contradiction" in heroic society; a great hero becomes a bad king who risks his people pursuing honor.

1965: George Clark suggests that arms and armor in the poem become means to discover an indissoluble union of order and violence in the heroic world.

1965: Kenneth Sisam suggests that the poem was composed to entertain but idealizes aristocratic values and represents a golden age of heroism.

1966: E. G. Stanley believes that the poet presents the heroic ideal "lovingly," though it is "in conflict with the ascetic idea of Christianity" and thus "not worth ambition."

1966: John Halverson finds that Beowulf's virtues and ethical standards are secular, heroic, and political, not Christian or religious.

1967: Charles Moorman argues that the poem creates a guilty hero and a pagan worldview in which man's lot is futile struggle and defeat.

1968: Edward B. Irving Jr. argues that a humanized and admirable Beowulf sustains heroic values despite the world's instability and, though conscious of his mortality, lives an exemplary life.

1968: Jeffrey Helterman argues that in defeating Grendel, Beowulf reenacts the creation but "externalizes" the conflict of order and chaos; entering Geatish history, the hero cannot reenact the creation.

1969: John Halverson finds that Beowulf's flaw is social in origin, the hero "moulded gloriously and inflexibly by his world."

1970: John C. Pope notes that in the hero's final speech his will at last exerts itself so powerfully that his "astonishing hardihood" seems to come more from within than from above.

1970: Fred C. Robinson finds that the poem's last word, "lofgeornost," has a "bad sense" contrasting the Christian superlatives eulogizing Beowulf.

1970: A. D. Horgan concludes that Beowulf, a noble pagan practising natural religion, rightly seeks "glory, and honor and immortality" (Saint Paul) and may be saved. The last word is an honorific.

1970: Margaret E. Goldsmith characterizes Beowulf as "a just man who nobly fought a losing battle against the evil powers"; though the hero errs, "deluded by the Dragon's gold," he is saved. She parallels Christ and Beowulf.

1972: T. A. Shippey argues that the poem illustrates laudable responses to the uncertainties of life and certainty of death in a heroic culture whose values strikingly differ from ours.

1972: Alvin Lee claims that the poem metaphorically reworks the war of hell against heaven, that its characters are social archetypes in a myth of human society ending with "hell's possession of middle-earth."

1973: Mary P. Richards argues that all four superlatives of Beowulf's eulogy describe him as an excellent Christian.

1973: Stephen C. Bandy notes that Augustine saw giants as God's enemies, that the *Liber Monstrorum* calls Hygelac a giant, that the coast guard describes Beowulf as gigantic—and asks if the hero is of the devil's party.

1974: Harry Berger and H. Marshall Leicester find that heroic society in *Beowulf* self-destructs because of inner contradictions the poem's characters cannot perceive or rectify.

1974: Marion L. Huffines argues that in his three fights Beowulf becomes more monster-like, the monsters less clearly evil.

1975: Andreas Haarder concludes that the poem contrasts the hall and the world of monsters, finds the meaning of life in heroic action, and closes with both "sadness" and "exultation" at Beowulf's funeral. Conflict of man and monster, not character, is central.

1975: Mary C. Wilson Tietjen argues that a "blind and whimsical" *wyrd* and God jointly rule mankind; *wyrd* ignores men's worthiness (heroically defined), which God rewards with "grace and guidance."

1975: Kathryn Hume finds the subject of *Beowulf* to be neither the hero nor the action but "threats to social order."

1976: Stanley B. Greenfield finds that the poem's "authenticating voice" sometimes separates, sometimes unites pagan and Christian worlds and reveals the "limitations of human knowledge."

1977: John Miles Foley argues that Beowulf overcomes the "Terrible Father" (Unferth, Grendel) and "Terrible Mother" (Grendel's), masters his maleness (giant sword, adoption by Hrothgar) in a Jungian myth.

1977: Charles Donahue finds the social and literary value of the poem in its positive representation of the "values of ancient Germanic society" to an Christian Anglo-Saxon world.

1978: Whitney F. Bolton claims that an Alcuinian reading reveals a Christian text but a spiritually "lost" pagan hero who failed his king.

1978: Marijane Osborn argues that the hero's three great fights are part of the "Great Feud" between the forces of good and evil, as the audience recognizes and the poem's characters cannot.

1979: John M. Hill argues that the poet "repeatedly asserts the continuity of time and values between his present and a heroic past."

1981: Martin Camargo asserts that Beowulf, an "exemplary pagan," falls as far short of the Christian ideal as Grendel falls short of Beowulf.

1981: W. G. Busse and R. Holtei find Beowulf an example of "social advancement" won by praiseworthy deeds, but *oferhygd* (pride) leads him to believe he could fight the dragon alone.

1982: David Williams sees Cain as a central symbol in the poem which reveals the Geats are doomed because "pagan social institutions" cannot "guarantee peace and order."

1982: James W. Earl finds that in *Beowulf* the Christian Anglo-Saxon world mourns for its heroic past and so completes the separation of the pagan and Christian cultures.

1982: John M. Hill argues that Beowulf threads his way among opposed political moves by Hrothgar and Wealhtheow (an offer of succession, a splendid farewell gift) to reaffirm his loyalty to Hygelac.

1982: Samuel M. Riley argues that the superlatives closing the poem describe the hero as combining "the two best traits of an ideal Germanic ruler—generosity and bravery."

1983: James W. Earl argues that the poem implies movement from a tribal culture to one of lordship, thence to or toward a state fusing Christianity and lord's hall and instituting the superego and the church.

1983: John D. Niles finds *Beowulf* a "history of spiritual development" and an affirmation of the values of community and human solidarity achieved in battles against the monstrous in us all.

1984: Laurence N. de Looze sees Beowulf's last speech as a creative work enabling the hero to act rightly in his battle against the dragon.

1984: Edward B. Irving Jr. argues that Beowulf's religious statements reveal his modesty, his sense that God judges human actions; the poem's close represents Beowulf's struggle against mortality and oblivion.

1985: Fred C. Robinson argues that the poet juxtaposes his Christian worldview and the ethos of his characters to create a noble past from which he and his audience are forever alienated.

1985: Hiroto Ushigaki rebuts Leyerle (1965) and Goldsmith (1962); poet pities a good pagan dying without "sure hope" of an afterlife.

1986: Norma Kroll argues that the poem values "a practical politics of civilization," not an otherworldly virtue; Beowulf and Grendel share a destructive potential and instinct, which the hero controls.

1987: Linda Georgianna believes that Hrethel's "immobilizing sorrow" at Herebeald's death "threaten[s] the coherence of the heroic world," but Beowulf's final "heroic choice" proves equally futile.

1989: Tomoaki Mizuno asserts that Beowulf, a "terrible stranger" (like his father), brings disaster on the Geats by his complicity in the murder of Herebeald and betrayal of Hygelac in Frisia.

1990: George Clark argues that the narration of the hero's three battles moves from optimistic certainty that the world order is knowable and benevolent to doubt, leaving fame as the only sure value.

1992: Clark finds that the superlatives eulogizing Beowulf are honorifics reflecting the values of a heroic society.

1993: John D. Niles (1993a) argues that the poem integrates "Germanic culture and Christian faith" into a single worldview and the peoples of Saxon England into one nation under the West-Saxon dynasty.

1993: Fred C. Robinson (1993a) claims that Beowulf's funeral may hint the hero's deification, crowning the poem's tension between heroism and the "sad shame of paganism."

1993: Michael R. Near asserts that the poem depicts an oral society whose culture is threatened by the literacy the text posits.

In the study of *Beowulf,* the character of the hero and the theme of the poem seem both to require and to resist separate analyses. Edward B. Irving Jr. makes theme and character one when he claims that "to write of the hero in *Beowulf* is to write of everything in the poem" (1968, 43). Peter Clemoes concurs: "in an important sense, the hero *is* the poem" (1979, 167). In contrast, Kathryn Hume separates the poem's representation of the hero and its essential meaning: "were the poem centered on Beowulf himself, we would expect to learn something about him as a person." She claims that the poem gives us Beowulf's deeds and public speeches but no "private thoughts or personal hopes or misgivings," not even "characterizing features," save for "extraordinary strength" (1975, 1–2). Similarly, John Niles argues that the poem's audience "cannot really identify itself with Beowulf the man. . . . He outdistances us and becomes part of the marvelous machinery of the plot, like Grendel or the dragon. We know too little of his everyday humanity, his normal human feelings, to be able to see him as an extension of ourselves" (1983, 29; see also Lee 1972, 175).

The poem teases us with the sense that its hero is a real person, though we know him almost entirely from the outside. The audience continually gains a sense of Beowulf, his "characterizing features," and his involvement in human contexts. What we lack, and miss, are direct, detailed, and extended representations of Beowulf's inner life. No interior monologues or authorial descriptions of the hero's states of mind open up Beowulf's consciousness for our direct observation. The representation of Beowulf is severely "dramatic," his part has no soliloquies; he addresses audiences within the poem, not us. Even his long speech before the dragon fight, perhaps his "death song," has an audience of several persons. Until the final scene with Wiglaf, Beowulf never speaks privately to one listener. His words are consistently heard and overheard in a public world. Within the constraints imposed by a largely dramatic form and the narrator's general impassivity, the poem constructs Beowulf, the hero, as a person, not simply an Everyman or a model for emulation or of what should be avoided.

Oddly enough, Hume's remarks very nearly imply that Beowulf has a human reality that includes "private thoughts . . . hopes or misgivings," although such individual characteristics remain just outside our field of vision. Some of the hero's human qualities seem visible to Margaret Pepperdene, who credits Beowulf with tact and courtesy and describes him as "mild and gentle and kind" (1966, 409–19). In a deeper reading, Irving first comments on some of Beowulf's discernible qualities and the audience's reaction to them: the hero is "attractive" in part because of his "sense of humor, . . . [his] friendship with Breca, and the way he seems to perform acts of public service by casual instinct" (1968, 63). Irving then shows that Beowulf can be seen as a person interacting with others when he examines Beowulf's interview with Hygelac as a social drama, an encounter between two realized persons, and observes that the hero's cool "acumen" in foretelling the failure of Hrothgar's hope to end a war by a diplomatic marriage may have astonished Hygelac (1982, 138). John Leyerle clearly assumes that we can understand Beowulf as a person seen in a continuous process of development. Leyerle faults Beowulf's concern for honor as excessive rather than appropriate but gives the hero's alleged fault a human and understandable origin: chagrin at the low esteem the Geats accorded him in his youth rather has made Beowulf too eager for fame (1965, 94). One might object that a prince born into a shame culture should exhibit a stronger concern for honor than might be appropriate or prudent for less aristocratic persons, but to raise the objection is to accept Leyerle's assumption that the poem presents Beowulf as a person formed in part by social expectations, childhood experience, and so on.

Seth Lerer tacitly assumes Beowulf can be understood as a consistently realized person when he characterizes the hero's taste in poetry and argues that that taste reappears in Beowulf's own narrative relating the Danish adventure to Hygelac. Lerer claims that Beowulf omits the content of poetry in Heorot and "focuses solely on form and quality. The songs are true, sad, strange, and rightly or traditionally put. . . . Song is more a ritual than an art for Beowulf" (1991, 191). Lerer contrasts Beowulf's critical formalism with the narrator's interest in the substance of the Danish scop's song of creation sung in Heorot before Grendel's first attack. In objecting that Lerer has given "rightly or traditionally put" the emphasis and marginalized "sad" (perhaps "painful" or even "tragic"), we would again, as with Leyerle (see above), be granting the critic's unstated premise while qualifying his conclusion. Beowulf's critical emphasis seems to center the emotional power of the poetry of Heorot since he begins with "soð ond sarlic" ("true" and therefore powerful, "sad" arousing the emotions of pity and fear, "tragic"). What songs and singers Beowulf heard in Heorot makes a difficult question but is not past all conjecture.

Francis P. Magoun Jr. detailed the differences between the narrator's account (A) of the poetry in Heorot following Beowulf's victory over Grendel and the hero's own, later, account (A') of that evening's poetry: "[in A'] as in A there is said to have been singing but in A there is mention only of one particular song, the Finn episode, while in A' there seem to be both traditional songs (l. 2106b) and lyrics (ll. 2108b–09). This last is a small matter, but not small at all is the difference in the identification of the singer who in A is "Hrothgar's court scop (l. 1066b), and in A' the Scielding king himself" (1958, 97). A scholarly reader like Magoun would notice the inconsistencies in the two accounts of poetry in Heorot, but the *Beowulf* poet might expect that a thousand lines later his audience would remember the Finnsburg matter better than the identity of its singer. Indeed, the poet himself might have unconsciously reattributed the Finnsburg matter to Hrothgar. The needs of the artistic moment, creating the scene in which Beowulf reports on his Danish adventure to his uncle and king, Hygelac, would dominate the poet's practice (Kinney 1985), not a tidy consistency.

A listening audience could easily refer Beowulf's characterization of Hrothgar's "traditional songs" to the story of Finnsburg, which they heard along with Beowulf and should have recognized as a well-known story in a new setting. The audience has, after all, no other site for Beowulf's description of Heorot's and Hrothgar's songs as "soð ond sarlic" (true and tragic, 2109), as a "syllic spell" (a wonderful story, 2109), which Hrothgar "rehte æfter rihte" (recited correctly, 2110). In Hrothgar's hall, Beowulf heard the Finnsburg song, which the Danes greeted with joy as the story of a great victory that saved their endangered honor. If in Hygelac's hall the hero described the Finnsburg song as a tragic story, he reads the song, like most modern critics, as Hildeburh's tragedy, and not like Hrothgar's followers, who receive it as Hengest's triumph (Clark 1990, 80–82). Beowulf's account of narrative poetry in Heorot omits its content in part so that the audience can impose its memory of the Finnsburg song on Hrothgar's true and tragic story.

Of course Beowulf as a teller of stories should not summarize the Finnsburg song: he has grasped its truth, which informs his narrative report on Hrothgar's diplomacy. Lerer's account of Beowulf as critic rather neglects the other songs the hero claims to have heard in Heorot:

hwilum eft ongan   eldo gebunden,
gomel guðwiga   gioguðe cwiðan,

hildestrengo;   hreðer inne weoll,
þonne he wintrum frod   worn gemunde. (2111–14)

[at other times the old warrior hobbled by age lamented the passing of his
youth and strength in battle; his heart surged within him as the man who had
experienced many years recalled the past.]

The poet must be Hrothgar himself (see Klaeber 1950a, line 2105n) whose reported
poetic expression of the sorrows of old age reminds us of his "sermon," with its
warning to Beowulf that he too will grow old, fail, and die. In Denmark, Beowulf
did not reply to the "sermon," but the hero's précis of Hrothgar's elegies responds
to and comments on the old king's words of self-conscious wisdom. Beowulf's
account of poetry in Heorot reminds us again of his empathy for suffering. As he
speaks to Hygelac, the audience realizes how clearly Beowulf understood
Hrothgar's warning that death comes to us all. Beowulf understands Hrothgar's
wisdom—a wisdom born of experience, age, and awareness of mortality—and
understands the limitations of Hrothgar's power. Beowulf's account of the poetry
of Heorot illustrates his acute perception of the old king's dilemma: the Finnsburg
story illustrates that a diplomatic marriage of Hrothgar's daughter, Freawaru, and
the young king of the Heathobards, Ingeld, will not succeed, but Hrothgar's elegiacs
feelingly reveal that the unpromising attempt must be made. Beowulf's version of
the Ingeld story, a prophecy to Hygelac but history to the poem's audience (Clark
1965, 410–11), dovetails philosophically and artistically with the Finnsburg song,
which he heard in Heorot along with the audience of the poem. That story opens the
morning after a battle whose immediate cause remains unstated. In effect, a brief
and violent incident has terminated the peace achieved by a diplomatic marriage.
The truce lasted long enough that a son born to that marriage is among the warriors
slain in the sudden renewal of hostility. Beowulf's re-creation of the traditional
Ingeld matter can be read as his reconstruction of the unstated cause of the first fight
at Finnsburg and his realization that the Finnsburg principle will apply to
Freawaru's marriage.

Beowulf's "personal characteristics" include a basically cheerful tempera-
ment, as the narrator implies when observing that the hero's "dark thoughts"
occasioned by the dragon's raids were unusual for him (cf. Robinson 1984, 119).
Lerer has acutely remarked on the verbal play by which Beowulf transforms the
horrifying story of the death of Hondscio—the warrior eaten by Grendel—into an
unfrightening "social performance" for his king and queen at home (1991, 184–85).
In the same vein of humor, Beowulf jokes cheerfully in Heorot that if Grendel wins
the coming battle, Hrothgar will not have to feed his guest any longer because the
guest will be feeding Grendel, whose eating habits are sloppy (445–51). Beowulf's
seemingly neutral statement that the winner of the battle will be able to go to the
mead the next morning (603–06) lightly disguises his optimism with irony: Grendel

goes to Heorot only at night, drinks no mead, and his tomorrow will not dawn. Despite his imaginative power to enter into the suffering and pain of others, Beowulf's sense of humor can have a hard edge. After the battle in Heorot, he tells Hrothgar that though the monster escaped

> . . . he his folme forlet
> to lifwraþe   last weardian,
> earm ond eaxle. . . . (970—72)

[he left his hand (*folme*) behind to save his life, his arm (*earm*) and shoulder (*eaxle*).]

Beowulf's nice separation—getting a whole line between Grendel's hand and the rest of him—capped by the brisk movement from "arm" to "shoulder"—makes a black joke of Grendel's dismemberment. The narrator anticipated Beowulf in the hand, arm, shoulder sequence (834–35), but without the exquisite timing of Beowulf's "hand . . . / . . . arm and shoulder," which moves with ironic satisfaction from the extremity to the body, from injury to death.

Despite the possibilities, few critics have set out to examine Beowulf as an imagined person. The most influential critical essay on the poem, Tolkien's "*Beowulf*: The Monsters and the Critics" (1936), left no room for the project. Tolkien foregrounds the monsters and the monstrous, thereby leaving Beowulf at the poem's periphery. For Tolkien, theme, not the character of the hero, is central, and the poem's theme is the threat to human order posed by the monstrous, as illustrated in the hero's battle against Grendel and the dragon. For Tolkien, the poem is about the onslaught of the monsters—not quite allegorized into transparent representations of Christian notions of evil—against mankind, whose champion is an Everyman without personal qualities or human contexts, a hero with "no enmeshed loyalties, nor hapless love"—"*He is a man, and that for him and many is sufficient tragedy*" (260). Tolkien's Beowulf is "something more significant than a standard hero, a man faced with a foe more evil than any human enemy . . . is before us" (259). Tolkien's Beowulf is significant and signifies, but has no character at all.

Others have found the poem's central theme in Beowulf's *meaning* rather than his *being*. Although a strong critical movement followed Klaeber in taking Beowulf as a Christian hero or even Christ figure, the most numerous and influential body of postwar critics, including Margaret Goldsmith (1960, 1962, 1970), read the poem as faulting the hero for moral failures according to one or another Christian standard of judgment (see also Bolton 1978). The poem became a neo-Aristotelian tragedy in which the hero's flaw could be identified as a sin, greed, or pride. In 1936, Tolkien rather surprisingly foreclosed such interpretations, arguing that the idea driving *Beowulf* is "doom" rather than ἁμαρτία (*hamartia*), a tragic flaw or error (256). The poem, Tolkien seems to argue, creates a myth of humanity's fate, not a tragedy of character. This critical position seems strongly influenced by W. P. Ker's praise of the northern heroic spirit manifested by mortal gods who are finally "defeated" but "think" that defeat is not refutation (1904, 58).

Most *Beowulf* critics would identify Tolkien as the most influential of the authors who turned the postwar critical consensus away from Klaeber's suggestion that Beowulf was a Christian hero and perhaps even a Christ figure to a conviction that he is represented as a tragic and flawed character. Tolkien's 1936 reading of *Beowulf* ran counter to the usual tenor of his criticism. In his 1953 essay on *The Battle of Maldon,* Tolkien implicitly corrects the lecture of 1936 by appending a note on the meanings of "ofermod" (in *Maldon*) and "lofgeornost" (closing *Beowulf*). His remarks became an important source or stimulus for the moralizing and antiheroic movements of postwar *Beowulf* criticism. *Doom* disappears from Tolkien's postwar critical vocabulary. He regards the defeat at Maldon as proof of Byrhtnoth's flaw or error, and so too with Beowulf's death beneath Eagles' Cape. Failure to survive the dragon fight seems to Tolkien in 1953 a proof of Beowulf's inner failure. After the war, Tolkien saw defeat as a moral refutation.

Tolkien reopened in 1953 the critical approach he had foreclosed in 1936. In treating *The Battle of Maldon,* he identified Byrhtnoth's fault or flaw as "chivalry"—adding that this was also Beowulf's flaw. But in anatomizing the heroes' common flaw, Tolkien noted that this defect of character arose partly from their nurture as well as their natures—this "chivalric" character was "moulded also by 'aristocratic tradition'" (1953, 15). These brief remarks opened the way for critics to read the poems as tragedies of character or to shift the fatal flaw from Byrhtnoth or Beowulf to the heroic world and its institutions. The poem could then be reread as a cultural tragedy (Berger and Leicester 1974), social criticism (Leyerle 1965; Halverson 1969), or an indictment of pagan society judged from a triumphal Christian perspective (D. Williams 1982).

Tolkien stripped the hero of an individual character much as he deprived the poem of an action, a story. The *Beowulf* poem became a lyric balancing "comprehensive opposites," for example, a beginning and an end (cf. Sisam 1965, 18–19); the hero's life was reduced to a balance of youth and age, initial success and final defeat (Tolkien 1936, 271). Despite Tolkien's claim, the poem gives us unexpected glimpses of Beowulf as a youth and even as a child and creates a sense of a whole life resembling other human lives. Again and again, we see him caught up in the basic human context of family. His father recurs repeatedly in the poem, his relationship with his uncle, Hygelac, is central to our idea of Beowulf, and his relationship with his grandfather, founder of the dynasty of which the hero is a part, reminds us how often males find their grandfathers more comfortable than their fathers.

Beowulf's introduction into the poem and subsequent arrival at the Danish court swiftly juxtapose his present with his earlier life. On hearing the newcomer's name, Hrothgar announces that he knew this now-towering figure "cnihtwesende" (as a boy, 372), the son of the late Ecgtheow, once a fugitive or political refugee in Hrothgar's protecting court. The powerful hero has known the vulnerability of a political refugee's child. Hrothgar, however, remarks (377–81) that seafarers returning from the Geats have reported that the hero has the strength of thirty men. That observation links the vulnerable child and the powerful young hero. Moreover, this touch hints that Hrothgar has followed his child guest's growth with interest. On greeting Hrothgar—without reference to their former acquaintance—Beowulf introduces himself as Hygelac's kinsman and liegeman and as one who in his youth ("on geogoþe," 409) did great deeds, including winning victories over "eotenas" and "nicoras" who had grieved the Geats in ways not specified. In one of the poem's most celebrated passages, still another version of young Beowulf appears: Unferth asks, "Are you the Beowulf who lost a swimming contest with Breca?" (506–10). Beowulf—not Unferth, who leaves the adventure or contest un-dated—refers the event to his and Breca's boyhoods. Breca and Beowulf, "cnihtwesende," dared one another to swim a monster-infested sea (535–38). The same adjective, in Hrothgar's story and in Beowulf's account of his venture with Breca, becomes part of two strikingly different images of the hero's boyhood.

As he prepares to challenge the dragon, Beowulf recalls the battles of his youth: "Fela ic on giogoðe / guðræsa genæs, // orleghwila; / ic þæt eall gemon" (in my youth I survived many charges, hours of pitched battles; I remember it all, 2426–27). As he speaks, however, Beowulf's memory reaches beyond that youth to his childhood: "Ic wæs syfanwintre, / þa mec sinca baldor, // freawine folca / æt minum fæder genam" (I was seven years old when the ruler of treasures and noble lord of peoples received me from my father, 2428–29). Beowulf's memory of his childhood almost reaches back to the time of Hrothgar's memory of Beowulf, Ecgtheow's child. Rather than exile in Denmark, however, Beowulf recalls his grandfather's court, where he was no less favored than his young uncles, the king's sons, "Herebeald ond Hæðcyn / oððe Hygelac min" (2434). In the landscape of Beowulf's memory, his uncles seem giants, but the traditional triad of names ends "Hygelac min" (my beloved Hygelac). After more than fifty years, the long-dead Hygelac is still Beowulf's beloved lord. The narrator calls Beowulf "Higelaces þegn" (Hygelac's noble follower, 194); in Denmark Beowulf first introduces himself and his troop saying "We synt gumcynnes / Geata leode // ond Higelaces / heorðgeneatas" (We are of the Geatish nation and Hygelac's companions, 260–62); arriving at the door of Heorot, he announces "We synt Higelaces // beodgeneatas . . . " (We are Hygelac's companions, 342–43). Near the end of his long kingship, Beowulf still knows himself as "Higelaces retainer." Tolkien claimed that Beowulf had "no enmeshed loyalties, nor hapless love" (1936, 260), but this enduring love, and lasting sorrow for the dashing figure of young Beowulf's admiration, seems as poignant as any hapless love (see Brodeur 1959, 78–81).

The poem attests Beowulf's humanity in his grief for Hygelac's death, still fresh a long lifetime later. His empathy for others' sorrows appears in his lyric evocation of an imagined father's lament for his hanged son. In that elegiac fiction, Beowulf makes real and tangible his perception of his grandfather's grief for the death of Herebeald, Hygelac's brother. The mourning father of Beowulf's story summons up archetypal images of paternal loss, possibly suggesting Odin's grief at the death of Baldr. Beowulf's relationship with his late father similarly invites the audience to see the hero as a real person. When Beowulf and his followers arrive on the Danish shore and answer the coast guard's queries, the hero reveals his father's name, not his own, and sums up the late Ecgtheow's status in the heroic world:

> Wæs min fæder   folcum gecyþed,
> æþele ordfruma,   Ecgþeow haten;
> gebad wintra worn,   ær he on weg hwurfe,
> gamol of geardum;   hine gearwe geman
> witena welhwylc   wide geond eorþan. (262–66)

> [My father, a noble commander named Ecgtheow, was known in many nations; he lived long before he departed, old, from human dwellings; every wise councillor over the wide earth remembers him well.]

In a poem that begins and ends with "lof" (praise, fame, good report, 24, 3182) and finds in "lof" and "dom" a lasting value, Ecgtheow left his son a formidable challenge. In his son's eyes, Ecgtheow reached the pinnacle of "lof." His heroic achievement was remembered among many nations, while his renown became part of the consciousness of wise men generally. Like many men in the poem's probable audiences, the young Beowulf seems aware of the necessity and difficulty of living up to a father's status.

Hrothgar's account of Ecgtheow suggests that Beowulf's idea of his father's status may be subjective, exaggerated. On learning that a stranger named Beowulf has come seeking an audience, Hrothgar identifies the visitor as the son of Ecgtheow to whom the king of the Geats married his only daughter. When Beowulf has announced his purpose, Hrothgar tells his story: Ecgtheow came to the Danish court as an exile after killing Heatholaf of the Wylfings; Hrothgar settled the feud, ending Ecgtheow's exile, and received unspecified oaths from him. Ecgtheow's renown does not enter into Hrothgar's account of Beowulf's late father, and the different views we get of the late Ecgtheow tease us into considering the relationships among all three parties—Ecgtheow, Hrothgar, and Beowulf. Hrothgar has his own agenda; if Beowulf's help is an appropriate exchange for benefits extended to Ecgtheow, Hrothgar can accept that succor as his due. Hrothgar notes that Hrethel gave his only daughter to Ecgtheow without commenting on the reasons for that match. A royal marriage traditionally rewards heroes. Eofor won Hygelac's only daughter, for example, by killing Ongentheow, the great warrior-king of the Swedes (2991–98). We cannot know how Ecgtheow won King Hrethel's daughter, Beowulf's mother, since Hrothgar, the person (Beowulf excepted?) most likely to know the story, chooses not to tell it.

Hrothgar's story of Ecgtheow's difficulties brings Beowulf's gigantic father figure into human compass; Beowulf's idea of his father makes him, in that domestic context, recognizably human. Nine instances of the formula "Beowulf maþelode, / bearn Ecgþeowes" (Beowulf, Ecgtheow's son, spoke, 529, 631, 957, 1383, 1473, 1651, 1817, 1999, 2425) keep Beowulf's father at least formally in the audience's mind. In five other passages Beowulf is Ecgtheow's "bearn," "sunu," or "mæg" (child, son, or kinsman) and each of these might recall Hrothgar's depiction of Ecgtheow as a man in difficulties. Beowulf is "sunu Ecgþeowes" at the moment he seems most likely to lose his life in the struggle with Grendel's mother (1550–51), when (as an "earm anhaga" [unhappy loner]) he swims or sails back from the defeat in Frisia (2367–68), and when, as the survivor of many hard battles, he sets out for the one he will not survive (2397–2400). During the dragon fight, the hero is "maga Ecgðeowes" when the narrator predicts his death (2586–87). The hero is "bearn Ecgðeowes" (2177) immediately after giving Hygd the neck ring, Wealhtheow's gift, and three horses. A few lines later Beowulf is said to have suffered an "inglorious youth" (2183–89), a detail with ample precedent in the analogues, but one that seems belated and intrusive in our poem.

If Beowulf's relationships with his late father, the far-famed (but unlucky?) Ecgtheow, and with Hygelac, who died young in Frisia, prompt the audience to regard the hero as a person, so does the son Beowulf never had. That missing kinsman makes a void in the hero's life revealed and filled as Beowulf at the last moment adopts Wiglaf. The dying hero first laments that he has no son to receive his arms and armor, then orders Wiglaf—"Wiglaf leofa" (beloved Wiglaf, 2745)—to enter the dragon's tomb and bring out a portion of the treasure. On his return, Wiglaf again revives Beowulf, whose first words thank God for the treasures that, he believes, will benefit the Geats after his death (2800–1). Victorious and dying, Beowulf contemplates the ancient tomb and treasures, monuments of past greatness and of mortality (Pope 1982), and attends to his hopes for the future of the Geats by designating Wiglaf as his successor and leaving the dragon's treasure to his people. The poem's recurring periphrases identify good kings as protectors of their people and givers of treasure. In his last great battle, Beowulf fulfills both of these royal duties to the ultimate limit of his obligation.

The poem announces its theme, fame (honor, the praise of one's peers and posterity), before introducing its hero, keeps the theme of fame in view throughout the narrative, and reasserts that theme in its closing episode and in its final word. The impassive narrator acknowledges the gulf of past time that separates him and his audience from the poem's actors, hints at the difference in religion that separates them too, but makes the actors and the audience members of the same culture, holders of the same values, admirers of the same conduct. At the poem's end, the story has brought its audience and the Geats together in doubt as to the meaning of death and of life and yet in certainty that for the departed warrior a worthy fame is best and is the one sure reality in the world's darkness. In *Beowulf,* fame and the pursuit of fame become an ethical and moral ideal, an answer to a problem of evil when evil becomes recognizable as part of the inescapable nature of things. The sea of stories making up *Beowulf* create a meaning that ultimately converges with the poem's repeated theme of fame. In the first major episode of the poem, the telling of the story seems to distance the narrator and his audience from the poem's actors by suggesting that evil has an origin the audience can comprehend and the actors cannot (cf. Grundtvig 1817; Helterman 1968; Osborn 1978). The audience seems to enjoy a superior knowledge of the origin and nature of evil and, therefore, a better understanding of a divine and ultimately benevolent plan governing the world. The ironic perspective in the story of the first great battle enhances the philosophical optimism the defeat of Grendel communicates. The stories of Finnsburg, of Grendel's mother, of the wars of the Swedes and Geats and Franks, and of Beowulf's fatal battle with the dragon subvert the philosophical optimism the Grendel story suggests but affirm the triumph of fame over time, the brevity of human life, and even the specter of oblivion and forgetting, the black hole haunting the heroic imagination.

Beowulf begins with a brief sketch of the history of the Scylding dynasty in Denmark, which we may take as a brief illustration of the reading or hearing that will discover the poem's meaning. Scyld, the founder of the Danish line, rose from adversity to greatness by war and valor and receives the poet's praise: "þæt wæs god cyning!" (that was a good king, 11). Scyld's career seems to end with the birth of his son and with his son's fame, but to close this illustrative prologue, the narrator generalizes "lofdædum sceal // in mægþa gehwære / man geþeon" (in every nation one can prosper only by praiseworthy deeds, 24b–25). As the good king recedes into the past, the narrator universalizes on the meaning of his story, its themes of good kingship and of fame won by deeds of courage. In that heroic aphorism, the meaning of Scyld's life retains its validity, its compelling truth, down to a present moment in which the narrator begins his story (Greenfield 1976).

Scyld's funeral follows the narrator's aphoristic statement of the poem's theme and poses the ultimate challenge to human aspiration, death. The narrator observes at Scyld's funeral that no one, neither councillors in the hall nor warriors in the field, knew who received the cargo of Scyld's funeral ship, his body and grave goods. Scyld's praiseworthy deeds won his prosperity, but his death leaves warriors and councillors in doubt. At the poem's end, the narrator reports the praise brave and noble warriors sang at Beowulf's funeral. The last word of the poem praises Beowulf for being "lofgeornost" (most eager for praise). The last word on Beowulf reaches back to the poem's opening and the sole means, "lofdædum" (24) by which one prospers, in all nations, at all times (Clark 1992, 15–30).

The poem's last word, echoing its first universalizing comment on what constitutes the good, confronts us with an ethical system that, though not completely alien to us, is not our own. *Beowulf,* like the *Chanson de Roland,* assumes and expresses the values of a "shame culture," a moral universe whose vital principle is the pursuit of honor and avoidance of shame (Jones 1963, 96–158). Interpretation has customarily made the poet, audience, and modern reader part of a Christian community separated from the pagan actors within the poem (see esp. Robinson 1985). In cultural terms, however, the poet, the Anglo-Saxon audience, and the poem's actors belong to a world that rewards right conduct with honor and punishes wrong conduct with shame. The conclusion of Wiglaf's speech to Beowulf's retainers who valued their lives above their moral obligations—"Deað bið sella // eorla gehwylcum / þonne edwitlif" (For any nobleman death is better than a life of shame, 2890b–91)—illustrates the dynamics of an ethical system not entirely foreign to us even now. The introduction of a new state-sanctioned (or ruler-sanctioned) religion does not necessarily effect radical changes in a culture's basic structure of values. Not only *Beowulf* but the *Maxims* of the Exeter Book—"Dom biþ selast" (Fame is best, 80)—and *The Battle of Maldon* attest to the vitality of the shame culture and its values in Anglo-Saxon England long after the Conversion. The theme of "worship" (i.e., Anglo-Saxon *weorðscipe* [honor]) running through Malory's stories suggests that the ethos of the shame culture survived both the Conversion and the Conquest. Fred C. Robinson assumes that the Conversion produced a prompt cultural shift and that therefore the poem represents "a shame culture viewed through the eyes of a guilt culture" (1984, 119). Robinson cites Beowulf's unaccustomed "dark thoughts," occasioned by fears that some unknown fault of his own may have called up the dragon's wrath, as evidence for the hero's sense of guilt, an anachronistic imposition of the poet's culture on the poem's heroic (and pagan) world: "The heroic world is a world of action and of public recognition for deeds performed, not of brooding and soul searching" (119). Beowulf's unaccustomed gloom need not be taken as arising from a sense of guilt inappropriate to a shame culture: after all, the dragon's raids and wrath scourge the Geats, whose prosperity Beowulf must assure. His honor is at stake.

Interpretation has characteristically found its meaning for *Beowulf* in the Grendel story and has read that meaning into the story of Grendel's mother and thence into the story of the dragon. This convenient approach is faulty. W. P. Ker asserted long ago that the three stories have vastly differing characters, tones, and feelings (1904, 253), but he did not characterize the differences he found in the three great battles. Among many others, H. L. Rogers (1955) directly engaged the problem of meaning in *Beowulf* and concluded in apparent despair that the poet was unable to reshape the second and third great battles to fit his intended meaning, though he had succeeded with the first. In short, the poet meant what the Grendel story means, despite the difficulty of deriving that meaning from the battles with

Grendel's mother and the dragon. Rogers did not take up the possibility that the meaning of *Beowulf* arises from the contradictions the three stories pose.

The form of *Beowulf* taken as a whole suggests both the "Bear's Son" folktale type (especially as we find it in Scandinavia) and the "combat myth" analyzed by Fontenrose (1959, 524–34; see also Chadwick 1959, 171–203; Clark 1973, 66–87; Clark 1990, 30–33). The hero fights successively against three nonhuman and apparently supernatural enemies, forces of elemental or archetypal disorder. The first enemy, Grendel, can be taken as a chaos monster in a diminished, almost humanized form resembling the troll or *draugr* (revenant) of the Scandinavian analogues, but he seems clearly associated with the force of evil in a Christian mythology. The story juxtaposes Grendel's rage and the scop's song in Heorot celebrating God's creation of the world; subsequently, the narrator traces Grendel's descent back to Cain. The monster might seem an enemy of any order, pagan or Christian, but at this point the narrator distances the audience from the actors. The audience can apprehend Grendel intellectually by his descent from Cain, whereas even Hrothgar, the wisest of the Danes, cannot account for Grendel's origins and thus, in a sense, for the nature and origin of evil. The audience enjoys an insight denied Hrothgar, the Danes, and the Geats, and that superiority of vision makes the actors in the poem liable to irony. Like the audience, Hrothgar knows God can easily end Grendel's raids (478–79), and he sees God's benevolent plan in Beowulf's appearance in Denmark (381–84), hence he shares much of the audience's insight and implied optimism. Hrothgar's wisdom thus partly shields him from the audience's ironic vision; Beowulf's easy indifference to Grendel's origins and confidence as to the monster's destination do as much. The full weight of irony in the first great battle falls on Grendel. Before the battle, Beowulf is clearly confident of success, Hrothgar hopeful, and Beowulf's companions apprehensive, but the narrator envelopes Grendel's ill-fated march on Heorot in irony (Ringler 1966).

Irony dominates the story of Beowulf's first great battle. Grendel's famous approach to Heorot, often treated as a "design for terror," deliberately traces his course from the mere to the hall: "Com on wanre niht . . . Ða com of more . . . Wod under wolcnum . . . Com þa to recede / rinc siðian // dreamum bedæled" (He came in the dark night . . . then he came from the moor . . . he advanced beneath the clouds . . . then the joyless warrior came moving to the hall, 702–21a). The narrator punctuates Grendel's progress with comments contrasting the unsuspecting monster's intentions to feast his fill on the hall's sleepers with God's power to thwart him, with Beowulf's battle mood, with God's anger (which Grendel bears to Heorot), and with the tough luck and tough warrior awaiting him there (718–19). The story's ironic perspective enhances its dominant optimism.

In Beowulf's first great battle, the issues seem clear-cut. Hero is pitted against monster, a descendant of Cain against an idealized champion of right. The outcome seems an instance of poetic justice, proof that God's benevolent plan embraces mankind and stands between Grendel and his monstrous desires. The celebration of Beowulf's victory includes the scop's song of the battles at Finnsburg in which a party of Danes first suffers the loss of their leader but subsequently gains a great victory over Finn and his followers. In this reversal of fortune from humiliation to triumph, Finn's Danish wife, Hildeburh, loses her brother and son in the Danes' defeat and her husband in their victory. The Danes receive the song joyfully, yet Beowulf apparently recalls the poetry of Heorot as if he understood its tragedy. The battles in Finn's hall create a world of moral uncertainty where poetic justice has no place, and no benevolent plan leaves its trace on events.

The beginning, climax, and close of the second great fight, the battle with Grendel's mother, surprise and even shock the audience of the poem and the actors. The narrative style becomes strikingly abrupt. Grendel's mother reaches the hall suddenly—"Com þa to Heorote, / ðær Hring-Dene // geond þæt sæld swæfun" (Then she came to Heorot, where the Danes were sleeping throughout the hall, 1279–80a)—but Grendel's fateful coming occupies nearly twenty lines. In Heorot, the issue of battle never seems in doubt; Grendel apprehends his doom when he first feels Beowulf's grip. The climax of the battle at the bottom of the mere suddenly reverses the flow of a battle the hero has almost lost. Pinned down and almost knifed, Beowulf regains his feet, sees and seizes a gigantic sword, and decapitates Grendel's mother with one blow. One instant brings victory and exultation. For the Danes, who left the mere assuming Beowulf's defeat, Beowulf's return (with Grendel's awesome head carried into the hall it had visited so often before) provides still another surprise accompanied by a touch of terror.

Brusque movements, surprises, and suspense characterize the story of the second great battle. The Danes receive a number of shocks: the unexpected raid, the discovery of Æschere's death, then the sudden horror when they see an appalling sight at the edge of the mere—Æschere's severed head. As Beowulf and Hrothgar stand at the mereside, Beowulf specifies the arrangements to be made if he does not return—enhancing the power of suspense in the narrative—then suddenly plunges in without waiting for Hrothgar's answer or agreement.

The narrative preface to the story of Grendel's mother ironically indicates the Danes' ignorance both of man's dark fate generally and of the particular doom hanging over one of them, then reports that an avenger survived Grendel, reminds us of Grendel's origins and deeds, and closes with two and one-half lines stating Grendel's mother's intention to avenge his death. After this brief excursion into irony, the narration creates and sustains its suspense, its abrupt turns, and its cruel surprises. The narrator never anticipates the outcome of the battle at the bottom of the mere, its sequence of events is never predictable, and suspense rather than irony characterizes the telling. The narrator does not identify Grendel's mother as a figure of evil, nor does he explicitly link her to Cain. She attacks Heorot to avenge her son's death, a motive that Beowulf and the heroic world accept and that Anglo-Saxon culture continued to accept long after the conversion (Whitelock 1951, 14–17).

Grendel's mother must avenge her son, while Beowulf must champion Hrothgar and take revenge for Æschere's death. The narrative does not invite the audience to see the conflict as one between moral evil and good.

The ironic vision reporting Beowulf's first great battle thus suggests an essential stability, a grand and benevolent design, governing in the world of the audience's experience, but the recurring surprises and the pervasive suspense characterizing the story of the second battle threaten the moral assurance that was previously proposed. In the first battle, the audience clearly understands Grendel's origins, the meaning of the battle, and its inevitable outcome better than do the actors, but, in the second, the audience's higher perspective is eroded by a tumultuous narrative that takes its decisive turn too quickly for anticipation, irony, or assurance.

In the story of Beowulf's last great battle, the tactics of narration consistently retake any high ground the audience may briefly occupy, thus defeating irony's brief sallies, which are sometimes against Beowulf and sometimes against the dragon. At the beginning of the action, the audience knows, as Beowulf does not, the cause of the dragon's anger: the theft of a precious object from the treasure the dragon guards. Thus, the audience's better understanding of the scourge that has descended on the Geats briefly sustains an ironic view of the hero who fears that some fault of his has summoned up the dragon's wrath. Unaccustomed dark thoughts oppress Beowulf as he contemplates his failure in the kingly duty of protecting the Geats. But the audience's potentially ironic superiority in knowledge disappears as Beowulf deduces what the audience has been told, immediately understands the cause of the Geats' affliction, and devises a weapon for confronting the enemy. Irony loses its position as the audience's knowledge and Beowulf's coincide. Indeed, the audience is left to admire the acuity and alacrity of Beowulf's understanding rather than its own inside knowledge.

Achieving non-ironic equipoises out of potentially ironic situations and constructing a narrative of discoveries in which the audience, hero, and actors come to the same understanding of truth characterize the final part of *Beowulf*. Before they confront each other directly, the dragon counts—in vain—on his prowess and his stronghold, while Beowulf relies—also in vain—on his long experience of victory in every kind of battle. Irony is at first neutralized in this balance of hero and monster and then dismissed as the two great enemies face each other in complete equality and both experience a chill of fear at the sight of the other: "æghwæðrum wæs // bealohycgendra / broga fram oðrum" (each of them felt a chill of fear at the sight of the other, 2564b–65). As the battle begins, the narrator makes clear that both adversaries are doomed; an even-handed representation of the two great enemies allows irony no purchase on either.

The narrator treats the battle as inevitable and its outcome as predetermined, yet Beowulf can challenge his enemy only after he has addressed a formal speech to his followers and reviewed his life and place in Geatish history. Beowulf's long speech becomes part of the construction of the history of the Geats and a significant part of the poem's creation of its hero. In the first two major episodes of the poem, narrative digressions drawn from what seems the whole history of the Germanic peoples generally illuminate the central action or comment on it thematically, but, in part 2, the digressions reflect—and create—just two stories, the history of the dragon's treasure and the history of the Geatish people in the time of the Hrethlings.

The Geatish digressions in the last episode of the poem take the audience from Hrethel's death to the deaths of all his sons and the succession of his grandson, Beowulf, though not in chronological order. Moreover, Geatish dynastic history is related to the dynastic history of the Swedes and the recurring wars of the two peoples. All these matters are presumptively better known to the actors than to the audience. The audience, to be sure, initially knows the history of the treasure, the other thread making up the digressive matter of the dragon story, better than the actors, but Beowulf, on seeing the cup and hearing the informer (and thief?), at once apprehends the origin of the dragon's raids. The two threads of Geatish history and the history of the treasure lead the audience through a labyrinthine series of narrative fragments ultimately revealing how Beowulf and the dragon became, respectively, the protector of the treasure and the guardian of the Geats. The two threads join the history of the Geats (and the Swedes) and humanity. Geatish history manifests the mortality of kings and the brevity of dynasties, while the history of the treasure manifests the mortality of peoples in the huge expanse of time. Though the Geats seem part of a distant past, their story is both fresh and brief. The Geatish dynasty reaches back only to Hrethel, Beowulf's grandfather, but the audience learns the name and death, apparently, of every male royal from Hrethel to Beowulf and in the Swedish dynasty from Ongentheow to Eadgils. The "last survivor" who consigns the treasure to its tomb, and his vanished people remain nameless, lost in oblivion.

A king must protect his people; a dragon must keep guard over a treasure. The wars of the Franks, Swedes, and Geats and the deaths of Hrethel and his successors make Beowulf the protector of the Geats; the extinction of an ancient race commits the tomb and treasure to the dragon's keeping. The narrator, Beowulf, Wiglaf, and an anonymous messenger all relate episodes from the wars of the Swedes and Geats without identifying either side as representing moral good or evil. Ongentheow and Onela (quite possibly the "god cyning" of 2390) are not traced to the lineage of Cain, nor is the dragon. The enemies of the Geats, including the dragon, are nowhere identified as God's enemies. Every event detailed in the many stories of the last great episode is part of the pattern of history and of nature leading to the mortal battle between Beowulf and the dragon. At Beowulf's cremation, the audience of the poem and the mourners within it view the hero's departure in the same state of doubt that closed Scyld Scefing's ship burial. Beowulf's funeral includes both uncertain signs of divine favor as the smoke from Beowulf's funeral pyre ascends to the heavens and the winds grow still (Taylor 1966), and a clear statement of heroic fame won in ancient times and renewed with every retelling of the hero's story. In his youth, Beowulf asserted the doctrine that for the dead warrior, a living fame is best. In his age he summons up his will for the battle against the dragon in a speech that reviews his life and his place in Geatish history (Pope 1970; de Looze 1984). Beowulf defines himself as one of the Hrethelings, as Hygelac's champion and at last his avenger. Beowulf finds his resolve in the memory of his heroic service to his beloved king, Hygelac, then vows to perform deeds meriting fame in the battle (2514), to act as becomes a noble warrior (2535). The poem's theme and the hero's goal are one.

Chapter 15

Beowulf and Archaeology

by Catherine M. Hills

Summary: Archaeology has been deployed since the nineteenth century to illustrate the artifacts and burial rites described in *Beowulf*. Parallels for helmet, sword, and hall, for cremation and ship burial, can be found in Britain and Scandinavia at various times and places during the first millennium A.D. Archaeology can also illustrate the kinds of society and the relationships between peoples that existed in northern Europe at this time. New Danish evidence can be added to well-known material from sixth- to seventh-century England and Sweden, such as that found at Sutton Hoo. A ninth- to tenth-century context for the poem is not incompatible with the archaeological evidence.

Chronology

1852: Charles Roach-Smith discusses the Benty Grange boar helmet and Anglo-Saxon shields and swords in connection with *Beowulf*.

1855: John Yonge Akerman quotes the account of Beowulf's burial and says it throws little light on the urn burial of the Anglo-Saxon tribes.

1863: John M. Kemble discusses excavated Anglo-Saxon cremations and accounts of cremation in Beowulf as a "noble" rite. As cremation is not mentioned in the "mass" of Anglo-Saxon legislation he concludes it was a strictly pagan rite.

1881: Discovery of boat burials at Vendel, Uppland, Sweden, dating to the seventh to the tenth centuries.

1908: Knut Stjerna describes recent archaeological finds in Scandinavia, including Vendel, as a context for *Beowulf*.

1913: Birger Nerman uses *Beowulf* to identify the occupants of the burial mounds at Uppsala.

1915: G. Baldwin Brown repeats references to helmet and sword, refers to Offa of Angeln as ruler of a territory near to the homeland of the Anglo-Saxons, and argues for composition of *Beowulf* at the court of King Offa of Mercia.

1928: Discovery and excavation of boat graves at Valsgärde, Sweden.

1936: E. T. Leeds says the northern sagas are "boastful" and add little to our understanding of archaeology. No halls such as Heorot have been found, only small, squalid huts full of rubbish.

1936: Sune Lindqvist compares burial mounds at Uppsala and Ottarshögen to Beowulf's burial mound.

1936: R. G. Collingwood and J. N. L. Myres identify Hengest in *Beowulf* with the Hengest who is said to have invaded England in the fifth century.

1939: Discovery of the ship burial in Mound I at Sutton Hoo.

1940: Publication of volume of *Antiquity* devoted to reports and discussion of Sutton Hoo. H. M. Chadwick identifies occupant of Mound I as Rædwald.

1948: Lindqvist claims Sutton Hoo and *Beowulf* "both become the clearer by comparison."

1953: Start of excavations by Brian Hope-Taylor at Yeavering, near Wooler, Northumbria. Site identified as Ad Gefrin, *villa regalis* of King Edwin of Northumbria.

1957: Rosemary Cramp publishes paper on *Beowulf* and archaeology, including discussion of literary and archaeological evidence for swords and helmets and the Yeavering halls.

1959: C. L. Wrenn relates Sutton Hoo to *Beowulf* in chapter included in Chambers (1959).

1960: David M. Wilson, in his general introduction to Anglo-Saxons, discusses weapons, halls, etc., as found in archaeology and in *Beowulf.*

1965–70: Reexcavation of Sutton Hoo Mound I, record of now damaged impression of ship, and recovery of more fragments.

1969: J. N. L. Myres suggests that pottery found in Kent includes Frisian and Jutish elements, as might be expected as a reflection of the career of Hengest.

1969: Michael Müller-Wille publishes survey of boat-grave burials in northern Europe.

1971: Rupert Bruce-Mitford adds archaeological discussion, drawing on Sutton Hoo, to reissue of Girvan's *Beowulf and the Seventh Century.*

1974–88: Martin Biddle and Birthe Kjølbye Biddle excavate at Repton, where they find remains of mass grave and other burials of Viking date.

1975: Publication of volume 1 of the Sutton Hoo Ship Burial report by Rupert Bruce-Mitford. Accounts of excavation, ship, coins, date, and the identity of the person commemorated or buried in Mound I.

1976: David M. Wilson edits volume on Anglo-Saxon archaeology; *Beowulf* mentioned in relation to iron fittings on buildings and pattern welding of swords, also in chapter by Rahtz on settlements and buildings.

1977: Publication of Yeavering report by Hope-Taylor, who claims that "*Beowulf* is more strikingly illustrated by Sutton Hoo but it is Yeavering that exemplifies that aspiration to an ideally majestic hall . . . expressed in the poem."

1978: Publication of volume 2 of the Sutton Hoo Ship Burial report: arms, armor and regalia.

1980: George Speake explores possible symbolism of boar and serpent images in Anglo-Saxon animal ornament with quotations from *Beowulf.*

1982: Discovery of Anglo-Saxon helmet at Coppergate, York.

1983: Publication of Sutton Hoo Ship Burial volume 3, Bruce-Mitford and Care-Evans. Bronze and silver vessels, lyre, textiles, and other objects.

1983–91: Renewed investigations at Sutton Hoo, directed by Martin Carver.

1984: Continuing excavations at Gudme, on Fyn, Denmark, and at nearby contemporary port and market at Lundborg.

1986–88: Excavation at Lejre, Seeland, Denmark, traditional home of early Danish kings, of large timber hall dating from seventh to tenth centuries.

1988: C. J. Arnold calls on archaeologists to abandon the *"Beowulf* and brooches" approach to archaeology.

1989: Richard Hodges argues for the origin of the Anglo-Saxon kingdoms in military and political takeover, not mass migration. Offa's court still likely context for composition of *Beowulf.*

1992: Publication of York helmet by D. Tweddle.

1992: Publication of three volumes of papers relating to Sutton Hoo, including interim reports on recent work at Sutton Hoo by Carver, on Snape by Filmer-Sankey, and on Asthall by Dickinson and Speake, papers on the coins by Stahl and Oddy, on early Anglo-Saxon East Anglia by Scull, on Denmark by Hedeager, and paper by Roberta Frank casting doubt on closeness of connection between Sutton Hoo and *Beowulf.*

1993: Sam Newton restates arguments for seeing *Beowulf* and Sutton Hoo as reflections of the same society.

The history of the relation between archaeology and *Beowulf* begins in the mid-nineteenth century. J. M. Kemble edited and translated the poem, and discussed the accounts of burial practice it contains in connection with the excavated cremations he knew from England and Germany. He was struck by the accounts in *Beowulf* of cremation as a "noble" rite whereas "in all the mass of legislation" from Anglo-Saxon England he could not find one mention of it, and concluded that cremation was a strictly pagan rite, expunged from Christian record (1863, 96). J. Y. Akerman also quoted from *Beowulf* in his discussion of early Anglo-Saxon burial rites (1855, xv), and Charles Roach-Smith added detailed consideration of artifacts (1852, 237, 240, 247). The helmet, then recently found at Benty Grange in Derbyshire, surmounted by the figure of a boar, seemed to provide illustration of the boar helmets in *Beowulf.* Similarly, Anglo-Saxon swords, seaxs, and shields were compared with the poem's descriptions of weapons. This approach, of direct comparison between actual ancient artifacts and descriptions in the poem, has remained dominant. Even the choice of topics has remained constant. Baldwin Brown (1915, 194–95, 206), repeated Roach-Smith's boar helmet discussion, adding swords and noting that mail coats, mentioned in *Beowulf,* had not been found in graves. The Swedish archaeologist Knut Stjerna, in "Essays on *Beowulf,*" expanded the discussion through Swedish archaeological material, which, when he wrote, offered far more possibilities for comparison.

Burial rites, boar helmet, sword, and shield reappear more recently in, among others, D. M. Wilson (1960, 115–16, 128; and 1976, 254, 266), Speake (1980, 80–81), and Welch (1992, 89, 93). These authors had the benefit of two remarkable archaeological excavations, which seemed to put the reality of the things and places described in *Beowulf* beyond doubt. The discovery of the treasure in Mound I at Sutton Hoo in 1939 provided the arms, armor, regalia, gold, and silver to match any poet's imagination. The author of *Beowulf* need not have been fantasizing. It all really existed, in Suffolk in the seventh century. What Roberta Frank has termed the "marriage" between *Beowulf* and Sutton Hoo has certainly seemed an indissoluble union to most people who have thought about the subject for the past fifty years. Even if the story of the recital of the poem at the coroner's inquest is, sadly, apocryphal, it was not long before popular and scholarly writing had connected the two with ever more circumstantial detail. The Swedish archaeologist Sune Lindqvist wrote a paper on "Sutton Hoo and *Beowulf*" in 1948 in which he argued strongly that the burial and the poem "complement one another admirably" and "both become the clearer by the comparison" (140). This sets the scene for most subsequent writing on the subject. In volume 1 of the report on Sutton Hoo Mound I, Rupert Bruce-Mitford quotes the account of Scyld's funeral and includes other references to *Beowulf* as possibly relevant to his interpretation (1975–83, 716–17).

Hope-Taylor's excavations at Yeavering in the 1950s gave further "proof" of the reality of *Beowulf*. Here were large timber halls from the days of Edwin and Oswald of Northumbria, confirmation that buildings like Hrothgar's Heorot could and did exist in England as early as the seventh century. Hope-Taylor himself drew the parallels: "*Beowulf* is more strikingly illustrated by Sutton Hoo, but it is Yeavering that exemplifies that aspiration to an ideally majestic hall 'lofty and wide-gabled' which is repeatedly expressed in the poem" (1977, 315).

The best expression of this approach to the subject is the paper "*Beowulf* and Archaeology" by Rosemary Cramp (1957). Cramp possesses a knowledge of the poem in the original, lacking to most archaeologists, and her arguments are expressed with more subtlety, and also more caution, than usual. Parts of the present chapter are no more than an update on Cramp, to take account of more than thirty years further digging in Anglo-Saxon grave fields (and elsewhere) since she wrote.

A secondary strand of research has been the attempt to use *Beowulf* and archaeology to write history. From Stjerna onwards Swedish archaeologists have tried to use *Beowulf* to attach names to the kings buried at Uppsala and elsewhere. Baldwin Brown noted the reference to Offa of Angeln in *Beowulf* and suggested it was a "reasonable theory" that *Beowulf* received its present form at the court of King Offa of Mercia in the eighth century (1915, 566–67). This idea was developed in Whitelock's influential *The Audience of Beowulf* and is still favored by Hodges (1989, 145). J. N. L. Myres identified the Hengest of the Finnsburg fragment with the Hengest who came to conquer Kent in the fifth century (Collingwood and Myres 1936, 346). In his account of Anglo-Saxon pottery, Myres identified a type he called "Anglo-Frisian" and suggested that "if one had been asked to guess the style of pottery which a Jutish chieftain with Frisian contacts (i.e., Hengest) would have used towards the middle of the fifth century" it would be very like some of the earliest Anglo-Saxon pottery from Kent (1969, 96–97).

Other archaeologists either make very little reference to *Beowulf* or have actually expressed doubt as to its relevance to Anglo-Saxon archaeology. E. T. Leeds felt that attempts to correlate the two, as exemplified by Stjerna's essays, "leave the reader with a certain sense of unfulfilment" and "do little more than dot the i's and cross the t's of the deductions of archaeological research" (1936, xi). Leeds also found his opinion of the "boastfulness" and exaggeration of northern sagas amply confirmed by comparison of the evidence for Anglo-Saxon houses, much of it from his own excavations, with the description of Heorot. Excavation showed miserable hovels, or, at best, simple farmsteads, but not great halls. Yeavering might have changed Leeds's mind on that point (the excavations at Yeavering were in progress but not published at the time of his death in 1955), but his endeavor to "treat the material purely from an archaeological standpoint" has found successors.

Arnold calls on us to abandon the *"Beowulf* and brooches" approach (1988, 16) and resolutely eschews any reference to the poem in his account of Anglo-Saxon archaeology. He belongs to a generation of archaeologists who have come to the Anglo-Saxons by way of prehistoric archaeology or practical fieldwork, and not through history, art history, or literature. Because the theoretical underpinnings of prehistory derive from anthropology rather than from history, it has an emphasis on social and economic structure rather than on specific events and named people. Thus, it is well suited to the kind of evidence archaeology is capable of providing. In the past few decades, the increase both in excavation and in the capacity to extract information from unpromising data like seeds, soil stains, and animal bones has encouraged archaeologists in their own capacity to reconstruct the past, whether of early Anglo-Saxon England or elsewhere, without reference to written sources. Arnold is consistent in his view that *Beowulf* has little to do with modern archaeology. Richard Hodges, however, although also trained in anthropological theory, has remained surprisingly enamored of named historical figures—Ine, Offa, Alfred—and deploys *Beowulf* in a fairly traditional manner (1989, 58, 88–89).

In the 1980s, renewed excavation at Sutton Hoo, directed by Martin Carver, gave rise to research that takes account of archaeological realignment away from attempts to write history from artifact typologies and towards socioeconomic issues and ideology. Three collections of papers appeared in 1992 that show the range of traditional and new thinking now being applied to Sutton Hoo, most obviously its location in a wider context (Carver 1992c; Kendall and Wells 1992; Farrell and de Vegvar 1992). This is not just one rich burial but a whole burial ground, to be understood in relation to contemporary East Anglia, early Anglo-Saxon society as a whole, and the North Sea and beyond. Among these papers are both direct and indirect attacks on the relevance of *Beowulf* to archaeology as well as others that maintain a more traditional line.

One surprising lacuna in almost all the works so far cited is any serious discussion of Danish archaeology. Sweden got into the picture long ago, chiefly at the instigation of Swedish scholars, and Carver has tried to put Sutton Hoo in a wider, North Sea perspective, but using Swedish and Norwegian, more than Danish, evidence. Danish buildings and pottery have occasionally put in an appearance, but in general little attention has been devoted, by English-speaking scholars, to the possibility of illuminating *Beowulf* through the archaeology of the country where the most famous events of that poem are supposed to have happened. This used to be partly excusable on the grounds that the archaeology of the migration period in Denmark was very unimpressive. Little sign of kings, treasure, or even monsters could be found. This is no longer the case. Discoveries and research in recent years now allow Denmark a position of central importance in the North during the Roman Iron Age and later, and, if one wishes to seek a real historical context for the story of *Beowulf,* one could do worse than look at the archaeology of fifth- to sixth-century Denmark (for an introduction to this, see Hedeager 1992b).

A fresh appraisal of the relation between archaeology and *Beowulf* needs to take account of Denmark as well as new evidence from England and elsewhere. Also, the possibility that the poem may have been composed, or written in its final form, as late as the end of the tenth century extends the chronological range of the evidence to be surveyed. We must also consider the fundamental problem of the difference between the two types of source material, epic poetry and archaeological remains, and ask the heretical question, Is there after all any real connection between *Beowulf* and archaeology?

Beowulf is not the only epic to have inspired archaeologists. Homer's Troy and King Arthur's Camelot have both been pursued through excavation, and we have learned much about the Aegean Bronze Age and ancient Britain as a result. Archaeologists should not look gift horses in the mouth, and the motivation to dig up Hissarlik in Turkey, or South Cadbury in Somerset, was the popular identification of those places as, respectively, Troy and Camelot. But Moses Finley (1964) argued long ago that such identifications may be chimeras. The *Iliad* and *Beowulf* are works of fiction. Epics based on historical events for which we have alternative sources, like the *Song of Roland,* show how cavalier the treatment of historical fact can and could be. Minor figures could assume central importance; battles could change their date, their location, and even their protagonists. This could very easily have happened with *Beowulf*: indeed, it seems quite likely since, although minor figures, notably Hygelac, seem to have some historical basis for their existence, Beowulf himself is notably lacking from any other historical or literary account. There may be a considerable kernel of historical fact embedded in *Beowulf,* or we may be wasting our time looking for a "real" Heorot. Another point made by Finley is that we are very selective in our search for history in epics. Schliemann set out to find Troy and claimed to have looked on the face of Agamemnon. He did not climb up Mount Olympus to look for Zeus. Similarly, we have looked for the hall at Heorot, for helmets and swords and even for Beowulf's grave. No one has tried to dig up Grendel, his mother, or the dragon. Can we be sure we have distinguished correctly between the mythical and the historical?

Perhaps it does not matter whether Troy, Camelot, Heorot, or any of the people who are said to have built, lived in, or destroyed those places ever really existed. Audiences for the poems, including ourselves, may have always preferred to believe they are about people who once existed—and perhaps they are—but they are just as "true" as illustrations of the human condition or as good stories.

I could stop this chapter here and argue, like Arnold, that archaeologists should have nothing to do with *Beowulf*. There are, however, positive and negative reasons for continuing. Archaeology is often deployed optimistically by non-archaeologists—just as archaeologists use history—to fill in gaps and provide support for weak arguments. In particular, it has been suggested that if precise dates could be given for all the features of *Beowulf* likely to have provided physical remains (not including the dragon), it would help date the poem. But most of those features—cremation, ship burial, large timber halls, lavish treasure, helmets, swords, mail coats—can be found somewhere in the northern world throughout most of the first millennium A.D. I shall set out some of the evidence for this below.

The fictional element in the poem is often thought less likely to have extended to physical objects—helmets or halls—than to personalities and events. Author and audience will have imagined these from their own experience, which will limit their possibilities and allow us to partially reconstruct their world. Beowulf had no guns, and Heorot was not built of concrete. It is also true that, even if a conscious effort was made to describe something from the past, not the present, an ancient sword unlike any owned by the listeners, the attempt would not have been entirely successful. Contemporary features would have crept in. In this century, many reconstructions of Anglo-Saxon and Viking period houses have been drawn and sometimes actually built. The longer these exist, the more clearly we can see that they belong as much to the 1930s or the 1970s, 1980s, or 1990s, when they were created, as to the period they are meant to represent. An early medieval poet would have had neither the ability nor the inclination to produce accurate historical descriptions. One might hope therefore that the things described are essentially what poet and audience knew. Specific artifactual details therefore probably can be used, with due caution, recognizing that many of the descriptions given are sufficiently vague for anyone to hang his or her own imagined picture on the words. I shall examine some of this material, before concluding, by looking at how archaeological evidence can be used more widely in the reconstruction of early medieval society.

I. Funeral Rites

Accounts of burials and funeral rites in *Beowulf* have been used to show both how unfamiliar and how familiar the poet was with pagan practices. The Swedish burial mounds at Uppsala, from around 500, and the ship burials at Vendel,

Valsgärde, and Sutton Hoo, from the sixth and seventh centuries, have been cited as more or less corresponding to aspects of the funeral rites of either Scyld Scefing or Beowulf himself.

Near the beginning of *Beowulf,* we are told that when Scyld Scefing died, he was laid in a ship heaped with treasure and weapons, which was then sent off on the open sea to an unknown destiny. If this type of burial really took place, it is not one easily to be recovered by archaeologists, although underwater exploration might one day reveal the remains of such a ship. We can, however, look for parallels among the burials interred in ships on land, some famously equipped with treasure.

The Finnsburg episode includes an account of the mass cremation of Finn's slaughtered warriors, put on the pyre with mail coats and gold. At the end of the poem there is the story of Beowulf's last battle, his death, and his burial. This involves the construction of a funeral pyre, on which the body was laid, which had helmets, shields, and mail coats hung around or laid on it. All this was consumed by fire. Then a mound was built, to be a landmark, apparently on top of the remains of the pyre, and into this mound the dragon's treasure, unburned, was put. This offers several features for investigation: cremation, including the burning of weaponry, the construction of a mound on top of the pyre as a landmark, and further deposits of unburned treasure in the mound.

Cremation burial was practiced throughout Europe at the start of the first millennium. Within the Roman Empire, including Britain, inhumation became the dominant rite by the fourth century, but elsewhere cremation remained common much later, in northern Scandinavia as late as 1000. It has sometimes been thought that all Christian burials were unfurnished inhumations while all other burial rites can be identified as pagan, but the situation is not so simple. The coincidence of the spread of unfurnished inhumation and the adoption of Christianity as the official religion of the Roman Empire in the fourth century led to a connection between the two that found justification in Christian doctrine about the resurrection. This had not originally been the case: the cremated bones of purportedly no less a person than Saint Peter are displayed beneath his church in Rome today. Nor was conversion to Christianity followed automatically by abandonment of the practice of putting grave goods with the dead: a number of well-equipped early medieval graves have been excavated from beneath churches. Many medieval ecclesiastics were buried with vestments and liturgical vessels that, in a prehistoric context, would be interpreted as grave goods. There are no hard and fast rules according to which pagan burials can always be distinguished from those of Christians, although there may be a balance of probability in one direction or the other.

In the fifth century, cremation was reintroduced to Britain from northern Germany and Scandinavia. Both rites were practiced throughout Anglo-Saxon England during the fifth and sixth centuries, but cremation was predominant only in eastern England and was even there replaced once more by inhumation during the sixth century (before conversion to Christianity). Anglo-Saxon cremation involved the construction of a funeral pyre on top of which the body was laid. Women wore their jewelery, burnt fragments of which were buried with the bones, but men were seldom cremated with their weapons. Glass, bronze, and pottery vessels might also be put on the pyre. Animals were often also cremated. The bones and the remains of the burned objects were collected up, not always very carefully, and put into decorated pots. Unburned objects, mostly toilet implements such as tweezers and shears, were sometimes added. The pot was then buried in a pit in a cemetery, often a large burial ground with many graves. Small mounds or cairns may have been commonly raised over these cremations, but few of these have survived centuries of subsequent ploughing. Points of contact with *Beowulf* are the rite of cremation and the deposit of both burned and unburned objects, but otherwise these burial practices do not provide very close models for the poem's burials.

These cremations do vary in their relative wealth, but they are not usually distinguished by very lavish grave goods (Hills 1994; McKinley 1994). Occasional exceptions come from the later sixth or seventh centuries, when inhumation had otherwise become the norm. Bronze bowls were used as containers for these elaborately equipped cremations, instead of pots, as at Coombe in Kent (Davidson and Webster 1967) or Sutton Hoo, where one cremation contained a sword (Carver 1992c, 368).

After the seventh century, Anglo-Saxons did not cremate their dead, although they continued to bury grave goods occasionally into the eighth century. Elsewhere the practice lasted much longer, and it could have been known in England as a current contemporary foreign ritual rather than an ancient, discarded native one. In Denmark, graves of the sixth through the eighth centuries are rare. Those that have been found include both inhumations and cremations, neither richly equipped. In the Viking period, there are rich inhumation burials.

In Norway and Sweden, cremation remained common until the tenth century or even later. Many burials consist of a mound or cairn of stones heaped over the funeral pyre, and although most are poorly equipped, some were more elaborate. Rich cremations can be found in Sweden as late as the tenth century, for example, at Skopintull, near Birka, not far from modern Stockholm (Roesdahl 1992, 157). This burial contained fragments of gold, mounts for a horse harness, and possibly even a boat. Burials such as this must have been public events, and accounts of them could have traveled far, as did the famous account of the cremation in a ship witnessed by the Arab traveler Ibn Fadlan in Russia in the 920s. At Birka, more than a thousand burials of ninth- and tenth-century date have been excavated, including cremations and inhumations of various types. Some of these were probably graves of visiting merchants, who might have been English or have traveled to England.

But in the ninth century, and possibly into the tenth, there was no need for an Anglo-Saxon to go abroad to experience pagan burials. There are not many recorded pagan Viking burials in Britain, a fact usually explained as the result of rapid conversion and use of Christian cemeteries. But there are some. Particularly striking is the evidence from Repton in Derbyshire (Biddle and Kjolbye-Biddle 1992). Here, what had been an important Mercian church, the site of a royal mausoleum, was taken over by the Viking army in 873–74 as a fortified base. As well as there being several burials with Viking artifacts in the churchyard, there was an extraordinary assemblage nearby, associated with coins of the 870s, that included the bones of least 249 individuals, 80 percent males, buried in an earlier stone building. Over these a mound had been raised, into which further burials had been cut. These bodies were not cremated, but they offer some parallel for the mass cremation of the Finnsburg episode. Only four kilometers from Repton is Ingleby, where there is another Viking cemetery. Some of these burials were cremations, with mounds raised over pyres and remains of weapons. The events surrounding these burials, especially the mass grave at Repton, would have impressed themselves on the memory of any local survivors.

Ship burial is found in Britain and Scandinavia, and hardly anywhere else in Europe, in the first millennium (Schönbäck 1983, Müller-Wille 1968–69). The earliest examples known so far are from Slusegard, Bornholm, Denmark, dating to the second and third centuries. These do not seem to have any immediate successors, although recently excavated sixth-century boats from Snape, Suffolk, seem very similar (Filmer-Sankey 1992). Better known are the larger ships from Snape, from Sutton Hoo Mound I, and from the series of graves from Sweden, especially from Vendel and Valsgärde. These contained burials of unusual wealth, including weapons, drinking vessels, and the remains of animals. At Sutton Hoo, there is both the large ship from Mound I, with its famous treasure, and another burial in a wooden chamber underneath a ship. Recent research has emphasized the variety of burial rite in contemporary use amongst the pagan Anglo-Saxons. At Sutton Hoo, there was inhumation in a ship, in a chamber, under a ship, next to a horse, in a coffin, as sacrificial victims around a cremation, and possibly also around a tree. Cremations were contained in bronze bowls, on a wooden tray or boat, in a pot, or simply put in the ground. Men, women, and children were among the burials (Carver 1992a, 367–71). At Snape, there was inhumation in a ship, in boats, on biers, or in coffins, cremations in pots, one in a bronze bowl, and some possibly left to be buried on the pyre (Filmer-Sankey 1992, 47–49). Commentators who have felt that the *Beowulf* poet was confusing accounts of burial rites he did not know of at firsthand to create impossible rituals were not aware of this considerable contemporary variation. If those burying their dead at Sutton Hoo could call on such a range of practice, so could a poet.

Rich ship burials occur again in the Viking period. A recent program of tree-ring dating has produced precise dates for some of the Norwegian ships (Bonde and Christensen 1993). Timbers from the grave chambers, constructed specifically for the burials, were examined, because the ships themselves could have been old when buried. At Oseberg some timbers had sapwood and bark, allowing the calculation of a precise date, 834, for their felling and the construction of the grave chamber. The ships at Gokstad and Tune have slightly less precise dates of shortly after 900. In Denmark, the ship at Ladby, on Fyn, was buried in an existing cemetery during the tenth century (Roesdahl 1992, 162).

Attention has usually focused on the rich burials listed above, but there are probably many more burials in boats that have left no trace, because they had no metal fittings and the wood has entirely disappeared after burial in the ground, or because they were cremated. Many cremations from Scandinavia have left behind iron rivets of the kind used to build ships, in some cases in such quantity that they are reasonably interpreted as the remains of cremation in ships. In the British Isles, Viking burials in boats have been found on the Isle of Man.

The raising of a mound as a landmark above a burial is a feature found in Britain in the Bronze Age and again among the Anglo-Saxons. In Scandinavia, it is a feature of both the Migration and the Viking periods. Most of the burials already discussed as either rich cremations or ship burials had large mounds raised over them, on sites chosen for their visibility, like Beowulf's barrow. Particularly towards the end of the sixth century and into the seventh, when otherwise burials are ceasing to contain many finds, there are a few strikingly rich burials, marked out by large and prominent mounds. Besides those located at Sutton Hoo, Snape, and Asthall, there are others to be found at places such as Taplow or Broomfield. One explanation for this final pagan outburst is that it is a defiant gesture in the face of advancing Christianity. Another is that these burials reflect increasing social inequality and were constructed by new dynasties, who had acquired increased power over larger kingdoms than had existed before. A large public funeral, involving feasting, sacrifice, and the deliberate burial and/or destruction of great treasures, all commemorated by a large visible monument, was a means of asserting control and authority, perhaps for people whose hold on that authority was still somewhat new and insecure. Later Anglo-Saxon kings had a more established basis for their power and had also converted to Christianity, so they were normally buried—and commemorated—in churches they had built themselves partly for that purpose.

In *Beowulf,* the dragon guards a hoard in an ancient barrow, described variously as of earth and of stone. Knowledge of ancient barrows and stone tombs could hardly have been avoided from their prominence in the landscape both in the British Isles and in Scandinavia. Early Anglo-Saxon cemeteries sometimes had Bronze Age barrows as their initial focal point, and "heathen burials" provided landmarks for boundaries in late Saxon land charters. Prehistoric burials did sometimes contain gold, as might have been known or suspected by later people. The stone tomb at Maes Howe, on Orkney, was broken into by Scandinavians who left runic graffiti as witness of their presence, including a reference to treasure carried off from the mound. Maes Howe, or the passage graves of the Boyne Valley d, would provide fitting homes for a dragon—both places possibly known to Vikings but not to Anglo-Saxons.

II. Halls

Until the 1950s, Anglo-Saxon houses in England were represented only by sunken huts, dismissed as squalid hovels. This changed with the discoveries at Yeavering. This site has been identified as a residence of the sixth- and seventh-century kings of Northumbria. The most massive hall and a timber amphitheater are attributed to the time of King Edwin, when Bede tells us Paulinus preached at a *villa regalis* of Edwin at "Ad Gefrin" and converted and baptized many people (*Eccl. Hist.* 2.14). Hope-Taylor's 1977 analysis of the buildings showed that complex and sophisticated carpentry techniques had been used in their construction. There were even a few surviving iron fittings, unusual for excavated timber buildings, which produce mainly foundation plans, to set beside the iron fittings that are said to have made fast the walls and door of Heorot. This discovery spurred a search for other, comparable buildings. Air photographs produced other sites in the same area—Sprowston and Millfield, the latter identified as Bede's Mælmin—and also in southern England (Welch 1992, 43–49; Scull 1991; Rahtz 1976). At more ordinary settlements, smaller "halls" have appeared beside the huts. At Cowderys Down near Basingstoke, a series of buildings were excavated, including one measuring twenty-two meters by nine meters, which showed a sophistication of carpentry comparable to that of Yeavering (Millett and James 1983).

At Cheddar in Somerset, historically a residence of the West Saxon kings, excavation showed a tenth-century timber hall twenty-four meters long (Rahtz 1979). In Northampton, a large timber structure was replaced in the ninth century by a stone hall (Williams, Shaw, and Denham 1985), although this could have been part of a religious complex. Otherwise, we have very little evidence for urban royal palaces. We do not know what Offa's palace in Tamworth was like or the late Saxon palaces in Winchester, Gloucester, or London. So we do not know when it would have ceased to be normal for an Anglo-Saxon king to have as his major residence a timber hall rather than a stone palace. The concept and techniques of building in stone returned to England with the Christian mission, and from the seventh century some ecclesiastical buildings were constructed in stone, although they were not normally very large. Anglo-Saxons traveled to Rome and saw the great buildings there, and they also knew the palace of Charlemagne at Aachen. A king like Offa is likely to have emulated his Continental contemporaries in palace building as in other activities, and others would have followed him. Cheddar was not the main residence of the West Saxon kings. By the late eleventh century, Edward the Confessor and William of Normandy were certainly building in stone.

The evidence is still lacking, but it is likely that an English poet describing a contemporary royal residence would not have imagined it as a timber hall after the eighth century. This does not, however, give us a defining date for the poem's composition, as long as we allow the poet to draw on Danish evidence for details, as he obviously did for the main story. In Denmark, there is good archaeological evidence for the construction of great timber halls from as early as the second century to well into the tenth century and later. Extensive excavations of settlements from the pre-Roman Iron Age to the Viking period have given a clear picture of the range of buildings, their construction, and their development. Timber was the universal building material. Farmhouses took the form of "long houses" with animal stalls at one end, human habitation at the other. In the Viking period, there was a tendency for buildings to widen in the middle to produce a "boat-shaped" plan. These last were sometimes quite large, but not spectacularly so (Hedeager 1992a, 180–223; Randsborg 1991, 76–78). However, there are two recent finds in Denmark of halls far larger than anything so far excavated in England.

Lejre, near Roskilde Fjord on Seeland, has been said to be the site of an early capital of Denmark since at least the early eleventh century. Here, between 1986 and 1988, remains of several buildings were excavated, including one massive structure 48.5 meters by 10 meters wide, twice as long as the large halls at Yeavering (Christensen 1991). This building had been rebuilt on more than one occasion, and the range of carbon 14 dates for it runs from the end of the seventh into the tenth century. The Danes who came to England in the ninth and tenth centuries would have known Lejre and would have portrayed great deeds and kings in a hall like the one there, or even at that very place—some Danes have not hesitated to put *Beowulf* there. In fact, they would have been justified in setting much earlier exploits in such a hall. In 1993 at Gudme on Fyn, a huge hall was excavated (Nielsen and Sørensen 1993). It was forty-seven meters long by nine meters wide, constructed of timbers seventy centimeters in diameter. It seems to have been built in the third century. There was no sign of repair or rebuilding, but such massive timbers could have lasted a long time: medieval barns in Essex have stood since the thirteenth century.

If a hall this big could be built in the third century, it is perfectly reasonable to set a king of the fifth or sixth centuries in one of equal size and magnificence. Hrothgar's Heorot is not at all implausible at the time or place it is supposed to have existed. This does not necessarily mean that the author of *Beowulf* used accurate early sources for his poetic background: if he had any knowledge of Denmark, it would have been natural to put a king in a great timber hall up to the millennium or beyond. By that date, it would probably not have been normal for an English king to have such a hall as his principal, most magnificent, residence. The archaeological evidence for buildings allows either for a poet drawing on English experience, which puts composition early, or for someone who reported faithfully a much earlier account—or who knew of Danish kings and courts at any time up to the eleventh century, the latest possible date for the poem. One detail that seems rather English than Danish is the "stræt . . . stanfah" (320a) that leads to Heorot: stone-paved Roman roads were widespread, if disused, in England, but not in Denmark.

III. Arms and Armor

Weapons could be heirlooms, and royal treasuries and armories still preserve arms and weapons from earlier days, so imagination in this area need not be confined to contemporary artifacts. Parts of the *Beowulf* descriptions could refer generally to any elaborate arms from the Roman period to the end of the Middle Ages, but other details seem more specific.

Helmets are the most dramatic and often quoted item of armor found in *Beowulf.* Less than a hundred early medieval helmets have been found in Europe altogether, mostly dating to the sixth and seventh centuries. There are three main types, two of them descended from late Roman parade armor. Later Roman emperors were often portrayed wearing helmets, and this, combined with elaborate decoration of helmets, their rarity, and burial in unusually rich graves, has led to the conclusion that at this date helmets were a symbol of royalty, related to later medieval crowns.

Helmets found in England and Scandinavia usually have a central ridge or comb running from between the eyes to the back of the head. Thirty-seven helmets of this type could be listed in 1992 (Tweddle 1992, 1082–1132), the majority from Sweden, mostly fragmentary, including a group from Gotland that were buried in cremations. Thirteen are reconstructable, the best known being those from Vendel, Valsgärde, and Sutton Hoo. In England, only three Anglo-Saxon helmets have been found: from Benty Grange in Derbyshire, probably of seventh-century date; from Sutton Hoo Mound I, probably sixth century; and a more recent find from York, of eighth-century date. The publication of *The Anglian Helmet* (Tweddle 1992) includes a detailed survey of helmets and of chain mail, because a section of mail was found attached as a neck guard to the York helmet.

Representations of armed men wearing helmets were included in the ornament of actual helmets. Some of these have exaggerated crests in the form of birds' heads or boars, and such designs have been seen as the origin for the references to boar ornaments on the helmet in *Beowulf*. There is also the Benty Grange boar, and there are boars' heads on the eyebrows of the Sutton Hoo helmet.

The York helmet, from the second half of the eighth century, seems to be the latest surviving example. It has a Christian inscription and zoomorphic ornament on the nose and eyebrows. Although it is not so elaborate as some of the earlier helmets, analysis of its manufacture shows a very high level of technical skill. Occasional representations of helmets in sculpture or in manuscripts show that crested helmets continued in use through the tenth century. By the eleventh century, helmets had become the plain, conical objects we see on the Bayeux tapestry, and, by this date also, they seem to have been in wider use than before, although possibly still confined to an aristocratic warrior group. Elaborate, ornamented helmets belong to a period before 1000: but not necessarily very long before. In *Beowulf,* helmets are worn by the retinues of Beowulf and Hrothgar, not just by the leaders, as would fit a time when they had become more common than in the seventh century, when they seem to have belonged only to kings and war leaders.

Chain mail is first found in Europe in the pre-Roman Iron Age and remained in use until the end of the Middle Ages. Most surviving early examples are heavily corroded and fragmentary, including those from Sutton Hoo, Vendel, and Vals-gärde. Examination of the chain mail neck guard from the York helmet showed that this was a product involving considerable skill and time (O'Connor 1992). Again, mail was at first rare and valuable, possibly owned only by leaders, so that its possession by retinues as well as kings in *Beowulf* might indicate a relatively later date.

The most important weapon referred to in *Beowulf* is the sword. Beowulf's own sword, which fails him in the fight with Grendel's mother, and the ancient sword he finds in her lair, with which he kills her, are both described in vivid but confusing detail. Cramp has explored these passages and points out the difficulties involved in using poetic terms as precise technical descriptions (1957, 63–67). The term *wyrmfah*, for instance, might refer to the serpentine patterns produced on iron blades by the technique known as pattern welding. This technique develops from the third century to reach a peak of popularity in the sixth to the seventh centuries and then declines in the face of competition from good-quality Frankish blades in the ninth and tenth centuries (Lang and Ager 1989). One would expect an eighth-century poet to think of pattern welding in connection with famous swords, whereas by the tenth century the best swords were not being made this way. But it could still have seemed appropriate for famous ancient swords to have had such blades. In any case, some of the decoration belonged to the hilt: the blade of the ancient sword melted away in the blood of Grendel's mother, leaving a golden hilt that carried the story of the Flood and a runic inscription. Elaborate golden sword hilts, inlaid with garnets, can be found from the fifth century onward, and occur at Sutton Hoo. But later Saxon and Viking period swords had decorated hilts as well, some with patterns of wyrm-like twisted beasts. There are, however, no hilts with biblical scenes.

Runic inscriptions are known from a few early Anglo-Saxon sword hilts, but knowledge and use of runes continued in England long after the introduction of the Latin alphabet, while in Scandinavia they remained the dominant script throughout the Viking period (Page 1987).

References to rings in connection with swords in *Beowulf* may relate to the practice of attaching rings to hilts. Ring swords have been found in England, Scandinavia, the Rhineland, and Italy. The earlier examples, with pairs of movable rings, looped into each other and riveted to the sword hilt, date to the early sixth century and come from Frankish areas and Kent. Later pairs of rings are cast as one object and, in some of the latest examples, from Finland, are cast in one with the hilt (Steuer 1987). Even the earlier, movable, rings allow little space for a strap and probably had no practical function, and the later ones clearly did not. Some swords show signs of having once had a ring, later removed, and rings have been found attached to other objects, such as the shield at Sutton Hoo, or separately, as from a hoard at Gudme. About eighty ring swords have been found, made from gold or silver. They are depicted on helmets but are not often found in graves together with actual helmets. The rings have been interpreted as symbolic of membership in a warrior band or the retinue of a king or of a war leader. As such they fit well into the world of *Beowulf* and for once provide a more limited date range, of the sixth to the seventh centuries.

IV. Treasure

Treasure is too widespread a concept to be useful in contextual definition. Valuables have been buried in the ground, put in graves, or thrown into lakes and rivers, and later dug up again, at many times and places in the past. Stories of its existence, or of the circumstances of its discovery, still cause excitement. Viking period hoards contained more silver than gold, but that might have made it all the more likely that famous ancient treasures would be pictured as of gold.

V. Monsters

Zoomorphic ornament, complicated patterns of twisted beasts and men, forms the most distinctive feature of Germanic art from the fifth century to the end of the Viking period. Its complexity and ambiguity has obvious parallels in the language of Old English poetry, and it clearly had importance and meaning to those who created and used it, though most of this significance is now lost to us. The animals depicted include both naturalistic and fantastic creatures, and the human figures could have been gods, men, or monsters. Such ornament is found especially on high-status objects, like the gold buckle and the shield from Sutton Hoo, the latter decorated with an appliqué often described as a dragon. Animal ornament takes on new forms in England after the conversion, under Celtic and Mediterranean influence, and is found most often as an element of manuscript art, but in Scandinavia its development continues on the old lines through the Viking age.

VI. Early Medieval Society

In this context, we must begin with Denmark. The only generally accepted link between *Beowulf* and historically recorded events is the raid by Hygelac on the Franks, equated with a raid by a Danish king, Chochilaicus, recorded by Gregory of Tours as having happened in the early sixth century. This is the reason for looking to the decades around 500 for the origin of the stories, but given the nature of epic poetry perhaps we should not draw our chronological limits too precisely.

Danish archaeology of the migration period has suffered from a lack of remarkable burials. Around 200, there were rich burials equipped with imported Roman silver and glass, but subsequently the burial record is not impressive until the Viking period. This has led to a mistaken downplaying of the importance of this region. Societies do not all, always, demonstrate their wealth or their social hierarchy in their burials. It has been argued that lavish display is in fact a mark of instability. Excavation has shown that throughout the first millennium A.D., Denmark was, as now, a settled country of farmers, some living where their descendants live today.

There were also warriors. A dramatic feature of the archaeology of this period is the deposit of huge quantities of weapons, and sometimes ships, in what are now bogs, which may then have been lakes. Currently, these are interpreted as the sacrificed weapons of defeated armies, a celebration, therefore, of native victories (Hines 1989; Ilkjær and Lønstrup 1982).

The zoomorphic ornament discussed above probably developed first in Denmark. The discovery of rich, complete objects in graves elsewhere has partly obscured the pattern shown by overall distributions and by evidence for manufacture. If this very influential art style did develop and spread from Denmark, it is a strong indicator of the cultural importance of this area.

Although there are few rich burials, gold and silver objects have been found in increasing quantities in recent years as a result of the activities of metal detector users. There is a remarkable concentration of such finds on the island of Fyn, at Gudme, in an area where there are a number of place names interpreted as religious, relating specifically to the worship of Odin. The name *Gudme* itself has been interpreted as meaning something like "Home of the Gods" (Randsborg 1990). Among these finds are gold pendants; bracteates, derived from Roman imperial medallions, with symbolic designs; and also tiny gold plaques with pictures of human or divine couples. Not just one hoard but lots of separate large and small finds of gold and silver single out this part of Denmark, including neck rings, finger rings, sword rings, and scabbard mounts, all of solid gold, as well as gold and silver coins and quantities of silver. Objects found at Gudme came from far afield, from the Rhineland, Italy, and Byzantium. They arrived by sea and were unloaded on the coast, a few miles away at Lundborg, where there was a market where people brought, and made, their wares to buy and sell.

Excavations at Gudme reveal the presence of an extensive settlement of large farmhouses from around 200–600. Some of the gold finds came from the foundations of the houses. In 1993, the very large house at Gudme of Fyn, described above, was found, and others like it could well lie in unexcavated areas.

At the time when the story of *Beowulf* was set, there was a rich and prosperous society in Denmark, one that was also successful in war. It had a center at Gudme with both religious and secular importance, the focus of people and treasure from across the northern world and beyond. The finds of detached gold rings suggest this was a place where such rings were given out, as Hrothgar did at Heorot. Gudme was occupied for many years and included at least one memorably large and magnificent hall. Neither Lundborg nor Gudme have yet produced evidence for defensive structures. It is during the seventh century, when Gudme was in decline, that the first rich burial was made at Lejre, perhaps a sign that authority had passed to a new dynasty with a new center.

There are many ways in which the archaeology of Gudme provides a remarkably plausible context for the Danish episodes in *Beowulf*. This is not to say that the historicity of *Beowulf* has been, or could be, proved by archaeology. But the poem's, set in a famous past, could have continued to be part of living Danish traditions.

In later centuries, there continued to be strong rulers in Denmark capable of conducting engineering works at home and trade and warfare abroad (Roesdahl 1982, 134–58). Initial phases of the Danevirke, the boundary across Jutland between Denmark and north Germany, and of the trading centers at Ribe and Hedeby, near Schleswig, belong to the eighth century. King Godfred of Denmark, murdered in 810, was taken seriously when he attacked Charlemagne's empire. In the tenth century, there are the complex of church and burial mounds at Jellinge, new forts, town defenses, and reconstruction of the Danevirke to put to the credit of Harold Bluetooth and his descendants, who were to add England to their empire. In some ways, tenth- and fifth-century Denmark were not dissimilar. Kings fought rivals at home and abroad, with their retinue of warriors. However, many other people lived lives as merchants or farmers. Tenth-century Denmark seems an ideal context for telling the story of *Beowulf*, for much the same reasons as used to be adduced for its composition in seventh- to eighth-century England: a society still close to its heroic pagan past, but newly converted, with an aristocratic culture where status was achieved through warfare and conspicuous consumption.

But the poem is written in Old English, not Old Danish. How, when, and why did the story cross the North Sea? Connections between England and Denmark can be traced throughout the early medieval period, although it is not easy to use archaeological evidence to distinguish between trade, migration, invasion, or the spread of ideas. In the fifth and sixth centuries, elements of English material culture can be traced to Scandinavia, including Denmark. From the later seventh century, ports like Ipswich were part of a North Sea trading network that allowed movement of people, goods, and ideas all around northern Europe. Finally, from the end of the eighth to the early eleventh centuries, Viking raids and settlement culminating in the Danish conquest of England provided many opportunities for transmission of Danish traditions to England.

The sixth and seventh centuries have long attracted the attention of English and Swedish scholars in connection with *Beowulf*, and it is not hard to see why. The princely burials of that date contain all the ingredients found in *Beowulf*: elaborate funeral rituals involving ships, cremation, burnt and unburnt treasure, great memorial mounds, and the objects themselves, elaborately decorated weapons, gold and silver vessels, horse trappings, drinking horns, harps, and chain mail. Investigation of all these, their ornament and symbolism, seems to lead directly to *Beowulf*, as Newton (1993) has most recently argued. The complexity of ritual and ornament provide a visual version of the poetic imagery. Martin Carver has described Sutton Hoo as itself a form of epic poem—an ideological statement by a pagan dynasty at bay against encroaching southern Christianity (Carver 1992c, 151).

But however close some of the parallels between poem and burial may be, the Christian elements of *Beowulf* show that in its present version it could not be contemporary with Sutton Hoo. The eighth century in England was a time of expansion and prosperity. Against a background of conflict, larger and more stable political units were carved out, culminating in Mercia under Offa. This period saw the expansion of towns, long-distance trade, and diplomatic contacts on a scale lost since the Roman Empire, while royal and ecclesiastical patronage saw the growth of art, literature, and church building. It has seemed to some the ideal context for the composition of a great English poem, embodying recollections of times past yet not entirely forgotten, composed in an age when there were still great halls, jeweled swords and helmets, and folk memory or travelers' tales of pagan burials. Alternatively, it has been suggested that the "exciting picture" of kingship found in *Beowulf* was composed as compensation for the mundane reality of state formation in the eighth century (Bassett 1989a, 4). This persuasive scenario may have prevented even a search for alternative contexts. Since archaeologists have tended to follow current consensus among literary scholars, a date later than the eighth century has not seemed a serious proposition until recently.

The ninth or tenth centuries are not impossible in archaeological terms. At first, *Beowulf* seems alien to what we know of later Anglo-Saxon England. Ring swords, pattern-welded swords, boar-crested helmets, lavish burials in ships or as cremations, and royal halls of timber would by then be memories from the past. By King Alfred's time, bands of warriors traveling with heroic war leaders were found only among enemies: the English had an organized army. But much of this description does of course fit the Vikings, in England as well as in Scandinavia. Vikings did still bury dead rulers in ships or cremate them on funeral pyres, with weapons ornamented with fantastic beasts. Their kings feasted in great timber halls and heard stories and poems of their own and their ancestors' heroic deeds. They did all of this in the parts of Britain they conquered, as much as at home.

The capacity for the Vikings to become assimilated into Anglo-Saxon society is witnessed archaeologically by the way a mixed Anglo-Scandinavian culture flourished in the Danelaw (J. Richards 1991) and by their conversion to Christianity. The sculptured stone crosses from northern England (Bailey 1980) provide a vivid illustration of the ways in which the two cultures met. The Christian, Anglo-Saxon stone cross was taken up as a medium for Viking art. It is still Christian, but on it are Viking beasts and mythology, somehow integrated into the Christian message. The cultural processes that allowed Odin to appear on Christian crosses could also underlie the creation of an Old English epic poem from Danish traditions.

In conclusion, I think the archaeological evidence is at least partly compatible with a later date of composition for *Beowulf* than that usually suggested by reference to Sutton Hoo. It also provides a richer understanding of the various societies among which both the original stories and their later literary elaboration were produced and allows a better assessment of the importance of early medieval Denmark.

Chapter 16

Gender Roles

by Alexandra Hennessey Olsen

Summary: Scholarly approaches to the depiction of women in *Beowulf* have changed substantially over the years. Until about 1970, most Anglo-Saxonists assumed that, since men were responsible for public functions like king, warrior, and avenger, and since women held roles viewed as purely private such as hostesses, peaceweavers, and ritual mourners, women were passive in the social world depicted in *Beowulf*. Anglo-Saxonists also assumed that women were therefore marginalized by the poet. After 1970, women in the poem and in Anglo-Saxon society have more often been viewed as active and powerful figures who function on a nearly equal footing with men. Among the several women of the poem, Grendel's mother, Wealhtheow, and Hygd have attracted the most critical attention.

Chronology

1895: Richard Burton argues that Wealhtheow, Hygd, Hildeburh, and Freawaru represent the ideal woman as a dignified queen and peaceweaver and that Thryth is the negative of the ideal.

1909: Grace Fleming von Sweringen believes that *Beowulf* is a poem without genuine women characters and that Wealhtheow and the other women do not play an active role in the story except as characters of passion, imagination, and courage.

1936: J. R. R. Tolkien argues that the poem has two major structural divisions, youth and age. He treats Grendel's mother as secondary to her son.

1938: Henry Bosley Woolf makes an onomastic study of the significance of alliteration in the names of fathers and daughters, arguing that Freawaru was a nickname for Hrothgar's daughter Hrut.

1940: Kemp Malone suggests that the name Freawaru evokes mythical characters and was invented by the *Beowulf* poet to give the Ingeld episode a legendary character.

1941: Malone suggests that the contrasting characterizations of Hygd and Thryth were inspired by the meanings of their names, "Thought" and "Power."

1949: Adrien Bonjour argues that the fight with Grendel's mother is critical to the organic unity of *Beowulf* because it suggests the possibility that the hero may be defeated.

1963: Robert E. Kaske suggests that Hygd's name (Thought) reflects her role in *Beowulf* and was created by wordplay on the name of Hygelac (Lack of Thought).

1967: Tauno F. Mustanoja studies the funeral lament sung for Beowulf by a nameless woman in the context of ritual lamentation for the dead practiced worldwide.

1970: L. John Sklute examines the role of Wealhtheow as a peaceweaver and argues that the term has diplomatic connotations.

1971: Janet T. Buck argues that male bonding excludes women from decision making. She maintains that in societies that practice exogamy, peaceweavers often become "foreign-captive[s]."

1974: Elizabeth Judd argues that Anglo-Saxon women were both independent and influential.

1976: Elaine Tuttle Hansen emphasizes two aspects of the historical Germanic woman, her inferior status vis-à-vis a man and her greater share of suffering.

1977: Bernice C. Kliman asserts that women in *Beowulf* are inferior to men because of their lack of physical strength in a society devoted to war but that they achieve status as wives, mothers, and peaceweavers.

1979: Sheila C. Dietrich reexamines primary sources and suggests that historical Anglo-Saxon women possessed considerable rights and privileges, discussing women in *Beowulf* as peaceweavers.

1979: Audrey L. Meaney analyzes the word "ides" (lady) in *Beowulf* and argues that the word is used of high-born women, especially "the exemplary queens Wealhtheow and Hygd."

1980: Jane Chance (Nitzsche) discusses the structural unity of *Beowulf* focusing on Grendel's mother, whom she considers an antitype of the feminine ideal of woman as cup passer and peace weaver.

1981: Gale R. Owen studies archaeological, historical, and literary evidence to develop a picture of religion and ritual in Anglo-Saxon England in both pagan and Christian times. The evidence sheds light on the women of *Beowulf,* Wealhtheow, Hildeburh, and the mourner at Beowulf's funeral.

1983: James W. Earl sees Grendel's mother as a symbol of the threat that women and kinship ties pose to male warrior society.

1983: Jane-Marie Luecke uses modern anthropology to suggest that *Beowulf* reflects an early Germanic matrilocal or matrician culture rather than the patriarchal society in which it was composed.

1983: John D. Niles argues that *Beowulf* displays evidence of ring composition and that the battle with Grendel's mother is the center of the poem.

1983: Richard J. Schrader in "God's Handiwork" examines the principal women of *Beowulf* and argues that their roles are derived from those of Eve and Mary.

1984: Stephen C. B. Atkinson studies the monsters of *Beowulf* as reversals of the roles expected to be played by thane, avenger, and king and discusses the "precariousness of . . . peacemaking" in the poem.

1984: Helen Damico studies the Scandinavian tradition of the battle maiden and interprets Wealhtheow as an active figure.

1984: Kevin S. Kiernan discusses the actions of Grendel's mother in terms of Germanic feud structure.

1984: Alexandra Hennessey Olsen discusses the women of *Beowulf,* arguing against interpretations of them as passive.

1985: Eugene Green suggests that naming patterns in *Beowulf* exclude women and argues that royal women who marry men other than kings remain anonymous.

1985: Michael Murphy points out that women in Germanic literature played the role of goaders who spurred men into action and suggests that this role underlies the scene between Wealhtheow and Beowulf.

1986: Jane Chance discusses the social role of women as peaceweavers in Anglo-Saxon society and identifies two literary types, Mary (who underlies the conventional queens) and Eve (who underlies Grendel's mother and Thryth).

1986: Setsuko Haruta reviews the women in *Beowulf* as passive sufferers and peaceweavers, concluding that they help enhance the poem's worldview by depicting the side of society that complements the warriors.

1986: Judith Weise reiterates Kaske's point that the name of Hygd provides contrast to that of Hygelac and relates it to "the Christian tradition of onomastics."

1988: Michael J. Enright examines the relationship of Wealhtheow and Hygd to king and *comitatus* to conclude that the queen helps establish rank and succession.

1990: Joyce Hill reexamines the stereotype of the "geomoru ides" (mournful lady) along with new historical evidence to show how the stereotype works with women like Hildeburh.

1990: Gillian Overing examines Wealhtheow, Hildeburh, and Thryth, arguing that women have no place in the masculine, death-centered world of *Beowulf.*

1992: Helen Bennett suggests that the mourner at Beowulf's funeral has been created by emendation of the manuscript. The mourner has traditionally been interpreted as a "passive victim," but Bennett argues that analogues can help us visualize her as "strong and enduring."

Traditionally, the study of gender roles in *Beowulf* has been based on the assumption that, since men were responsible for public functions like king, warrior, and avenger, they also held the power in the world of the poem. Women, it was assumed, held more passive and private roles as hostesses, peaceweavers, and ritual mourners and were therefore marginalized by the poet. Critics of *Beowulf* have tended to minimize the importance of women in the poem because of the obvious importance of male heroism. This view is widespread. Setsuko Haruta, for example, says that "our attention is first attracted to the male characters in the poem since, in that masculine-oriented society, only men can assert themselves in dramatic moments, as warriors and decision-makers" (1986, 1). Janet T. Buck speaks of "the *Beowulf* poet's vision of a warrior-lord bond entered by men . . . and not by women" (1971, 47) and of the "attractively tragic and pathetic women" (51) of *Beowulf,* and Elaine Tuttle Hansen argues that the women provide "a poetic voice for all lonely and innocent victims of fate, and an apt symbol . . . of the weakness inherent in the human condition" (1976, 117). Several critics (Schrader 1983a and Chance 1986) have argued that the roles for women are archetypal and derive from traditional representations of Mary and Eve.

In recent years, the accuracy of such views has been challenged by both men and women, in a way that parallels similar revaluations in social history, anthropology, and the study of other Germanic literatures. Carol J. Clover argues that we misinterpret gender roles in Germanic society by viewing them in the light of beliefs developed in the late eighteenth century (1993, 377). She suggests that these roles should be viewed in terms of power and the lack thereof rather than in terms of biological sex. In all medieval studies, the view of "power as public authority" has discouraged the "investigation of women's actions in society as seemingly inconsequential" (Erler and Kowaleski 1988, 1). A more inclusive view of power in general and in *Beowulf* in particular helps us appreciate the actual social order presented by the poem.

Women are not excluded from the world of *Beowulf*. They play important roles that are public and active rather than merely private and passive. Three roles that have traditionally been identified are those of *hostess* (ceremonial cup passer and gift giver), *peaceweaver*, and *ritual mourner* (see, e.g., Schrader 1983a). Two others that have been discussed only recently are *goader* and *counselor*.[1] Those who accept the presence of these five roles for women in *Beowulf* acknowledge that the social order of Anglo-Saxon England included women in what Michael J. Enright calls "a significant if subordinate" position (1988, 171). Each of the roles is worth examining in turn.

The role of hostess has two aspects, cup passer and gift giver, and it has often been seen as passive and domestic, despite the fact that *Beowulf* depicts public roles and behavior and devotes no space to the domestic. At the first banquet, when Wealhtheow, Hrothgar's queen, says, "Onfoh þissum fulle" (Receive this cup, 1169a), she acts in a public rather than a private way insofar as she addresses Hrothgar before the court. She subsequently encourages all the men, not just her husband, to enjoy the feast. Enright observes that most scholars "have traditionally underrated the significance of the scene" (1988, 174) by ignoring its ritualistic significance. Sandra Gilbert and Susan Gubar have argued that *Beowulf* depicts women as "servants to men" (1985, 5), but the role of the cup passer is in fact an active one, more suggestive of a person who serves communion than a servant.

Enright reinterprets both the nature of the *comitatus* and the role of the cup passer. He questions the idealized portrait of the *comitatus* as a society of men happy because of the absence of women. James W. Earl, operating from Freudian assumptions, argues that *Beowulf*'s world is exclusively that of the *comitatus*, represented by the hall and its masculine warrior values, and that women represent a threat "to the civilizing work of men" (1983, 153). By asking us to view the *comitatus* in a new way, Enright is calling for a fresh understanding of female and male gender roles and by implication criticizes Earl's contrast of the masculine hall and the feminine hut. He asks us to reconceptualize the social and cultural implications of the Anglo-Saxon division of humanity into male and female, a different matter from considering the biological determinants we term *sex*. His examination of the queens in Germanic history as well as in *Beowulf* leads him to conclude that women indeed played a significant role in preserving social order: "The queen's activities within the group are too thoroughly integrated, too nicely interwoven, to consider her any longer as an attending but essentially extraneous figure . . . Although she does not fight, . . . her ritual and ministrations would seem to be too closely tied to the maintenance and thus existence of the group to view her as a total outsider and too functional during successions to describe her as really extraneous. The mortar that cements the bricks must be regarded as part of the building" (1988, 202). Enright's study reinforces a point made separately by Helen Damico and Gale R. Owen, that women play an integral role in what Owen terms "the most significant communal rituals" of society (1981, 175).

A hostess also gives gifts. Enright calls gift giving one of the "essential gestures of the society" (1988, 174), and John M. Hill analyzes gifts and accompanying speech making in detail, pointing out that "gift giving establishes an important reciprocity" and plays an especially important part in "dynastic succession" (1982, 177). At the second banquet in Heorot, Wealhtheow gives Beowulf "healsbeaga mæst" (the greatest of neck-rings, 1195b). Likewise, Hygd "ne to gneað gifa / [wæs] Geata leodum // maðmgestreona" (was not too niggardly of gifts of precious treasures to the Geats, 1930–31a). In a thoughtful piece informed by recent historical research, Joyce Hill (1990) analyzes filiations between historical and literary women in order to place Hrothgar's daughter Freawaru, for example, in the setting of a period in which marriages were arranged to form alliances. She also shows that both Wealhtheow and Hygd, queen of the Geats, "participate in the public ceremonies of gift-exchange which are so bound up, in heroic poetry as in early medieval history, with loyalty, status, and honour" (1990, 237). She deals with the public roles that women may play. Her analysis has more depth and persuasive power than analyses based solely on the poetry, and gift giving is one of the public roles played by women and men alike. Her analysis leads to emphasis on the poet's power to employ stereotypes for particular thematic ends: "To acknowledge the force of the stereotype is not, however, to conclude that for women the patterns of heroic poetry are necessarily reductive. . . . If the processes which transform history into legend tend to marginalize the women of the heroic world, judged from the viewpoint of 'story,' the sophistication of certain Anglo-Saxon poets' responses to that legendary material give women a position of ethical and imaginative importance" (1990, 244). Enright, John Hill, and Joyce Hill ask us to understand the society in which *Beowulf* was composed and view woman's role as hostess within that society rather than extrapolating from the role of hostess in the modern world.

The second important role of women in Anglo-Saxon society is that of the *freoðuwebbe* (peaceweaver). It has been argued that the word may be viewed as describing "the primary, if not the only, designated female role" in *Beowulf* (Overing 1990, xxiv). In 1895, Richard Burton suggested that the word *freoðuwebbe* refers "to the frequent part played by woman when given in marriage between hostile tribes" (6). Jane Chance concurs: "The Anglo-Saxon social ideal of the aristocratic woman . . . depended upon her role as a peacemaking queen, which was achieved fundamentally through her function as a mother" (1986, 1). This idea appears often in Anglo-Saxon studies. In a study of Branwen in the second branch of the *Mabinogion,* Andrew Welsh assumes its validity. He says, "The role of the Germanic peaceweaver is twofold: to create by her marriage peaceful bonds between two previously or potentially hostile kin-groups, or tribes, and after her marriage to encourage and support peaceful and harmonious relations among the members of the kin-group, especially the comitatus, that she has joined" (1991, 7). The role of the peaceweaver has usually been viewed as passive and ineffective (see Chance 1986, 7). Schrader (1983a) notes that the peace that women ensure by their attention to communal rituals is a fragile one. Generalizing from the characters in the poem to the position of women in Anglo-Saxon society, Chance interprets Wealhtheow, Freawaru, and the Danish princess/Frisian queen Hildeburh as failed peaceweavers who "convey dialectically the idea that woman cannot ensure peace in the world" (1986, 106).

The use of the term *peaceweaver* requires caution, however. It is the concept of peaceweaving rather than the word *freoðuwebbe* itself that is important in *Beowulf,* because the word is used only three times in Old English poetry. In *Beowulf,* the term is used of Offa's queen, Thryth (1942a), and not of the women who are presented positively, although an analogous term, *friðusibb* (peace-pledge, 2017a), is used of Wealhtheow. Audrey L. Meaney relates the term *freoðuwebbe* to the word *ides,* which "appears . . . to mean 'noble woman, lady'" (1979, 159–60) and seems to connote "woman in her sacral and mysterious aspect" (158)—that is, in her powerful aspect. In *Elene,* as L. John Sklute points out, the word *freoðuwebbe* is used of an angel, who does not match the stereotypical picture of woman as peaceweaver. Sklute's article is important because it suggests that *freoðuwebbe* "is a poetic metaphor referring to the person whose function it seems to be to perform openly the action of making peace by weaving to the best of her art a tapestry of friendship and amnesty" (1970, 208). He goes on to say that if the word "reflects anything of the social system of the Anglo-Saxons, it is that of the diplomat" (208). He thus revisions the role of the *freoðuwebbe* as more public and more active than it has traditionally been viewed.

It is helpful to consider the role of the peaceweaver in its historical rather than its merely literary setting. Part of this role involves the giving of the peaceweaver in marriage outside her tribe, through the custom of exogamy. Critics who view exogamy negatively would agree with Buck that when it was practiced, a peaceweaver often became a "foreign-captive" (1971, 48). Exogamy may, however, be viewed more positively, because it "begins with the incest taboo of very early peoples, and then seems to continue as a political maneuver for furthering the alliance between hostile groups" (Luecke 1983, 195). In *Beowulf,* both Hildeburh and Freawaru and, possibly, Wealhtheow exemplify this custom. One digression concerns Freawaru, who is married to the Heathobard king Ingeld in order to bring peace. Beowulf himself points out the limitations of this custom: "Oft seldan hwær // æfter leodhryre / lytle hwile // bongar bugeð, / þeah seo bryd duge!" (As a rule, the deadly spear rests only a little while after the fall of a prince, although the bride is good, 2029b–31b). Frederic Seebohm points out that there was "no blood relationship between husband and wife" (1911, 498), a fact that sheds light on the Finn digression and the role of Hildeburh. This digression tells the story of a two-stage battle between the Frisian king, Finn, and his Danish brothers-in-law, Hnæf and Hengest. As a result of this combat, Hildeburh loses her son, her brother, and her husband, and she is returned to her homeland. She has failed as a peaceweaver. The traditional picture of the peaceweaver leads to a tendency to view Hildeburh (and Anglo-Saxon women in general) as victims. Martin Camargo, for example, calls Hildeburh "tragic," "destitute," and "helpless" (1981, 126), and Chance speaks of her as "torn between the pulls of two tribes" (1986, 10). Although her marriage may have been intended to weave peace between the Danes and the Frisians, when peace fails, her loyalty lies with her "bearnum ond broðrum" (sons and brothers, 1074a) rather than with her husband. Anglo-Saxonists tend to forget that given the nature of a feud society, Hildeburh would be obligated to avenge her brother Hnæf. From a Danish perspective, the slaying of her husband Finn could be considered as a kind of triumph, but the poet emphasizes only the deed, not Hildeburh's view of it.

The third women's role is that of the ritual mourner, summed up by the phrase "geomuru ides" (mournful lady, 1075b), which the poet applies to Hildeburh on the occasion of the funeral of her son and brother. Tauno F. Mustanoja studies the occasion of Beowulf's death, when a "meowle" (maiden, 3150b) sings "sorgcearig" (sorrowful, 3152a). He links this mourning woman to an international tradition of ritual mourning, "an essential traditional feature in the funeral ceremony" (1967, 27). Bennett, however, objects that "the passage in *Beowulf* dealing with the female mourner . . . does not actually exist" (1992, 35); the existence of the mourner is problematic because "almost all that is legible in this page [has been] freshened up in a late hand" (Julius Zupitza, quoted in Klaeber 1950a, 118). The scholarly acceptance of the traditional text reinforces the idea that women are passive because, as Bennett notes, traditional interpretations have viewed the mourner as "another example of the passive female victim in Old English poetry" (1992, 35). Analogues, however, "can produce a quite opposite picture of the female mourner as strong and enduring" (35).

The role of mourner overlaps with a fourth role, the woman as goader (see Murphy 1985). The presence of a female mourner in *Beowulf* need not be denied, but her role needs to be rethought. Mourning may not be as passive an experience as it is in contemporary American society. Reinterpreting female characters in *Beowulf* who have traditionally been viewed as passive brings the poem into line with Barrie Ruth Strauss's interpretation of *The Wife's Lament,* in which "women act by using words as weapons" (1981, 281). Assuming that *Beowulf* does not reflect an exclusively Christian ethos, it would follow that Hildeburh's mourning is a form of *hvǫt* ("whetting," an Old Norse noun cognate with the Old English verb *hwettan,* "to incite") that has the function of inciting Hengest to take revenge. The image of the woman who incites the men to action has been much studied in Old Norse but far less in Old English. Although Old Norse evidence has sometimes been misapplied, cautiously used, it can provide a helpful analogy to Old English. Clover cites a passage from *Hárvarðar saga* to the effect that "it is manly for those unfit for vigorous deeds to be unsparing in their use of the tongue in saying things that may avail" (1986, 144–45). She goes on to say that "in the feud situation, women's (and old men's) words are *the equivalent of* men's deeds; it is as incumbent on a woman to urge vengeance as it is incumbent on a man to take it" (145; emphasis added). Michael Murphy (1985) suggests that the role of the goader informs the scene between Wealhtheow and Beowulf in Heorot. In his view, her speech is active and public, not merely ornamental.

The fifth role, that of the counselor, has often been overlooked by critics who view the peaceweaver as passive. Damico presents the picture of the peaceweaver as gold adorned and wise in speech, a picture seconded by Enright (1988, 175). In Damico's view, a woman's advice is important—and heeded. In a related argument, Owen mentions historical Anglo-Saxon queens who counseled their husbands (1981, 61). When Wealhtheow appears, she is "wisfæst wordum" (wise in her words, 626a) and gives counsel, advising Hrothgar, "Bruc þenden þu mote // manigra medo, / ond þinum magum læf // folc ond rice, / þonne ðu forð scyle" (Enjoy many rewards as long as you can, and leave the people and kingdom to your sons when you must go forth, 1177b–79b). When we perceive the importance of the counselor's act and the importance of speech in Anglo-Saxon society, we get a balanced appreciation of Wealhtheow's active role in the poem.

When we turn from the general roles of women in the poem to the depiction of particular women, *Beowulf* scholarship is similarly uneven. The one female in *Beowulf* whom one might think no reader could ignore is Grendel's mother. Many scholars, however, do. J. R. R. Tolkien sets the pattern by making the poem bipartite and subsuming the fight against Grendel's mother under that against Grendel. In appendix A, he says (in a parenthetical remark) that "Grendel's mother is naturally described, when separately treated, in precisely similar terms" to those describing Grendel (1936, 44). By overlooking the significance of Grendel's mother as an independent figure, Tolkien established a fashion of misreading *Beowulf* that has been hard to escape. Part of the misreading is influenced by translations. "Grendles modor" (Grendel's mother, 1282a) is often translated as "Grendel's *dam.*" This translation enables the critic to ignore her humanity and her womanness by equating her with animals, just as the monstrous nature of Grendel rather than his humanity has often been stressed. By implication, this stance devalues all the women of the poem. Other critics view *Beowulf* as basically tripartite and the fight with Grendel's mother as important (see Sisam 1965; Bonjour 1949; and Rogers 1955). John D. Niles (1983), for example, argues that *Beowulf* displays evidence of ring composition and that the battle with Grendel's mother is the center of the poem. Chance makes an analogous point, viewing the episode as "medial and transitional" (1986, 108) and crucial to understanding the role of women in the poem.

Chance reviews studies of Grendel's mother that preceded the publication of her "Structural Unity of *Beowulf*" in 1980. She points out that "early *Beowulf* studies . . . ignored Grendel's mother or treated her as a type of Grendel" and that "recent interpretations have stressed her significance in Germanic social terms, but without developing the implications of such insights" (1980, 390). Since 1980, two scholars have studied Grendel's mother in Germanic social terms. In his study of the psychological development of Anglo-Saxon society, Earl (1983) argues that Grendel's mother as an avenger poses a threat to civilizing warrior values. Kevin S. Kiernan suggests that Grendel's mother's revenge taking resembles that of heroes but that "because she is a monster, . . . her case turns out to be an indictment of the kind of heroism she represents" (1984, 194). Mary Kay Temple analyzes Grendel's mother from another angle, pointing out that the word *ides* is not always positive but is associated with Eve and the wives of Cain. Grendel's mother is a "caricature of the cup-bearing hostess" (1986, 14). The most thorough literary study of Grendel's mother remains that of Chance, who suggests that Grendel's mother is not a caricature but an "antitype . . . of the peace-weaving queen" (1986, 106) exemplified by Wealhtheow.

Wealhtheow has generally attracted more attention than Grendel's mother in the critical literature. Many scholars study Wealhtheow as a passive, tragic, and sorrowing queen. George Clark, for example, speaks of "the nearly distraught urgency of Wealhtheow's appeal to Beowulf for his favor for her sons" (1990, 89). In contrast, Kenneth Sisam asserts that the scene of "national rejoicing" (1965, 39) makes it unlikely that Wealhtheow is sorrowful and resembles Hildeburh, and Damico argues that "the queen's status in the narrative, her association with the other female figures in Germanic heroic tradition, and her proposed legendary identity, preclude a tragic dimension" (1984, 20). Certainly, the poet says nothing about her place in an impending tragedy. Wealhtheow is not passive; she is a peaceweaver in respect to her sons but goads Beowulf to kill Grendel: "Gode þancode // wisfæst wordum / þæs ðe hire se willa gelamp, // þæt heo on ænigne eorl gelyfde / fyrena frofre" (wise in words, she thanked God that her will had come to pass, that she could count on any man for help for wicked deeds, 625b–28a). Her speech throughout the banquet scenes seems urgent but not distraught as she incites Beowulf to slay the son who is in a way the rival of her own sons for control of Heorot.

Many scholars have been more concerned with Wealhtheow's name than with her role in the poem. Such arguments tend to treat a character less as a realistic representation of a woman than as a figure of symbolic interest to the poet. The various interpretations of Wealhtheow's name imply the various critics' views of the roles of women in *Beowulf*. The traditional etymology of her name is "foreign captive" (see Klaeber 1950a, 440) or "foreign slave" (see Björkman 1919). Although this etymology may be valid,[2] scholarly reliance on it devalues the woman of highest social station in *Beowulf* and implies that women in the poem are merely servants in a patriarchal society. In 1935, Eric V. Gordon argued that *wealh* does not mean "foreign"; rather, *Wealhtheow* is cognate with Old Norse *Valþjófr* and means chosen servant, that is, "'servant' of a god" (171). Damico argues that there is "an etymological connection between *Wealhþeow* and the name of the valkyries" (1984, 66). By attributing to Wealhtheow such status, Gordon and Damico suggest that the *Beowulf* poet viewed the position of women as powerful. Their point can be compared to Meaney's attribution of semidivine status to the *ides* (1979, 158–59).

Scholarship on Hildeburh is dominated by discussion of her as the image of the "geomuru ides" (mournful lady, 1075b), an image that Joyce Hill (1990) has reexamined. In particular, some critics view Hildeburh as passive *because* she mourns—"Ides gnornode, // geomrode giddum" (the lady lamented, mourned with songs, 1117b–18a)—and Chance believes that she mourns in part her own failure as a peaceweaver (see Chance 1986, 100). In contrast to scholars like Enright who view women as playing an important role in the hierarchical Anglo-Saxon society, Overing argues that Hildeburh, like the classical Helen, is "the designated female focal point of a masculine system of exchange" (1990, 81). She embraces the critical idea that Hildeburh and the female mourner are passive lamenters (82). Bennett's study (1922) disputes the grounds on which such interpretations are made by arguing that mourning is an active role.

Like studies of Wealhtheow, studies of Hygd, Freawaru, and Thryth have often concentrated on onomastics. *Hygd*, for example, definitely means "Thought." Robert E. Kaske (1963) therefore argues that her role in the poem is to provide a contrast to her husband, a point reiterated by Judith Weise (1986). Kaske speculates that *Hygelac* must mean "Lack of Thought," citing an unattested Old English form *læc* and ignoring names like *Guthlac*, or "War-play," that suggests that *Hygelac* may mean "Mind-play" (1963, 204). In contrast, Chance views her as contributing to the literary effect of the poem because Wealhtheow and Hygd are "the two major queens of *Beowulf*" (1986, 111) and are important in the two halves of the poem. The name *Freawaru* provides a scholarly problem because "it departs from the alliterative pattern otherwise characteristic of the name-giving of this dynasty" (Malone 1940, 39). Henry Bosley Woolf suggests that it is "a complimentary title used by the English poet instead of Hrut, the true name of Hrothgar's daughter" (1938, 115). Kemp Malone seconds his point, theorizing that, since Ingeld's wife Hrut in Saxo Grammaticus plays "an active (and villainous) part" (1940, 43), the *Beowulf* poet deliberately omitted her name. Saxo wrote in the thirteenth century, two centuries after even Kiernan's date of 1026 for *Beowulf* (see Kiernan 1981a), and his legendary history does not seem likely to shed light on the earlier text. Chance studies the literary position of Freawaru: "In this second part of the adventure of Grendel's Mother, Hygd and Freawaru as queens or cup-passers contrast with the *wif* just as Hildeburh and Wealhtheow as mothers were contrasted with Grendel's dam in the first part" (1986, 105). As for Offa's queen, there are many arguments about whether her name is properly *Thryth, Thrytho, Modthryth,* or *Modhrytho.* The name is used only once; the manuscript reads "mod þryðo wæg," and it is unclear how the line should be interpreted. Friedrich Klaeber interprets the name as "Modthrytho" (1931b), while Malone opts for "Thrytho" (Malone 1941b, 356); the former name would mean "Mind-Power" and the latter "Power." Critics usually contrast the woman to Hygd; Malone, for example, contrasts "the moderate, reasonable, reflective Hygd" with "the reckless, impulsive, cruel Thrytho" (Malone 1941b, 357). Working from a Lacanian perspective, Overing interprets the passage that says that Offa's queen executes each man "þæt hire an dæges / eagum starede" (that stared at her with his eyes by day, 1935) in psychological terms, arguing that she "rejects objectification . . . by refusing to be held in the masculine 'gaze'" (1990, 104).

Some critics use the nameless women of *Beowulf* to prove the validity of critical arguments. An example is Eugene Green's 1985 article, which equates power with having a name (an even narrower view than equating power with public authority) and women's lack of power with their anonymity. Readers who remember the many nameless men of *Beowulf,* including the coastguard, the messenger, and the nameless thief, thane of a nameless chieftain, are not likely, however, to overgeneralize about the namelessness of women. Critics who provide a name, *Yrse,* for Healfdene's nameless daughter follow Malone (1929), who uses late Old Norse sources (*Hrólfs saga kraka* is fifteenth century) to provide the name, pointing out that Yrse was Healfdene's daughter-in-law rather than daughter. With the exception of the ritual mourner if she really exists, the nameless women neither act nor speak in the poem, but arguments about the position of all women based on these minor figures are untenable. Many nameless people of both sexes play secondary roles in the poem.

Research by social historians has produced subtle work on Anglo-Saxon women that suggests that their social position (as shown by laws, charters, and wills) was comparatively strong. Mary P. Richards and B. Jane Stanfield point out that what "Old English laws tell us about the lives and legal status of women in

Anglo-Saxon England . . . depends upon the way in which these curious, quasi-historical materials are analyzed" (1990, 89). They maintain that "from the laws we receive hints about the kinds of situations involving women conveyed elsewhere in Old English literature" (1990, 97). Arlene Walsh suggests that the poetry reinforces the view of historians that "Anglo-Saxon women were esteemed, honoured, and revered" (1991, 6). Sheila C. Dietrich observes that we must study primary sources in a fresh light in order to understand historical women: "The disparity of modern treatments underscores the necessity of going directly to the primary sources. In some cases this involves stripping away the accretions of another writer's bias or orientation, and asking new questions of very old records. In other cases it involves merely supplementing or complementing the partial picture already obtained" (1979, 33). The most comprehensive social history of Anglo-Saxon women (Fell 1984) surveys both historical and fictional sources. Fell's research leads her to a conclusion that is useful for *Beowulf* studies as well: "Scholarship does not require us to read only, always and inevitably a history of oppression and exploitation of the female sex. The real evidence from Anglo-Saxon England presents a more attractive and indeed assertive picture" (1984, 21). Such a conclusion lends support to scholars like Enright, John Hill (1982), and Joyce Hill (1990), who argue that the women in *Beowulf* play an important (albeit secondary) role.[3]

Recent research in Old Norse (see Clover 1993) has clarified gender roles in early Germanic societies. It is reasonable to suppose that the Anglo-Saxons conceived of gender in terms similar to those of the Icelanders. Scholars who, influenced by modern ideas about gender, view women in Anglo-Saxon England as passive cannot fit Grendel's mother into their paradigm, because as an avenger, she acts. Stephen C. B. Atkinson argues that Grendel's mother plays an important *masculine* role by acting as an avenger (1984, 61–62). Grendel's mother is best understood in terms of the asexual model for gender, and it is intriguing that Grendel's mother actually performs the actions that the goader only inspires. In the Old Norse context, it is clear from portraits like Aud in *Laxdœla saga*, Hervor in *The Waking of Angantyr*, and Guthrun in *Atlaqviða* that women are expected to act in the absence of male relatives (see Olsen 1984, 153–54; and Clover 1993, 371–72), so that when necessary the role of avenger is played by women as well as men. A more extreme example is Signy from *Vǫlsunga saga,* who, in order to gain vengeance on her husband, sacrifices four of her five sons and lies with her brother in order to bear a full-blooded Volsung son as avenger. Grendel's mother as "wrecend" (avenger, 1256b) is not playing a purely masculine role.

A promising approach to *Beowulf* involves the use of speech act theory to analyze the poem from an angle hitherto little utilized.[4] Speech act theory has limitations as a tool of literary criticism, especially when applied to premodern texts like *Beowulf.* It is still valuable, however, because "the older heroic societies valued acts of speech" (Strauss 1981, 280), and it helps us appreciate that speech can be a form of heroic action. T. A. Shippey argues that speech act theory has an "analytical approach" that "bring[s] out some distinctive qualities in the speech of Old English characters" (1993a, 110). Manuel José Gómez Lara agrees, suggesting that speech act theory "can provide the critic and the student of Anglo-Saxon literature with a different apparatus to focus on certain traditional cruxes" (1988, 269). The analytic approach of speech act theory may help us achieve an accurate picture of gender roles in *Beowulf*. In 1981, Barrie Ruth Strauss noted that "speech itself is action, belying its own apparent passivity" (269), and this approach helps us perceive the speakers of *Beowulf*, including the women, as active and powerful. However, speech acts are difficult to interpret; for example, Overing observes that "analyzing the truth value of representatives is to some degree another way of talking about irony" (1990, 98).[5] Our understanding of whether speech acts are ironic depends on our critical preconceptions.

Speech acts have been defined as "goal-directed actions" (Traugott and Pratt 1980, 10), and when we consider them in that light, even the role of hostess appears as a public and influential one. Both when she exercises her diplomatic function and at other times, the peaceweaver uses speech acts of the class of directives, which are "designed to get the addressee to do something" (Traugott and Pratt 1980, 229). During the second banquet, Wealhtheow acts as more than a hostess when she reminds Hrothulf of the debt that he owes her and Hrothgar. This speech has often been viewed as the utterance of a desperate woman trying to protect her sons. We should view it as a perlocutionary act: that is, Wealhtheow is persuading Hrothulf to act ethically. As a powerful speech intended to influence masculine action, its emotional tone is not desperate.

Just as the role of avenger is not dependent on gender, male and female speech acts are often remarkably similar. Hrothgar has frequently been denigrated as passive (see Cramer 1977, 40) just as women have been; Edward B. Irving Jr. calls him "both impotent and honorable, incompetent and magnificent" (1989, 37). Like those of the women, however, his speech acts are active. Hrothgar laments after Æschere's death, for example, but his lamentation serves to goad Beowulf to avenge Æschere. His lamentation, resembling that ascribed to the ritual mourner at Beowulf's funeral, contradicts the assumption of some scholars that only women in *Beowulf* are the passive victims of fate. After the dragon destroys the Geats' dwellings, Beowulf also laments. A third lamenting man is Hrethel, who cannot avenge a son killed by his own brother. Hrothgar, Beowulf, and Hrethel have all been heroic figures who are now old. Irving notes that "in any tradition-directed oral society, old people must be accorded the highest respect" because "age is power" (1989, 47). The power is different from that of a young hero but is like that of a woman. Clover cites evidence that "link[s] the condition of old men with femaleness" (1993, 383), and the laments of Hrothgar and Hrethel resemble those of Egill Skalla-Grimsson after the death of his son. Haruta argues that "after the hero is dead, . . . the only role left for a woman is to mourn his death" (1986, 15), and under the right circumstances this is the only role available to a man.

In general, the men in *Beowulf* both act and speak, while the women use speech acts that influence male action, but these gender roles can overlap and dovetail. There are women who play a normally male role and men who play a normally female role. As Mary Erler and Maryanne Kowaleski have argued, while it is important for critics not to "deny the powerful advantages or greater prestige enjoyed by men in the Middle Ages," it is equally essential for them to recognize "how and when women wielded power" (1988, 10). The conclusion reached by Erler and Kowaleski is that studying women and power will force scholars "to rethink such issues as . . . the centrality of public authority and military might in history writing" (10). An appreciation of gender roles in *Beowulf,* likewise, will force us to reassess the role of heroism in this seemingly most heroic of poems.

Notes

1. Not all women's roles depicted in the poem are positive, of course. Two women, Grendel's mother and Offa's queen, represent the negation of the ideal woman. Grendel's mother inverts hospitality and adopts the usually masculine role of *avenger* (see Chance 1986, 101–06). Thryth could be called a *negative peaceweaver* who has men killed and who does not work for what Enright (1988) calls "cohesion and unity of purpose" until after her marriage.

2. In 1990, Thomas D. Hill cited Frankish evidence of kings who married slaves and argued that Wealhtheow does indeed mean "foreign slave."

3. John Hill analyzes the gift giving in *Beowulf* and suggests that it shows "something of the likely scope actual Anglo-Saxon gift giving had in aristocratic contexts" (1982, 193). His literary analysis helps us understand the role of historical Anglo-Saxon women.

4. Speech act theory was developed in the 1960s by J. L. Austin and other British language philosophers. Elizabeth Closs Traugott and Mary Louise Pratt provide a "working classification" (1980, 229) of speech acts, dividing illocutionary acts (or "attempt[s] to accomplish some communicative purpose" [229]) into six categories, namely representatives, expressives, verdictives, directives, commissives, and declarations. Another form of speech act is a perlocutionary act, aimed at "achieving certain intended effects in . . . [the] hearer in addition to those achieved by the illocutionary act" (1980, 81).

5. Representatives are "illocutionary acts that undertake to represent a state of affairs" (Traugott and Pratt 1980, 229).

Chapter 17

Beowulf and Contemporary Critical Theory

by Seth Lerer

Summary: Since the early 1980s, approaches drawn from deconstruction, semiotics, cultural studies, and psychoanalysis have sought to relocate *Beowulf* in the shifting canons of contemporary academic debate. This chapter offers a review of these approaches, while locating their polemics in the traditions of Old English criticism established in Tolkien's classic *"Beowulf*: The Monsters and the Critics." There is a rhetoric of salvation that controls criticism on the poem, and this chapter illustrates the ways in which recent writers have invoked literary theory to rescue *Beowulf* from traditional Anglo-Saxon scholarship and to secure its place in the modern curriculum.

Chronology

1936: J. R. R. Tolkien seeks to rescue *Beowulf* from archaeological and philological study by defining its aesthetic qualities and its moral voice.

1983: James W. Earl constructs a Freudian psychoanalytic anthropology to define the ritual space of the hall in *Beowulf* and in Anglo-Saxon society in general.

1985: Jonathan D. Evans uses semiotic theory to define the "codes" that underlie medieval dragon tales and to argue that Beowulf's fight with the dragon deploys these codes to critique the heroic ethic.

1986: Martin Irvine seeks to recover a theory of signification in the cultural practices of Anglo-Saxon grammatical education and vernacular poetics.

1987: Linda Georgianna analyzes Beowulf's last speech to posit the poet's "modern or postmodern taste for subversive elements in narratives."

1989: John P. Hermann draws on the work of Derrida, Lacan, and Paul de Man to associate the violence of spiritual warfare with the violence of writing in Old English religious poetry.

1989: John M. Hill draws on psychoanalytic theory to define the poem's heroic world as caught in tensions between the Oedipal and the pre-Oedipal stages of development.

1989: Rosemary Huisman relies on M. A. K. Halliday's social-semiotic language theory to understand the development of Beowulf's three versions of his fight with Grendel's mother.

1990: Gillian Overing draws together deconstruction, semiotics, and feminist psycho-analysis to understand the poem's representations of manhood, its figurations of women's power, and its methods of social and linguistic signification.

1990: Allen J. Frantzen draws on modern cultural studies to critique the traditions of Old English scholarship, criticism, teaching, and editing (chapter 6 is on *Beowulf*).

1991: James W. Earl posits a poem constructed, through its act of reading and interpretation, out of the psyches of the poem's heroic male and its Oedipalized reader.

1991: Seth Lerer draws on Derrida's critique of writing and orality to analyze the representations of reading in Anglo-Saxon literature and to define a literate culture for the period (chapter 5 is on *Beowulf*).

1993: Michael Near seeks to define the nature of the poem's literary allegory (after the fashion of Paul de Man) by showing how the inscribed sword hilt that Beowulf recovers from Grendel's mere presents, to the poem's audience, "a world in transition" from orality to literacy.

1994: James W. Earl brings together his earlier psychoanalytic studies into a book about the nature of the epic in both traditional and modern cultures.

1994: Seth Lerer uses modern theories of the cultural display and dismemberment of the body, together with anthropological researches into human sacrifice, to find the workings of corporeal allegory and a theory of representation in Beowulf's account of Grendel's glove and its Scandinavian analogues.

At first glance, a contribution to *A Beowulf Handbook* titled *"Beowulf and Contemporary Critical Theory"* should pose little problem for its writer or its reader. Like other, pedagogically minded reviews of historical and modern opinion, this essay should aspire to present an overall conspectus of the various relations between the two nominal terms of its title. What are, one might ask, the various approaches to the poem that critical theory offers? How do the disciplines of deconstruction, semiotics, feminism, psychoanalytic theory, or cultural studies angulate the meaning and the mode of *Beowulf*? Is there a case to be made for a specificity of theoretical engagement, an argument, in other words, that *Beowulf* invites distinctive applications of a unique theoretical approach?

But, on even brief reflection, the task of this chapter, either as a chronicle of views or as an advocacy of approach, is less transparent. Such questions as the ones above carry with them the burden of contemporary academic history. After the theory wars of the last two decades—in which the challenges, if not the practitioners, of deconstruction were condemned as antihumanist—one may query the existence of a commonly agreed upon, self-evident "critical theory" of this chapter's title.[1] Moreover, as medieval studies continue to be marginalized in the academy—as requirements for Old English dissolve and as the dissolution of traditional historical periods leaves, as its curricular precipitate, a tripartite arrangement of the premodern, the modern, and the postmodern—one may question the utility of bringing *Beowulf* into the critical canon at all. Finally, as Old English scholarship revels in its revived turn towards the empirical and the philological—exemplified in the *fontes Anglo-Saxonici* project, the spate of recent studies of Old English meter, and the revival of paleography as a constitutive discipline of professional Anglo-Saxonism—reactions against theoretical endeavors have become particularly sharp.[2] The very verbal gestures that derive from this chapter's title suggest that what is at stake here is an unnatural affiliation of two things: as if (depending on one's metaphors) the union of *Beowulf* and critical theory would be an academic miscegenation of monstrous proportions, or as if the poem and the theory offered up the matter and the antimatter of an academic cosmos whose untimely union would result in the assured destruction of both.

Much recent work in the historiography of medieval studies, however, suggests that such reactions are neither new nor unique to Old English. From Lee Patterson's narrative of the tensions between Exegetics and New Criticism in Chaucer studies, through the accounts of the nationalist projects of Romance philology charted by R. Howard Bloch and Hans-Ulrich Gumbrecht, to Allen Frantzen's deconstructions of the history of Anglo-Saxon scholarship, there has emerged a new consensus that an academic discipline is constructed through its institutional and political history (see Bloch 1990; Frantzen 1990; Gumbrecht 1986; Patterson 1987, 3–40). To understand the possible pitfalls and promises of *Beowulf* and critical theory, therefore, it will be necessary to expose some of the history that shaped Anglo-Saxon studies generally. In the process, what will emerge is not just a chronicle of theoretical approaches to a poem but a study of the rhetoric of theory in the discourse of professional Old English studies. This chapter's argument will be that Old English scholarship has been and continues to be citational and eulogistic and that what critical theory does is not so much to undermine familiar philological approaches or New Critical verities as to threaten the very structure of professional Anglo-Saxonism by undermining the authority of scholarly *auctores* and by revealing *as rhetoric* the citational and celebratory language of those *auctores*.

This chapter is not, therefore, a review of critical approaches to *Beowulf*. Such assessments have recently been made in articles by Douglas Short (1980b) and Edward B. Irving Jr. (1990) and by R. D. Fulk (1991) in his preface to *Interpretations of Beowulf*—a collection designed specifically, its subtitle notes, as *A Critical Anthology*. And Clare Lees, in her annual reviews for the *Year's Work in English Studies*, has shown particular sensitivity to theoretically minded readings of Old English writing in general and of *Beowulf* in particular. Furthermore, this chapter does not limit itself to work on *Beowulf* alone. Many of the most adventurous of recent Anglo-Saxon forays into theory have been charted through texts other than the epic's, in particular the saints' lives, biblical narratives, and prose histories and sermons.

The reader of this chapter should also recognize that contemporary theory does not necessarily produce the kinds of readily identifiable, autonomous "contributions" to scholarship central to the positivist traditions of critical historiography. What has been advanced as theory in the university is, in the end, not so much a unifying method as it is an attitude. Theory is less a practice than it is a kind of metalanguage that describes the rhetorical phenomena controlling literary discourse. As one critic has put it, surveying the twenty or so years of theoretical ascendancy in literary studies, "theory . . . must be equated with a certain conception of rhetoric, in which the privileged trope is irony, defined as the indeterminacy or the undecidability of meaning" (Kahn 1986, 373). Theory thus calls into question the very stability of language, both the language of literature and that of criticism, and in the process it potentially undermines the very practices of those who would attempt to deploy it.

In Old English studies, the resistance to theory is played for the highest stakes, as both the theorists and their opponents take as their *telos* nothing less than the salvation of the field and the rescuing of literary artifacts from those who would destroy them. Indeed, the rhetoric of salvation controls much of the criticism of the past decade. Theory, in one view, is potentially destructive, as the poetry is wrenched, forced, or disfigured to conform to certain prearranged agendas. For the "survival of the field," as one reviewer notes, "philology and basic historical, including exegetic, scholarship will obviously remain logically prior to theory" (J. Harris 1992b, 984).[3] In the other view, the goals of theory are precisely to revive the field: to save it from the ministrations of philology or the encrustings of archaeology. One recent avowal speaks of the "new thinking that has revived Anglo-Saxon studies," where the successes of such a revival would be measured in the "integration of contemporary criticism into Anglo-Saxon studies" (Frantzen and Overing 1993, 1177–78).

This chapter traces the rhetoric of salvation in three ways. First, it locates the origins of the salvific trope in what may well be the originary piece of modern *Beowulf* criticism, J. R. R. Tolkien's "*Beowulf*: The Monsters and the Critics." Second, it locates the urge to revivify Old English studies in a range of theoretical and critical accounts drawn from work of the past decade. Third, it suggests that the current critical fascination with the sword hilt that Beowulf recovers from Grendel's mere is itself something of an allegory of the history of *Beowulf* and critical theory. By rescuing a written artifact from the mere of the poem's narrative, such approaches relocate the place of the literate in *Beowulf*'s construction and, in the process, ironically recapitulate the central tropes of salvation and loss controlling the history of Old English studies.

I. Tolkien's Legacy
J. R. R. Tolkien's Sir Israel Gollancz Memorial Lecture to the British Academy of 1936, "*Beowulf*: The Monsters and the Critics," sought to save the

literary integrity of the poem from the hands of dismembering historians. Responding to a half century of philological and archaeological inquiries, "The Monsters and the Critics" redefined *Beowulf* as both an object of inquiry and a subject of professional discourse. The poem stands not as a repository of information but as an aesthetic whole. Powerful verse overshadows historical content (5), the thrill of the imagination overtakes our resistance to the improbable (see esp. 13, 19), deep themes replace superficial plots, the artifice of form effaces the artifacts of archaeology. Monsters are good, critics bad; monsters are poets, critics historians; monsters bring the poem to life, critics kill it.

This is the received version of Tolkien's account and its reception—an account that is as much a central myth of Anglo-Saxon studies as, say, the saving of the poem from the Cotton fire or the superiority of Klaeber's edition over all others. By calling these phenomena myths I do not, of course, query either their occasion or their import. What I do claim, though, is that they have been elevated to the great salvational moments in *Beowulf* scholarship, moments when the poem has been rescued or restored. This is the narrative of Old English studies, and it is a narrative whose origins need to be exposed. Take, for example, Tolkien's own initiatory gestures in his essay, where he begins by noting that "the original books [i.e., in the Anglo-Saxon tongue] are nearly buried" and goes on:

> Of none is this so true as of *The Beowulf*, as it used to be called. I have of course read *The Beowulf*, as have most (but not all) of those who have criticized it. But I fear that, unworthy successor and beneficiary of Joseph Bosworth, I have not been a man so diligent in my special walk as duly to read all that has been printed on, or touching on, this poem. But I have read enough, I think, to venture the opinion that *Beowulfiana* is, while rich in many departments, specially poor in one. It is poor in criticism, criticism that is directed to the understanding of a poem as a poem. It has been said of *Beowulf* itself that its weakness lies in placing the unimportant things at the centre and the important on the outer edges. This is one of the opinions that I wish specially to consider. I think it profoundly untrue of the poem, but strikingly true of the literature about it. *Beowulf* has been used as a quarry of fact and fancy far more assiduously than it has been studied as a work of art. (3–4)

Tolkien begins, first and foremost, by recovering the proper name of the poem itself. Instead of calling it *The Beowulf*, "as it used to be called," he silently renames it simply *Beowulf*, thus stripping the poem of its classicizing patina (as we call Homer's works *The Iliad* and *The Odyssey* and Virgil's *The Aeneid*), eponymizing its title (the poem and the hero become interchangeable), and encapsulating both its plot and its theme in such eponymy. It is a poem about *"man on earth,"* a poem about its hero. Names and naming are a controlling strategy of Tolkien's argument. Not only do we now have a new poem, but we have the name of the originary figure of Old English studies, Joseph Bosworth, the original chaired professor of Anglo-

Saxon. By contrast, we have only the anonymities of writing on the poem, the unnamed critics who, between Bosworth and Tolkien, are lumped together under the distancing epithet of *Beowulfiana.* "It has been said of *Beowulf . . . ,*" but we dare not ask who had said it.

For Tolkien, most writing on the poem has been marginal. It fails to recognize the poem as a poem, fails to study it as a work of art. Now, what precisely Tolkien means by these terms—*poem, art, criticism*—will become clear by his essay's end, and one could well argue that the business of "The Monsters and the Critics" is as much to define these key terms as it is to appreciate the poem through them. To understand the poem as a poem is to find its value in the unity of form and content: "*Beowulf* is indeed the most successful Old English poem because in it the elements, language, metre, theme, structure, are all most nearly in harmony" (31). Its status as a work of art is thus a statement of the autonomy of aesthetic creation: the sense that literary artifacts are artifacts, whose transhistorical appreciation outweighs whatever narrowly historical conditions fostered their creation and transmission. The purpose of criticism, then, is to define the poem's formal unity, to celebrate its quality as an aesthetic object, and—this, it seems to me, is the real legacy of Tolkien's essay—to construct a way of writing about it. "The Monsters and the Critics" creates the rhetoric of *Beowulf* criticism. The strategies of celebration and citation, of elegiac tone and eulogistic purpose, are all presented here for the first time, and they control the fundamental assumptions of Old English scholarship for the next fifty years.

These fundamental assumptions, however, are not those defining the position of a critic or the constructions of a method. They are, instead, those of a genealogy of critical *auctores,* and when Stanley Greenfield and Fred Robinson published their *Bibliography of Publications on Old English Literature* (1980) they sustained this notion of the field as an inheritance. They offer this obeisance, complete with untranslated German, to define the scope of their project: "In deciding what constitutes Old English 'literature' as opposed to other types of writing in the vernacular, we have in general been guided by the formulation of Richard Wülker in his *Grundriss* of 1885: 'Ausgeschlossen habe ich alle Denkmäler, welche man in einer Literaturgeschichte ausschliessen würde, weil sie kein selbstständiges Interesse haben' (p.vi)" (xii). What are the theoretical presuppositions behind this avowal? On the one hand, they purport to eschew self-conscious reflection on the definitions of the subject or the methodology of study in favor of intuition and common sense: a privileging of the "selbstständiges Interesse," those things of self-apparent interest. Literary works for Wülker, much as for Tolkien, are *Denkmäler,* monuments or memorials, with an aesthetic autonomy from cultural conditions or social production. But note that this is not a guide to understanding but a principle of exclusion, and Greenfield and Robinson announce that they have occasionally departed from its strictures. Their *Bibliography* includes entries on Ælfric's *Grammar,* "since it is a work by the leading literary figure of his age," as well as sections on Old English scientific writings and late Old English texts, "including a few which some scholars have preferred to call early Middle English (e.g., 'The Grave' and 'William the Conqueror'), but nothing that is generally regarded as Middle English has been included." Finally, they announce, again with an untranslated appeal to German authority, "The distinction between literary and historical scholarship is not always clear. . . . As Wülker ruefully remarked, 'Überhaupt liess sich die Grenze zwischen dem, was aufzunehmen, und dem, was wegzulassen war, nicht immer so scharf ziehen'" (xii).

Rhetorically, these statements from the Greenfield-Robinson *Bibliography* sustain the citational and patrimonial program of Tolkien. Wülker stands in relationship to the modern bibliographers as Bosworth stands for Tolkien, as the originary (and, thus, only named) authority to whom one constructs appeals of control. Both Tolkien and Greenfield-Robinson hold to the fundamental, and therefore tacit, assumptions of the autonomy of the literary text; indeed, it is that very autonomy that defines something as a literary text and thus enables one to demarcate that *Grenze* between it and the "historical." In these terms, literature as well as literary scholarship is to be distinguished from history—a position that much of the polemic of the 1980s was to react against—but also, it is to be associated with certain social values or, even, ethical positions. The tone of Tolkien, much like the tone of Greenfield and Robinson, is always recuperative. For the latter, Ælfric is recuperated as "the leading literary figure of his age," a named author in a world of anonymous scops. Similarly, certain texts such as "The Grave" and "William the Conqueror" are retrieved from that unsure mid-world between Old and Middle English, though by whom such texts have been "generally regarded as Middle English" is never made explicit.

Tolkien's criticism and Greenfield-Robinson's bibliographical scholarship are linked not just in their rhetoric or in their celebration but in their sense of an institutional purpose. Though the former may be grounded in the legacy of Edwardian middlebrow tastes and the latter in the habits of mid-century American New Criticism, both share a fundamentally Arnoldian position on the nature of literary study. As Lee Patterson has pointed out, the origins of much institutional-ized early English literary study are to be found in the ideals that F. J. Furnivall inherited from Matthew Arnold, in particular, "that the study of the literature of the English past could serve to recover the organic unity that the class-divided society of the nineteenth century had lost" (1987, 10). Patterson recognizes that, "For all its celebration of the work of art as a value in and for itself, New Criticism never abandoned the Romantic and Arnoldian claim that literature offers the alienated reader a saving knowledge" (18–19). These terms precisely characterize both the rhetoric and the reaction of a century of Old English studies, a century that, from Wülker, through Tolkien, to Greenfield and Robinson, to the theoretically minded critics of the 1980s and early 1990s, still commits itself to defining the reader of Old English literature as alienated and to characterizing its mission as salvific.

This is what marks the contemporary debate on Old English literature and theory and, in particular, that distinguishes a clutch of recent forays into the union of *Beowulf* and critical theory. At stake is not the ahistoricism of the theoretical agenda, or even the local interpretive successes or failures of its practitioners, but rather its institutional missions. The motivation for the theoretical approach to Anglo-Saxon studies is to rescue it: to revive the field for a generation of new students, to save it from philologists and exegetes, and to maintain a primacy of place in the divisive world of the academy.

II. Recent Theoretical Approaches

Broadly speaking, recent attempts to yoke together *Beowulf* and critical theory have fallen into three categories, each grounded in particular presuppositions about the nature of the poetic text, the social function of the critic, and the relation between formalism and historicism in literary study.[4] For the first group, the awareness that earlier literatures can respond effectively to theoretical responses has grown out of the recognition that medieval cultures, and in particular Anglo-Saxon culture, share with our own a preoccupation with language and its forms, with the nature of signification, and with the institutionalizations of authority in narrative and in politics. For the second, Anglo-Saxon literature is more a social practice than a surviving autonomous discourse, and thus it may respond effectively to an approach grounded in "cultural studies": a way of getting beyond both the textual formalisms of close reading and the institutional abstractions of traditional analysis to understand the "material reality" of the societies that produced both the literary work and the interpreting and teaching reader. Finally, for yet a third group, Old English literature provides a provocation for political analysis and action, as its representations of women or constructions of the psyche generate feminist and psychoanalytic studies that seek dialogue with modern movements of reform and restitution as much as they seek an understanding of an Anglo-Saxon public or interior life.

Since the mid-1980s, critics have tried variously to apply contemporary semiotic theory to Old English texts and, more generally, to conceive of Anglo-Saxon culture as a whole in terms of problems of signification and interpretation. Early assays of the semiotic were primarily concerned with understanding the identifying "codes" behind the folkloric motifs and ancient narratives inherited by *Beowulf*. Articles by Jonathan D. Evans (1985) and Rosemary Huisman (1989) sought to clarify problems of narratorial structure by explicating the social codes of verbal conduct in the poem, and both locate those problems in the encounters of the human with the monstrous. Recently Martin Irvine (1986b) has discerned in the tradition of *grammatica*—the institutionalized study and teaching of the *auctores* of grammatical practice and literary commentary that flourished in the Anglo-Saxon schools—what might be thought of as a culture of the sign: a way, not only, of disseminating Christian doctrine but of understanding the key texts of pagan

Latinity (Ovid, Virgil, Terence, etc.) and, perhaps, of applying that understanding to the making of vernacular literature as well. In a telling summary of his position, he locates both the historical reality of Anglo-Saxon grammatical thinking and the critical positioning of modern theory in a rhetorical move designed to validate both the past and his own position: "Grammatical culture in the early middle ages is thoroughly text-centered and bears the marks of the semiotic orientation to texts that recent scholars like Umberto Eco have developed largely from medieval principles, into a modern method of cultural analysis. . . . In this text-centered culture, grammatical texts and commentaries, even when attributed to an author, bear a mark of anonymity: the text, as signifying vehicle, was the focus of the reader's activity, not the historical circumstances or personalities of authors" (1986b, 40–41). Irvine here validates the project of a semiotics of Anglo-Saxon culture by both appealing to its academic timeliness and, furthermore, arguing implicitly that the very project of modern semiotics owes its origins to explicating certain "medieval principles." By paradoxically invoking the name of the *auctor* of modern semiotics, Umberto Eco, and simultaneously denying the possibilities of author-centered criticism for the Anglo-Saxons, Irvine constructs a theoretical position that mimes the central tensions of poststructuralist academic life.

Though Irvine does not discuss *Beowulf,* his concern with recovering a signifying way of life for Anglo-Saxon literary culture is shared by—and, to a certain extent, provides some historical grounding for—the work of Gillian Overing in the second chapter of her *Language, Sign, and Gender in Beowulf* (1990, based on articles of 1986 and 1987). Drawing primarily on the semiotic theory of Charles S. Peirce, Overing interprets the swords of the poem through what Peirce would call an "index" of signification for the poem's society. Her argument is that the meaning of the sword lies not in any specificity of symbolism or historical usage (the purview, e.g., of allegorical or archaeological approaches) but rather in the ways in which its recurrence throughout the poem signifies relationships of power and control among the poem's characters. The meaning of the sword is therefore something of a cipher, as it takes on different interpretations throughout the poem. Thus, the sword will function differently as a gift (as when Unferth presents the hero with his sword), as a relic (as when Hrothgar meditates on the recovered hilt from Grendel's mere), or as an object of masculine power (as in its successful decapitation of the monsters or its failure in the final dragon fight). Overing sees the other central objects of the poem—especially rings and cups—as working similarly in this process of signification. Rather than construing a distinctive set of references for these objects, Overing views their function in the poem as part of a larger process of the poem's making meaning: "The repetitions, convolutions, and wanderings of theme and structure might suggest that the entire poem is 'about' process—the nature of continual questioning and examination of values, heroic and Christian" (1990, 65).

Overing's book appeared only a year after John P. Hermann's *Allegories of War,* a study that, while not explicitly discussing *Beowulf,* proposed a theoretical approach to pre-Conquest literature that has had an immense impact on current criticism of the poem and its milieu. By focusing on the poetic transformations of the psychomachia tradition, Hermann's book argues that the violence of spiritual warfare leads to an appreciation of the violence of the letter—that nexus of the bodily and the interpretive that, in the work of Derrida and Lacan, stands for (among other things) the disarticulation of the Enlightenment ideal of the self and the critique of a reading, writing subject controlling the production of discourse. For Hermann, these approaches enable a "[re]construction of society and psyche in Anglo-Saxon England" (1989, 2)—a project thus concerned with both the historical understanding of a state of mind and the theoretical appreciation of the difficulties of such understanding.

Hermann's book also figures prominently in what I have characterized as the second set of critical directions of contemporary Anglo-Saxonism: the critique of the profession of Old English studies itself and, in turn, the attempt to historicize the institutions and practitioners of the discipline. In part, as he states, his goal is to understand the "institutional positioning of the reader of Old English poetry" (118), in other words, to expose and to explicate the provocations to the modern reader of a literature preoccupied with problems of linguistic signification, social violence, and psychological tension. His interest is thus calibrated to the impact of contemporary theory on the study of historical literature. But his book, too, concerns itself with the impact of studying Old English on the hegemonies of the critical academy. The act of historicizing such theoretical concerns as the relations between violence and signification generates what Hermann sees as a "critical reflexivity" (200)—a double focus, both on the cultural institutions that produced a literary form and on those that shape its readers.

The double focus of *Allegories of War* resonates with the projects of Allen Frantzen, who, in the late 1980s and early 1990s, sought to reconsider the profession of the Anglo-Saxonist as a species of "cultural studies." During the 1980s, this phrase emerged as convenient way of characterizing the varied disaffections with the formalisms of Derridean analysis and, too, the reductivism of some forms of academic Marxism (see Johnson 1986). At times, the phrase has defined a materialist approach to historical *epistemes*: the "cultural poetics" of New Historicism and its preoccupations with the display of the body as the locus of force relations and with the writing of a history of the subject for premodern English communities. In Anglo-Saxon studies, Frantzen has sought to apply some of these various approaches to an understanding, not just of the historical culture that produced the documents of literary form, but of the history of the profession that described, and may have even helped constitute, those documents. The cultural studies model has helped Frantzen redefine, for example, the place of archaeology in *Beowulf* scholarship, has offered ways of exposing the past century's fascination with the aristocracy of Anglo-Saxon England, and has helped unmask the pose of scholarly objectivity in the empiricist and positivist traditions of Old English study. As Frantzen puts it, in his opening manifesto to the collection *Speaking Two Languages*: "Cultural studies focus on the political nature of the structural, structuring effects of the relationship between scholars and their subjects. . . . In order to see medieval studies as a form of cultural studies, it is necessary to look from the uniform rules of disciplines to the moments of their formation and institutionalization of the preferences and interests of those who created them. Exploration of the history of the disciplines is, I submit, the only way to balance the power of these founding scholars and to make their paradigms responsive to the interests of new readers" (1991b, 22–23). The goal here, as elsewhere, is to expose the power politics of the profession—not to condemn the motives of its practitioners, but to affirm the ways in which that politics constructed the canonical approaches of a discipline. The vision of a *Beowulf* produced by the aristocratic world of Sutton Hoo-like inhumators (a vision constructed out of a possibly unwitting collaboration between gentlemen archaeologists and Oxbridge critics of the 1930s) may reflect more the power of the discipline's founding scholars than the interests of the poetry's new readers.

The fissures between founding scholars and new readers opened here become the points of historical entry in Frantzen's *Desire for Origins,* a full-scale engagement with the history of the discipline of Anglo-Saxon studies. While offering capsule accounts of the development of Old English lexicography and the applications of classical textual criticism to vernacular editorial practice, the primary goal of this book is, like many of the other works discussed here, pedagogic and recuperative. What Frantzen seeks to recover here, however, is not the authentic text of *Beowulf,* or an Old English literature mired in the ministrations of philologists, but rather the unarticulated history of Anglo-Saxon studies itself. Frantzen proposes "a reversal of the causal relationship of Anglo-Saxon studies to Anglo-Saxon England" (1990, 111). His claim is that the profession constructs the subject of its study, not that there is some historically autonomous subject that invites observation and response, and Frantzen's claim is bolstered by an eclectic blend of critical approaches. What deconstruction does, for example, is offer up not another way of reading the poetry but a way of understanding the self-mythologizing nature of professional Old English studies, thus offering "an ongoing challenge to the hermeneutic mission of philology" (1990, 114). What cultural studies does is not so much illuminate the objects of professional study as enlighten the practitioners of such a study to the worldly implications of their work and, in the process, enable them to restore its place in the academy (1990, 201, 224). Frantzen's goal is thus something of a dialogue between the objects of our study and the professional subjects constituted by that study. His is a claim, in short, for reviving Anglo-Saxon by reviving Anglo-Saxonists—by acknowledging the "personal investment in the issues we study" and, as a consequence, placing our own lives at the center of professional experience (1991b, 30).

Placing our own lives at the center of professional experience has informed the third set of contemporary theoretical approaches to Old English literature: those shaped by feminism and psychoanalysis. The traditional approach to *Beowulf* as a heroic poem—with its celebrations of the *comitatus,* its attempts to explain or to explain away ritual drinking, and its depictions of the poem's women as either negotiated brides or monstrous mothers—has excluded an analysis of women's roles and sensibilities in this as well as other documents of pre-Conquest narrative. To a certain extent, feminist approaches to Old English literature in general, and *Beowulf* in particular, have recapitulated the history of academic feminism generally. The first stage was recuperative and historical, and to a certain extent the goals of early feminist approaches to *Beowulf* were to identify a female presence in the poem, to relate the literary presentation of women to the recoverable facts of social life, and thus to restore a certain balance to the cultural and literary emphases of Anglo-Saxon England (see Damico and Olsen 1990). The work of Helen Damico, Jane Chance, and Alexandra Hennessey Olsen during the 1980s was devoted to such projects. Damico sought to place *Beowulf*'s queens in the literary traditions of the valkyrie. Chance argued that the notion of the woman as "peace-weaver" informed both the normative and the transgressive depictions of the females in the poem. Olsen advocated an understanding of the female voice of the Old English elegies and gnomic poems as offering a social gloss on the "duties of Anglo-Saxon femininity" (Olsen 1984, 155).

The second stage of academic feminism has been to move beyond the pointings of identification to analyses of female subjectivity, and, in particular, to understandings of the ideological construction of the female body. Work on the "male gaze," developed in the film criticism of Laura Mulvey and Teresa De Lauretis, as well as theorizings of the body by French feminists such as Hélène Cixous, Luce Irigaray, and Julia Kristeva, has found its venue for Old English studies in the work of Gillian Overing. In the third chapter of *Language, Sign, and Gender in Beowulf,* Overing studies the figures of Hildeburh, Wealhtheow, and Thryth to characterize the poem's presentation of idealized, or condemned, females who, in their participation in the poem's patterns of desire and control, may subvert expectations of female behavior shaped both by historical generics (e.g., those of saint's life and martyrology) and by contemporary institutional norms. And in her subsequent article on *Genesis B*—a reading that, while not explicitly addressing *Beowulf,* has profound implications for any subsequent narratological work on the poem—Overing seeks to ground Eve as a figure in a complex of desires, here, one shaped by feminist theoretical associations between Oedipal desire and Western narrative form.

As Overing's work recognizes, the line between gender studies and psychoanalytic criticism is an artificial one, and James W. Earl (1991) has sought a *Beowulf* constructed out of the psyches of the heroic male and the Oedipalized reader. The double focus of his project concerns itself with understanding the heroic ethos of the poem's age—the nexus of a Christian psychology and an epic sensibility—as well as the cultural condition of the modern reader. By stressing individual responses to the poem's presentations of male action, public mourning, and monstrous female rapacity, Earl seeks to restore a personal response to epic: whether it lies in the imagined possibility of *The Battle of Maldon*'s Byrhtnoth as a reader of *Beowulf,* or in the self-analyzing discourses of the modern academic as the poem's teacher.[5]

III. The Hilt as Critical Nexus

If the foregoing review has demonstrated anything, it is the recognition that the history of Anglo-Saxon studies is a history of definitions. From Wülker onward, it has been essential to define the canon of Old English texts, to locate philologically, historically, and critically the primary documents, narrative moments, and key passages that constitute just what is "central" in the study of the literature. Tolkien's sense of the marginal's relation to the center is as much a statement of aesthetic taste as it is an ideology of form. At stake is not so much identifying what is central to a poem or a passage but rather the very valorization of the central. If critical theory has done anything, it has challenged this fundamental hierarchization, from Derrida's reversal of familiar polarities such as man/woman and oral/written, through the New Historicism's supposition that the culturally marginal is the symbolically central.

In these terms, then, it may seem little wonder that foci of Old English criticism have changed. The sword hilt that the hero recovers from Grendel's mere, for example, has stood for Overing, Frantzen, Lerer, and, most recently, Michael Near, as the key artifact of *Beowulf*: an object whose uniquely written character stands in relation to the oral texture of the poem. For Overing, the sword constitutes the image of male power and the inscribed hilt a version of the phallologocentrism of Western metaphysics (1990, 33–67). For Frantzen, the hilt stands as the nexus of writing and death in the poem, a moment when the "suppressed textuality" of *Beowulf* comes through in ways that both query the nature of authorship and literary authority within the poem's fiction and thematize the status of the text of *Beowulf* within the history of its scholarly reception (1990, 184–90). For Lerer, the hilt stands as a figure for the poem itself, one that provides the opportunity for Hrothgar to function as a kind of reader and that enables *Beowulf*'s own meditations on the social function of literature, the nature of performance, and the tensions between *run* and *ræd* that are alliteratively linked throughout Germanic poetry and that suggest something of a hermeneutic impulse in craft-literate societies (1991, 158–94). For Michael Near, the hilt's literacy intrudes into a predominantly oral performance, not simply challenging the poem's traditional mode of presentation, but presenting to its own audience "a world in transition" from orality to literacy, "a world that looks back in nostalgic longing for an already absent past and forward with marked hesitation to the final voices in song" (1993, 321).

The sword hilt thus seems the ideal nexus for the productive meeting of *Beowulf* and critical theory. As the only piece of writing in the poem—however obliquely envisioned—its entry into the narrative performs what might be thought of as a Derridean twist of its own: a replacement of the primacy of speech with the originality of writing, a challenge to the authoritative presence of performance by the authorial absence of the incised text. The hilt becomes the object of critical analysis, the metonymy for the poem as a whole, the center of the story. It is the ideal place to locate the textualization of Anglo-Saxon culture, the place to link the inheritances of the Germanic and the ministrations of the Christian, and the place to begin a substantial query of the oral-formulaic quality of early English verse and its embracing by professional Old English scholars. Yet the modern theoretical enticement with the hilt ironically reenacts the very narrative of Anglo-Saxon scholarship itself. By making it the center of the poem, the critic replaces a performance with an artifact. As the recovered object from the mere, the hilt stands as the embodiment of that controlling myth of scholarly recovery that has so dominated discourse on the poem. For, by miming Beowulf 's own act of retrieval and Hrothgar's own act of interpretation, the modern theoretically minded interpreter projects a heroic hermeneutic all his or her own. The true act of recovery here, the true act of salvation, is the act of theoretically locating the poem. For unlike the situation in Tolkien's age, the critics are the monsters now, and theorists, much like Beowulf himself, must set themselves the task of rescuing a legacy and literature from their omnivorous grasp.

What, in the end, does current critical theory contribute to the study of *Beowulf?* On the one hand, it provides the modern student with a way of understanding our relationships both to the past texts and to the present contexts in which scholarship and criticism transpire. But, on the other hand, it exposes for scholarly investigation certain aspects of the poem adumbrated or neglected by earlier approaches. The function of the sword hilt as a written object and its challenges to a culture of oral performance; the role of women in defining relations of gender and power; the figurations of the body and the place of the heroic self in complex patterns of desire and representation; the thematics of signification and the ways in which the poem signals moments of interpretation both for its fictional characters and its historical audience—all represent the problems of the poem raised by recent theoretical inquiries.[6] It is true that an attention to such problems challenges the humanist inheritance of moral reading and the New Critical verities of formal and thematic unity. Yet, in the process, theoretical approaches may help relocate the poem in the shifting canons of contemporary pluralist discourse. They may reveal what in the end may be the truly human quality of *Beowulf*: its recognition that the open-endedness and ambiguity of language mark us as creatures of the historical moment and that such a language gives voice to the social worlds in which our literature is made and understood.

Notes

1. For a convenient popular account, see Lehman (1991); for a scholarly assessment from within the legacy of Paul de Man, see Esch (1990).

2. For an account of the archival turn in Old English studies, see Biggs, Thomas Hill, and Szarmach (1990); for the paleographic turn, see Robinson's seminal article (1980) and O'Brien O'Keeffe's book (1990); for the metrical turn, see Kendall (1991).

3. Among many such reviews, see Joyce Hill (1993) and Olsen (1992). See, too, the characterization of the field by Shippey (1993b), and Overing's response (1993).

4. Influential studies that sought to recover a literary theory for the Middle Ages and to reset the study of medieval literature in the poststructuralist concern with language and interpretation include Bloch (1983), Gellrich (1985), and Vance (1985). For the potential applicability of this work to Anglo-Saxon literary culture, see Lerer (1991, 5–18).

5. Among other specifically psychoanalytic approaches to the poem (as distinguished from those generally concerned with a psychology of character or motivation), mention should be made of those by John M. Hill (1989), who locates the poem's tensions in the shifts between the Oedipal and the pre-Oedipal stages of human development, and Paul Beekman Taylor (1990), who relies on Lacan's idea of countertransference to explain Wealhtheow's use of epithets.

6. Some of these issues are raised, in the context of contemporary theoretical speculations on the body and the poetics of dismemberment, in Lerer (1994).

Chapter 18

Translations, Versions, Illustrations

by Marijane Osborn

Summary: Attempts to make *Beowulf* accessible abound. Mainly producing in the nineteenth century summaries and translations, this quest for familiarization, joined by a desire for the exotic, thereafter proliferated into a broad range of presentations in modern English and many foreign languages. The chronology below gives special attention to first translations into any given language, unusual versions, and recent items. The essay that follows discusses the earliest translations, translations into a wider range of languages, adaptations, illustrations, and a selection of relatively faithful, currently available translations into modern English.

Chronology

1805: First mentioning the poem in 1803, Sharon Turner includes several passages from *Beowulf* in English verse in his 1805 edition of *The History of the Anglo-Saxons*, expanding these in later editions, though never achieving accuracy.

1814: John Josias Conybeare publishes the Finnsburg materials in Latin verse translation and English paraphrase.

1815: Grímur Jónsson Thorkelin publishes the first complete, often mistaken, translation of *Beowulf*. Thorkelin, who thought *Beowulf* was itself a translation, made in the court of King Alfred, of an original "Scyldingid" (1815b), translated the poem into Latin.

1815: P. E. Müller (probably: he signs himself "Pem") translates passages of *Beowulf* in his review of Thorkelin, arguing for an Old Norse original.

1816: William Taylor presents in his review of Thorkelin the first attempt at English verse translation meant to appeal to a wider audience.

1818: Ebenezer Henderson translates passages from Thorkelin's Latin.

1820: N. F. S. Grundtvig offers the first complete, though periphrastic, translation into any modern language, in Danish verse.

1826: Conybeare includes sustained passages of *Beowulf* and *Finnsburg* in his *Illustrations of Anglo-Saxon Poetry*.

1830: Alfred Lord Tennyson puts a few lines of *Beowulf* into modern verse, marking the first interest in the poem by a distinguished poet.

1833: Giuseppe Pecchio publishes a partial translation into Italian.

1837: J. M. Kemble publishes his translation with copious glossary, preface, and notes.

1840: Ludwig Ettmüller publishes in German the first complete translation into a foreign language not Scandinavian, motivated by a desire to separate earlier ("pure") and later (Christian) layers of the text.

1855: Benjamin Thorpe provides the first facing-page edition and English translation of *Beowulf,* full of errors and long in use.

1857: C. W. M. Grein's literal line-for-line alliterative translation makes *Beowulf* available in a German translation based on his own dependable text.

1857: John Earle publishes a paraphrase in Charles Dickens's magazine, *Household Words.*

1859: Karl Simrock publishes his German translation in imitative meter.

1863: Moritz Heyne publishes a fourth German translation, in iambic pentameter.

1895: A. J. Wyatt and William Morris cooperate in translating *Beowulf.*

1896: L. Simons publishes a Dutch translation of *Beowulf,* with extensive notes.

1901: J. R. Clark Hall publishes his scholarly English prose translation. Revised in 1940 by C. L. Wrenn and with a preface by J. R. R. Tolkien, it was still the "crib of choice" in Oxford in the 1960s.

1909: Francis Gummere publishes his English translation, still in use.

1925: Howard Hanson's symphonic "Lament for Beowulf," with chorus using the Wyatt-Morris translation, marks the poem's first notable adaptation to another art form.

1941: Enrico Basari publishes in Italian the first comic strip loosely based on *Beowulf,* calling it a "cineepopeia."

1948: Richard Wilbur publishes the first original poem by a distinguished modern poet drawing clearly on a *Beowulf* theme.

1952: Scottish poet Edwin Morgan publishes his translation in modern imitative verse.

1963: Burton Raffel publishes his loose (and provocative) translation into modern poetry.

1966: E. Talbot Donaldson publishes his literal prose translation of *Beowulf,* one that still serves to introduce most newcomers to the poem.

1968: Kevin Crossley-Holland publishes his English verse translation.

1971: John Gardner makes the villain sympathetic in his novel *Grendel.*

1973: Michael Alexander publishes his popular Penguin translation.

1974: Betty Jane Wylie retells *Beowulf* as a rock musical.

1977: Howell D. Chickering Jr. publishes his useful facing-page translation.

1978: Michael Crichton publishes *Eaters of the Dead,* the first thriller based on *Beowulf.*

1982: S. A. J. Bradley includes *Beowulf* among his prose translations of most of the poetic corpus in his volume *Anglo-Saxon Poetry.*

1982: Stanley B. Greenfield publishes the first translation based on syllabic meter.

1983: Raymond P. Tripp Jr. reedits and translates lines 2208b–3182 of *Beowulf,* attempting to express its punning quality and to demonstrate that the dragon is a transformed human; he publishes a translation of the entire poem in 1991.

1984: Bernard F. Huppé translates and provides a reading of *Beowulf* to demonstrate its "inescapable Augustinian frame of reference."

1984: Marijane Osborn publishes her verse translation accompanied by photographs of artifacts.

1988: Poul Anderson weaves *Beowulf* into his spirited retelling of *Hrólfs saga kraka*.

1988: Ruth Lehmann attempts an exactly imitative verse form.

1990: Marc Hudson translates *Beowulf* with a careful elegance emphasizing the meditative quality of the verse.

1990: Randolph Swearer, Raymond Oliver, and Marijane Osborn together produce *Beowulf: A Likeness,* representing the world of the poem in photographs and in Oliver's modern yet formal poetry.

1994: Fordította Szegő György publishes a complete Hungarian translation of the poem.

Since the first translation of passages from *Beowulf* into English prose by Sharon Turner in 1805 and the first complete translation by Thorkelin into Latin in 1815, both versions imaginative enough to provoke angry responses from scholars more skilled in philology (notably Grundtvig, Conybeare, Kemble, and Thorpe), literally hundreds of complete and partial translations and retellings have appeared in a surprising array of the world's languages. These exist in such expected languages as modern English, Swedish, and German and in those less expected, for example, Bulgarian, Serbo-Croatian, Hungarian, archaic Japanese, and even Old English prose. Although some readers may first encounter Beowulf in modern fictions like John Gardner's *Grendel* and Michael Crichton's *Eaters of the Dead* (both distort the hero into a "Buliwulf," as Crichton renames him), virtually every modern reader finds initial serious entry into the poem by way of anthologized excerpts, retellings of lesser or greater complexity, or full-fledged translations, the latter usually providing some supporting material such as introduction and notes. After that, either before moving to the text itself or simultaneously, the more interested reader is likely to consult a guide, trusting that the guide will offer a reliable account of the poem.

Yet all that even the most canonically established translation or guide is able to offer is an account of the poem consistent with the current state of scholarship and the currently valued modes of reception at the time of writing (Lefevere 1992; see also Niles 1993b). The historically arranged commentaries in this book have made that fact richly clear, and the present essay will elaborate it by listing and commenting on the way that translations and paraphrases of the poem have served as acts of literary criticism, continually reinterpreting *Beowulf* in the currently or locally acceptable idiom. The discussion of illustrations culled from both English and non-English texts offers fascinating and often amusing examples of how either the culture or a particular segment within the culture will make visual commentary on the original it seeks to possess (Bassnett 1980, 2). Any author might say of his or her work what the *Beowulf* poet says of the launching of Scyld's treasure ship onto the world's seas:

> No one can know
> for certain, either hall-councillors or heroes under
> the heavens, whose hands will receive that cargo. (cf. 50b–52)

I. Understanding the Poem: The Earliest Translations to Kemble

No one knows, though many are eager to imagine, the nature of the first Anglo-Saxon audience of *Beowulf*. Certainty about that audience would profoundly affect the interpretation and hence translation of the poem. The second or modern audience of *Beowulf* first gained access to the poem through an edition with Latin translation that placed it squarely in the hands of the international community of scholars. In 1815, a translation into Thorkelin's adopted Danish or his native Icelandic would have been far less generally accessible than the Latin one. It was read avidly, the first series of reviewers attacking with a vengeance Thorkelin's text, translation, and discussion and elaborating their own views (see Haarder 1975, 13–28). Kemble's dismissive response is representative and undoubtedly valid: "And for a translation—God in Heaven" (R. A. Wiley 1981, 27). One feels sympathy, however, for this pioneer who traveled to England and painstakingly copied out the text himself (paying a scribe to make a second copy), who prepared an edition and saw much of his work go up in flames when, ironically, the English bombarded Copenhagen in 1807, and who stalwartly undertook it again. Because of the crumbling of the edges of the manuscript after the Ashburnham House fire of 1731 (Klaeber 1950a, xcvi), Thorkelin's copies are invaluable, and his translation at least launched efforts to get at a more accurate understanding of the text.

Influenced by earlier Danish suggestions of what the poem might be about (summarized in Cooley 1940), Thorkelin's translation reveals the following plot. The Jutes and Frisians, united under the leadership of Grendel, mount a raid on the Scyldings, ruled by Hrothgar. Beowulf comes to Hrothgar's support and has three battles with Grendel, wounding him in the second and finally killing him in the third (the Sigemund/Heremod episode). But Grendel comes back to life and again attacks, with his mother aiding him in a naval battle, which Beowulf again wins. Beowulf goes home laden with treasures, becomes Thorkelin's king, rules fifty years, and in his old age slays a dragon. When looking at his Old English text (sample in Tinker 1903, 18–19), one may be astonished that the translation achieved even this much accuracy.

Some stalwart souls, however, tried to work with this text and translation. In 1818, Ebenezer Henderson published an English translation of the harp-song passages with Thorkelin's version of the Old English printed alongside, and the American poet Longfellow speaks two decades later of how anyone attempting to read *Beowulf* in the original will "find it no child's play, particularly if he undertakes, at the same time, the Latin version of Grim. Johnson Thorkelin" (1838, 102).

After Thorkelin, the next notable translator is N. F. S. Grundtvig, a young divine at the time he encountered *Beowulf* but destined to become one of Denmark's greatest educators and arbiters of "taste" (a favorite concept of his). While immediately recognizing that Thorkelin's presentation of the poem was faulty, he was fascinated by that scholar's edition and translation. In order to get a firmer grip on *Beowulf,* he studied Old English with the philologist Rask and memorized the entire poem (1861, introduction). This "oral" access granted him a holistic view that Thorkelin appears to have lacked. Moreover, because Grundtvig was familiar with Danish antiquities and history and Germanic folklore, he was able to correct many of Thorkelin's errors, becoming, as Tinker says, "the first [modern person] to understand the story of *Beowulf* " (1903, 23). He filled in a number of the thirty-nine proper names that Thorkelin did not recognize as such (Cooley 1940, 50); he deduced, without even having access to the manuscript, that a folio leaf was misplaced; and he made the enormously important association of Beowulf's lord Hygelac with the historical Chochilaicus, whose raid on the Frisians in the early sixth century links the poem to a verifiable event. This discovery is universally acclaimed, Chambers assessing it as "the most important discovery ever made in the study of *Beowulf* " (1959, note 4).

Scholarly assessment of Grundtvig's translation of 1820 is less enthusiastic, however, partly because in those early years of discovery scholars wanted access to the literal contents of the poem, whereas Grundtvig's purpose was to offer the youth of his country "a little common Homer for England and the North" (Cooley 1940, 54–55; my translation). In an introduction echoing his earlier 1815 assessment, he praises the poem as a potential work of art, "boldly laid out, beautifully expressed, and in many ways gloriously executed, but nevertheless half-miscarried if taken as a unit" (1820, xlix; translated by Malone 1941a, 133). Despite what he sees as the poem's artistic failure, Grundtvig finds it possible to project upon *Beowulf* a moral or symbolic unity that accords with his own neo-Aristotelian "taste," and anticipating reception theory he suggests in a later work that each age takes different pleasures in a text (1832, 593). His translation, which according to Tinker "may properly be called nothing more than a paraphrase" (1903, 27), is in fact a considered attempt to rectify what seemed from his neoclassicist point of view the poem's weaknesses and to present it in a form more suitable to his period and his own nationalistic purpose. The extract presented by Tinker (25–26) displays the kinds of liberty Grundtvig took. As Tinker justly says, "He has popularized the story, and he has cheapened it," although "in many places it reads well" (27). Many who admired Grundtvig's other work comment on his translation with equally faint praise. In 1865, he published a revision where he defends himself and his theory of translation against those "deficient in knowledge or sense, or both," who have dared to criticize his style (Tinker 1903, 24).

Although Sharon Turner had published his first translation of passages from *Beowulf* in 1805, he "did not at that time sufficiently comprehend" the poem. Most notoriously, the famous misplaced leaf led him to interpret Beowulf's fight with Grendel as Hrothgar committing a murder. When he was preparing the third edition of his *History,* published in 1820, Turner came back to the poem. This time he got the outlines of the story right and offered further selections. His translation continues, however, to be replete with errors, uncorrected in later editions. Tinker gives extracts from all three editions and censures Turner "for allowing an account of *Beowulf* so full of inaccuracy to be reprinted year after year" (15). Pecchio's Italian version (see below) is simply a translation of Turner's abbreviated and inadequate account of *Beowulf* in this third edition of the *History*.

If we can accept the word of its author, the first attempt in English to understand the poem as a whole was completed in the same year as Grundtvig's translation and Turner's third edition, 1820, though it was not published until 1826 (Conybeare 1826, 29). The Oxford Professor of Anglo-Saxon and Poetry, John Josias Conybeare, revised Thorkelin's texts against the original manuscript and based his partial translation, into English blank verse and literal Latin prose, on those revisions of the text. Unaware of the advances already made by Grundtvig, he perpetuated some of Thorkelin's errors and produced a poetry "freighted with Miltonic phrase" (Tinker 1903, 32). Unlike Grundtvig, who found the poem a work of beauty and passion, if wrongly put together, Conybeare found it of value chiefly as an antiquarian document.

This prevailing attitude was expressed in the earliest account of *Beowulf* in a Romance language, a summary with extracts in Giuseppe Pecchio's 1833 *Storia critica della poesia inglesi*. Basing his work on Sharon Turner's *History* (1820), Pecchio evaluates the poem as the most important work known in Anglo-Saxon, valuable presumably for its representation of antiquities since he does not consider it worth much as literature. He offers an almost word-for-word translation of Turner's partial version, duplicating the mistakes found in his original, sometimes adding more, and burdening Italy with an erroneous impression of *Beowulf* for the next eighty years.

This dismal picture changes with the advent upon the *Beowulf* scene of John Mitchell Kemble (related to Kemble the actor), who published an edition of the poem in 1833, improved it greatly in a second edition of 1835, and followed this with a prose translation in 1837. He dedicated his work to Jacob Grimm, who received it with pleasure (Wiley 1981, 10). This alone is a recommendation. With no pretentions whatever to artistry but a firm conviction "that knowledge ought not to be made the property only of a learned class" (letter to Grimm in Wiley 1981, 293), Kemble translated the poem into an English prose as literal as he could make it while remaining comprehensible. He says, "I might have made it smoother, but

I purposely avoided doing so, because had the Saxon poet thought as we think, and expressed his thoughts as we express our thoughts, I might have spared myself the trouble of editing or translating his poem" (quoted in Tinker 1903, 36). The statement is that of a romantic who admires the alterity of his subject, but the effect of his principle of translation, along with his careful editing, was to give the world *Beowulf* in the form of a readable Old English text, a literal translation of that text ("as a part of the apparatus for interpreting the poem" [Tinker 1903, 36]), and the first usable glossary to link the two. "After publication of Kemble's translation, interest in *Beowulf* becomes common," says Chambers (1959, 586). Kemble's scholarly rendering is the first strictly literal translation to succeed, and the last in modern English that was needed in order for non-Anglo-Saxonists to have access to the poem, though of course other translations proliferated and improved as the text was better understood. From Kemble's time on, opportunities for manipulating the poem increased, offering the possibility of making *Beowulf* available in other languages or to specific nonspecialist audiences and of creating new works based on the old one.

II. Dispersing the Poem: Foreign Translations

"You were born in Greece," proclaims the Greek national tourist authority in a widely published advertisement of recent vintage, exploiting "the doctrine that 'western society' derives, by unbroken tradition, from Graeco-Roman origins" (Fernández-Armesto 1987, 1). Many of us may have had to deal with suggestions that we were betraying our "natural" culture by going off on the Anglo-Saxon tangent; I certainly did. Yet romantics prefer the tangential, and others, aware that they were *not* "born in Greece," seek roots in the spaces marginalized by the *mare nostrum* doctrine. These two impulses, the romantic and the genealogical or racial, were important motivations for most of the early translating of *Beowulf.* Apparently among the first things perceived as needed when escaping the false claim of Greek heritage is one's "own" national epic, and *Beowulf,* as the earliest extant warrior narrative in a Germanic language, was appropriated to that purpose, even nationalized according to the politics of the translator. Thorkelin interprets the poem as a Scyldingid or "[Epic] Song of the Scyldings," opposing it thereby to the *Aeneid,* and he believes it to be an Anglo-Saxon translation from Danish; Leo, whose study of 1839 with interspersed translation was "the first German book to give any extended account of the poem" (Tinker 1903, 121), titles his work *Bëówulf, dasz älteste deutsche Heldengedicht* (Beowulf, the oldest German hero poem). Translators of other nationalities, as will be seen later in this essay, lay claim to the poem by other, sometimes more subtle, means. The epic question was debated from the first. In an 1816 review of Thorkelin, the Danish critic "Pia" argued that the poem was not an epic (Haarder 1975, 17), whereas, as we have seen, Grundtvig imagined his 1820 translation as a "simple little Homer" for young people. This question of epic genre, one that continues to be debated even today, is relevant only to how we situate ourselves in relation to the claim that "You were born in Greece."

Related to the need for an epic to validate a nonclassical native culture was the desire to extricate the "real" *Beowulf* from the tampering of Christian redactors, or at least to determine which part of the poem was which. This was one motivation for Ettmüller's 1840 translation, the first complete German translation and the first significant translation after Kemble's work of 1835, on which it is based. In his later edition of 1875, Ettmüller omits the passages he considers the work of a Christian interpolator. Ironically, even Ettmüller's desire to excise Mediterranean Christianity from the poem takes its impetus from the so-called "higher criticism" of the Bible as well as Friedrich Wolf 's dissection of Homer to separate earlier from later layers in the text, an effort that in turn inspired Karl Lachmann to attempt a similar analysis of the "inner history" of the *Nibelungenlied.* All were seeking "original" texts (see Haarder 1975, 93–94; Frantzen 1990, 50–71), and to this end Ettmüller offers the closest translation he can give within the constraints of an imitative alliterative meter. Tinker criticizes the translation for "its numerous strange word-combinations" (1903, 40), these often being simply the original Old English words with footnoted explanations. But Ettmüller brought the poem, along with his theory of multiple authorship, into the German sphere, where for the rest of the century the most progress in its interpretation was made.

Although Thorpe published his facing-page English translation in 1855, in the scholarly sphere the most influential translation after Kemble was C. W. M. Grein's literal German version of 1857, improved in a second edition of 1863, and revised by Richard Paul Wülker *nach Greins Handexemplar* ("following Grein's handwritten notes") in 1883. Tinker assesses the value of this translation in imitative meter as "one with the superiority of the text on which it is founded" (1903, 59); Grein's was a reliable text and translation. In 1859, Karl Simrock (translator of the *Nibelungenlied* and other works) produced a third German translation, in an imitative meter and using mainly simple diction, but attempting to retain the heavy compounding of Old English to which Tinker strongly objects in any translation (61). Then the *Beowulf* scholar Heyne offered a fourth German translation in a free and readable iambic meter (1863; 2nd ed. 1898), so that now trustworthy versions were available in that language for scholars and public alike.

Meanwhile in England translators were busy also. In 1857, John Earle published an unsigned paraphrase of *Beowulf* titled "A Primitive Old Epic" in Charles Dickens's magazine *Household Words,* and many years later, in 1892, he published his translation, *The Deeds of Beowulf: An English Epic of the Eighth Century Done into Modern Prose.* The word *primitive* in the 1857 title denies the poem's artistry, but the term *epic* in both titles directs attention to what Earle probably thought more worthy than mere art, the heroic values of men of old. The diction he uses suggests that he aims to be nobly "antique": "Ye twain in the realm of waters toiled a se'nnight; he at swimming outvied thee." The acme of archaic diction, however, must be the Morris and Wyatt translation of 1895. In this cooperative effort, Wyatt was the scholar, William Morris the poet. Morris himself said that he "rhymed up" (he must mean "alliterated") a prose draft that Wyatt made for him on the basis of Wyatt's own 1894 text (Tinker 1903, 104–05): "Ye twain in the waves' might/ For a seven nights swink'd. He outdid thee in swimming," etc. This passage is relatively successful compared to many others in this version, the poet merely being led into "swink'd" by the alliterative "swimming."

The rest of this section will draw brief attention to the first partial or full translations into any foreign language and others of special interest or recent date, in order to offer an idea of how access to the poem has spread through the international community.

The first partial but scholarly prose translation into *French* was by Botkine in 1877. Pierquin published a complete prose translation side by side with the original in 1912. André Crépin published his long-awaited verse translation in 1991.

Although Pecchio had offered extracts and a summary of the poem in *Italian* as early as 1833 (following Turner 1820), a fuller and more correct translation of passages linked by paraphrase was published by Giuseppe Schuhmann in 1882. That one was immediately superseded in 1883 by a more scholarly and literary translation in imitative meter by Grion. In 1934, Olivero published a literal prose translation with Chambers's text on the facing page, thus offering full access to the poem for Italian readers.

The first *Swedish* translation, avoiding alliteration but otherwise in imitative meter aspiring to be "readable and modern," was published by Wickberg in 1889. In 1954, the philologist Björn Collinder published an imitative verse translation of more value, and, in 1958, the archaeologist Sune Lindqvist published a work titled *Beowulf Dissectus,* regrouping the various parts of the poem according to kind, excising all references to Christianity, and translating into Swedish those passages most like chronicle.

The most recent *Danish* translation is by Andreas Haarder, 1984.

The first *Dutch* translation, in iambic pentameter and aiming at accuracy, was published by Simons in 1896; another followed in 1930, a third, in prose, by Jonk in 1977.

The first *Norwegian* (Landsmaal; alliterative) translation was by Rytter, in 1921.

The first *Finnish* translation, of substantial passages in alliterative verse, was published by Dillström in 1927.

The first *Japanese* translation was into the archaic prose of a Biwa romance, by Kuriyagawa in 1931. Recently, translations into Japanese have proliferated, and more, the *Beowulf* translator Tsunenori Karibe tells me, are in progress, by Professors Ogawa, Hasegawa, and Yamaguchi. Professor Karibe and others have referred me to the translation in a "rather archaic literary style" by Kinshiro Oshitari (1990), which I take therefore to be the approved one in Japanese.

The first passages in *Russian,* in alliterative meter, were published by IArkho in 1934, a more complete translation by V. Tikhomirova in 1975.

The first account of *Beowulf* in *Spanish* was a retelling for children by Vallvé published in 1934. The first direct translation of passages was published by Manent in 1947. Orestes Vera Pérez produced the first full Spanish translation, in prose, in 1959, republishing it in 1962. The most recent Spanish translation was by Lerate and Lerate, in 1986.

In 1937, Kalma published passages translated into *Frisian,* those recounting the fight at Finnsburg in Frisia. A full prose translation by Krol and van der Zee appeared in 1984.

The first passages translated into *Bulgarian* were published by R. Rusev in 1937; in his introduction, Rusev compares *Beowulf* to the narrative poems of Byron.

The first, and probably only, passage in *Scots* dialect was published by the well-known Scottish poet Edwin Morgan in 1953.

The first *Portuguese* version, wildly distorted, appeared in 1955 in an anonymous Brazilian comic book, discussed in the next section.

The first *Arabic* translation was published by Wahba in 1964.

The first *Polish* version was Przedpelska-Trzeciakowska's translation of Rosemary Sutcliff's 1961 retelling of the story for children, published in 1966.

The first *Icelandic* translation, in close imitative meter, was by Halldóra B. Björnsson, posthumously edited from her manuscripts by Pétur Knútsson Ridgewell and published in 1983. Björnsson imitates in Icelandic the surface structures of the Old English, often preferring an inexact translation in order to capture the sound of the original.

The first *Hungarian* translation was by Fordította Szegő György in 1994.

In languages producing the most activity, I have noted sixty-four substantial or complete translations into modern English, fifteen into German, and eight (so far) into Japanese. The modern European language most notably lacking a translation of *Beowulf* is Greek.

III. Shape Shiftings: *Beowulf* in New Forms

"There is . . . a difference between a monument in stone and a monument in language. Of the latter we can at least say to what race it belongs, it bears in each lineament the family stamp." Allen J. Frantzen quotes these words from John Earle's introduction to his 1892 translation of *Beowulf* (xviii) in an argument about "the reconstructive dangers of the discipline," adding that Earle "did not equate documents and monuments as indices of Anglo-Saxon culture: for him, the document was familiar, the monument strange" (Frantzen 1991b, 19). *Beowulf* scholars may find the two sections that follow equally strange, or strange in the context of our discipline, because they demonstrate how incapable the discipline is of holding onto this poem that we tend to think of as ours. As *Beowulf* is adapted in different ways, as T. A. Shippey has pointed out, these new forms cater to a third audience of the poem, and Shippey asks, "How does that tertiary audience relate to the secondary one of the scholars and translators, or the primary and equally unscholarly audience of Anglo-Saxons?" (Shippey 1975, 974).

The story of Beowulf was retold with relatively tame intentions in the nineteenth century, as a native fairy tale, or a narrative sample from the barbarian past, or a model of behavior for young people. But from the beginning translators experimented creatively if mainly unsuccessfully with various meters, Grundtvig with Danish ballad meter in 1820, Lumsden with English ballad meter in 1881, Hoffmann in German (1893) and William Ellery Leonard in English (1923) with Nibelung couplets. Actual creative adaptation of *Beowulf* into other genres seems to have begun around the turn of the century.

The first notable creative work based on *Beowulf* is a symphony, Howard Hanson's 1925 "Lament for Beowulf" (opus 25), in which a chorus chants passages from the Morris and Wyatt translation of the poem, supported by a full orchestra. In the same year, a parody of *Beowulf* by "Mr. Beach" (Henry Cecil Wyld) appeared in the *Oxford Magazine,* confirming the poem's canonical status among the intelligensia.

In 1927, Otto Brüder adapted the poem to startlingly political ends in a play for German youth, *Beowulf: Ein heldisches Spiel* (for a description of the second edition of 1931, see Osborn [1969, 233]); and in 1933, in *Beowulf: A Paraphrase,* Harry Morgan Ayres retells the poem as a saga in the Icelandic manner. John O. Beaty, the first scholar to write about "The Echo-Word in *Beowulf*" (1934), incorporated the Finnsburg materials into a rousing adventure novel, *Swords in the Dawn* (1937), as Gillian Paton Walsh does again in her novel *Hengest's Tale* (1966). But by far the most "creative" adaptation of the poem before the coming of Gardner's *Grendel* is Enrico Basari's highly Catholicized Italian comic-book version published in 1941 and anonymously translated into Brazilian Portuguese in 1955 as *O Monstro de Caim,* "The Monster of Cain."

This work, of which I possess both the Italian and the Portuguese versions, is described in detail by Francis Peabody Magoun Jr. in a festschrift article titled "*Beowulf* in Denmark: An Italo-Brazilian Variant" (1959). I consider the plot worth retelling; it may have been influenced by Turner's early account. The story begins with pagan Rogar (Hrothgar) killing his good Christian brother Etheow (Ecgtheow) in a territorial feud sponsored by the evil spirit Grendel; Beowulf as son of the slain king is then obliged to serve Rogar to repay him for the funeral rites. Fearing Beowulf will usurp his throne, Rogar orders him in a runic message to go out and slay Grendel. Grendel intercepts and reads this message and vows to kill Beowulf, mentioning his mother Frotha's magic. An enormous battle pits Ringuedanos (Ring Danes) against Geatos, but Beowulf and Grendel, the latter under Frotha's protective magic, meet at a distance from the battle. As they fight, Beowulf's Christian blood spurts onto the monster, counteracting the pagan enchantment, and Beowulf is able to cut off Grendel's head, which he takes back to Rogar. Rogar falsely accuses him of black magic and orders him burned at the stake. Frotha kidnaps Rogar's (good) son Gunar in order to use his blood to revive Grendel. As the flames mount around Beowulf, Rogar hears of his son's abduction and frees the hero, vowing to do anything in exchange for the safe return of his son. Beowulf dutifully goes to confront Frotha in her lair. As they fight, Frotha suddenly merges with her son's corpse to become a seven-headed dragon (representing the Seven Deadly Sins) and coils around Gunar and Beowulf. When Beowulf nevertheless succeeds in slaying the dragon, Envy and Wrath vanish from Rogar's soul. Rogar becomes a penitent monk. Leaving the kingdom to Gunar, the dying Beowulf is carried up to heaven like Galahad, by chanting archangels—but on the throne of Thor.

Tennyson translated some lines in 1830 (see Tennyson 1969, 1235 [Harvard notebook 4]), and Longfellow published a selection of passages in 1838, but on the whole famous poets did not turn their hands to the poem until the mid-twentieth century. Then suddenly several do. Richard Wilbur published a brief translation and an original poem in 1948, Wallace Stevens his allusive poem "The Auroras of Autumn" in a book of that title in 1950 (see Stevens 1961), Edwin Morgan his Scots "Auld Man's Coronach" in 1953 ("The Father's Lament," *Beowulf* 2444–62a), Kingsley Amis a satirical poem in 1957, and Auden a Beowulfian praise poem for Tolkien in 1962. The famous poet displaying the most excitement about *Beowulf,* however, was Jorge Luis Borges, who published an essay about the poem in 1951 and a poem about reading *Beowulf* in 1967, both in Spanish. In 1965, Kenneth Rexroth movingly retold the story of Beowulf in the *Saturday Review.* In 1987, after referring to Old English etymologies for several years, Seamus Heaney translated the Scyld passage about "The Ship of Death" in *The Haw Lantern.* This poem is in the current (sixth) edition of *The Norton Anthology of English Literature,* volume 2. Modern poets who use Anglo-Saxon meter and/or themes have received attention lately from Fernando Galván (1992), Fred C. Robinson on Pound (1982, 1993a), and Nicholas Howe (1997) on Auden, Hill, and Gunn. The relatively unexplored interest of modern poets in *Beowulf* seems a subject ripe for much more extended inquiry.

Novelists and short-story writers also took up *Beowulf* in mid-century. In addition to the two versions of the Finnsburg story mentioned above are retellings, often radical revisions, by, among others, Canaway (1958), Sutcliff (for children, 1961), Nye (for children, 1968), Gardner (1971), Hart (short story, 1974), Crichton (1976), the team of Niven, Pournelle, and Barnes (1987), Anderson (1988), and Holt (1988). Of these, I like Gardner's *Grendel* and Anderson's *Hrolf Kraki's Saga* best and the Niven-Pournelle-Barnes science fiction thriller, *The Legacy of Heorot,* least. Most readers will remember how Gardner turns the cannibalistic monster into "poor Grendel," a personage to whom I return below with the film version. Since Poul Anderson's subject is Hrolf Kraki (Hrothulf), Beowulf makes only brief appearances in his novel, but the materials are excellently combined into a compelling narrative based on *Beowulf* and its analogues; this specialist novel must have been totally perplexing to Anderson's usual science fiction audience. Despite his title, *Who's Afraid of Beowulf,* Tom Holt (another writer best known for his science fiction) also focuses on themes from *Hrólfs saga kraka,* but includes a Beowulfian beginning and ending and turns the whole into hilarious slapstick located mainly in contemporary Scotland. The two thrillers by Crichton and Niven's team each introduce contemporary issues into the Beowulfian material. Crichton's *Eaters of the Dead* is based on the Arab Ibn Fadlan's report on his historical mission from Bagdad to the king of the Bulgars; on this journey, he encounters a tribe of Swedish merchants and records the lifestyle and ceremonies he witnesses (see Smyser 1965). In Crichton's novel, the Grendel folk who invade the hall are apparently Neanderthals, who worship a mother goddess. A Scandinavian tribe has taken over their territory, and "Buliwulf" comes to the colonizing tribe's defense when the displaced Grendel folk try to get their homeland back. In the science fiction novel by Niven, Pournelle, and Barnes, saurian "grendels" appear when humans destroy the ecological balance of the planet. Cadmann Wayland (equals Beowulf) comes to the rescue. Gore wells forth. (A previous hero invented by Niven, Beowulf Shaeffer, reappears in "Procrustes," an insert story in the May 1993 issue of *Omni*.)

The blood-drenched thriller reminds one of B movies, and indeed *Beowulf* has been adapted for radio, television, and screen. I will mention only three such adaptations. The first screenplay of which I have record is my own Stanford University M.A. thesis (written under the name Allen), which won an American Screenwriters' Award in 1966. Perhaps the most intriguing script actually produced is MGM's 1981 *Clash of the Titans,* an amazingly star-cast but somewhat stilted film "based on centuries-old Greek and Nordic legends" (videotape cover), in which Beverley Cross, an Englishman, remolds the myth of Perseus into the shape of *Beowulf*. The hero, exposed at sea as an infant like Scyld, grows up to fight three successive monsters, first a man turned swamp monster, then a terrifying cave-woman (the Medusa; in Nye's 1966 novel Grendel's mother is also a medusa), and finally the titanic sea dragon. Andromeda in chains provides the damsel in distress motif that *Beowulf* so notably, from the Hollywood perspective, lacks. The most amusing script is that for the Australian animated cartoon version of Gardner's novel: *Grendel, Grendel, Grendel,* a musical by Bruce Sweaton with the theme-song "Mother Loves You." Because the visuals take some getting used to, I had to watch the video twice to get many of the jokes—such as the fact that the humans have Aussie workingman accents while the dragon, who discourses in Peter Ustinov's voice, and Grendel, whether feeling sorry for himself or discussing philosophy with the dragon, both talk "posh." I would like to see the same delightful filmscript remade with better animation over the same soundtrack. Betty Jane Wylie's Canadian "musical epic" was recorded in 1974 and a lively rock musical produced in 1977, but neither proved so enjoyable as the Australian animated film, probably because Gardner's reinterpreted Grendel lends himself better to the modern media than Beowulf does.

Animation brings us to comic books, of which the Italo-Brazilian version described above was but the first. In the past two decades, two comic-book approaches to *Beowulf* have appeared, Uslan's in 1975 and Bingham's in 1984. In the first of their six issues, Uslan and his team more or less follow the story of Beowulf, who fights the monsters with his feisty girlfriend Nanzee at his side; then the writers bundle the pair off to sail with Odysseus, encounter von Däniken's *Chariots of the Gods*, and so forth. Jerry Bingham, on the other hand, attempts to offer his readers the real story as he understands it, complete with alliterative speech balloons and narration boxes. While the presentation falters, as when Hrothgar, slumped with despair in his hall, is served by half-naked wenches in harem costume, the graphics are technically excellent, and the dragon, zapping Beowulf like a ray gun, is one of the best I have seen.

For all Bingham's seriousness, however, this comic-book version will seem like a parody to anyone familiar with the original. A genuine parody comes from the hand of Bruce Blackistone in 1977 (republished 1983), *Beowabbit*. Purporting to be "translated from a recently discovered runic document that was conveniently burned thereafter [by a] well-intentioned arsonist," it is "attributed to Æthelstan of Devonshire." Fortunately, the first page was saved to be the frontispiece; it is in a fake Old English script that does at first glance resemble the real (not runic) manuscript. *Beowabbit* abounds in allusions to popular culture, as the beginning of the Unferth (Uncouth) episode demonstrates. He was under

> Hogrower's heel   official footstool.
> "Thay, arn't you   the Beowabbit
> who with Thumper   thwam in contetht
> thoppily thloshed   in thalt thea scum?"

These lines will not please those who must take their *Beowulf* straight. The only other "attributed" version I know is that by a modern German translator who is serious about it: Wilhelm Tegethoff's 1971 *Der altangelsächsische Beowulf: Ein Werk Adalberts von Bremen* (The Old Anglo-Saxon *Beowulf*: A Work by Adalbert von Bremen). In the much the same mold as Beowabbit with very clever punning is Beocat, hero of the one-page epic about "Grendel's Dog" in Henry Beard's 1994 *Poetry for Cats*.

Seriousness marks the creative adaptation most recent at the time of this essay, *Beowulf: A Likeness* (1990), in which I had a hand. Randolph Swearer's evocative photographs of place and artifact realize—and fantasize—the world of the poem through graphic expression, and the poem by Raymond Oliver, in a variety of formal meters, adopts the realistic techniques of the historical novel to "add to the poem's human, affective dimension as well as its linguistic texture" (Niles 1993b, 874).

IV. Illustrations of *Beowulf*

Swearer manipulates his photographs to achieve just the combination of mood and style that he wants. He even had me find the exactly correct manuscript page to go with particular passages of text on the "shadow-pages" he designed, a detail I am glad to be able to mention because few, I am certain, will have noticed. Such scrupulous attention to textual detail is unusual for an artist, but Swearer as a designer is conscious of his work having the same weight as Oliver's poem rather than merely decorating it. Most artwork in connection with literature is conceived of as secondary, dependent on the words, and this has the peculiar effect of cutting it loose from a need for authenticity. Yet illustrations should not be regarded lightly, for as well as revealing a bias and ignorance about the material that is often symptomatic of the larger society, the art that accompanies a text affects how we read that text.

Art can, for example, determine literary genre. The effect of Virgil Burnett's two-tone illustrations for Crossley-Holland's translation, published by the Folio Society in 1968, is to turn *Beowulf* into a fairy tale. The reader recognizes the style, perhaps especially that of Wealhtheow's dress (plate 1), and responds to the text accordingly. The art is familiar and soothing even when the action is violent (as in plate 2), and the English audience will read the poem as native, making Beowulf an English hero.

The English reviewers of Collinder's 1954 Swedish translation, on the other hand, found Per Engström's highly stylized linoleum prints too "primitive" for *Beowulf,* speaking of "the delicate tracery of the originals" and declaring that "linoleum is no substitute for gold" (Ross and Stanley 1960, 112). The comment reveals their ignorance about early Scandinavian material culture. Engström based his illustrations specifically on designs on the circa eighth-century carved stones found throughout Sweden, but especially on the island of Gotland. The allusion implicit in the artwork brings Beowulf back to his native land.

Herrera's 1965 Spanish *Beowulfo* won a prize for the illustrations by Julio Castro that again appropriate the poem. One might well call the quixotic hero "Don Beowulfo," as in fifteenth-century armor he spars with a mildly cubist brachiosaurus that serves as the dragon (plate 3). In other pictures, Grendel is a hulking Moorish wrestler, and cacti stud the landscape of Grendelsmere, that desert lake.

I find these three nationalistic appropriations both attractive and amusing, the two that follow less so. "Lynd Ward is a name you know, of course," says the editor of the Limited Editions Club, which reissued in 1952 William Ellery Leonard's 1923 translation. Ward's illustrations first accompanied Leonard's translation in 1939. This famous mid-century American illustrator created the engravings on wood after studying at the Academy of Graphic Arts in Leipzig. They are technically perhaps the most beautiful of all illustrations of *Beowulf*. The editor goes on to say, "The Viking folk in *Beowulf* seem ideally suited to Lynd Ward's personal art, their square jaws and granite eyes and flowing hair and outsize anatomies." But then one pauses to examine the meaning of this Aryan art, *Jugendstil* at its finest and its most disturbing. Ward's arrogant blond Beowulf is indeed a suitable protagonist for the work that Leo had labeled as *dasz älteste deutsche Helden-gedicht* (the oldest German hero poem) (plate 4).

For a different reason, I admire yet dislike Leonard Baskin's 1971 illustrations for Burton Raffel's (1963) translation. As in the case of Lynd Ward, one cannot fault the art. Baskin's drawings are technically excellent, and he is deservedly famous for his sensitive portraiture elsewhere. His "work is represented in the permanent collections of the major museums and art galleries in America" (flap copy), and Raffel says that he had long hoped for his illustrations (xix). But Baskin makes the young Beowulf look like an amiable dolt (plate 5) and the old Beowulf a whiskey priest; his Grendel flaunts as many phallus-like protuberances as the Diana of Ephesus has "breasts" (plate 6); and his dragon looks like some aged auntie's cast-off fox fur. The flap copy claims that Baskin was impressed by the "grotesque majesty" of the poem. *Majesty* would not be my choice of those two words to describe his illustrations. Others' opinions may differ.

When I show my *Beowulf* slides to students, at this point I insert the unarguably most grotesque of the illustrations, the cover for the Brazilian comic book of which the story content is described above. Against a yellow background, the huge, taloned, slimy-green hand of Froda (Grendel's mother) reaches up from the blood-red mere to clutch a Beowulf struggling like a mouse. Then we move to the amused, extravagant art of Ricardo Villamonte in the comic book designed by Michael Uslan. The cover picture parodies the modern idea of a Viking as Beowulf, long, steely horns extending from his helmet, single-handedly holds open the dragon's jaws (plate 7). Next I show the serious art of Bingham in *Beowulf: Dragon Slayer,* whose hero has the fierce but sensitive intentness of Clint Eastwood: "He was of a noble breed. He was . . . BEOWULF!" In their very different ways, Baskin, Uslan, and Bingham all make Beowulf into the great American hero; any one of these three Beowulfs could easily don football gear or become ace jet pilots. But only Bingham's might willingly pick up a book or guide a community in his later years.

The Icelander Flóki's Beowulf in Björnsson's 1983 translation, with his sensitive, thoughtful (Icelandic) face, might well be a potential reader had he time to indulge in such pleasures. Like others, the artist appropriates the poem by referring through art to his own culture. As Beowulf dives into Grendel's mere, he passes monsters with their mouths frozen in the Norwegian artist Munch's famous "Scream" (plate 8). Grendel's big-breasted mother is a she-troll lurking beneath the wreathed roots overhanging her lake, glaring out of the picture like a Medusa, broad nosed and vampire toothed, yet she is clearly akin to Maurice Sendak's monsters, in a not-so-friendly mood (plate 9). On page 77, she leaps on Beowulf, dagger uplifted, huge breasts flopping in his face: "Ðæt nis heore ides!" (That is not a nice lady!) Her only rival in awfulness is J. H. F. Bacon's Blakean "demon of evil," the huge-jowled saurian Grendel illustrating M. I. Ebbutt's 1910 version of the demon tale for children—who must have been scared out of their wits (plate 10).

Two of my personal favorites come last. Brian Froude's "Native-American" Beowulf (plate 11) stands sternly over the anonymous *Childcraft Annual* retelling of the story, a true warrior, with the interior of a wooden Heorot behind him decorated with carvings based on Celtic and Scandinavian art, some being exact replicas of those intricate designs. In another illustration (plate 12), Froude's ravening Grendel, clawed and clad, lurches convincingly into Heorot, the only artist-imagined monster that succeeds in "scrithing" (the poet's word for his motion, line 650). Charles Keeping's ink-and-wash drawings for Kevin Crossley-Holland's 1982 version lend a brooding atmosphere somewhat at variance with the lively text for children. The monsters, their mouths agape with rotting teeth when dead (32–33), are terrifyingly alive with a nightmare indeterminacy when they come raiding or wrestle with the hero. In plate 13, the skeletal mother, shawled with spidery black wisps of hair, clutches Beowulf to her breast in a deadly, erotic embrace.

V. Recent or Currently Available Modern English Translations

The following selective list is alphabetized in order to minimalize preferential treatment, but the reader should be forewarned that my commentary expresses bias. For example, some of the available translations are quite old, and their dated style and diction will disturb many readers more than it does me. Full citations appear in the list of "Works Cited" at the end of this volume.

Alexander, Michael (1973). This taut, gritty imitative translation influenced by Ezra Pound, of whom Alexander is a scholar, is the one most easily available in England.

Bradley, S. A. J. (1982; pp. 408–94). Presenting a literal prose translation, Bradley elaborates from the commentary of Grundtvig (1820), whom he quotes extensively, to commend a reading in accordance with "the larger philosophy of Christianity" (411).

Chickering, Howell D., Jr. (1977). This line-for-line, facing-page translation in a literal, moderately imitative verse, accompanied by an elegant essay, is the choice of many scholars who teach the poem.

Crossley-Holland, Kevin (1968). A readable and mainly dependable translation in four-stress verse, this receives an approving and informative introduction by one of the major scholars of Old English, Bruce Mitchell.

Donaldson, E. Talbot (1966). Because it appears in *The Norton Anthology of English Literature,* many students first encounter *Beowulf* in this version. The somewhat old-fashioned prose dense on the page gives the impression that the poem is a barrier to be mounted, yet Donaldson has produced a good, literal translation.

Gordon, R. K. (1923). This mainly close prose translation comes in a Dover Thrift Edition, the most inexpensive version now available.

Greenfield, Stanley B. (1982). This translation by one of the most sensitive literary critics of Anglo-Saxon poetry is, as advertised, readable. Greenfield's main innovations are a syllabic verse of mainly nine syllables per line and an effort to incorporate wordplay comparable to what he finds in the original.

Hieatt, Constance B. (1967). Also inexpensively priced, Hieatt's is a readable prose translation in which, the translator says, "I have taken a great many liberties in rearranging sentences, and have simply discarded some minor details" (v).

Hudson, Marc (1990). "Liberal paraphrase might describe the path I took" (17). Hudson's chapter title, "The Syntax of Contemplation," tells us much about the effect he strives for in this fine verse translation.

Huppé, Bernard F. (1984). Huppé writes that his aim is "to present a coherent view of the theme and structure of the poem in the context of the poet's inescapable Augustinian frame of reference" (ix). The careful alliterative translation on pages 105–92 furthers that (questionable) aim with its marginal notes referring back to previous commentary.

Kennedy, Charles W. (1940). Many are critical of this extremely alliterative, rhythmic translation, but it was the form in which I first read *Beowulf,* and I remember being swept along through the narrative.

Lehmann, Ruth P. M. (1988). While succeeding in a faithful rendition of the text and more precise attention to meter than any previous translation, the book abounds in misprints and errors of fact surprising both from this scholar and from this press.

Morgan, Edwin (1952). In a loosely alliterative four-stress verse by a well-known Scottish poet, this slim and inexpensive paperback translation, though somewhat dated in diction, nevertheless achieves some dazzling effects. Kenneth Rexroth acclaimed it as the most elegant translation he knew (Rexroth 1963, 27).

Osborn, Marijane (1984). In imitative verse aiming at clarity and readability, this translation is illustrated with an array of artifacts and related images.

Raffel, Burton (1963). This rendering into an extremely free imitative verse is probably, as Raffel claims, the liveliest translation of *Beowulf.* My misgivings echo those of many reviewers: in its freedom this translation often misrepresents the poem.

Rebsamen, Frederick R. (1991). My quick reading finds this alliterative verse translation adequate among those striving for faithfulness, though the punctuation is so odd as sometimes to be disturbing. Rebsamen earlier experimented with *Beowulf* in a prose retelling of the poem as if by Beowulf himself (*Beowulf Is My Name,* 1971).

Swanton, Michael (1978). Claiming that *"Beowulf* is to English what the *Odyssey* and *Iliad* are to Greek language and literature" (i), Swanton compactly presents text and facing page prose translation in a handy format, with notes.

Tripp, Raymond P., Jr. (1991). Incorporating material from *More about the Fight with the Dragon* (1983), in which "an entirely different story emerges" (ix), this translation reflects the most extreme textual reinterpretation produced by a cholar in this century and is mentioned here for that reason.

The previous chapters of this book show how the perception of *Beowulf* shifts with time, often radically, and they record the scholarly conversations that have marked those shifts. This chapter adds a geographical and ethnic dimension to the conversation, showing how different nationalities and groups have perceived or taken possession of the poem. My personal list of translations, independent partial translations, and versions of *Beowulf,* of which the texts mentioned here are only a representative sample, contains more than three hundred items. Each one of these, at some time, has brought the poem alive to a different audience. The latest news is that Nobel Prize winner Seamus Heaney has embarked upon a complete translation (personal communication, 8 June 1995).

Your fame has spread
throughout the wide world, Beowulf my friend . . . . (ll. 1703b–04)

Plate 1. *Weahltheow.* Lithograph by Virgil Burnett for *Beowulf,* trans. Kevin Crossley-Holland (London: Folio Society, 1971), 53. © The Folio Society Ltd.

Plate 2. *Grendel's Mother.* Lithograph by Virgil Burnett for *Beowulf,* trans. Kevin Crossley-Holland (London: Folio Society, 1971), 64. © The Folio Society Ltd.

Plate 3. *Don Beowulfo*. Cover by Julio Castro reprinted from José Luis Herrera's *Beowulfo* (Madrid: Aguilar, 1965).

Plate 4. *Young Beowulf.* Drawing by Lynd Ward reprinted from William Ellery
Leonard's *Beowulf* (New York: Century, 1952), 19.

Plate 5. *Young Beowulf*. Drawing by Leonard Baskin reprinted from *Beowulf*, trans. with an introduction and afterword by Burton Raffel (Amherst: University of Massachusetts Press, 1971), opposite p. 12. Copyright © 1963, 1971 by Burton Raffel and copyrighted © 1971 by The University of Massachusetts Press.

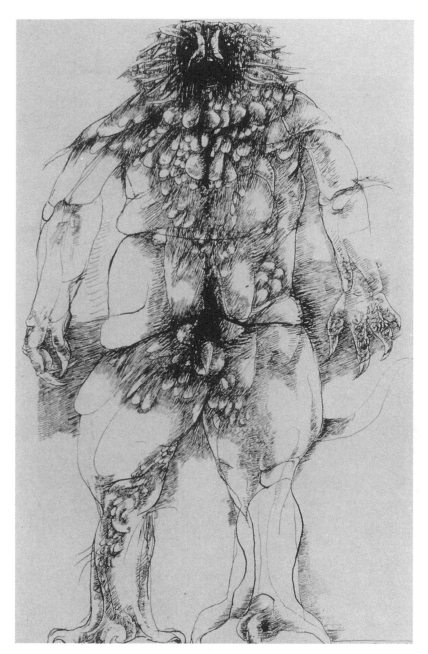

Plate 6. *Grendel*. Drawing by Leonard Baskin reprinted from *Beowulf*, trans. with an introduction and afterword by Burton Raffel (Amherst: University of Massachusetts Press, 1971), opposite p. 36. Copyright © 1963, 1971 by Burton Raffel and copyrighted © 1971 by The University of Massachusetts Press.

Plate 7. *Beowulf and Nan-Zee*. Cover drawing by Richardo Villamonte reprinted from "Beowulf" No. 3, © 1975 DC Comics. All rights reserved. Used with permission.

Plate 8. *Dive with Monsters.* Drawing by Flóki reprinted, with permission, from Halldóra B. Björnsson's *Bjólfskviða* (Reykjavík: Fjölvi, 1983), 73.

Plate 9. *Grendel's Mother.* Drawing by Flóki reprinted, with permission, from Halldóra B. Björnsson's *Bjólfskviða* (Reykjavík: Fjölvi, 1983), 61.

Plate 10. *Grendel Devouring*. Drawing by J. H. F. Bacon reprinted from M. I. Ebbutt's *Hero-Myths and Legends of the British Race* (London: G. G. Harrup, 1910), opposite p. 4.

Plate 11. *Native-American Beowulf.* Illustration by Brian Froude reprinted from "Be-owulf and Grendel" in *The Magic of Words: The 1975 Childcraft Annual*, 77. © 1975 Field Enterprises Educational Corporation. By permission of World Book Inc.

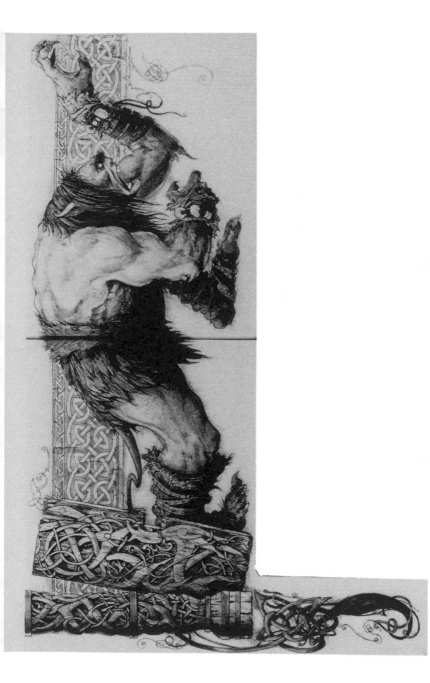

Plate 12. *Grendel's Coming*. Illustration by Brian Froude reprinted from "Beowulf and Grendel" in *The Magic of Words: The 1975 Childcraft Annual*, 80–81. © 1975 Field Enterprises Educational Corporation. By permission of World Book Inc.

Plate 13. *Grendel's Ma & Beowulf.* Drawing by Charles Keeping reprinted from
Kevin Crossley-Holland's *Beowulf* (Oxford: Oxford University Press, 1982), 31.
By permission of Oxford University Press.

Abbreviations

ABR	*American Benedictine Review*
AfNF	*Arkiv för nordisk filologi*
Age of Sutton Hoo	*The Age of Sutton Hoo.* Ed. Martin Carver. Woodbridge: Boydell, 1992.
An Med	*Annuale Mediaevale*
AN&Q	*American Notes and Queries*
Anthology	*An Anthology of Beowulf Criticism.* Ed. Lewis E. Nicholson. Notre Dame IN: University of Notre Dame Press, 1963.
Antiquity	*Antiquity: A Quarterly Journal of Archaeology*
Archiv	*Archiv für das Studium der neueren Sprachen und Literaturen*
ASE	*Anglo-Saxon England*
ATfS	*Antikvarisk tidskrift för Sverige*
Basic Beowulf	*Beowulf: Basic Readings.* Ed. Peter S. Baker. Basic Readings in Anglo-Saxon England 1. New York and London: Garland, 1995.
Beowulf Poet	*The Beowulf Poet: A Collection of Critical Essays.* Ed. Donald K. Fry. Englewood Cliffs NJ: Prentice-Hall, 1968.
BGdSL	*Beiträge zur Geschichte der deutschen Sprache und Literatur*
BJRL	*Bulletin of the John Rylands Library*
Brodeur	*Studies in Old English Literature in Honor of Arthur G. Brodeur.* Ed. Stanley B. Greenfield. Eugene: University of Oregon Press, 1963.
Cambridge Companion	*Cambridge Companion to Old English Literature.* Ed. Malcolm Godden and Michael Lapidge. Cambridge: Cambridge University Press, 1991.
CE	*College English*
CL	*Comparative Literature*
Dating of Beowulf	*The Dating of Beowulf.* Ed. Colin Chase. Toronto: University of Toronto Press, 1981.
Donaldson	*Acts of Interpretation: The Text in Its Contexts, 700–1600: Essays on Medieval and Renaissance Literature in Honor of E. Talbot Donaldson.* Ed. Mary J. Carruthers and Elizabeth D. Kirk. Norman OK: Pilgrim, 1982.

E&S	*Essays and Studies by Members of the English Association*
EETS	Early English Text Society
EGS	*English and Germanic Studies*
ELH	*ELH*, or *Journal of English Literary History*
ELN	*English Language Notes*
ES	*English Studies*
ESC	*English Studies in Canada*
Essential Articles	*Essential Articles for the Study of Old English Poetry.* Ed. Jess B. Bessinger Jr. and Stanley J. Kahrl. Hamden CT: Archon, 1968.
EStn	*Englische Studien*
GRM	*Germanisch-romanische Monatsschrift*
Interpretations	*Interpretations of Beowulf: A Critical Anthology.* Ed. R. D. Fulk. Bloomington: Indiana University Press, 1991.
JEGP	*Journal of English and Germanic Philology*
Klaeber	*Studies in English Philology: A Miscellany in Honor of Frederick Klaeber.* Ed. Kemp Malone and Martin B. Ruud. Minneapolis: University of Minnesota Press, 1929.
Leeds Studies	*Leeds Studies in English and Kindred Languages*
Lord	*Oral Traditional Literature: A Festschrift for Albert Bates Lord.* Ed. John Miles Foley. Columbus OH: Slavica, 1981.
MÆ	*Medium Ævum*
Magoun	*Franciplegius: Medieval and Linguistic Studies in Honor of Francis Peabody Magoun, Jr.* Ed. Jess B. Bessinger Jr. and Robert F. Creed. New York: New York University Press, 1965.
McGalliard	*Anglo-Saxon Poetry: Essays in Appreciation for John C. McGalliard.* Ed. Lewis E. Nicholson and Dolores Warwick Frese. Notre Dame IN: University of Notre Dame Press, 1975.
Meritt	*Philological Essays: Studies in Old and Middle English Language and Literature in Honor of Herbert Dean Merrit.* Ed. James L. Rosier. The Hague and Paris: Mouton, 1970.
MH	*Medievalia et Humanistica*
MLN	*Modern Language Notes*

MLQ	*Modern Language Quarterly*
MLR	*Modern Language Review*
MP	*Modern Philology*
MRTS	Medieval and Renaissance Texts and Studies
N&Q	*Notes and Queries*
Neophil	*Neophilologus*
New Readings	*New Readings on Women in Old English Literature.* Ed. Helen Damico and Alexandra Hennessey Olsen. Bloomington: University of Indiana Press, 1990.
NM	*Neuphilologische Mitteilungen*
OEL in Context	*Old English Literature in Context.* Ed. John D. Niles. Cambridge: D. S. Brewer, 1980.
OEL: 22 Essays	*Old English Literature: Twenty-two Analytical Essays.* Ed. Martin Stevens and Jerome Mandel. Lincoln: University of Nebraska Press, 1968.
OE Poetry	*Old English Poetry: Essays on Style.* Ed. Daniel G. Calder. Berkeley and Los Angeles: University of California Press, 1979.
PBA	*Proceedings of the British Academy*
PLL	*Papers on Language and Literature*
PMLA	*PMLA,* or *Publications of the Modern Language Association of America*
Pope	*Old English Studies in Honour of John C. Pope.* Ed. Robert B. Burlin and Edward B. Irving Jr. Toronto: University of Toronto Press, 1974.
PQ	*Philological Quarterly*
RES	*Review of English Studies*
RUO	*Revue d'Université d'Ottawa*
SBVS	*Saga-Book* (Viking Society for Northern Research)
SEL (Tokyo)	*Studies in English Literature*
SN	*Studia Neophilologica*
SP	*Studies in Philology*
SS	*Scandinavian Studies*
TCAAS	*Transactions of the Connecticut Academy of Arts and Sciences*
Tolkien	*English and Medieval Studies Presented to J. R. R. Tolkien on the Occasion of His Seventieth Birthday.* Ed. Norman Davis and C. L. Wrenn. London: Allen & Unwin, 1962.
TSLL	*Texas Studies in Literature and Language*

UTQ	*University of Toronto Quarterly*
ZfdA	*Zeitschrift für deutsches Altertum und deutsche Literatur*
ZfdP	*Zeitschrift für deutsche Philologie*

Works Cited

In five sections: bibliographies, editions and facsimiles, translations, imaginative re-creations, and all other works cited.

I. Bibliographies

Fry, Donald K. 1969. *Beowulf and the Fight at Finnsburh: A Bibliography*. Charlottesville: University Press of Virginia.

Greenfield, Stanley B., and Fred C. Robinson. 1980. *A Bibliography of Publications on Old English Literature to the End of 1972*. Toronto: University of Toronto Press.

Hasenfratz, Robert J. 1993. *Beowulf Scholarship: An Annotated Bibliography, 1979–1990*. New York: Garland.

———. 1994. *A Bibliography of Beowulf Criticism, 1979-94* [database online]. Available from http://www.georgetown.edu/labyrinth/labyrinth-home.html.

Short, Douglas. 1980a. *Beowulf Scholarship: An Annotated Bibliography*. New York: Garland.

Tinker, Chauncey B. 1903. *The Translations of Beowulf: A Critical Bibliography*. New Haven: Yale University Press. Republished 1974 with an updated bibliography by Marijane Osborn and a new foreword by Fred C. Robinson. Hamden CT: Archon.

II. Editions and Facsimiles

Arnold, Thomas. 1876. *Beowulf: A Heroic Poem of the Eighth Century*. London: Longmans, Green.

Chickering, Howell D., Jr. 1977. *Beowulf: A Dual-Language Edition*. Garden City NY: Anchor.

Crépin, André. 1991. *Beowulf: Édition diplomatique et texte critique, traduction française, commentaires et vocabulaire*. Goppingen: Kummerle.

Dobbie, Elliott Van Kirk. 1953. *Beowulf and Judith*. Anglo-Saxon Poetic Records 4. New York: Columbia University Press.

Ettmüller, Ludwig. 1875. *Carmen de Beovulfi Gautarum regis rebus praeclare gestis atque interitu, quale fuerit ante quam in manus interpolatoris, monachi Vestsaxonici, inciderat*. Zürich: Zürcher & Fürrer.

Grundtvig, N. F. S. 1861. *Beowulfes beorh eller Bjovulfs-drapen, det old-angelske helte digt, paa grund-sproget*. Copenhagen: K. Schönberg.

Heyne, Moritz. 1863. *Beowulf: Mit ausführlichem Glossar*. Paderborn: F. Schöningh. 1888: 5th ed., rev. Adolf Socin. 1908: 8th ed., rev. Levin L. Schücking. 1940: 15th ed., rev. Else von Schaubert as *Heyne-Schückings Beowulf*. 3 pts. [text, commentary, glossary]. 1961: 17th ed., rev. Else von Schaubert.

Holder, Alfred. 1881. *Beowulf. I: Abdruck der Handschrift im British Museum*. Freiburg im Breslau: J. C. B. Mohr.

Holthausen, Ferdinand. 1905–06. *Beowulf nebst dem Finnsburg-Bruchstück*. 2 vols. Heidelberg: Winter.

Jack, George. 1994. *Beowulf: A Student Edition*. Oxford: Clarendon.

Kemble, John M. 1833. *The Anglo-Saxon Poems of Beowulf, The Travellers Song, and The Battle of Finnesburh*. Vol. 1. 1835: 2nd ed., issued along with vol. 2, *Translation* [1837; see section III, below]. London: Wm. Pickering.

Kiernan, Kevin. 1993–. *The Electronic Beowulf* [facsimile of specimens from Cotton Vitellius A. xv.; Thorkelin's transcripts, edition, translation; Conybeare's and Madden's collations]. Available from http://www.uky.edu/~kiernan/BL/kportico.html (U.S.) or http://portico.bl.uk/access/electronic-beowulf.html (outside U.S.).

Klaeber, Friedrich. 1922a. *Beowulf and The Fight at Finnsburg.* 1950a: 3rd ed., with first and second supplements. Boston: D. C. Heath.

Kuriyagawa, Fumio. 1931–32. *Beowulf and the Fight at Finnsburg* [English text and Japanese translation]. *English Literature and Philology* 3: 1–283.

Malone, Kemp. 1951. *The Thorkelin Transcripts of Beowulf in Facsimile.* Early English Manuscripts in Facsimile 1. Copenhagen: Rosenkilde & Bagger.

———. 1963. *The Nowell Codex: British Museum Cotton Vitellius A.xv, Second MS.* Early English Manuscripts in Facsimile 12. Copenhagen: Rosenkilde & Bagger.

Sedgefield, Walter J. 1910. *Beowulf.* 1935: 3rd. ed. Manchester: University of Manchester Press.

Thorkelin, Grímur Jónsson. 1815a. *De Danorum rebus gestis seculi III & IV: Poëma Danicum dialecto Anglo-Saxonica.* Copenhagen: Th. E. Rangel.

———. 1815b. "'Greetings to the Reader' from *De Danorum rebus gestis seculi III & IV.*" Trans. Taylor Corse and Robert E. Bjork. *SS* 68.3 (1996): forthcoming.

Thorpe, Benjamin. 1855. *The Anglo-Saxon Poems of Beowulf, The Scop or Gleeman's Tale, and The Fight at Finnesburg.* Rpt. 1962 with introduction by V. F. Hopper. Woodbury NY: Barron's Educational Series.

Trautmann, Moritz. 1904. *Das Beowulflied: Als Anhang das Finn-Bruchstück und die Waldhere-Bruchstücke. Bonner Beiträge zur Anglistik* 16. Bonn: P. Hanstein.

Tripp, Raymond P., Jr. 1983. *More about the Fight with the Dragon: Beowulf 2208b–3182.* New York: University Press of America.

———. 1991. *Beowulf: An Edition and Literary Translation in Progress.* Denver: Society for New Language Study.

von Schaubert, Else. See Heyne 1863, above.

Wrenn, C. L. 1953. *Beowulf with the Finnesburg Fragment.* London: Harrup.

Wyatt, A. J. 1894. *Beowulf: Edited with Textual Foot-Notes, Index of Proper Names, and Alphabetical Glossary.* Cambridge: Cambridge University Press.

———. 1914. *Beowulf with the Finnsburg Fragment.* 2nd ed., rev. R. W. Chambers. Cambridge: Cambridge University Press.

Zupitza, Julius. 1882. *Beowulf: Autotypes of the Unique Cotton MS. Vitellius A. XV in the British Museum, with a Transliteration.* EETS 77. London. 1959 [for 1958]: 2nd ed., rev. Norman Davis. EETS 245. London: Oxford University Press.

III. Translations

Alexander, Michael. 1973. *Beowulf: A Verse Translation.* Harmondsworth: Penguin.

Ayres, Harry Morgan. 1933. *Beowulf: A Paraphrase.* Williamsport PA: Bayard.

Björnsson, Halldóra B. 1983. *Bjólfskviða.* Ed. Pétur Knúttson Ridgewell. Reykjavík: Fjölvi.

Botkine, L. 1876. *Beowulf, épopée anglo-saxonne.* Le Havre: Imprimerie Lepelletier.

Bradley, S. A. J. 1982. *Anglo-Saxon Poetry.* London: Dent.

Clark Hall, John R. 1901. *Beowulf and the Fight at Finnsburg: A Translation into Modern English Prose.* 1950: 2nd edition, ed. C. L. Wrenn, with a preface by J. R. R. Tolkien. London: Allen and Unwin.

Collinder, Björn. 1954. *Beowulf översatt i originalets versmått.* Stockholm: Natur och Kultur.

Crossley-Holland, Kevin. 1968. *Beowulf.* London: Farrar Straus Giroux. London: Folio Society, 1973.

———. 1982. *Beowulf.* Illustrated by Charles Keeping. Oxford: Oxford University Press.

———. 1987. *Beowulf: The Poetry of Legend.* Woodbridge, Suffolk: Boydell.

Dillström, R. 1927. "*Beowulf.*" *Laivastolehti* 2: 35–40, 73–78, 137–44, 176–80, 201–4, 243–46, 284–89, 316–21, 349–56.

Donaldson, E. Talbot. 1966. *Beowulf.* New York: W. W. Norton.

Earle, John. 1857–58. "A Primitive Old Epic." *Household Words* 17: 459–64.

———. 1892. *The Deeds of Beowulf: An English Epic of the Eighth Century Done into Modern Prose.* Oxford: Clarendon.

Ebbutt, Maude Isabel. 1910. *Hero-Myths and Legends of the British Race.* London: G. G. Harrup. Republished as *Myths and Legends Series: The British.* New York: Avenel, 1986.

Ettmüller, Ludwig. 1840. *Beowulf: Heldengedicht des achten Jahrhunderts.* Zürich: Meyer & Zeller.

Garmonsway, G. N., and Jacqueline Simpson, trans. 1968. *Beowulf and Its Analogues.* Including "Archaeology and *Beowulf* " (rev. 1980) by Hilda Ellis Davidson. London: Dent.

Gordon, Robert K. 1923. *The Song of Beowulf.* London: Dent. Rpt. 1926 in his *Anglo-Saxon Poetry Selected and Translated.* 1954: Rev. ed. London: Dent.

Greenfield, Stanley B. 1982. *A Readable Beowulf: The Old English Epic Newly Translated.* Carbondale: Southern Illinois University Press.

Grein, C. W. M. 1857. *Dichtungen der Angelsachsen, stabreimend übersetzt.* 2 vols. Göttingen: G. H. Wigand.

Grion, Giusto. 1883. "*Beowulf:* Poema epico Anglosassone del vii secolo." *Atti della Real Accademia lucchese di scienze, lettere ed arti* 22: 197–379.

Grundtvig, N. F. S. 1820. *Bjowulfs drape: Et gothisk helte-digt.* Copenhagen: A. Seidelin.

Gummere, Francis B. 1909. *The Oldest English Epic: Beowulf, Finnsburg, Waldere, Deor, Widsith, and the German Hildebrand.* New York: Macmillan.

György, Fordította Szegő. 1994. *Beowulf.* Budapest: Eötvös Loránd Tudományegyetem, Anglisztika Tanszék.

Haarder, Andreas. 1984. *Sangen om Bjovulf.* Copenhagen: G. E. C. Gad.

Heaney, Seamus. 1987. "A Ship of Death." *The Haw Lantern.* New York: Noonday. 20.

Herrera, José Luis. 1965. *Beowulfo.* Madrid: Aguilar.

Hieatt, Constance B. 1967. *Beowulf and Other Old English Poems.* New York: Odyssey.

Hoffmann, P. 1893. *Beowulf: Aeltestes deutsches Heldengedicht.* 1900: 2nd ed. Hanover: M. & H. Schaper.

Hudson, Marc. 1990. *Beowulf: A Translation and Commentary.* Lewisburg PA: Bucknell University Press.

IArkho, Boris I. 1934. *Saga o Vol'sungakh [The Volsunga Saga].* Moscow.

Jonk, Jan. 1977. *Beowulf, een prosavertaling.* Amsterdam: Bert Bakker.

Kalma, Douwe. 1937. *Kenning Finn.* Frisia Rige 3. Snits, Netherlands.

Kemble, John M. 1837a. *A Translation of the Anglo-Saxon Poem of Beowulf, with a Copious Glossary, Preface, and Philological Notes.* Vol. 2 of Kemble's 1835 edition. London: Wm. Pickering.

Kennedy, Charles W. 1940. *Beowulf: The Oldest English Epic, Translated into Alliterative Verse.* New York: Oxford University Press.

Krol, Jelle, and Popke van der Zee. 1984. *Beowulf, in proaza-oersetting út it Aldingelsk.* Boalsert: Koperative Utjourwerij.

Lehmann, Ruth P. M. 1988. *Beowulf: An Imitative Translation.* Austin: University of Texas Press.

Leonard, William Ellery. 1923. *Beowulf: A New Verse Translation for Fireside and Classroom.* New York: Century. Rpt. 1939, New York: New York Heritage Press. Also rpt. 1952, New York: New York Limited Editions Club.

Lerate, Luis, and Jesus Lerate. 1986. *Beowulf y otros poemas anglosajones (siglos VII–X).* Madrid: Alianaza.

Lindqvist, Sune. 1958. *Beowulf Dissectus: Snitt ur fornkvädet jämte svensk tydning.* Uppsala: Almqvist & Wiksell.

Lumsden, Henry W. 1881. *Beowulf, an Old English Poem.* 1883: 2nd ed. London: K. Paul, Trench.

Manent, Maria. 1947. *La Poesía ingelsa, de los primitivos a los neoclásicos.* Barcelona: Ediciones Lauro. 20-25.

Morgan, Edwin. 1952. *Beowulf: A Verse Translation into Modern English.* Aldington, Kent: Hand and Flower. Rpt. 1962, Berkeley: University of California Press.

————. 1953. "Auld Man's Coronach" ["The Father's Lament" from *Beowulf* translated into Scots]. *Glasgow Herald,* 8 August.

Morris, William, and Alfred J. Wyatt. 1895. *The Tale of Beowulf, Sometime King of the Weder Geats.* Hammersmith: Kelmscott.

Nye, Robert. 1968. *Beowulf: A New Telling.* New York: Hill and Wang.

Olivero, Federico. 1934. *Beowulf.* Turin: Edizioni dell' "Erma."

Osborn, Marijane. 1984. *Beowulf: A Verse Translation with Treasures of the Ancient North.* Berkeley and Los Angeles: University of California Press.

Oshitari, Kinshiro. 1990. *Beowulf.* Tokyo: Kenkyusha.

Pierquin, Hubert. 1912. *Le poème anglo-saxon de Beowulf.* Paris: Picard.

Polevoy, P. N. 1993. *Legendy i skrazanyja staoj Evropy: Pod zvon mechej, Pesni Eddy, Pesn' o Nibelungakh, Skazanie o Beovul'fe.* Smolensk: Smiadyn'.

Raffel, Burton. 1963. *Beowulf.* New York: New American Library. Rpt. 1971, Amherst: University of Massachusetts Press.

Rebsamen, Frederick R. 1971. *Beowulf Is My Name, and Selected Translations of Other Old English Poems.* San Francisco: Rinehart.

————. 1991. *Beowulf: A Verse Translation.* New York: Harper-Collins.

Rytter, Henrik. 1921. *Beowulf og striden um Finnsborg fra angelsaksisk.* Oslo: Det Norska Samlaget.

Schuhmann, Giuseppe. 1882. *"Beowulf,* Antichissimo poema epico de' popoli germanici." *Giornale Napoletano di Filosofia e Lettere, Scienze morali e politiche* 7: 25–36, 175–90.

Simons, L. 1896. *Beowulf: Angelsaksisch Volksepos vertaald in stafrijm en met inleidung en aanteekeningen.* Ghent: A. Siffer.

Simrock, Karl. 1859. *Beowulf: Das älteste deutsche Epos.* Stuttgart: J. G. Cotta.

Swanton, Michael. 1978. *Beowulf: Edited with an Introduction, Notes and New Prose Translation.* Manchester: Manchester University Press.

Tharaud, Barry. 1990. *Beowulf.* Illustrations by Rockwell Kent. Niwot: University Press of Colorado.

Tikhomirova, V. 1975. *Beowulf, Starshaia Edda, Pesnia o Nibelungakh* [*Beowulf, Elder Edda, Song of the Nibelungen*]. Ed. M. I. Steblin-Kamenskii. Biblioteka vsemirnoi literatury [Library of World Literature], ser. 1, vol. 9. Moscow: Khudozhestvennaia literatura.

Vera Pérez, Orestes. 1959. *Beowulf: Traducción, en prosa, del anglosajón al español.* Madrid: Aguilar.

Wahba, Y. Magdi M. 1964. *Qudamā' al-Injilīz wa-malhamat Biyūlf* [*A Study of Beowulf.*] Cairo.

Wickberg, Rudolf. 1889. *Beovulf, en fornengelsk hjeltedikt.* Westervik: C. O. Ekblad.

IV. Imaginative Re-creations

Allen, Marijane [Marijane Osborn]. 1965. "Beowulf: A Screenplay." M.A. thesis, Stanford University, Department of English.

Amis, Kingsley. 1957. "Anglo-Saxon Platitudes." *Spectator* 198: 445.

Anderson, Poul. 1988. *Hrolf Kraki's Saga.* New York: Baen.

Auden, W. H. 1962. "A Short Ode to a Philologist." In *Tolkien,* 11–12.

Basari, Enrico. 1940–41. *"Beowulf:* Leggenda cristiana dell' antica Danimarca, cineepopea eroica." *Il Vittorioso* [Rome, periodical].

Beard, Henry. 1994. *Poetry for Cats: The Definitive Anthology of Distinguished Feline Verse.* New York: Villard.

Beaty, John O. 1937. *Swords in the Dawn: A Story of the First Englishmen.* New York: Longmans, Green.

"Beowulf." 1984. *Great Myths and Legends.* Childcraft Annual. Chicago: Field Enterprises.

Bingham, Jerry. 1984. *Beowulf, Adapted from the 8th Century Epic Poem.* Chicago: First Comics.

Blackistone, Bruce Edward. 1977. *Beowabbit: Facsimile from the Collection of Raymond Palmer, Attributed to Æthelstan of Devonshire.* Avenue, MD: Bruce Blackistone.

Borges, Jorge Luis. 1951. "La Gesta de Beowulf." *Antiguas Literaturas Germánicas.* México: Fondo de Cultura Económica. 18–25.

———. 1967. "Poem Written in a Copy of *Beowulf.*" Trans. Alastair Reid. *A Personal Anthology.* Ed. Anthony Kerrigan. New York: Grove. 202. [The Spanish originals of this poem and others on Anglo-Saxon subjects appear in *Obras Completas 1923–1972.* Buenos Aires: Emecé Editores, 1974. 902–06.]

———. 1983. *Obras completas en colaboración.* Madrid: Alianza. 307–21.

Brüder, Otto. 1927. *Beowulf, ein heldisches Spiel*. Munich: Chr. Kaiser.

Canaway, W. H. 1958. *The Ring Givers*. London: Michael Joseph.

Crichton, Michael. 1976. *Eaters of the Dead: The Manuscript of Ibn Fadlan Relating His Experiences with the Northmen in A.D. 922*. New York: Knopf.

Cross, Beverley. 1981. *Clash of the Titans* [script for Charles H. Schneer's MGM movie].

Gardner, John. 1971. *Grendel*. New York: Knopf.

Hanson, Howard. 1925. *Symphony No. 2 ("Romantic"): "The Lament for Beowulf." Opus 25*. Victor Masterworks VM 889. Victor 11-8114/6, set M889. Mercury Records SR90192.

Hart, Joseph. 1974–75. "Wiglaf " [short story]. *Prairie Schooner* Winter: 283-95.

Holt, Tom. 1988. *Who's Afraid of Beowulf?* London: Macmillan.

Niven, Larry. 1966. *World of Ptavvs*. New York: Ballantine.

———. 1993. "Procrustes." *Omni* May

Niven, Larry, Jerry Pournelle, and Steven Barnes. 1987. *The Legacy of Heorot*. New York: Simon and Schuster.

Nye, Robert. 1966. *Beowulf*. London: Arrow.

"O Monstro de Caim" 1955. [Based on Basari]. *Epopéia* 33: 3–20.

Przedpelska-Trzeciakowska, Anna. 1966. *Beowulf*. Warsaw. [Polish translation of Sutcliff.]

Stevens, Wallace. 1961. "The Auroras of Autumn." *The Collected Poems of Wallace Stevens*. New York: Knopf. 411–21.

Sutcliff, Rosemary. 1961. *Beowulf*. Oxford: Bodley Head. Reissued as *Dragon Slayer: The Story of Beowulf*. London: Puffin, 1966.

Swearer, Randolph, Raymond Oliver, and Marijane Osborn. 1990. *Beowulf: A Likeness*. New Haven: Yale University Press.

Sweaton, Bruce. 1982. *Grendel, Grendel, Grendel* [Animated film]. Satori Films, Australia.

Tennyson, Alfred Lord. 1969. *Tennyson: A Selected Edition Incorporating the Trinity College Manuscripts*. Ed. Christopher Ricks. Berkeley and Los Angeles: University of California Press.

Uslan, Michael. 1975–76. *Beowulf, Dragon Slayer*. New York: D.C. Quality Magazine.

Vallvé, Manuel. 1934. *Beowulf*. Barcelona: Araluce.

Walsh, Gillian Paton. 1966. *Hengest's Tale*. London: Macmillan.

Wilbur, Richard. 1948. "Notes on Heroes (I–IV)." *Wake* 6: 80–81. Rpt. 1963 in *The Poems of Richard Wilbur*. New York: Harvest. 148–49.

Wyld, Henry Cecil. 1925. "Gothique" [by "Mr. Beach"]. *Oxford Magazine* 12 March: 367.

Wylie, Betty Jane. 1974. *Beowulf: A Musical Epic*. Composed by Victor Davies. Toronto: Golden Toad Music.

V. All Other Works Cited

Akerman, John Yonge. 1855. *Remains of Pagan Saxondom*. London: J. R. Smith.

Amos, Ashley Crandall. 1981. *Linguistic Means of Determining the Dates of Old English Literary Texts*. Cambridge MA: Medieval Academy of America.

———. 1982. "An Eleventh-Century *Beowulf?*" *Review* 4: 335–45.

Anderson, Benedict. 1983. *Imagined Communities: Reflections on the Origin and Spread of Nationalism*. London: Verso.

Anderson, Earl R. 1972. "A Submerged Metaphor in the Scyld Episode." *Yearbook of English Studies* 2: 1–4.

———. 1978. "Treasure Trove in *Beowulf:* A Legal View of the Dragon's Hoard." *Mediaevalia* 3: 141–64.

———. 1980. "Formulaic Typescene Survival: Finn, Ingeld, and the Nibelungenlied." *ES* 61: 293–301.

———. 1981. "*Beowulf*'s Retreat from Frisia: Analogues from the Fifth and Eighth Centuries." *ELN* 19: 89–93.

———. 1982. "Grendel's *glof* (*Beowulf* 2085b–88) and Various Latin Analogues." *Mediaevalia* 8: 1–8.

Andersson, Theodore M. 1976. *Early Epic Scenery: Homer, Virgil, and the Medieval Legacy*. Ithaca: Cornell University Press.

———. 1980. "Tradition and Design in *Beowulf*." In *OEL in Context*, 90–106. Rpt. in *Interpretations*, 219–34.

———. 1983. "The Dating of *Beowulf*." *UTQ* 52: 288–301.

———. 1985. "Heathen Sacrifice in *Beowulf* and Rimbert's *Life of Ansgar*." *MH* 13: 65–74.

———. 1992. "The Speeches in the *Waldere* Fragments." *De Gustibus: Essays for Alain Renoir*. Ed. John Miles Foley. New York: Garland. 21–29.

Andrew, Malcolm. 1981. "Grendel in Hell." *ES* 62: 401–10.

Andrew, Samuel O. 1940. *Syntax and Style in Old English*. Cambridge: Cambridge University Press.

———. 1948. *Postscript on Beowulf*. Cambridge: Cambridge University Press. 1969: 2nd ed. New York: Russell and Russell.

Arent, A. Margaret. 1969. "The Heroic Pattern: Old Germanic Helmets, *Beowulf,* and *Grettis saga*." *Old Norse Literature and Mythology: A Symposium*. Ed. Edgar C. Polomé. Austin: University of Texas Press. 130–99.

Arnold, C. J. 1988. *An Archaeology of the Early Anglo-Saxon Kingdoms*. London: Routledge.

Atkinson, Stephen C. B. 1984. "Beowulf and the Grendel-Kin: Thane, Avenger, King." *Publications of the Missouri Philological Association* 9: 58–66.

Aurner, Nellie S. 1917. *An Analysis of the Interpretations of the Finnsburg Documents*. University of Iowa Humanistic Studies 1. 6: 1–36.

Ayres, Harry M. 1917. "The Tragedy of Hengest in *Beowulf*." *JEGP* 16: 282–95.

Babb, Terry A. 1970. "*Beowulf,* Myth, and Meaning." *Arlington Quarterly* 2: 15–28.

Bachlechner, Joseph. 1849. "Die Merovinge im *Beowulf*." *ZdfA* 6: 524–26.

———. 1856. "Eomær and Heming (Hamlac)." *Germania* 1: 297–303, 455–61.

Bailey, Richard. 1980. *Viking Age Sculpture in Northern England*. London: Collins.

Baird, Joseph L. 1970. "Unferth the Þyle." *MÆ* 39: 1–12.

Baker, Peter S. 1988. "Beowulf the Orator." *Journal of English Linguistics* 21: 3–23.

Bakhtin, M. M. 1981. *The Dialogic Imagination: Four Essays.* Trans. Caryl Emerson and Michael Holquist. Austin: University of Texas Press.

Baldwin Brown, G. 1915. *The Arts in Early England.* Vol. 3. London: J. Murray.

Ball, Christopher J. E. 1971. "*Beowulf* 99–101." *N&Q* n.s. 18: 163.

Bammesberger, Alfred. 1990. "Die Lesart in *Beowulf* 1382a." *Anglia* 108: 314–26.

Bandy, Stephen C. 1973. "Cain, Grendel, and the Giants of *Beowulf.*" *PLL* 9: 235–49.

———. 1976. "Christliche Eschatologie und altenglische Dichtung, dargestellt am Beispiel des *Beowulf.*" Trans. Wolfgang Heuss. *GRM* 26: 14–25.

Barakat, Robert A. 1967. "John of the Bear and *Beowulf.*" *Western Folklore* 269: 1–11.

Barnes, Daniel R. 1970. "Folktale Morphology and the Structure of *Beowulf.*" *Speculum* 45: 416–34.

Bartlett, Adeline Courtney. 1935. *The Larger Rhetorical Patterns in Anglo-Saxon Poetry.* New York: Columbia University Press. Rpt. 1966, New York: AMS.

Bassett, Steven. 1989. "In Search of the Origins of Anglo-Saxon Kingdoms." *The Origins of Ango-Saxon Kingdoms.* Ed. Steven Bassett. London: Leceister University Press. 3–27.

Bassnett, Susan. 1980. *Translation Studies.* London: Methuen.

Batchelor, C. C. 1937. "The Style of the *Beowulf:* A Study of the Composition of the Poem." *Speculum* 12: 330–42.

Bately, Janet. 1985. "Linguistic Evidence as a Guide to the Authorship of Old English Verse: A Reappraisal, with Special Reference to *Beowulf.*" *Learning and Literature in Anglo-Saxon England: Studies Presented to Peter Clemoes on the Occasion of His Sixty-Fifth Birthday.* Ed. Michael Lapidge and Helmut Gneuss. Cambridge: Cambridge University Press. 409–31.

Baugh, A. C. 1959. "Improvisation in the Middle English Romance." *Proceedings of the American Philosophical Society* 103: 418–54.

———. 1967. "The Middle English Romance: Some Questions of Creation, Presentation, and Preservation." *Speculum* 42: 1–31.

Baum, Paull F. 1948–49. "The Meter of the *Beowulf.*" *MP* 46: 73–91, 145–62.

———. 1960. "The *Beowulf* Poet." *PQ* 39: 389–99. Rpt. in *Anthology,* 353–65.

Bauschatz, Paul C. 1982. *The Well and the Tree: World and Time in Early Germanic Culture.* Amherst: University of Massachusetts Press.

Beaty, John O. 1934. "The Echo-Word in *Beowulf* with a Note on the *Finnsburg Fragment.*" *PMLA* 49: 365–73.

Belden, H. M. 1913. "Onela the Scylfing and Ali the Bold." *MLN* 28: 149–53.

———. 1918. "Scyld Scefing and Huck Finn." *MLN* 33: 315.

Bellman, James Fredrick, Jr. 1985. "The Institutional Environment of *Beowulf.*" Diss. University of Nebraska.

Benediktsson, Jakob. 1957–61. "Icelandic Traditions of the Scyldings." *SBVS* 15: 48–66.

Bennett, Helen. 1992. "The Female Mourner at Beowulf's Funeral: Filling in the Blanks/ Hearing the Spaces." *Exemplaria* 4: 35–50.

Benson, Larry D. 1966. "The Literary Character of Anglo-Saxon Formulaic Poetry." *PMLA* 81: 334–41. Rpt. in Benson 1995, 1–14.

———. 1967. "The Pagan Coloring of *Beowulf.*" *Old English Poetry: 15 Essays.* Ed. Robert P. Creed. Providence: Brown University Press. 193–213. Rpt. in Benson 1995, 15–31. Also rpt. in *Basic Beowulf,* 35–50.

———. 1970. "The Originality of *Beowulf.*" *The Interpretation of Narrative: Theory and Practice.* Ed. Morton W. Bloomfield. 1–43. Harvard English Studies 1. Cambridge MA: Harvard University Press. Rpt. in Benson 1995, 32–69.

———. 1995. *Contradictions: From Beowulf to Chaucer: Selected Studies of Larry D. Benson.* Ed. Theodore M. Andersson and Stephen A. Barney. Aldershot, Hants, and Brookfield VT: Scolar.

Berendsohn, Walter A. 1915. "Altgermanische Heldendichtung." *Neue Jahrbücher* 18: 633–48.

———. 1932. "Hrolfssaga kraka und Beowulf-Epos." *Niederdeutsche Studien. Festschrift für Conrad Borchling.* Neumünster: Karl Wachholtz. 328–37.

———. 1935. *Zur Vorgeschichte des Beowulf.* Copenhagen: Levin & Munksgaard.

Berger, Harry, Jr., and H. Marshall Leicester Jr. 1974. "Social Structure as Doom: The Limits of Heroism in *Beowulf.*" In *Pope,* 37–79.

Bessinger, Jess B., Jr. 1958. "*Beowulf* and the Harp at Sutton Hoo." *UTQ* 27: 148–68.

———, and Robert Y. Yeager, eds. 1984. *Approaches to Teaching Beowulf.* New York: Modern Language Association.

Biddle, Martin, and Birthe Kjolbye-Biddle. 1992. "Repton and the Vikings." *Antiquity* 66: 36–51.

Biggs, Frederick M., Thomas D. Hill, and Paul E. Szarmach. 1990. *Sources of Anglo-Saxon Literary Culture: A Trial Version.* MRTS 74. Binghamton: State University of New York.

Binns, Alan L. 1953–57. "The Story of Þorsteinn uxafót." *SBVS* 14: 36–60.

Binz, Gustav. 1895. "Zeugnisse zur germanischen Sage in England." *BGdSL* 20: 141–223.

Bjork, Robert E. 1980. "Unferth in the Hermeneutic Circle: A Reappraisal of James L. Rosier's 'Design for Treachery: The Unferth Intrigue.'" *PLL* 16: 133–41.

———. 1994. "Speech as Gift in *Beowulf.*" *Speculum* 69: 993–1022.

———. 1997. "Nineteenth-Century Scandinavia and the Birth of Anglo-Saxon Studies." *Anglo-Saxonism: The Idea of Anglo-Saxon England from the Anglo-Saxons to the Present Day.* Ed. Allen J. Frantzen and John D. Niles. (Forthcoming).

Björkman, Erik. 1919. "Zu einigen Namen im *Beowulf: Breca, Brondingas, Wealhþeo(w).*" *Beiblatt zur Anglia* 30: 170–80.

Black, Vaughan, and Brian Bethune. 1984. "*Beowulf* and the Rites of Holy Week." *Scintilla* 1: 5–23.

Blackburn, F. A. 1897. "The Christian Coloring in the *Beowulf.*" *PMLA* 12: 205–25. Rpt. in *Anthology,* 1–21.

Blake, Norman F. 1962. "The Heremod Digressions in *Beowulf.*" *JEGP* 61: 278–87.

Bliss, Alan J. 1958. *The Metre of Beowulf.* Rpt. 1967, Oxford: Blackwell.

———. 1962a. "The Appreciation of Old English Metre." In *Tolkien,* 27–40.

———. 1962b *An Introduction to Old English Metre.* Oxford: Blackwell.

———. 1972. "The Origin and Structure of the Old English Hypermetric Line." *N&Q* n.s. 19: 242–48.

———. 1979. "*Beowulf,* Lines 3074–3075." *J. R. R. Tolkien, Scholar and Storyteller: Essays in Memoriam.* Ed. Mary Salu and Robert T. Farrell. Ithaca: Cornell University Press. 41–63.

Bloch, R. Howard. 1983. *Etymologies and Genealogies: A Literary Anthropology of the French Middle Ages.* Chicago: University of Chicago Press.

———. 1990. "New Philology and Old French." *Speculum* 65: 38–58.

Blomfield, Joan. 1938. "The Style and Structure of *Beowulf.*" *RES* 14: 396–403. Rpt. in *Beowulf Poet,* 57–65. See also Joan E. Turville-Petre.

Bloomfield, Morton W. 1949–51. "*Beowulf* and Christian Allegory: An Interpretation of Unferth." *Traditio* 7: 410–15. Rpt. in *Anthology,* 155–64. Also rpt. in *Beowulf Poet,* 68–75.

———. 1959. "Beowulf, Byrthnoth, and the Judgment of God: Trial by Combat in Anglo-Saxon England." *Speculum* 44: 545–59.

———. 1970. "Episodic Motivation and Marvels in Epic and Romance." *Essays and Explorations: Studies in Ideas, Language, and Literature.* Cambridge MA: Harvard University Press. 96–128.

———. 1986. "'Interlace' as a Medieval Narrative Technique with Special Reference to *Beowulf.*" *Magister Regis: Studies in Honor of Robert Earl Kaske.* Ed. Arthur Groos. New York: Fordham University Press. 49–59.

Boberg, Inger M. 1942–43. "Die Sage von Vermund und Uffe." *Acta Philologica Scandinavica* 16: 129–57.

Boer, Richard C. 1898. "Zur Grettissaga." *ZfdP* 30: 1–71.

———. 1903–04. "Finnsage und Nibelungensage." *Anzeiger für deutsches Altertum* 47: 125–60.

———. 1909. "Die Sigmundsage." *Untersuchungen über den Ursprung und die Entwicklung der Nibelungensage.* Vol. 3. Halle: Buchhandlung des Waisenhauses. 75–94.

———. 1912. *Die altenglische Heldendichtung. 1: Beowulf.* Germanistische Handbibliothek 11. Halle: Buchhandlung des Waisenhauses.

———. 1923. Rev. of *"Beowulf": An Introduction to the Study of the Poem,* by R. W. Chambers. *ES* 5: 105–18.

Bolton, Whitney F. 1978. *Alcuin and Beowulf: An Eighth-Century View.* New Brunswick: Rutgers University Press.

———. 1979. "Boethius and a Topos in *Beowulf.*" *Saints, Scholars and Heroes: Studies in Medieval Culture in Honour of Charles W. Jones.* Ed. Margot H. King and Wesley M. Stevens. Vol. 1. Collegeville MN: Hill Monastic Manuscript Library, St. John's Abbey and University. 15–43.

Bond, George. 1943. "Links between *Beowulf* and Mercian History." *SP* 40: 481–93.

Bonde, Niels, and Arne Emil Christensen. 1993. "Dendrochronological Dating of Viking Ship Burials." *Antiquity* 67: 575–83.

Bonjour, Adrien. 1940. "The Use of Anticipation in *Beowulf.*" *RES* 16: 290–99. Rpt. 1962 with additional comments in his *Twelve Beowulf Papers, 1940–1960, with Additional Comments.* Université de Neuchâtel Recueil de travaux publiés par la faculté des lettres 30. Geneva: E. Droz; Neuchâtel: Faculté des lettres. 11–28.

———. 1949. "Grendel's Dam and the Composition of *Beowulf.*" *ES* 30: 113–24.

———. 1950. *The Digressions in Beowulf.* Rpt. 1965, Oxford: Blackwell. "Finn and the Heathobards" (56–63) rpt. in *OEL: 22 Essays,* 319–27.

———. 1953. "Monsters Crouching and Critics Rampant, or the *Beowulf* Dragon Debated." *PMLA* 68: 304–12.

———. 1957a. "*Beowulf* and the Beasts of Battle." *PMLA* 72: 563–73.

———. 1957b. "*Beowulf* and the Snares of Literary Criticism." *Études Anglaises* 10: 30–36. Rpt. 1962 in his *Twelve Beowulf Papers, 1940–1960, with Additional Comments.* Université de Neuchâtel Recueil de travaux publiés par la faculté des lettres 30. Geneva: E. Droz; Neuchâtel: Faculté des lettres. 121–33.

―――. 1967. "Jottings on *Beowulf* and the Aesthetic Approach." *Old English Poetry: Fifteen Essays.* Ed. R. P. Creed. Providence: Brown University Press. 179–92.

Bonner, Joshua H. 1975–76. "Toward a Unified Critical Approach to Old English Poetic Composition." *MP* 73: 219–28.

Bosse, Roberta Bux, and Jennifer Lee Wyatt. 1987. "Hrothgar and Nebuchadnezzar: Conversion in Old English Verse." *PLL* 23: 257–71.

Bouman, A. C. 1959. "Beowulf's Song of Sorrow." *Mélanges de linguistique et de philologie Fernand Mossé in memoriam.* Paris: Didier. 41–43.

Boyle, Leonard. 1981. "The Nowell Codex and the Dating of *Beowulf.*" In *Dating of Beowulf,* 23–32.

Bracher, Frederick. 1937. "Understatement in Old English Poetry." *PMLA* 52: 915–34. Rpt. in *Essential Articles,* 228–54.

Bradley, Henry. 1910. "Beowulf." *Encyclopedia Britannica.* 11th ed. Vol. 3. London and New York: Encyclopedia Britannica. 758–61.

―――. 1915–16. "The Numbered Sections in Old English Poetical MSS." *PBA* 7: 165–87.

―――. 1929. "Beowulf." *Encyclopedia Britannica.* 14th ed. Vol. 3. London and New York: Encyclopedia Britannica. 424–26.

Bradley, S. A. J. 1993. "'The First New-European Literature': N. F. S. Grundtvig's Reception of Anglo-Saxon Literature." *Heritage and Prophecy: Grundtvig and the English-Speaking World.* Ed. A. M. Allchin et al. Aarhus: Aarhus University Press. 45–72.

Brady, Caroline. 1952. "The Synonyms for 'Sea' in *Beowulf.*" *Studies in Honor of Albert Morey Sturtevant.* Humanistic Studies 29. University of Kansas Publications. 22–46.

―――. 1979. "'Weapons' in *Beowulf:* An Analysis of the Nominal Compounds and an Evaluation of the Poet's Use of Them." *ASE* 8: 79–141.

―――. 1983. "'Warriors' in *Beowulf:* An Analysis of the Nominal Compounds and an Evaluation of the Poet's Use of Them." *ASE* 11: 199–246.

Brandl, Alois. 1908a. "Die Angelsächsische Literatur." *Grundriss der germanischen Philologie.* Ed. Hermann Paul. Vol. 2, pt. A. 2nd ed. Strassburg: Trübner. 980–1024.

―――. 1908b. *Geschichte der altenglischen Literatur.* Strassburg: Trübner.

―――. 1928. "Hercules und Beowulf." *Sitzungsberichte der Preussischen Akademie der Wissenschaften, Philosophisch-historische Klasse* 14: 161–67.

―――. 1929. "*Beowulf* und die Merowinger." In *Klaeber,* 182–88.

―――. 1932. "Zur Entstehung der germanischen Heldensage, gesehen vom angelsächsischen Standpunkt." *Archiv* 162: 191–202.

―――. 1936. "Das Beowulfepos und die mercische Königskrisis um 700." *Forschungen und Fortschritte* 12: 165–68. Trans. as "The *Beowulf* Epic and the Crisis in the Mercian Dynasty about the Year 700 A.D." *Research and Progress* 2: 195–203.

―――. 1937. "Beowulf-Epos und Aeneis in systematischer Vergleichung." *Archiv* 171: 161–73.

Bremmer, Rolf H., Jr. 1980. "The Importance of Kinship: Uncle and Nephew in *Beowulf.*" *Amsterdamer Beiträge zur älteren Germanistik* 15: 21–38.

Brennan, Malcolm M. 1985. "Hrothgar's Government." *JEGP* 84: 3–15.

Britton, G. C. 1971. "Unferth, Grendel and the Christian Meaning of *Beowulf.*" *NM* 72: 246–50.

Brodeur, Arthur G. 1943a. "The Climax of the Finn Episode." *University of California Publications in English* 3: 285–361.

————. 1943b. "Design and Motive in the Finn Episode." *University of California Publications in English* 14: 1–42.

————. 1953. "The Structure and the Unity of *Beowulf.*" *PMLA* 68: 1183–95. [Rev. and expanded as chapter 3 of Brodeur 1959].

————. 1959. *The Art of Beowulf.* Berkeley: University of California Press. Chapter 2, "Variation," rpt. in *Interpretations,* 66–87.

————. 1968. "A Study of Diction and Style in Three Anglo-Saxon Narrative Poems." *Nordica et Anglica: Studies in Honor of Stefán Einarsson.* Ed. Allan H. Orick. The Hague: Mouton. 97–114.

————. 1970. "*Beowulf:* One Poem or Three?" *Medieval Literature and Folklore Studies: Essays in Honor of Francis Lee Utley.* Ed. Jerome Mandel and Bruce Rosenberg. New Brunswick: Rutgers University Press. 3–28.

Brooke, Stopford A. 1921. *English Literature from the Beginnings to the Norman Conquest.* London: Macmillan.

Brooks, Kenneth R., ed. 1961. *Andreas and the Fates of the Apostles.* Oxford: Clarendon.

Brooks, Peter. 1994. "The Storyteller." *Psychoanalysis and Storytelling.* Oxford: Blackwell.

Brown, Alan K. 1980. "The Firedrake in *Beowulf.*" *Neophil* 64: 439–60.

Bruce-Mitford, Rupert, et al. 1975–83. *The Sutton Hoo Ship-Burial.* London: British Museum.

Bryan, William F. 1929. "Epithetic Compound Folk–Names in *Beowulf.*" In *Klaeber,* 120–34.

Brynjúlfsson, Gísli. 1852–54. "Oldengelsk og oldnordisk." *ATfS* 4: 81–143.

Buchloh, P. G. 1966. "Unity and Intention in Beowulf." *English Studies Today, 4th Series: Lectures and Papers Read at the Sixth Conference of the International Association of University Professors of English Held at Venice, August 1965.* Ed. Ilva Cellini and Giorgio Melchiori. Rome: Edizioni di Storia e Letteratura. 99–120.

Buck, Janet T. 1971. "Pre-Feudal Women." *Journal of the Rutgers University Library* 34: 46–51.

Bullough, Donald A. 1993. "What Has Ingeld to Do with Lindisfarne?" *ASE* 22: 93–125.

Burlin, Robert B. 1974. "Inner Weather and Interlace: A Note on the Semantic Value of Structure in *Beowulf.*" In *Pope,* 81–89.

————. 1975. "Gnomic Indirection in *Beowulf.*" In *McGalliard,* 41-49.

Burton, Richard. 1895. "Woman in Old English Poetry." *Sewanee Review* 4: 1–14.

Busse, Wilhelm. 1981. "Assumptions in the Establishment of Old English Poetic Texts: P. J. Lucas's Edition of 'Exodus.'" *Arbeiten aus Anglistik und Amerikanistik* 6: 197–219.

————. 1987. *Altenglische Literatur und ihre Geschichte: Zur Kritik des gegenwärtigen Deutungssystems.* Düsseldorf: Droste.

————, and R. Holtei. 1981. "*Beowulf* and the Tenth Century." *BJRL* 63: 285–329.

Butts, Richard. 1987. "The Analogical Mere: Landscape and Terror in *Beowulf.*" *ES* 68: 113–21.

Bynum, David E. 1978. *The Dæmon in the Wood: A Study in Oral Narrative Patterns.* Cambridge MA: Center for Studies in Oral Tradition, Harvard University.

Cabaniss, Allen. 1955. "*Beowulf* and the Liturgy." *JEGP* 54: 195–201. Rpt. in *Anthology,* 223–32.

Cable, Thomas M. 1971. "Clashing Stress in the Meter of *Beowulf.*" *NM* 72: 42–50.

————. 1974. *The Meter and Melody of Beowulf.* Urbana: University of Illinois Press.

———. 1981. "Metrical Style as Evidence for the Date of *Beowulf*." In *Dating of Beowulf*, 77–82.

———. 1991. *The English Alliterative Tradition*. Philadelphia: University of Pennsylvania Press.

———. 1994. "Syllable Weight in Old English Meter: Grids, Morae, and Kaluza's Law." *Diachronica* 11.1: 1–11.

Calder, Daniel G. 1972. "Setting and Ethos: The Pattern of Measure and Limit in *Beowulf*." *SP* 69: 21-37.

———. 1979. "The Study of Style in Old English Poetry: A Historical Introduction." In *OE Poetry*, 1–65.

———. 1981. "Histories and Surveys of Old English Literature." *ASE* 10: 201–44.

Caldwell, James Ralston. 1940. "The Origin of the Story of Bǫthvar-Bjarki." *AfNF* 55: 223–75.

Camargo, Martin. 1981. "The Finn Episode and the Tragedy of Revenge in *Beowulf*." *SP* 78: 120–34.

Cameron, Angus F. 1969. "Saint Gildas and Scyld Scefing." *NM* 70: 240–46.

———, Ashley Crandell Amos, and Gregory Waite, with the assistance of Sharon Butler and Antonette DiPaolo Healey. 1981. "A Reconsideration of the Language of *Beowulf*." In *Dating of Beowulf*, 33–75.

Campbell, A. P. 1974. "The Death of Beowulf: Please Indicate Church Affiliation." *RUO* 44: 539–42.

———. 1975a. "The Decline and Fall of Hrothgar and His Danes." *RUO* 45: 417–29.

———. 1975b. "Physical Signs of Spiritual Cleansing in Old English Poetry." *RUO* 45: 382–91.

Campbell, Alistair. 1962. "The Old English Epic Style." In *Tolkien*, 13–26.

———. 1971. "The Use in *Beowulf* of Earlier Heroic Verse." *England before the Conquest: Studies in Primary Sources Presented to Dorothy Whitelock*. Ed. Peter Clemoes and Kathleen Hughes. Cambridge: Cambridge University Press. 283–92.

Campbell, Jackson J. 1966. "Learned Rhetoric in Old English Poetry." *MP* 63: 189–201.

———. 1967. "Knowledge of Rhetorical Figures in Anglo-Saxon England." *JEGP* 65: 1–20.

———. 1978. "Adaptation of Classical Rhetoric in Old English Literature." *Medieval Eloquence: Studies in the Theory and Practice of Medieval Rhetoric*. Ed. James J. Murphy. Berkeley: University of California Press. 173–97.

Campbell, Joseph. 1972. *Myths to Live By*. New York: Viking.

Canitz, A. E. C. 1986. "Kingship in *Beowulf* and the *Nibelungenlied*." *Mankind Quarterly* 27: 97–119.

Carney, James. 1955. "The Irish Elements in *Beowulf*." *Studies in Irish Literature and History*. Dublin: Dublin Institute for Advanced Studies. 77–128.

Carrigan, Eamonn. 1967. "Structure and Thematic Development in *Beowulf*." *Proceedings of the Royal Irish Academy* 66 section c, no. 1: 1–51.

Carsley, Catherine A. 1992. "Reassessing Cultural Memory in Beowulf." *Assays* 7: 31–41.

Carver, Martin. 1989. "Kingship and Material Culture in Early Anglo-Saxon East Anglia." *The Origins of Ango-Saxon Kingdoms*. Ed. Steven Bassett. London: Leicester University Press. 141–58.

———. 1992a. "The Anglo-Saxon Cemetery at Sutton Hoo: An Interim Report." In *Age of Sutton Hoo*, 343–71.

————. 1992b. "Ideology and Allegiance in East Anglia." *Sutton Hoo: Fifty Years After.* Ed. Robert T. Farrell and Carol Neumann de Vegvar. Kalamazoo MI: Medieval Institute. 173–82.

————, ed. 1992c. *The Age of Sutton Hoo.* Woodbridge: Boydell.

Cassidy, Frederic G. 1965. "How Free Was the Anglo-Saxon Scop?" In *Magoun,* 75–85.

————. 1982. "Knowledge of *Beowulf* in Its Own Time." *Yearbook of Research in English and American Literature* 1: 1–12.

Chadwick, Hector M. 1907. "Early National Poetry." *The Cambridge History of English Literature.* Ed. A. W. Ward and A. R. Waller. Vol. 1. Cambridge: Cambridge University Press. 21–41.

————. 1912. *The Heroic Age.* Cambridge: Cambridge University Press. Excerpt rpt. in *Anthology,* 23–33.

————, and N. Kershaw. 1932, 1936, 1940. *The Growth of Literature.* 3 vols. Cambridge: Cambridge University Press.

————. 1940. "Who Was He?" *Antiquity* 14: 76–87.

Chadwick, Nora K. 1959. "The Monsters and Beowulf." *The Anglo-Saxons: Studies in Some Aspects of Their History and Culture Presented to Bruce Dickins.* Ed. Peter Clemoes. London: Bowes and Bowes. 171–203.

Chambers, R. W. 1921. *Beowulf: An Introduction to the Study of the Poem with a Discussion of the Stories of Offa and Finn.* 1959: 3rd ed., with a supplement by C. L. Wrenn. Cambridge: Cambridge University Press.

————. 1925. "Foreword." *Beowulf Translated into Modern English Rhyming Verse.* Trans. Archibald Strong. London: Constable. xii–xxxii. Rpt. 1939 as "*Beowulf* and the 'Heroic Age' in England" in his *Man's Unconquerable Mind.* London and Toronto: J. Cape. 53–59.

————. 1929. "Beowulf's Fight with Grendel, and Its Scandinavian Parallels." *ES* 11: 81–100.

Chance (Nitzsche), Jane. 1980. "The Structural Unity in *Beowulf:* The Problem of Grendel's Mother." *TSLL* 22: 287–303.

————. 1986. *Woman as Hero in Old English Literature.* Syracuse: Syracuse University Press.

Chaney, William A. 1961. "Grendel and the *Gifstol:* A Legal View of Monsters." *PMLA* 77: 513–20.

————. 1970. *The Cult of Kingship in Anglo-Saxon England: The Transition from Paganism to Christianity.* Berkeley: University of California Press.

Chapman, Coolidge Otis. 1931. "*Beowulf* and *Apollonius of Tyre.*" *MLN* 46: 439–43.

Chase, Colin. 1981a. "Opinions on the Date of *Beowulf.*" In *Dating of Beowulf,* 3–8.

————. 1981b. "Saints' Lives, Royal Lives, and the Date of *Beowulf.*" In *Dating of Beowulf,* 161–71.

————. 1985. "*Beowulf,* Bede, and St. Oswine: The Hero's Pride in Old English Hagiography." *The Anglo-Saxons: Synthesis and Achievement.* Ed. J. Douglas Woods and David A. E. Pelteret. Waterloo ON: Wilfrid Laurier University Press. 37–48. Rpt. in *Basic Beowulf,* 181–93.

Cherniss, Michael D. 1968. "The Progress of the Hoard in *Beowulf.*" *PQ* 47: 473–486.

————. 1970. "*Beowulf:* Oral Presentation and the Criterion of Immediate Rhetorical Effect." *Genre* 3: 214–28.

————. 1972. *Ingeld and Christ: Heroic Concepts and Values in Old English Christian Poetry.* The Hague: Mouton.

Christensen, T. 1991. "Lejre beyond Legend—the Archaeological Evidence." *Journal of Danish Archaeology* 10: 163–85.

Clark, Francelia. 1981. "Flyting in *Beowulf* and Rebuke in *The Song of Bagdad:* The Question of Theme." In *Lord,* 164–93.

Clark, George. 1964. "Beowulf and Bear's Son in the *Vishnu Purana.*" *PQ* 43: 125–30.

————. 1965. "Beowulf 's Armor." *ELH* 32: 409–41.

————. 1973. "*Beowulf* and *Njálssaga.*" *Proceedings of the First International Saga Conference, University of Edinburgh, 1971.* Ed. Peter Foote, Hermann Pálsson, and Desmond Slay. London: Viking Society for Northern Research. 66–87.

————. 1990. *Beowulf.* Boston: Twayne.

————. 1992. "*Beowulf:* The Last Word." *Old English and New.* Ed. Joan H. Hall et al. New York and London: Garland. 15–30.

Clark Hall, J. R., ed. 1894. *A Concise Anglo-Saxon Dictionary.* 1960: 4th ed., with a supplement by Herbert D. Meritt. Rpt. 1984, Toronto and London: University of Toronto Press.

Claudel, Calvin. 1952. "Some Comments on the Bear's Son Tale." *Southern Folklore Quarterly* 16: 186–91.

Clemoes, Peter. 1979. "Action in *Beowulf* and Our Perception of It." In *OE Poetry,* 147–68.

————. 1981. "Style as the Criterion for Dating the Composition of *Beowulf.*" In *Dating of Beowulf,* 173–85.

Clover, Carol J. 1980. "The Germanic Context of the Unferþ Episode." *Speculum* 55: 444–68. Rpt. in *Basic Beowulf,* 127–54.

————. 1986. "Hildigunnr's Lament." *Structure and Meaning in Old Norse Literature: New Approaches to Textual Analysis and Literary Criticism.* Ed. John Lindow, Lars Lönnroth, and Gerd Wolfgang Weber. Odense: Odense University Press. 141–83.

————. 1993. "Regardless of Sex: Men, Women, and Power in Early Northern Europe." *Speculum* 68: 363–87.

Clunies Ross, Margaret. 1989. "Two of þórr's Great Fights According to *Hymiskviða.*" *Leeds Studies* n.s. 20: 7–27.

Colgrave, Bertram. 1951. "A Mexican Version of the 'Bear's Son' Folk Tale." *Journal of American Folklore* 64: 109–13.

Colgrave, Bertram, and R. A. B. Mynors, eds. and trans. 1969. Bede's *Ecclesiastical History of the English People.* Oxford: Clarendon.

Collingwood, R. G., and J. N. L. Myres. 1936. *Roman Britain and the English Settlements.* Oxford: Clarendon.

Collins, Douglas C. 1959. "Kenning in Anglo-Saxon Poetry." *E&S* n.s. 12: 1–17.

Conquergood, Dwight. 1981. "Boasting in Anglo-Saxon England: Performance and the Heroic Ethos." *Literature in Performance* 1: 24–35.

Conybeare, John J. 1826. *Illustrations of Anglo-Saxon Poetry.* Ed. William D. Conybeare. London. Rpt. 1964, New York: Haskell House.

————, ed. 1814. "Anglo-Saxon Poem on the Battle of Finsborough." *The British Bibliographer.* By Sir Egerton Brydges and Joseph Haslewood. Vol. 4. Rpt. 1966, New York: AMS.

Cook, Albert S. 1899. "An Irish Parallel to the *Beowulf* Story." *Archiv* 103: 154–56.

————. 1902. "Old English Notes: I. *Beowulf* 1408ff." *MLN* 17: 209–10.

————. 1907. "Various Notes: *Beowulf* 1408ff." *MLN* 22: 146–47.

————. 1921–22. "The Possible Begetter of the OE *Beowulf* and *Widsith.*" *TCAAS* 25: 281–346.

————. 1922–24. "The Old English *Andreas* and Bishop Acca of Hexham." *TCAAS* 26: 245–332.

————. 1924. "*Beowulf* 1422." *MLN* 39: 77–82.

————. 1925a. "Aldhelm and the Source of *Beowulf* 2523." *MLN* 40: 137–42.

————. 1925b. "*Beowulf* 159–163." *MLN* 40: 352–54.

————. 1925c. "Cynewulf 's Part in Our *Beowulf.*" *TCAAS* 27: 385–406.

————. 1926a. "Beowulfian and Odyssean Voyages." *TCAAS* 28: 1–20.

————. 1926b. "The Beowulfian *maðelode.*" *JEGP* 25: 1–6.

————. 1926c. "Greek Parallels to Certain Features of the *Beowulf.*" *PQ* 5: 226–34.

————. 1926d. "Hellenic and Beowulfian Shields and Spears." *MLN* 41: 360–63.

————. 1928. "*Beowulf* 1039 and the Greek *archibasileus.*" *Speculum* 3: 75–81.

Cooley, Franklin. 1940. "Early Danish Criticism of *Beowulf.*" *ELH* 7: 45–67.

Cornelius, Roberta D. 1927. "Palus inamabilis." *Speculum* 2: 321–25.

Cosmos, Spencer. 1976. "Kuhn's Law and the Unstressed Verbs in *Beowulf.*" *TSLL* 18: 306–28.

Cramer, Carmen. 1977. "The Voice of Beowulf." *Germanic Notes* 8: 40–44.

Cramp, Rosemary J. 1957. "*Beowulf* and Archaeology." *Medieval Archaeology* 1: 57–77. Rpt. in *Beowulf Poet,* 114–40.

Crawford, Samuel John, ed. 1922. *The Old English Version of the Heptateuch.* EETS 160. London. Rpt. 1969, London: Oxford University Press.

————. 1928a, "*Beowulf,* ll. 168–69." *MLR* 23: 336.

————. 1928b. "Grendel's Descent from Cain." *MLR* 23: 207–8.

————. 1929. "Grendel's Descent from Cain: *Beowulf,* ll. 107–14, etc." *MLR* 24: 63.

Creed, Robert P. 1955. "Studies in the Techniques of Composition of the "Beowulf" Poetry in British Museum MS. Cotton Vitellius A. xv." Diss. Harvard University.

————. 1957. "The *Andswarode*-System in Old English Poetry." *Speculum* 32: 523–28.

————. 1959. "The Making of an Anglo-Saxon Poem." *ELH* 26: 445–54. Rpt. in *Beowulf Poet,* 141–53. Also rpt. in *Essential Articles,* 363–73; *OEL: 22 Essays,* 52–72.

————. 1961. "On the Possibility of Criticizing Old English Poetry." *TSLL* 3: 97–106.

————. 1962. "The Singer Looks at His Sources." *CL* 14: 44–52.

————. 1966a. "A New Approach to the Rhythm of *Beowulf.*" *PMLA* 81: 23–33.

————. 1966b. "'. . . Wél-hwelć Gecwæþ . . .': The Singer as Architect." *Tennessee Studies in Literature* 11: 131–43.

————. 1981. "The *Beowulf*-Poet: Master of Sound Patterning." In *Lord,* 194–216.

————. 1986. "The Remaking of *Beowulf.*" In *Oral Tradition in Literature: Interpretation in Context.* Ed. John Miles Foley. Columbia: University of Missouri Press. 136–46.

————. 1989. "*Beowulf* and the Language of Hoarding." *Medieval Archaeology.* Ed. Charles L. Redman. MRTS 60. Binghamton: State University of New York.

————. 1990. *Reconstructing the Rhythm of Beowulf.* Columbia: University of Missouri Press.

Crépin, André. 1983. "La Conscience de soi héroïque: L'Exemple de Beowulf." *Genèse de la conscience moderne: Études sur le développement de la conscience de soi dans les littératures du monde occidentale.* Ed. Robert Ellrodt. Publications de la Sorbonne, Série Littérature, 14. Paris: Presses Universitaires de France. 51–60.

————. 1987. "L'Espace du texte et l'esprit liturgique dans la civilisation vieil-anglaise." *Liturgie et espace liturgique.* Ed. André Crépin. Paris: Didier Erudition. 49–58.

Crook, Eugene J. 1974. "Pagan Gold in *Beowulf.*" *ABR* 25: 218–34.

Crowne, David K. 1960. "The Hero on the Beach: An Example of Composition by Theme in Anglo-Saxon Poetry." *NM* 61: 362–72.

Cunningham, Maurice P., ed. 1966. *Aurelii Prudentii Clementis Carmina.* Corpus Christianorum Series Latina 126. Turnholt: Brepols.

Cygan, Jan. 1968. "A Critique of the Sieversian Theory of Old Germanic Alliterative Verse." *Germanica Wratislaviensia* 12: 147–60.

Dahlberg, Charles R. 1988. *The Literature of Unlikeness.* Hanover NH: University Press of New England.

Daldorph, Brian [= Charles R. Dahlberg]. 1986. "Mar-Peace, Ally: Hunferth in *Beowulf.*" *Massachusetts Studies in English* 10: 143–60.

Damico, Helen. 1983. "Sörlaþáttr and the Hama Episode in *Beowulf.*" *SS* 55: 222–35.

————. 1984. *Beowulf's Wealhtheow and the Valkyrie Tradition.* Madison: University of Wisconsin Press.

————, and Alexandra Hennessey Olsen. 1990. "Introduction." In *New Readings,* 1–28.

Damon, Phillip. 1980. "The Middle of Things: Narrative Patterns in the *Iliad, Roland,* and *Beowulf.*" In *OEL in Context,* 107–16.

Danielli, Mary. 1945. "Initiation Ceremonial from Norse Literature." *Folk-Lore: Transactions of the Folk-Lore Society* 56: 229–45.

Daunt, Marjorie. 1946. "Old English Verse and English Speech Rhythm." *Transactions of the Philosophical Society:* 56–72. Rpt. in *Essential Articles,* 289-304.

Davidson, Hilda Ellis, and L. Webster. 1967. "The Anglo-Saxon Burial at Coombe, Kent." *Medieval Archaeology* 11: 1–41.

Davis, Craig R. 1992. "Cultural Assimilation in the Anglo-Saxon Royal Genealogies." *ASE* 21: 23–39.

Dederich, Hermann. 1877. *Historische und geographische Studien zum angelsächsischen Beowulfliede.* Cologne: C. Römke.

Dehmer, Heinz. 1927. *Primitives Erzählungsgut in den Íslendinga-Sögur.* Leipzig: J. J. Weber.

————. 1928. "Die Grendelkämpfe Beowulfs im Lichte moderner Märchenforschung." *GRM* 16: 202–18.

Delasanta, Rodney, and James Slevin. 1968. "*Beowulf* and the Hypostatic Union." *Neophil* 52: 409–16.

de Looze, Laurence N. 1984. "Frame Narratives and Fictionalization: Beowulf as Narrator." *TSLL* 26: 145–56. Rpt. in *Interpretations,* 242–50.

Derolez, René. 1986. "Focus on *Beowulf:* Variation or Meaning." *Essays in Honour of Kristian Smidt.* Ed. Peter Bilton et al. Oslo: University of Oslo, Institute of English Studies. 9–16.

Detter, Ferdinand. 1893. "Zur Ynglingasaga." *BGdSL* 18: 72–105.

Deutschbein, Max. 1909. "Die sagenhistorischen und literarischen Grundlagen des Beowulfepos." *GRM* 1: 103–19.

De Vries, Jan. 1953. "Die Beiden Hengeste." *ZfdP* 72: 125–43.

Diamond, Robert E. 1961. "Theme as Ornament in Anglo-Saxon Poetry." *PMLA* 76: 461–68. Rpt. in *Essential Articles,* 374–92.

Dietrich, Franz E. 1859. "Rettungen." *ZfdA* 11: 409–48.

Dietrich, Sheila C. 1979. "An Introduction to Women in Anglo-Saxon Society (c. 600–1066)." *The Women of England from Anglo-Saxon Times to the Present: Interpretive Bibliographic Essays.* Ed. Barbara Kanner. Hamden: Archon. 32–56.

Diller, Hans-Jürgen. 1984. "Contiguity and Similarity in the *Beowulf* Digressions." *Medieval Studies Conference, Aachen, 1983.* Ed. Wolf-Dietrich Bald and Horst Weinstock. Bamberger Beiträge zur englischen Sprachwissenschaft 15. New York: Peter Lang. 71–83.

Doane, A. N., ed. 1978. *Genesis A.* Madison: University of Wisconsin Press.

———. 1991. "Oral Texts, Intertexts, and Intratexts: Editing Old English." *Influence and Intertextuality in Literary History.* Ed. Jay Clayton and Eric Rothstein. Madison: University of Wisconsin Press. 75–113.

——— and Carol Braun Pasternack, eds. 1991. *Vox Intexta: Orality and Textuality in the Middle Ages.* Madison: University of Wisconsin Press.

Donahue, Charles. 1949–51. "Beowulf, Ireland and the Natural Good." *Traditio* 7: 263–77.

———. 1950. "Grendel and the *Clanna Cain.*" *Journal of Celtic Studies* 1: 167–75.

———. 1965. "*Beowulf* and Christian Tradition: A Reconsideration from a Celtic Stance." *Traditio* 21: 55–116.

———, with William Whallon, Margaret E. Goldsmith, et al. 1973. "Allegorical, Typological or Neither: Three Short Papers on the Allegorical Approach to *Beowulf* and a Discussion." *ASE* 2: 285–302.

———. 1975. "Potlatch and Charity: Notes on the Heroic in *Beowulf.*" In *McGalliard,* 23–40.

———. 1977. "Social Function and Literary Value in *Beowulf.*" *The Epic in Medieval Society: Aesthetic and Moral Values.* Ed. Harald Scholler. Tübingen: Niemeyer. 382–90.

Donoghue, Daniel. 1987. "On the Classification of B–Verses with Anacrusis in *Beowulf* and *Andreas.*" *N&Q* 34: 1–5.

Dow, Janet H. 1970. "Beowulf and the 'Walkers in Darkness.'" *Connecticut Review* 4: 42–48.

Dragland, S. L. 1977. "Monster-Man in *Beowulf.*" *Neophil* 61: 606–18.

Dronke, Ursula. 1969. "*Beowulf* and Ragnarǫk." *SBVS* 17: 302–25.

Du Bois, Arthur E. 1934. "The Unity of *Beowulf.*" *PMLA* 49: 374–405.

Duff, J. Wight. 1905–6. "Homer and *Beowulf.*" *SBVS* 4: 382–406.

Dumézil, Georges. 1973. *Gods of the Ancient Northmen.* Trans. Einar Haugen. Berkeley: University of California Press.

———. 1988. *Mitra-Varuna: An Essay on Two Indo-European Representatives of Sovereignty.* Trans. Derek Coltman. New York: Zone.

Dumville, David N. 1977. "Kingship, Genealogies and Regnal Lists." *Early Medieval Kingship.* Ed. P. H. Sawyer and I. N. Wood. Leeds: Leeds University Press. 72–104.

———. 1981. "*Beowulf* and the Celtic World: The Uses of Evidence." *Traditio* 37: 109–60.

———. 1988. "*Beowulf* Come Lately: Some Notes on the Palaeography of the Nowell Codex." *Archiv* 225: 49–63.

Duncan, Edwin. 1993. "Weak Stress and Poetic Constraints in Old English Verse." *JEGP* 92: 495–509.

Duncan, Ian. 1987. "Epitaphs for Æglæcan: Narrative Strife in *Beowulf.*" *Beowulf.* Ed. Harold Bloom. New York: Chelsea. 111–30.

Dundes, Alan, ed. 1984. *Sacred Narrative: Readings in the Theory of Myth.* Berkeley and Los Angeles: University of California Press.

Earl, James W. 1979. "The Necessity of Evil in *Beowulf.*" *South Atlantic Bulletin* 44: 81–98.
———. 1982. "Apocalypticism and Mourning in *Beowulf.*" *Thought* 57: 362–70. Rpt. with revisions as part of chapter 1 of Earl 1994.
———. 1983. "The Role of the Men's Hall in the Development of the Anglo-Saxon Superego." *Psychiatry* 46: 139–60. Rpt. with revisions as chapter 4 of Earl 1994.
———. 1987. "Transformation of Chaos: Immanence and Transcendence in *Beowulf* and Other Old English Poems." *Ultimate Reality and Meaning* 10: 164–85. Rpt. with revisions as chapter 2 of Earl 1994.
———. 1991. "*Beowulf* and the Origins of Civilization." *Speaking Two Languages: Traditional Disciplines and Contemporary Theory in Medieval Studies.* Ed. Allen J. Frantzen. Albany: State University of New York Press. 65–89. Rpt. with revisions as chapter 6 of Earl 1994.
———. 1994. *Thinking about Beowulf.* Stanford: Stanford University Press.
Earle, John. 1884. "The *Beowulf.*" *The Times,* 25 August: 6.
———. 1885a. "*Beowulf* I." *The Times,* 30 September: 3.
———. 1885b. "*Beowulf* II." *The Times,* 29 October: 3.
Ebenauer, Alfred. 1976. "Fródi und sein Friede." *Festgabe für Otto Höfler zum 75. Geburtstag.* Ed. Helmut Birkhan. Vienna: Wilhelm Braunmüller. 128–81.
Eco, Umberto. 1979. *The Role of the Reader: Explorations in the Semiotics of Texts.* Bloomington: Indiana University Press.
———. 1986. *Art and Beauty in the Middle Ages.* Trans. Hugh Bredin. New Haven: Yale University Press.
Einarsson, Stefán. 1934. "Old English *Beot* and Old Icelandic *Heitstrenging.*" *PMLA* 49: 99–103. Rpt. in *Essential Articles,* 99–123.
Eliason, Norman E. 1963. "The Þyle and Scop in *Beowulf.*" *Speculum* 38: 267–84.
———. 1965. "The 'Thryth-Offa' Digression in *Beowulf.*" In *Magoun,* 124–38. Rpt. 1975 in his *English Essays Literary and Linguistic.* Ed. Robert G. Benson and Erika C. D. Lindemann. Grand Prairie TX: Scholars Guild. 83–98.
———. 1979. "Beowulf's Inglorious Youth." *SP* 76: 101–8.
———. 1980. "The Burning of Heorot." *Speculum* 55: 75–83.
Emerson, Oliver F. 1921. "Grendel's Motive in Attacking Heorot." *MLR* 16: 113–19.
Engelhardt, George J. 1955. "*Beowulf:* A Study in Dilatation." *PMLA* 70: 825–52.
Enright, Michael J. 1988. "Lady with a Mead-Cup: Ritual, Group Cohesion and Hierarchy in the Germanic Warband." *Frühmittelalterliche Studien* 22: 170–203. Rpt. 1996 in his *Lady with a Mead Cup: Ritual, Prophecy and Lordship in the European Warband from La Tène to the Viking Age.* Portland OR and Dublin: Four Courts. 1–37.
Erler, Mary, and Maryanne Kowaleski, eds. 1988. "Introduction." *Women and Power in the Middle Ages.* Athens: University of Georgia Press.
Esch, Deborah. 1990. "The Work to Come." *Diacritics* 20: 28–49.
Ettmüller, Ludwig. 1850. *Engla and Seaxna Scôpas and Bôceras.* Quedlinburg: G. Basse.
Evans, Jonathan D. 1985. "Semiotics and Traditional Lore: The Medieval Dragon Tradition." *Journal of Folklore Research* 22: 85–112.
———. 1986. "Episodes in Analysis of Medieval Narrative." *Style* 20: 126–41.
Fahlbeck, Pontus. 1884. "Beovulfskvädet såsom källa för nordisk fornhistoria." *ATfS* 8.2: 1–88.
Fakundiny, Lydia. 1970. "The Art of Old English Verse Composition." *RES* n.s. 21: 129–42, 257–66.

Farrell, Robert T. 1972. *Beowulf, Swedes and Geats.* London: Viking Society for Northern Research.

———. 1982. "Beowulf and the Northern Heroic Age." *The Vikings.* Ed. Robert T. Farrell. London: Phillimore. 180–216.

——— and Carol Neumann de Vegvar. 1992. *Sutton Hoo: Fifty Years After.* Kalamazoo MI: Medieval Institute.

Fast, Carl Otto [Svionum]. 1929. *Beowulf, germanernas äldsta epos.* Stockholm: Kurt Lindberg.

———. 1944. *Svenska rikets ursprung.* Göteborg: Aktiebolaget Götatryckeriet.

Fast, Lawrence. 1971. "Hygelac: A Centripetal Force in *Beowulf.*" *An Med* 12: 90–99.

Feldman, Thalia Phillies. 1979. "The Taunter in Ancient Epic: The *Iliad, Odyssey,* and *Beowulf.*" *PLL* 15: 3–16.

———. 1981. "Grendel and Cain's Descendants." *Literary Onomastics Studies* 8: 71–87.

Fell, Christine. 1984. *Women in Anglo-Saxon England.* Oxford: Blackwell.

Fernández-Armesto, Felipe. 1987. *Before Columbus: Exploration and Colonisation from the Mediterranean to the Atlantic, 1229-1492.* London: Macmillan.

Filmer-Sankey, William. 1992. "Snape Anglo-Saxon Cemetery: The Current State of Knowledge." In *Age of Sutton Hoo,* 39–51.

Finley, Moses. 1964. "The Trojan War." *Journal of Hellenic Studies* 84: 1–9.

Finnegan, Robert Emmett. 1978. "Beowulf at the Mere (and Elsewhere)." *Mosaic* 11.4: 45–54.

Fisher, Peter F. 1958. "The Trials of the Epic Hero in *Beowulf.*" *PMLA* 73: 171–83.

Florey, Kenneth. 1988. "Grendel, Evil, 'Allegory,' and Dramatic Development in *Beowulf.*" *Essays in Arts and Sciences* 17: 83–95.

Foley, Joanne De Lavan. 1981. "Feasts and Anti-Feasts in *Beowulf* and the *Odyssey.*" In *Lord,* 235–61.

Foley, John Miles. 1976. "Formula and Theme in Old English Poetry." *Oral Literature and the Formula.* Ed. Benjamin A. Stolz and Richard S. Shannon. Ann Arbor: Center of Coordination of Ancient and Modern Studies, University of Michigan. 207–32.

———. 1977. "*Beowulf* and the Psychohistory of Anglo-Saxon Culture." *American Imago* 94: 133–54.

———. 1980. "*Beowulf* and Traditional Narrative Song: The Potential and Limits of Comparison." In *OEL in Context,* 117–36.

———. 1981. "The Oral Theory in Context." In *Lord,* 1981b, 27–122.

———. 1982. "The Scansion of *Beowulf* in Its Indo-European Context." *Approaches to Beowulfian Scansion.* Ed. Alain Renoir and Ann Hernandez. Old English Colloquium. Berkeley: Department of English, University of California, Berkeley. 7–17.

———. 1990. *Traditional Oral Epic: The Odyssey, Beowulf, and the Serbo-Croatian Return Song.* Berkeley and Los Angeles: University of California Press.

———. 1991. *Immanent Art: From Structure to Meaning in Traditional Oral Epic.* Bloomington: Indiana University Press.

Fontenrose, Joseph. 1959. *Python: A Study of Delphic Myth and Its Origins.* Berkeley: University of California Press.

Foucault, Michel. 1972. *"The Archaeology of Knowledge" and "The Discourse on Knowledge."* Trans. A. M. Sheridan Smith. New York: Pantheon.

———. 1973. *The Order of Things: An Archaeology of the Human Sciences.* New York: Vintage.

Frank, Roberta. 1981. "Skaldic Verse and the Date of *Beowulf.*" In *Dating of Beowulf,* 123–99. Rpt. in *Basic Beowulf,* 155–80.

———. 1982a. "The *Beowulf* Poet's Sense of History." *The Wisdom of Poetry: Essays in Early English Literature in Honor of Morton W. Bloomfield.* Ed. Larry D. Benson and Siegfried Wenzel. Kalamazoo MI: Medieval Institute Publications, Western Michigan University.

———. 1982b. "Old Norse Memorial Eulogies and the Ending of *Beowulf.*" *The Early Middle Ages. Acta* 6: 1–19.

———. 1986. "'Mere' and 'Sund': Two Sea-Changes in *Beowulf.*" *Modes of Interpretation in Old English Literature: Essays in Honour of Stanley B. Greenfield.* Ed. P. R. Brown, G. R. Crampton, and F. C. Robinson. Toronto and London: University of Toronto Press. 153–72.

———. 1987. "Did Anglo-Saxon Audiences Have a Skaldic Tooth?" *SS* 59: 338–55.

———. 1992. "*Beowulf* and Sutton Hoo: The Odd Couple." *Voyage to the Other World: The Legacy of Sutton Hoo.* Ed. Calvin B. Kendall and Peter S. Wells. Medieval Studies at Minnesota 5. Minneapolis. 47–64.

Frantzen, Allen J. 1990. *Desire for Origins: New Language, Old English, and Teaching the Tradition.* New Brunswick: Rutgers University Press.

———. 1991a. "Writing the Unreadable *Beowulf:* 'Writan' and 'Forwritan,' the Pen and the Sword." *Exemplaria* 3: 327–57.

———, ed. 1991b. *Speaking Two Languages: Traditional Disciplines and Contemporary Theory in Medieval Studies.* Albany: State University of New York Press.

———, and Gillian Overing. 1993. Letter to the Editor. *PMLA* 108: 1177–78.

Frazer, Sir James. 1890. *The Golden Bough: A Study in Magic and Religion.* 2 vols. 1911–15: 3rd ed. 12 vols. London: Macmillan.

Freud, Sigmund. 1900. *The Interpretation of Dreams.* In *The Standard Edition of the Complete Psychological Works of Sigmund Freud.* Ed. James Strachey. Trans. James Strachey et al. 24 vols. London: Hogarth, 1953–74. Vols. 4, 5.

———. 1930. *Civilization and Its Discontents.* In *The Standard Edition of the Complete Psychological Works of Sigmund Freud.* Ed. James Strachey. Trans. James Strachey et al. 24 vols. London: Hogarth, 1953–74. 21: 64–145.

Fritzsche, Arthur. 1879. "Das angelsächsische Gedicht *Andreas* und Cynewulf." *Anglia* 2: 441–96.

Fry, Donald K. 1967. "Old English Formulas and Systems." *ES* 48: 193–204.

———. 1968a. "Old English Formulaic Themes and Type-Scenes." *Neophil* 52: 48–54.

———. 1968b. "Variation and Economy in *Beowulf.*" *MP* 65: 53–56.

———. 1974a. "*Finnsburh:* A New Interpretation." *Chaucer Review* 9: 1–14.

———, ed. 1974b. *Finnsburh: Fragment and Episode.* London: Methuen.

Fulk, R. D. 1982. "Dating *Beowulf* to the Viking Age." *PQ* 61: 341–59.

———. 1987. "Unferth and His Name." *MP* 85: 113–27.

———. 1989. "An Eddic Analogue to the Scyld Scefing Story." *RES* 40: 313–22.

———, ed. 1991. *Interpretations of Beowulf: A Critical Anthology.* Bloomington: Indiana University Press.

———. 1992. *A History of Old English Meter.* Philadelphia: University of Pennsylvania Press.

Fuss, K. 1963. "Der Held: Versuch einer Wesensbestimmung." *ZfdP* 82: 295–312.

Gahrn, Lars. 1986. "The Geatas of Beowulf." *Scandinavian Journal of History* 11: 95–113.

Gaidoz, Henri. 1921. "Cûchulainn, Béowulf et Hercule." *Cinquantenaire de l'École Pratique des Hautes Études: Mélanges publiés par les directeurs d'études de la section des sciences historiques et philologiques.* Paris: Champion. 131–56.

Galloway, Andrew. 1990. *"Beowulf* and the Varieties of Choice." *PMLA* 105: 197–208.

Galván, Fernando. 1992. "Rewriting Anglo-Saxon: Notes on the Presence of Old English in Contemporary Literature." *SELIM: Journal of the Spanish Society for Medieval English Language and Literature* 2: 70-90.

Gang, T. M. 1952. "Approaches to *Beowulf." RES* 33: 1–12.

Garbáty, Thomas J. 1959. "Feudal Linkage in *Beowulf." N&Q* 6: 11–12.

Gardiner-Stallaert, Nicole. 1988. *From the Sword to the Pen: An Analysis of the Concept of Loyalty in Old English Heroic Poetry.* New York: Peter Lang.

Gardiner-Stallaert, Nicole. 1988. *From the Sword to the Pen: An Analysis of the Concept of Loyalty in Old English Heroic Poetry.* New York: Peter Lang.

Gardner, John. 1970. "Fulgentius's *Expositio Vergiliana Continentia* and the Plan of *Beowulf:* Another Approach to the Poem's Style and Structure." *PLL* 6: 227–62.

———. 1975. *"Beowulf."* In *The Construction of Christian Poetry in Old English.* Carbondale: Southern Illinois University Press. 54–84.

Gardner, Thomas. 1969–70. "The OE Kenning: A Characteristic Feature of Germanic Poetical Diction?" *MP* 67: 109–17.

———. 1972. "The Application of the Term 'Kenning'." *Neophil* 56: 464–68.

———. 1973. "How Free Was the *Beowulf* Poet?" *MP* 71: 111–27.

———. 1993. "Compositional Techniques of the *Beowulf* Poet." *Anglo-Saxonica: Beiträge zur Vor- und Frühgeschichte der englischen Sprache und zur altenglischen Literatur: Festschrift für Hans Schabram.* Ed. Klaus R. Grinda and Claus-Dieter Wetzel. Munich: Fink. 209–23.

Garmonsway, G. N. 1965. "Anglo-Saxon Heroic Attitudes," In *Magoun,* 139–46.

Gattiker, Godfrey L. 1962. "The Syntactic Basis of the Poetic Formula in *Beowulf."* Diss. University of Wisconsin.

Gauger, Hans-Martin. 1992. "Zur Frage des Stils." *Stilfragen.* Ed. Willi Erzgräber and H.-M. Gauger with Eugen Bader and Sabine Habermalz. ScriptOralia 38. Tübingen: Gunter Narr. 9–27.

Geertz, Clifford. 1988. *Works and Lives: The Anthropologist as Author.* Stanford: Stanford University Press.

Gellrich, Jesse. 1985. *The Idea of the Book in the Middle Ages.* Ithaca: Cornell University Press.

Genzmer, Felix. 1950. "Die skandinavischen Quellen des Beowulfs." *AfNF* 65: 17–62.

Georgianna, Linda. 1987. "King Hrethel's Sorrow and the Limits of Heroic Action in *Beowulf." Speculum* 62: 829–50.

Gering, Hugo. 1880. "Der Béowulf und die isländische Grettissaga." *Anglia* 3: 74–87.

Gerritsen, Johan. 1989. "Have With You to Lexington! The *Beowulf* Manuscript and *Beowulf." Other Words: Transcultural Studies in Philology, Translation, and Lexicology Presented to Hans Heinrich Meier on the Occasion of His Sixty-Fifth Birthday.* Ed. J. Lachlan Mackenzie and Richard Todd. Dordrecht: Foris. 15–34.

Gilbert, Sandra M., and Susan Gubar, eds. 1985. *The Norton Anthology of Literature by Women: The Tradition in English.* New York: W. W. Norton.

Gingher, Robert S. 1974. "The Unferth Perplex." *Thoth* 4: 19–28.

Girvan, Ritchie. 1935. *Beowulf and the Seventh Century: Language and Content.* London: Methuen. Rpt. 1971 with essay "Sutton Hoo and the Background to the Poem" by Rupert L. S. Bruce-Mitford.

———. 1940. "Finnsburuh." *Proceedings of the British Academy* 26: 327–60.

Glass, Sandra A. 1982. "The Saxonists' Influence on Seventeenth-Century English Literature." *Anglo-Saxon Scholarship: The First Three Centuries.* Ed. Carl T. Berkhout and Milton McC. Gatch. Boston: Hall. 91–106.

Glosecki, Stephen O. 1989. *Shamanism and Old English Poetry.* New York and London: Garland.

Goebel, Julius. 1897. "On the Original Form of the Legend of Sigfrid." *PMLA* 12: 461–74.

Goffart, Walter. 1981. "*Hetware* and *Hugas:* Datable Anachronisms in *Beowulf.*" In *Dating of Beowulf,* 83–100.

Golden, John Thomas. 1970. "Societal Bonds in Old English Heroic Poetry: A Legal and Typological Study." Diss. Cornell University.

———. 1976. "A Typological Approach to the *Gifstol* of *Beowulf* 168." *NM* 77: 190–204.

Goldsmith, Margaret E. 1960. "The Christian Theme of *Beowulf.*" *MÆ* 29: 81–101.

———. 1962. "The Christian Perspective in *Beowulf.*" *CL* 14: 71–90. Rpt. in *Anthology,* 373–86. Also rpt. in *Interpretations,* 103–19.

———. 1964. "The Choice in *Beowulf.*" *Neophil* 48: 60–72.

———. 1970. *The Mode and Meaning of Beowulf.* London: Athlone.

Gordon, Eric V. 1935. "*Wealhþeow* and Related Names." *MÆ* 4: 169–75.

Gough, Alfred Bradley. 1902. "The Thrytho Saga, and Offa and Cynethryth of Mercia." *The Constance Saga.* Palaestra 23. Berlin: Mayer & Müller. 53–83.

Gould, Kent. 1985. "*Beowulf* and Folktale Morphology: God as Magical Donor." *Folklore* 96: 98–103.

Gradon, Pamela. 1971. *Form and Style in Early English Literature.* London: Methuen.

Graff, Gerald. 1987. *Professing Literature: An Institutional History.* Chicago: University of Chicago Press.

Green, Alexander. 1916. "The Opening of the Episode of Finn in *Beowulf.*" *PMLA* 31: 759–97.

Green, D. H. 1965. *The Carolingian Lord: Semantic Studies on Four Old High German Words: Balder, Fro, Truhtin, Herro.* Cambridge: Cambridge University Press.

Green, Eugene. 1985. "Power, Commitment, and the Right to a Name in *Beowulf.*" *Persons in Groups: Social Behavior as Identity Formation in Medieval and Renaissance Europe.* Ed. Richard C. Trexler. MRTS 36. Binghamton: State University of New York. 133–40.

Green, Martin. 1975. "Man, Time, and Apocalypse in *The Wanderer, The Seafarer,* and *Beowulf.*" *JEGP* 74: 502–18.

Greenfield, Stanley B. 1955. "The Formulaic Expression of the Theme of 'Exile' in Anglo-Saxon Poetry." *Speculum* 30: 200–06. Rpt. in *Essential Articles,* 352–62. Also rpt. in Greenfield 1989, 125–31.

———. 1963. "Geatish History: Poetic Art and Epic Quality in *Beowulf.*" *Neophil* 47: 211–17. Rpt. in Greenfield 1989, 19–26. Also rpt. in *Interpretations,* 120–26.

———. 1965. *A Critical History of Old English Literature.* New York: New York University Press.

———. 1966. "*Beowulf* 207b–228: Narrative and Descriptive Art." *N&Q* n.s. 13: 86–90. Rpt. in Greenfield 1989, 27–32.

————. 1967a. "Grammar and Meaning in Poetry." *PMLA* 82: 377–87.

————. 1967b. "Grendel's Approach to Heorot: Syntax and Poetry." *Old English Poetry: Fifteen Essays.* Ed. Robert P. Creed. Providence: Brown University Press. 275–84.

————. 1972. *The Interpretation of Old English Poems.* London: Routledge and Kegan Paul.

————. 1974. "'Gifstol' and Goldhoard in *Beowulf.*" In *Pope,* 107–17. Rpt. in Greenfield 1989, 33–42.

————. 1976. "The Authenticating Voice in *Beowulf.*" *ASE* 5: 51–62. Rpt. in Greenfield 1989, 43–54. Also rpt. in *Basic Beowulf,* 97–110.

————. 1985. "Beowulf and the Judgement of the Righteous." *Learning and Literature in Anglo-Saxon England: Studies Presented to Peter Clemoes on the Occasion of His Sixty-Fifth Birthday.* Ed. Michael Lapidge and Helmut Gneuss. Cambridge: Cambridge University Press. 393–408. Rpt. in Greenfield 1989, 75–89.

————, and Daniel G. Calder. 1986. *A New Critical History of Old English Literature.* New York: New York University Press.

————. 1989. *Hero and Exile: The Art of Old English Poetry.* Ed. George H. Brown. London and Ronceverte: Hambledon.

Grein, C. W. M. 1857a. *"Beùvulf." Dichtungen der Angelsachsen, stabreimend übersetzt.* Vol. 1. Göttingen: Wigand.

————. 1857b. *Bibliothek der angelsächsischen Poesie.* Vol. 1. Göttingen: Georg H. Wigand. 1881: 2nd ed., rev. Richard Paul Wülcker. Kassel: Wigand.

————. 1862. "Die historischen Verhältnisse des Beowulfliedes." *Jahrbuch für romanische-englische Literatur* 4: 260–85.

Grimm, Jacob. 1835. *Deutsche Mythologie.* Göttingen: Dieterichsche Buchhandlung.

————. 1856. "Der Le am Seestrande." *Germania* 1: 235–36.

————, and Wilhelm Grimm. 1826. *Irische Elfenmärchen.* Leipzig: Fr. Fleischer. Rpt. 1881 in *Werke.* Ed. Otfrid Ehrismann. Vol. 31. Also rpt. 1992 in *Kleinere Schriften.* Vol. 1. Hildesheim: Olms Weidman. 405–90.

Grimm, Wilhelm. 1829. *Die deutsche Heldensage.* Göttingen: Dieterichschen Buchhandlung.

Grønbech, Vilhelm. 1909–1912. *Vor Folkeæt i Oldtiden.* 4 vols. Trans. William Worster as *Culture of the Teutons.* 3 vols. Oxford: Oxford University Press, 1931.

Grundtvig, N. F. S. 1815a. "Et Par Ord om Bjovulfs Drape." *Nyeste skilderie af Kjøbenhavn.* Nos. 60: cols. 945–52; 64: cols. 1009–15; 65: cols. 1025–30; 66: cols. 1045–47.

————. 1815b. "Nok et Par Ord om Bjovulfs Drape." *Nyeste Skilderie af Kjøbenhavn.* Nos. 70: cols. 1105–09; 71: cols. 1121–25; 72: cols. 1139–45.

————. 1817. "Om Bjovulfs Drape eller det af Hr. Etatsraad Thorkelin 1815 udgivne angelsachsiske Digt." *Danne-Virke, et Tids-Skrift* 2: 207–89.

————. 1832. *Nordens Mythologi.* 2nd ed. Copenhagen: J. H. Schubothes. Rpt. 1983, Copenhagen: Samleren.

————. 1841. "Bjovulfs Drape eller det Oldnordiske Heltedigt." *Brage og Idun* 4: 481–538.

Guðnason, Bjarni. 1963. *Um Skjöldunga sögu.* Reykjavik: Bókaútgafa Menningarsjóðs.

Gumbrecht, Hans-Ulrich. 1986. "'Un souffle d'Allemagne ayant passé': Friedrich Diez, Gaston Paris, and the Genesis of National Philologies." *Romance Philology* 40: 1–37.

Haarder, Andreas. 1975. *Beowulf: The Appeal of a Poem.* Copenhagen: Akademisk Forlag.

Haber, Tom Burns. 1931. *A Comparative Study of the Beowulf and the Aeneid.* Princeton: Princeton University Press.

Hagen, Sivert N. 1904. "Classical Names and Stories in the *Beowulf*." *MLN* 19: 65–74.

Haigh, Daniel H. 1861. *The Anglo-Saxon Sagas: An Examination of Their Value as Aids to History*. London: John Russell Smith.

Hall, J. R. 1995a. "The First Two Editions of *Beowulf*: Thorkelin's (1815) and Kemble's (1833)." *Editing Old English Texts: Proceedings of the 1990 Manchester Conference*. Ed. Donald K. Scragg and Paul E. Szarmach. Cambridge: Boydell and Brewer. 239–50.

———. 1995b. "Old English Editing." *Scholarly Editing: An Introduction to Research*. Ed. D. C. Greetham. New York: Modern Language Association. 149–83.

Halverson, John. 1966. "*Beowulf* and the Pitfalls of Piety." *UTQ* 35: 260–78.

———. 1969. "The World of *Beowulf*." *ELH* 30: 593–608.

Hamilton, Marie P. 1946. "The Religious Principle in *Beowulf*." *PMLA* 61: 309–30. Rpt. in *Anthology*, 105–35.

Hanning, Robert W. 1974. "*Beowulf* as Heroic History." *MH* 5: 77–102.

Hansen, Adolf. 1901. "Oldengelsk Litteratur." *Illustreret Verdens-Litteraturhistorie*. Ed. Julius Clausen. Copenhagen.

Hansen, Elaine Tuttle. 1976. "From *freolicu folccwen* to *geomuru ides*: Women in Old English Poetry Reconsidered." *Michigan Academician* 9: 109–17.

Hardy, Adelaide. 1969. "The Christian Hero Beowulf and Unferð þyle." *Neophil* 53: 55–69.

Harris, A. Leslie. 1982. "Techniques of Pacing in *Beowulf*." *ES* 63: 97–108.

———. 1988. "Litotes and Superlative in *Beowulf*." *ES* 69: 1–11.

———. 1990. "The Vatic Mode in *Beowulf*." *Neophil* 74: 591–600.

Harris, Joseph. 1979. "The *Senna*: From Description to Literary Theory." *Michigan Germanic Studies* 5: 65–74.

———. 1982. "*Beowulf* in Literary History." *Pacific Coast Philology* 17: 16–23. Rpt. in *Interpretations*, 235–41.

———. 1985. "Die altenglische Heldendichtung." *Neues Handbuch der Literaturwissenschaft*. Vol. 6. *Europäisches Frühmittelalter*. Ed. Klaus von See. Wiesbaden: AULA. 237–76.

———. 1992a. "Beowulf's Last Words." *Speculum* 67: 3–32.

———. 1992b. Rev. of *Allegories of War*, by John P. Hermann. *Speculum* 67: 983–86.

Harris, Richard L. 1973. "The Death of Grettir and Grendel: A New Parallel." *Scripta Islandica* 24: 25–53.

Hart, Thomas E. 1972. "Tectonic Design, Formulaic Craft, and Literary Execution: The Episodes of Finn and Ingeld in *Beowulf*." *Amsterdamer Beiträge zur älteren Germanistik* 2: 1–61.

———. 1981. "Calculated Casualties in *Beowulf*: Geometrical Scaffolding and Vertical Symbol." *SN* 53: 3–35.

Hart, Walter Morris. 1907. *Ballad and Epic: A Study in the Development of the Narrative Art*. Rpt. 1967, New York: Russell and Russell.

Haruta, Setsuko. 1986. "The Women in *Beowulf*." *Poetica* (Tokyo) 23: 1–15.

Haudry, Jean. 1984. "*Beowulf* dans la tradition indo-européenne." *Études Indo-Européennes* 9: 1–56.

Hauer, Stanley R. 1983. "Thomas Jefferson and the Anglo-Saxon Language." *PMLA* 98: 879–98.

Hedeager, Lotte. 1992a. *Iron Age Societies*. Oxford: Blackwell.

————. 1992b. "Kingdoms, Ethnicity and Material Culture: Denmark in a European Perspective." In *Age of Sutton Hoo,* 279–300.

Heinemann, Fredrik J. 1983. *"Ealuscerwen-Meoduscerwen,* the Cup of Death and *Baldrs Draumar." SN* 55: 3–10.

————. 1987. *"Beowulf* 665b–738: A Mock Approach-to-Battle Type Scene." *Perspectives on Language in Performance: Studies in Linguistics, Literary Criticism, and Language Teaching and Learning to Honour Werner Hüllen on the Occasion of His Sixtieth Birthday.* Ed. Wolfgang Lörscher and Rainer Schulze. Tübingner Beiträge zur Linguistik 317. Tübingen: Gunter Narr. 677–94.

Heinzel, Richard. 1875. *Über den Stil der altgermanischen Poesie.* Strassburg: Trübner.

————. 1884. Rev. of *Beovulfs-kvadet: En literær-historisk undersøgelse,* by Frederik Rönning. *Anzeiger für deutsches Altertum* 10: 233–39.

Helder, Willem [William]. 1977. "Beowulf and the Plundered Hoard." *NM* 78: 317–25.

————. 1987. "The Song of Creation in *Beowulf* and the Interpretation of Heorot." *ESC* 13: 243–55.

Helterman, Jeffrey. 1968. *"Beowulf:* The Archetype Enters History." *ELH* 35: 1–20.

Henderson, Ebenezer. 1818. *Iceland, or the Journal of a Residence between 1814 and 1815.* Edinburgh: Oliphant, Waugh and Innes.

Henige, David P. 1974. *The Chronology of Oral Tradition: Quest for a Chimera.* Oxford: Clarendon.

Herben, Stephen J. 1938. "Beowulf, Hrothgar, and Grendel." *Archiv* 173: 24–30.

Hermann, John P. 1989. *Allegories of War: Language and Violence in Old English Poetry.* Ann Arbor: University of Michigan Press.

Herrmann, Paul. 1905. *Die Geschichte von Hrolf Kraki.* Torgau: Friedr. Jacobs Buchhandlung.

Heusler, Andreas. 1889. "Zur Geschichte der altdeutschen Verskunst." Diss. University of Leipzig. Rpt. 1891 as "Zur Metrik des altsächsischen und hochdeutschen Alliterations-Verses." *Germania* 36: 139–79, 279–307.

————. 1905. *Lied und Epos in germanischer Sagendichtung.* Dortmund: F. W. Ruhfus.

————. 1929. *Die altgermanische Dichtung.* 1941: 2nd ed. Potsdam: Athenaion.

Hickes, George. 1703–1705. *Linguarum Veterum Septentrionalium Thesaurus Grammatico-Criticus et Archaeologicus.* Rpt. 1970, Hildesheim and New York: Georg Olms.

Hieatt, Constance B. 1969. "A New Theory of Triple Rhythm in the Hypermetric Lines of Old English Verse." *MP* 67: 1–8.

————. 1972. "Prosodic Analysis of Old English Poetry: A Suggested Working Approach with Sample Applications." *RUO* 42: 72–82.

————. 1975. "Envelope Patterns and the Structure of *Beowulf." ESC* 1: 249–65.

————. 1984. "Modþryðo and Heremod: Intertwined Threads in the *Beowulf*-Poet's Web of Words." *JEGP* 83: 173–82.

Hill, John M. 1979. *"Beowulf,* Value, and the Frame of Time." *MLQ* 40: 3–16.

————. 1982. "Beowulf and the Danish Succession: Gift Giving as Occasion for Complex Gesture." *MH* n.s. 11: 177–97.

————. 1989. "Revenge and Superego Mastery in *Beowulf." Assays* 5: 3–36.

————. 1991. "Hrothgar's Noble Rule: Love and the Great Legislator." *Social Approaches to Viking Studies.* Ed. Ross Samson. Glasgow: Cruithne. 169–78.

————. 1995. *The Cultural World in Beowulf.* Toronto: University of Toronto Press.

Hill, Joyce M. 1975. "Figures of Evil in Old English Poetry." *Leeds Studies* 8: 5–19.

———. 1990. "'Þæt Wæs Geōmuru Ides!': A Female Stereotype Examined." In *New Readings*, 235–47.

———. 1993. Rev. of *Desire for Origins: New Language, Old English, and Teaching the Tradition*, by Allen J. Frantzen. *Anglia* 111: 161–64.

Hill, Thomas D. 1966. "Two Notes on Patristic Allusion in *Andreas*." *Anglia* 84: 156–62.

———. 1982. "The Confession of Beowulf and the Structure of *Vǫlsunga saga*." In *The Vikings*. Ed. Robert T. Farrell. London: Phillimore. 165–79.

———. 1986. "Scyld Scefing and the 'Stirps Regia': Pagan Myth and Christian Kingship in *Beowulf*." *Magister Regis: Studies in Honor of Robert Earl Kaske*. Ed. Arthur Groos. New York: Fordham University Press. 37–47.

———. 1990. "'Wealhþeow' as a Foreign Slave: Some Continental Analogues." *PQ* 69: 106–12.

Hills, Catherine, K. Penn, and R. Rickett. 1987. "The Anglo-Saxon Cemetery at Spong Hill, North Elmham. Part IV." *East Anglian Archaeology*, Report no. 34.

———. 1994. "The Chronology of the Anglo-Saxon Cemetery at Spong Hill, Norfolk." *Prehistoric Graves as a Source of Information*. Ed. Berta Stjernqvist. Konferenser 29. Stockholm: Kungliga Vitterhets Historie och Antikvitets Akademie. 41–49.

Hines, John. 1989. "The Military Contexts of the Adventus Saxonum: Some Continental Evidence." *Weapons and Warfare in Anglo-Saxon England*. Ed. Sonia Chadwick Hawkes. Monograph 21. Oxford: Oxford University Committee for Archaeology. 25–48.

Hintz, Howard W. 1934. "The 'Hama' Reference in *Beowulf*: 1197–1201." *JEGP* 33: 98–102.

Hodges, Richard. 1989. *The Anglo-Saxon Achievement*. London: Duckworth.

Hollowell, Ida M. 1976. "Unferth the *Þyle* in *Beowulf*." *SP* 73: 239–65.

Hoops, Johannes. 1932a. *Beowulfstudien*. Heidelberg: Winter.

———. 1932b. *Kommentar zum Beowulf*. Heidelberg: Winter.

———. 1940. "Time and Place in the Ingeld Episode of *Beowulf*." *JEGP* 39: 76–92.

Hoover, David L. 1985. *A New Theory of Old English Meter*. New York: Peter Lang.

Hope-Taylor, Brian. 1977. *Yeavering*. London: HMSO.

Horgan, A. D. 1970. "Religious Attitudes in *Beowulf*." *Essays and Poems Presented to Lord David Cecil*. Ed. W. W. Robson. London: Constable. 9–17.

Hornburg, Johannes. 1877. *Die Komposition des Beowulf*. Programm des Kaiserlichen Lyceums zu Metz 411. Metz.

Horowitz, Sylvia Huntley. 1978. "Beowulf, Samson, David and Christ." *Studies in Medieval Culture* 12: 17–23.

———. 1981. "The Ravens in *Beowulf*." *JEGP* 80: 502–11.

Horsman, Reginald. 1981. *Race and Manifest Destiny: The Origins of American Racial Anglo-Saxonism*. Cambridge MA: Harvard University Press.

Howe, Nicholas. 1989. *Migration and Mythmaking in Anglo-Saxon England*. New Haven: Yale University Press.

———. 1997. "The Afterlife of Anglo-Saxon Poetry: Auden, Hill and Gunn." *Words and Works: Studies in Medieval English Language and Literature in Honour of Fred C. Robinson*. Ed. Nicholas Howe and Peter S. Baker. Toronto: University of Toronto Press (forthcoming).

Howlett, David. 1974. "Form and Genre in *Beowulf*." *SN* 46: 309–25.

Hübener, Gustav. 1927–28. "Beowulf und nordische Dämonenaustreibung (Grettir, Heracles, Theseus usw.)." *EStn* 62: 293–327. Trans. 1935 as *"Beowulf* and Germanic Exorcism." *RES* 11: 163–81.

Huffines, Marion L. 1974. "OE *aglæce*: Magic and Moral Decline of Monsters and Men." *Semasia* 1: 71-81.

Hughes, Geoffrey. 1977. "Beowulf, Unferth and Hrunting: An Interpretation." *ES* 58: 385–95.

Huisman, Rosemary. 1989. "The Three Tellings of Beowulf's Fight with Grendel's Mother." *Leeds Studies* n.s. 20: 217–48.

Hulbert, James R. 1951a. "The Genesis of *Beowulf:* A Caveat." *PMLA* 66: 1168–76.

———. 1951b. "Surmises Concerning the *Beowulf* Poet's Source." *JEGP* 50: 11–18.

Hume, Kathryn. 1974. "The Concept of the Hall in Old English Poetry." *ASE* 3: 63–74.

———. 1975. "The Theme and Structure of *Beowulf.*" *SP* 72: 1–27.

Huppé, Bernard F. 1975. "The Concept of the Hero in the Early Middle Ages." *Concepts of the Hero in the Middle Ages and the Renaissance.* Ed. Norman T. Burns and Christopher R. Reagan. Albany: State University of New York Press. 1–26.

———. 1984. *The Hero in the Earthly City: A Reading of Beowulf.* MRTS 33. Binghamton: State University of New York Press.

Hutcheson, B. R. 1991. "Quantity in Old English Poetry: A Classical Comparison." *Geardagum* 12: 44–53.

———. 1993. "Stress of Quantitative Adjectives and Some Common Adverbs in Old English Poetry: An Alternative to Kuhn's Law." *Leeds Studies* n.s. 24: 27–56.

———. 1994. "The Realizations of Tertiary Stress in Old English Poetry." *SP* 91.1: 13–34.

———. 1995. *Old English Poetic Metre.* London: Boydell and Brewer.

Ilkjær, Jon, and Jørgen Lønstrup. 1982. "Interpretation of the Great Votive Deposits of Iron Age Weapons." *Journal of Danish Archaeology* 1: 95–103.

Imelmann, Rudolf. 1920. *Forschungen zur altenglischen Poesie.* Berlin: Weidmannsche Buchhandlung.

Irvine, Martin. 1986a. "Anglo-Saxon Literary Theory Exemplified in Old English Poems: Interpreting the Cross in *The Dream of the Rood* and *Elene.*" *Style* 20: 157–81.

———. 1986b. "Bede the Grammarian and the Scope of Grammatical Studies in Eighth-Century Northumbria." *ASE* 15: 15–44.

Irving, Edward B., Jr. 1968. *A Reading of Beowulf.* New Haven: Yale University Press. Chapter 1, "The Text of Fate," rpt. in *Interpretations,* 168–93.

———. 1982. "Beowulf Comes Home: Close Reading in Epic Context." In *Donaldson,* 129–43.

———. 1984. "The Nature of Christianity in *Beowulf.*" *ASE* 13: 7–21.

———. 1989. *Rereading Beowulf.* Philadelphia: University of Pennsylvania Press.

———. 1990. *"Beowulf."* *AN&Q* n.s. 3: 65–69.

Irving, Edward B., Jr., ed. 1953. *The Old English Exodus.* New Haven: Yale University Press.

Jacobs, Nicolas. 1978. "Anglo-Danish Relations, Poetic Archaism and the Date of *Beowulf:* A Reconsideration of the Evidence." *Poetica* (Tokyo) 8: 23–43.

Jager, Eric. 1990. "Speech and Chest in Old English Poetry: Orality or Pectorality?" *Speculum* 65: 845–59.

Jauss, Hans Robert. 1982. *Toward an Aesthetic of Reception.* Trans. Timothy Bahti. Minneapolis: University of Minnesota Press.

Jellinek, M. H., and Carl Kraus. 1891. "Die Widersprüche im *Beowulf.*" *ZfdA* 35: 265–81.

John, Eric. 1974. "Beowulf and the Margins of Literacy." *BJRL* 56: 388–422. Rpt. in *Basic Beowulf,* 51–77.

Johnson, Richard. 1986. "What Is Cultural Studies Anyway?" *Social Text* 16: 38–80.

Johnson, Samuel F. 1951. "Beowulf." *Explicator* 9.7 (May): item no. 52.

Jones, George Fenwick. 1963. *The Ethos of the Song of Roland.* Baltimore: Johns Hopkins University Press.

Jones, Gwyn. 1972. *Kings, Beasts and Heroes.* London: Oxford University Press.

Jordan, Richard. 1906. *Eigentümlichkeiten des anglischen Wortschatzes.* Anglistische Forschungen 17. Heidelberg: Winter.

Jorgensen, Peter A. 1973. "Grendel, Grettir and Two Skaldic Stanzas." *Scripta Islandica* 24: 54–61.

———. 1975. "The Two-Troll Variant of the Bear's Son Folktale in *Hálfdanar saga Brönufóstra* and *Gríms saga loðinkinna.*" *Arv: Journal of Scandinavian Folklore* 31: 35–43.

———. 1978. "Beowulf's Swimming Contest with Breca: Old Norse Parallels." *Folklore* 89: 52–59.

———. 1979. "The Gift of the Useless Weapon in *Beowulf* and the Icelandic Sagas." *AfNF* 94: 82–90.

———. 1986. "Additional Icelandic Analogues to *Beowulf.*" *Sagnaskemmtun: Studies in Honour of Hermann Pálsson on His 65th Birthday, 26th May 1986.* Ed. Rudolf Simek, Jónas Kristjánsson, and Hans Bekker-Nielsen. Vienna: Hermann Böhlaus Nachfolger. 201–08.

Joseph, Brian D. 1982–83. "Using Indo-European Comparative Mythology to Solve Literary Problems: The Case of Old English Hengest." *Papers in Comparative Studies* 2: 177–86.

———. 1983. "Old English Hengest as an Indo-European Twin Hero." *Mankind Quarterly* 24: 105–15.

Judd, Elizabeth. 1974. "Women before the Conquest: A Study of Women in Anglo-Saxon England." *Papers in Women's Studies* 1: 127–49.

Jung, Carl G. 1916. *Psychology of the Unconscious.* In *Collected Works.* Ed. Herbert Read, Michael Fordham, and Gerhard Adler. 20 vols. London: Routledge and Kegan Paul, 1953–79. 7:1–119.

Kahn, Victoria. 1986. "Humanism and the Resistance to Theory." *Literary Theory/Renaissance Texts.* Ed. Patricia Parker and David Quint. Baltimore: Johns Hopkins University Press. 373–96.

Kahrl, Stanley J. 1972. "Feuds in *Beowulf:* A Tragic Necessity?" *MP* 69: 189–98.

Kail, Johannes. 1889. "Über die Parallelstellen in der angelsächsischen Poesie." *Anglia* 12: 21–40.

Kaluza, Max. 1894. *Der altenglische Vers: Eine metrische Untersuchung.* Vol. 1. *Kritik der bisherigen Theorien.* Vol. 2. *Die Metrik des Beowulfliedes.* Berlin: E. Felber.

———. 1896. "Zur Betonungs- und Verslehre des Altenglischen." *Festschrift zum siebzigsten Geburtstage Oskar Schades.* Königsberg: Hartung. 101–34.

Karkov, Catherine, and Robert T. Farrell. 1990. "The Gnomic Passages in *Beowulf.*" *NM* 91: 295–310.

Kasik, Jon C. 1979. "The Use of the Term 'Wyrd' in *Beowulf* and the Conversion of the Anglo-Saxons." *Neophil* 63: 128–35.

Kaske, Robert E. 1958. *"Sapientia et Fortitudo* as the Controlling Theme of *Beowulf." SP* 55: 423–56. Rpt. in *Anthology,* 269–310.

———. 1959. "The Sigemund-Heremod and Hama-Hygelac Passages in *Beowulf." PMLA* 74: 489–94.

———. 1960. "Weohstan's Sword." *MLN* 75: 465–68.

———. 1963. "'Hygelac' and 'Hygd'." In *Brodeur,* 200–06.

———. 1968. *"Beowulf." Critical Approaches to Six Major English Works: Beowulf through Paradise Lost.* Ed. Robert M. Lumiansky and Herschel Baker. Philadelphia: University of Pennsylvania Press. 3–40.

———. 1971. *"Beowulf* and the Book of Enoch." *Speculum* 46: 421–31.

Kellogg, Robert L. 1965. "The South Germanic Oral Tradition." In *Magoun,* 66–74.

Kelly, Birte. 1982. "The Formative Stages of *Beowulf* Textual Scholarship: Part I." *ASE* 11: 247–74.

———. 1983. "The Formative Stages of *Beowulf* Textual Scholarship: Part II." *ASE* 12: 239–75.

Kemble, John Mitchell. 1834. Letter of 17 July. *John Mitchell Kemble and Jakob Grimm: A Correspondence, 1832–1852.* 1971: Ed. and trans. Raymond A. Wiley. Leiden: Brill. 61–68.

———. 1836. *Über die Stammtafel der Westsachsen.* Munich.

———. 1837. "Postscript to the Preface." *A Translation of the Anglo-Saxon Poem of Beowulf.* Vol. 2 of Kemble's 1835 edition. London: Wm. Pickering.

———, ed. 1839–48. *Codex diplomaticus aevi Saxonici.* 6 vols. London: English Historical Society.

———. 1863. *Horae Ferales: Studies in the Archaeology of the Northern Nations.* Ed. R. G. Latham and A. W. Franks. London: Wm. Pickering.

Kendall, Calvin B. 1983. "The Metrical Grammar of *Beowulf:* Displacement." *Speculum* 58: 1–30.

———. 1991. *The Metrical Grammar of Beowulf.* Cambridge: Cambridge University Press.

———, and Peter S. Wells, eds. 1992. *Voyage to the Other World: The Legacy of Sutton Hoo.* Medieval Studies at Minnesota 5. Minneapolis: University of Minnesota Press.

Kennedy, Charles. 1943. *The Earliest English Poetry.* London: Oxford University Press.

Ker, Neil R. 1968. "The Manuscript." In *The Will of Æthelgifu,* trans. Dorothy Whitelock. Oxford: Roxburghe Club. 45–48.

Ker, W. P. 1897. *Epic and Romance: Essays on Medieval Literature.* Rpt. 1957, New York: Dover.

———. 1904. *The Dark Ages.* Rpt. 1955, New York: Scribner.

———. 1912. *Medieval English Literature.* New York: Holt.

Keyser, Samuel J. 1969. "Old English Prosody." *CE* 30: 331–56.

Kiefer, Thomas M. 1972. *The Tausug: Violence and Law in a Philippine Moslem Society.* New York: Holt, Rinehart and Winston.

Kier, Christian. 1915. *Beowulf: Et Bidrag til Nordens Oldhistorie.* Copenhagen: V. Thaning & Appels.

Kiernan, Kevin S. 1981a. *Beowulf and the Beowulf Manuscript.* New Brunswick: Rutgers University Press.

———. 1981b. "The Eleventh-Century Origin of *Beowulf* and the *Beowulf* Manuscript." In *Dating of Beowulf,* 9–22. Rpt. 1994 in *Anglo-Saxon Manuscripts: Basic Readings,* ed.

Mary P. Richards. Basic Readings in Anglo-Saxon England 2. New York and London: Garland. 277–99.

———. 1983. "The Legacy of Wiglaf: Saving a Wounded *Beowulf.*" Rev. and rpt. in *Basic Beowulf*, 195–218.

———. 1984. "Grendel's Heroic Mother." *Geardagum* 6: 13–33.

———. 1986. *The Thorkelin Transcripts of Beowulf.* Anglistica 25. Copenhagen: Rosenkilde & Bagger.

Kindrick, Robert L. 1981. "Germanic *Sapientia* and the Heroic Ethos of *Beowulf.*" *MH* n.s. 10: 1–17.

King, Richard John. 1850. "Traces of Sigmund the Wælsing in Popular Tradition." *Athenaeum:* 636–37.

Kinney, Clare. 1985. "The Needs of the Moment: Poetic Foregrounding as a Narrative Device in *Beowulf.*" *SP* 82: 295–314.

Kittredge, George Lyman. 1903. "Arthur and Gorlagon." *Harvard Studies and Notes in Philology and Literature* 8: 149–275.

Klaeber, Friedrich. 1910. "Die *Ältere Genesis* und der *Beowulf.*" *EStn* 42: 321–38.

———. 1911a. "Aeneis und Beowulf." *Archiv* 126: 40–48, 339–59.

———. 1911b, 1912. "Die christlichen Elemente im *Beowulf.*" *Anglia* 35: 111–36, 249–70, 453–82; 36: 169–99.

———. 1915. "Observations on the Finn Episode." *JEGP* 14: 544–49.

———. 1918. "Concerning the Relation between *Exodus* and *Beowulf.*" *MLN* 33: 218–24.

———. 1922b. "Der Held Beowulf in deutscher Sagenüberlieferung." *Anglia* 46: 193–201.

———. 1926. "Beowulfiana." *Anglia* 50: 107–22, 195–244.

———. 1927. "Attila's and Beowulf's Funerals." *PMLA* 42: 255–67.

———. 1938–39. "*Beowulf* 769 und *Andreas* 1526ff." *EStn* 73: 185–89.

———. 1950b. "Noch einmal *Exodus* 56–58 und *Beowulf* 1408–10." *Archiv* 187: 71–72.

———. 1951. "Anmerkungen zum Beowulftext." *Archiv* 188: 108–9.

Klein, Thomas. 1988. "Vorzeitsage und Heldensage." *Heldensage und Heldendichtung im Germanischen.* Ed. Heinrich Beck. Berlin: de Gruyter. 115–47.

Kleinschmidt, Harald. 1991. "Architecture and the Dating of *Beowulf.*" *Poetica* 34: 39–56.

Kliman, Bernice W. 1977. "Women in Early English Literature, *Beowulf* to the *Ancrene Wisse.*" *Nottingham Mediaeval Studies* 21: 32–49.

Kluge, Friedrich. 1896. "Der *Beowulf* und die *Hrolfs Saga Kraka.*" *EStn* 22: 144–45.

Köhler, Artur. 1870a. "Die beiden Episoden von Heremod im Beovulfliede." *ZfdP* 2: 314–21.

———. 1870b. "Die Einleitung des Beovulfliedes: Ein Beitrag zur Frage über die Liedertheorie." *ZfdP* 2: 305–14.

Kölbing, Eugen. 1876. "Zur Beowulfhandschrift." *Archiv* 56: 91–118.

Krapp, George Philip, and Elliott Van Kirk Dobbie, eds. 1931–53. *The Anglo-Saxon Poetic Records.* 6 vols. New York: Columbia University Press.

Krappe, Alexander Haggerty. 1927. "Eine mittelalterlich-indische Parallele zum *Beowulf.*" *GRM* 15: 54–58.

———. 1937. "The Offa-Constance Legend." *Anglia* 61: 361–69.

Krishna, Valerie. 1982. "Parataxis, Formulaic Density, and Thrift in the *Alliterative Morte Arthure.*" *Speculum* 57: 63–83.

Kroll, Norma. 1986. "Beowulf: The Hero as Keeper of Human Polity." *MP* 84: 117–29.

Krüger, Thomas. 1884. "Über Ursprung und Entstehung des Beowulfliedes." *Archiv* 71: 129–52.

Krutch, Joseph Wood. 1929. "The Tragic Fallacy." *The Modern Temper.* New York: Harcourt. Rpt. 1970 in *A Krutch Omnibus: Forty Years of Social and Literary Criticism.* New York: William Morrow. 14–27.

Kuhn, Hans. 1933. "Zur Wortstellung und betonung im Altgermanischen." *BGdSL* 57: 1–109.

Kuhn, Sherman M. 1969. "*Beowulf* and the Life of Beowulf: A Study in Epic Structure." *Studies in Language, Literature and Culture of the Middle Ages and After.* Ed. E. B. Atwood and A. A. Hill. Austin: University of Texas Press. 243–64.

Kuryłowicz, Jerzy. 1948–49. "Latin and Germanic Metre." *EGS* 2: 34–39.

––––––. 1950. "Problems of Germanic Quantity and Meter." *Biuletyn Polskiego Towarzystwa Jezykoznawczego* 10: 25–44.

––––––. 1970. *Die sprachlichen Grundlagen der altgermanischen Metrik.* Innsbruck: Institut für vergleichende Sprachwissenschaft der Universität Innsbruck.

––––––. 1979. "Linguistic Fundamentals of the Meter of *Beowulf.*" *Linguistic and Literary Studies in Honor of Archibald A. Hill.* Ed. Mohammad Ali Jazayery, Edgar C. Polomé, and Werner Winter. Trends in Linguistics: Studies and Monographs 10. The Hague: Mouton. 111–20.

Laistner, Ludwig. 1889. *Das Rätsel der Sphinx: Grundzüge einer Mythengeschichte.* 2 vols. Berlin: Wilhelm Hertz.

Lancaster, Lorraine. 1958. "Kinship in Anglo-Saxon Society." *British Journal of Sociology* 9: 230–50, 359–77.

Lang, Janet, and Barry Ager. 1989. "Swords of the Anglo-Saxon and Viking Periods in the British Museum: A Radiographic Study." *Weapons and Warfare in Anglo-Saxon England.* Ed. Sonia Chadwick Hawkes. Monograph 21. Oxford: Oxford University Committee for Archaeology. 85–122.

Langebek, Jakob, ed. 1772. *Scriptores Danicarum Rerum Medii Ævi.* Vol. 1. Rpt. 1969, Nendeln, Liechtenstein: Kraus.

Langenfelt, Gösta. 1961. "*Beowulf* och Fornsverige: Ett försök till datering av den fornengelska hjältedikten. 1." *Ortnamnssällskapet i Uppsala årsskrift:* 35–55. "Tillägg," 37–38.

––––––. 1962. "*Beowulf* och Fornsverige: Ett försök till datering av den fornengelska hjältedikten. 2." *Ortnamnssällskapet i Uppsala årsskrift:* 23–36.

Lapidge, Michael. 1982. "*Beowulf,* Aldhelm, the *Liber Monstrorum* and Wessex." *Studi Medievali* 3rd ser. 23: 151–92.

––––––. 1991. "Textual Criticism and the Literature of Anglo-Saxon England." *BJRL* 73: 17–45.

––––––. 1993. "The Edition, Emendation and Reconstruction of Anglo-Saxon Texts." *The Politics of Editing Medieval Texts.* Ed. Roberta Frank. New York: AMS. 131–57.

Lara, Manuel José Gómez. 1988. "The Death of Anglo-Saxon Secular Heroes: A Linguistic Discussion on *Beowulf* and *The Battle of Maldon.*" *Revista Canaria de Estudios Ingleses* 17: 269–80.

Lass, Roger. 1992. "Phonology and Morphology." *The Cambridge History of the English Language.* Vol. 2. Cambridge: Cambridge University Press. 23–156.

Laur, Wolfgang. 1954. "Die Heldensage vom Finnsburgkampf." *ZfdP* 85: 107–36.

Lawrence, R. F. 1966. "The Formulaic Theory and Its Application to English Alliterative Poetry." *Essays on Style and Language: Linguistic and Critical Approaches to Literary Style.* Ed. Roger Fowler. New York: Humanities Press. 166–83.

Lawrence, William W. 1909. "Some Disputed Questions in Beowulf-Criticism." *PMLA* 24: 220–73.

———. 1912. "The Haunted Mere in *Beowulf.*" *PMLA* 27: 208–45.

———. 1913. "The Breca Episode in *Beowulf.*" *Anniversary Papers by Colleagues and Pupils of George Lyman Kittredge.* Boston: Harvard University Press. 359–66.

———. 1915. "*Beowulf* and the Tragedy of Finnsburg." *PMLA* 30: 372–432.

———. 1928. *Beowulf and Epic Tradition.* Cambridge MA: Harvard University Press.

———. 1929. "*Beowulf* and the *Saga of Samson the Fair.*" In *Klaeber,* 172–81.

———. 1939. "Grendel's Lair." *JEGP* 38: 477–80.

Leake, Jane Acomb. 1967. *The Geats of Beowulf: A Study in the Geographical Mythology of the Middle Ages.* Madison: University of Wisconsin Press.

Lee, Alvin A. 1972. *The Guest-Hall of Eden: Four Essays on the Design of Old English Poetry.* New Haven: Yale University Press.

———. 1975. "Old English Poetry, Mediaeval Exegesis, and Modern Criticism." *Studies in the Literary Imagination* 8: 47–73. Rpt. 1992 in *Typology and English Medieval Literature.* Ed. Hugh T. Keenan. New York: AMS. 43–70.

———. 1993. "Gold-Hall and Earth-Dragon, *Beowulf* and 'First-Phase' Language." *ESC* 19: 201–08.

Lee, Donald W. 1972. "Lactantius and *Beowulf.*" *Studies in Linguistics in Honor of Raven I. McDavid, Jr.* Ed. Lawrence M. Davis. Birmingham: University of Alabama Press. 397–413.

Leeds, E. T. 1936. *Early Anglo-Saxon Art and Archaeology.* Rpt. 1968, Oxford: Oxford University Press.

Lees, Clare. 1988, 1989, 1990, 1991. "Old English Literature." *Year's Work in English Studies* 69: 115–34; 70: 151–71; 71: 177–204; 72: 70–96.

Lefevere, André. 1992. *Translating Literature: Practice and Theory in a Comparative Literature Context.* New York: Modern Language Association.

Lehman, David. 1991. *Signs of the Times: Deconstruction and the Fall of Paul De Man.* New York: Poseidon.

Lehmann, Winfred P. 1956. *The Development of Germanic Verse Form.* Austin: University of Texas Press.

———, and Takemitsu Tabusa. 1958. *The Alliterations of the Beowulf.* Austin: University of Texas Press.

———. 1982. "Drink Deep!" *Approaches to Beowulfian Scansion.* Ed. Alain Renoir and Ann Hernandez. Old English Colloquium. Berkeley: Department of English, University of California, Berkeley. 18–26.

Leisi, Ernst. 1952–53. "Gold und Manneswert im *Beowulf.*" *Anglia* 71: 259–73.

Leo, Heinrich. 1839. *Bëówulf, dasz älteste deutsche, in angelsächsischer Mundart erhaltene Heldengedicht nach seinem Inhalte, und nach seinen historischen und mythologischen Beziehungen betrachtet.* Halle: Eduard Anton.

Le Page, R. B. 1957. "A Rhythmical Framework for the Five Types." *EGS* 6: 92–103.

———. 1959. "Alliterative Patterns as a Test of Style in Old English Poetry." *JEGP* 58: 434–41.

Lerer, Seth. 1991. *Literacy and Power in Anglo-Saxon Literature.* Lincoln: University of Nebraska Press.

———. 1994. "Grendel's Glove." *ELH* 61: 721–51.

Levander, Lars. 1908. "Sagotraditioner om sveakonungen Adils." *ATfS* 18.3: 1–55.

Levine, Robert. 1971. "Ingeld and Christ: A Medieval Problem." *Viator* 2: 105–28.

Lévi-Strauss, Claude. 1978. *Myth and Meaning.* Toronto: University of Toronto Press.

Lewis, I. M. 1976. *Social Anthropology in Perspective.* Cambridge: Cambridge University Press.

Leyerle, John. 1965. "Beowulf the Hero and the King." *MÆ* 34: 89–102.

———. 1967. "The Interlace Structure of *Beowulf.*" *UTQ* 37: 1–17. Rpt. in *Interpretations,* 146–67.

Liberman, Anatoly. 1986. "Beowulf—Grettir." *Germanic Dialects: Linguistic and Philological Investigations.* Amsterdam Studies in the Theory and History of Linguistic Science 38. Ed. Bela Brogyanyi and Thomas Krömmelbein. Amsterdam: John Benjamins. 353–401.

Liebermann, Felix. 1920. "Ort und Zeit der Beowulfdatierung." *Nachrichten von der Königlichen Gesellschaft der Wissenschaften zu Göttingen, philosophisch-historische Klasse:* 255–76.

Liestøl, Knut. 1930. "Beowulf and Epic Tradition." *American-Scandinavian Review* 18: 370–73.

Liggins, Elizabeth M. 1973. "Revenge and Reward as Recurrent Motives in *Beowulf.*" *NM* 74: 193–213.

Lindow, John. 1993. "Sailing and Interpreting the Ships on the Gotland Stones." *American Neptune* 53: 39–50.

Lindqvist, Sune. 1936. *Uppsala Högar och Ottarshögen.* Stockholm: Wahlström & Widstrand.

———. 1948. "Sutton Hoo and Beowulf." *Antiquity* 22: 131–40.

Locherbie-Cameron, Margaret. 1978. "Structure, Mood and Meaning in *Beowulf.*" *Poetica* (Tokyo) 10: 1–11.

Longfellow, Henry Wadsworth. 1838. "Anglo-Saxon Literature." *North American Review* 47: 90–143. Rpt. 1845 in his *Poets and Poetry of Europe.* Philadelphia: Carey and Hart.

Lönnroth, Lars. 1969. "The Noble Heathen: A Theme in the Sagas." *SS* 41: 1–29.

Lord, Albert Bates. 1960. *The Singer of Tales.* Harvard Studies in Comparative Literature 24. Rpt. 1965, New York: Atheneum.

———. 1965. "Beowulf and Odysseus." In *Magoun,* 86–91.

———. 1974. "Perspectives on Recent Work on Oral Literature." *Forum for Modern Language Studies* 10: 187–210.

———. 1980. "Interlocking Mythic Patterns in *Beowulf.*" In *OEL in Context,* 137–42.

———. 1991. *Epic Singers and Oral Tradition.* Ithaca: Cornell University Press.

Luecke, Jane-Marie. 1978. *Measuring Old English Rhythm: An Application of the Principles of Gregorian Chant Rhythm to the Meter of Beowulf.* Literary Monographs 9. Madison: University of Wisconsin Press.

———. 1983. "*Wulf and Eadwacer:* Hints for Reading from *Beowulf* and Anthropology." *The Old English Elegies: New Essays in Criticism and Research.* Ed. Martin Green. Rutherford NJ: Fairleigh Dickinson University Press. 190–203.

Luehrs, Phoebe M. 1904. "A Summary of Sarrazin's *Studies in Beowulf.*" *Western Reserve University Bulletin* 7: 146–65.

Lutz, Angelika. 1993. "Lautwandel und paläographische Evidenz für die Wiedergabe von /h/ (<Germ. /x/) in der Lindisfarne-Glosse." *Anglia* 111: 285–309.

Mackie, William S. 1938. "The Demons' Home in *Beowulf.*" *JEGP* 37: 455–61.

Maeth, Ch. Russell. 1987. "El cuento de Zhou Chu: ¿Un precursor sino-tibetano de la edad media temprana de *Beowulf*?" *Estudios de Asia y Africa* 22: 535–46.

Magennis, Hugh. 1985. "The *Beowulf* Poet and His *druncne dryhtguman.*" *NM* 86: 159–64.

———. 1986. "*Monig Oft Gesæt:* Some Images of Sitting in Old English Poetry." *Neophil* 70: 442–52.

Magoun, Francis P., Jr. 1953. "The Oral-Formulaic Character of Anglo-Saxon Narrative Poetry." *Speculum* 28: 446–67. Rpt. in *Anthology,* 189–221. Also rpt. in *Essential Articles,* 319–51; in *Beowulf Poet,* 83–113; and in *Interpretations,* 45–65.

———. 1954. "Béowulf and King Hygelác in the Netherlands: Lost Anglo-Saxon Verse-Stories about This Event." *ES* 35: 193–204.

———. 1958. "'*Béowulf A':* A Folk-Variant." *Arv: Journal of Scandinavian Folklore* 14: 95–101.

———. 1959. "*Beowulf* in Denmark: An Italo-Brazilian Variant." *Mélanges de linguistique et de philologie Fernand Mossé in Memoriam.* Paris: Didier. 247–55.

———. 1960. "Conceptions and Images Common to Anglo-Saxon Poetry and the *Kalevala.*" *Britannica: Festschrift für Hermann M. Flasdieck.* Ed. Wolfgang Iser and Hans Schabram. Heidelberg: Winter. 80–91.

———. 1961. "Some Notes on Anglo-Saxon Poetry." *Studies in Medieval Literature in Honor of Albert Croll Baugh.* Ed. MacEdward Leach. Philadelphia: University of Philadelphia Press. 273–83.

———. 1963a. "*Béowulf B:* A Folk-Poem on Beowulf's Death." *Early English and Norse Studies Presented to Hugh Smith in Honour of His Sixtieth Birthday.* Ed. Arthur Brown and Peter Foote. London: Methuen. 127–40.

———, trans. 1963b. *The Kalevala.* Cambridge MA: Harvard University Press.

Malinowski, Bronislaw. 1926. "The Role of Myth in Life." *Psyche* 24: 29–39. Rpt. 1984 in *Sacred Narrative: Readings in the Theory of Myth,* ed. Alan Dundes. Berkeley and Los Angeles: University of California Press. 193–206.

———. 1932. *Argonauts of the Western Pacific.* Rpt. 1961, New York: E. P. Dutton.

———. 1935. *Coral Gardens and Their Magic.* 2 vols. New York: American Book.

Malmberg, Lars. 1977. "Grendel and the Devil." *NM* 78: 241–43.

Malone, Kemp. 1925. "King Alfred's Geatas." *MLR* 20: 1–11.

———. 1926. "The Finn Episode in *Beowulf.*" *JEGP* 25: 157–72.

———. 1927. "Hrethric." *PMLA* 42: 268–313.

———. 1929. "The Daughter of Healfdene." In *Klaeber,* 135–58.

———. 1930. "Ingeld." *MP* 27: 257–76.

———. 1939. "Swerting." *Germanic Review* 14: 235–57.

———. 1939–40. "Hygelac." *APS* 21–22: 108–19.

———. 1940. "Freawaru." *ELH* 7: 39–44.

———. 1941a. "Grundtvig as *Beowulf* Critic." *RES* 17: 129-38.

———. 1941b. "Hygd." *MLN* 56: 356–58.

———. 1942. "Grendel and Grep." *PMLA* 57: 1–14.

———. 1943. "Hildeburg and Hengest." *ELH* 10: 257–84.

———. 1948. "*Beowulf.*" *ES* 29: 161–72. Rpt. 1953 in *Literary Masterpieces of the Western World.* Ed. F. H. Horn. Baltimore: Johns Hopkins University Press. Also rpt. in *Anthology,* 137–54.

———. 1954. "Epithet and Eponym." *Names* 2: 109–12.

———. 1958. "Grendel and His Abode." *Studia Philologica et Litteraria in Honorem L. Spitzer.* Ed. A. G. Hatcher and K. L. Selig. Bern: Francke. 297–308.

———. 1959. "The Tale of Ingeld." *Studies in Heroic Legend and in Current Speech.* Ed. Stefán Einarsson and Norman E. Eliason. Copenhagen: Rosenkilde & Bagger. 1–62.

———. 1960. "Words of Wisdom in *Beowulf.*" *Humanoria.* Ed. W. D. Hayland and G. O. Arlt. Locust Valley NY: Augustin. 180–94.

Marquardt, Hertha. 1940. "Zur Entstehung des *Beowulf.*" *Anglia* 64: 152–58.

Martin-Clarke, Daisy E. 1936. "The Office of Thyle in *Beowulf.*" *RES* 12: 61–66.

Matthes, Heinrich C. 1953. "Beowulfstudien." *Anglia* 71: 148–90.

Mauss, Marcel. 1922–23. *The Gift: Forms and Functions of Exchange in Archaic Societies.* Trans. 1967, Ian Cunnison. New York: Norton.

Mazzuoli Porru, Giulia. 1985. "*Beowulf,* v. 33: *isig ond utfus.*" *Studi linguistici e filologici per Carlo Alberto Mastrelli.* Pisa: Pacini. 263–74.

McConchie, R. N. 1982. "Grettir Ásmundarson's Fight with Kárr the Old: A Neglected *Beowulf* Analogue." *ES* 63: 481–86.

McCone, Kim. 1990. *Pagan Past and Christian Present in Early Irish Literature.* Maynooth: An Sagart.

McCully, Christopher. 1988. Rev. of *Old English Meter and Linguistic Theory,* by Geoffrey Russom. *Lingua* 75: 379–83.

McGalliard, John C. 1967. "*Beowulf* and Bede." *Life and Thought in the Early Middle Ages.* Ed. Robert S. Hoyt. Minneapolis: University of Minnesota Press. 101–21.

———. 1978. "The Poet's Comment in *Beowulf.*" *SP* 75: 243–70.

McGann, Jerome J. 1983. *A Critique of Modern Textual Criticism.* Chicago: University of Chicago Press.

———. 1985. "The Monks and the Giants: Textual and Bibliographical Studies and the Interpretation of Literary Works." *Textual Criticism and Literary Interpretation.* Ed. Jerome J. McGann. Chicago: University of Chicago Press. 180–99.

———. 1991. *The Textual Condition.* Princeton: Princeton University Press.

McHugh, Maire. 1987. "The Sheaf and the Hound: A Comparative Analysis of the Mythic Structure of *Beowulf* and *Táin Bó Cúalnge.*" *La narrazione: Temi e tecniche dal medioevo al nostri giorni.* Quaderni del dipartimento di lingue e letterature straniere moderne, Università di Genova, 1. Abano Terme: Piovan. 9–43.

McKinley, J. 1994. "The Anglo-Saxon Cemetery at Spong Hill, Norfolk. Part VIII. The Cremations." *East Anglian Archaeology,* Report no. 69.

McNamee, Maurice B. 1960a. "Beowulf, a Christian Hero." *Honor and the Epic Hero: A Study of the Shifting Concept of Magnanimity in Philosophy and Epic Poetry.* New York: Holt, Rinehart and Winston. 86–117.

———. 1960b. "*Beowulf*—An Allegory of Salvation?" *JEGP* 59: 190–207. Rpt. in *Anthology,* 331–52. Also rpt. in *Interpretations,* 88–102.

McNeill, William H. 1986. *Mythistory and Other Essays.* Chicago: University of Chicago Press.

McTurk, Rory. 1981. "Variation in *Beowulf* and the Poetic *Edda:* A Chronological Experiment." In *Dating of Beowulf,* 141–60.

Meaney, Audrey L. 1979. "The *Ides* of the Cotton Gnomic Poem." *MÆ* 48: 23–39. Rpt. in *New Readings,* 158–75.

———. 1989. "Scyld Scefing and the Dating of *Beowulf*—Again." *BJRL* 75: 7–40.

Meigs, Karl. 1964. "*Beowulf,* Mythology and Ritual: A Common-Reader Exploration." *Xavier University Studies* 3: 89–102.

Mellinkoff, Ruth. 1979. "Cain's Monstrous Progeny in *Beowulf:* Part I, Noachic Tradition." *ASE* 8: 143–62.

———. 1981. "Cain's Monstrous Progeny in *Beowulf:* Part II, Post-Diluvian Survival." *ASE* 9: 183–97.

Menéndez Pidal, Ramón. 1959. *La Chanson de Roland y el neotradicionalismo.* Madrid: Espasa-Calpe.

Meroney, Howard. 1949. "Full Name and Address in Early Irish." *Philologica: The Malone Anniversary Studies.* Ed. Thomas A. Kirby and Henry Bosley Woolf. Baltimore: Johns Hopkins University Press. 124–31.

Meyer, Richard M. 1889. *Die altgermanische Poesie nach ihren formelhaften Elementen beschrieben.* Berlin: Wilhelm Hertz.

Miletich, John S. 1988. "Muslim Oral Epic and Medieval Epic." *MLR* 83: 911–24.

Millett, Martin, and Simon James. 1983. "Excavations at Cowdery's Down, Basingstoke, Hants." *Archaeological Journal* 140: 151–279.

Mitchell, Bruce. 1963. "'Until the Dragon Comes . . . ': Some Thoughts on *Beowulf.*" *Neophil* 47: 126–38. Rpt. in Mitchell 1988a 3–15.

———. 1975. "Linguistic Facts and the Interpretation of Old English Poetry." *ASE* 4: 11–28. Rpt. in Mitchell 1988a, 152–71.

———. 1980. "The Dangers of Disguise: Old English Texts in Modern Punctuation." *RES* n.s. 31: 385–413. Rpt. in Mitchell 1988a, 172–202.

———. 1985. *Old English Syntax.* Oxford: Oxford University Press.

———. 1988. "1987: Postscript on *Beowulf.*" In Mitchell 1988a, 41-54.

———. 1988a. *On Old English: Selected Papers.* Oxford: Blackwell.

——— and Fred C. Robinson. 1992. *A Guide to Old English.* 5th ed. Oxford: Blackwell.

Mizuno, Tomaki. 1989. "Beowulf as a Terrible Stranger." *Journal of Indo-European Studies* 17: 1–46

Moffat, Douglas. 1992. "Anglo-Saxon Scribes and Old English Verse." *Speculum* 67: 805–27.

Moisl, Hermann. 1981. "Anglo-Saxon Genealogies and Germanic Oral Tradition." *Journal of Medieval History* 7: 215–48.

Möller, Hermann. 1883. *Das altenglische Volksepos in der ursprünglichen strophischen Form.* Vol. 1. *Abhandlungen.* Kiel: Lipsius & Tischer.

Mone, F. J. 1836. *Untersuchungen zur Geschichte der teutschen Heldensage.* Quedlinburg & Leipzig: G. Basse.

Montrose, Lewis Adrian. 1983. "'Shaping Fantasies': Figurations of Gender and Power in Elizabethan Culture." *Representations* 2: 61–94. Rpt. 1988 in *Representing the English Renaissance.* Ed. Stephen Greenblatt. Berkeley and Los Angeles: University of California Press. 31–64.

Moore, Arthur K. 1968. "Medieval English Literature and the Question of Unity." *MP* 65: 285–300.

Moore, Bruce. 1976. "The Relevance of the Finnsburh Episode." *JEGP* 75: 317–29.

———. 1980. "The Thryth-Offa Digression in *Beowulf.*" *Neophil* 64: 127–33.

Moorman, Charles. 1967. "The Essential Paganism of *Beowulf.*" *MLQ* 28: 3–18.

Morrison, Stephen. 1980. "*Beowulf* 698a, 1273a: 'Frofor ond fultum.'" *N&Q* 225: 193–96.

Morsbach, Lorenz. 1906. "Zur Datierung des Beowulfepos." *Nachrichten von der Königlichen Gesellschaft der Wissenschaften zu Göttingen, philosophisch-historische Klasse:* 251–77.

Mossé, Fernand. 1945. *Manuel de l'anglais du Moyen Age des origines au XIVᵉ siècle.* Pt. 1. *Viel-anglais.* Paris: Aubier Montaigne.

Müllenhoff, Karl. 1844. "Die deutschen Völker an Nord- und Ostsee in ältester Zeit: Eine Kritik der neueren Forschungen mit besonderer Rücksicht auf Tacitus, *Beovulf,* und Scopevidsith." *Nordalbingische Studien: Neues Archiv der Schleswig-Holstein-Lauenburgischen Gesellschaft für vaterländische Geschichte* 1: 111–74.

———. 1849a. "Der Mythus von *Beovulf.*" *ZfdA* 7: 419–41.

———. 1849b. "Sceaf und seine Nachkommen." *ZfdA* 7: 410–19.

———. 1868. Letter to Wilhelm Scherer. 12th May. *Briefwechsel zwischen Karl Müllenhoff und Wilhelm Scherer.* 1937: Ed. Albert Leitzmann. Berlin and Leipzig: W. de Gruyter.

———. 1869. "Die innere Geschichte des *Beowulfs.*" *ZdfA* 14: 193–244.

———. 1879. "Die alte Dichtung von den Nibelungen: I. Von Sigfrids Ahnen." *ZfdA* 23: 113–73.

———. 1889. *Beovulf: Untersuchungen über das angelsächische Epos und die älteste Geschichte der germanischen Seevolker.* Berlin: Weidmann.

Müller, P. E. 1815. Rev. of *De Danorum rebus gestis seculi III & IV: Poëma Danicum dialecto Anglo-Saxonica,* by Grímur Jónsson Thorkelin. *Dansk-Litteratur-Tidende:* 401–32, 437–46, 461–62.

Müller-Wille, Michael. 1968–69. "Bestattung im Boot: Studien zu einer nordeuropäischen Grabsitte." *Offa 1968–1969.* 25/26. Neumünster. 1–203.

Murphy, Michael. 1985. "Vows, Boasts and Taunts, and the Role of Women in Some Medieval Literature." *ES* 66: 105–12.

Murray, Alexander Callander. 1981. "Beowulf, the Danish Invasions, and Royal Genealogy." In *Dating of Beowulf,* 101–12.

Musgrove, S. 1945. "*Beowulf* on Perelandra." *N&Q* 188: 140–42.

Mustanoja, Tauno F. 1967. "The Unnamed Woman's Song of Mourning over Beowulf and the Tradition of Ritual Lamentation." *NM* 68: 1–27.

Myres, J. N. L. 1969. *Anglo-Saxon Pottery and the Settlement of England.* Oxford: Oxford University Press.

Nader, E. 1888, 1889. "Tempus und Modus im *Beowulf.*" *Anglia* 10: 542–563; 11: 444–499.

Nagler, Michael N. 1980. "*Beowulf* in the Context of Myth." In *OEL in Context,* 143–56.

Nagy, Joseph F. 1982. "Beowulf and Fergus: Heroes of Their Tribes?" *Connections between Old English and Medieval Celtic Literature.* Ed. Patrick K. Ford and Karen G. Borst. Old English Colloquium Series 2. Berkeley: Old English Colloquium, Department of English, University of California; Lanham MD: University Press of America. 31–44.

Near, Michael. 1993. "Anticipating Alienation: *Beowulf* and the Intrusion of Literacy." *PMLA* 108: 320–32.

Neckel, Gustav. 1910. "Scyld Scefing." *GRM* 2: 678–79.

———. 1920a. "Sigemunds Drachenkampf." *Edda* 13: 122–40, 204–9.

———. 1920b. *Die Überlieferungen vom Gotte Balder dargestellt und vergleichend untersucht.* Dortmund: F. W. Ruhfus.

Nerman, Birger. 1913a. *Studier över Svärges hedna litteratur.* Uppsala: Appelbergs Boktryckeri.

———. 1913b. *Vilka konungar ligga i Uppsala högar?* Uppsala: Appelbergs Boktryckeri.

Newton, Sam. 1993. *The Origins of Beowulf and the Pre-Viking Kingdom of East Anglia.* Cambridge: D. S. Brewer.

Nicholson, Lewis E. 1964. "The Literal Meaning and Symbolic Structure of *Beowulf.*" *Classica et Mediaevalia* 25: 151–201.

———. 1975. "Hunlafing and the Point of the Sword." In *McGalliard,* 50–61.

———. 1980. "The Art of Interlace in *Beowulf.*" *SN* 52: 237–49.

Nielsen, P., and P. Sørensen. 1993. "Jernalderhal udgravet i Gudme." *Nyt fra National-museet* 59: 4–5.

Niles, John D. 1979. "Ring Composition and the Structure of *Beowulf.*" *PMLA* 94: 924–35.

———. 1981a. "Compound Diction and the Style of *Beowulf.*" *ES* 62: 489–503.

———. 1981b. "Formula and Formulaic System in *Beowulf.*" In *Lord,* 394–415.

———. 1983. *Beowulf: The Poem and Its Tradition.* Cambridge MA: Harvard University Press.

———. 1991. "Pagan Survivals and Popular Belief." In *Cambridge Companion,* 126–41.

———. 1992. "Toward an Anglo-Saxon Oral Poetics." *De Gustibus: Essays for Alain Renoir.* Ed. John Miles Foley. New York: Garland. 359–77.

———. 1993a. "Locating *Beowulf* in Literary History." *Exemplaria* 5: 79–109.

———. 1993b. "Rewriting *Beowulf:* The Task of Translation." *CE* 55: 858–78.

———. 1993c. "Understanding *Beowulf:* Oral Poetry Acts." *Journal of American Folklore* 106: 131–55.

———. 1994. "Editing *Beowulf:* What Can Study of the Ballads Tell Us?" *Oral Tradition* 9: 440–67.

Nist, John A. 1957. "Textual Elements in the *Beowulf* Manuscript." *Papers of the Michigan Academy of Science, Arts, and Letters* 42: 331–38. [Incorporated as chapter 8 in Nist 1959].

———. 1958. "The Structure of *Beowulf.*" *Papers of the Michigan Academy of Science, Arts, and Letters* 43: 307–14. [Incorporated as chapter 1 in Nist 1959].

———. 1959. *The Structure and Texture of Beowulf.* São Paulo, Brazil: University of São Paulo.

———. 1963. "Beowulf and the Classical Epics." *CE* 24: 257–62.

Nitzsche, Jane. See Chance, Jane.

Nolan, Barbara, and Morton W. Bloomfield. 1980. "*Beotword, Gilpcwidas,* and the *Gilphlæden* Scop of *Beowulf.*" *JEGP* 79: 499–516.

North, Richard. 1990. "Tribal Loyalties in the Finnsburh Fragment and Episode." *Leeds Studies* 21: 13–43.

———. 1991. *Pagan Words and Christian Meanings.* Amsterdam: Rodopi.

O'Brien O'Keeffe, Katherine. 1981. "*Beowulf,* Lines 702b–836: Transformations and the Limits of the Human." *TSLL* 23: 484–94.

———. 1990. *Visible Song: Transitional Literacy in Old English Verse.* Cambridge: Cambridge University Press.

———. 1991. "Heroic Values and Christian Ethics." In *Cambridge Companion,* 107–25.

Obst, Wolfgang. 1987. *Der Rhythmus des Beowulf: Eine Akzent- und Takttheorie.* Anglistische Forschungen 187. Heidelberg: Winter.

————. 1989. Rev. of *Old English Meter and Linguistic Theory,* by Geoffrey Russom. *Anglia* 107: 506–10.

O'Connor, Sonia. 1992. "Technology and Dating of the Mail." *The Anglian Helmet from Coppergate.* Ed. Dominic Tweddle. The Archaeology of York, The Small Finds 8. York Archeological Trust. 1057–75.

Ogilvy, J. D. A. 1964. "Unferth: Foil to Beowulf?" *PMLA* 79: 370–75.

O'Loughlin, J. L. N. 1952. "*Beowulf*—Its Unity and Purpose." *MÆ* 21: 1–13.

Olrik, Axel. 1903. *Danmarks heltedigtning: En oldtidsstudie.* Vol. 1. *Rolf Krake og den ældre skjoldungrække.* 1919: Trans. (and rev. in collaboration with the author) by Lee M. Hollander as *The Heroic Legends of Denmark.* New York: American-Scandinavian Foundation. Rpt. 1971, New York: Kraus.

Olsen, Alexandra Hennessey. 1984. "Women in *Beowulf.*" *Approaches to Teaching Beowulf.* Ed. Jess B. Bessinger Jr. and Robert F. Yeager. New York: Modern Language Association. 150–56.

————. 1992. Rev. of *Language, Sign, and Gender in Beowulf,* by Gillian Overing. *Speculum* 67: 1024–26.

Olson, Oscar L. 1913–14. "*Beowulf* and *The Feast of Bricriu.*" *MP* 11: 1–21.

————. 1916. *The Relation of the Hrólfs saga kraka and the Bjarkarímur to Beowulf.* Chicago: University of Chicago Libraries. Also published in *Publications of the Society for the Advancement of Scandinavian Studies* 3: 1–104.

Ong, Walter J. 1962. *The Barbarian Within.* New York: Macmillan.

Opland, Jeff. 1973. "A *Beowulf* Analogue in *Njálssaga.*" *SS* 45: 54–58.

————. 1976. "*Beowulf* on the Poet." *Mediaeval Studies* 38: 442–67.

————. 1980. *Anglo-Saxon Oral Poetry: A Study of the Traditions.* New Haven: Yale University Press.

Osborn, Marijane. 1969. "Foreign Studies of *Beowulf.*" Diss. Stanford University.

————. 1978. "The Great Feud: Scriptural History and Strife in *Beowulf.*" *PMLA* 93: 973–81. Rpt. in *Basic Beowulf,* 111–25.

Oshitari, Kinshiro. 1974. "The Shift of Viewpoint in *Beowulf.*" *Poetica* (Tokyo) 1: 106–13.

————. 1988. "A Japanese Analogue of *Beowulf.*" *Philologia Anglica: Essays Presented to Professor Yoshiro Terasawa on the Occasion of His Sixtieth Birthday.* Ed. Kinshiro Oshitari et al. Tokyo: Kenkyusha. 259–69.

Outzen, N. 1816. "Das angelsächsische Gedicht *Beowulf,* als die schätzbarste Urkunde des höchsten Alterthums von unserem Vaterlande." *Kieler Blätter* 3: 307–27.

Overing, Gillian R. 1986. "The Object as Index: A Peircean Approach to *Beowulf.*" *Semiotics 1985.* Ed. John Deely. Lanham MD: University Press of America. 569–83. Expanded in chapter 2 of Overing 1990.

————. 1987. "Swords and Signs: A Semiotic Perspective on *Beowulf.*" *American Journal of Semiotics* 5: 35–57. Rev. as chapter 2 of Overing 1990.

————. 1990. *Language, Sign, and Gender in Beowulf.* Carbondale: Southern Illinois University Press. Last chapter rev. and rpt. as "The Women of *Beowulf:* A Context for Interpretation" in *Basic Beowulf,* 219–60.

————. 1991. "On Reading Eve: *Genesis B* and the Reader's Desire." *Speaking Two Languages: Traditional Disciplines and Contemporary Theory in Medieval Studies.* Ed. Allen J. Frantzen. Albany: State University of New York Press. 35–64.

————. 1993. "Recent Writing on Old English." *Æstel* 1: 135–49.

————, and Marijane Osborn. 1994. *Landscape of Desire: Partial Stories of the Medieval Scandinavian World.* Minneapolis: University of Minnesota Press.

Owen, Gale R. 1981. *Rites and Religions of the Anglo-Saxons.* Newton Abbot: David and Charles.

Paetzel, Walther. 1913. *Die Variationen in der altgermanischen Alliterationspoesie.* Palaestra 48. Berlin: Mayer & Müller.

Page, Amy, and Vincent H. Cassidy. 1969. "*Beowulf:* The Christologers and the Mythic." *Orbis Litterarum* 24: 101–11.

Page, R. I. 1981. "The Audience of *Beowulf* and the Vikings." In *Dating of Beowulf,* 113–22.

————. 1987. *Runes.* London: British Museum.

Palmer, Richard Barton. 1973. "The Moral Portrait of the Hero: A Study of Three Ethical Questions in *Beowulf.*" Diss. Yale University.

————. 1976. "In His End Is His Beginning: *Beowulf* 2177–99 and the Question of Unity." *An Med* 17: 5–21.

Panzer, Friedrich. 1910. *Studien zur germanischen Sagengeschichte, I: Beowulf.* Munich: Beck.

Parker, Mary A. 1987. *Beowulf and Christianity.* New York: Peter Lang.

Parks, Ward. 1986. "Flyting and Fighting: Pathways in the Realization of the Epic Contest." *Neophil* 70: 292–306.

————. 1988. "Ring Structure and Narrative Embedding in Homer and *Beowulf.*" *NM* 89: 237–51.

————. 1989. "Interperformativity and *Beowulf.*" *Narodna umjetnost* 26: 25–35.

————. 1990. *Verbal Dueling in Heroic Narrative: The Homeric and Old English Traditions.* Princeton: Princeton University Press.

Parry, Milman. 1980. *The Making of Homeric Verse: The Collected Papers of Milman Parry.* Ed. Adam Parry. New York: Arno.

Patterson, Lee. 1987. *Negotiating the Past: The Historical Understanding of Medieval Literature.* Madison: University of Wisconsin Press.

Payne, Richard C. 1982. "The Rediscovery of Old English Poetry in the English Literary Tradition." *Anglo-Saxon Scholarship: The First Three Centuries.* Ed. Carl T. Berkhout and Milton McC. Gatch. Boston: Hall. 149–66.

Pearsall, Derek. 1985. "Editing Medieval Texts: Some Developments and Some Problems." *Textual Criticism and Literary Interpretation.* Ed. Jerome J. McGann. Chicago: University of Chicago Press. 92–106.

Pearson, Michael P., Robert van de Noort, and Alex Woolf. 1993. "Three Men and a Boat: Sutton Hoo and the East Saxon Kingdom." *ASE* 22: 27–50.

Pecchio, Giuseppe. 1833. *Storia critica della poesia inglese.* Lugano: Ruggia.

Peltola, Niilo. 1972. "Grendel's Descent from Cain Reconsidered." *NM* 73: 284–91.

Pepperdene, Margaret W. 1955. "Grendel's *Geis.*" *Journal of the Royal Society of Antiquarians of Ireland* 85: 188–92.

————. 1966. "Beowulf and the Coast-guard." *ES* 47: 409-19.

Peters, F. J. J. 1989. "The Wrestling in *Grettis saga.*" *PLL* 25: 235–41.

Peters, Leonard J. 1951. "The Relationship of the Old English *Andreas* to *Beowulf.*" *PMLA* 66: 844–63.

Phillpotts, Bertha S. 1928. "Wyrd and Providence in Anglo-Saxon Thought." *E&S* 13: 7–27. Rpt. in *Interpretations,* 1–13.

Pigg, Daniel F. 1990. "Cultural Markers in *Beowulf:* A Re-Evaluation of the Relationship between Beowulf and Christ." *Neophil* 74: 601–17.

Pilch, Herbert. 1970. "Syntactic Prerequisites for the Study of Old English Poetry." *Language and Style* 3: 51–61.

Pizzo, Enrico. 1916. "Zur Frage der ästhetischen Einheit des *Beowulf.*" *Anglia* 39, n.s. 27: 1–15.

Polanyi, Livia. 1977. "Lexical Coherence Phenomena in Beowulf's Debate with Unferth." *Rackham Literary Studies* 8: 25–37.

Polomé, Edgar C. 1989. *Essays on Germanic Religion.* Journal of Indo-European Studies Monograph No. 6.

Pope, John C. 1942. *The Rhythm of Beowulf: An Interpretation of the Normal and Hypermetric Verse-Forms in Old English Poetry.* 1966: 2nd ed. New Haven: Yale University Press.

———. 1970. "Beowulf's Old Age." In *Meritt,* 55-81.

———. 1981. "On the Date of Composition of *Beowulf.*" In *Dating of Beowulf,* 187–96.

———. 1982. "The Existential Mysteries as Treated in Certain Passages in Our Older Poets." In *Donaldson,* 345–56.

Poussa, Patricia. 1981. "The Date of *Beowulf* Reconsidered: The Tenth Century?" *NM* 82: 276–88.

Pratt, Mary Louise. 1977. *Toward a Speech-Act Theory of Literary Discourse.* Bloomington: Indiana University Press.

Princi Braccini, Giovanna. 1984. "Tra folclore germanico e latinità insulare: Presenze del *Liber monstrorum* e della *Cosmographia* dello Pseudo-Etico nel *Beowulf* e nel cod. Nowell." *Studi medievali* 25: 681–720.

Puhvel, Martin. 1965. "Beowulf and Celtic Under-Water Adventure." *Folklore* 76: 254–61. Also in Puhvel 1979, 73–81.

———. 1966. "Beowulf's Slaying of Daghræfn—a Connection with Irish Myth?" *Folklore* 77: 282–85. Also in Puhvel 1979, 82–85.

———. 1969. "The Melting of the Giant-Wrought Sword in *Beowulf.*" *ELN* 7: 81–84. Also in Puhvel 1979, 39–44.

———. 1971. "The Swimming Prowess of Beowulf." *Folklore* 82: 276–80. Also in Puhvel 1979, 55–60.

———. 1979. *Beowulf and Celtic Tradition.* Waterloo ON: Wilfrid Laurier University Press.

———. 1980. "A Scottish Analogue to the Grendel Story." *NM* 81: 395–98.

———. 1983. "The Ride around Beowulf's Barrow." *Folklore* 94: 108–12.

Pulsiano, Phillip. 1985. "*Cames cynne*: Confusion or Craft?" *Proceedings of the PMR Conference* 7 (1985 for 1982): 33–38.

———, and Joseph McGowan. 1990. "*Fyrd, here* and the Dating of *Beowulf.*" *Studia Anglica Posnaniensia* 23: 3–13.

Quine, W. V. 1987. *Quiddities: An Intermittently Philosophical Dictionary.* Cambridge MA: Harvard University Press.

Quirk, Randolph. 1963. "Poetic Language and Old English Metre." *Early English and Norse Studies Presented to Hugh Smith in Honour of His Sixtieth Birthday.* Ed. Arthur Brown and Peter Foote. London: Methuen. 150–71.

Rahtz, Philip. 1976. "Buildings and Rural Settlement." *The Archaeology of Anglo-Saxon England.* Ed. David M. Wilson. London: Methuen. 49–98.

———. 1979. *The Saxon and Medieval Palaces at Cheddar.* British Archaeological Reports

65. Oxford: British Archaeological Reports.

Randsborg, Klaus. 1990. "Beyond the Roman Empire: Archaeological Discoveries in Gudme on Fünen." *Oxford Journal of Archaeology* 9: 355–66.

———. 1991. *The First Millennium* A.D. *in Europe and the Mediterranean.* Cambridge: Cambridge University Press.

Reichl, Karl. 1987. "Beowulf, Er Töstük und das Bärensohnmärchen." *Asiatische Forschungen: Monographienreihe zur Geschichte, Kultur und Sprache der Völker Ost- und Zentralasiens,* 101. Ed. Walther Heissig. Wiesbaden: Harrassowitz. 321–50.

Reidinger, Anita. 1985. "The Old English Formula in Context." *Speculum* 60: 294–317.

Reino, Joseph. 1972. "The 'Half-Danes' of Finnsburg and Heorot Hall." *Modern Language Studies* 2: 29–43.

Renoir, Alain. 1963. "The Heroic Oath in *Beowulf,* the *Chanson de Roland,* and the *Nibelungenlied.*" In *Brodeur,* 237–66.

———. 1966. "Originality, Influence, Imitation: Two Mediaeval Phases." *Actes du IVe Congrès de l'Association Internationale de Littérature Comparée, Fribourg 1964/ Proceedings of the IVth Congress of the International Comparative Literature Association.* Ed. François Jost. The Hague: Mouton. 737–46.

———. 1974. "The Terror of the Dark Waters: A Note on Virgilian and Beowulfian Techniques." *The Learned and the Lewed: Studies in Chaucer and Medieval Literature.* Harvard English Studies 5. Ed. Larry D. Benson. Cambridge MA: Harvard University Press. 147–68.

———. 1986. "Old English Formulas and Themes as Tools for Contextual Interpretation." *Modes of Interpretation in Old English Literature: Essays in Honour of Stanley B. Greenfield.* Ed. P. R. Brown, G. R. Crampton, and F. C. Robinson. Toronto: University of Toronto Press. 65–79.

Rexroth, Kenneth. 1965. "Classics Revisited— IV: *Beowulf.* " *Saturday Review* (London). 10 April: 27. Rpt. in *Beowulf Poet* 167–69.

Reynolds, Robert L. 1957. "Note on *Beowulf*'s Date and Economic-Social History." *Studi in onore di Armando Sapori.* Vol. 2. Milan: Istituto editoriale Cisalpino. 175–78.

Richards, Julian D. 1991. *Viking Age England.* London: English Heritage, Batsford.

Richards, Mary P. 1973. "A Reexamination of *Beowulf* ll. 3180-3182." *ELN* 10: 163-67.

———, and B. Jane Stanfield. 1990. "Concepts of Anglo-Saxon Women in the Laws." In *New Readings,* 89–99.

Rickert, Edith. 1904–05. "The Old English Offa Saga." *MP* 2: 29–76, 321–76.

Rieger, Friedrich M. 1876. "Die alt- und angelsächsische Verskunst." *ZfdP* 7: 1–64.

Rieger, Max. 1871. "Zum *Beowulf.*" *ZfdP* 3: 381–416.

Rigg, A. G. 1982. "*Beowulf* 1368–72: An Analogue." *N&Q* 227: 101–12.

Riley, Samuel M. 1982. "*Beowulf,* Lines 3180-82. *Explicator* 40: 2–3.

Ringler, Richard N. 1966. "*Him Seo Wen Geleah:* The Design for Irony in Grendel's Last Visit to Heorot." *Speculum* 41: 49–67.

Roach-Smith, Charles. 1852. *Collectanea Antiqua.* Vol. 2. London: J. R. Smith.

Roberts, Jane. 1980. "Old English *Un-* 'Very' and Unferth." *ES* 61: 289–92.

Robertson, Durant W., Jr. 1951. "The Doctrine of Charity in Mediaeval Literary Gardens: A Topical Approach through Symbolism and Allegory." *Speculum* 26: 24–49. Rpt. in *Anthology,* 165–88.

Robinson, Fred C. 1962. "Variation: A Study in the Diction of *Beowulf.*" Diss. University of North Carolina.

————. 1970a. "Lexicography and Literary Criticism: A Caveat." In *Meritt,* 99–110. Rpt. in Robinson 1993b, 140–52.

————. 1970b. "Personal Names in Medieval Narrative and the Name of Unferth in *Beowulf.*" *Essays in Honor of Richebourg Gaillard McWilliams.* Ed. Howard Creed. Birmingham AL: Birmingham-Southern College. 43–48. Rpt. in Robinson 1993b, 219–23.

————. 1974. "Elements of the Marvellous in the Characterization of Beowulf: A Reconsideration of the Textual Evidence." In *Pope,* 119–37. Rpt. in Robinson 1993b, 20–35. Also rpt. in *Basic Beowulf,* 79–96.

————. 1979. "Two Aspects of Variation in Old English Poetry." In *OE Poetry,* 127–45. Rpt. in Robinson 1993b, 71–86.

————. 1980. "Old English Literature in Its Most Immediate Context." In *OEL in Context,* 11–29. Rpt. 1994 in Fred C. Robinson, *The Editing of Old English.* Oxford: Blackwell. 3–24. Also rpt. 1994 in *Old English Shorter Poems: Basic Readings.* Ed. Katherine O'Brien O'Keeffe. Basic Readings in Anglo-Saxon England 3. New York and London: Garland. 3–29.

————. 1982. "'The Might of the North': Pound's Anglo-Saxon Studies and *The Seafarer.*" *Yale Review* 71: 199–224. Rpt. in Robinson 1993b, 239–58.

————. 1984. "History, Religion, and Culture." *Approaches to Teaching Beowulf.* Ed. Jess B. Bessinger Jr. and Robert F. Yeager. New York: Modern Language Association. 107–22.

————. 1985. *Beowulf and the Appositive Style.* Knoxville: University of Tennessee Press.

————. 1990. "Old English Poetry: The Question of Authorship." *AN&Q* 3: 59–64. Rpt. in Robinson 1993b, 164–69.

————. 1993a. "Ezra Pound and the Old English Translational Tradition." Robinson 1993b, 259-74.

————. 1993b. *The Tomb of Beowulf and Other Essays on Old English.* Oxford: Blackwell.

Robinson, Rodney P., ed. 1935. *The Germania of Tacitus: A Critical Edition.* Middletown CT: American Philological Association.

Rönning, Frederik. 1883. *Beovulfs-kvadet: En literær-historisk undersøgelse.* Copenhagen: Rasmussen & Olsen.

Roesdahl, Else. 1982. *Viking Age Denmark.* London: British Museum.

————. 1992. "Princely Burial in Scandinavia at the Time of the Conversion." *Voyage to the Other World: The Legacy of Sutton Hoo.* Ed. Calvin B. Kendall and Peter S. Wells. Medieval Studies at Minnesota 5. Minneapolis: University of Minnesota Press. 155–70.

Rogers, H. L. 1955. "Beowulf's Three Great Fights." *RES* n.s. 6: 339–55. Rpt. in *Anthology,* 233–56.

————. 1966. "The Crypto-Psychological Character of the Oral Formula." *ES* 47: 89–102.

Rollason, David. 1989. *Saints and Relics in Anglo-Saxon England.* Oxford: Blackwell.

Rollinson, Philip. 1970. "Some Kinds of Meaning in Old English Poetry." *An Med* 11: 5–21.

————. 1973. "The Influence of Christian Doctrine and Exegesis on Old English Poetry: An Estimate of the Current State of Scholarship." *ASE* 2: 271–84.

Rose, Nancy. 1967. "Hrothgar, Nestor, and Religiosity as a Mode of Characterization in Heroic Poetry." *Journal of Popular Culture* 1: 158–65.

Rosenberg, Bruce A. 1969. "The Necessity of Unferth." *Journal of the Folklore Institute* 6: 50–60.

———. 1975. "Folktale Morphology and the Stucture of *Beowulf:* A Counter-Proposal." *Journal of the Folklore Institute* 11: 199–209.

———. 1991. *Folklore and Literature: Rival Siblings.* Knoxville: University of Tennessee Press.

Rosier, James L. 1962. "Design for Treachery: The Unferth Intrigue." *PMLA* 77: 1–7.

———. 1963. "The Uses of Association: Hands and Feasts in *Beowulf.*" *PMLA* 78: 8–14.

———. 1977. "Generative Composition in *Beowulf.*" *ES* 58: 193–203.

Ross, A. S. C., and E. G. Stanley. 1960. Rev. of *Beowulf översatt i originalets versmått,* by Björn Collinder. *EGS* 6: 10–12.

Routh, James Edward. 1905. *Two Studies of the Ballad Theory of the Beowulf Together with an Introductory Sketch of Opinion.* Baltimore: J. H. Furst.

Rowland, Jenny. 1990. "OE *Ealuscerwen/Meoduscerwen* and the Concept of 'Paying for Mead'." *Leeds Studies* n.s. 21: 1–12.

Rue, Loyal D. 1989. *Amythia: Crisis in the Natural History of Western Culture.* Tuscaloosa: University of Alabama Press.

Rusev, R. 1937. *"Beowulf."* Godišnik na Sofiiskiya Universitet, Istoriko-filologičeski Fakultet 33.

Russell, James C. 1994. *The Germanization of Early Medieval Christianity.* Oxford: Oxford University Press.

Russom, Geoffrey R. 1978. "Artful Avoidance of the Useful Phrase in *Beowulf, The Battle of Maldon,* and *Fates of the Apostles.*" *SP* 75: 371–90. Rpt. in *Interpretations,* 206–18.

———. 1987a. *Old English Meter and Linguistic Theory.* Cambridge: Cambridge University Press.

———. 1987b. "Verse Translations and the Question of Literacy in *Beowulf.*" *Comparative Research on Oral Traditions.* Ed. John Miles Foley. Columbus OH: Slavica. 567–80.

———. 1990. "A New Kind of Metrical Evidence in Old English Poetry." *Papers from the 5th International Conference on English Historical Linguistics.* Ed. Sylvia Adamson et al. Amsterdam: Benjamins. 435–57.

Ruthven, K. K. 1976. *Myth.* London: Methuen.

Said, Edward. 1978. *Orientalism.* New York: Vintage.

Samuel, Raphael, and Paul Thompson, eds. 1990. *The Myths We Live By.* London: Routledge.

Sarrazin, Gregor. 1886a. "Altnordisches im Beowulfliede." *BGdSL* 11: 528–41.

———. 1886b. *"Beowulf* und Kynewulf." *Anglia* 9: 515–50.

———. 1886c. "Der Schauplatz des ersten Beowulfliedes und die Heimat des Dichters." *BGdSL* 11: 159–83.

———. 1888. *Beowulf-Studien: Ein Beitrag zur Geschichte altgermanischer Sage und Dichtung.* Berlin: Mayer & Müller.

———. 1889. "Die *Fata Apostolorum* und der Dichter Kynewulf." *Anglia* 12: 375–87.

———. 1892. "Die Abfassungszeit des Beowulfliedes." *Anglia* 14: 399–415.

———. 1897. "Neue Beowulf-Studien." *EStn* 23: 221–67.

———. 1905. "Neue Beowulf-Studien." *EStn* 35: 19–27.

———. 1910. "Neue Beowulf-Studien." *EStn* 42: 1–37.

Schaar, Claes. 1956. "On a New Theory of Old English Poetic Diction." *Neophil* 40: 301–15.

Schabram, Hans. 1965a. "*Andreas* und *Beowulf:* Parallelstellen als Zeugnis für literarische Abhängigkeit." *Nachrichten der Giessener Hochschulgesellschaft* 34: 201–18.

———. 1965b. *Superbia: Studien zum altenglischen Wortschatz.* Vol. 1. *Die dialektale und zeitliche Verbreitung des Wortguts.* Munich: Fink.

Schaefer, Ursula. 1992. *Vokalität: Altenglische Dichtung zwischen Mündlichkeit und Schriftlichkeit.* ScriptOralia 39. Tübingen: Gunter Narr.

Schemann, Karl. 1882. *Die Synonyma im Beowulfliede mit Rücksicht auf Composition und Poetik des Gedichtes.* Hagen: G. Butz.

Schichler, Robert Lawrence. 1986. "Heorot and Dragon-Slaying in *Beowulf.*" *Proceedings of the PMR Conference* 11: 159–75.

Schick, J. 1929. "Die Urquelle der Offa-Konstanze-Sage." *Britannica: Max Förster zum sechzigsten Geburtstage.* Leipzig: Tauchnitz. 31–56.

Schlauch, Margaret. 1927. *Chaucer's Constance and Accused Queens.* New York: Gordian.

———. 1930. "Another Analogue of *Beowulf.*" *MLN* 45: 20–21.

Schneider, Hermann. 1934. "Englische Heldensage." Vol. 2, pt. 2 of *Germanische Heldensage. Grundriss der germanischen Philologie* 10:3. Berlin: W. de Gruyter.

Schneider, Karl. 1986. *Sophia Lectures on Beowulf.* Ed. Shoichi Watanabe and Norio Tsuchiya. Tokyo: Taishukan for the Japan Science Society.

Schönbäck, Bengt. 1983. "The Custom of Burial in Boats." *Vendel Period Studies.* Ed. J. P. Lamm and H. A. Nordström. Museum of National Antiquities Studies 2. Stockholm. 123–32.

Schrader, Richard J. 1972. "*Beowulf*'s Obsequies and the Roman Epic." *CL* 24: 237–59.

———. 1980. "Cædmon and the Monks, the *Beowulf*-Poet and Literary Continuity in the Early Middle Ages." *ABR* 31: 39–69.

———. 1983a. *God's Handiwork: Images of Women in Early Germanic Literature.* Contributions in Women's Studies 41. Westport CT: Greenwood.

———. 1983b. "Sacred Groves, Marvellous Waters, and Grendel's Abode." *Florilegium* 5: 76–84.

———. 1984. "The Deserted Chamber: An Unnoticed Topos in the 'Father's Lament' of *Beowulf.*" *Journal of the Rocky Mountain Medieval and Renaissance Association* 5: 1–5.

Schröbler, Ingeborg. 1939. "*Beowulf* und Homer." *BGdSL* 63: 305–46.

Schröder, Edward. 1921–22. "Die Leichenfeier für Attila." *ZfdA* 59: 240–44.

Schrøder, Ludvig. 1875. *Om Bjovulfs-drapen: Efter en række foredrag på folkehöjskolen i Askov.* Copenhagen: Karl Schønberg.

Schück, Henrik. 1907. *Folknamnet Geatas i den fornengelska dikten Beowulf.* Uppsala: Uppsala Universitets Årsskrift.

———. 1909. *Studier i Beowulfsagan.* Uppsala: Uppsala Universitets Årsskrift.

Schücking, Levin L. 1905. *Beowulfs Rückkehr: Eine kritische Studie.* Studien zur englischen Philologie 21. Halle.

———. 1908. "Das angelsächsische Totenklagelied." *EStn* 39: 1–13.

———. 1915. *Untersuchungen zur Bedeutungslehre der angelsächsischen Dichtersprache.* Heidelberg: Winter.

———. 1917. "Wann entstand der *Beowulf?* Glossen, Zweifel und Fragen." *BGdSL* 42: 347–410.

———, ed. 1919. *Kleines angelsächsiches Dichterbuch: Lyrik und Heldenepos.* Cöthen: O. Schulze.

————. 1923. "Die Beowulfdatierung: Eine Replik." *BGdSL* 47: 293–311.

————. 1929a. "Das Königsideal im *Beowulf.*" *Bulletin of the Modern Humanities Research Association* 3: 143–54. Rpt. as "The Ideal of Kingship in *Beowulf*" in *Anthology,* 35–49.

————. 1929b. "Noch einmal: 'enge anpaðas, uncuð gelad.'" In *Klaeber,* 213–16.

————. 1933. *Heldenstolz und Würde im Angelsächsischen.* Leipzig: S. Hirzel.

Scowcroft, Richard Mark. 1982. "The Hand and the Child: Studies of Celtic Tradition in European Literature." Diss. Cornell University.

Scull, C. J. 1991. "Post-Roman Phase 1 at Yeavering: A Reconsideration." *Medieval Archaeology* 25: 51–63.

————. 1992. "Before Sutton Hoo: Structures of Power and Society in Early East Anglia." In *Age of Sutton Hoo,* 3–23.

Seebohm, Frederick. 1911. *Tribal Custom in Anglo-Saxon Law.* New York: Longmans, Green.

Shaw, Brian A. 1978. "The Speeches in *Beowulf:* A Structural Study." *Chaucer Review* 13: 86–92.

Shippey, T. A. 1969. "The Fairy-Tale Structure of *Beowulf.*" *N&Q* 214: 2–11.

————. 1972. *Old English Verse.* London: Hutchinson. Part of chapter 2 rpt. as "The Ironic Background" in *Interpretations,* 194–205.

————. 1975. "Connecting with Beowulf" [review article]. *Times Literary Supplement* (London), 29 August: 974.

————. 1978. *Beowulf.* London: Edward Arnold.

————. 1993a. "Principles of Conversation in Beowulfian Speech." *Techniques of Description: Spoken and Written Discourse: A Festschrift for Malcolm Coulthard.* Ed. John M. Sinclair, Michael Hoey, and Gwyneth Fox. London: Routledge. 109–26.

————. 1993b. "Recent Writing on Old English." *Æstel* 1: 111–34.

Short, Douglas D. 1980b. "*Beowulf* and Modern Critical Tradition." *A Fair Day in the Affections: Literary Essays in Honor of Robert B. White, Jr.* Ed. Jack D. Durrant and M. Thomas Hester. Raleigh: Winston. 1–23.

Shuman, Baird, and H. Charles Hutchings. 1960. "The *Un-* Prefix: A Means of Germanic Irony in *Beowulf.*" *MP* 57: 217–22.

Sieper, Ernst. 1915. *Die altenglische Elegie.* Strassburg: Trübner.

Sievers, Eduard. 1885. "Zur Rhythmik des germanischen Alliterationsverses." *BGdSL* 10: 209–314, 451–545.

————. 1886. "Die Heimat des Beowulfdichters." *BGdSL* 11: 354–62.

————. 1893. *Altgermanische Metrik.* Halle: M. Niemeyer.

————. 1904. "Zum *Beowulf.*" *BGdSL* 29: 305–31.

————. 1925. "Zu Cynewulf." *Neusprachliche Studien: Festgabe Karl Luick. Die Neuere Sprachen* 33: 60–81.

Silber, Patricia. 1980. "Unferth: Another Look at the Emendation." *Names* 28: 101–11.

————. 1981. "Rhetoric Powers in the Unferth Episode." *TSLL* 23: 471–83.

Sisam, Kenneth. 1953a. "Notes on Old English Poetry: The Authority of Old English Poetical Manuscripts." *Studies in the History of Old English Literature.* Oxford: Clarendon. 29–44. Rpt. in *OEL: 22 Essays,* 36–51.

————. 1953b. "MSS. Bodley 340 and 342: Ælfric's *Catholic Homilies.*" *Studies in the History of Old English Literature.* Oxford: Clarendon. 148–98.

————. 1965. *The Structure of Beowulf.* Oxford: Clarendon.

Sklute, L. John [Larry M.]. 1970. "'Freoðuwebbe' in Old English Poetry." *NM* 71: 534–41. Rpt. in *New Readings,* 204–20.

Smith, Arthur H. 1938. "The Photography of Manuscripts." *London Mediaeval Studies* 1: 179–207.

Smith, J. C., and E. De Selincourt, eds. 1952. *The Poetical Works of Edmund Spenser.* London: Oxford University Press.

Smith, Lewis W. 1917. "Race Permanence and the War." *Sewanee Review* 25: 187–92.

Smith, Roger. 1990. "Ships and the Dating of *Beowulf.*" *AN&Q* 3: 99–103.

Smithers, George V. 1961. *The Making of Beowulf: Inaugural Lecture of the Professor of English Language Delivered . . . on 18 May, 1961.* Durham: University of Durham.

———. 1966. "Four Cruces in *Beowulf.*" *Studies in Language and Literature in Honor of Margaret Schlauch.* Ed. Mieczysław Brahmer, Stanisław Helsztynski, and Julian Krzyżanowski. Warsaw: Polish Scientific Publishers. 413–30.

———. 1970. "Destiny and the Heroic Warrior in *Beowulf.*" In *Meritt,* 65–81.

Smithson, George A. 1910. *The Old English Christian Epic: A Study in the Plot Technique of Juliana, the Elene, the Andreas, and the Christ, in Comparison with the Beowulf and with the Latin Literature of the Middle Ages.* University of California Publications in Modern Philology 1: 303–400.

Smyser, H. M. 1965. "Ibn Fadlan's Account of the Rus with Some Commentary and Some Allusions to *Beowulf.*" In *Magoun,* 92–119.

Sontag, Susan. 1966. *Against Interpretation.* New York: Farrar Straus Giroux.

Sorrell, Paul. 1992. "Oral Poetry and the World of *Beowulf.*" *Oral Tradition* 7: 28–65.

Southward, Elaine C. 1946. "The Knight Yder and the *Beowulf* Legend in Arthurian Romance." *MÆ* 15: 1–47.

Speake, George. 1980. *Anglo-Saxon Animal Art.* Oxford: Oxford University Press.

Spolsky, Ellen. 1977. "Old English Kinship Terms and *Beowulf.*" *NM* 78: 233–38.

Standop, Ewald. 1969. "Formen der Variation im *Beowulf.*" *Festschrift für Edgar Mertner.* Ed. Bernhard Fabian and Ulrich Suerbaum. Munich: Fink. 55–63.

Stanley, Eric G. 1956. "OE Poetic Diction and the Interpretation of *The Wanderer, The Seafarer,* and *The Penitent's Prayer.*" *Anglia* 73: 413–66. Rpt. in *Essential Articles,* 458–514. Also rpt. in Stanley 1987, 234–80.

———. 1963. "Hæþenra Hyht in *Beowulf.*" In *Brodeur,* 136–51. Rpt. in Stanley 1987, 192–208.

———. 1966. *"Beowulf." Continuations and Beginnings.* London: Thomas Nelson. 104–41. Rpt. in Stanley 1987, 139–69. Also rpt. in *Basic Beowulf,* 3–34.

———. 1974. "Some Observations on the A3 Lines in *Beowulf.*" In *Pope,* 139–64.

———. 1975. *The Search for Anglo-Saxon Paganism.* Cambridge: D. S. Brewer.

———. 1979. "Two Old English Poetic Phrases Insufficiently Understood for Literary Criticism: *Þing Gehegan* and *Seoneþ Gehegan.*" In *OE Poetry,* 76–82. Rpt. in Stanley 1987, 298–317.

———. 1980. "The Narrative Art of *Beowulf.*" *Medieval Narrative: A Symposium.* Ed. Hans Bekker-Nielsen et al. Odense: Odense University Press. 16–23. Rpt. in Stanley 1987, 170–91.

———. 1981a. "The Date of *Beowulf:* Some Doubts and No Conclusions." In *Dating of Beowulf,* 197–211. Rpt. in Stanley 1987, 209–31.

———. 1981b. "The Scholarly Recovery of the Significance of Anglo-Saxon Records in Prose and Verse: A New Bibliography." *ASE* 9: 223–62. Rpt. in Stanley 1987, 3–48.

————. 1982. "Translation from Old English: 'The Garbaging War-Hawk' or, The Literal Materials from Which the Reader Can Re-Create the Poem." In *Donaldson*, 67–101. Rpt. in Stanley 1987, 83–114.

————. 1984. "Unideal Principles of Editing Old English Verse." *PBA* 70: 231–73.

————. 1986. "Rudolf 1986 von Raumer: Long Sentences in *Beowulf* and the Influence of Christianity on Germanic Style." *N&Q* 33: 434–38.

————. 1987. *A Collection of Papers with Emphasis on Old English Literature*. Toronto: Pontifical Institute of Mediaeval Studies.

————. 1990. "'Hengestes heap,' *Beowulf* 1091." *Britain, 400–600: Language and History*. Ed. Alfred Bammesberger and Alfred Wollmann. Anglistische Forschungen 205. Heidelberg: Winter. 51–63.

————. 1993. "'Ἀπὸ κοινοῦ,' Chiefly in *Beowulf.*" *Anglo-Saxonica: Beiträge zur Vor- und Frühgeschichte der englischen Sprache und zur altenglischen Literatur: Festschrift für Hans Schabram*. Ed. Klaus R. Grinda and Claus-Dieter Wetzel. Munich: Fink. 181–207.

Steadman, J. M., Jr. 1930. "The Ingeld-Episode in *Beowulf:* History or Prophecy?" *MLN* 45: 522–25.

Stedman, Douglas. 1913–14. "Some Points of Resemblance between *Beowulf* and the *Grettla* (or *Grettis saga*)." *SBVS* 8: 6–28.

Stefanović, Svetislav. 1934. "Zur Offa-Thryðo-Episode im *Beowulf.*" *EStn* 69: 15–31.

Steuer, Heiko. 1987. "Helm und Ringschwert: Prunkbewaffnung und Rangabzeichen germanischer Krieger: Eine Übersicht." *Studien zur Sachsenforschung* 6: 189–236.

Stevens, Martin. 1978. "The Structure of *Beowulf:* From Gold-Hoard to Word-Hoard." *MLQ* 39: 219–38.

Stevick, Robert D. 1962. "The Oral-Formulaic Analyses of Old English Verse." *Speculum* 37: 382–89. Rpt. in *Essential Articles*, 393–403. Also rpt. in *OEL: 22 Essays*, 62–72.

————. 1963. "Christian Elements and the Genesis of *Beowulf.*" *MP* 61: 79–89.

————. 1992. "Representing the Form of *Beowulf.*" *Old English and New: Studies in Language and Linguistics in Honor of Frederic G. Cassidy*. Ed. Joan H. Hall, Nick Doane, and Dick Ringler. New York: Garland. 3–14.

Stitt, Michael J. 1992. *Beowulf and the Bear's Son: Epic, Saga, and Fairytale in Northern Germanic Tradition*. New York: Garland.

Stjerna, Knut. 1908. *Essays on Questions Connected with the Old English Poem of Beowulf.* 1912: Trans. and ed. J. R. Clark Hall. London: Curtis and Beamish.

Storms, Godfrid. 1963. "The Subjectivity of the Style of *Beowulf.*" In *Brodeur*, 171–86. Rpt. in *OEL: 22 Essays*, 301–18.

————. 1974. "The Author of *Beowulf.*" *NM* 75: 11–39.

Strauss, Barrie Ruth. 1981. "Women's Words as Weapons: Speech as Action in 'The Wife's Lament.'" *TSLL* 23: 268–85.

Suchier, Hermann. 1877. "Über die Sage von Offa und Þrytho." *BGdSL* 4: 500–21.

Sutherland, Raymond C. 1964. *The Celibate Beowulf, the Gospels, and the Liturgy*. Georgia State College School of Arts and Sciences, Research Papers 2. Atlanta: Georgia State College. iii–48.

Swanton, Michael J. 1982. *Crisis and Development in Germanic Society, 700–800: Beowulf and the Burden of Kingship*. Göppinger Arbeiten zur Germanistik 333. Göppingen: Kümmerle.

Szövérffy, Joseph. 1956. "From *Beowulf* to the *Arabian Nights* (Preliminary Notes on Aarne-Thompson 301)." *Midwest Folklore* 6: 89–124.

Taglicht, Josef. 1961. "*Beowulf* and Old English Verse Rhythm." *RES* n.s. 12: 341–51.

Takayanagi, Shunichi. 1961. "*Beowulf* and Christian Tradition." *SEL* (Tokyo) 37: 149–63.

Talbot, Annelise. 1983. "Sigemund the Dragon-Slayer." *Folklore* 94: 153–62.

Tanselle, G. Thomas. 1986. "Historicism and Critical Editing." *Studies in Bibliography* 39: 1–46.

Tarzia, Wade. 1989. "The Hoarding Ritual in Germanic Epic Tradition." *Journal of Folklore Research* 26: 97–121.

Taylor, A. R. 1952. "Two Notes on *Beowulf*." *Leeds Studies* 7–8: 5–17.

Taylor, Paul Beekman. 1964–65. "Snorri's Analogue to Beowulf's Funeral." *Archiv* 201: 349–51.

———. 1966. "Heorot, Earth, and Asgard: Christian Poetry and Pagan Myth." *Tennessee Studies in Literature* 11: 119–30.

———. 1967. "The Theme of Death in *Beowulf*." *Old English Poetry: Fifteen Essays*. Ed. Robert P. Creed. Providence: Brown University Press. 249–74.

——— and R. Evan Davis. 1982. "Some Alliterative Misfits in the *Beowulf* MS." *Neophil* 66: 614–21.

———. 1986. "The Traditional Language of Treasure in *Beowulf*." *JEGP* 85: 191–205.

———. 1990. "The Epithetical Style of *Beowulf*." *NM* 91: 195–206.

Taylor, William. 1816. [Anon. rev. of Thorkelin 1815.] *Monthly Review* 71: 516-23. Rpt. 1830 in his *Historic Survey of German Poetry, Interspersed with Various Translations*. 3 vols. Vol. 1. London: Treuttel and Wurtz. 788–90.

Tegethoff, Wilhelm. 1971. *Der altangelsächsiche Beowulf: Ein Werk Adalberts von Bremen*. Osnabrück: Self-published.

Tejera, Dionisia. 1979. "Date and Provenance of *Beowulf*." *Letras de Duesto* 9: 165–76.

Temple, Mary Kay. 1986. "*Beowulf* 1258–1266: Grendel's Lady-Mother." *ELN* 3: 10–15.

ten Brink, Bernhard. 1877. *Geschichte der englischen Literatur*. Vol. 1. *Bis zu Wiclifs Auftreten*. Berlin: Oppenheim.

———. 1888. *Beowulf: Untersuchungen*. Quellen und Forschungen 62. Strassburg: Trübner.

——— and Alois Brandl. 1891. "Fragment über altenglische Literatur" [written 1891–92]. *Geschichte der englischen Literatur*. Vol. 1. *Bis zu Wiclifs Auftreten*. 1899: 2nd ed. Ed. Alois Brandl. Strassburg: Trübner. App. 1. 431–78.

Thorkelin, Grímur Jónsson. 1816. "Svar til 'Et Par Ord om det nys udkomne angelsaxiske Digt' i Skilderiets No. 60." *Nyeste Skilderie af Kjøbenhavn* nos. 67–68.

Thornton, Harry, and Agathe Thornton. 1962. *Time and Style: A Psycho-Linguistic Essay in Classical Literature*. London: Methuen.

Thorpe, Benjamin, ed. 1844–46. *The Homilies of the Anglo-Saxon Church: The First Part, Containing the Sermones Catholici, or Homilies of Ælfric*. 2 vols. London: Printed for the Ælfric Society.

Thundy, Zacharias P. 1973. "Doctrinal Influence of *Ius Diaboli* on *Beowulf*." *Christian Scholar's Review* 3: 150–69.

———. 1983a. "*Beowulf*: Geats, Jutes, and Asiatic Huns." *Littcrit* 17: 1–8.

———. 1983b. "*Beowulf*: Meaning, Method, and Monsters." *Greyfriar: Siena Studies in Literature* 24: 5–34.

———. 1986. "*Beowulf*: Date and Authorship." *NM* 87: 102–16.

Tietjen, Mary C. Wilson. 1975. "God, Fate, and the Hero of *Beowulf.*" *JEGP* 74: 159–71.

Tolkien, J. R. R. 1936. *"Beowulf:* The Monsters and the Critics." *PBA* 22: 245–95. Rpt. 1958 as separate pamphlet, Oxford: Oxford University Press. Also rpt. in *Anthology,* 51–103; *Beowulf Poet,* 8–56; *Interpretations,* 14–44.

———. 1950. Preface. *Beowulf and the Fight at Finnsburg.* Trans. J. R. Clark Hall. 2nd edition, ed. C. L. Wrenn. London: Allen and Unwin. ix–xliii.

———. 1953. "The Homecoming of Beorhtnoth Beorhthelm's Son." *E&S* 6: 1–18.

———, ed. 1982. *Finn and Hengest: The Fragment and the Episode.* Ed. A. J. Bliss. London: Allen and Unwin.

Tonsfeldt, H. Ward. 1977. "Ring Structure in *Beowulf.*" *Neophil* 61: 443–52.

Traugott, Elizabeth Closs, and Mary Louise Pratt. 1980. *Linguistics for Students of Literature.* New York: Harcourt.

Tripp, Raymond P., Jr. 1953. "The Exemplary Role of Hrothgar and Heorot." *PQ* 56: 123–29.

———. 1992. *Literary Essays on Language and Meaning in the Poem Called "Beowulf":Beowulfiana Literaria.* Lewiston: Mellon Press.

Trnka, Bohumil. 1981. "The *Beowulf* Poem and Virgil's *Aeneid.*" *Poetica* 12: 50–56.

Tupper, Frederick. 1911. "The Philological Legend of Cynewulf." *PMLA* 26: 235–79.

Turner, Sharon. 1799–1805. *The History of the Manners, Landed Property, Government, Laws, Poetry, Literature, Religion, and Language of the Anglo-Saxons.* Vol. 4. London: Longman, Hurst, Rees, and Orme.

Turville-Petre, E. O. G. 1964. *Myth and Religion of the North: The Religion of Ancient Scandinavia.* New York: Holt, Rinehart and Winston.

Turville-Petre, Joan E. 1953–57. "Hengest and Horsa." *SBVS* 14: 273–90. See also Joan Blomfield.

Turville-Petre, Joan E. 1977. *"Beowulf* and *Grettis saga:* An Excursion." *SBVS* 19: 347–57. See also Joan Blomfield.

Tweddle, Dominic, ed. 1992. *The Anglian Helmet from Coppergate.* The Archaeology of York, The Small Finds 8. York Archeological Trust.

Uhland, Ludwig. 1857. "Zur deutschen Heldensage, I: Sigemund und Sigeferd." *Germania* 2: 344–63.

Ushigaki, Hiroto. 1982. "The Image of 'God Cyning' in *Beowulf:* A Philological Study." *SEL* (Tokyo) 58 (English no.): 63–78.

———. 1985. "The Image of Beowulf as King and Hero: Some Interpretative and Critical Problems." *SEL* (Tokyo) 61 (English no.): 13-20.

Vance, Eugene. 1985. *Mervelous Signals.* Lincoln: University of Nebraska Press.

van Meurs, Jan. 1955. *"Beowulf* and Literary Criticism." *Neophil* 39: 114–30.

Vaughan, M. F. 1976. "A Reconsideration of 'Unferð.'" *NM* 77: 32–48.

Veeser, H. Aram, ed. 1989. *The New Historicism.* New York: Routledge.

———, ed. 1994. *The New Historicism Reader.* New York: Routledge.

Vaught, Jacqueline. 1980. *"Beowulf:* The Fight at the Center." *Allegorica* 5: 125–37.

Vickery, John B., ed. 1966. *Myth and Literature: Contemporary Theory and Practice.* Lincoln: University of Nebraska Press.

Vickman, Geoffrey, 1990. *A Metrical Concordance to Beowulf.* Old English Newsletter. Subsidia 16. Binghamton: State University of New York Press.

Vickrey, John F. 1974. *"Egesan Ne Gymeð* and the Crime of Heremod." *MP* 71: 295–300.

———. 1977. "The Narrative Structure of Hengest's Revenge in *Beowulf.*" *ASE* 6: 91–103.

Vigfússon, Guðbrandur. 1878. "Prolegomena." *Sturlunga saga.* 2 vols. Oxford: Clarendon.

————, and F. York Powell, eds. 1883. *Corpus Poeticum Boreale: The Poetry of the Old Northern Tongue from the Earliest Times to the Thirteenth Century.* 2 vols. Rpt. 1965, New York: Russell and Russell.

Vogt, Walther H. 1927. *Stilgeschichte der eddischen Wissensdichtung.* Vol. 1. *Der Kultredner (Þulr).* Breslau: Ferdinand Hirt.

von Sweringen, Grace Fleming. 1909. "Women in the Germanic Hero-Sagas." *JEGP* 8: 501–12.

von Sydow, C. W. [Carl Wilhelm]. 1914. "Irisches in *Beowulf.*" *Verhandlungen der 52. Versammlung deutscher Philologen und Schulmänner in Marburg, 1913.* Ed. Rudolf Klee. Leipzig: Trübner. 177–80.

————. 1923a. "Beowulf och Bjarke." *Studier i Nordisk Filologi* 14, no. 3.

————. 1923b. "Beowulfskalden och nordisk tradition." *Vetenskaps-societeten i Lund Årsbok:* 79–91.

————. 1924. "Scyld Scefing." *Namn och Bygd* 12: 63–95.

Wachsler, Arthur A. 1985. "Grettir's Fight with a Bear: Another Neglected Analogue of *Beowulf* in the Grettis Sage [*sic*] Asmundarsonar." *ES* 66: 381–90.

Wackernagel, Wilhelm. 1848. *Geschichte der deutschen Literatur.* 2nd ed. 1879. 2 vols. Basel: Schweighäuserische Buchhandlung.

Walsh, Arlene. 1991. "The Depiction of Secular Women in Early Old English Poetry." *Unisa English Studies* 29: 1–7.

Wanley, Humphrey. 1705. *Librorum Veterum Septentrionalium, qui in Angliae Bibliothecis extant, nec non multorum Veterum Codicum Septentrionalium alibi extantium Catalogus Historico-Criticus, cum totius Thesauri Linguarum Septentrionalium sex Indicibus.* Vol. 2 of Hickes 1703–5.

Ward, Gordon. 1949. "Hengest." *Archaeologia Cantiana* 61: 77–97.

Watts, Ann Chalmers. 1969. *The Lyre and the Harp: A Comparative Reconsideration of Oral Tradition in Homer and Old English Epic Poetry.* New Haven: Yale University Press.

Webb, Bernice Larson. 1968. "James Bond as Literary Descendant of *Beowulf.*" *South Atlantic Quarterly* 67: 1–12.

Weinstock, Horst. 1982. "Comment on 'Knowledge of *Beowulf* in Its Own Time' by Professor Frederic G. Cassidy." *Yearbook of Research in English and American Literature* 1: 13–25.

Weise, Judith. 1986. "The Meaning of the Name 'Hygd': Onomastic Contrast in *Beowulf.*" *Names* 34: 1–10.

Welch, Martin. 1992. *Anglo-Saxon England.* London: Batsford.

Wells, David M. 1976. "The Sections in Old English Poetry." *Yearbook in English Studies* 6: 1–4.

Welsh, Andrew. 1991. "Branwen, *Beowulf,* and the Tragic Peaceweaver Tale." *Viator* 22: 1–13.

Wentersdorf, Karl P. 1981. "*Beowulf:* The Paganism of Hrothgar's Danes." *SP* 78: 91–119.

Westphalen, Tilman. 1967. *Beowulf 3150–55: Textkritik und Editionsgeschichte.* 2 vols. Munich: Fink.

Wetzel, Claus-Dieter. 1985. "Die Datierung des *Beowulf:* Bemerkungen zur jüngsten Forschungsentwicklung." *Anglia* 103: 371–400.

Weyhe, Hans. 1908. "König Ongentheows Fall." *EStn* 39: 14–39.

Whallon, William. 1961. "The Diction of *Beowulf.*" *PMLA* 76: 309–19.

———. 1962. "The Christianity of *Beowulf.*" *MP* 60: 81–94.

———. 1965a. "Formulas for Heroes in the *Iliad* and in *Beowulf.*" *MP* 63: 95–104.

———. 1965b. "The Idea of God in *Beowulf.*" *PMLA* 80: 19–23. [Incorporated in Whallon 1969, chap. 4].

———. 1969. *Formula, Character, and Context: Studies in Homeric, Old English, and Old Testament Poetry.* Washington DC: Center for Hellenic Studies.

———, with Margaret E. Goldsmith, Charles J. Donahue et al. 1973. "Allegorical, Typological or Neither? Three Short Papers on the Allegorical Approach to *Beowulf* and a Discussion." *ASE* 2: 285–302.

Whitbread, L. 1945. "Three *Beowulf* Allusions." *N&Q* 189: 207–19.

———. 1968. "*Beowulf* and Archaeology: Two Further Footnotes." *NM* 69: 63–72.

Whitelock, Dorothy. 1949. "Anglo-Saxon Poetry and the Historian." *Transactions of the Royal Historical Society* 4th ser., 31: 75–94.

———. 1951. *The Audience of Beowulf.* Oxford: Clarendon. Pp.1–30 rpt. in *OEL: 22 Essays,* 279–300.

Whitman, F. H. 1975. "The Meaning of 'Formulaic' in Old English Verse Composition." *NM* 76: 529–37.

Whitman, Frank W. 1993. *A Comparative Study of Old English Metre.* Toronto: University of Toronto Press.

Wieland, Gernot. 1988. "*Manna mildost:* Moses and Beowulf." *Pacific Coast Philology* 23: 86–93.

Wiley, Raymond A., ed. 1981. *John Mitchell Kemble and Jakob Grimm: A Correspondence, 1832-1852.* Leiden: Brill.

Willard, Rudolph, and Elinor D. Clemons. 1967. "Bliss's Light Verses in the *Beowulf.*" *JEGP* 66: 230–44.

Williams, David. 1975. "The Exile as Uncreator." *Mosaic* 8.3: 1–14.

———. 1982. *Cain and Beowulf: A Study in Secular Allegory.* Toronto: University of Toronto Press.

Williams, John H., Michael Shaw, and Varian Denham. 1985. *Middle Saxon Palaces at Northampton.* Northampton Development Corporation, Archaeological Monograph 4.

Williams, R. A. 1924. *The Finn Episode in Beowulf: An Essay in Interpretation.* Cambridge: Cambridge University Press.

Wilson, David. 1992. *Anglo-Saxon Paganism.* London: Routledge.

Wilson, David M., 1960. *The Anglo-Saxons.* 1981: 3rd ed. London: Pelican.

———. ed. 1976. *The Archaeology of Anglo-Saxon England.* London: Methuen.

Witke, Charles. 1966. "*Beowulf* 2096b–2199: A Variant?" *NM* 67: 113–17.

Woolf, Henry Bosley. 1938. "The Naming of Women in Old English Times." *MP* 36: 113–20.

———. 1947. "Beowulf and Grendel: An Analogue from Burma." *MLN* 62: 261–62.

———. 1949. "Unferth." *MLQ* 10: 145–52.

Woolf, Virginia. 1925. "Modern Fiction." *The Common Reader.* Rpt. 1948, New York: Harcourt, Brace. 207–18.

Work, James A. 1930. "Odyssean Influence on the *Beowulf.*" *PQ* 9: 399–402.

Wormald, Patrick. 1978. "Bede, *Beowulf* and the Conversion of the Anglo-Saxon Aristocracy." *Bede and Anglo-Saxon England.* Ed. Robert T. Farrell. Oxford: British Archaeological Reports. 32–95.

———. 1991. "Anglo-Saxon Society and Its Literature." In *Cambridge Companion,* 1–22.

Wright, Charles D. 1993. *The Irish Tradition in Old English Literature.* Cambridge: Cambridge University Press.

Wright, Herbert. 1957. "Good and Evil; Light and Darkness; Joy and Sorrow in *Beowulf.*" *RES* n.s. 8: 1–11. Rpt. in *Anthology,* 257–67.

Wright, Louise E. 1980. "*Merewioingas* and the Dating of *Beowulf:* A Reconsideration." *Nottingham Mediaeval Studies* 24: 1–6.

Wülker, Richard P., ed. 1883–98. *Bibliothek der angelsächsischen Poesie.* Kassel: Wigand.

———. 1885. *Grundriss zur Geschichte der angelsächsischen Literatur.* Leipzig: Veit.

Wyld, Henry Cecil. 1925. "Diction and Imagery in Anglo-Saxon Poetry." *E&S* 11: 49–91. Rpt. in *Essential Articles,* 183–227.

Zappert, Georg. 1851. "Virgil's Fortleben im Mittelalter: Ein Beitrag zur Geschichte der classischen Literatur in jenem Zeitraume." *Denkschriften der Kaiserlichen Akademie der Wissenschaften,* Philosophisch-historische Klasse, 2. Vienna. 17–70.

Ziegelmaier, Gregory. 1969. "God and Nature in the *Beowulf* Poem." *ABR* 20: 250–58.

Zumthor, Paul. 1984. "The Text and the Voice." *New Literary History* 16: 67–92.

Index

Abel, 181, 188, 245; as type, 250

Abraham, 230

action, 60, 106, 110, 167, 168, 171, 189, 198, 207, 216, 218, 223, 225, 229, 246, 274, 337; feminine, 323; heroic, 259, 274; symbolic, 252

Adalbert of Bremen, 30, 354

Adam, 204, 244, 253

Adam of Bremen, 30

adaptations: adventure novel, 351; animated cartoon, 353; children's stories, 352; comic book, 342, 350, 351, 354, 356; fairy tales, 351; film, 353; Icelandic saga, 351; modern fiction, 343; novels, 342, 352–53; parody, 351, 354; poetry, 342, 352, 354, 355; rock musical, 342, 353; satire, 352; science fiction, 352, 353; short story, 352, 353; symphony, 342, 351; theater, 351

Ad Gefrin (Northumbria), 292, 302

Ælfric, 48, 52n. 1, 53n. 8, 331; *Catholic Homilies,* 48; *Grammar,* 330; "Preface to Genesis," 52n. 1; *Sermones,* 52n. 1

Ælfwald, 128

Aeneid. See Virgil

Æschere, 121, 222, 266, 287, 288, 323

aesthetics, 5, 6, 8, 85–87, 92, 94, 103, 106, 107, 110, 124, 189, 194, 196–200, 211, 214, 217, 325, 330, 337; Aristotelian, 198, 199, 211; non-Aristotelian, 193, 196, 201

Æthelred, 32

Æthelweard, 202

Æthelwulf, 25, 202

Ager, Barry, 305

aggression, 208, 252, 259

Akerman, John Yonge, 291, 293

Ála flekks saga, 134

Alcuin, 147, 185, 274

Aldfrith (King of Northumbria) 14, 20, 23, 126

Aldhelm, 13, 16, 17, 23, 28, 29; *De Virginitate,* 142

Alexander, Michael, 342, 357

Alfred the Great, 21, 25, 52, 181, 192, 203, 231, 233, 245, 249, 295, 341, 342, 357; Boethius translation, 151, 168

allegory, 6, 7, 23, 30, 33, 176, 183, 194, 206, 207, 208, 216n. 2, 232n. 2, 233, 238–44, 247–54, 279, 333; Christian, 207, 234, 245; conceptual, 233, 239–42, 247, 249–51; corporeal, 326; cultural, 239; doctrinal, 233, 243, 250; Fulgentian, 242, 245; function of, 251; heroic soul, 234; historical, 23, 145, 233, 239, 240, 242, 247–49; homily, 240; mythic, 155; political, 14, 15, 19; Prudentian, 185, 244; psychological, 233, 251, 252; secular, 235

Allen, Marijane, 353. *See also* Osborn, Marijane

alliteration, 38–43, 45–48, 55–61, 63, 64, 66–68, 71, 73, 75, 76, 79, 80, 83n. 20, 85, 88, 93, 100, 101, 106, 107, 110, 111, 202, 206, 208, 311, 321, 337, 349, 350, 354; double, 58, 73, 75; enjambed, 208; South Germanic tradition of, 86

Alliterative Morte Arthure, 88, 102

allusions, 154, 163, 165, 185; contrapuntal, 164; English, 22, 231

alterity, 264, 347

ambiguity, 6, 16, 168, 235, 252, 256, 261, 338

Ambrose, Saint, 250

Amis, Kingsley, 352

Amos, Ashley Crandall, 15, 24, 26, 27, 42, 46

analogues, 18, 125, 129, 283, 317, 353; Armenian, 146; classical, 125, 127, 141; Eddic, 128; Germanic, 18; *Grettis saga,* 126, 146; historical, 147; *Hrólfr kraki* legend, 126; Icelandic, 125, 165; Irish, 125, 128, 135, 138; Latin, 136; Norse, 125; Old English, 143; Old Icelandic, 134; Old Norse,

succession, 205, 224, 226, 262, 263, 267, 274, 283, 289, 313–15; royal 196
Suchier, Hermann, 194
suffering, 182, 235, 252, 278, 279, 312, 313
supernatural, 242, 243
Sutcliff, Rosemary, 352
Sutherland, Raymond C., 244
Sutton Hoo, 15, 19, 147, 166, 178, 179, 192n. 1, 228, 291–96, 298–301, 304–6, 309, 310, 335; date, 292; Mound I, 292, 294, 300, 304
Swanton, Michael J., 16, 21, 179, 257, 263, 359
Swearer, Randolph, 343, 355
Sweaton, Bruce, 353
Sweden, 19, 127, 128, 132, 145, 158, 173n. 6, 202, 213, 226–28, 291, 296, 299, 300, 304, 355; Swedes, 257, 266, 269n. 2; Swedish homeland, 230
Swift, Jonathon, 23
swimming, 127, 140, 211n. 7, 221, 281; contest, 145
sword hilt, 188, 305, 326, 328, 333, 337, 338; Finnish, 305; Frankish, 305; Kentish, 305; ornamentation, 305
swords, 95, 96, 117, 137, 168, 172, 173, 188, 221, 229, 274, 287, 291–93, 297, 299, 305–7, 309, 326, 328, 333, 337, 338, 351; Frankish, 305; Hrunting, 205; ornamentation, 305; pattern-welding, 292; ring, 305, 306, 309; Saxon, 305; symbolism, 333, 337; Viking Age, 305
syllables, 25, 40, 41, 55, 56, 60–62, 64–68, 70–74, 76, 78–81; expansion, 79; extrametrical, 72; heavy, 62, 64–66, 67; ictic, 65, 67, 68, 81n. 3; light, 62, 64–66; resolved, 66, 69; root, 85; stressed, 64, 66, 68, 71, 73, 78; strong, 68, 78; suppressed, 70; suppression, 56; syllabification, 64, 82n. 6; unstressed, 65, 66, 73, 81; weak, 70–73, 76–79, 81, 83n. 15; weak resolving, 65; weak-stressed, 73; weight, 64–67
symbols, 6, 223, 233, 234, 236, 240–42,

244, 250, 253, 272, 274, 304, 312, 313; biblical, 234, 250; Christological, 244; definition, 237; liturgical, 244; mythic, 234; psychological, 222; sacramental, 244; serpent, 292; symbolism, 6, 7, 23, 164, 173, 186, 203, 204, 206, 218, 222, 223, 227, 232, 234–37, 241, 244, 246, 250, 252, 274, 292, 308, 333
synaesthesia, 106
synonyms, 85, 88, 90, 93, 94, 99, 112, 116, 124, 208, 211
syntax, 45, 46, 56, 58, 59, 68, 69, 79, 80, 86, 90, 97, 98, 101, 102, 105–7, 110, 112–17, 122, 195, 208, 358; apo koinou constructions, 105, 107, 112, 113, 115; apposition, 87, 88, 90, 97, 98, 100, 106, 134, 152; asyndetic, 117; combinatives, 88; conjunctive order, 117; end-positioning, 117; genitives, 63, 88, 90, 93; hypotaxis, 118; parallelism, 97, 98; parataxis, 98, 110, 115–17; periodic sentences, 107; punctuation, 35, 50, 51, 106, 112, 113, 117, 118, 358; rhetorical, 117; sentences, periodic, 107; temporal clauses, 105
Szarmach, Paul E., 53n. 9, 339n. 2
Szövérffy, Joseph, 134
taboo, 243, 317
Tacitus, 145, 243, 261; Germania, 138, 230, 242, 243, 261
Taglicht, Josef, 57
Táin Bó Fraích (The Cattle Raid of Froech), 127, 136
Takayanagi, Shunichi, 243
Talbot, Annelise, 145, 256, 342, 357
Tanselle, G. Thomas, 50
Tarzia, Wade, 257, 260
Taylor, A. R., 127, 129
Taylor, Paul Beekman, 88, 97, 104n. 4, 133, 206, 214, 221, 289, 339n. 5
Taylor, William, 341
teaching, 251; teaching the poem, 52
Tegethoff, Wilhelm, 30
Temple, Mary Kay, 319
Tennyson, Alfred Lord, 341, 352